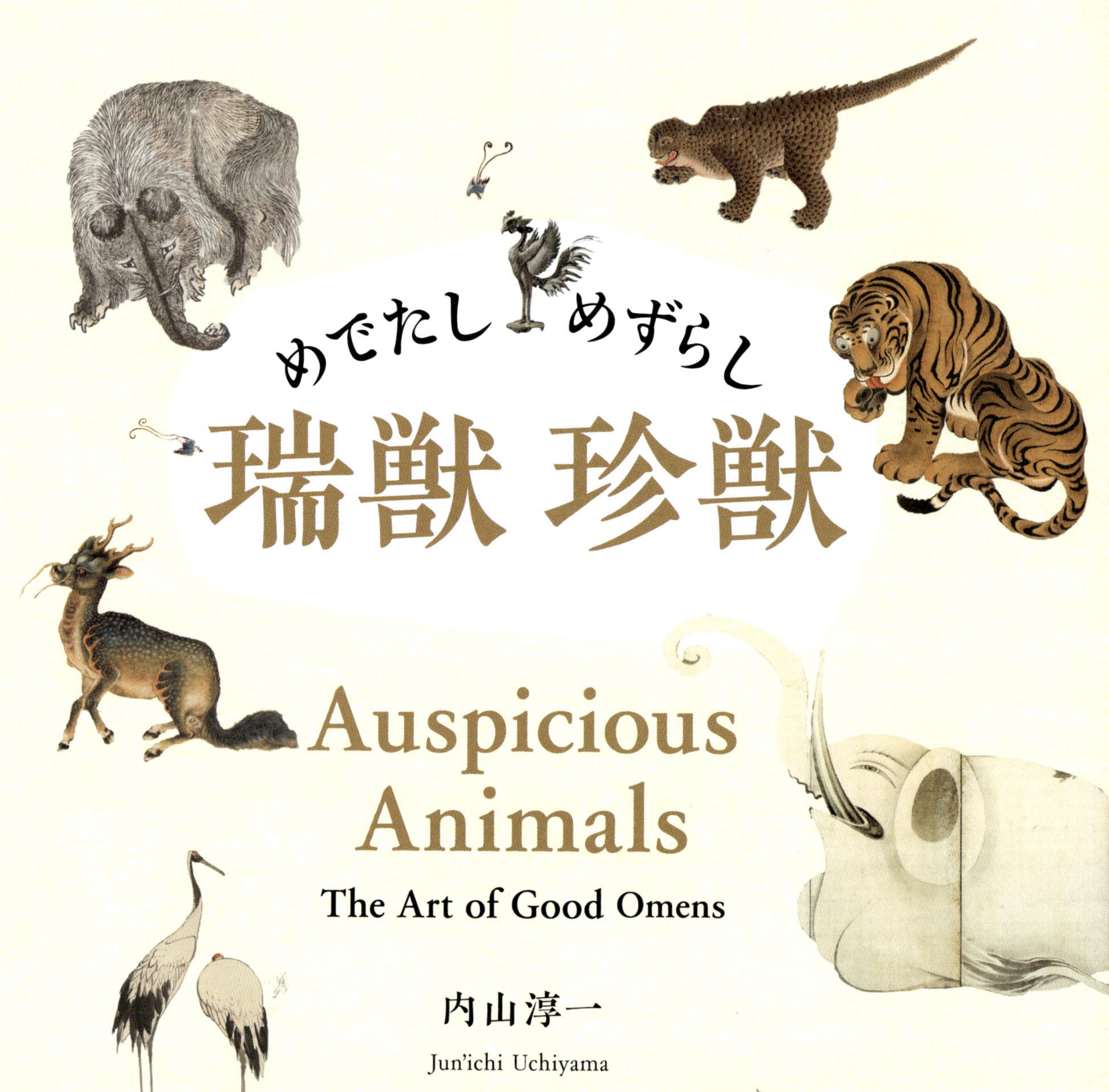

めでたし めずらし

瑞獣 珍獣

Auspicious Animals

The Art of Good Omens

内山淳一

Jun'ichi Uchiyama

Auspicious Animals
The Art of Good Omens

Japanese text by Jun'ichi Uchiyama
Translated and proofread by Sumishi Aran and Jeannine Mulnar
Designed by Yoko Hayashi
Illustrations by Chika Shibata
Edited by Eriko Hara

Published by PIE International Inc.

PIE International Inc.
2-32-4 Minami-Otsuka, Toshima-ku, Tokyo 170-0005 Japan
international@pie.co.jp

ISBN 978-4-7562-5429-0 (outside Japan)
Printed in Japan

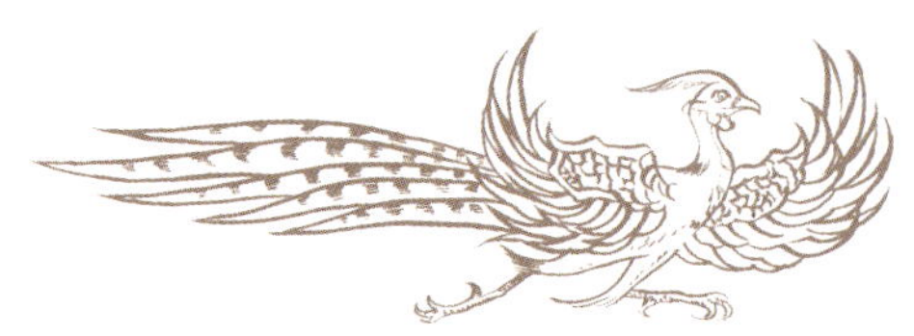

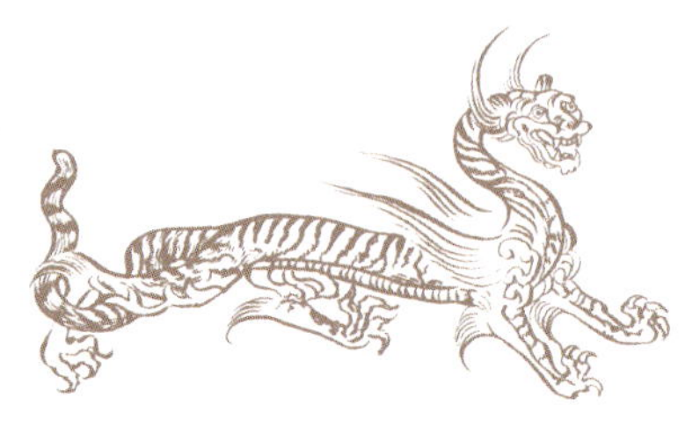

はじめに

瑞獣とは？
珍獣とは？

「瑞獣」という言葉から思い浮かべる動物は何だろうか。NHK大河ドラマ「麒麟がくる」で認知度が急上昇した「仁獣」麒麟だろうか。それとも伊達政宗の異名「独眼竜」の龍、あるいは「獅子の時代」の獅子か。相撲の世界でも、多くの四股名に鳳凰や龍・麒麟の文字が当てられている。この瑞獣の瑞とは、吉祥（めでたい）という意味で、歴史的には古代中国に発する「祥瑞」の思想が根底にある。天子の徳が高く、すぐれた政治が行われていると、それに感応して天が、麒麟や鳳凰・霊亀・龍などの霊獣をはじめとする珍しい動植物や天然現象を出現させるという思想（天命思想）にもとづくとされる。国家の命運をも左右する兆しを現わすものとして、これらの動物たちは時代を超えて崇敬されてきたのである。

日本では650年（大化6）、白雉が朝廷に献上されたことで改元に至った白雉改元の記事が、祥瑞の語が現れる最初という。やがて律令制のなかにその基準も定められ、中国の古制にならった10世紀の法令集「延喜式」に見えるリストには、大瑞59・上瑞38・中瑞33・下瑞15件が列挙された。大瑞の中の動物だけを抽出してみると、河精、麟（麒麟）、鳳（鳳凰）、鸞、比翼鳥、同心鳥、永楽鳥、富貴、吉利、神亀、龍、騶虞、白澤、神馬、周帀、角端、觧廌（解豸）、比肩獣、六足獣、茲白、白象、一角獣、天鹿、鼈封、酋耳、豹犬、露犬となる。麒麟や鳳凰・龍、さらには普賢菩薩が乗る白象など一部を除き、多くはほとんど馴染みのない名称であろう。さらに、これらに上瑞・中瑞・下瑞の動物たちが加わることになる。

瑞獣のなかでも別格とされてきたのが、儒教にもとづく「四霊」「四神」などと称される龍・鳳凰・麒麟・霊亀である。中国ではすべての動物を、魚のように鱗のある鱗蟲、鳥のように羽のある羽蟲、獣類のように毛のある毛蟲、甲殻類のように固い殻や甲羅のある甲蟲（各360種）に分類したのだが、この4つの動物世界に君臨する長としての特別な力をもち、吉兆を知らせる神秘的な存在として位置づけられてきた。一方、中国神話において四方を司る霊獣も四神と呼ばれ、東に青龍、南に朱雀、西に白虎、北に玄武が当てられるとともに、さらに五行説により中央に麒麟や黄龍を加えること

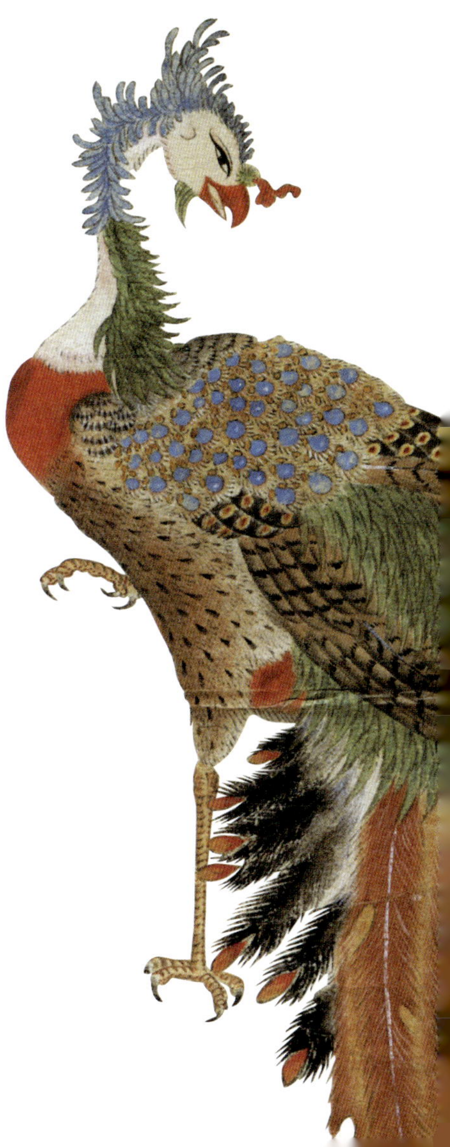

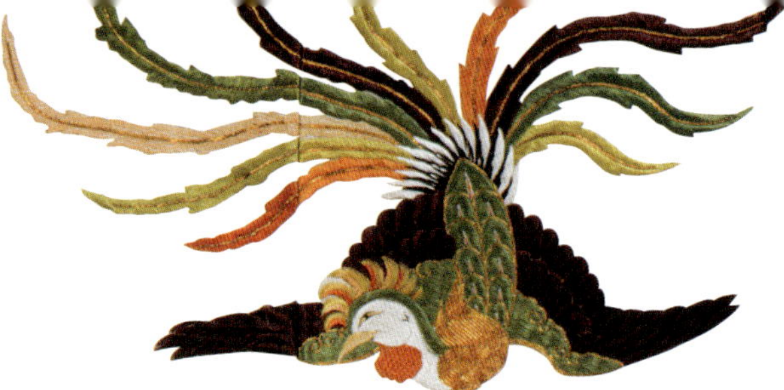

Introduction

What are Auspicious Beasts? What are Rare Creatures?

The Japanese word *zuijū* stands for auspicious beasts. The term's etymological origins can be traced back to ancient Chinese thought. It was believed that, if the imperial rule was full of virtue and excellent governance was conducted, auspicious creatures like *kirin* (C. *qilin*), phoenixes, turtles, and dragons would appear as harbingers of propitious natural phenomena. As time passed, these animals continued to be regarded as symbols of the nation's destiny.

A Japanese record dating to the year 650 (Taika 4) describes how a white pheasant was presented to the imperial court and provided the new era's name: Hakuchi, literally "white pheasant." This event marked the first recorded instance of a rare creature being used as a fortuitous omen in Japan. Following this precedent, auspicious symbolism was also included in Japan's system of governance, which was adopted on the basis of the ancient Chinese model. The tenth-century collection of laws and ordinances, *Engishiki*, includes a list with categories of auspicious beasts. Among the so-called "great omens" list we find the following creatures: an ancient Chinese deity said to inhabit the Yangtze River (J. Kasei; C. Hebo), *kirin* (a type of unicorn), phoenixes, *ran* (C. *luan*; a mythical bird akin to a peacock), *hiyokudori* (a fabled singing bird), two more avian creatures named *dōshinchō* and *eirakuchō*, *fūki* (C. *fugui*; literally "wealth and rank"), *kitsuri* (C. *jili*; literally meaning "lucky"), divine turtle (J. *jinki*), dragons, *sūgu* (C. *zouyu*; a creature likened to a panda), *hakutaku* (C. *bai ze*; an animal with a bovine body and the head of an old man), sacred horse (J. *shinba*), *shūsō* (C. *zhouza*; literally "walking around"), *kakutan* (C. *luduan*; a cross between a deer and a lion), *kaichi* (C. *xiezhi*; a type of horned lion type), *hikenjū* (literally "beast of equality"), *rokusokujū* (a mythical hexapod), *jihaku* (a kind of turtle), white elephant (J. *hakuzō*), *ikkakujū* (a type of unicorn), *tenroku* (a heavenly deer), *beppō* (another mythical turtle), *shūji* (a creature akin to a tiger), *hyōken* (a leopard-dog), and *rōken* (a hound type of creature). Apart from a handful of names, most of the creatures are probably unfamiliar to many Japanese today. In the tenth-century list, all the animals of the category mentioned above are joined by a plethora of others in two more subsections.

Among auspicious beasts, a special role is occupied by those tied to Confucian thought, such as dragons, phoenixes, *kirin*, and turtles. In China, animals are separated by identifying characteristics, namely scales, wings, fur, and shell. These four distinguishing traits were thought to carry special powers and imbue these creatures with mystical meaning. On the other hand, the four directions in Chinese mythology are occupied by four sacred animals that were considered deities in and of themselves: the Azure Dragon in the East (J. Seiryū), the Vermillion Bird in the South (J. Suzaku), the White Tiger in the West (J. Byakko) and the Black Tortoise

もあった。雲をつかむような話で何ともややこしいのだが、後者は高松塚古墳やキトラ古墳の壁画として、また奈良・薬師寺の金堂薬師如来坐像台座にも表現されている。

もとより、これらの動物のうち白鹿や白雉・白烏・白亀など、現代ではアルビノ(先天性色素欠乏症)として認知される一部の動物を除き、そのほとんどが実見されるはずもなく、空想の世界に埋没してゆく運命にあったのだろう。そのなかで生き残ったのが、神社仏閣の建築彫刻や障壁画などの絵画に今でも見ることができる霊獣(※)たちなのである。文殊菩薩の乗る獅子や普賢菩薩の乗る象など、仏教とともに入ってきた動物は多い。とりわけ密教の世界では、孔雀明王の孔雀をはじめ、大威徳明王(だいいとくみょうおう)や焔摩天(えんまてん)の水牛、摩利支天(まりしてん)の猪など、多様な乗り物が用意されている。一方、神道の世界においても、日吉山王(ひえ(ひよし)さんのう)と猿、春日神(かすがしん)と鹿、稲荷神(いなりしん)と狐、八幡神(はちまんしん)と鳩といった具合に、神の使い(神使(しんし)・眷属(けんぞく))として祀られる動物も少なくなかった。

さらに富貴や福徳、長寿を寿ぐ意味で鶴と亀、あるいは仲睦(なかむつ)まじい鴛鴦(おしどり)が婚礼の象徴として、また子孫繁栄を願って鼠や兎・犬など多産や安産を象徴する動物たちも造形化され続けていった。とりわけ後者については、いずれもが十二支に含まれることから、干支(えと)にあたる人々からの終生変わらぬ圧倒的支持を獲得することになったのである。それらを大量に描けば描くほど吉祥性は増幅することから「百〜図」がたびたび描かれ、また中国の吉祥主義ともいうべき音の語呂合(ごろあ)わせによる主題も、中国文化に傾倒した多くの知識人を通じて日本に定着していった。猿猴(えんこう)(=侯)と蜂(=封)とを描いて「封侯」(中国で諸侯に封ぜられること)、禄(ろく)に音が通じる鹿は仕官が叶い家栄えるの意、蝶と猫とで長寿を、また猪が臥す姿は天下泰平を表す語「撫綏(ぶすい)」に通じる「臥猪(ふすい)」と読み解かれた。

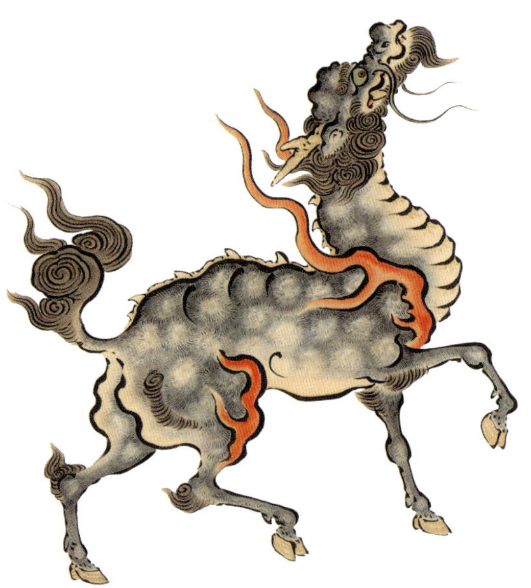

in the North (J. Genbu). At the center, a *kirin* or yellow dragon were frequently added, reflecting the five elements of ancient Chinese belief. Although the origins of this symbolism are murky, such images have been used in wall paintings of Japanese *kofun* tombs, such as the Takamatsuzuka and Kitora tombs. Later, the same imagery adorned the pedestal of the Bhaisajyaguru (J. Yakushi Nyorai) sculpture at Yakushiji temple in Nara.

From the beginning, animals like white tigers, white pheasants, white crows, and white turtles that are now understood as albinos were removed from the larger group of the animal kingdom and transplanted into the world of imagination. These sacred beasts existed in the pictorial arts, such as sculptures and wall paintings, many of which survive to this day. For example, the lion that carries the bodhisattva Manjusri (J. Monju) and the elephant which Samantabhadra (J. Fugen) is riding, illustrate how such animals entered the iconography of Buddhism. In esoteric Buddhism, mythical creatures are particularly numerous. Beginning with the peacock associated with Mahamayuri (J. Kujaku Myōō), the list continues with the water buffalo of Yamantaka (J. Taitoku Myōō) and Yama (J. Enmaten), as well as the wild boar of Marici (J. Marishiten). In the world of Shinto, animals play an equally central role. The deity Hiyoshi Sannō is associated with monkeys, while the Kasuga deity is attended by deer, the rice deity Inari by foxes, and the deity Hachiman by pigeons.

Animals like cranes and turtles came to be thought of as harbingers of fortune, luck, and long life. Similarly, the harmonious nature of mandarin duck couples rendered them into symbols of marital fortuity, whereas the many offspring born by mice, rabbits, and dogs made them emblems of fecundity and easy childbirth. The latter three animals are also part of the twelve zodiacs, leading them to occupy a pivotal role from the beginning to the end of a person's life cycle. In order to multiply their efficacy, such auspicious animals are sometimes depicted in large numbers and the Chinese characters used to write their names are often linked in shape to auspicious meaning. For example, the characters for monkey and bee were used as a portmanteau for "feudal enfeoffment," a term whose Chinese characters resemble those used for "monkey" and "bee." Phonetic associations were also drawn. Deer, whose character reads the same way as the character for "reward," came to denote success in government service. Butterflies and cats stand for long life and the bent shape of boars came to symbolize peace and prosperity in the realm.

江戸開幕後、泰平の世を迎えて1世紀余りが経過すると、本当の姿を知りたいという人々の欲求は次第に高まりを見せてゆく。とくに18世紀半ば以降に、動植物や鉱物などの万物を研究する博物学という学問が流行した。当初は本草学という薬用植物などを研究するものだったのだが、やがて実用から離れ興味は様々な文物へと拡大していったのである。

そうしたなか、海外からの知識の流入にともない、今まで実態が定かでなかった動物たちの実像が明らかになってくる。唐獅子からライオンへ、麒麟からキリン（ジラフ）へ、水犀からサイへとイメージの変革がなされつつあったと言えよう。とはいえ、その改変は蘭学者らを中心とする一部の知識人たちにとどまり、一般化は果たされなかったようである。日本各地で発見され治療用に用いられてきたトウヨウゾウの化石は「龍骨」とされ、龍の存在自体を疑う者はほとんどいなかったのである。

その一方で、人々の好奇心に応えるため、ヤマアラシ・ジャコウネコ・オランウータン・ロバ・ヒョウ・クジャク・ヒクイドリ・オウムなど多種多様な動物たちが、中国船やオランダ船に乗せられ長崎にやってきた。幕府への献上品や物好きな藩主をいただく諸藩からの注文に応じた鳥獣のほか、興行師の手にわたり江戸や京・大坂で見世物にされ、さらに全国巡回に至る動物も少なくなかった。なかでも人気の高かったのが象と駱駝で、一種の社会現象ともなった。そのようなブームの中で生み出された作品からは、人々の尽きることのない好奇心の発露を認めることができる。空想と現実とが入り交じった状況下、人々は見世物に刺激されつつ溢れんばかりの好奇心を解放し、かくも豊かな造形作品を残すことに成功したのである。

本書では、こうした人間のイマジネーション力の可能性を実感させてくれる、何とも恵まれた時代をめぐりながら、古代から連綿とつづく豊かな瑞獣と珍獣の世界を堪能していただきたい。

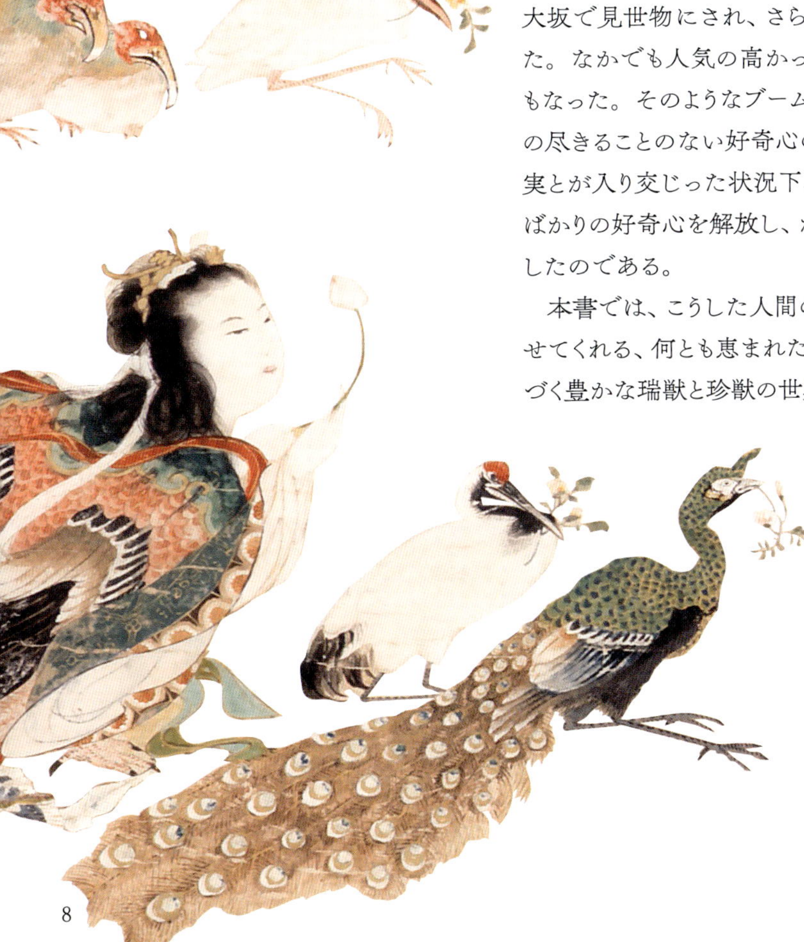

※これらの動物たちは瑞獣・霊獣・聖獣・神獣などと呼ばれるが、ニュアンスの差はみられるものの明確な区別があるわけでもなさそうである。そこで、本書においては霊獣の語を主に用い、吉祥性の顕著なものについては適宜、瑞獣と称することにしたい。また、「延喜式」の動物の読み方には推定のものも含まれる。

With the advent of the Edo period and the peace and prosperity that followed, voices inquiring into the actual physical shapes of mythical animals grew louder. The eighteenth century in particular saw a rising interest in the study of plants, animals, and natural history in general. Initially, this interest focused on medicinal herbs and botany, but it soon expanded into areas beyond practical use. Together with the influx of Western scientific knowledge, the actual shapes of animals that had previously existed only in the imagination became clear. Mythical creatures like guardian dogs now became lions, *kirin* became giraffes, and the horned creatures with shell-like armor called *suisai* became rhinoceroses. Be that as it may, such specified knowledge rarely exceeded the realm of Western-inspired science, the so-called "Dutch learning" (*rangaku*), and did not seep into the public realm. Fossils of the Asian elephant that were found throughout Japan and used as medicine were labeled as dragon bones. As a result, the existence of dragons was not questioned by many Japanese at the time.

Rare creatures, on the other hand, arrived on Chinese and Dutch ships at the port of Nagasaki. Porcupines, civet cats, orangutans, donkeys, leopards, peacocks, cassowaries, and parrots could be seen in the flesh. They were coveted gifts for the shogunal rulers and treasured possessions for regional lords. As a result, such animals were frequently ordered and made their way to Edo, Kyoto, and Osaka. Often animals were also paraded throughout the realm. Among this thriving interest in exotic creatures, a boom of their depictions occurred, often by showcasing an endearing affection for the animals. As fiction and reality coalesced, people were enthralled by the spectacle of rare animals, a fascination that spawned rich creativity.

This book seeks to convey the possibilities of the human imagination. From ancient days and throughout the ages, the fascination with the rich world of auspicious beasts and rare creatures continues to be unbroken.

These creatures are variously called auspicious beasts, sacred beasts, and divine beasts. For consistency and ease of understanding, the term sacred beasts (*reijū*) has been used throughout the book, while animals with propitious meaning are labeled as auspicious beasts (*zuijū*).

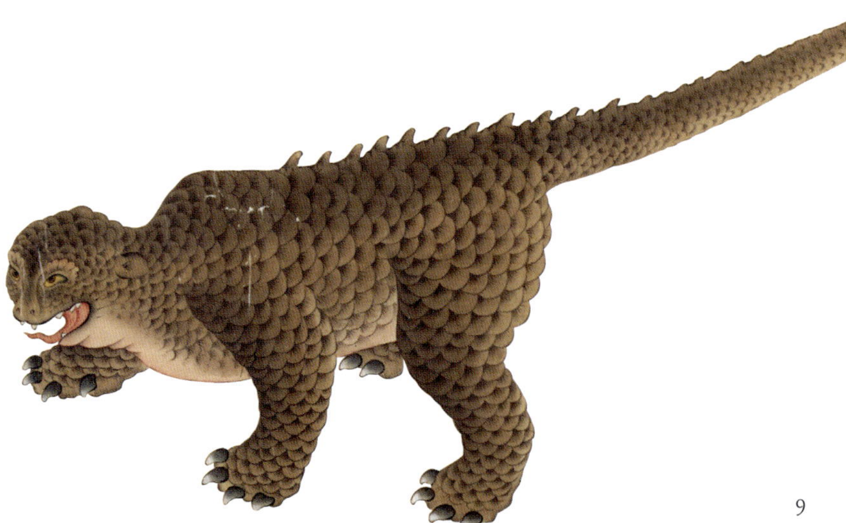

謝辞

作品掲載をお許しくださいました所蔵者各位、ならびにご協力たまわりました関係各位に対し、心より御礼申し上げます。また、東京国立博物館・田沢裕賀氏、府中市美術館・金子信久氏、十文字学園女子大学・樋口一貴氏、香雪美術館・勝盛典子氏からは貴重な情報のご提供を、仙台市博物館の諸氏からは多大なるご協力をいただきました。記してあつく御礼申し上げます。

著者

写真提供および協力者（五十音順、敬称略）

秋田市立千秋美術館
飛鳥園
安倍文殊院
板橋区立美術館
出光美術館
石清水八幡宮
ウィーン美術史美術館
Kunsthistorisches Museum Wien
エツコ＆ジョー・プライス
大阪歴史博物館
太田市立新田荘歴史資料館
沖縄県美ら島財団
金子信久
株式会社 千總
川越市立博物館
川越氷川神社
岩松院
関西大学図書館
木村比呂美
ギャラリー紅屋
熊本県立美術館
九州国立博物館
京都国立博物館
工藤恭二
宮内庁三の丸尚蔵館
宮内庁正倉院事務所
クリーブランド美術館
The Cleveland Museum of Art
群馬県立近代美術館
慶應義塾図書館
建仁寺
高山寺
高台寺
神戸市立博物館
国際日本文化研究センター
国立科学博物館
國立故宮博物院
国立国会図書館
国立歴史民俗博物館
古美術 瀬戸
Colbase
真田宝物館
静岡県立美術館
渋川市教育委員会
島根県立美術館
相国寺
相国寺承天閣美術館
真正極楽寺 真如堂
角匠
瑞龍寺
青雅堂
静嘉堂文庫美術館
仙台市博物館
雙林寺
DNPアートコミュニケーションズ
朝田寺
敦賀市博物館
摘水軒記念文化振興財団
東京国立博物館
東京文化財研究所
鳥取県立博物館
富山市郷土博物館
富山市佐藤記念美術館
長崎歴史文化博物館
内藤記念くすり博物館
名古屋城総合事務所
奈良県立美術館
奈良国立博物館
奈良文化財研究所
西尾市岩瀬文庫
日光東照宮
白鶴美術館
帆風美術館
兵庫県立美術館
平等院
福岡市美術館
文化庁
ベルリン州立図書館
Staatsbibliothek zu Berlin
北斎館
堀口晶夫
ボストン美術館
Museum of Fine Arts, Boston
本間美術館
松浦史料博物館
万葉洞
三重県総合博物館
MIHO MUSEUM
宮城県図書館
宮城県松島町
三芳野神社
無量寺・串本応挙芦雪館
メトロポリタン美術館
The Metropolitan Museum of Art
薬師寺
安村敏信
藪本公三
藪本太一
大和文華館
養源院
読売新聞東京本社
早稲田大学演劇博物館
早稲田大学図書館

凡例

- キャプションには、次の内容を記しました。
  作品名、作者名（不明のものは省略）、制作年代（和暦→西暦の順に記載。cは「世紀」の略記）、所蔵者（無記名も含む）
- 解説中は、西暦→和暦の順に記載しました。
- 解説中の人名のあとには可能な範囲で生没年を入れました。
  例：鄭和（1371〜1434）宋紫石（1715〜86）
- 西暦の期間は、下2桁のみで省略した場合もあります。
  例：1715〜86
- 本書は欧文併記のため左開きの仕様ですが、絵巻・版本・版画・屏風は、伝統的に向かって右から左に鑑賞されることを前提に制作されています。

Note to the reader

- The image caption contains the following information:
  Title, artist (except if unknown), date, collection (including unknown or unrecorded)
- For artists, dates of birth and death are included if known. Dates corresponding with the Gregorian Calendar are included except for select cases.
  For example:
  Sō Shiksei (1715-86)
- Japanese handscrolls, woodblock prints, and screens are viewed from right to left.

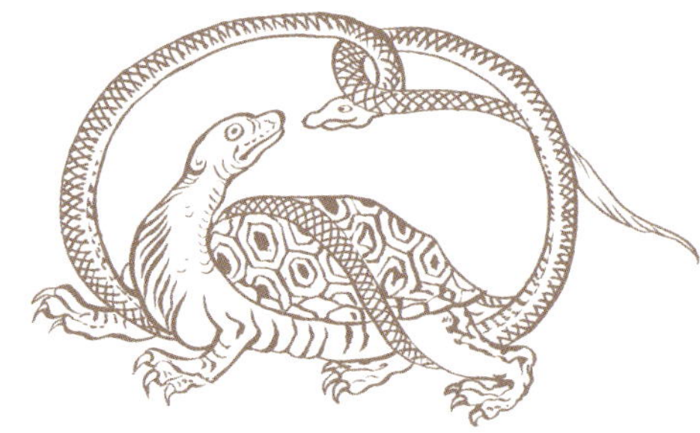

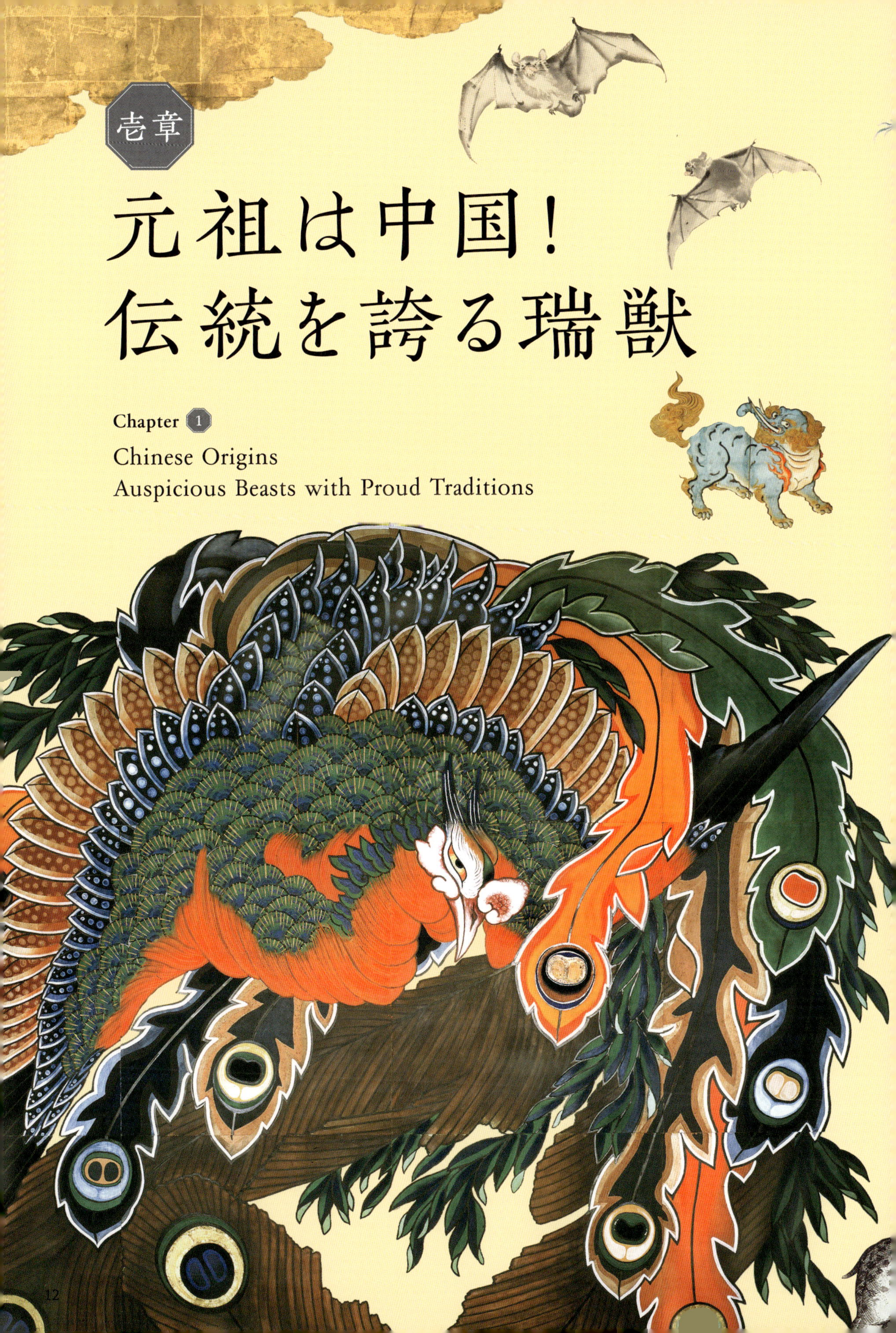

壱章

元祖は中国！伝統を誇る瑞獣

Chapter 1

Chinese Origins
Auspicious Beasts with Proud Traditions

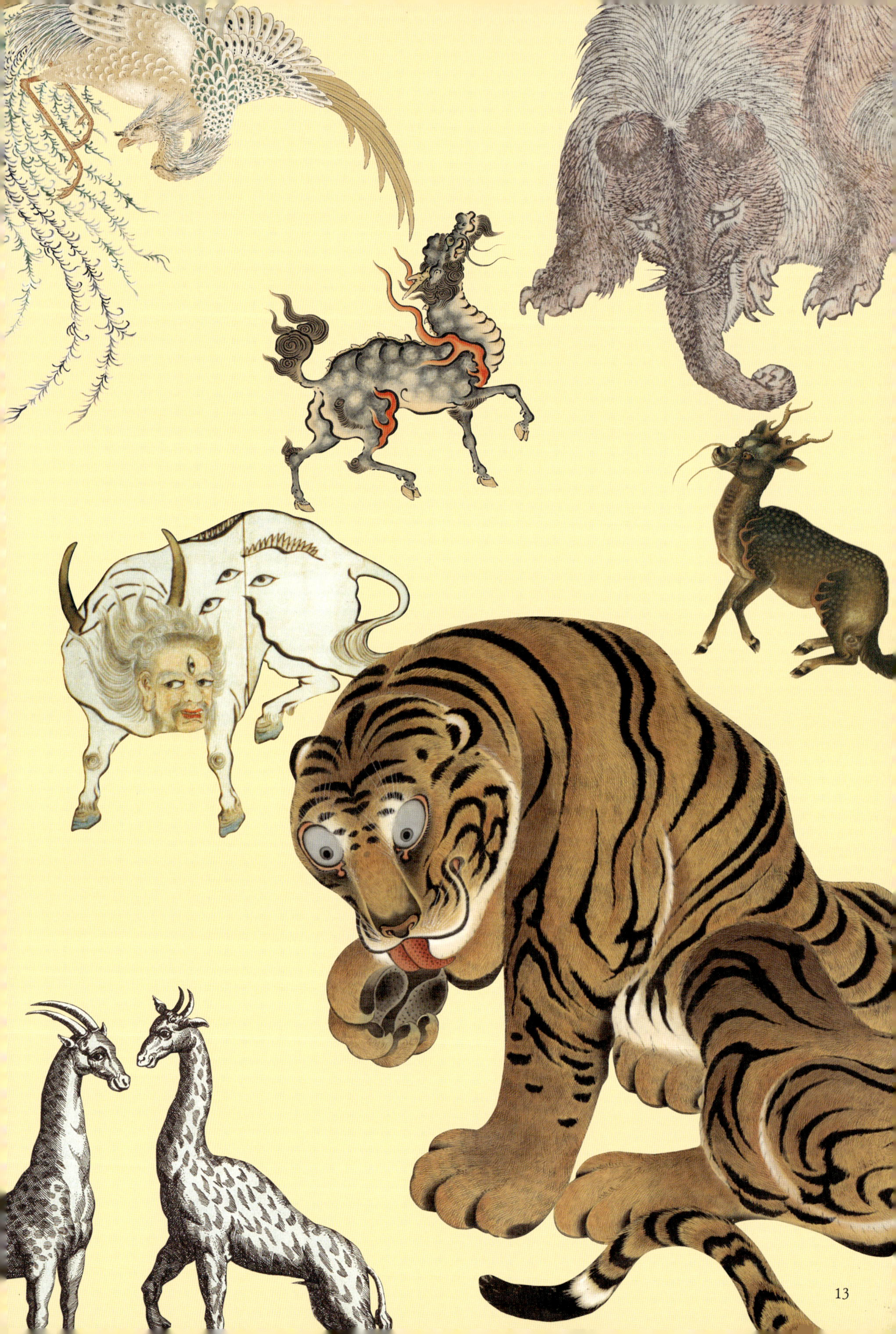

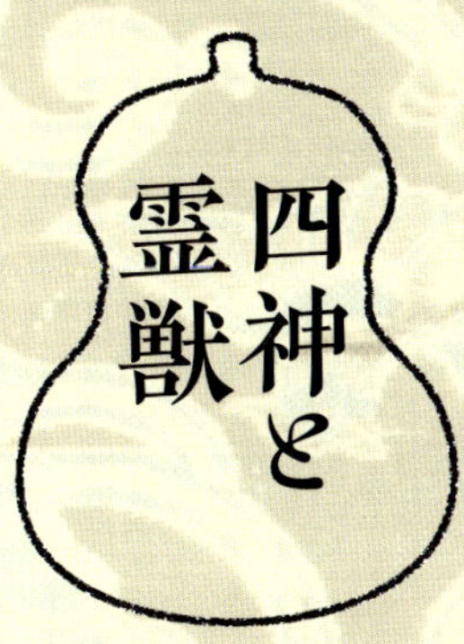

四神と霊獣

龍・鳳凰・麒麟・霊亀は、儒教(『礼記』)にもとづき「四霊」「四神」あるいは四大聖獣(神獣・瑞獣)などと称され、この世に存在するすべての動物たちの長として特別な力をもち、吉兆を知らせる神秘的な存在として位置づけられた。一方、中国神話のなかで四方を司る霊獣も四神と呼ばれ、東に青龍、南に朱雀、西に白虎、北に玄武が当てられるとともに、さらに五行説により中央に麒麟や黄龍を加えることもあった。

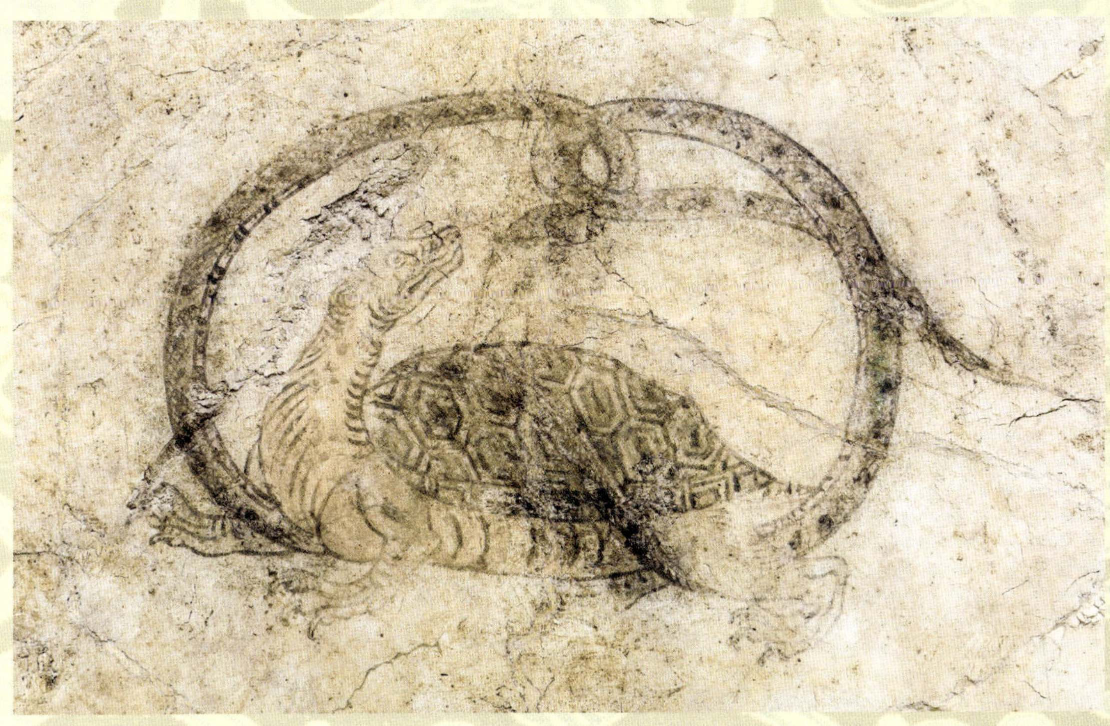

玄武　Genbu

The Four Guardians and the Sacred Beasts

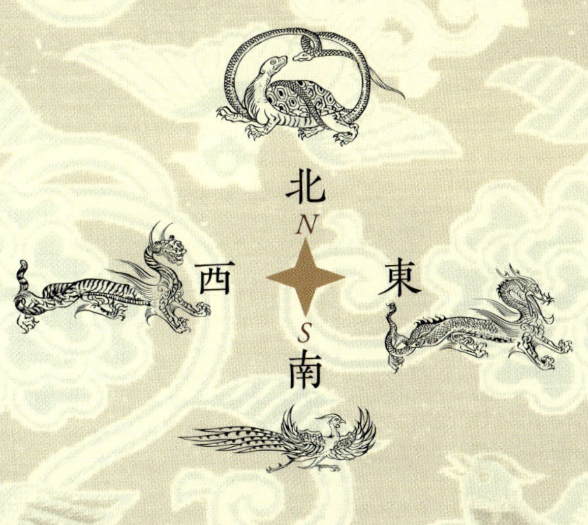

Based on Confucianism (especially the *Book of Rites*), the dragon, phoenix, *kirin*, and divine turtle are called the "Four Guardians," the "Four Holy Beasts," and "The Four Great Sacred Beasts." They have special powers as the lords of all the animals in the world, and are seen as mystical presences that foretell good fortune. Meanwhile, in Chinese myths, they are known as the Four Guardians or the Sacred Beasts that rule over the four cardinal directions. In addition to corresponding to the Azure Dragon in the East (J. Seiryū), the Vermillion Bird in the South (J. Suzaku), the White Tiger in the West (J. Byakko) and the Black Tortoise in the North (J. Genbu), sometimes a *kirin* or Yellow Dragon is added to the center in accordance with the *wuxing* Five Elements.

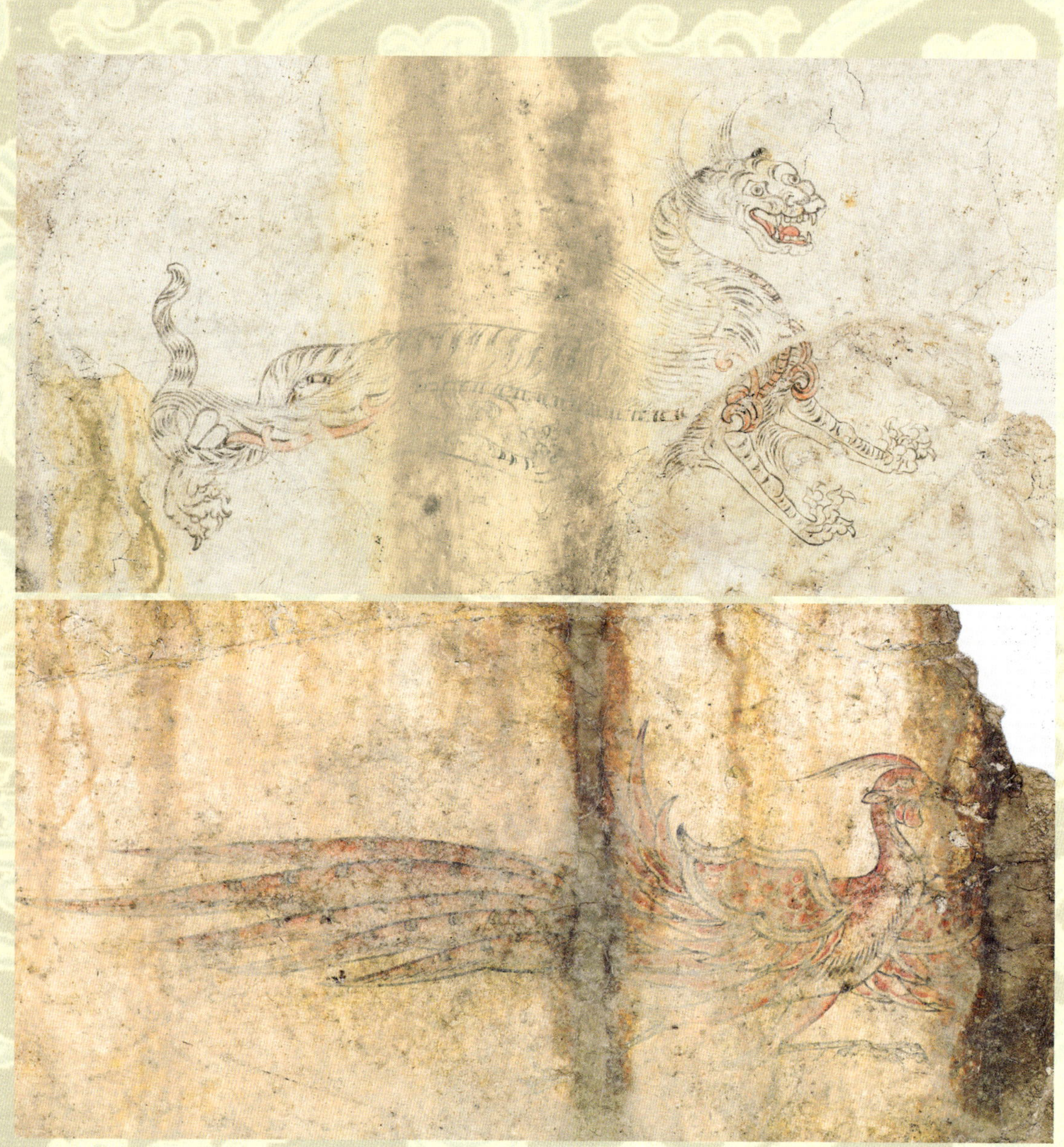

上：白虎 Byakko　下：朱雀 Suzaku

国宝

キトラ古墳壁画のうち朱雀・白虎・玄武

飛鳥時代(7c末～8c初頭)
国(文部科学省所管)

1983年に発見された円墳の石室を彩った壁画。高松塚古墳同様、四神(壁面)と太陽・月・星宿(天井)が描かれ、さらに四神の下には高松塚古墳になかった人身獣首の十二支像も加えられている。朱雀の脚の開きや白虎の流れる体毛にみる速度感、蛇と睨み合う耳付きの亀の緊張感が見事。

National Treasure

Suzaku, Byakko and Genbu from the Kitora Tomb Murals

Late 7th–early 8th century
Japan (Ministry of Education, Culture, Sports, Science and Technology)

This is a wall painting adorning the rock chamber of a burial mound discovered in 1983. Like the Takamatsuzuka Tomb, there are depictions of the Four Guardians (on the wall), as well as the sun, the moon, and the stars (on the ceiling). However, beneath the Four Guardians, there are also twelve zodiac figures with animal heads that do not appear in the Takamatsuzuka Tomb. Two high points of this work are the feeling of speed captured in the stretching of the Vermillion Bird's legs and the flowing of the White Tiger's fur, and the tension present in the way the tortoise with ears glares at the snake.

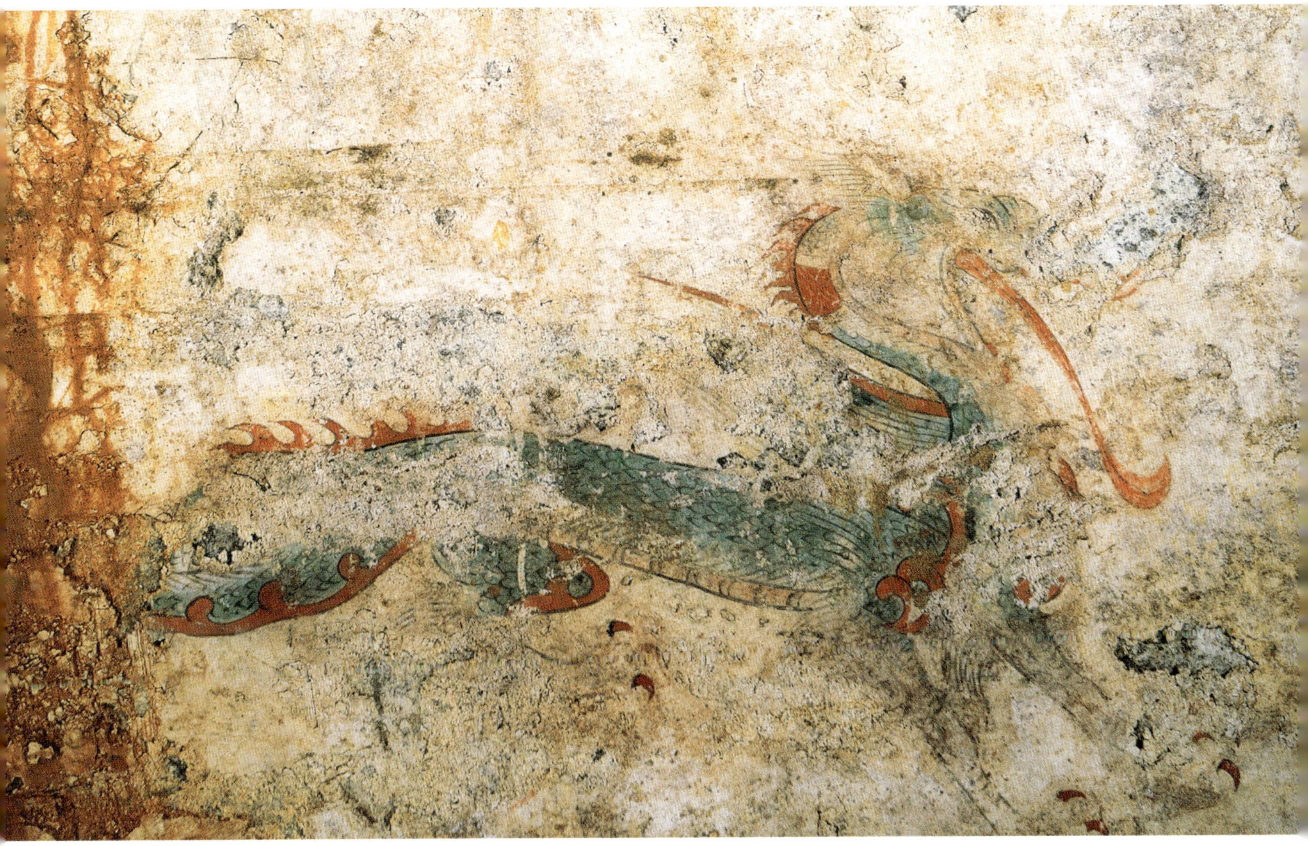

国宝

高松塚古墳壁画のうち青龍

飛鳥時代(8c初め)
国(文部科学省所管)

1972年に発見された古墳壁画のうち石室の東壁に、太陽とともに描かれた青龍。右脚(前後とも)の爪が3本、左脚は4本。この特徴はキトラ古墳や薬師寺金堂薬師如来坐像台座の白虎や青龍にもみられる。石室の壁面は、四神と太陽・月、男女の群像、天井北寄りには星宿図が描かれている。構成や群像表現には中国・唐代、8世紀初頭の墳墓壁画(陝西省の永泰公主墓706年、節愍太子墓710年)との親近性が認められる。壁画制作は、早くとも8世紀初め以降と考えられている。

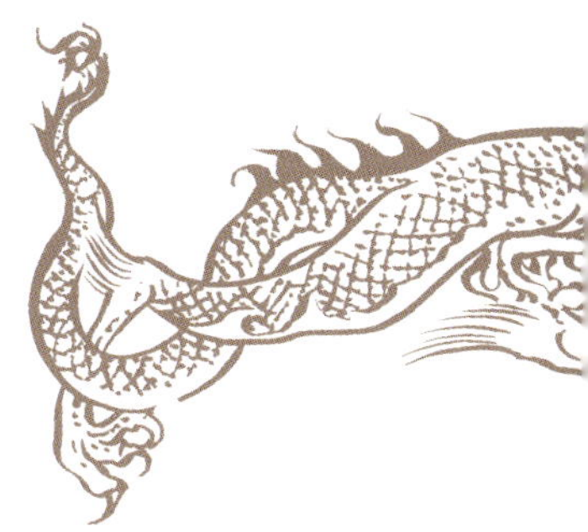

National Treasure

Seiryū from the Takamatsuzuka Tomb Murals

Early 8th century
Japan (Ministry of Education, Culture, Sports, Science and Technology)

This is a portrayal of the Azure Dragon with the sun that was painted on the eastern wall of the rock chamber of a burial mound discovered in 1972. His right feet (front and back) have three talons, while his left ones have four. This feature is also seen in the White Tiger and Azure Dragon from the Kitora Tomb murals and the pedestal of the seated Bhaisajyaguru in the main hall of Yakushiji. The wall paintings depict the Four Guardians, the sun, the moon, and a group of people; on the north side of the ceiling there is a painting of constellations. We can see the similarity with early eighth-century Tang dynasty tomb murals (e.g. the 706 grave of Princess Yongtai in Shaanxi and the 710 grave of Li Chongjun) in the depiction of the crowd, and the composition as a whole. It is thought that these murals were done in the beginning of the eighth century at the earliest.

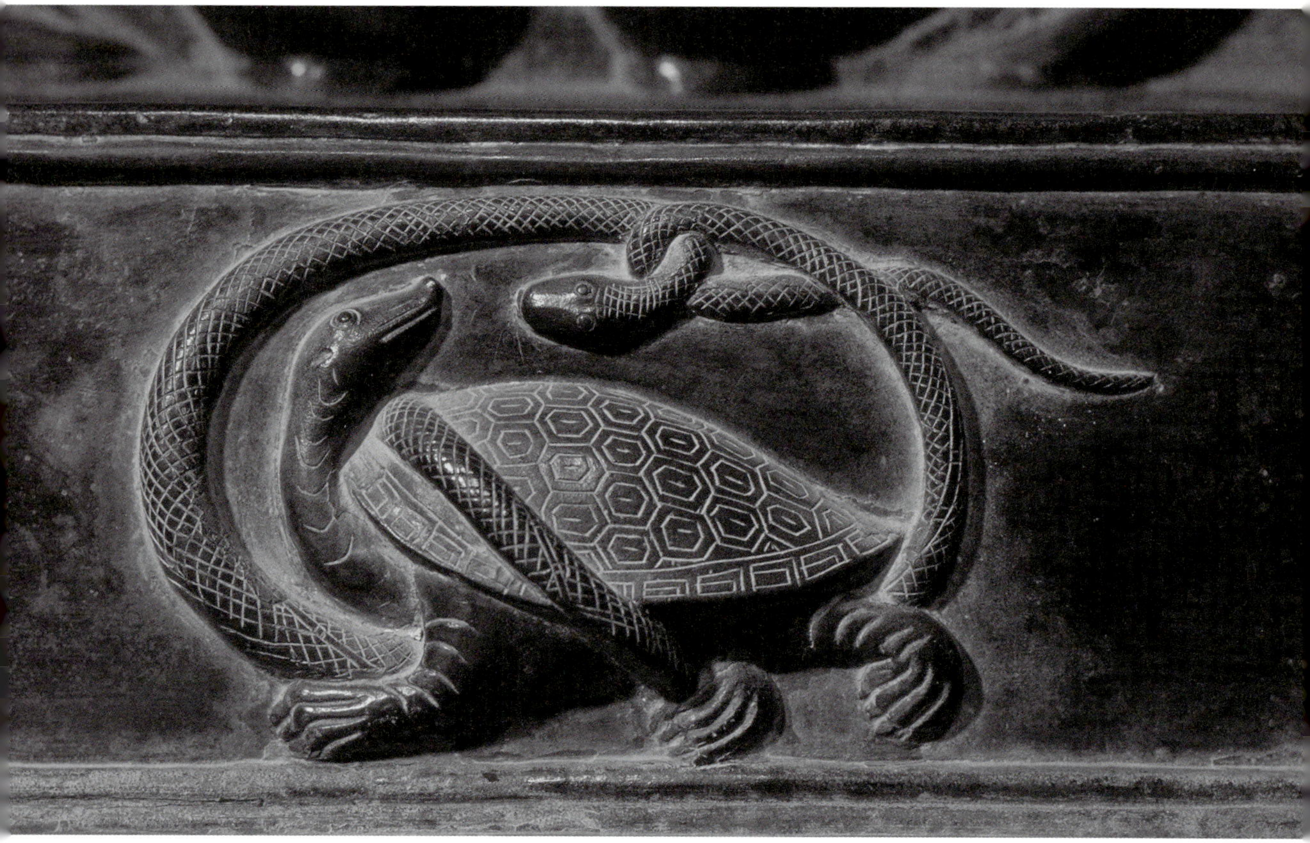

国宝

薬師寺金堂薬師如来坐像台座

白鳳時代（7c末〜8c初頭）
奈良・薬師寺

薬師寺の本尊、薬師如来の台座にも四神が表され、高松塚古墳やキトラ古墳の壁画の図像と類似している。玄武の図像は、中国・前漢時代にも遡り、南朝の影響を受けて多様な図案が北朝で登場し、隋・唐では様式化されていく。朝鮮半島でも、高句麗や百済などに玄武を含む四神の図像が伝わっている。

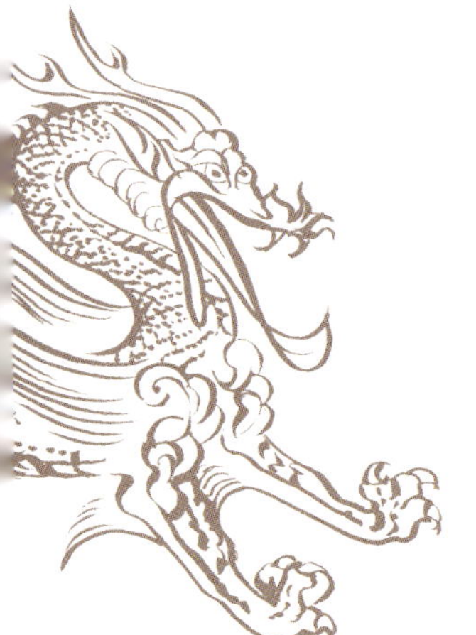

National Treasure

Pedestal of the Seated Bhaisajyaguru (J. Yakushi Nyorai) in the Main Hall of Yakushiji

Late 7th–early 8th century
Yakushiji, Nara

The Four Guardians are also depicted on the pedestal of Bhaisajyaguru, the main image of veneration at Yakushiji, and their portrayal is similar to that of the wall paintings in the Takamatsuzuka and Kitora Tombs. Images of the Black Tortoise go back as far as the Western Han dynasty in China, and due to influence from the Southern court, various depictions appear in the Northern court. By the Sui and Tang dynasties, depictions of the Black Tortoise come to be even more diversified. Images of the Four Guardians, including the Black Tortoise, spread as far as the kingdoms of the Korean peninsula, such as the Goguryeo and Baekje.

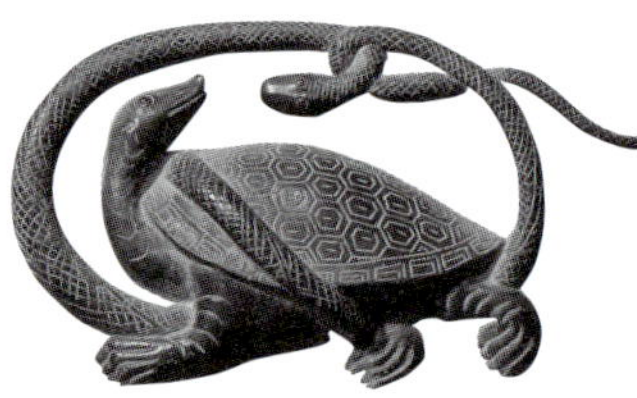

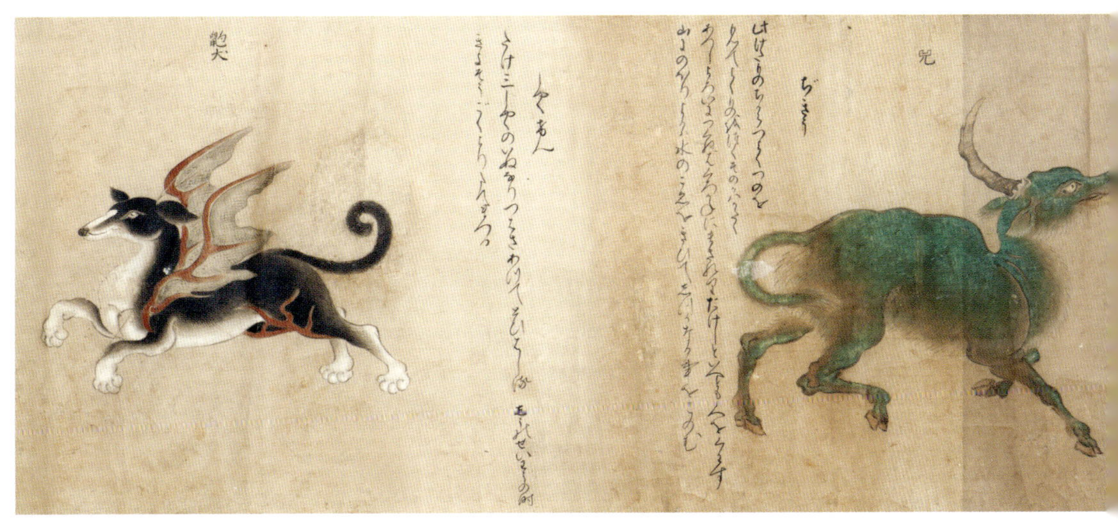

十二霊獣図巻（部分）

室町時代（16c）
静嘉堂文庫美術館

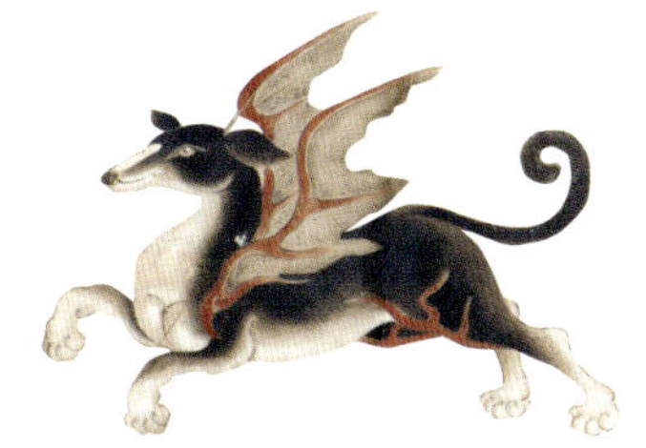

災いを除き、祥瑞（めでたい前兆）をもたらす中国伝来の12種の霊獣を図示したもの。描かれたすべての霊獣は、1607年（明・万暦35）に刊行された『三才図会』にその図様が掲載されている。作風から、中国の原本をもとに室町時代末期に模されたと考えられる。旧蔵者・田中秀相による1703年（元禄16）の跋文によれば、山城長岡藩主（のち摂津高槻藩主）永井直清（1591～1671）から、重臣の田中勝次（秀相の父）に下賜され、邪鬼を払うため子の秀相の部屋の屏風に貼付、後に巻子に改装された。中国での辟邪としての用法を日本でも踏襲していたことがうかがえ、霊獣図の受容の仕方を教えてくれる貴重な史料と言える。

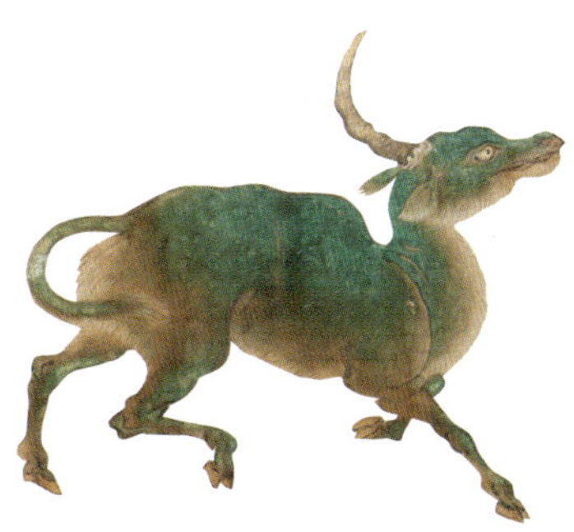

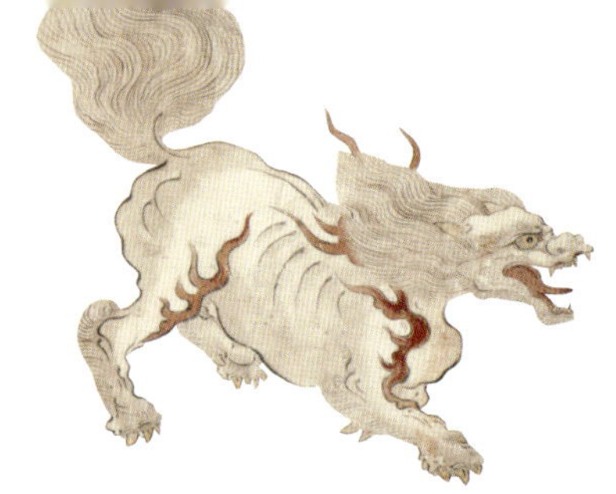

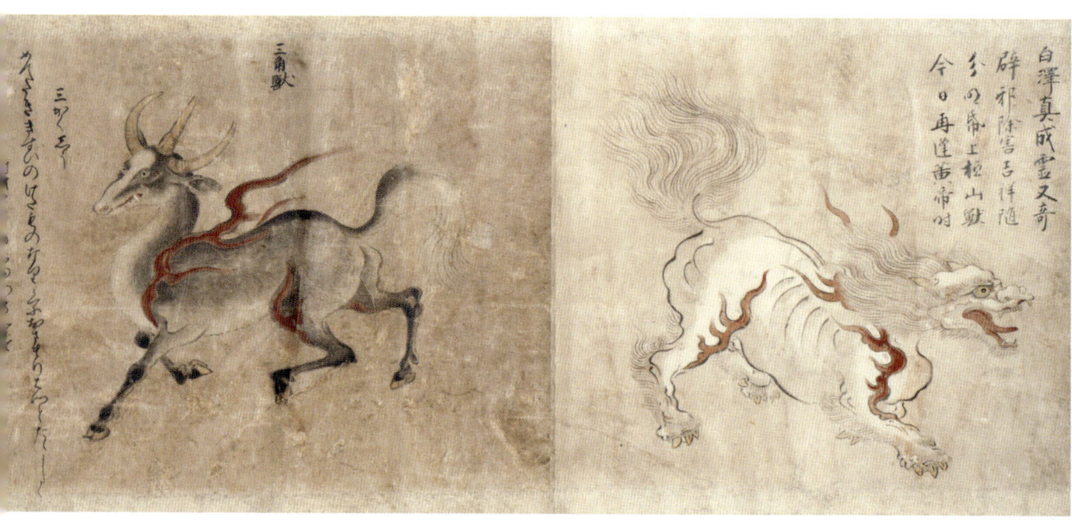

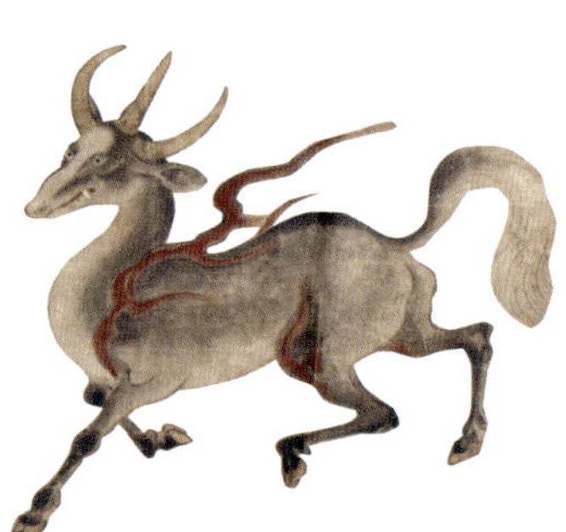

Twelve Sacred Beasts Handscroll (*detail*)

16th century
Seikadō Bunko Art Museum

This is a diagram of the twelve types of sacred beasts from China that bring good fortune and ward off disaster. All of the sacred beasts shown here were also depicted in the *Sancai Tuhui* (*Collected Illustrations of the Three Realms*) published in 1607 (Ming dynasty, Wanli 35). The style of this work suggests that it was copied from a Chinese original during the late Muromachi period. According to the 1703 (Genroku 16) postscript by the previous owner Tanaka Hidesuke, this work was a gift from Nagai Naokiyo (1591-1671), the daimyo of Nagaoka, Yamashiro (later the daimyo of Takatsuki, Settsu), to his chief vassal Tanaka Katsuji (Hidesuke's father). The images were pasted to a folding screen in young Hidesuke's room to drive away evil spirits, but were later remounted as a single handscroll. We can surmise that the Chinese use of these images as a means to banish evil spirits was continued in Japan, and this work can be seen as a valuable document that informs us about the reception of sacred beast images.

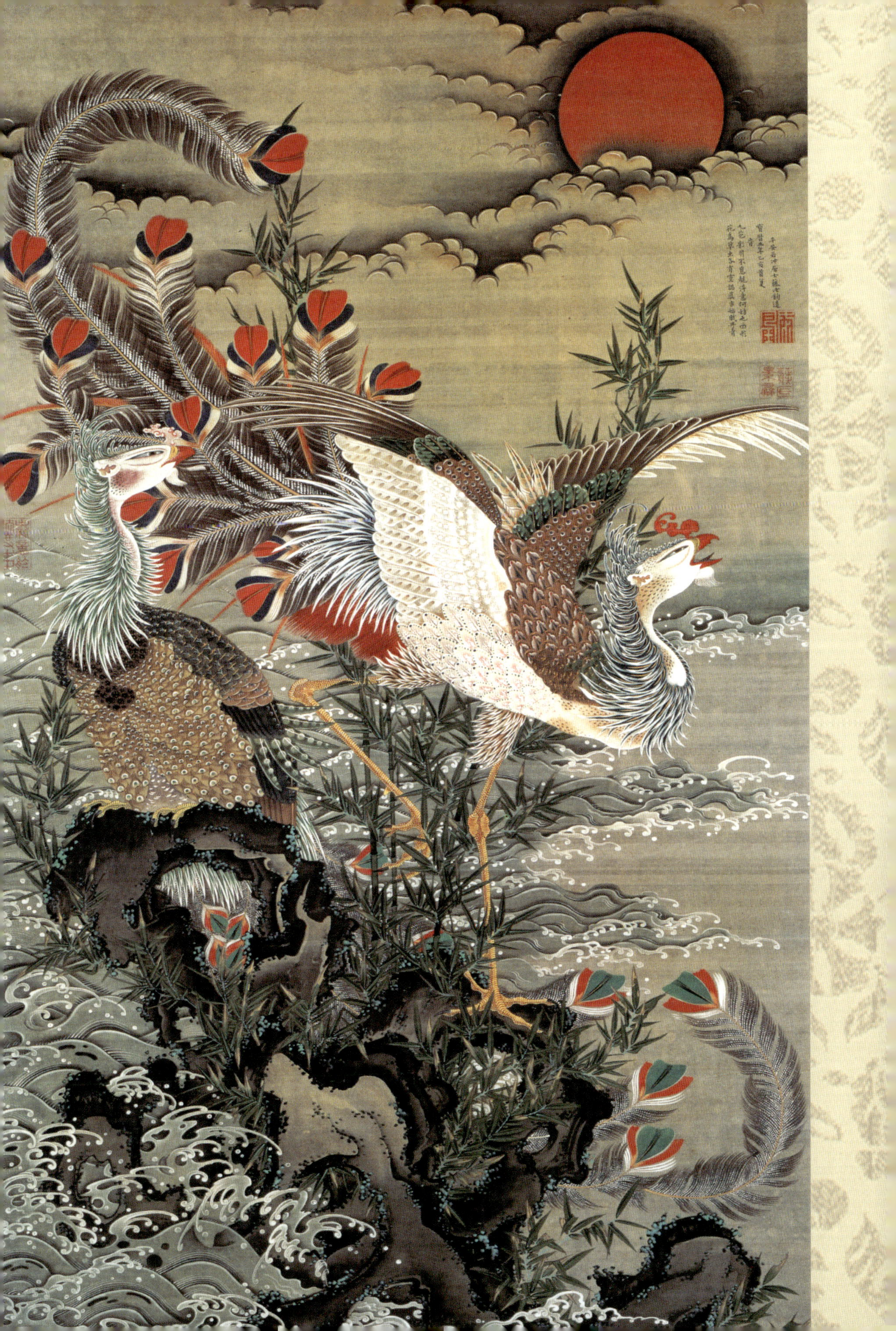

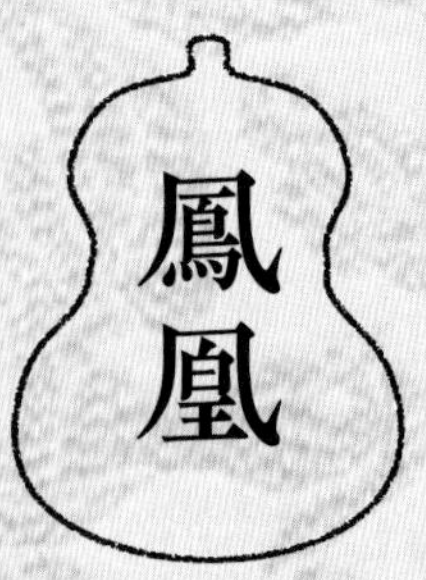

鳳凰

古代の中国思想に由来する瑞鳥で、羽蟲（鳥のように羽をもつ動物）360種の長である。雄を鳳、雌を凰という。南方に産する朱鳥で、朱雀と同じものとされる。前（半身）は鴻、後（半身）は麒（麒麟）、頷は燕、喙は鶏、頸は蛇、尾は魚、顙（額）は鸛、顋（あご）は鴛、文様は龍、背は亀に似たもので、羽には五彩を備え、高さは四、五尺あり、四海を飛びかけり、天下に道徳が行き渡っていれば姿を見せる。また生虫を啄まず、生草を折らず、という。「仁鳥」とされるゆえんであろう。梧桐（青桐）でなければ棲まず、竹の実以外は食べず、醴泉以外は飲まぬという。これを踏まえ、装飾彫刻や絵画などにおいて、桐や竹とともに表現される。日本には飛鳥時代に仏教とともに伝来したと伝えられる。鳳凰が出現する時、世に聖徳を持った天子が現れ、天下に泰平がもたらされると信じられた。

The Phoenix

This an auspicious bird that comes from ancient Chinese thought, and it is seen as the most excellent of all three hundred and sixty types of winged creatures. The male is called the *feng*, and the female is called the *huang*. The Red Bird, born in the South, is considered to be the same as Suzaku. The top half of the body is that of a large wild goose, and the bottom half is that of a *kirin*; the lower jaw is that of a swallow; the beak is that of a chicken; the neck is that of a snake; the tail is that of a fish; the forehead is that of a stork; the chin is that of a male mandarin duck; the pattern is that of a dragon; the back is like that of a turtle. The wings are made up of five colors, and its height is approximately four or five *shaku* (121cm to 151 cm); it flies across the seven seas, and it will appear if virtue prevails across the realm. Also, it is said that it will not eat living bugs or disturb any plant life – this is probably the reason that it is known as a “virtuous bird.” It is also said that the phoenix will only nest in Chinese parasol trees, will only eat bamboo fruit, and will only drink pure spring water. As a result, the phoenix is portrayed alongside paulownia or bamboo in decorative sculptures, paintings, and the like. These notions are thought to have reached Japan along with Buddhism in the Asuka period. It was also believed that a phoenix would appear during the reign of a virtuous ruler and there would be peace on earth.

旭日鳳凰図

伊藤若冲
江戸時代後期(18c)
宮内庁三の丸尚蔵館

旭日を背景に、波の打ち寄せる浜辺の岩上に雌雄の鳳凰がたたずむ。誠に豪華な祝祭の空間である。若冲40歳、「虎図」(p.69)と同年同月に描かれた作品だが、「虎図」で披瀝した自らの写生に対する態度は、鳳凰においてはどうだったのだろうか。

Phoenixes and Rising Sun

Itō Jakuchū
18th century
Sannomaru Shozokan
(The Museum of the Imperial Collections)

Against the background of a rising sun, male and female phoenixes perch on coastal rocks nestled against crashing waves. This is a truly luxurious festive space. This work was painted the same month as *Tiger* (p.69), done when Jakuchū was forty years old, but is his attitude regarding sketching from nature present in these phoenixes the way it is in *Tiger*?

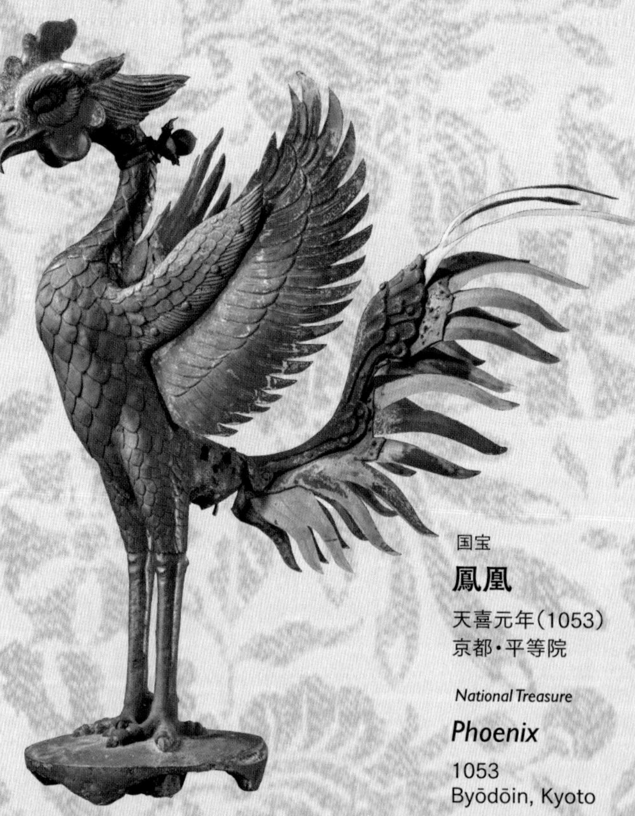

国宝
鳳凰
天喜元年(1053)
京都・平等院

National Treasure
Phoenix
1053
Byōdōin, Kyoto

八方睨み鳳凰図
（天井画）

葛飾北斎
嘉永元年（1848）頃
長野・岩松院

岩松院は、南北朝時代からの歴史をもつ古刹。現本堂は、1815年（文化12）に焼失後、1831年（天保2）に再建された。80代の老境を迎えた葛飾北斎（1760～1849）は、信州小布施の豪商で門人でもあった高井鴻山（1806～83）の招きで同地を訪れ、祭屋台の天井画などを制作した。1847年（弘化4）から翌年にかけ、鴻山の菩提寺でもあった岩松院本堂に、21畳分の大きさの天井画を見事に描ききった。北斎最晩年に手がけた畢生の大作であった。

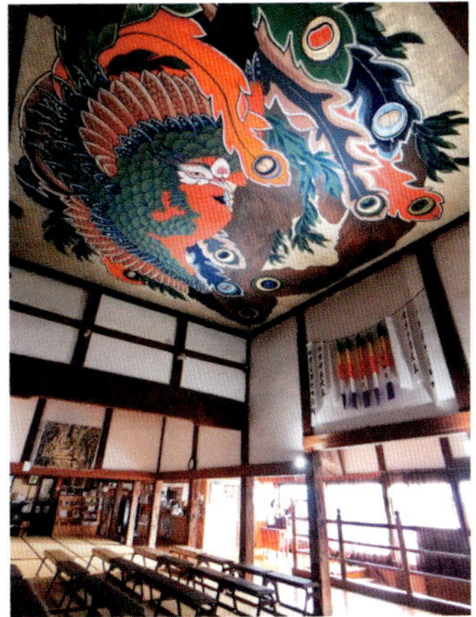

堂内　interior

Phoenix (*Ceiling Painting*)

Katsushika Hokusai
ca. 1848
Ganshōin, Nagano

Ganshōin is an ancient temple with a history that dates back to the Nanbokuchō period. The current main hall is an 1831 (Tenpō 2) rebuild, after the previous structure was lost in a fire in 1815 (Bunka 12). In 1847 (Kōka 4), Katsushika Hokusai (1760-1849), already an old man in his eighties, was invited to Obuse, Shinano by Takai Kōzan (1806-83), a wealthy local merchant who was also a student of Hokusai. For the next year, Hokusai produced works such as decorative ceiling paintings for the insides of festival floats, but in the main hall of Ganshōin, which was also Kōzan's family temple, Hokusai painted this exquisite ceiling mural that covered an expanse of twenty-one tatami mats. This is one of the great masterpieces of Hokusai's life.

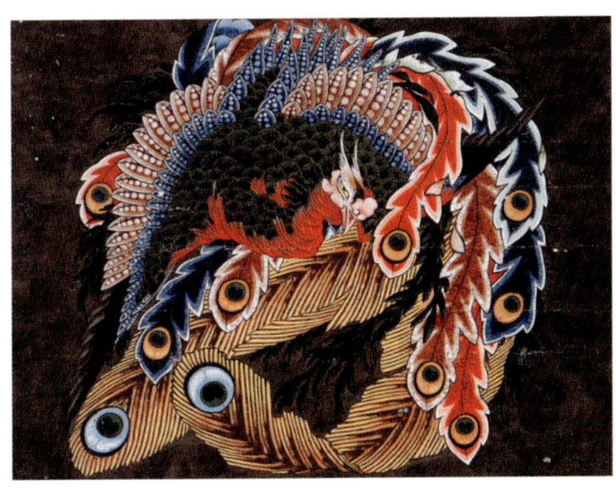

下図　sketch

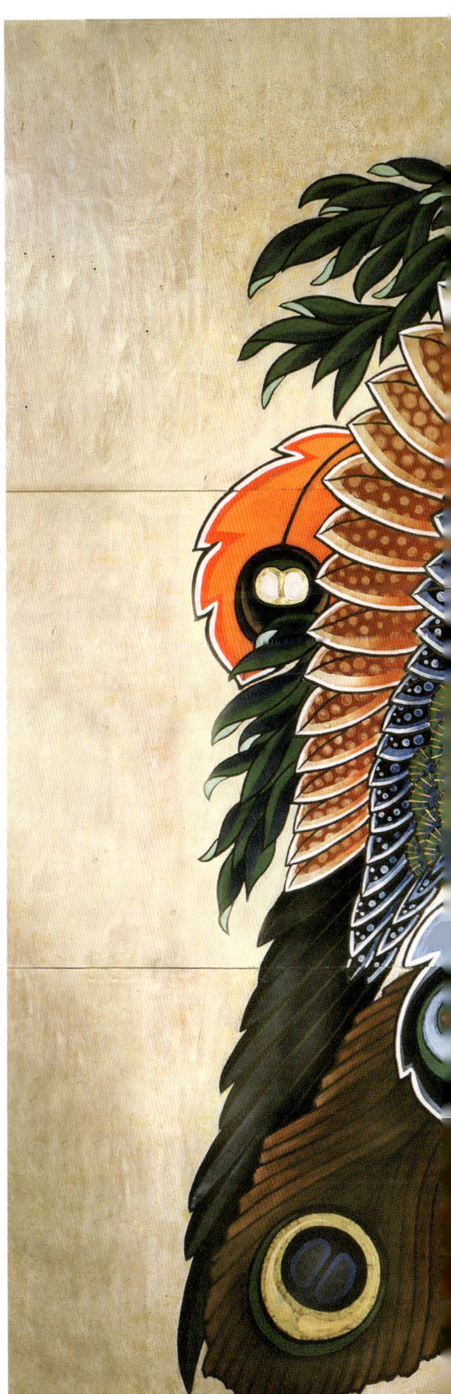

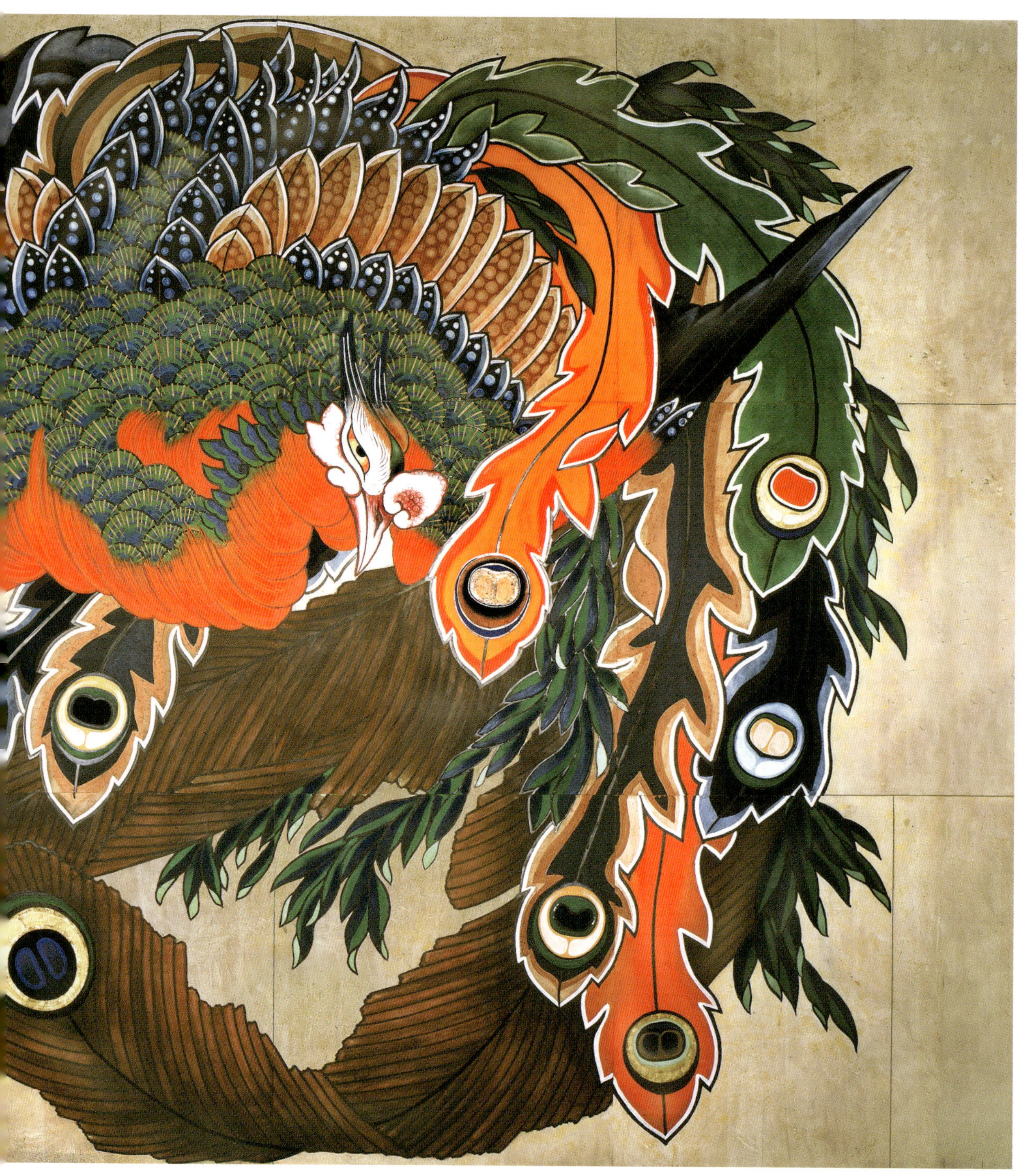

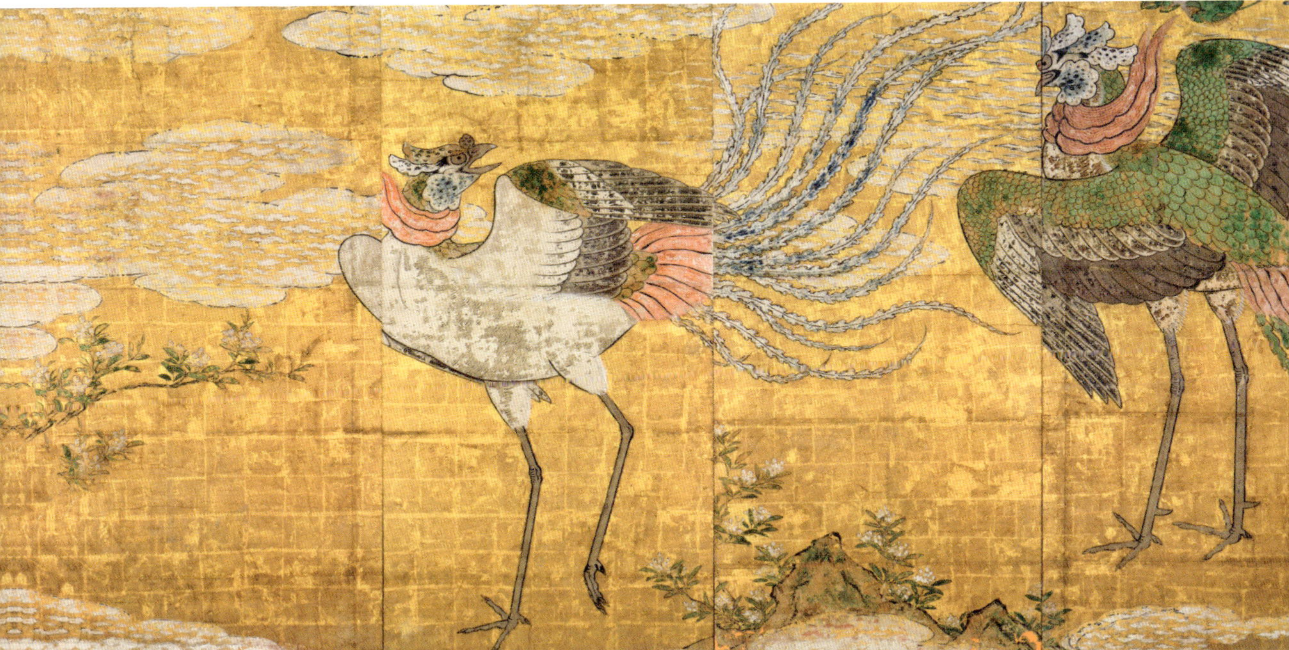

県指定文化財

鳳凰図屏風

狩野左京
慶長15年(1610)
宮城・松島町

この絵は現在屏風に改装されているが、もとは仙台城本丸大広間・上段の間の床貼付絵だったと考えられる。上段は、藩主が坐すための一段高くなった空間で、その前方に家臣などが控え謁見が行われた。すぐれた為政者の治世に出現するとされる瑞鳥の図は仙台藩主・伊達政宗(1567～1636)の背後を飾るにふさわしい画題であったと言える。実際の画面は上下左右にさらに展開していたはずで、その大きさが想像される。

Prefectural Cultural Property

Phoenixes Folding Screen

Kano Sakyō
1610
Matsushima-chō, Miyagi

This painting was remounted into its current state as a folding screen, but it is thought that this work was originally affixed to the alcove behind the raised reception hall of the inner bailey of Sendai Castle. The raised floor of the reception hall was an elevated space for the feudal lord to face his vassals when he granted them an audience as they sat below. You could say that this auspicious bird that appears during the reign of an outstanding statesman was a fitting subject for a painting that would decorate the space behind the lord of Yamashiro, Date Masamune (1567-1636). The actual dimensions of the image would have been even bigger on all sides, and we can imagine the magnitude of such an image.

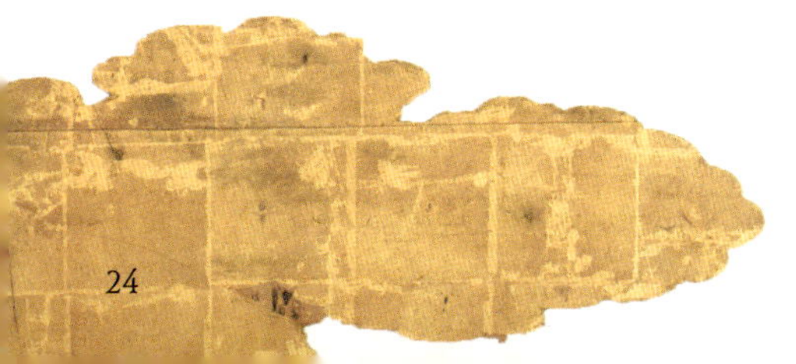

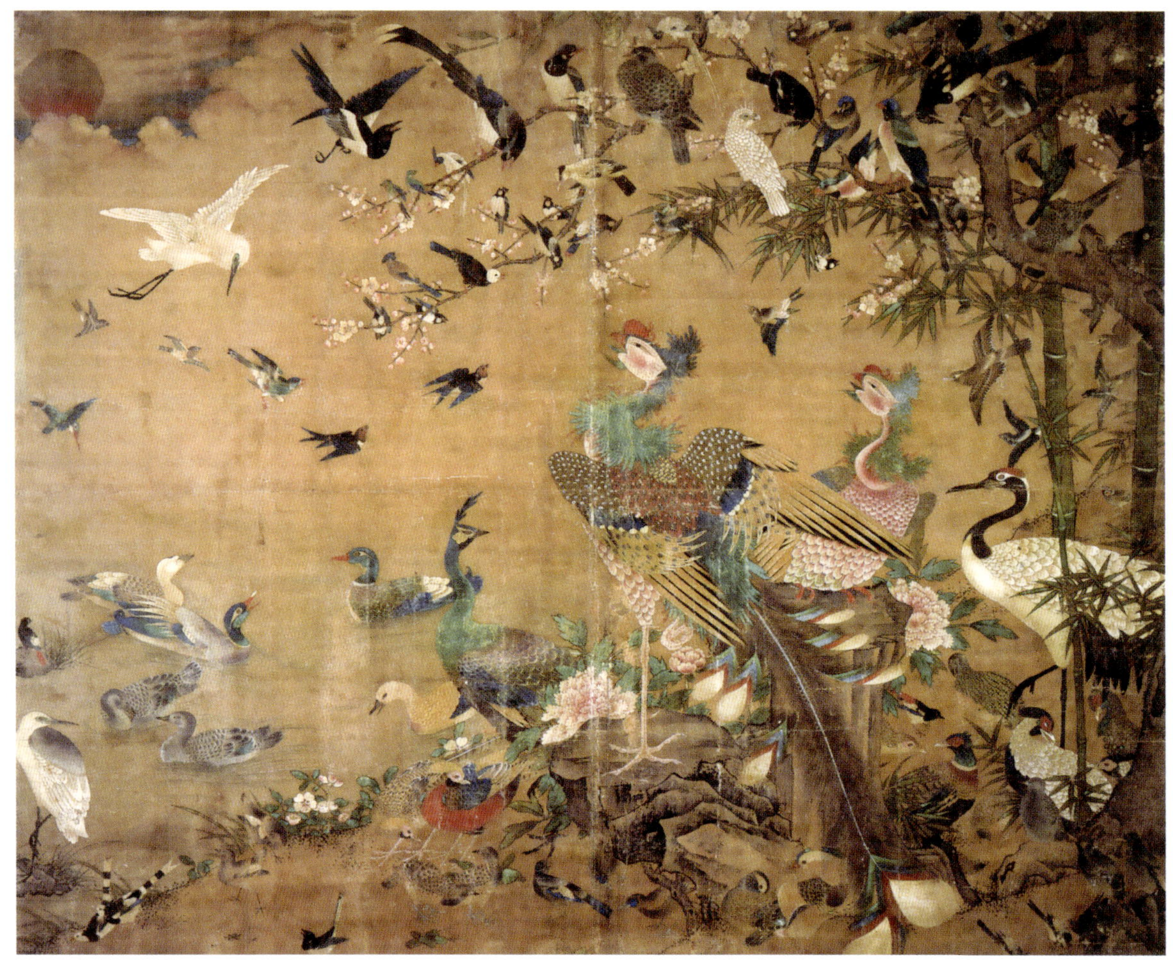

百鳥図

伝・銭選
中国・明時代(16c)
宮内庁三の丸尚蔵館

銭選(生没年不詳)は、宋末・元初に活躍した呉興(浙江省)出身の画人。字は舜挙。花鳥・山水を得意とし、わが国では南宋院体画風の写実的な花鳥画がもてはやされ伝承作も多い。本図は明時代の作で、旭日を見上げる雌雄の鳳凰を中心に、おびただしい鳥たちが画面を埋め尽くす。この種の図様は日本でも踏襲され、大名家の注文などにより狩野派画家を中心に多くの作例が残された。

Hundred Birds

Attributed to Qian Xuan
Ming dynasty, 16th century
Sannomaru Shozokan
(The Museum of the Imperial Collections)

Qian Xuan (dates unknown) was a painter from Wuxing (Zhejiang Province) who was active during the late Song and early Yuan dynasties. He was also known as Shunju. He was skilled at bird-and-flower paintings as well as landscapes, and in Japan there are many extant works influenced by the realistic bird-and-flower paintings of the Southern Song academic style. This work is from the Ming dynasty, and depicts a central pair of male and female phoenixes looking up at a rising sun as innumerable birds swarm the picture plane around them. This type of image was adopted by Japanese painters, especially from the Kano school, and many of the works that they produced for patrons such as daimyo are still extant.

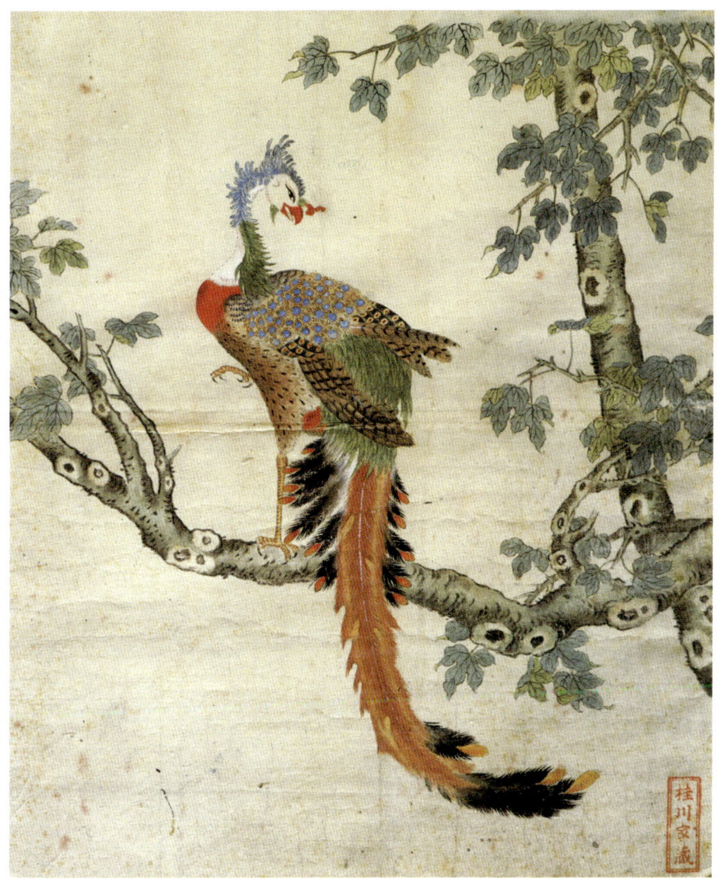

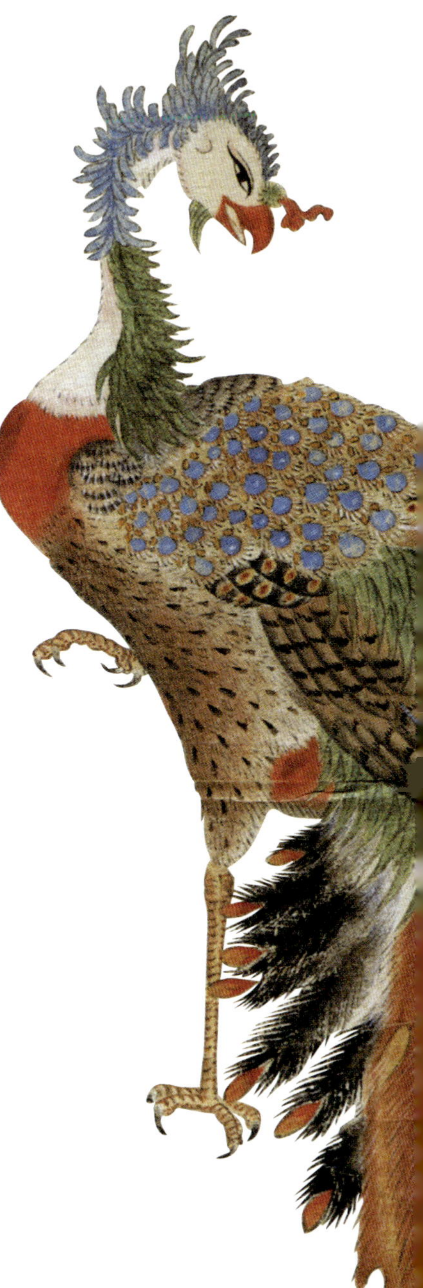

百鳥画冊

江戸時代後期(18c末〜19c前半)
ベルリン州立図書館

幕府奥医師でわが国の蘭学界を牽引した桂川家の旧蔵。原本は清の康熙帝(1654〜1722)の命で、余曽三が100種の鳥を描いたもの。1737年(元文2)に伝来し、「百鳥図」とも呼ばれ中国産鳥類図鑑として珍重された。伝本が少なく、中国には残存しないらしい。1836年(天保7)幕府の内庫に蔵されていたものを、尾張藩が藩絵師・神谷晴真と楠本雪渓(宋紫岡)に命じて写させた同図様の5巻本がある(徳川美術館蔵)。

Hundred Birds Booklet

Late 18th century–early 19th century
The Berlin State Library

This was formerly in the possession of the Katsura clan, shogunal doctors who opened up the world of Western studies to Japan. The original was produced during the lifetime of the Qing dynasty Kangxi Emperor (1654-1722), and was a depiction of a hundred types of birds by Yu Zhusan. Passed down in 1737 (Genbun 2), and also known as *The Hundred Birds*, it was prized as a Chinese manual for painting birds. There were not many copies to begin with, and it seems that there are no surviving copies in China at all. There is a version comprising five scrolls (Tokugawa Art Museum) that was a copy of one of these bird manuals in the possession of the shogunate, made by regional painters Kamiya Harumasa and Kusumoto Sekkei (Sō Shikō) under the orders of the Owari Domain in 1836 (Tenpō 7).

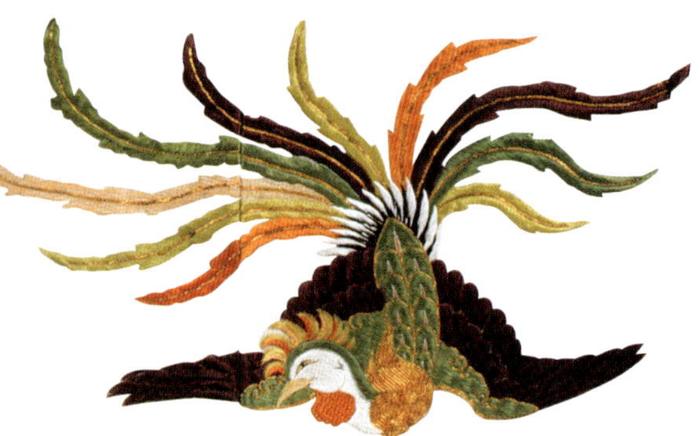

白麻地桐鳳凰文帷子

江戸時代（19c）
東京国立博物館

若い武家女性の夏の衣装。上質の麻布に描絵と刺繍、摺匹田（鹿の子絞りの模様を型紙で簡易に摺り出す方法）で模様を表わす。鳳凰は中国の伝説上の瑞鳥だが、吉祥文様として日本でも好まれた。

Katabira (Unlined Summer Kimono) with Phoenixes and Paulownia

19th century
Tokyo National Museum

This is a summer garment for a young lady from the warrior class. The composition is a mix of painting and embroidery, as well as stenciled "fawn spots" (a simple method of stenciling a fawn spot pattern onto fabric using paper) on fine quality linen. The phoenix is an auspicious bird from Chinese legend, but it was also enjoyed in Japan as a lucky visual motif.

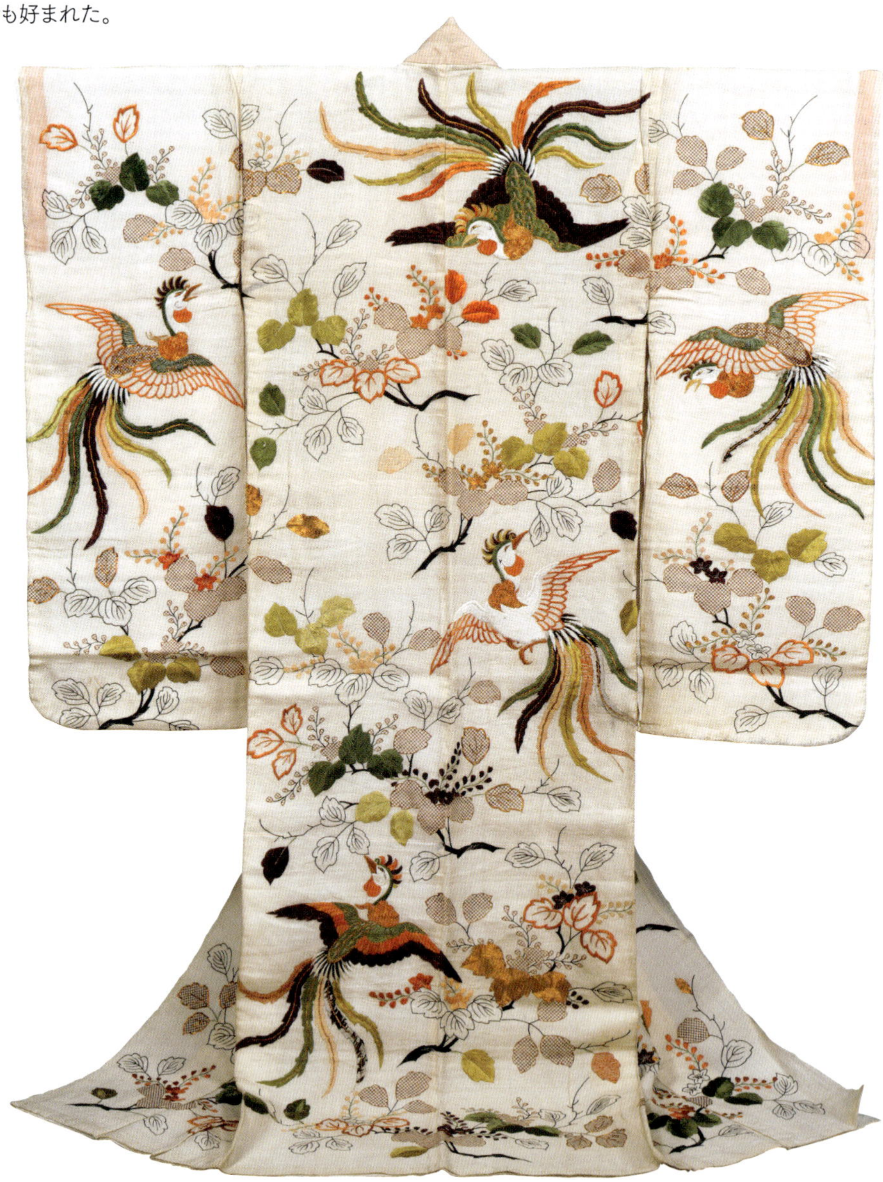

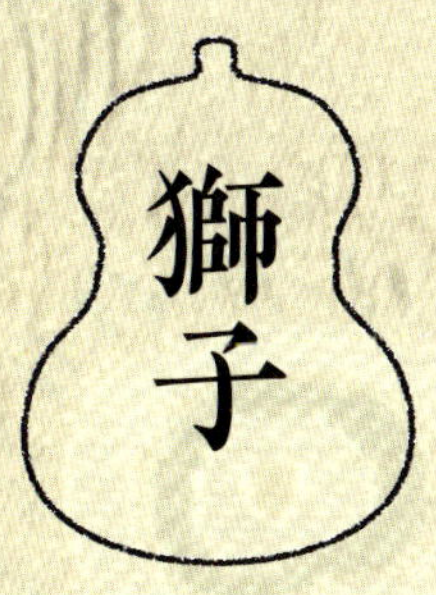

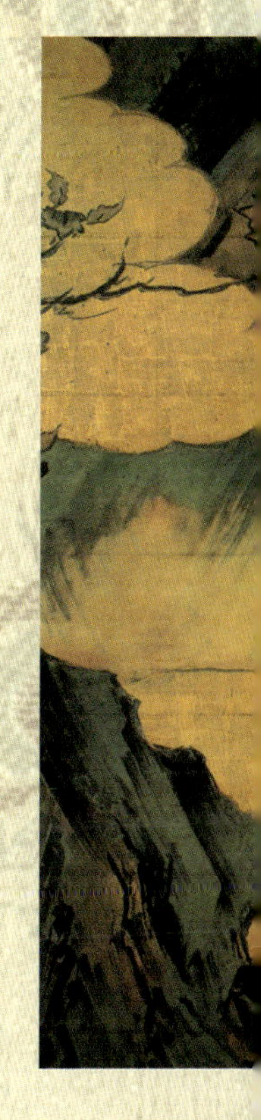

古代オリエント世界からインド経由で伝わったライオンのイメージにもとづき、古代中国で形成された想像上の瑞獣。生身のライオンは、87年（章和元）安息国（イラン高原のパルティア王国とされる）から献上された記録（『後漢書』西域伝）が最古というが、存在自体は前漢時代から知られたようだ。明時代の百科事典『本草綱目』によれば、別名を狻猊（さんげい）といい、百獣の長で西域に生息し、虎のようだが小さく黄色で、金色の猱狗（むくいぬ）のようでもあるが、頭が大きく尾が長い。青色のものもある。銅の頭、鉄の額、鉤の爪、鋸の牙、垂れた耳、盛り上がった鼻をもち、目の光は電（いなずま）、吼える声は雷のようである。頬ひげがあり、牡には尾の先に一斗升ほどの大きな茸毛（綿毛）があって、一日に五百里を走ることができる。毛蟲（獣のこと）の長で、一吼えすれば百獣はたじろぎ、馬は血尿を流す。虎をとり、豹を呑み、犀を裂き、象を真二つにする。その毛を牛馬や羊の乳中に入れるとみな水と化する、などとある。ライオンに関する虚実混在の情報をもとに形成されたイメージのようだ。仏教の伝来とともに神聖さを増し、仏法を守護する瑞獣として尊崇され、さらに邪を避ける（辟邪）役割を担う守護獣、さらには福を招き子孫繁栄をもたらす吉祥の意味も加えられた。釈迦の臨終の様子を描いた涅槃図には白象と対のように描かれ、寺社に施された建築彫刻や障壁画などの絵画作品でも馴染み深いものとなっていった。

The Lion

This is an imaginary auspicious beast that was created in ancient China based on the impression of lions that had been passed onto them from the world of the ancient Near East via India. Regarding flesh and blood lions being brought to China, it is thought that the oldest record we have is the account (from *Hon Hanshu*, or the *Book of the Later Han*; J. *Gokanjo*) of lions being gifted by Ānxī (the Parthian Empire of the Iranian Plateau) in 87 CE (Zhanghe 1). However, it seems that the Chinese had known of the existence of lions since the Western Han dynasty. According to the *Bencao gangmu* (*Compendium of Materia Medica*), another name for the lion is the *suan ni*, and it is the king of beasts. Inhabiting the Western regions of China, the body is like that of a tiger, but it is smaller and yellow; it is also like a golden shaggy dog, but it has a large head and a long tail. There are also blue lions. It has a head like copper, a brow like iron, claws like hooks, fangs like saws, drooping ears, and a protruding nose; the light in its eyes is like a lightning bolt, and its roar is like a clap of thunder. It has whiskers, and the male of the species has a large tuft at the tip of its tail that is one *to* in size, and it can run five hundred *li* in a single day. The lion is chief among the furry beasts, and if it lets out a single roar, all kinds of animals will recoil in fear, and horses will shed bloody urine. It will catch a tiger, overwhelm a leopard, rip open a rhinoceros, and tear an elephant right in half. If you put its fur in the milk of horses, cattle or sheep, everything will turn to water. These are the kinds of descriptions in the text. It seems that the image of lions that they came up with was based on a mixture of fact and fiction. The religious prestige of the lion increased along with the introduction of Buddhism, and it was venerated as an auspicious beast that was also a protector of the faith. Moreover, it later came to be seen as a guardian beast who warded off evil, as well as an auspicious beast that invited good fortune and brought about the perpetuation of one's descendants. In "Nirvana of the Historical Buddha" paintings depicting the death of Shakyamuni (J. Shaka), a lion is portrayed as being paired with a white elephant; lions also became extremely common in paintings like those on the wall partitions and architectural decorations added to temples and shrines.

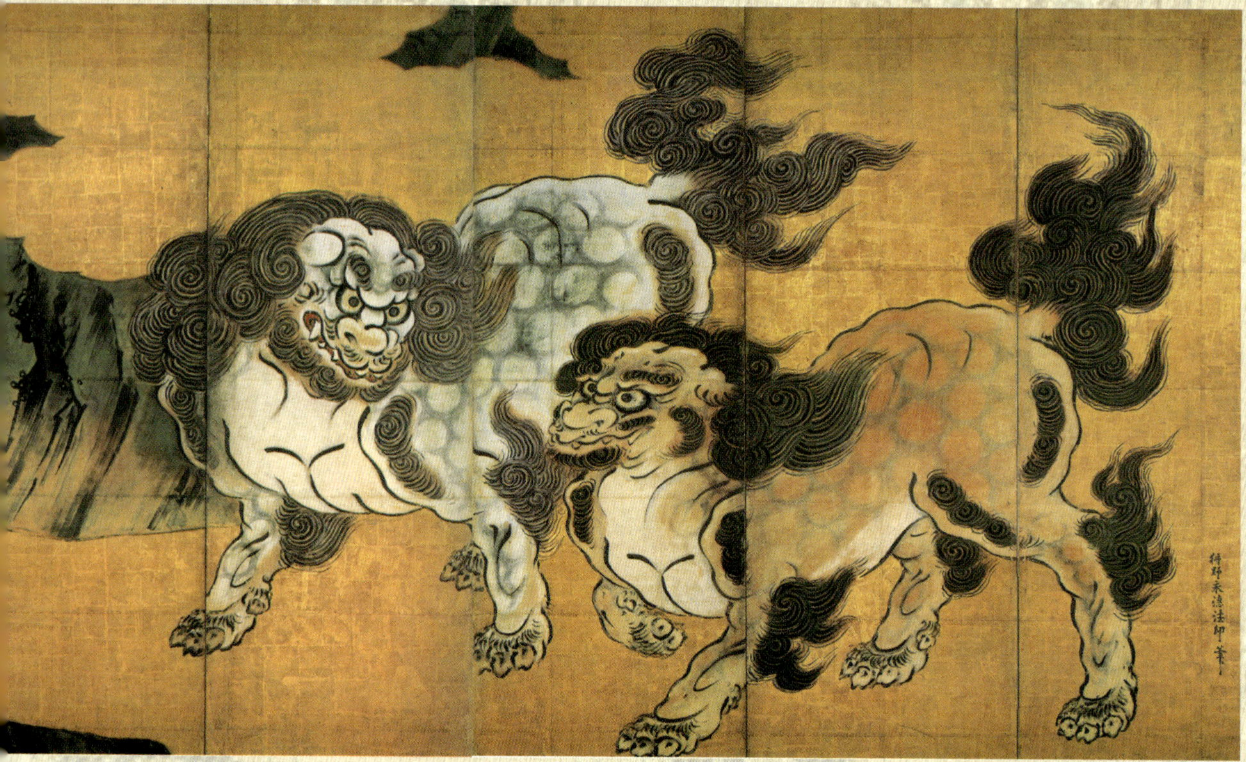

唐獅子図屏風

狩野永徳
桃山時代(16c)
宮内庁三の丸尚蔵館

長州毛利家に伝来した本作は豊臣秀吉が講和の記念に贈った陣屋屏風の伝承がある一方、当初の画面は上下左右に展開していたことは確実で、その破格の大きさと圧倒的な迫力から、聚楽第などの城郭御殿の床貼付だった可能性も指摘されている。2頭の獅子は雌雄ではなく親子と見る説もあり、王権の継承を寓意するものとなる。権力者の背後を飾るにふさわしい永徳の傑作である。

Chinese Lions Folding Screen

Kano Eitoku
16th century
Sannomaru Shozokan
(The Museum of the Imperial Collections)

This is a work that was passed down through the Chōshū Mōri clan until it was presented to the Imperial household in 1888 (Meiji 21). There is a theory that the two lions in this work are not male and female, but rather a parent and child pair. We can see how an image of this nature and stunning force was an appropriate choice to decorate the alcove behind a man of great power, and it is one of Eitoku's masterpieces.

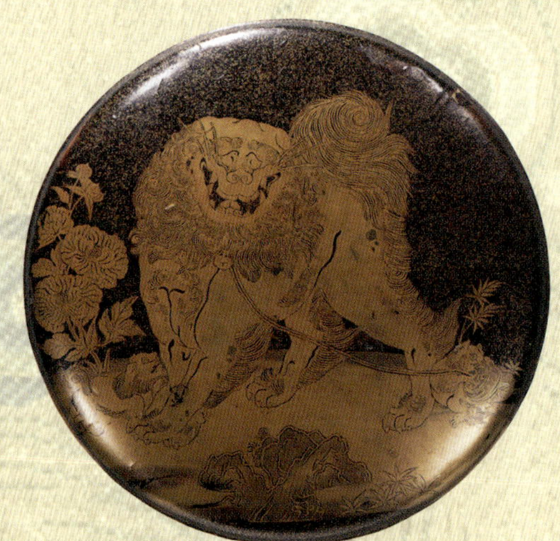

獅子牡丹蒔絵鏡箱

南北朝時代(14c)
東京国立博物館

Lion and Peony Maki-e Lacquered Mirror Box

14th century
Tokyo National Museum

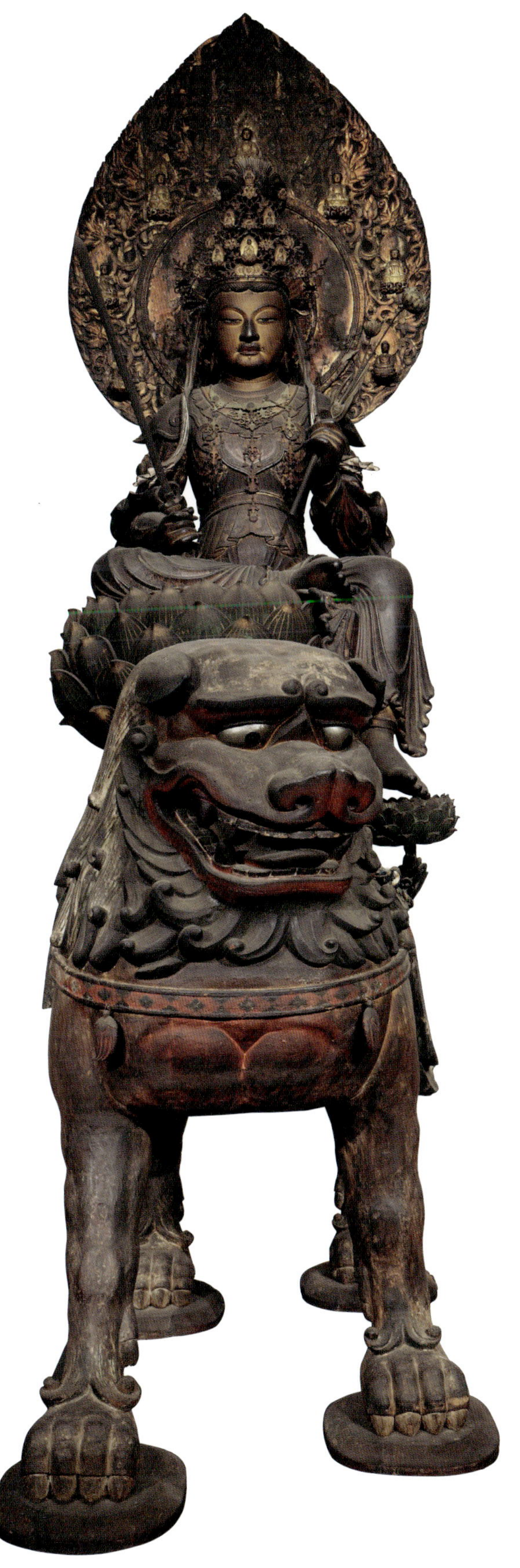

国宝

騎獅文殊菩薩像

快慶
建仁3年(1203)
奈良・安倍文殊院

東大寺の末寺だった崇敬寺文殊堂の後身で、「安倍の文殊」の名で知られる安倍文殊院の本尊。文殊菩薩が侍者をともない、雲に乗って大海原を渡る情景を表した渡海文殊の巨像である。像内に記された墨書銘から、仏師快慶の作と判明する。

National Treasure

Bodhisattva Manjusri Riding a Lion

Kaikei
1203
Abe-Monjuin, Nara

This work is known as "the Abe Manjusri," and it is the main object of veneration at the Abe Monjuin, the successor to the Manjusri (J. Monju) hall at Sūkeiji, which was a branch temple of Todaiji. It is a massive image of Manjusri crossing the sea, depicting the spectacle of him riding a cloud across the water, accompanied by attendants. The ink inscription recorded inside the sculpture identifies this as a work by the Buddhist artist Kaikei.

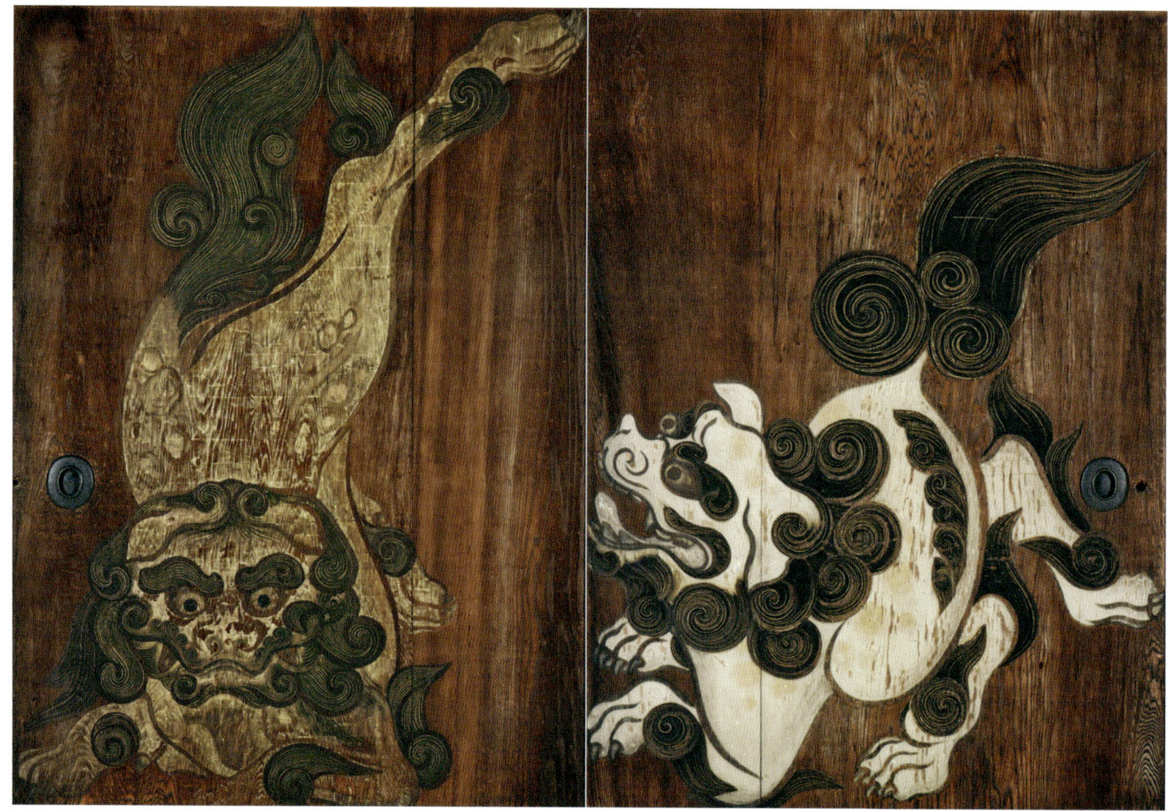

重要文化財

唐獅子図杉戸

俵屋宗達
元和7年(1621)以降
京都・養源院

養源院は、浅井長政(1545～73)の菩提を弔うため、長女淀殿が21回忌にあたる1594年(文禄3)に建立したが、1619年(元和5)火災に見舞われた。その2年後、長政の三女で2代将軍秀忠夫人となった江(崇源院)により伏見城の遺構を移して再建。当初、山楽ら狩野派が障壁画を手がけたが、何らかの事情で中断。その後を宗達が継承した。玄関を入ると出迎えるのが、杉戸に描かれた霊獣たちである。東西2枚ずつ、計4面に唐獅子が描かれ、その裏面に白象と麒麟(または水犀)が描かれる。画面の枠を意識しつつ、思い思いに体を展開させ躍動する様を大胆な筆致で描き出している。

Important Cultural Property

Chinese Lions Cedar Doors

Tawaraya Sōtatsu
After 1621
Yōgen'in, Kyoto

Yōgen'in was built by eldest daughter Yodo-dono in 1594 (Bunroku 3), corresponding to the twenty-first death anniversary of her father Asai Nagamasa (1545-73), in order to hold memorial services for his eternal happiness, but in 1619 (Genna 5) it suffered a major fire. Two years later, Gō (Sūgen'in), Nagamasa's third daughter and wife of the second shogun Hidetada, transferred the remains of Fushimi Castle and rebuilt the temple. Initially, Sanraku and the Kano School did the wall paintings, but for some reason the project was suspended. After that, Sōtatsu inherited the project. When you come through the entrance, you are greeted by the sight of auspicious beasts painted on the cedar doors. There are two lions each on the east and west, for a total of four Chinese lions; two white elephants and a pair of *kirin* (or water rhinoceros) are painted on the reverse. This work was executed in daring brushwork that depicts idiosyncratically expanded bodies that throb with energy, but still remain within the limits of the frame.

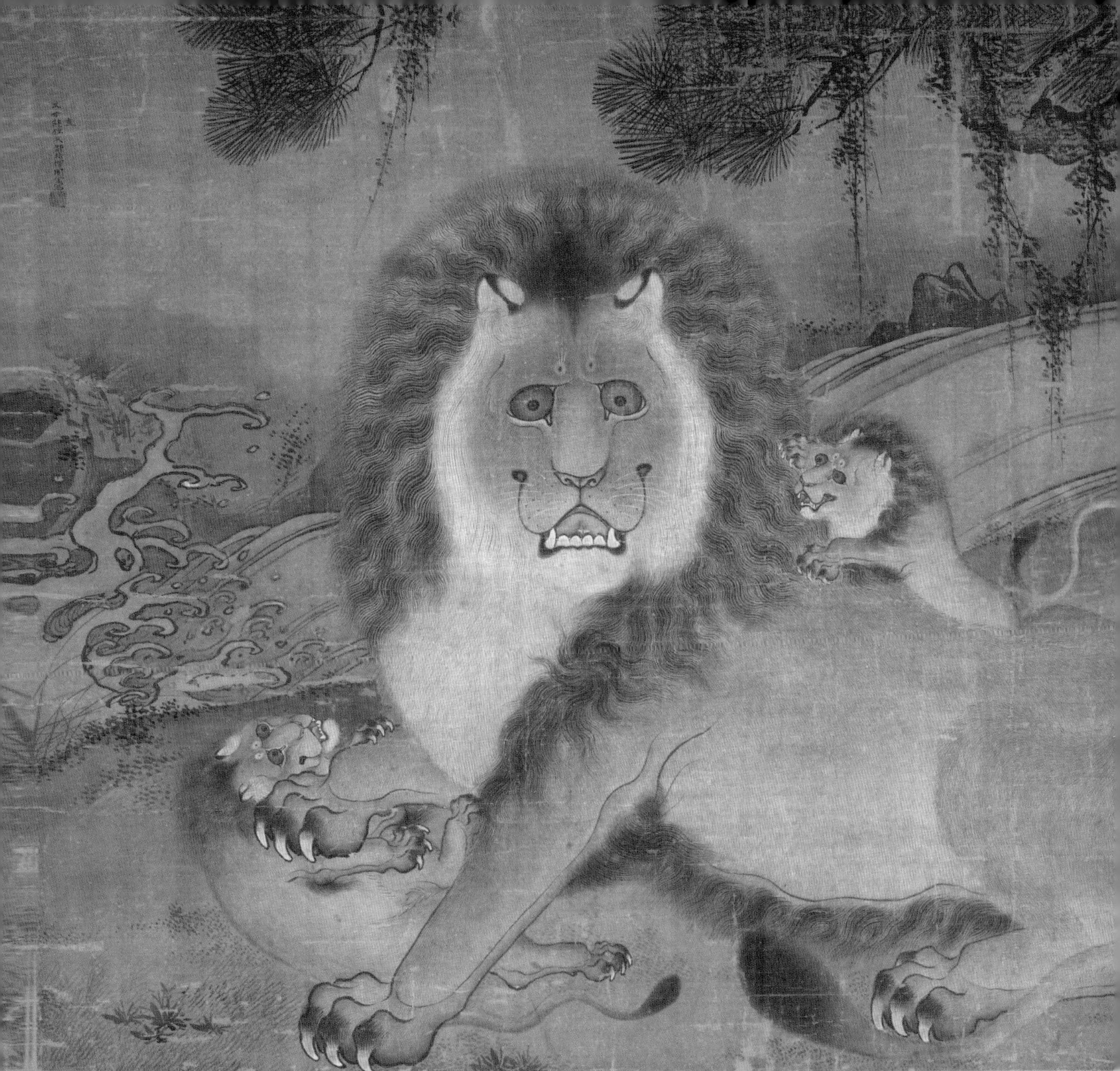

獅子図軸

周全
明時代(16c)
東京国立博物館

周全は15世紀後半に活躍した画院画家(宮廷画家)。奔流を背景に、獅子の親子が戯れる様子を描き出す。獅子は官位栄達を意味する吉祥画でもあったという。当時、明皇帝には南洋諸国から様々な文物とともに動物も献上され、なかでもライオンは頻繁にもたらされていたことが記録されている。本図の獅子には、実物のライオンの余韻が色濃く残されているようである。ただし、子ライオンがいずれも父ライオンをそのまま縮小コピーしたようにたてがみを蓄えているところをみると、画家が目にしたのは成獣の雄ライオンだけだったと見える。

Lions

Zhou Quan
Ming dynasty, 16th century
Tokyo National Museum

Zhou Quan was a court painter active during the late fifteenth century. This work depicts a parent and children group of lions frolicking in front of a rushing stream. It is thought that lion images signified good luck in having one's rank promoted. Around this time, it is recorded that the kingdoms of the South Seas would present animals, especially lions, to the Ming emperor, along with various other cultural products. The lions in this work seem to maintain the look and feel of actual lions. However, seeing that the lion cubs look just like smaller versions of their father, and somehow grow manes, it is clear that the artist had only ever seen adult male lions.

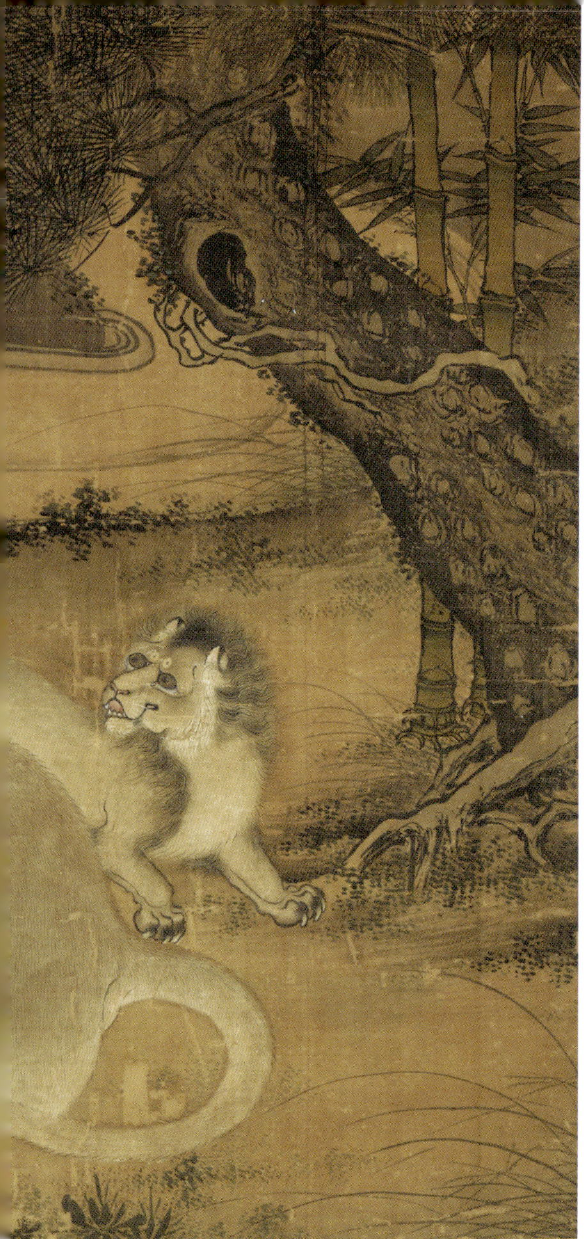

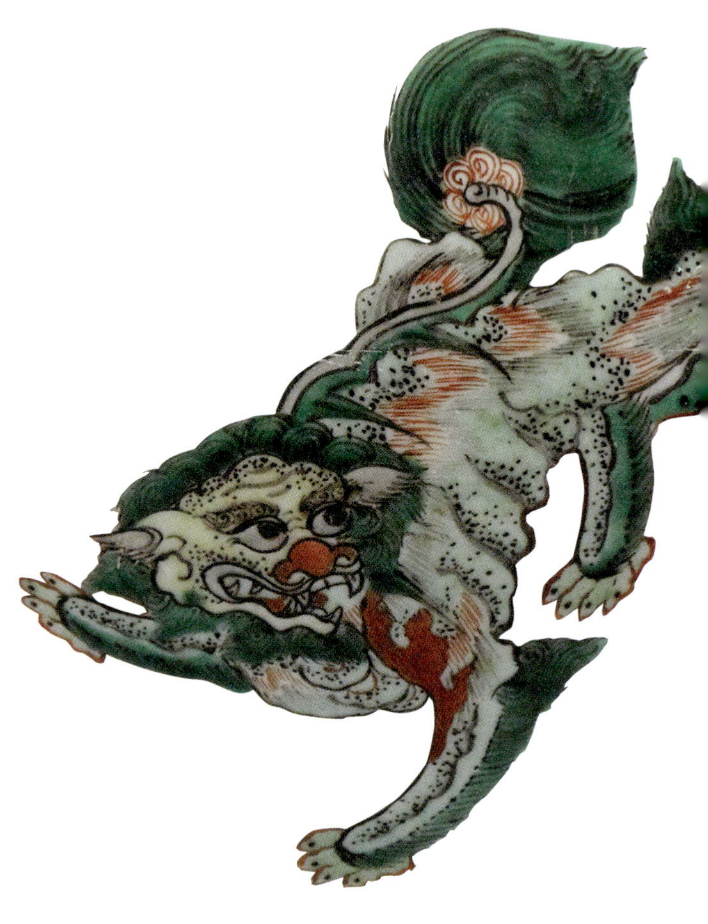

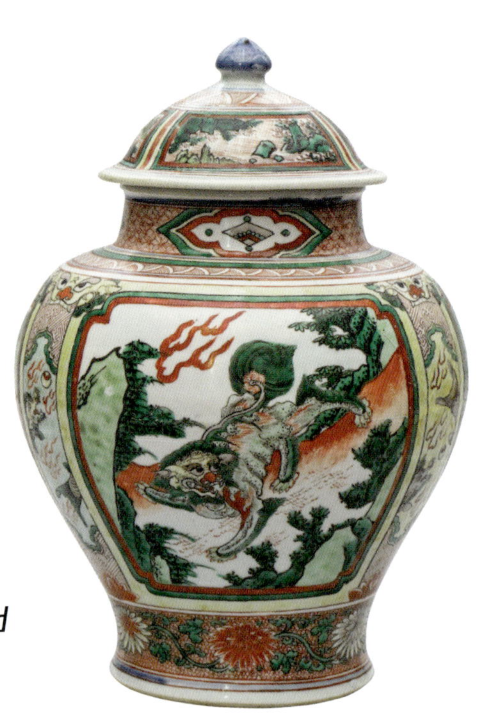

五彩獅子文有蓋壺（ごさいししもんゆうがいこ）

中国・景徳鎮窯
清時代（17～18世紀）
東京国立博物館

Colored Vase with a Lid

Jingdezhen porcelain, China
Qing dynasty, 17th–18th century
Tokyo National Museum

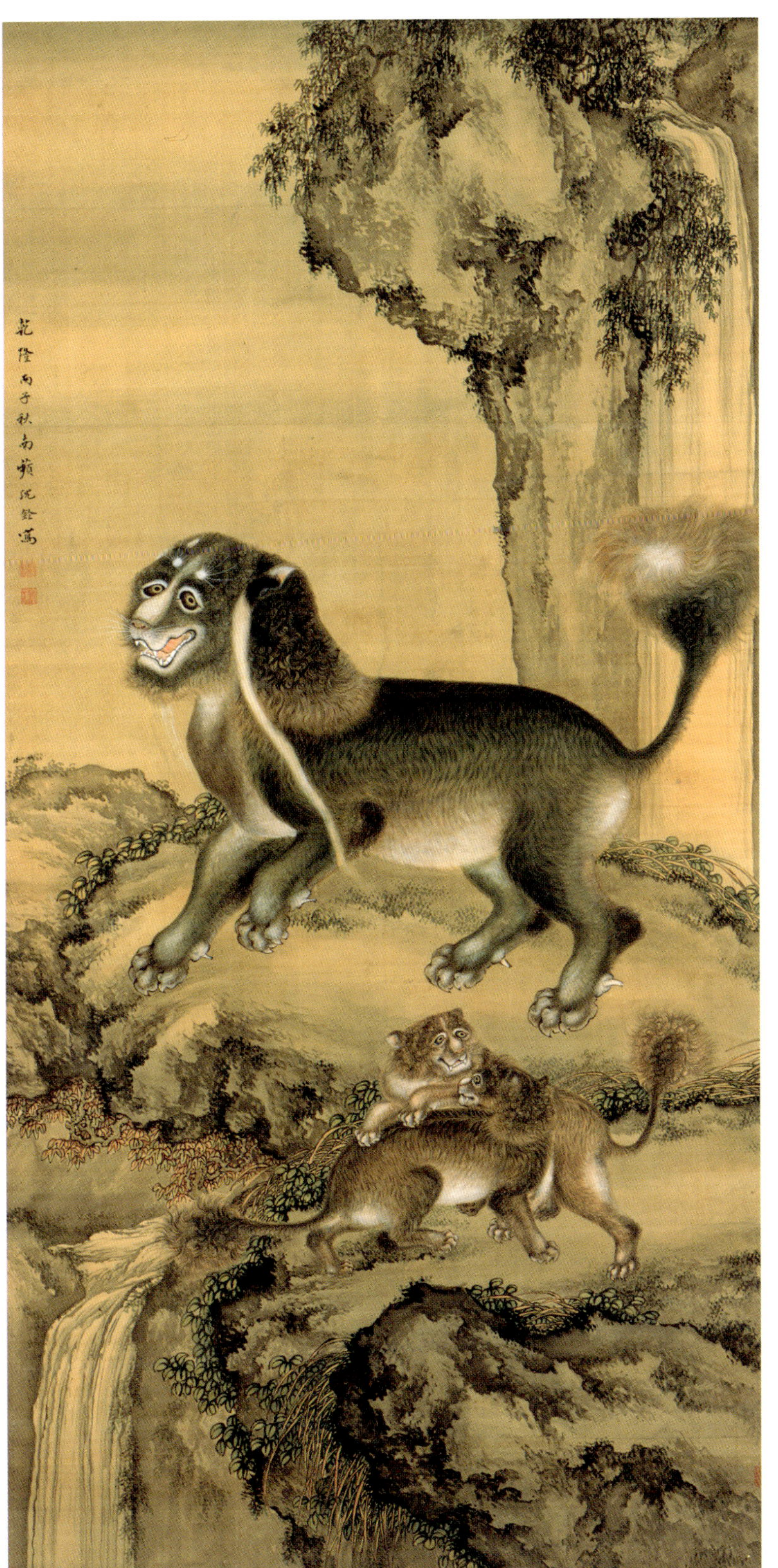

獅子戯児図

沈南蘋
中国・乾隆21年(1756)
神戸市立博物館

沈南蘋(1683～1760?)は中国・浙江省呉興の人。名は銓、字は衡斎、南蘋は号である。1731年(享保16)来日し、長崎滞在は2年に満たなかったが、その写生的で華やかな画風は江戸時代の画家たちに大きな影響を与えた。本図においては、宮廷画家が大画面に描き上げたライオンの片鱗こそ留めてはいるものの、たてがみや尾の形態は大きく変化してしまっていることがわかる。

Lion and Frolicking Cubs

Shen Nanpin
Qing dynasty, 1756
Kobe City Musum

Shen Nanpin (1683-1760?) was a Chinese painter from Wuxing in Zhejiang Province. Nanpin was his courtesy name, but his given name was Quan, and his sobriquet was Hengzhai. He came to Japan in 1731 (Kyōhō 16), and stayed in Nagasaki for less than two years, but his ornate style of creating realistic images left a huge impression on Edo-period painters. Even though this work retains the sense of large format lion paintings done by court artists, we can see that the shape of the mane and tail have been significantly altered.

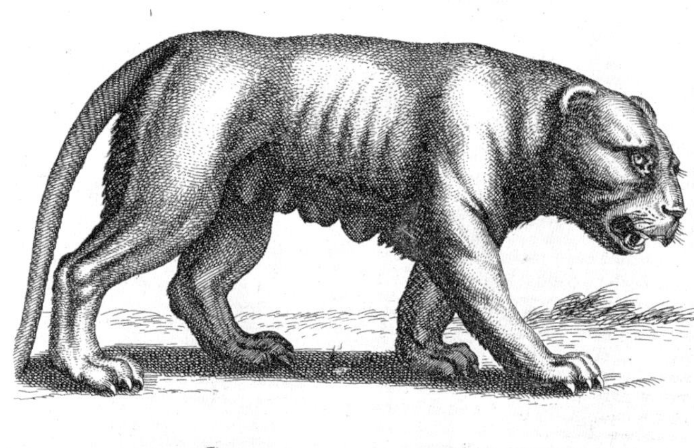

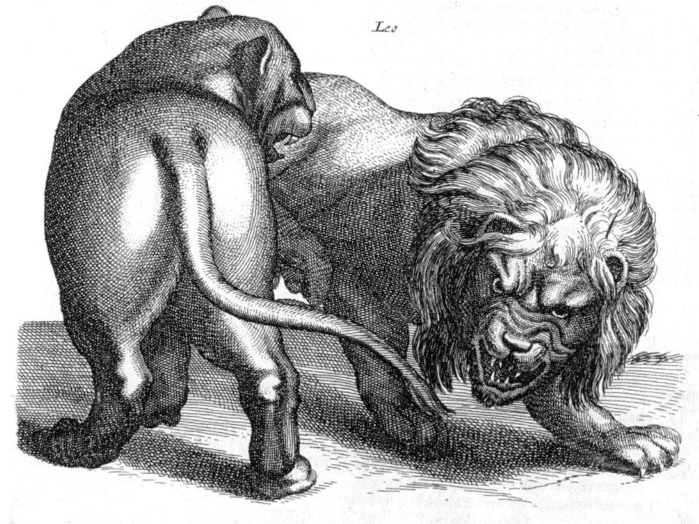

ライオン図
(『ヨンストン動物図譜』より)

ヤン・ヨンストン
1660年
仙台市博物館

オランダの動物学者ヤン・ヨンストン(1603～75)による本書は1660年にオランダ語版が出版された。哺乳類から鳥類・魚類・昆虫まで「世界中の生類を集めたる本にて、獅子、龍其外日本人見ざる所の物を生写にした」(司馬江漢の言)250枚もの銅版画が掲載された総合動物図鑑である。オランダ商館長から1663年(寛文3)に4代将軍家綱に献上され、のちに8代将軍吉宗が野呂元丈に翻訳させたことでも知られる。その書を1768年(明和5)、平賀源内が家財・夜具まで売り払って入手してくれた結果、江戸の学者や画家たちの目にも容易に届くようになったのである。

Lions (*from Historiae Naturalis*)

Johannes Jonston
1660
Sendai City Museum

This book by Dutch zoologist Johannes Jonston (1603-75) was published in Dutch in 1660. It was a comprehensive catalogue of animals including two hundred and fifty copperplate engravings that depicted everything from mammals to birds, fish, and insects, of which Shiba Kōkan said: "In this book covering animals from all over the world, there are exact depictions of lions, dragons and other creatures never seen by the Japanese." It is also known that the book, which had been presented to the fourth shogun Tokugawa Ietsuna by the visiting Dutch delegation in 1663 (Kanbun 3), was later translated by Noro Genjō under the orders of the eighth shogun Yoshimune. In 1768 (Meiwa 5), Hiraga Gennai sold all his household belongings, even his bedding, to obtain a copy; as a result, it became easy for Edo scholars and painters to also lay eyes on it.

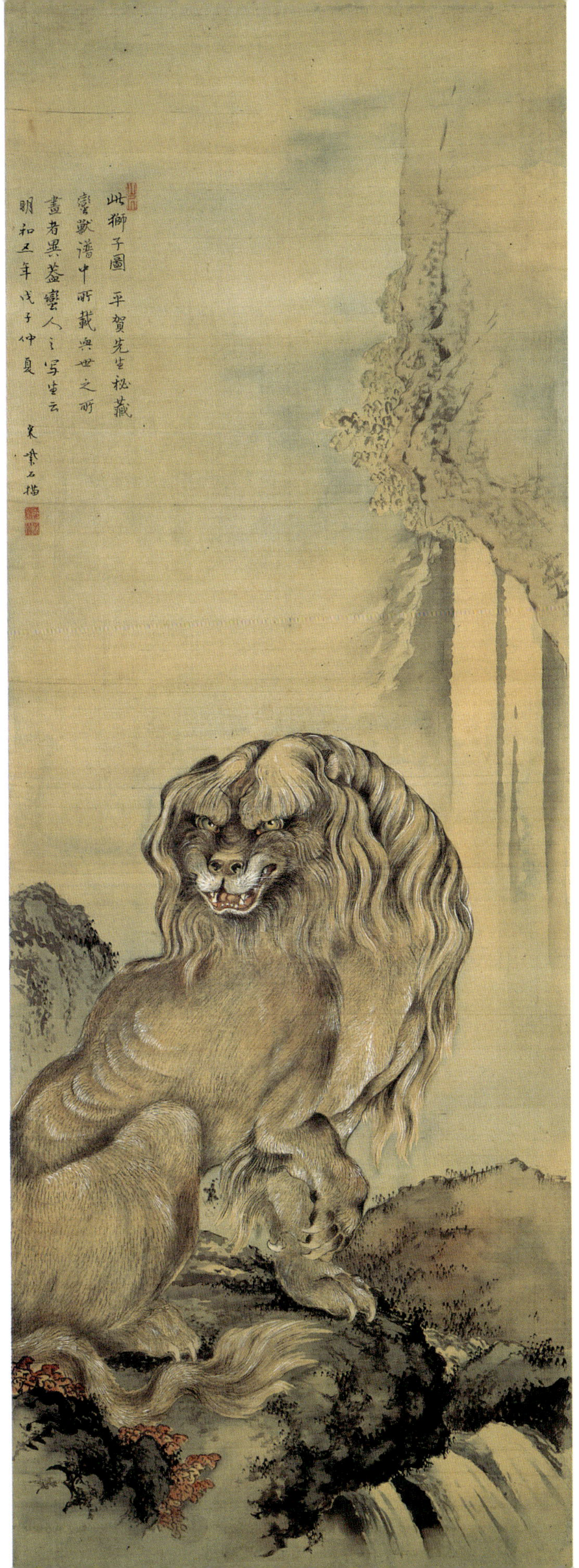

獅子図

宋紫石
明和5年(1768)
大和文華館

源内と親しかった宋紫石(1715〜86)が、『ヨンストン動物図譜』にもとづき描いた図。ふさふさの尾は狐や牛馬の尾に似、見得をきるように片足を上げたポーズは唐獅子や洋犬などの図に用いられた常套的表現だが、旧来の動物観から脱した自信作だったとみえ、画面上に自ら「世の獅子図とは違うものだ」と書き付けている。なお、紫石はこの蘭書によほど興味を抱いたらしく、2年後には絵手本『古今画藪』8冊中に、獅子・驢馬以下、象に至るまでの動物群を載せている。唐獅子とはまるで違った本物のライオン図が、ここに初めて出現したのである。

Lion

Sō Shiseki
1768
The Museum Yamato Bunkakan

This is a picture that Gennai and his longtime friend Shiseki (1715-86) did based on the Jonston *Historiae naturalis*. The fluffy tail is like that of a fox or horse, and the pose that it is striking with one leg raised is a visual convention that is used in images like those of Chinese lions and Western dogs. However, we can see that it is a work of art that deviates from the conventional perspective toward animals and that the creator took pride in; on the upper part of the image, he wrote "This is not like the other lion pictures in the world." Moreover, it seemed that Shiseki was engrossed in this Dutch book, and two years later, he included the lion, donkey, and even elephant in the eight booklets of his picture copybook *Kokon gasō* (*Thicket of Ancient and Modern Pictures*). The image of a real lion is completely different from a "Chinese lion," but it is the first time that it has appeared here.

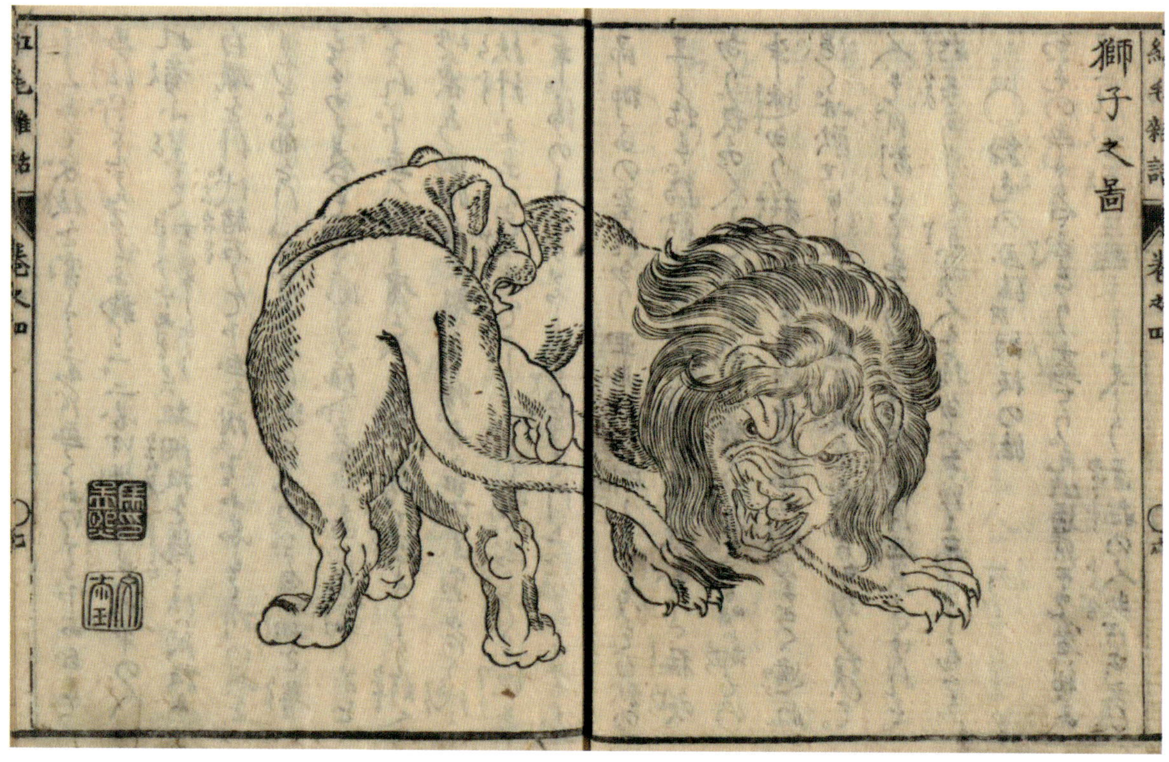

『紅毛雑話』

森島中良 編
天明7年(1787)刊
国立国会図書館

森島中良(1756?～1810)は幕府お抱えの蘭医・桂川甫周の実弟。平賀源内の戯作上の門人でもあった。蘭学に関わる情報に恵まれた環境をいかし、異国の興味あふれる話題をまとめ刊行したのが本書である。『ヨンストン動物図譜』掲載の銅版画を木版画にして、ライオンの姿を広く紹介した。

Kōmō zatsuwa (*Miscellany of Westerners*)

Edited by Morishima Chūryō
1787
National Diet Library, Japan

Morishima Chūryō (1756?-1810) was the younger brother of Katsuragawa Hoshū, a Western studies scholar and physician that was in the employ of the shogunal government. He was a student of *gesaku* popular literature under Hiraga Gennai. Chūryō made use of being in an environment where he was blessed with information about Western studies, and this book is a published collection of stories overflowing with interest in foreign countries. The copperplate engravings that appeared in the Jonston *Historiae naturalis* were reproduced as woodblock prints, and the image of the lion was widely shared.

サムソンと獅子図

岸駒
天明2年(1782)

岸駒(1749〜1838)は北陸出身で、虎絵の名人として京都で活躍した。本図は、『旧約聖書』に登場する怪力の持ち主サムソンが、目の前に現れたライオンを子ヤギでも裂くように引き裂いた、という場面を描いたもの。おそらく、舶載書(当時『旧約聖書』が禁教下のわが国にも入っていた)の挿図(銅版画)などに倣ったもので、どぎついまでの陰影表現が目を引く異色作と言える。ただし、描かれたライオンは、あまりにひ弱そうに見える。

Samson and Lion

Ganku
1782

Ganku (1749-1838), originally from the Hokuriku region, was a renowned tiger painter active in Kyoto. This is a depiction of the scene from the Old Testament where Samson, who had superhuman strength, came across a lion and tore it apart as one might rip apart a young goat. It is likely that Ganku imitated the illustrations (copperplate engravings) in books brought from overseas (at that time, the Old Testament had entered Japan as forbidden religious material), and as a result, you can say that this is a unique work whose extremely heavy shading draws our attention. However, the lion here looks rather sickly.

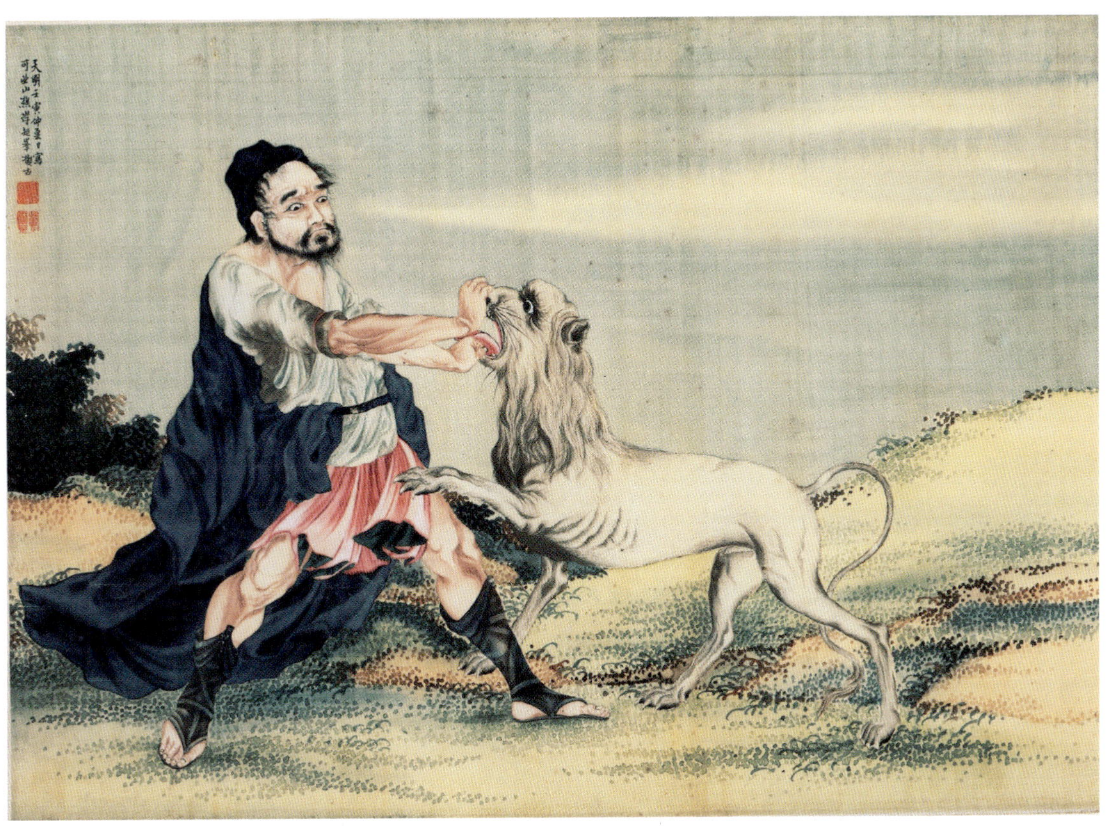

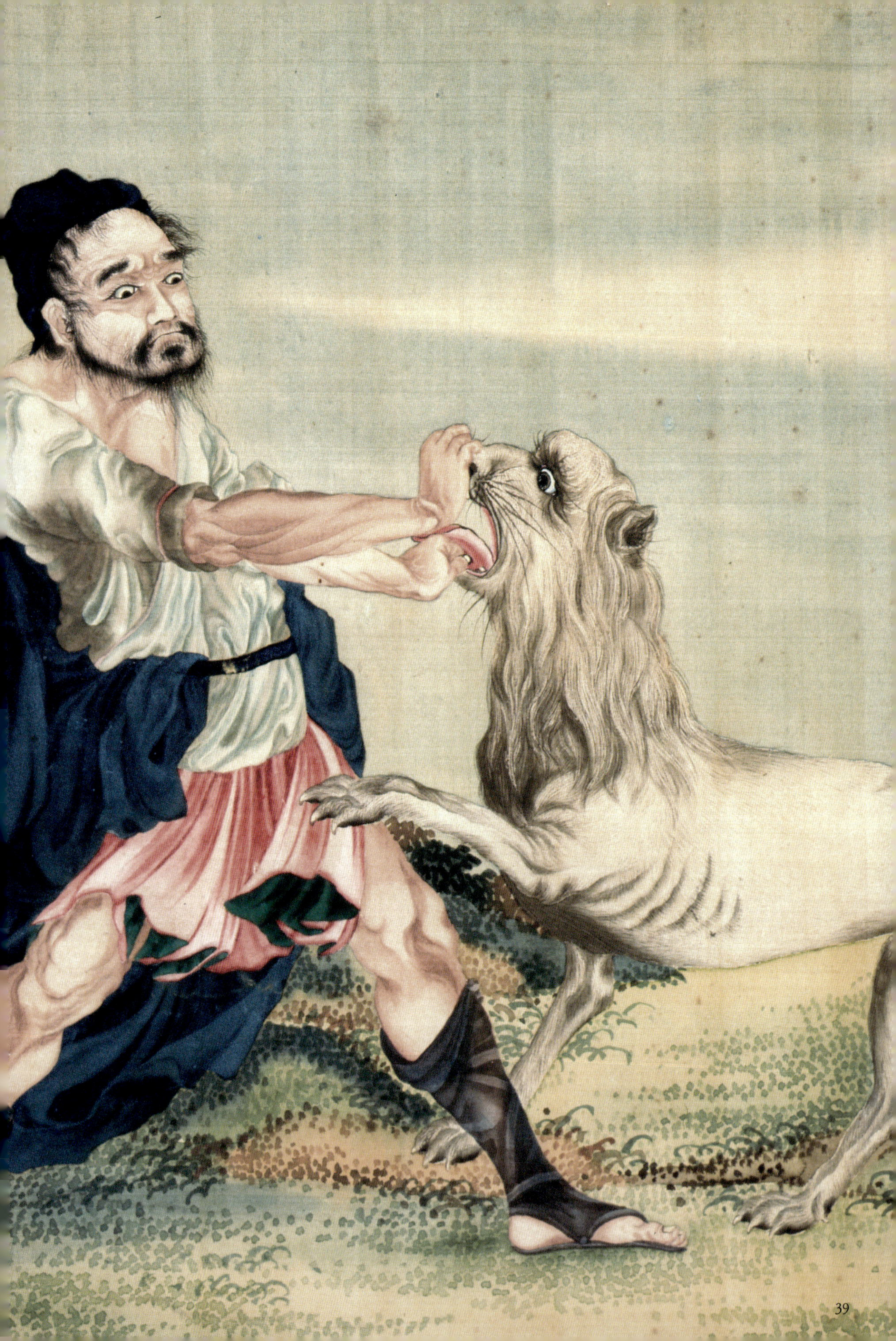

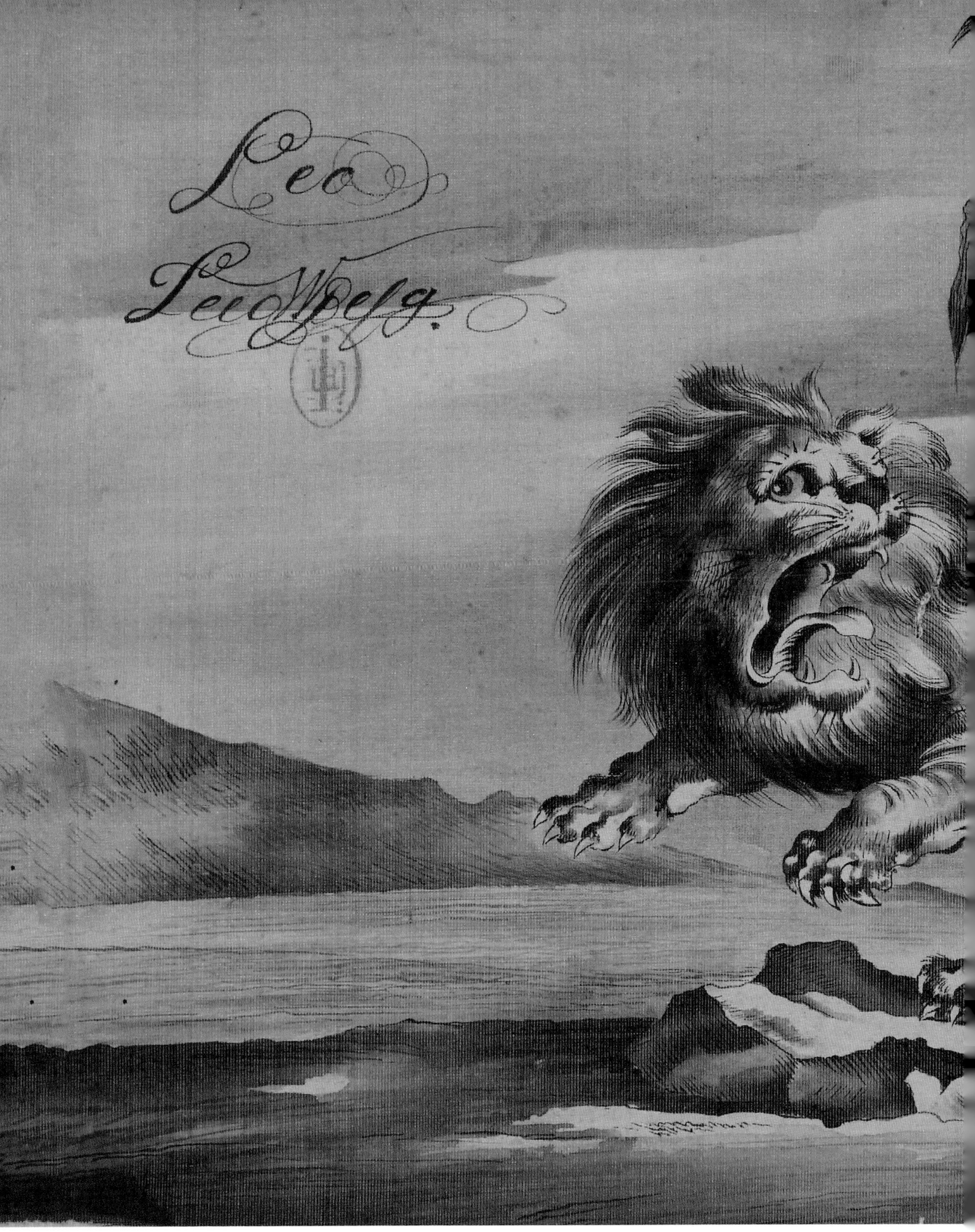

獅子図

石川孟高
江戸時代（19c）
歸空庵コレクション

石川孟高（1763～1826）は兄の大浪（1762～1817）とともに、蘭書挿絵などの銅版画から学び、洋風画を好んで描いた幕臣。銅版画に表現された細線を細筆で描き起こす。画面左上には、横文字で「レオ・レーウベルグ（獅子山）」と自らの蘭語名を記す。

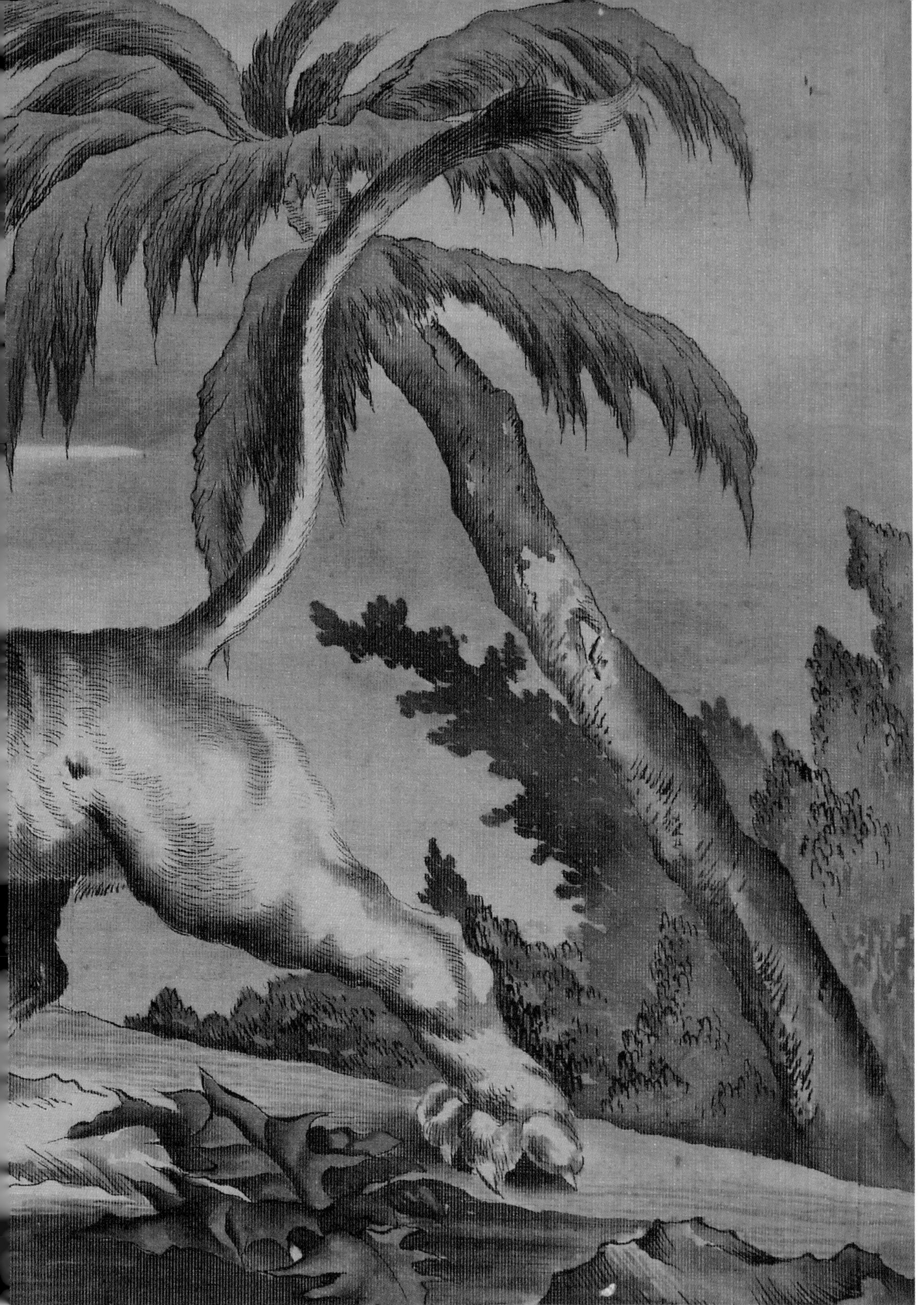

Lion

Ishikawa Mōkō
19th century
Kikūan Collection

Ishikawa Mōkō (1763-1826), along with his older brother Tairō (1762-1817), studied copperplate engravings like the ones that appeared as illustrations in Western books, and he was known as a shogunal retainer that enjoyed Western paintings. Mōkō painted with a fine brush and used the thin lines seen in copperplate engravings. On the upper left of the image, in horizontal letters, he signs his name in Dutch, "Leo, Leeuw Berg."

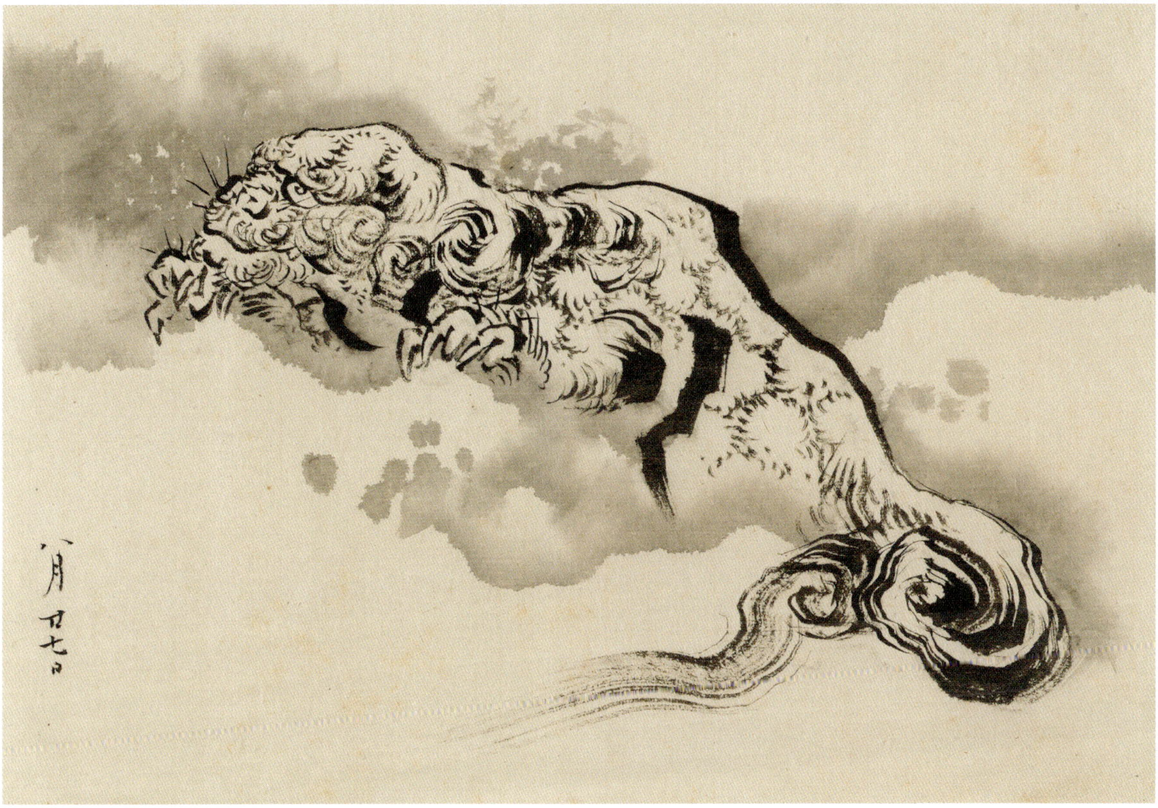

重要文化財

日新除魔図

葛飾北斎
天保13〜14年（1842〜43）
九州国立博物館

83〜84歳にかけて信州小布施に逗留していた葛飾北斎（1760〜1849）が、自身の長寿を祈願するため、毎朝の日課として描き続けたもの。様々な姿態の獅子や獅子舞の姿が登場する。信州松代藩士・宮本慎助が北斎に依頼していた掛軸の代わりに、北斎娘お栄（応為）の提案により彼女が保管していたこの219枚が送られた。

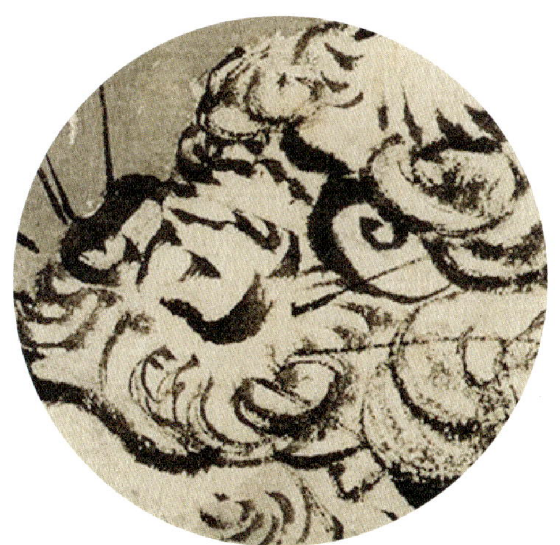

Important Cultural Property

Nisshin joma (*Daily Exorcisms*)

Katsushika Hokusai
1842-43
Kyushu National Museum

Katsushika Hokusai (1760-1849), who sojourned in Obuse, Shinano from when he was eighty-three to when he was eighty-four years old, continued drawing as part of his daily ritual every morning as a prayer for his longevity. In these drawings, we can see many different portrayals of lions and lion dances. Following the suggestion of Hokusai's daughter Oei (also known as her painter name Ōi), these two hundred and nineteen works were sent to Miyamoto Shinsuke, a warrior from Matsushiro, Shinano, instead of the hanging scroll that he had requested from Hokusai.

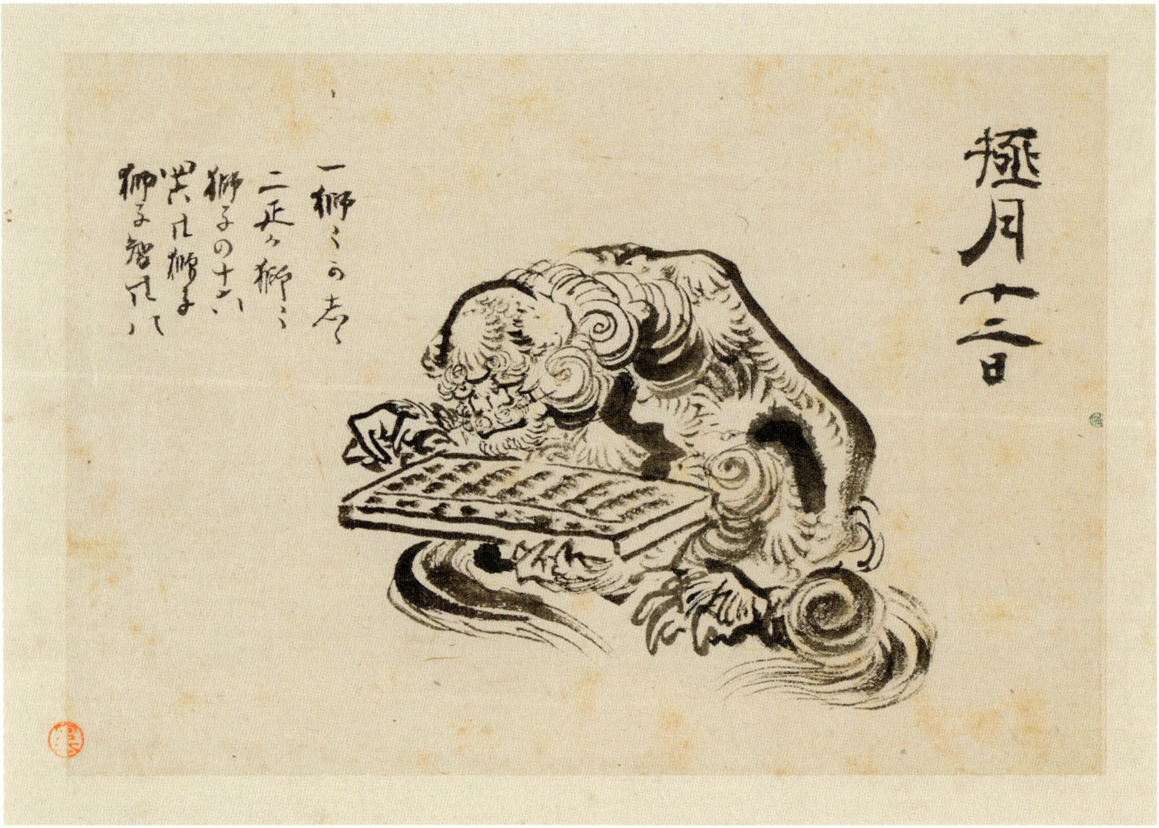

極月十三日

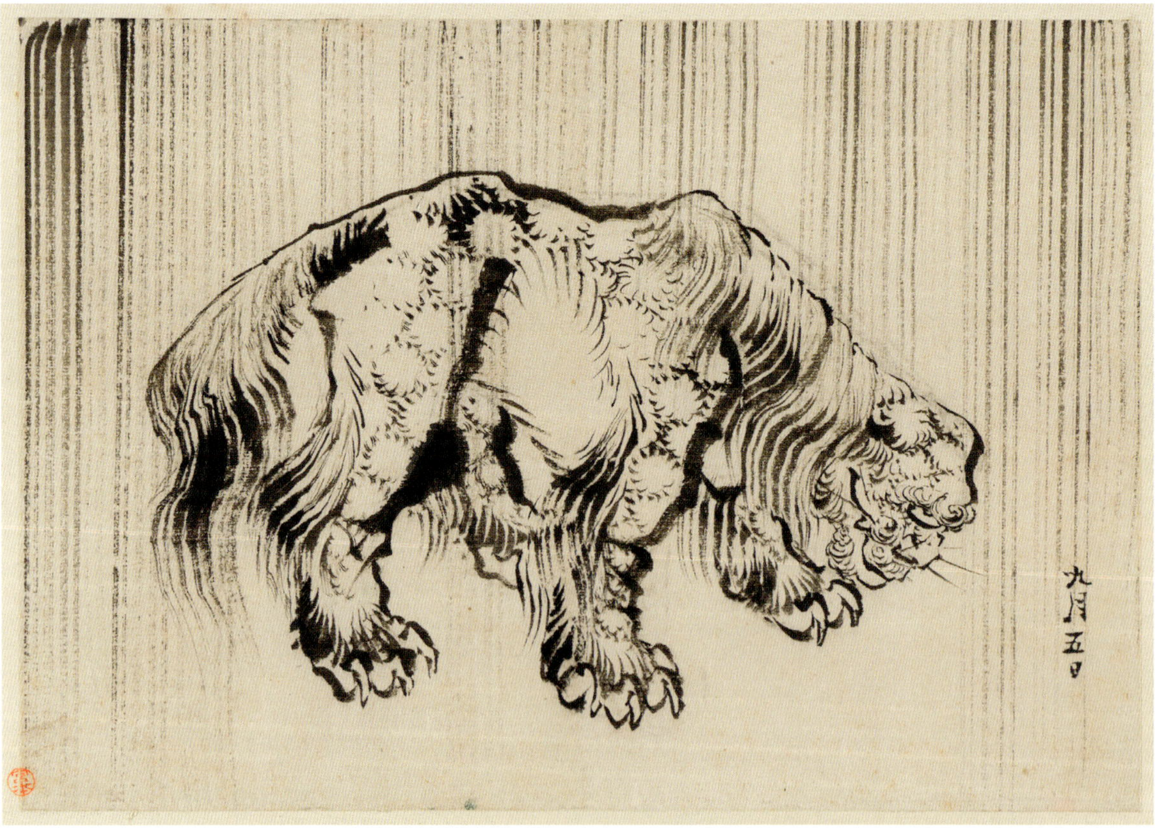

一獅々の声
二正々獅々
獅子の十六
其れ獅子
獅子智てハ

九月五日

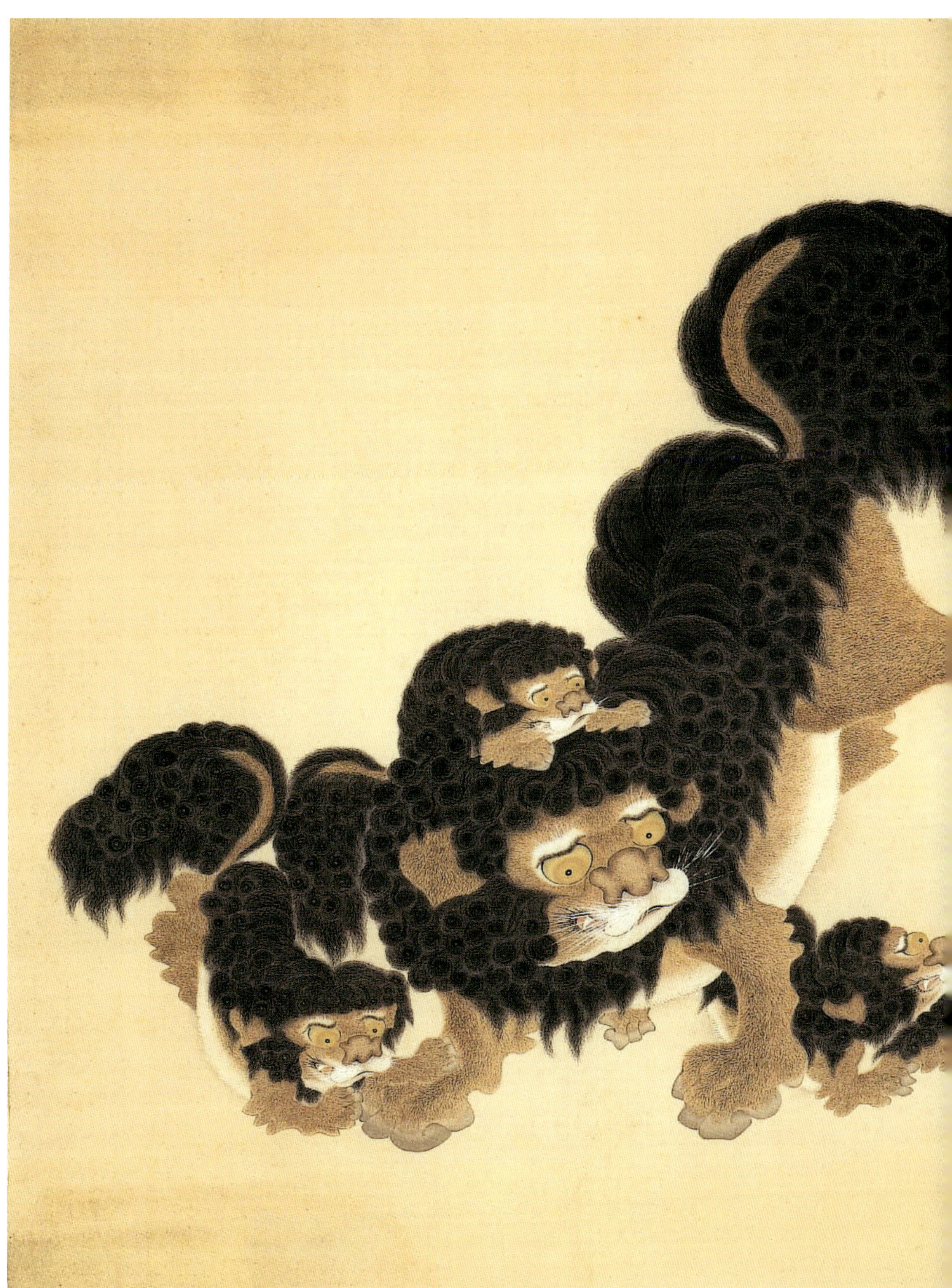

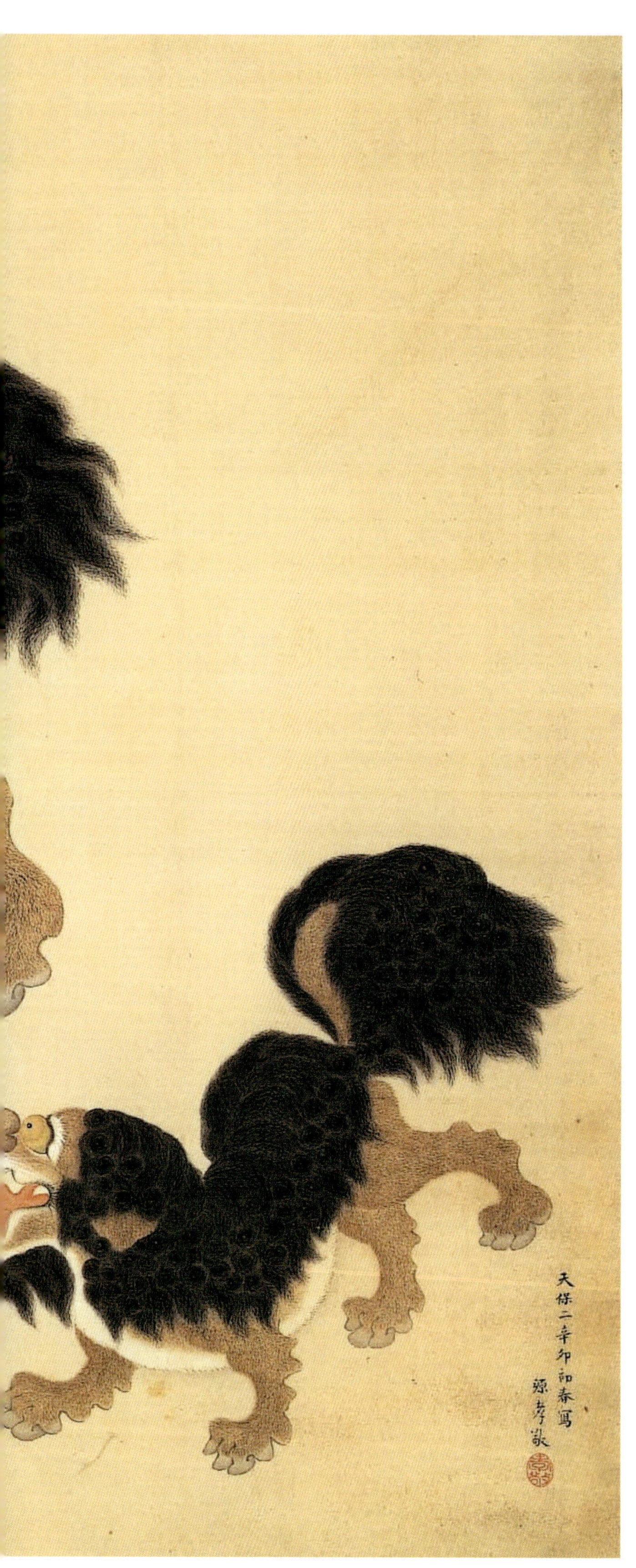

唐獅子図

吉村孝敬
天保2年(1831)
エツコ＆ジョー・プライスコレクション

吉村孝敬(1769～1836)は円山応挙の門人。周全や南蘋の作品同様、ライオン親子の仲睦まじい姿が表現されている。しかし、子ライオンが親と同じたてがみを蓄え、鼻が奇妙な形に変形してしまっているのはまだしも、四脚の鋭い爪が失われ蹄のような代物と化してしまったことはどう理解すべきなのだろうか。写生画に新生面を開いた円山派の画人にあるまじき仕業、とも言いたいところだが、縦横1mを超える大幅、何らかの意図があってのことだろうか。

Chinese Lions

Yoshimura Kōkei
1831
Etsuko and Joe Price Collection

Yoshimura Kōkei (1769-1836) was a student of Maruyama Ōkyo. Just like in the works of Zhou Quan and Nanpin, the harmonious figures of a lion and his cubs are depicted. However, how should we process the fact that each lion cub has the same mane as his father, the peculiar shape their noses have taken, and even more egregious, how the sharp claws on all four legs are gone, and have each changed into something almost like a hoof? I want to say that this work is unworthy of the painters of the Maruyama School, which was famous for pioneering new aspects of realistic pictures drawn from life, but is there not some sort of design in it, even just in the large scale of this work?

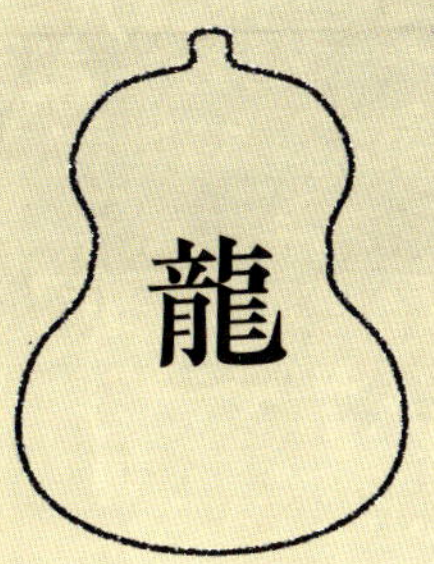

龍は鱗蟲（鱗のある動物）の長。雨を司る精霊とされ、思いのままに姿を変えることができ、春分に天に昇り、秋分に下って淵に入る。「九似」といわれるように、9種の動物に似たところがあり、頭は駱駝、角は鹿、目は鬼（一説に兎）、耳は牛、項は蛇、腹は蜃、鱗は鯉、爪は鷹、掌は虎のようだという。鱗の数は81枚で、九九の重陽にあたる。龍の原形は、人を欲望から救う神獣「夔」といわれる。中国では龍を、吉兆をもたらす霊獣として神聖視するとともに王権の象徴とした。とくに皇帝を表わす龍は5本爪と決められ、他の使用を厳しく制限された。

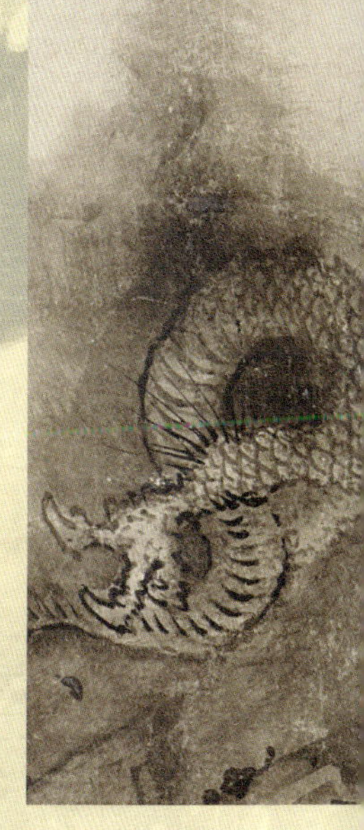

The Dragon

The dragon is the lord of the scaled beasts (creatures with scales). It is known as a spirit that controls the rain, and can shapeshift to its heart's content; it ascends to the heavens on the vernal equinox, and it descends into a deep pool on the autumnal equinox. The dragon is said to have "nine similarities," physical aspects that resemble nine different types of animals, and these are: a head like a camel, horns like a deer, eyes like a demon (or rabbit, depending on the source), ears like a cow, a neck like a snake, a belly like a clam-monster, scales like a carp, claws like a hawk, and paws like a tiger. The dragon has eighty-one scales, and they numerically correspond to the Double Ninth Festival. It is said that the original form of the dragon was a divine beast (the Kui) that saved people from their own desires. In China, along with being deified as a sacred beast that brings good fortune, the dragon was considered emblematic of royal authority. This was especially the case with the dragon that symbolized the emperor, which was determined to have five claws; other uses for this particular beast were strictly limited.

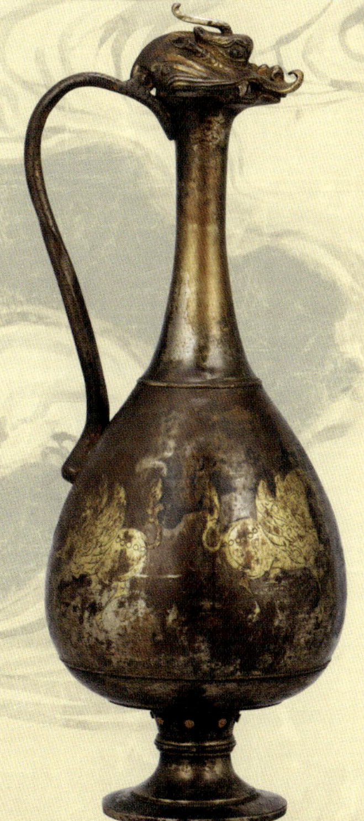

国宝

竜首水瓶（法隆寺献納宝物）

飛鳥時代（7c）
東京国立博物館

古代イランの地に栄えたササン朝ペルシャに源流を持つ形式の水差。胴に刻まれた4頭の天馬（ペガサス）には中国唐代と朝鮮・百済の美術の影響が見られ、これらを受容した日本で製作されたと考えられている。水の注ぎ口と把手は龍をかたどる。古代シルクロードに展開した壮大な国際交流の結晶といえる作。

National Treasure

Dragon-head Pitcher (*Hōryūji Treasure*)

7th century
Tokyo National Museum

This is a pitcher whose shape has its origins in the Sasanian Empire, which flourished in ancient Iran. We can see the influence of the visual culture of Tang dynasty China and Baekje Korea in the four flying horses (*pegasi*) carved into the main body, and it is thought that this work was produced in Japan, which had been the recipient of those continental influences. The water spout and the handle are modeled to look like dragons. You could say that this work is a result of the large-scale international exchange that flourished on the ancient Silk Road.

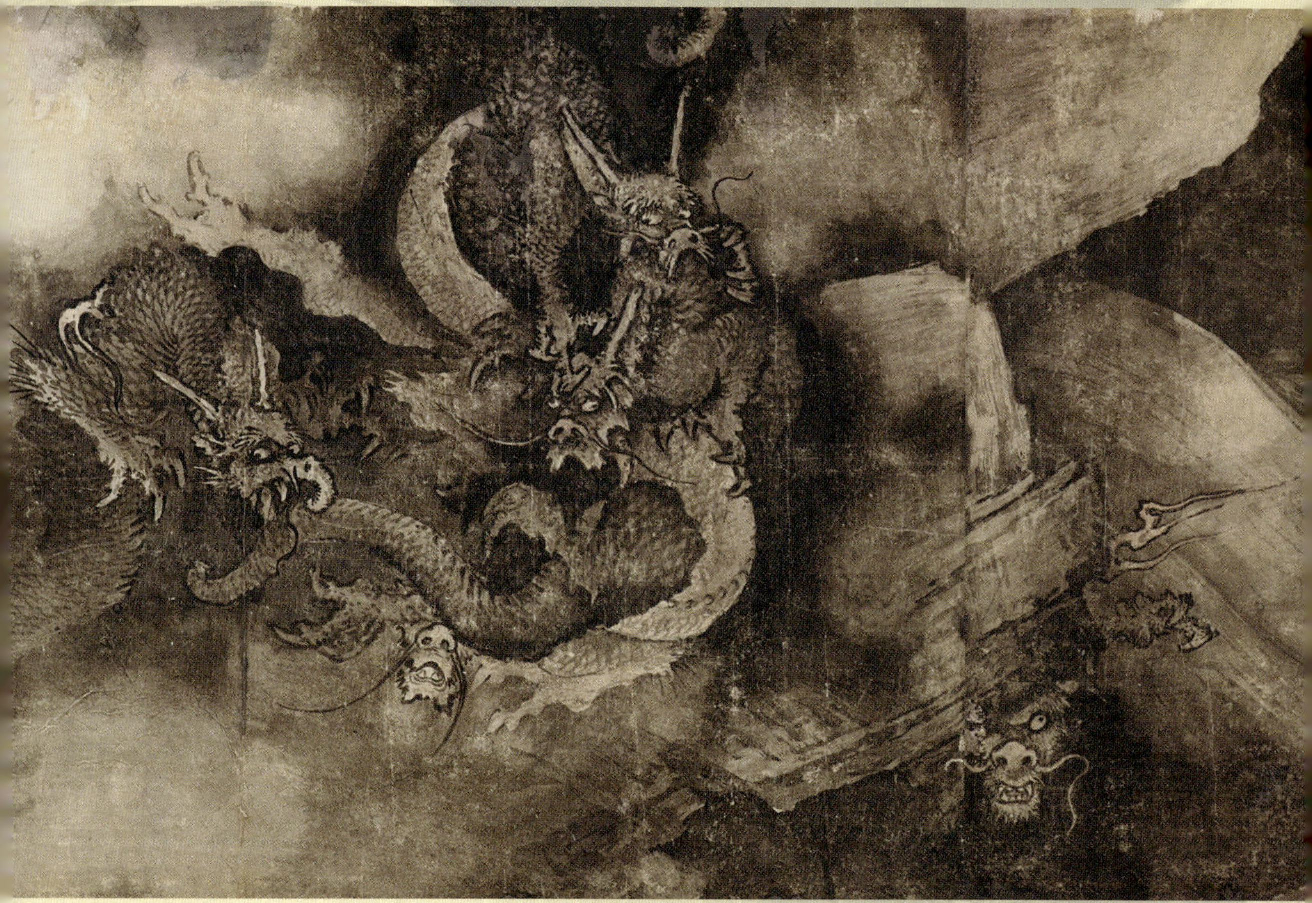

重要文化財

五龍図巻

伝・陳容
中国・南宋時代(13c)
東京国立博物館

陳容は中国・南宋末の文人画家。長楽(福建省)の人で、所翁と号した。詩文にすぐれるとともに、水墨の龍を得意とし、宝祐年間(1253～58)に画名が高かったという。

Important Cultural Property

Five Dragons Scroll

Attributed to Chen Rong
Southern Song dynasty, 13th century
Tokyo National Museum

Chen Rong was a late Southern Song Chinese literati painter. His style name was Suo Weng, and he was from Changle (Fujian Province). Along with his aptitude for poetry, he was skilled at painting monochrome ink dragons, and he was prominent during the Bao Diao era (1253-58).

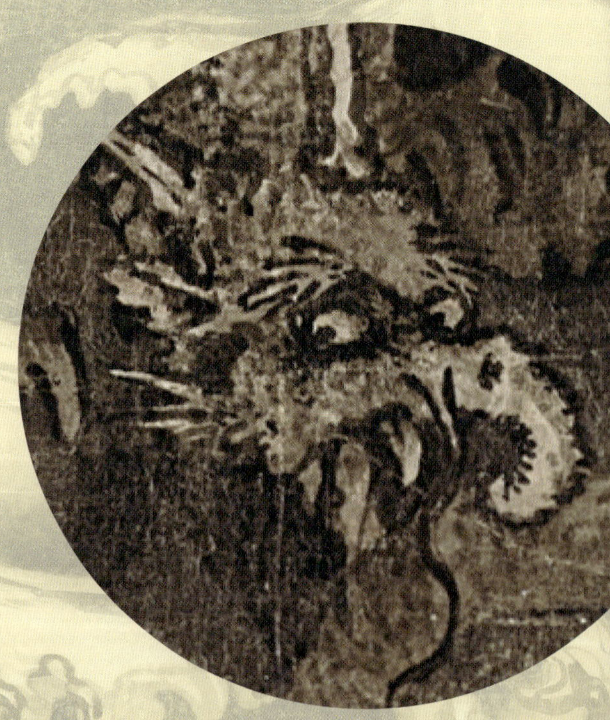

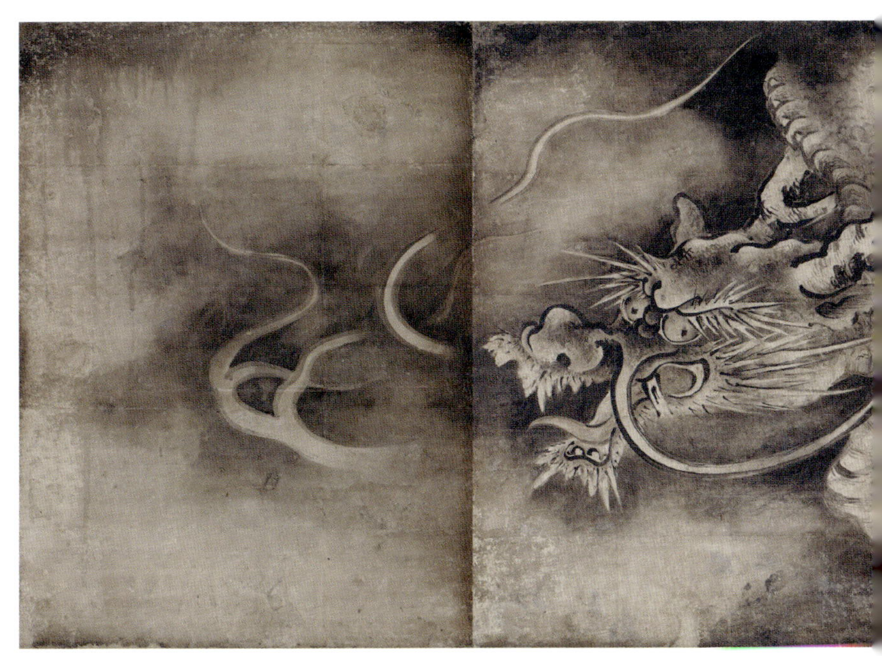

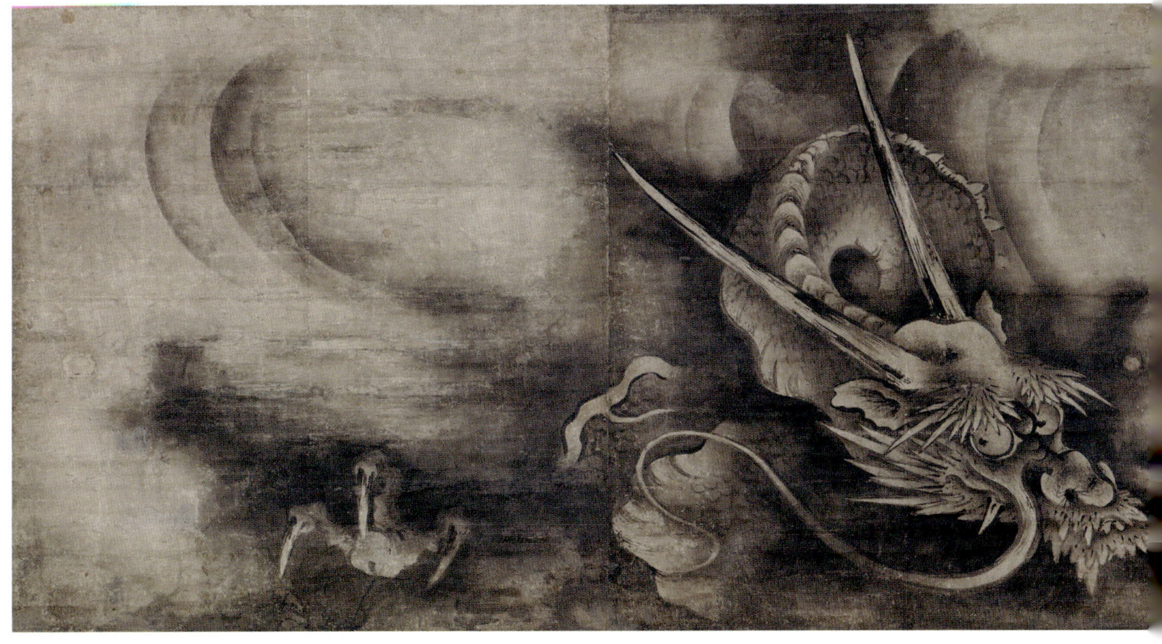

重要文化財

雲龍図　海北友松　慶長4年（1599）　京都・建仁寺

海北友松（1533～1615）は覇気あふれる水墨画で知られた桃山時代の武人画家。垂れ込めた暗雲のなかから姿を現した２頭の龍。一方は口を開けて躍動し、他方は口を閉じ静かにこちらを凝視する。動と静との対比は、昇り龍・降り龍の描き分けを意図したものかと思われる。友松の龍の絵は、朝鮮半島にも送られ評判になったと記録され、相当数の遺品も残されている。父の画風を受け継いだ子の友雪も同種の作品を手がけており、画龍が海北家のお家芸として広く認知されていたことがうかがえる。もと大方丈の礼之間を飾る８面の襖絵だったが、現在は掛軸に改装。

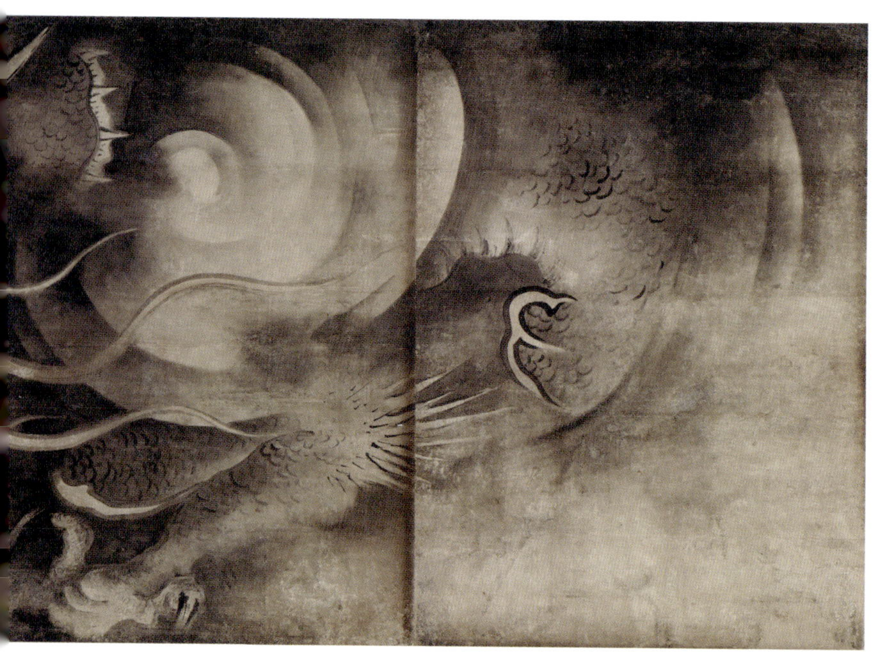

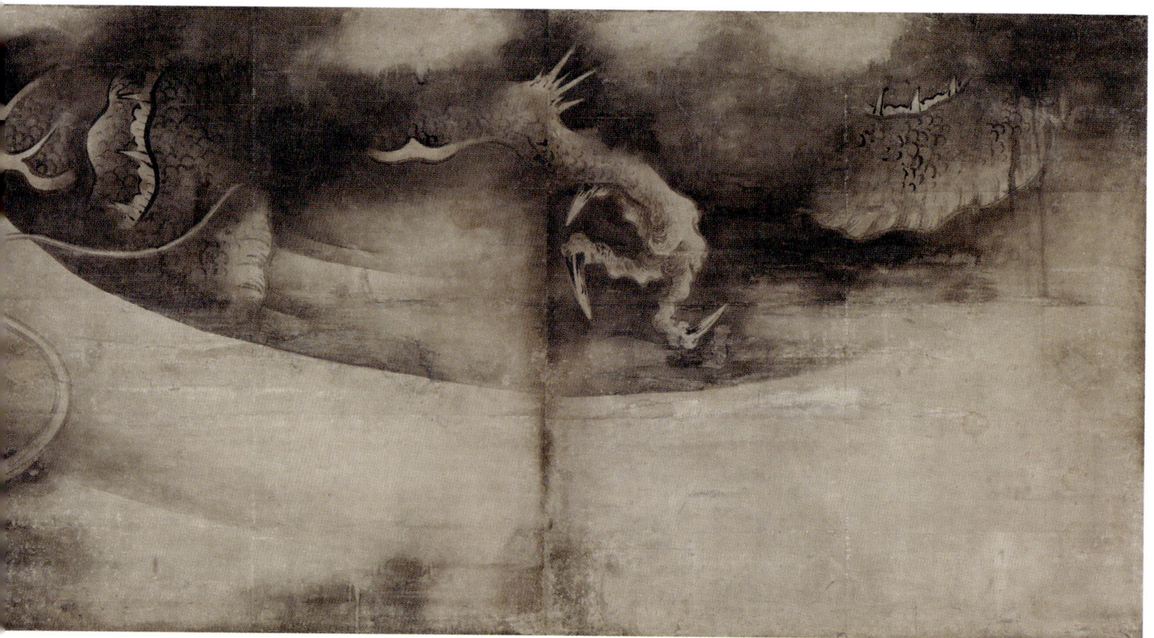

Important Cultural Property

Dragons and Clouds Kaihō Yūshō 1599 Kenninji, Kyoto

Kaihō Yūshō (1533-1615) was a Momoyama-period painter from a warrior house and is known for his monochrome ink paintings overflowing with vitality. This is an image of two dragons appearing from behind low-hanging dark clouds. One dragon has an open mouth and throbs with energy, while the other has a closed mouth and quietly looks on. It is thought that the contrast of motion and stillness was emphasized by the design choice to have one dragon ascending and one descending. It is recorded that Yūshō's dragon paintings were even sent to the Korean Peninsula, and he became famous there as well; a considerable number of his works still remain. Yūsetsu, who inherited his father's painting style, also did the same kinds of works, and we can surmise that dragon paintings were widely acknowledged to be a specialty of the Kaihō house. Originally this painting was bigger, and spanned eight sliding doors (*fusuma*) that decorated the waiting room for attendants (*reinoma*) of an abbot's chamber, but now it has been remounted into hanging scrolls.

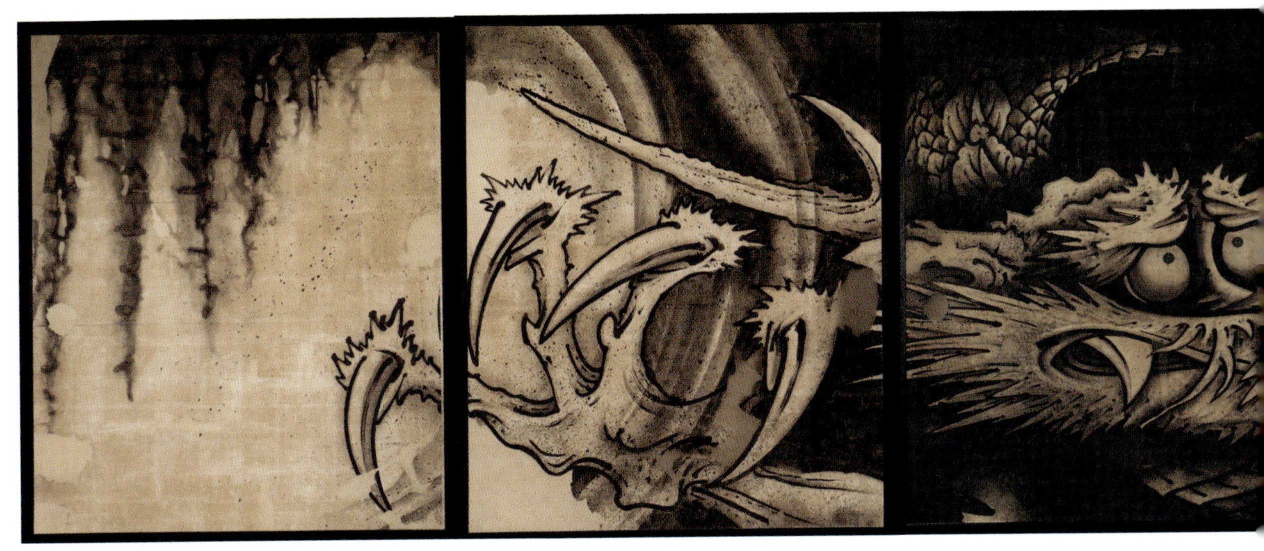

雲龍図襖（部分）

曾我蕭白
宝暦13年（1763）
ボストン美術館

襖８面に逆巻く波濤上の龍をクローズアップして描く。濃墨を垂れるにまかせたかのような雲気には、鬼気迫るものさえ感じられる。播州高砂付近の寺の襖に、黒々と２頭の龍が描かれていたとの伝えがあり、本図はその部分と考えられている。京都・建仁寺大方丈「雲龍図」（海北友松筆）の図様と類似性が認められることから、失われた方の龍は、口を開け下方を睥睨していたか。一般に龍は３本爪だが、本図は４本爪。中国では、皇帝およびその第１子・第２子を象徴する龍は５本爪、第３子・４子は４本爪、それ以下は使用を許されなかったとされる。「鷹図」（香雪美術館蔵）の落款「明大祖皇帝十四世玄孫」に見るように、蕭白は中国・明の皇帝太祖の血をひく者と標榜していたが、それと関係するのであろうか。

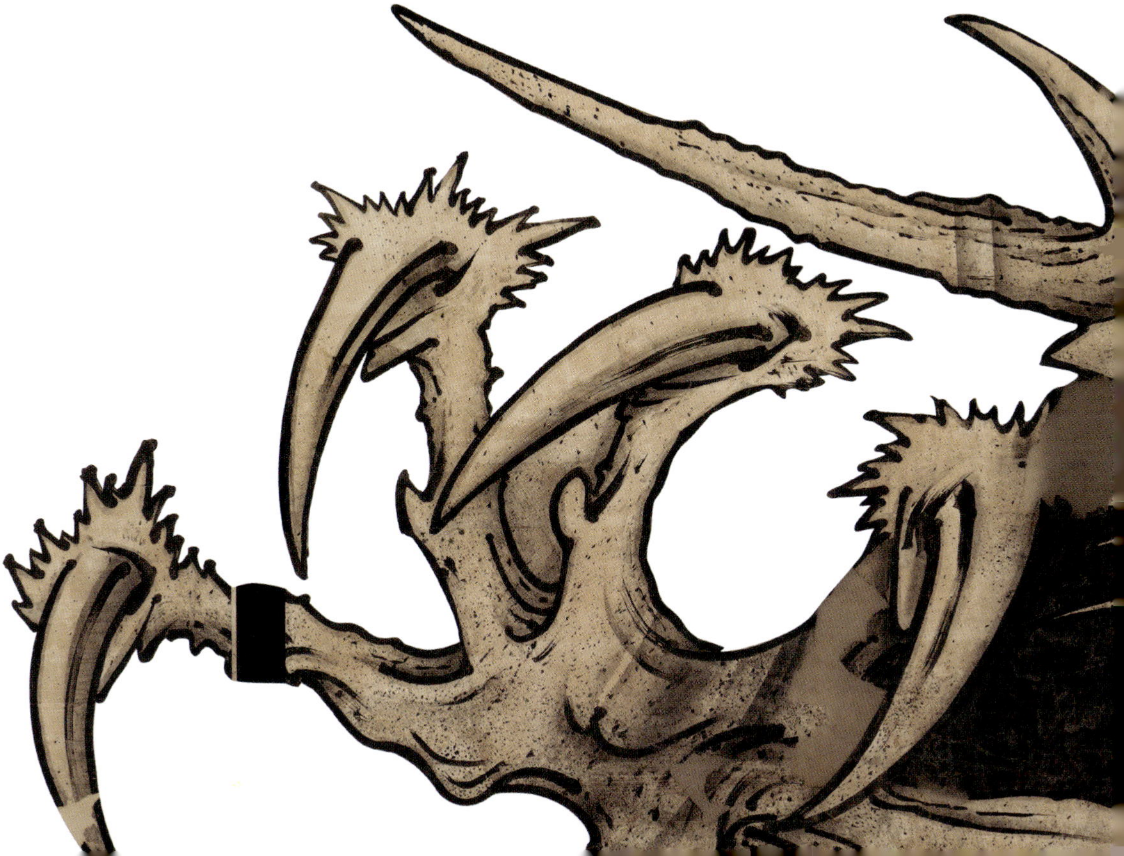

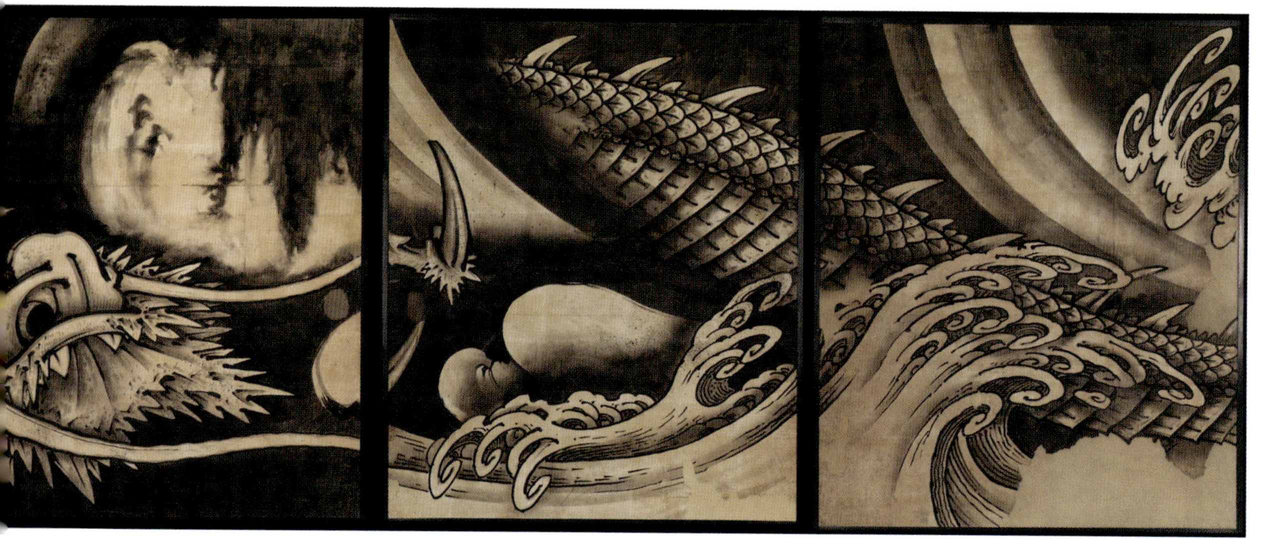

Dragon and Clouds Sliding Doors (detail)

Soga Shōhaku
1763
Museum of Fine Arts, Boston

This is a closeup image of a dragon over a tumultuous sea, the whole of which spanned eight sliding doors. We can feel the eeriness in the stormy clouds that look like they have been formed by letting dark ink drip down over the image. There is a story that Shōhaku painted two dragons in jet black on the sliding doors of a local temple in Takasago, Harima Province, and it is thought that this painting is taken from that larger work. The similarity to the painting *Dragons and Clouds* (Kaihō Yūshō) in the large abbot chambers of Kyoto's Kenninji is widely recognized, so it is likely that the missing dragon had an open mouth, and was glaring at the one on the bottom. Generally, dragons have three claws, but the one in this painting has four. In China, dragons that symbolize the emperor, as well as his first and second-born, have five claws; dragons symbolizing his third and fourth children have four claws—below that cutoff, they are not allowed to use the dragon imagery. As we can see in the signature reading "Fourteenth Great Grandchild of the Founding Emperor of the Ming Dynasty" on *Falcons* (Kosetsu Museum of Art), Shōhaku professed himself to be someone in whom flowed the blood of the founder of the Chinese Ming imperial line, so this is probably somehow related.

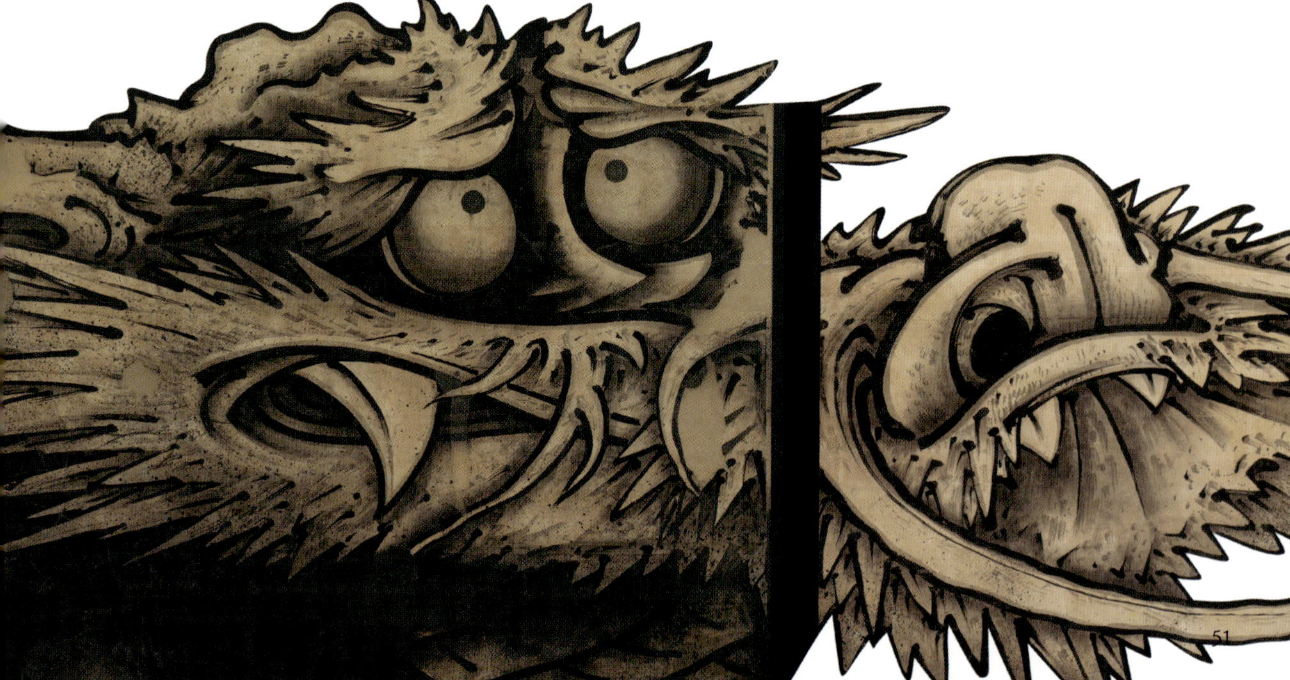

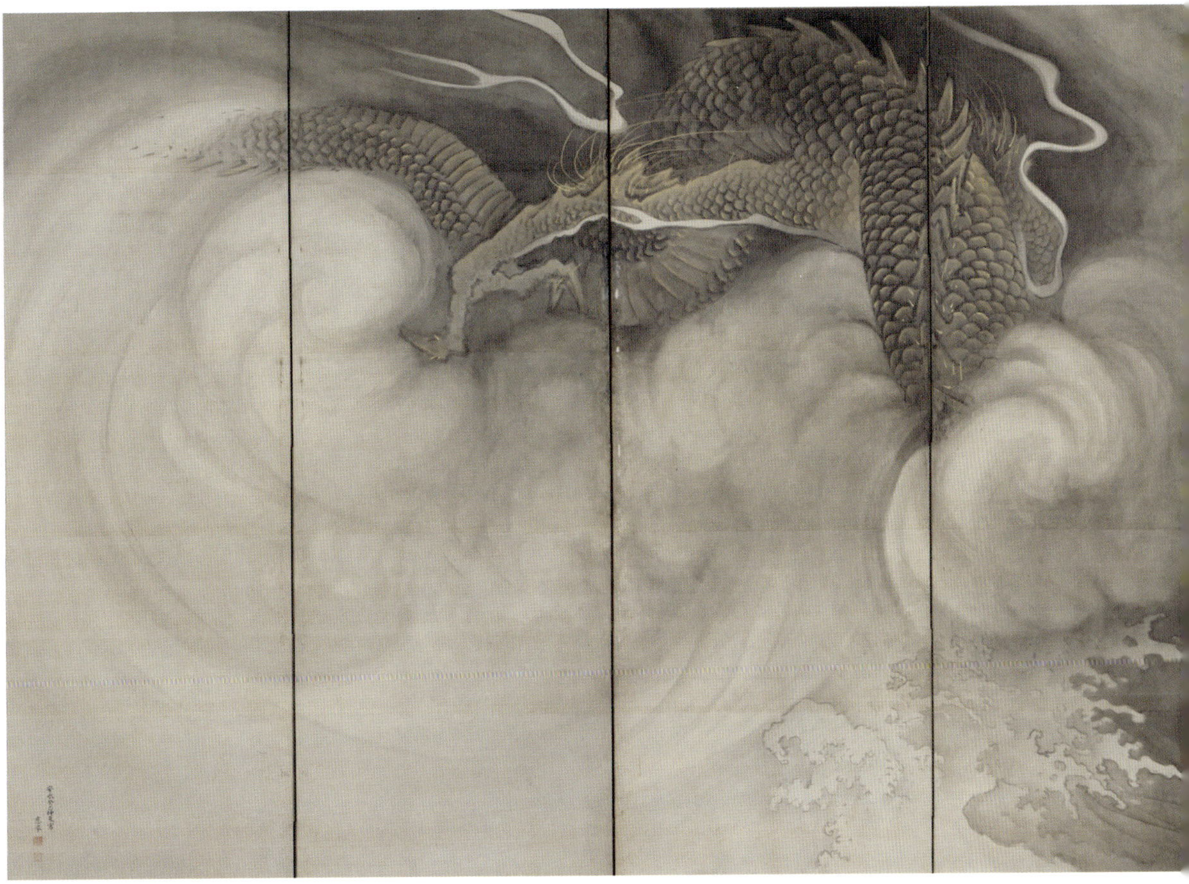

重要文化財

雲龍図屏風

円山応挙
安永2年(1773)

龍という霊獣にふさわしく鱗には金泥が施されるが、鯉に似るとされた形態の描写に当たっては実際の鯉が参考にされたに違いない。屏風の折り目がつくり出す凹凸にも配慮しながら、龍の動きには上下左右という平面上だけでなく前後の方向性までが加えられ、一種のバーチャルリアリティを実現させた。さらに、たらし込みや滲み、暈しといった多彩な墨技を駆使して、渦巻く雲気や逆巻く波濤にこの上ない現実感を与えている。日本絵画史上、これほどリアルな大気表現はかつて存在しなかったものであろう。もと東寺観智院の旧蔵で、灌頂の儀式に用いられたものという。

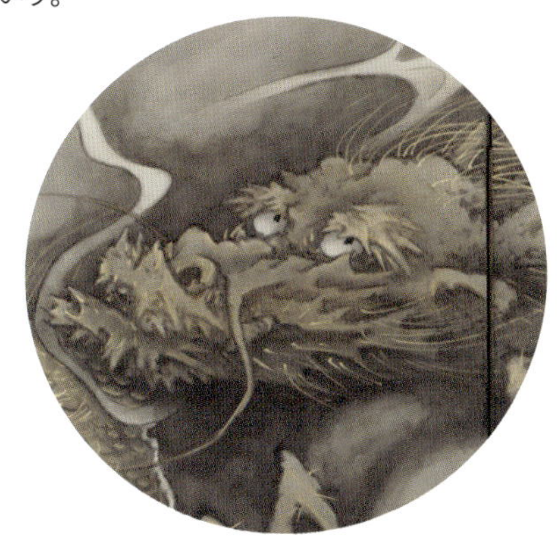

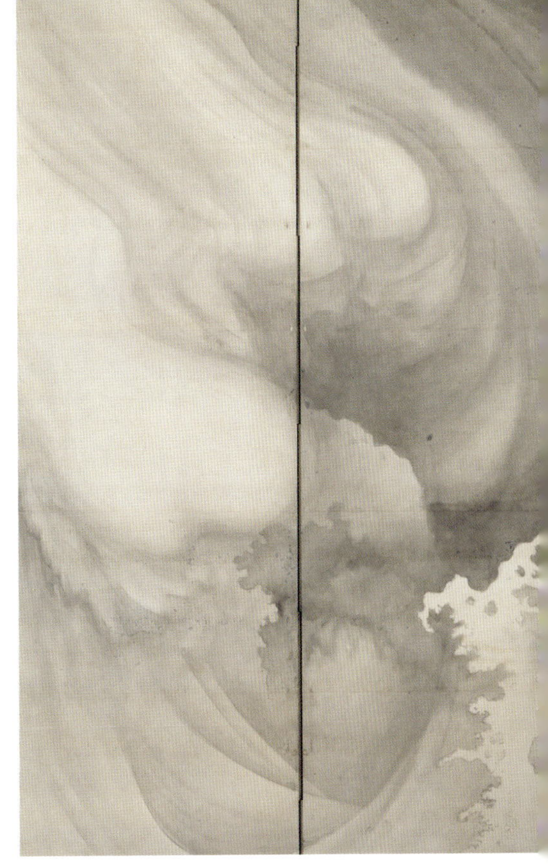

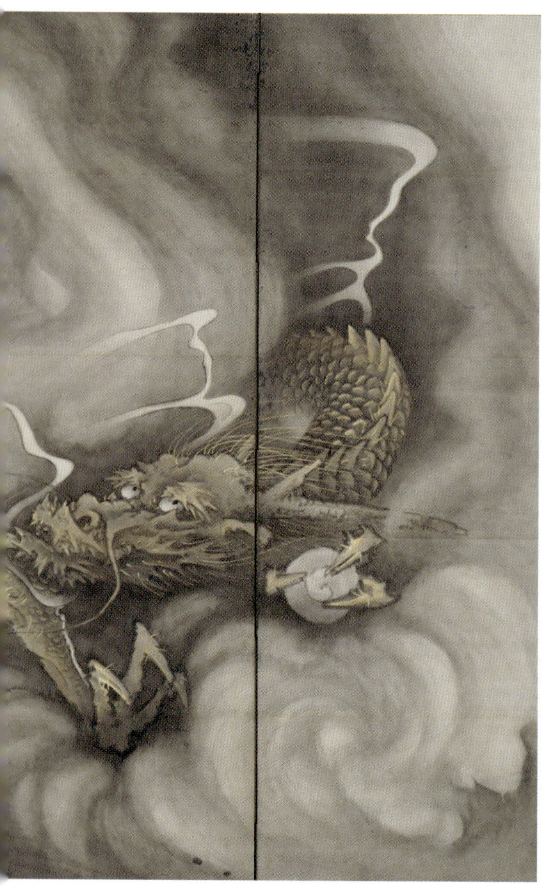

Important Cultural Property

Dragons and Clouds Folding Screens

Maruyama Ōkyo
1773

There is gold paint applied to each of the scales of the dragon, but judging from the body's correspondence to a shape that resembles a carp, it is unmistakable that this painter referred to an actual carp in completing this work. The movement of the dragon is not limited to just all the directions on a flat surface. Ōkyo manages to even add a sense of depth to the image while also taking into consideration the unevenness created by the seams of the folding screen. In doing so, he implements a type of virtual reality. Moreover, Ōkyo creates a sense of reality in the swirling clouds and surging waves by making effective use of various wet ink techniques such as *tarashikomi, nijimi*, and *bokashi*. In the history of Japanese painting, there has probably never been something that felt this real. Originally in the collection of Tōji Kanchi'in, this work was supposedly used for abhisheka (J. *kanjō*) ceremonies.

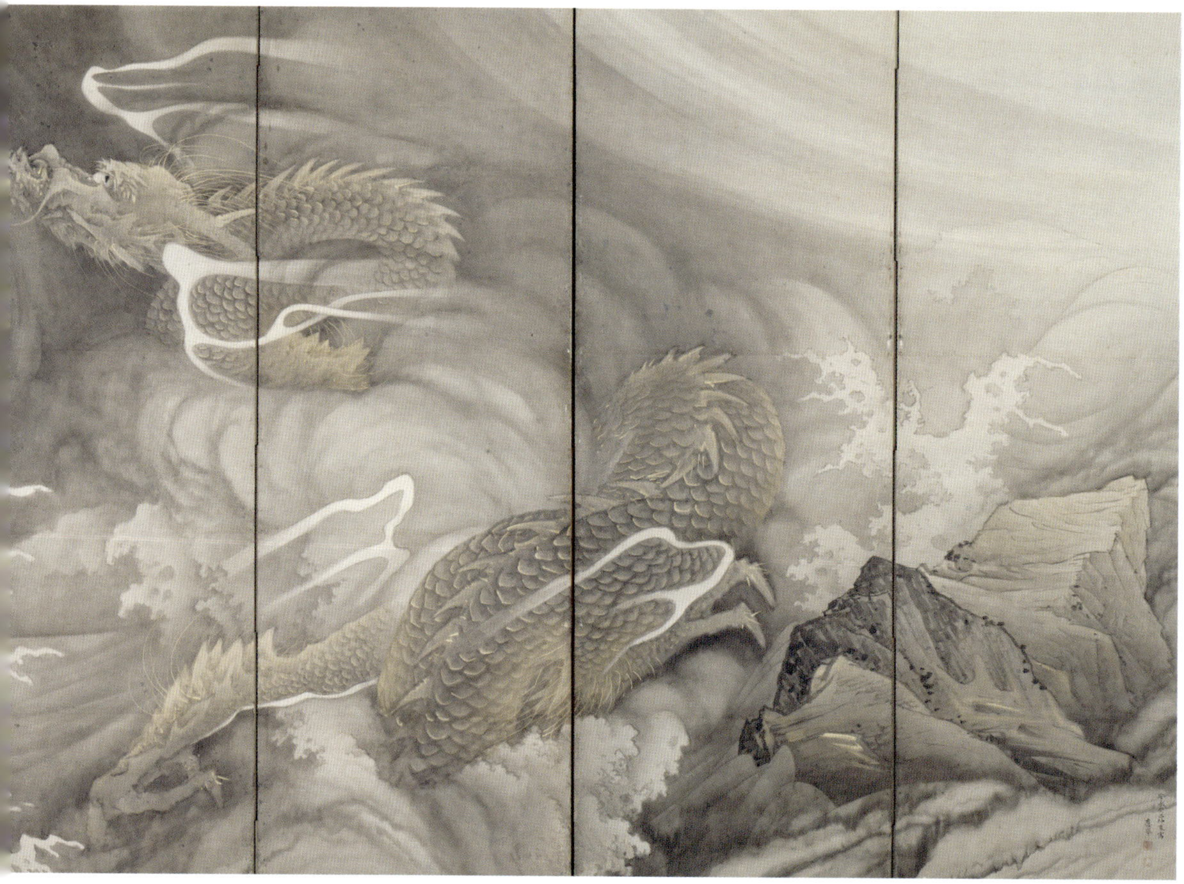

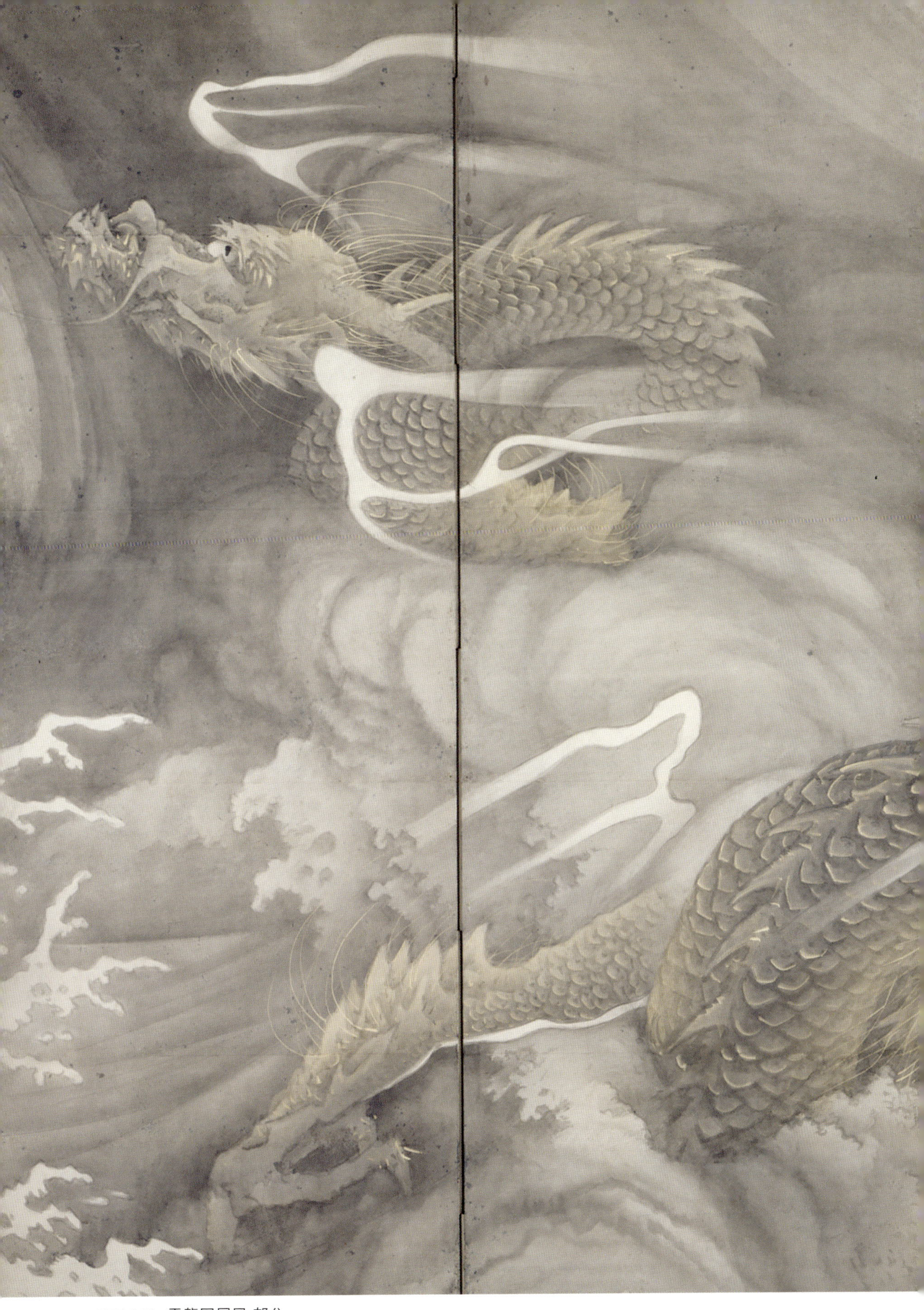

重要文化財　雲龍図屏風 部分
Important Cultural Property *Dragons and Clouds Folding Screens* (detail)

昇龍図

菅井梅関
天保6年(1835)
仙台市博物館

仙台出身の南画家・菅井梅関(1784〜1844)は1835年(天保6)松島を訪れた際に海上に龍を見、絵に描きとめた。当時の藩内は飢饉をもたらした不順な天候下にあり、梅関が見たものは竜巻だったのだろう。しかしながら、図中には「観龍記」が記され、龍を実見したことを疑う風はまったく見えない。この時代まで龍の実在が一般に信じられていたことがわかる。

Ascending Dragon

Sugai Baikan
1835
Sendai City Museum

Sugai Baikan (1784-1844), the *nanga* literati painter from Sendai, saw a dragon over the water when he visited Matsushima in 1835 (Tenpō 6), and painted it. However, around that time, there had been unfavorable weather that had caused a famine in that domain, and what Baikan saw was probably just a water tornado. Despite this, the painting reads "Record of the Dragon I Saw," and we get the sense that he was convinced he had seen a dragon with his own eyes. We can understand that the actual existence of dragons was generally believed in, up to and including that point in time.

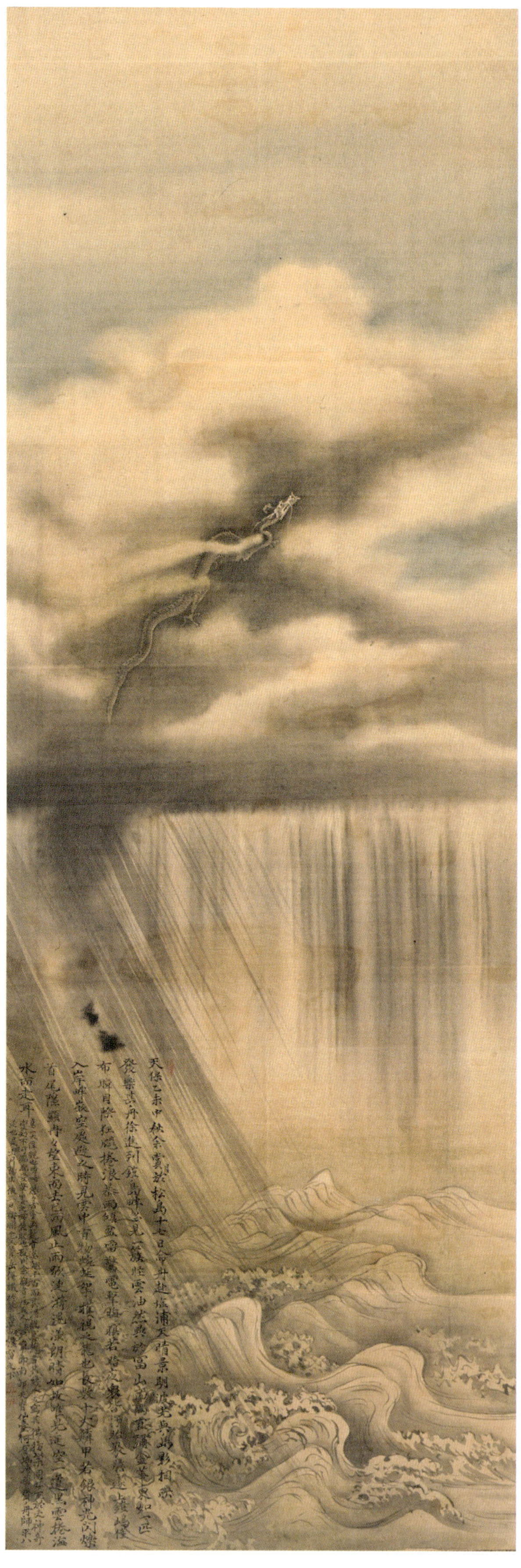

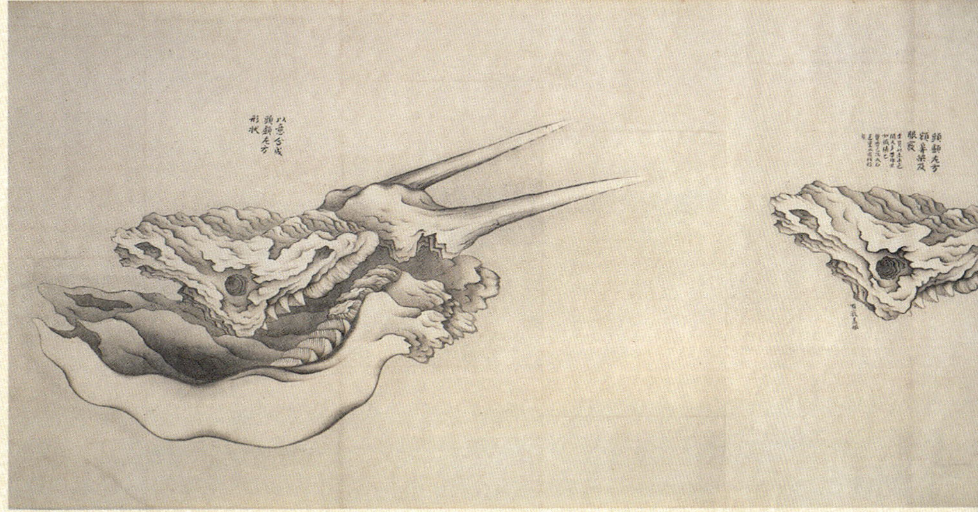

龍骨之図

上田耕夫筆、皆川淇園賛
文化2年(1805)賛

近江膳所藩で、ある出土品を識者に鑑定させたところ、龍骨と判明した。藩ではこれを祥瑞として、出土地を龍ケ谷と命名し伏龍祠なる祠を建て、その地の租税は免除、農民には龍の姓を与えたという。さらに上田耕夫(1760～1832)に写生させ、当代随一の文人・皆川淇園(1734～1807)にその由来を記させた。それが本図である。角に見立てた小さな牙は下あごと巧みに組み合わされ、見事な龍の頭部に作り上げられてしまった。その想像力のたくましさには驚くばかりだ。

Dragon Bones

Painted by Ueda Kōfu, Inscribed by Minagawa Kien
Inscribed in 1805

In Zeze Domain, Ōmi Province, when the excavated bones depicted here were appraised by an expert, they were identified as dragon bones. The domain took this as a good omen, and they named the archaeological site “Dragon Valley” (Tatsugaya). They also built the Crouching Dragon Shrine (Fukuryūshi), and it is said that this area was exempt from other taxes, and instead, the farmers offered them in the name of the dragon. Moreover, the domain had Ueda Kōfu (1760-1832) draw the bones, and they had the literatus Minagawa Kien (1734-1807) record their history from their origins to the present day—this is that record. Here, the bones have been skillfully put together so that the small tusks of the lower mandible look like horns, and they really look like a dragon’s head. Such robust power of imagination is truly amazing.

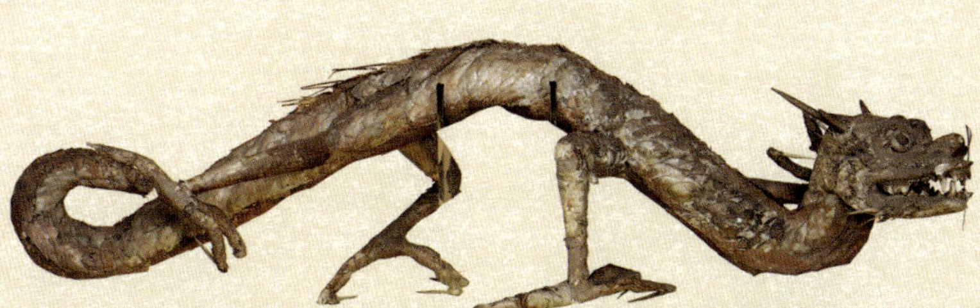

龍のミイラ

江戸時代(19c)
大阪・瑞龍寺

Dragon Mummy

19th century
Zuiryūji, Osaka

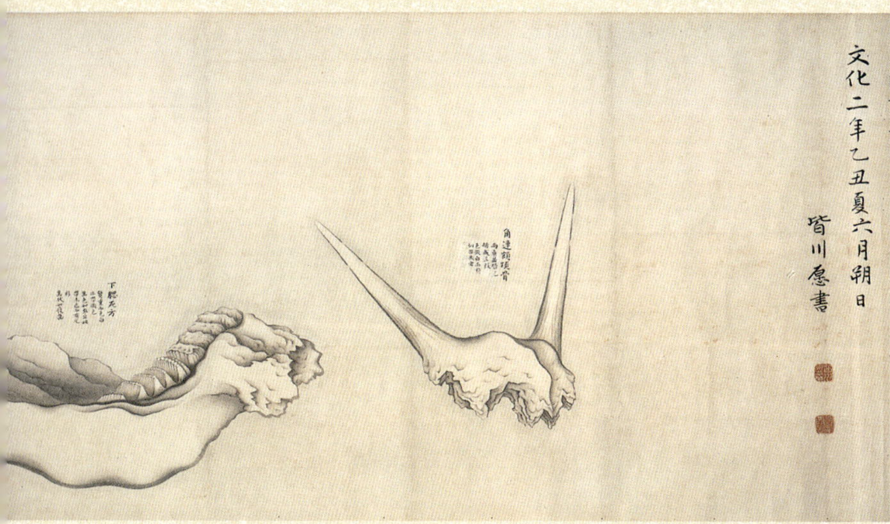

トウヨウゾウの化石

近江国滋賀郡南庄村出土
文化元年(1804)出土
国立科学博物館

琵琶湖付近の小丘から掘り出された、40万年前の象(トウヨウゾウ)の化石。発掘当時の認識は、龍骨－奈良時代の正倉院にも納められた薬の元－だった。郷里・小豆島の海中から得たものを平賀源内も所持し、物産会に出品したり、江戸参府中のオランダ商館長らに見せて驚かせたりした。弄石家として知られる木内石亭(1724～1808)の『雲根志』(1801年刊)にも、近江国などで採集された例がみえる。源内・石亭といった一部の学者や好事家たちは、その形状から象の骨の化石と予想していたようだが、日本には象が生息しないため疑問視されていたのである。阿波の小原峒山著『龍骨一家言』によって、龍骨の一部が象の骨の化石であることが結論づけられたのは1811年(文化8)。先の発掘から、わずか7年後のことであった。

Fossils of Asian Elephants

Archaeological Excavation in Minami Shōmura, Shiga, Ōmi Province
Excavated in 1804
National Museum of Nature and Science

These are the fossils of elephants (Asian elephants) from four hundred thousand years ago that were excavated from a small hill near Lake Biwa. The contemporary understanding of this excavation was that these were dragon bones, like the ones that had been stored in the Shōsōin as an ingredient for medicine in the Nara period. Hiraga Gennai also owned some bones that he had gotten from the beaches of his hometown in Shōdoshima, and he put them on display at a trade show, shocking the members of the Dutch trade delegation visiting Edo. Even in *Unkonshi* (published 1801), by Kiuchi Sekitei (1724-1808), an aficionado of collecting unusual stones and gems (*rōseki*), you can see examples that were gathered from places like Ōmi Province. It seems that dilettantes and some scholars like Gennai and Sekitei were conjecturing that, judging from this shape, dragon bones were the fossils of elephants. However, people were still skeptical since there were no elephants living in Japan, but in the 1811 (Bunka 8) *Ryūkotsu ikkagen* (*My Opinion on Dragon Bones*), Ohara Tōzan of Awa concluded that some dragon bones were indeed actually the fossilized bones of elephants. It was just seven years after the excavation.

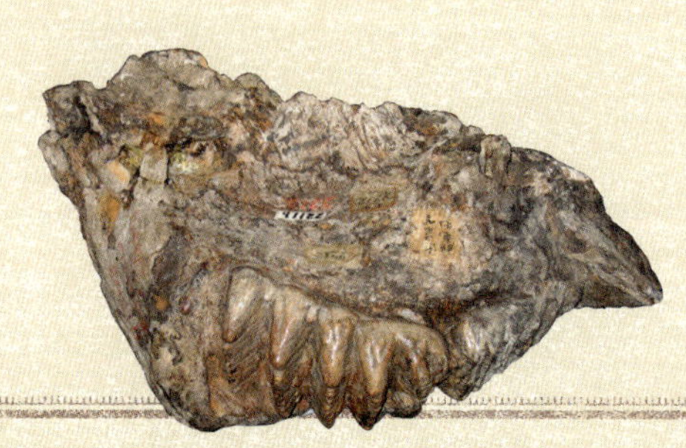

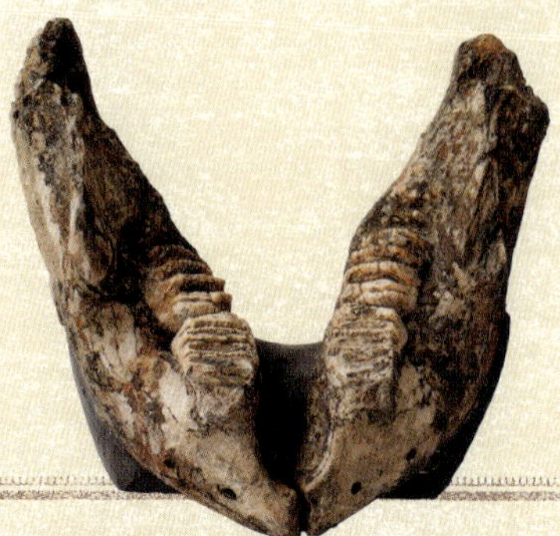

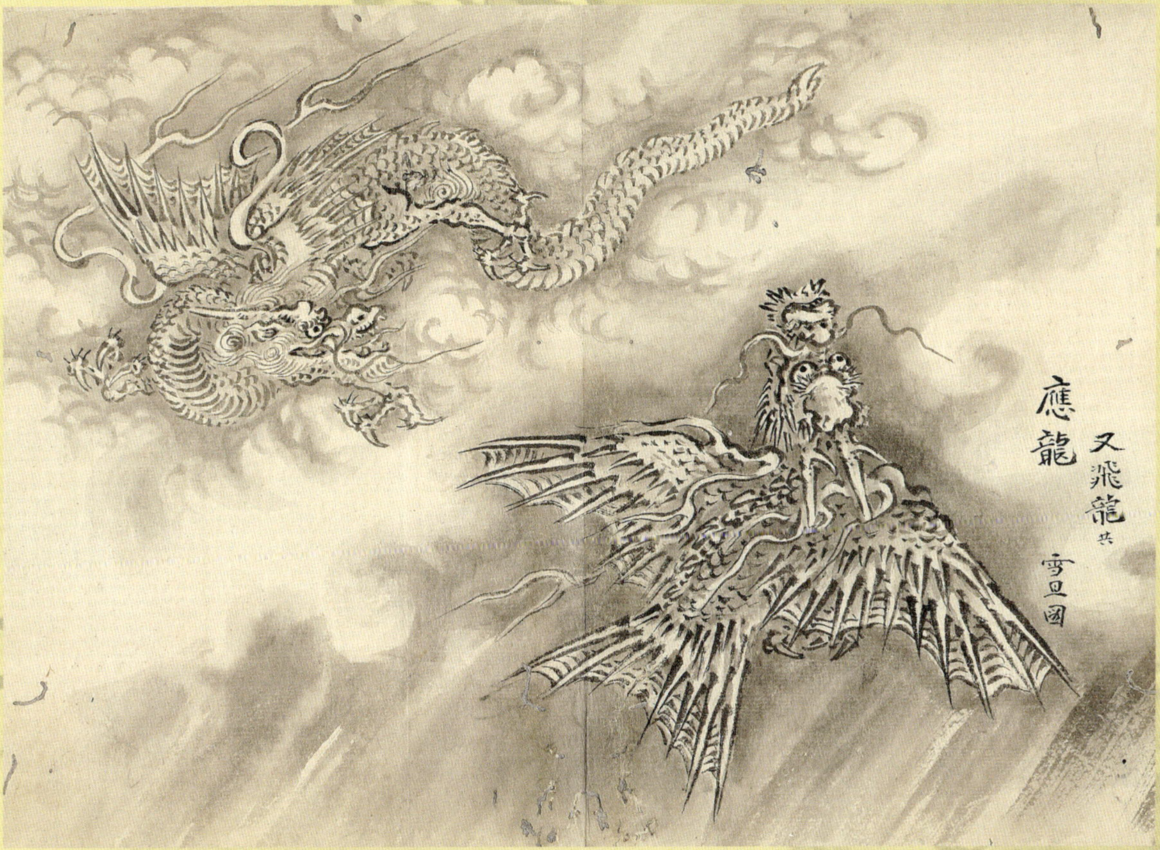

飛龍図(『魚類譜・魚介図』より)
長谷川雪旦・雪堤
江戸時代(18c〜19c)
国立公文書館

Flying Dragons (from *Genealogies of Fish*)
Hasegawa Settan and Settei
18th-19th century
National Archives of Japan

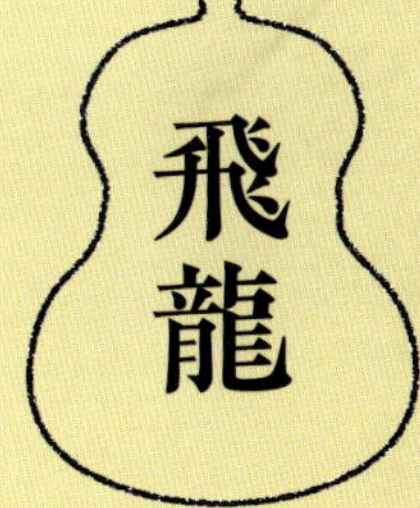

翼のある龍で、応龍とも言う。一般には龍の頭、魚のような胴体、翼のある姿で表現される。水や波との組み合わせで表現される場合が多く、火防の意味合いも担っていたものと考えられる。またその図様から、鯉が竜門の滝を昇り龍に変じる、との故事「登竜門」のイメージも付加されていたように思われる。

The Flying Dragon

This is a dragon with wings, and it is also known as the *yinglong* (J. *ōryū*). Generally, this creature is portrayed as having wings, the body of a fish, and the head of a dragon. There are many scenes where it is portrayed with waves or water of some sort, and it is thought that it also carries the connotation of fire prevention. Also, from this depiction, it seems that there is the added nuance of the story of the legendary gateway to success (*tōryūmon*), where the carp that swims up through the dragon-gate (*ryūmon*) waterfall becomes a dragon.

飛龍図

原在中
文政12年(1829)

原在中(1750～1837)は、石田幽汀・円山応挙ら写生画を得意とした画人に教えを受けるとともに、中国や日本の古画を幅広く学び、故実にも造詣が深かったという。長寿を保ち、晩年まで旺盛な制作活動を続けた。80歳の年記がある本図からは、筆力の衰えは全く感じられない。長寿の在中が描いた吉祥画には、さらに目出度さが加わり喜ばれたことであろう。

Flying Dragon

Hara Zaichū
1829

Hara Zaichū (1750-1837) learned from painters that were skilled at drawing from nature like Ishida Yūtei and Maruyama Ōkyo. He also widely studied the ancient paintings of China and Japan, and he was well-versed in ancient practices. Zaichū led a long life and continued actively painting until his final years. This work is dated to when he was eighty years old, and yet we cannot feel any weakening in the strength of his brushstrokes whatsoever. The auspicious paintings the long-lived Zaichū did were especially felicitous, and the recipients must have been delighted.

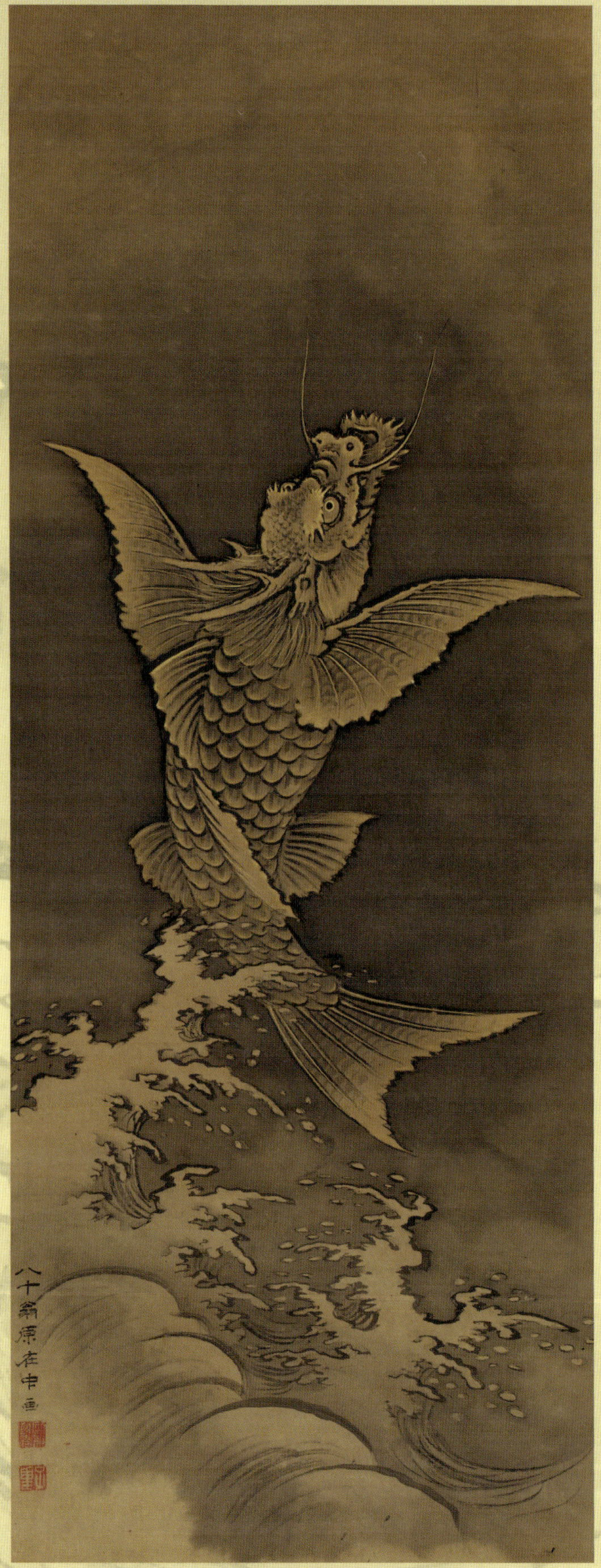

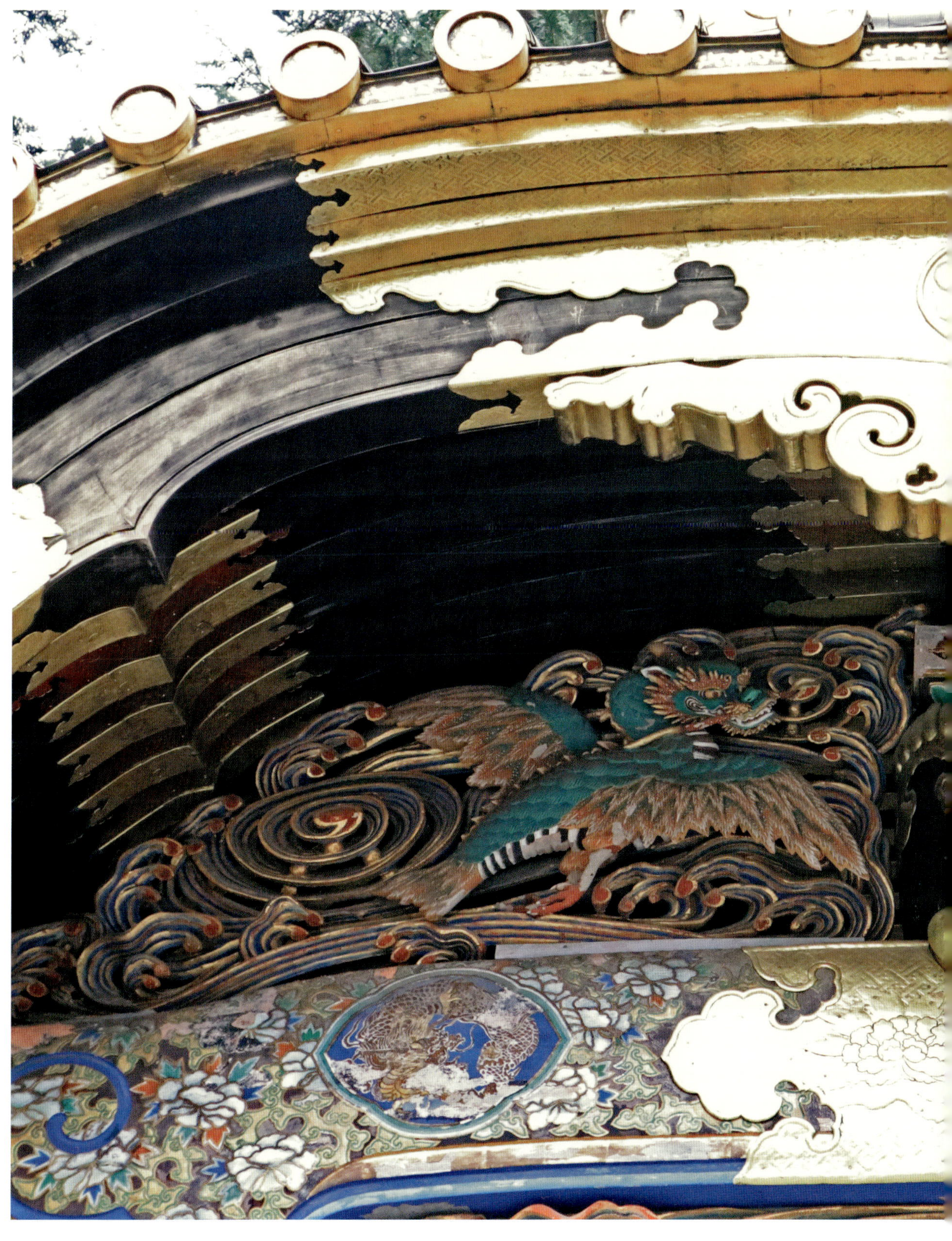

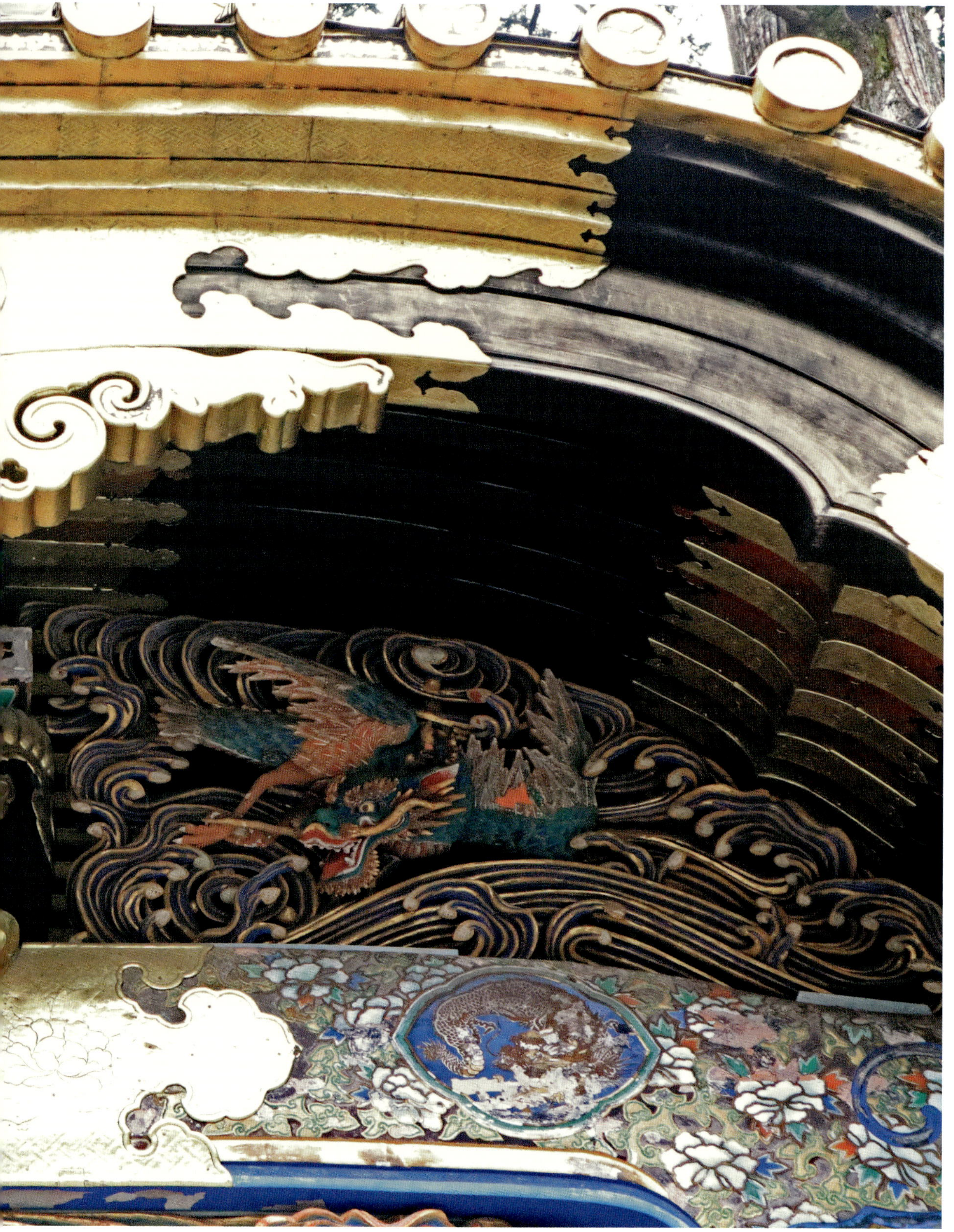

国宝
飛龍彫刻(御水舎)
寛永13年(1636)
日光東照宮

National Treasure
Flying Dragons Sculpture *(from Omizuya, Water Purification Building)*
1636
Nikkō Tōshōgū Shrine, Tochigi

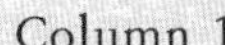

Column 1

実証の風、江戸に吹く

虎と龍

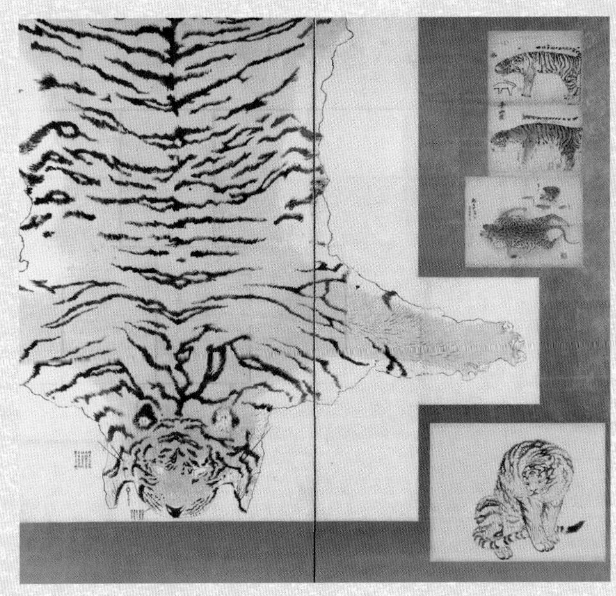

[1] 円山応挙「虎皮写生図」
Sketch of a Tiger Hide by Maruyama Ōkyo

「百聞は一見に如かず」という言葉がある。古代中国の『漢書』に由来するとのことだから、人は古くからこのことを認識し、また実践してきたのであろう。江戸時代の日本でも、先に記した博物学の隆盛に呼応するように、対象をよく観察し見たとおりに描くという、今ではあたりまえの写生が始まることになる。次第に台頭しつつあった実証主義的な精神(ものを実際に観察・記録し、その本質を見極めようとする科学的な態度)を背景に、絵画の世界でも写実的な表現が求められてきたのである。

この写生画[1]の確立者である円山応挙(1733～95)は、当時西洋から移入されつつあった銅版画などから遠近法や陰影法を習得していったのだが、その応挙に興味深い逸話が伝えられている。臥猪(寝そべった猪)の絵を注文された応挙は、知らずに病に伏した猪を写生したのだが、完成間近の絵を猪の生態に詳しい山中に暮らす老翁に見せたところ、病気の猪であると指摘されてしまった。応挙はそこで、この人物から教えてもらった元気な猪が寝そべる姿に描き直した。ちなみに最初に写生した猪は、指摘されたとおり間もなく死んでしまったという。滝沢馬琴(1767～1849)が1802年(享和2)京坂への旅中の伝聞として記録したもので、すでに応挙の生前から語られていた話のようだ。

この逸話が語るように、真に迫った動物画が求められる状況において、応挙門下やその周辺画家のなかから、描写そのものが名人芸の域に達するものが現われた。「一科の芸」ともいう画家の専売特許のようなものだが、虎を描かせればその右に出る者がなかったのが岸駒(1749～1838)である[2]。応挙が亡くなって3年後の1798年(寛政10)、岸駒は中国商人を通じて虎の頭骨を入手した。そこで虎の頭部の皮を知人から借り受け、この上にかぶせてみるとまるで生

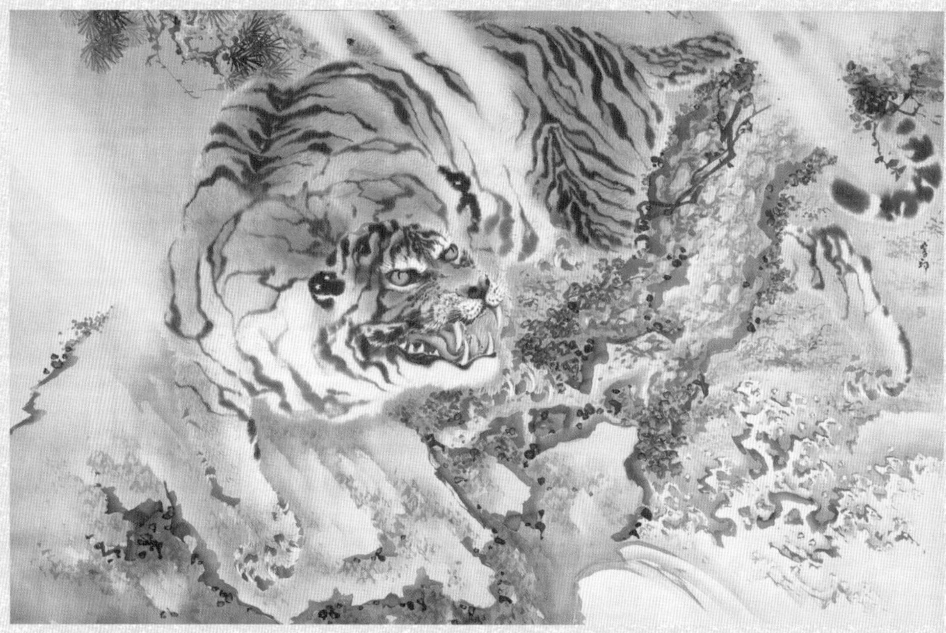

[2] 岸駒「猛虎図」
Fierce Tiger by Ganku

Winds of Authenticity in Edo:

Tigers and Dragons

There is a saying that "seeing is believing." The Japanese version of it finds its origins in the Chinese *Hanshu* (*Book of the Han;* J. *Kanjo*). Since ancient times, people have internalized this saying and acted upon it. The Edo period was a time with a pronounced interest in natural history. The era marked the beginning of the now-common practice of painting from life. The practice of observing a thing and recording it gained increasing prominence within the Edo period's tendency to verify the nature and shape of a given thing. As a result, it became a major tradition in painting.

The man who established the practice of painting from life in Japan was Maruyama Ōkyo (1733-95). He did so[1] by studying the modes of perspective and other conventions of Western painting by way of copperplate prints from Europe. When Ōkyo was asked to paint an image of a sleeping boar, he mistakenly rendered the animal as if looking sick. As Ōkyo was working on the image, he showed it to an old man living in the mountains who alerted the painter that he had painted a sick boar, not a sleeping one. "The boar you painted looks like it will die any minute," the old man said to Ōkyo. This episode is recorded in the 1802 travel diary of Takizawa Bakin, so it must have already circulated while Ōkyo was still alive.

This anecdote shows how Ōkyo and painters in his orbit had reached a new peak in their mastery of depicting animals. Naturalism became their trademark, but none other was more skilled at painting tigers than Kishi Ganku (1749-1838)[2]. Three years after Ōkyo died, in 1798 (Kansei 10), Ganku acquired a tiger skull from a Chinese merchant. Following that purchase, he quickly procured a tiger's hide which he laid on top of the skull as if the animal was still alive. That practice resulted in tiger paintings that differed markedly from those by other artists. Ganku paired his understanding of the animal's spirit with an intimate knowledge of its physique. Every inch is carefully laid out and every fang and tooth follows the creature's actual physiology. Ganku eventually also acquired four tiger legs, which allowed him to understand the positioning of its claws and feet, along with its movements. Truly, Ganku was more of a scientist than a painter.

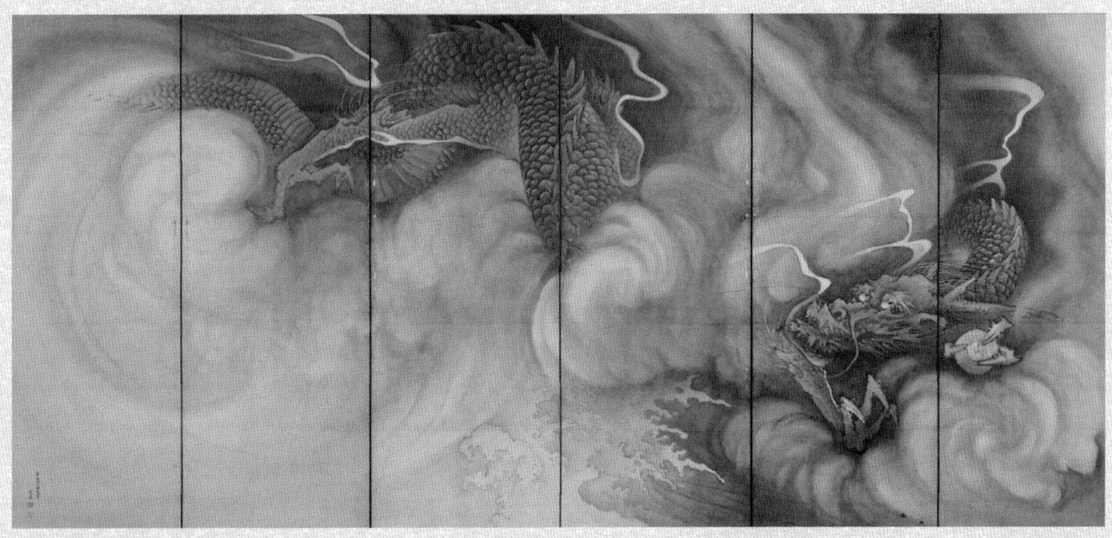

[3] 円山応挙「雲龍図屛風」部分
Dragons and Clouds (detail) by Maruyama Ōkyo

きているようだ。その表情や形態は、世間の画家が手がけるものとは全く違う。岸駒はさっそく筆をとり、あらゆる方向から精密な写生に精魂をかたむけるとともに各部の寸法を計測、牙と歯の本数や詳細な形状までも記録した。岸駒は続けて虎の四脚も手に入れ、指や爪の本数や位置関係はもちろん、関節の構造と動きの把握にまで努めている。その態度たるや、もはや画家ではなく科学者そのものであろう。

当時は解剖学が発展期を迎えており、人体描写に際し骨の構造自体を把握することの重要性が応挙らにより唱えられてもいた。従来の猫を手本としたような作とは打って変わったリアルな虎図の生み出された背景には、このような秘密があったわけである。

思えば、40歳を迎えた伊藤若冲（1716～1800）が、家業を弟に譲り画業を本格化させたのが1755年（宝暦5）。この年に手がけた「虎図」には、自分は本物でなければ描かないが、日本には虎がいないので（仕方なく）中国画に倣って模写した、と記されていた。現実に存在するものをしっかり観察して描くことを自らに課した、若冲の絵画観の逆説的な表明とも読み取れるものだったが、それからわずか半世紀足らずのうちに写生画は格段の進歩を遂げていたのである。

∽

それでは、しばしば虎と対で描かれる龍についてはどうだったろうか。中国明代の百科全書ともいうべき李時珍の『本草綱目』では、龍の姿を「形に九似あり」として、頭は駱駝、角は鹿、目は鬼、耳は牛、項は蛇、腹は蜃（みずち）、鱗は鯉、爪は鷹、掌は虎に似ると説明している。中国では王権の象徴でもあった龍は、鰐がモデルともいわれるが、日本にもたらされたそのイメージはほとんど形を変えることなく受け継がれてきた。[3] また、江戸時代になっても龍そのものの存在が疑われることはなかったようである。

博物学に熱中した藩主たちは、異国産のトカゲや鰐を龍の一種と見ていた[4] ようだし、応挙はスケッチ帳に摂津不動院の什物だった「龍の掌」を描写、皆川淇園（1734～1807）の詩文集には龍に化す前の蛇を見た体験談が綴られて

With the increased study of anatomy at the time, Ōkyo and other painters emphasized the importance bone structure for accurately representing the human body. The evolution of tiger pictures from enlarged cats to actual tigers initiated new developments in painting.

In 1755 (Hōreki 5), when Itō Jakuchū (1716-1800) reached age forty, he handed over the leadership of the family's greengrocer business to his younger brother and fully devoted himself to painting. As he created an image of a tiger that year, Jakuchū was conscious of the fact that tigers did not exist in Japan so he relied on a Chinese image as his model. Jakuchū represents a paradoxical case where he relied equally on printed or painted imagery as well as on the study of real things for his artworks. Nevertheless, it becomes clear from such stories that the practice of painting from life had made significant leaps within just fifty years' time.

∽

Here, we shall consider dragons which often flank tigers in Japanese painting. The Ming dynasty encyclopedia *Compendium of Materia Medica* records that dragons "resemble the letter 'nine.'" It goes on by explaining that their heads are similar to camels, their horns are like deer, their eyes like demons, their ears like cows, their napes like snakes, their bellies like clams, their scales like carps, their claws like falcons, and their palms like tigers. Dragons in China were symbols of imperial power and they may have been based on crocodiles. In Japan, the shape of Chinese dragons was adopted largely without changes.[3] Even during the Edo period the existence of dragons was not questioned.

Regional lords that had an interest in natural history acquired images or parts of lizards and crocodiles thinking they represented dragons. This misconception can be gleaned from such examples as Ōkyo's sketch of a "dragon's palm" from the collection of Fudōin in Settsu Province, and Minagawa Kien's (1734-1807) anecdote about seeing a snake that transformed into a dragon. The novella *Kōshi yawa* (*Nightly Chats in the Year of the Rat*) by the lord of Hirado Domain, Matsuura Seizan, records a passage about seeing an "actual dragon." The book says that in 1764 (Meiwa 1) a retainer of the lord of Iida Domain witnessed a towering creature with glowing eyes in the middle of a nocturnal rainstorm. The book goes on by saying that the creature was forty meters long. In 1835 (Tenpō 6), the Sendai-born literati painter Sugai Baikan (1784-1844) saw a dragon hovering above the ocean at Matsushima. In reality, he

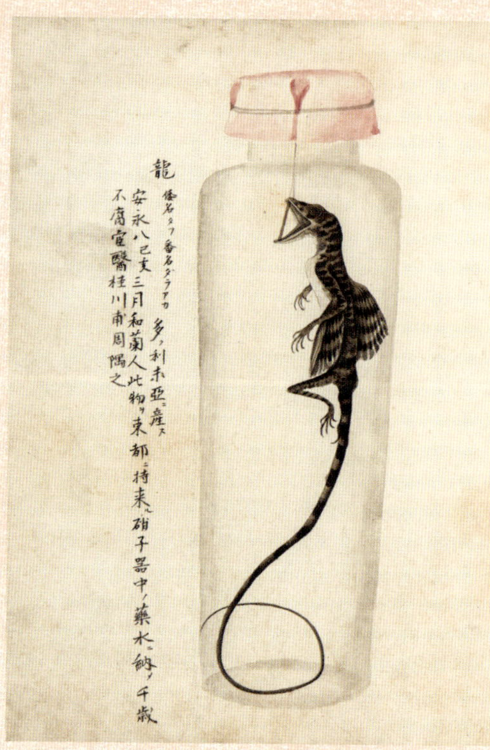

[4] 佐竹曙山「龍の図」(『佐竹曙山写生帖』より)
Dragon from *A Sketch Book* by Satake Shozan

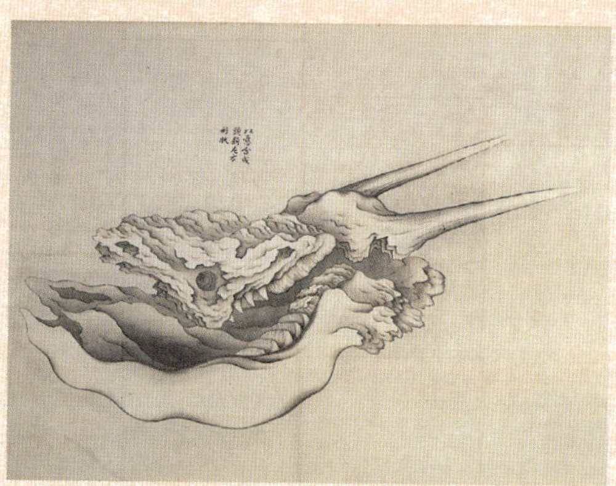

[5] 上田耕夫「龍骨之図」部分
Dragon Bones by Ueda Kōfu

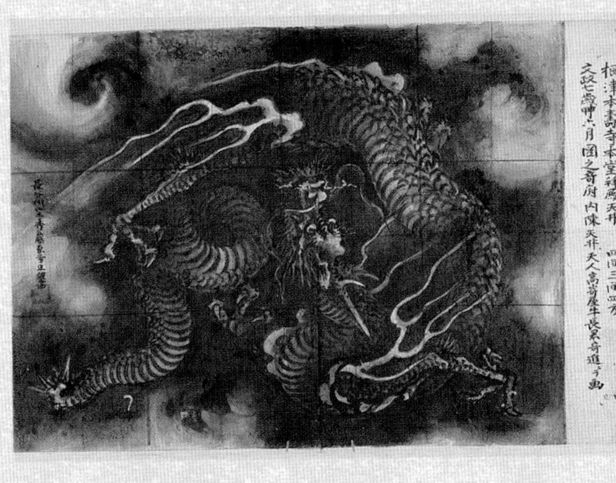

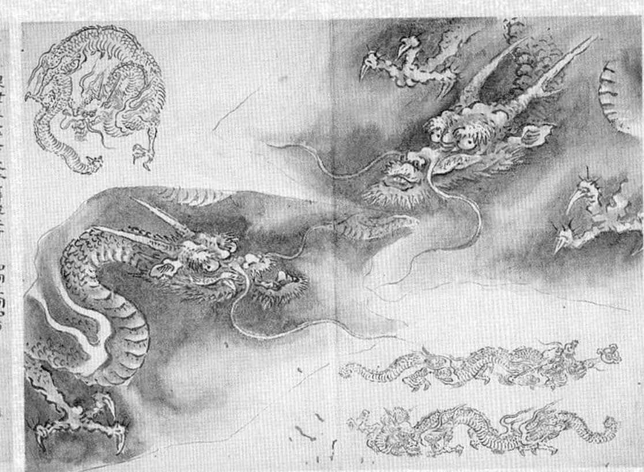

[7] 長谷川雪旦・雪堤『魚類譜・魚介図』より
Genealogies of Fish
by Hasegawa Settan and Settei

いる。さらに、平戸藩主・松浦静山は随筆『甲子夜話』に「真龍を見し事」として以下のような伝聞を記録した。1764年（明和元）江戸でのこと、飯田藩堀家の家臣が暴風雨の夜に、小ぶりな提灯ほどの大きさの眼を光らせた松の大木のようなものが、眼前を通過するのを見たというのである。長さ20余間というから、40メートル近くもあったようだ。また1835年（天保6）、仙台出身の南画家・菅井梅関（1784～1844）は松島を訪れた際、龍を海上に見た。もちろん竜巻だったのだろうが、その情景を描いた図上にしたためられた「観龍記」から、龍の実見を疑う風はまったくうかがえないのである。

そのような状況のなか、1804年（文化元）琵琶湖付近の小さな丘から不思議な石が掘り出された。農民は龍の骨と思い、さっそく藩主に献上。瑞祥（めでたいしるし）と見た藩は、この農民に褒美に加え龍の姓を下賜するとともに、絵師に写生させ当代一の文人にその由来を記させた[5]のであった。掛軸や巻物仕立てのものが少なからず制作されており、注目度も相当高かったものとみえる。実のところこの骨は、40万年前に日本に生息していたトウヨウゾウの下あごと牙部分の化石で、完全な骨格が出土したわけではなかったのだが、それらをうまく組み合わせ龍の頭部に作り上げてしまったのである。その想像力のたくましさには驚くばかりだ。

なお、『江戸名所図会』（1834～36刊）の絵師として知られる長谷川雪旦（1778～1843）と雪堤（1813～82）父子による『魚類譜・魚介図』（国立公文書館内閣文庫蔵）中に興味深い図がある。名家や諸寺院所蔵の龍図の模写や社寺の建築彫刻と思われる龍のスケッチ[6]と並んで、鰐の頭部（側面と上面からの写生図）[7]が収録されているのである。注記によれば雪堤が、1686年（貞享3）の古図を1832年（天保3）に模写したことが知れる。原図の由来は不明だが、19世紀を迎えて江戸の画人の間には、鰐と龍とは一連のものであるとの認識があった可能性が高い。まさに虚・実の間に翻弄された状況を、残された絵が物語ってくれているようである。

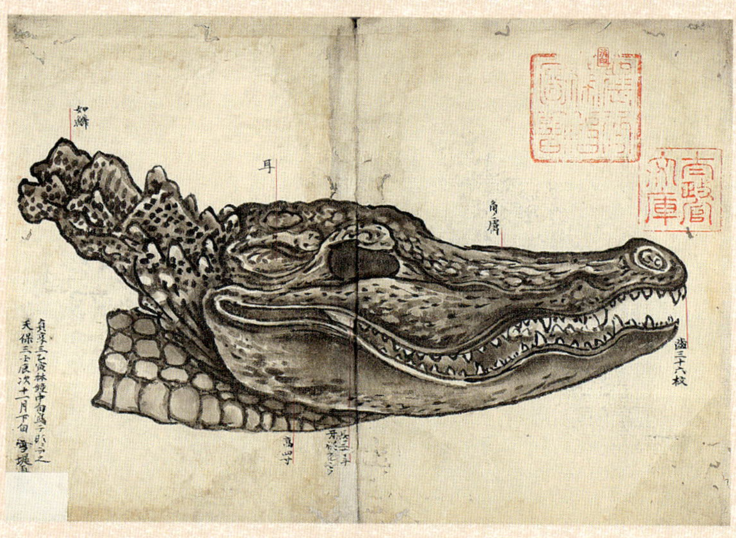

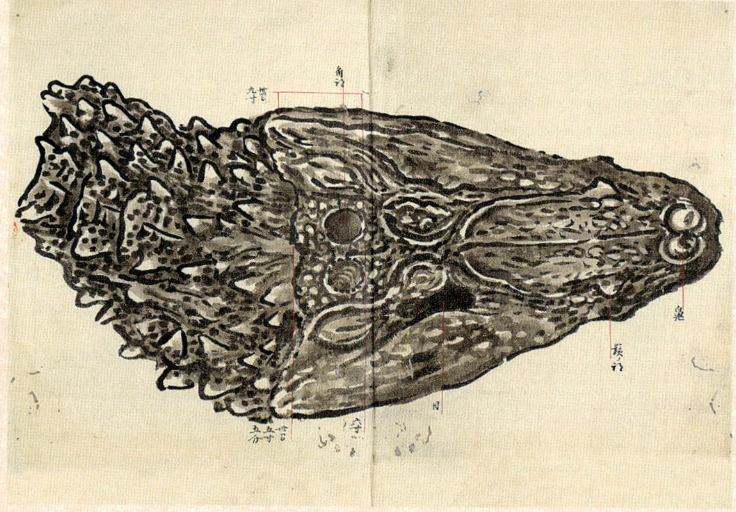

[7]
長谷川雪旦・雪堤『魚類譜・魚介図』より
Genealogies of Fish
by Hasegawa Settan and Settei

may have witnessed a tornado, as we can glean from his sketch of the event. But at the time, the existence of dragons was clearly never brought into question.

Within this context, in 1804 (Bunka 1), people dug up a number of strange bones from a hill near Lake Biwa. Thinking they excavated dragon bones, the peasants quickly brought them to the lord of the domain. The domain's leadership interpreted the finds as auspicious omens. After rewarding the finders and giving the dragon a name, a painter was tasked with drawing the bones and one of the greatest writers of the day was commissioned to compose the story of their discovery.[5] A great number of handscrolls and hanging scrolls were made with similar subjects, illustrating the extent of public interest in dragons. However, the bones were in fact remnants of the tusks of elephants that lived on the Japanese islands four hundred thousand years ago. The level of imagination and fantasy of people at the time is simply amazing.

Let us look at another interpretation of dragons. Hasegawa Settan (1778-1843) and his son Settei are best known for *Edo meisho zue* (*Famous Places of Edo*), published 1834-36. Their book *Genealogies of Fish* contains some curious images. Alongside a number of reproductions of dragon paintings from the collections of famous individuals, temples, and shrines,[6] the book illustrates a crocodile's skull.[7] According to Settei's explanatory note, the image was copied in 1832 (Tenpō 3) from an old work supposedly dating to 1686 (Jōkyō 3). The whereabouts of the original are unknown, but it appears that Edo period painters of the nineteenth century considered dragons and crocodiles to be one and the same thing. These works clearly illustrate the friction between imagination and reality in images of the time.

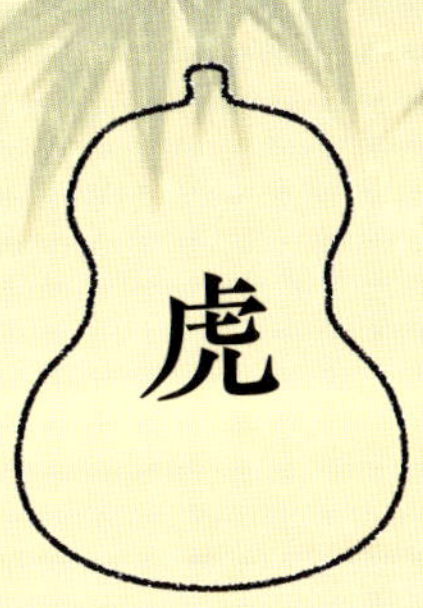

白虎は四神の一つであるが、虎は『本草綱目』によれば、山獣の君主で、形は猫のようで、大きさは牛ほど、黄の地色に黒い紋様がある。鋸のような牙、鉤爪、鬚は堅く尖り、舌は掌ほどの大きさで、刺が逆さまに生えている。項は短く、鼻は詰まり、夜間に物を視るには、一方の目で光を放ち、他方の目で物を見る。吼える声は雷のようで、吼えるに従い風が起こり、百獣は震え恐れる。あるいは、虎は犬を食えば酔う。犬は虎にとって酒なのである、ともいう。また、五百歳になると白く変ずるという。虎は、日本では縄文時代草創期に絶滅したらしいが、朝鮮半島には棲息しており、存在自体は古くから知られていた。勇猛と威厳のシンボルとして尊重され、仏教においては四天王のひとつ毘沙門天の使いであると考えられた。なお、生きた虎の初渡来は890年（寛平2）のことと伝えられる。さらに戦国時代以降、明船により度々もたらされ、文禄・慶長期の朝鮮出兵時（1592～98）に当地で捕獲された虎が秀吉のもとに何度か運ばれた。この際の加藤清正（1562～1611）による虎退治の話は有名。

The Tiger

Within tigers, the white tiger Byakko is one of the Four Guardians. According to the *Compendium of Materia Medica*, the tiger is the lord of the mountain beasts; its shape that of a cat, its size is that of an ox, and it has a pattern of black stripes on a yellow ground. It has claws and fangs like saws; its whiskers are stiffly tapered; its tongue is as big as the palm of a hand; and its spines grow in backwards. Its neck is short, and its nose is pushed in; when the tiger sees at night, one of its eyes emits light, and the other eye actually perceives the lit view. Its roar is like a clap of thunder, and following its roar there is a gust of wind, and all kinds of animals quake in fear. It is said that if a tiger eats a dog, it will get drunk, so perhaps dogs are like alcohol to tigers. The text also says that when a tiger turns five hundred, it will turn white. It seems that tigers in Japan went extinct during the early Jōmon period, but they were still living on the Korean Peninsula, and their existence was known of from very long ago. The tiger is regarded as a symbol of bravery and majesty, and in Buddhism, it is thought to be a messenger of Vaisravana (J. Bishamonten), one of the Four Heavenly Kings. Furthermore, it is also thought that the first living tigers that were brought to Japan were brought in 890 (Kanpyō 2). Moreover, after the Warring States period, tigers were often brought by ships from the Ming empire, and during the Korean expeditions (1592-1598) of the Bunroku and Keichō eras, tigers seized from Korea were brought before Hideyoshi several times. The story of Katō Kiyomasa (1562-1611) killing tigers during this time is famous.

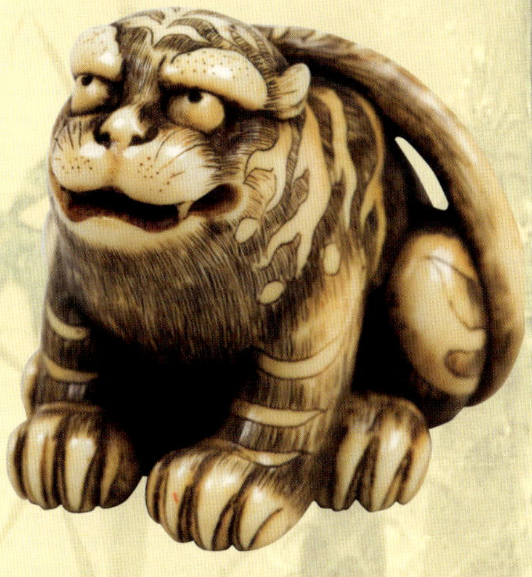

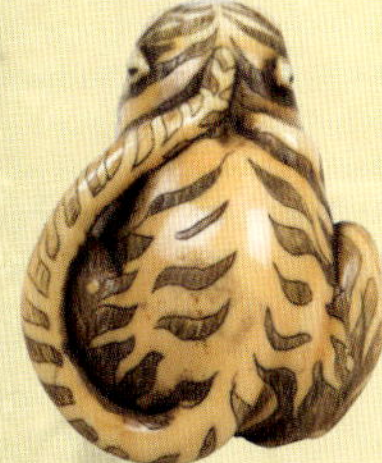

虎牙彫根付

江戸時代（19c）
メトロポリタン美術館

Netsuke of Seated Tiger

19th century
The Metropolitan Museum of Art

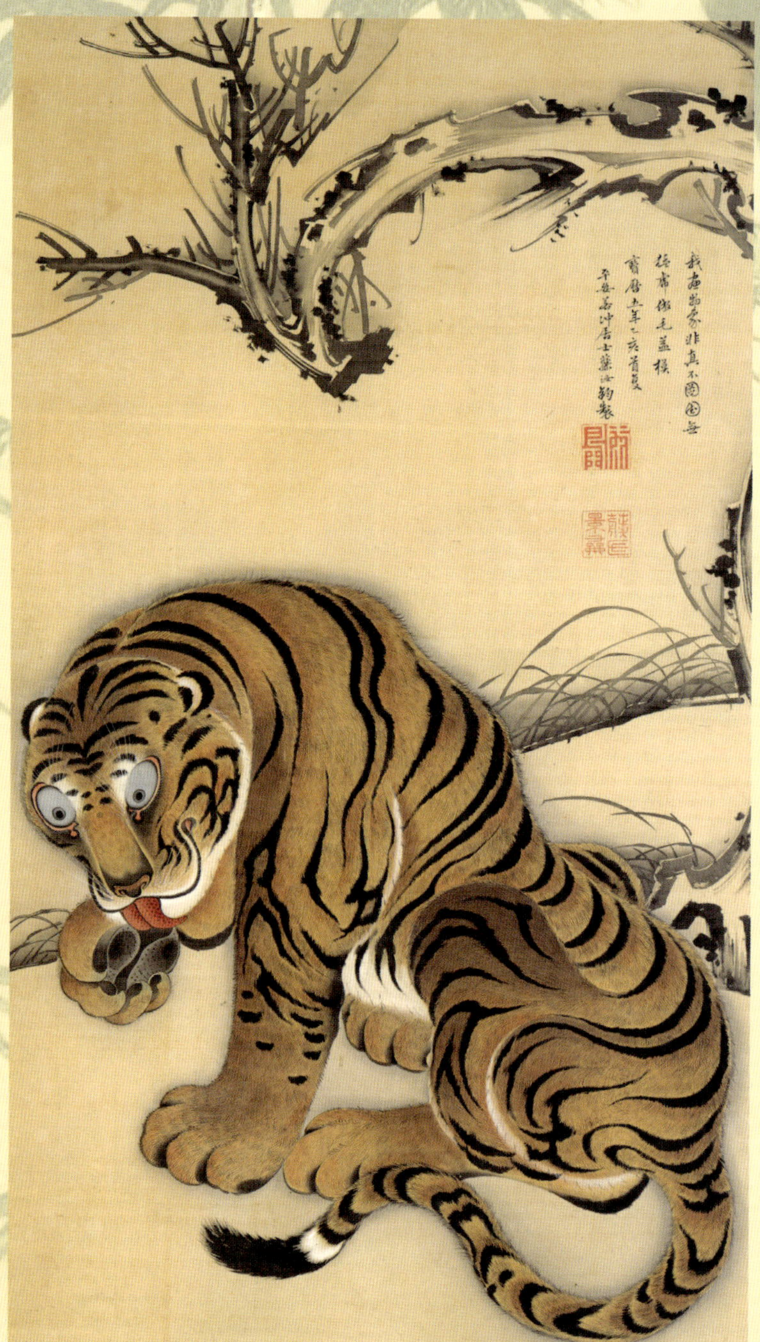

虎図

伊藤若冲
宝暦5年(1755)
エツコ&ジョー・プライスコレクション

1755年(宝暦5)、40歳の若冲(1716～1800)は家督を弟に譲って隠居し、念願の絵画制作に没頭した。その記念すべき年に手がけた本図は、京都・正伝寺に中国・北宋時代の作と伝わる(実は明代ないしは朝鮮画ともいわれる)「猛虎図」を模したもの。若冲の賛には、自分は本物でなければ描かないが、日本には虎がいないので(仕方なく)毛益(宋代の動物画を得意とした画家)の作に倣って模写した、とある。現実に存在するものをしっかり観察して描くことを自らに課した、若冲の絵画観の逆説的な表明とも読み取れるだろう。

Tiger

Itō Jakuchū
1755
Etsuko and Joe Price Collection

In 1755 (Hōreki 5), a forty-year-old Jakuchū (1716-1800) retired and handed over leadership of the family business to his younger brother, and he immersed himself in his long-cherished desire to make paintings. This work that he did from that memorable year was copied from *Ferocious Tiger*, a Chinese painting from the Northern Song dynasty handed down at Kyoto Shōdenji (however, in actuality, it is said to have been a Ming or Korean painting). Jakuchū's inscription reads: "I could not paint something like this without the real thing, but since there are no tigers in Japan (nothing to be done about it), I learned from copying the work of Mao Yi (the Song painter that was skilled at depicting animals)." We can probably infer that this was a paradoxical assertion of Jakuchū's view of painting, in which he challenged himself to draw things only after carefully observing them in real life.

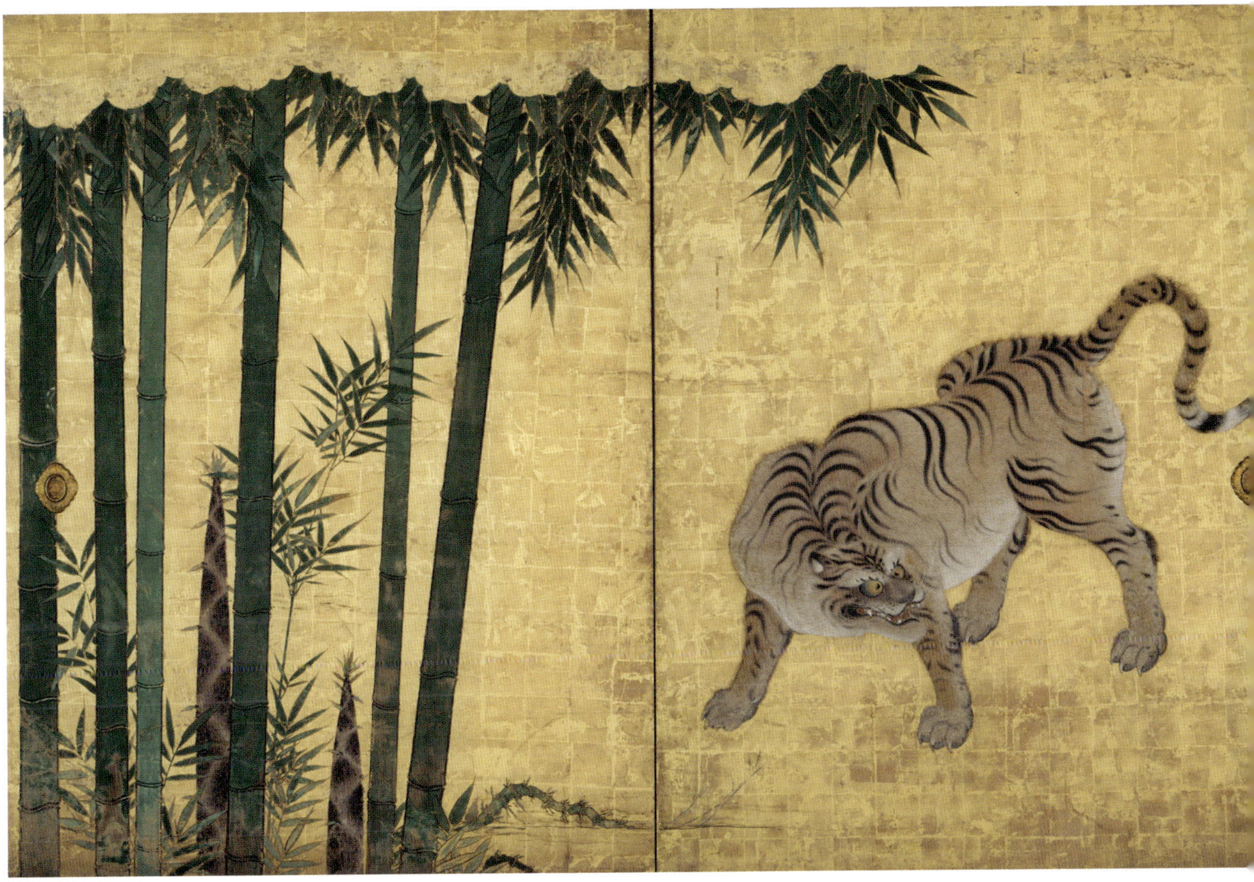

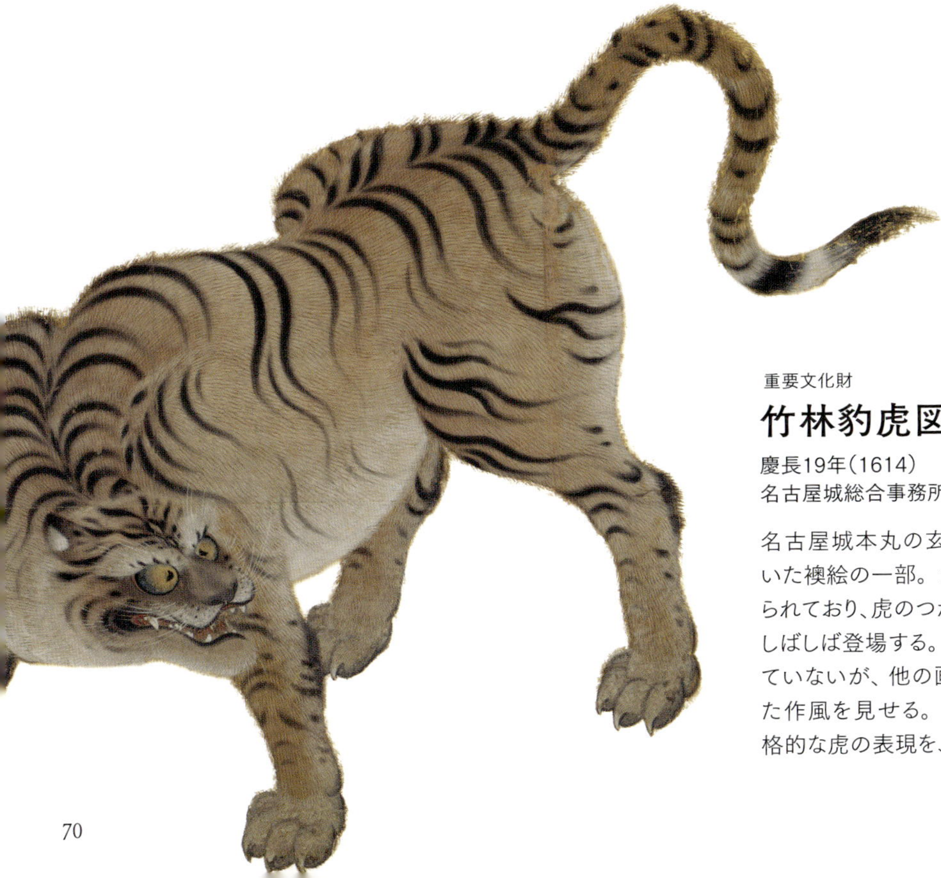

重要文化財

竹林豹虎図

慶長19年（1614）
名古屋城総合事務所

名古屋城本丸の玄関一之間にはめられていた襖絵の一部。当時、豹は虎の雌と考えられており、虎のつがいや親子の表現としてしばしば登場する。本図の筆者は特定されていないが、他の画面と比べひときわ優れた作風を見せる。当代の狩野派による本格的な虎の表現を、ここに見ることができる。

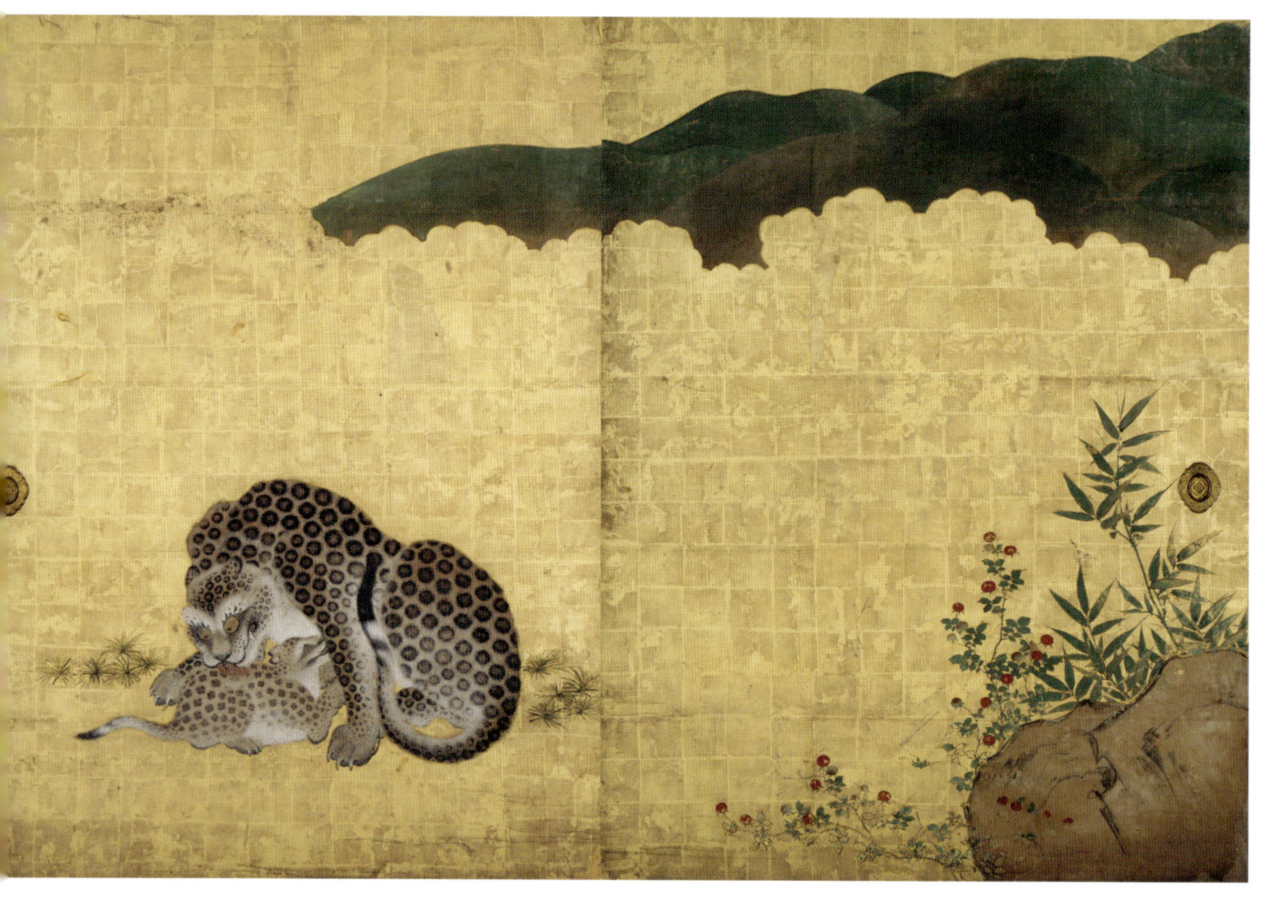

Important Cultural Property

Bamboo Grove, Leopards and Tigers

1614
Nagoya Castle Bureau

This is part of the set of sliding door paintings in the first room of the entrance of the inner citadel of Nagoya Castle. At the time, leopards were thought to be female tigers, and they often appear in mated pairs with tigers, in addition to scenes with tigers and their cubs. The painter of this image is undesignated, but comparing it to the other paintings, he seems particularly skilled. Here, we can see the typical way of painting a tiger in the style of the contemporary Kano school.

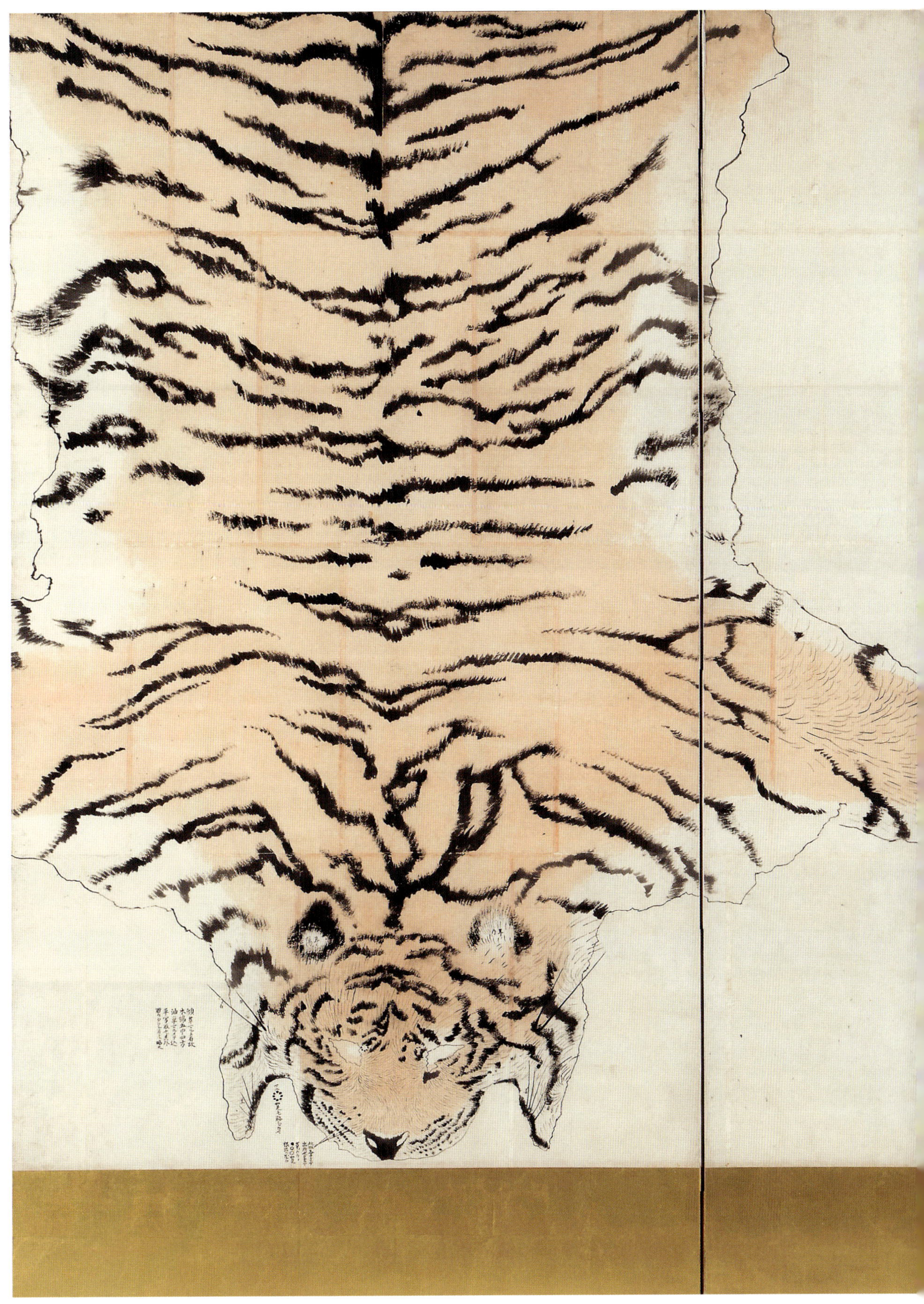

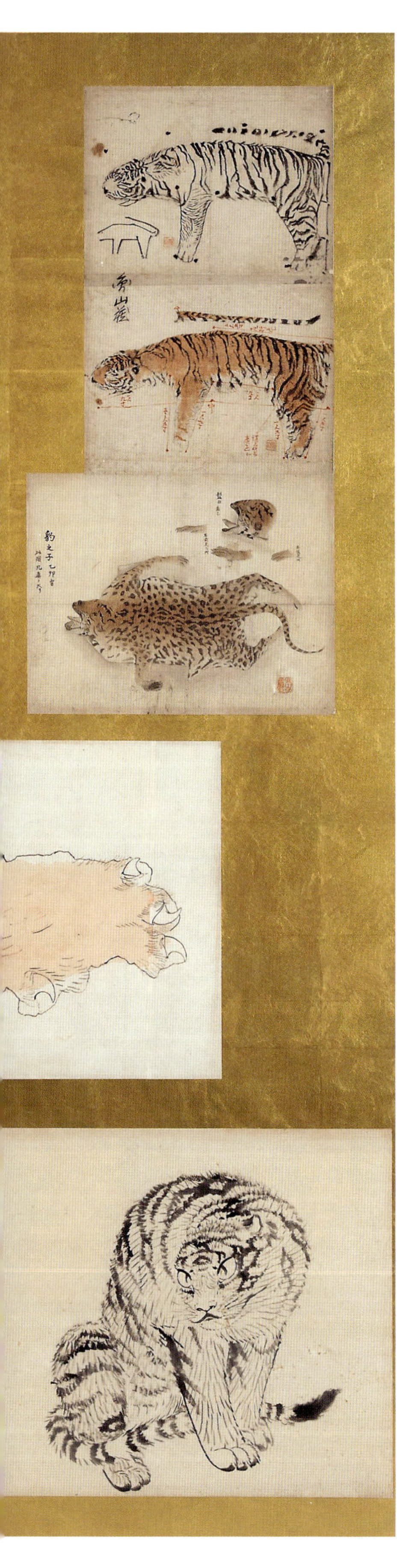

虎皮写生図

円山応挙
江戸時代後期(18c)
本間美術館

後年になって仕立てられた屛風には、1頭の虎の皮の原寸大とおぼしき写生図が添付されるのだが、そのあまりの大きさに前面だけでは足らず、背面(p.74)にまわして何とか収めたという代物である。図中の注記には寸法や模様についての記載もあり、虎の真の姿を捉えようとの意気込みが伝わってくる。

Sketch of a Tiger Hide

Maruyama Ōkyo
18th century
Homma Museum of Art

Mounted as a folding screen in later years, this is a work where a sketch that is apparently the actual size of a tiger pelt is attached to a screen. However, since the sketch was so big, the front of the screen was too small to display it in full, and the sketch was folded over onto the back (p.74). In the commentary on the work, there are records about the dimensions and pattern, and the enthusiasm for trying to catch the tiger's true form is conveyed.

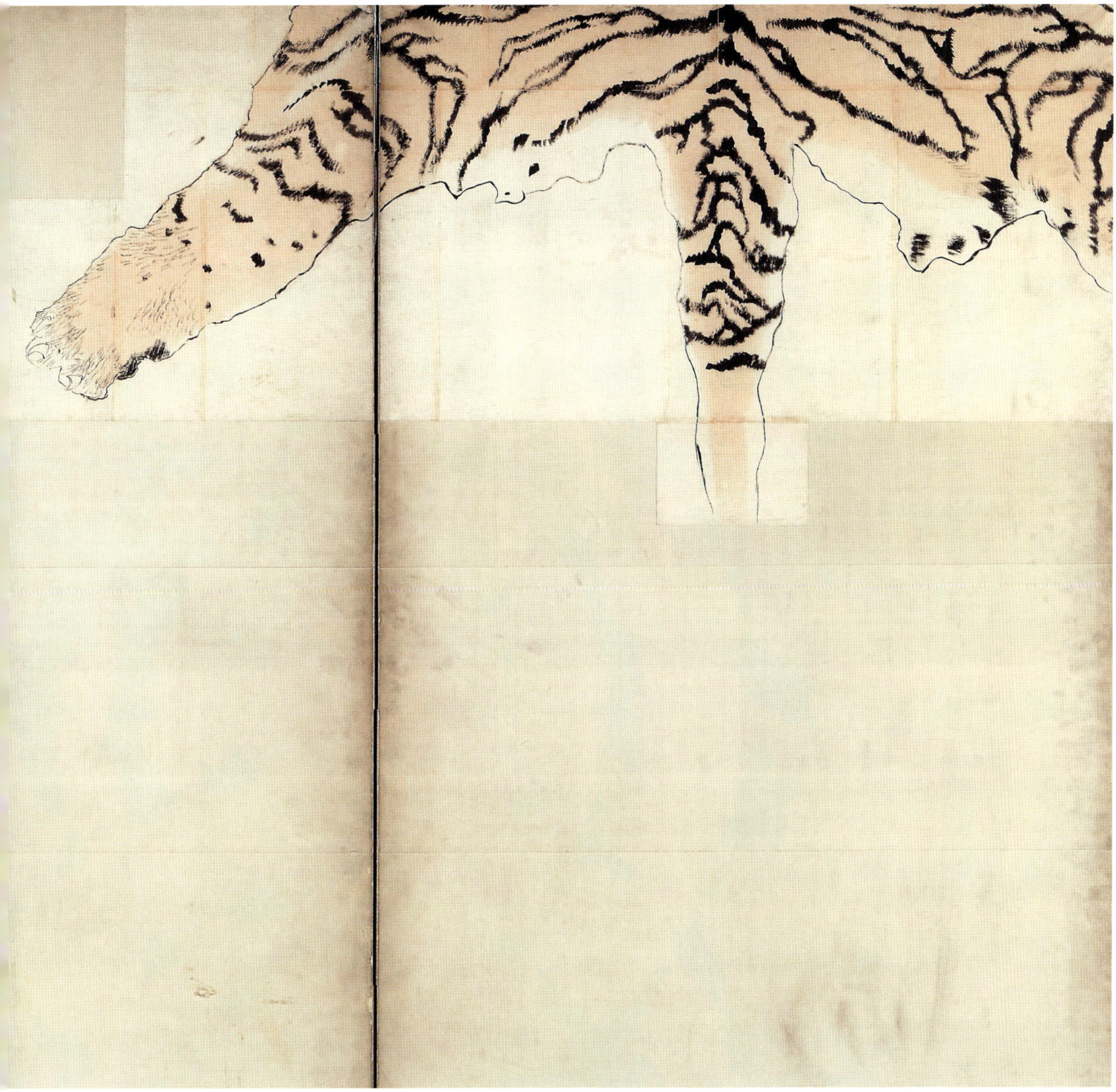

虎皮写生図（裏面）

円山応挙
江戸時代後期（18c）
本間美術館

Sketch of a Tiger Hide (back)

Maruyama Ōkyo
18th century
Homma Museum of Art

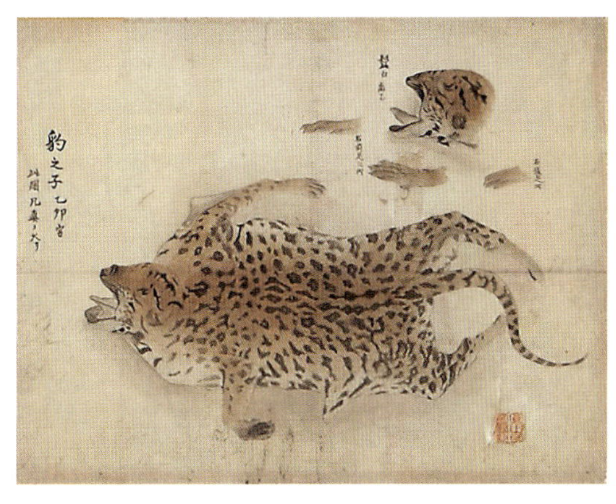

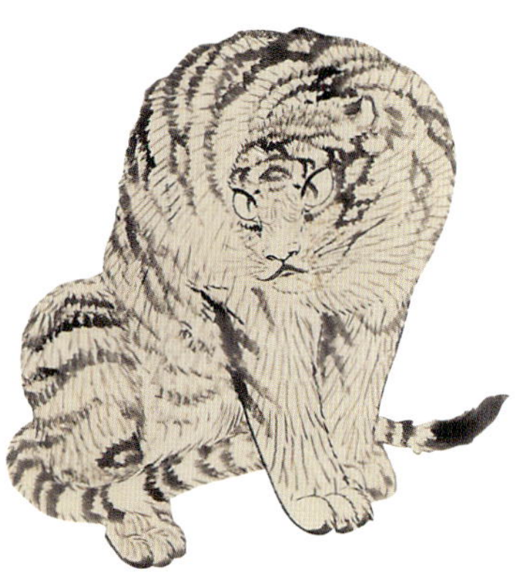

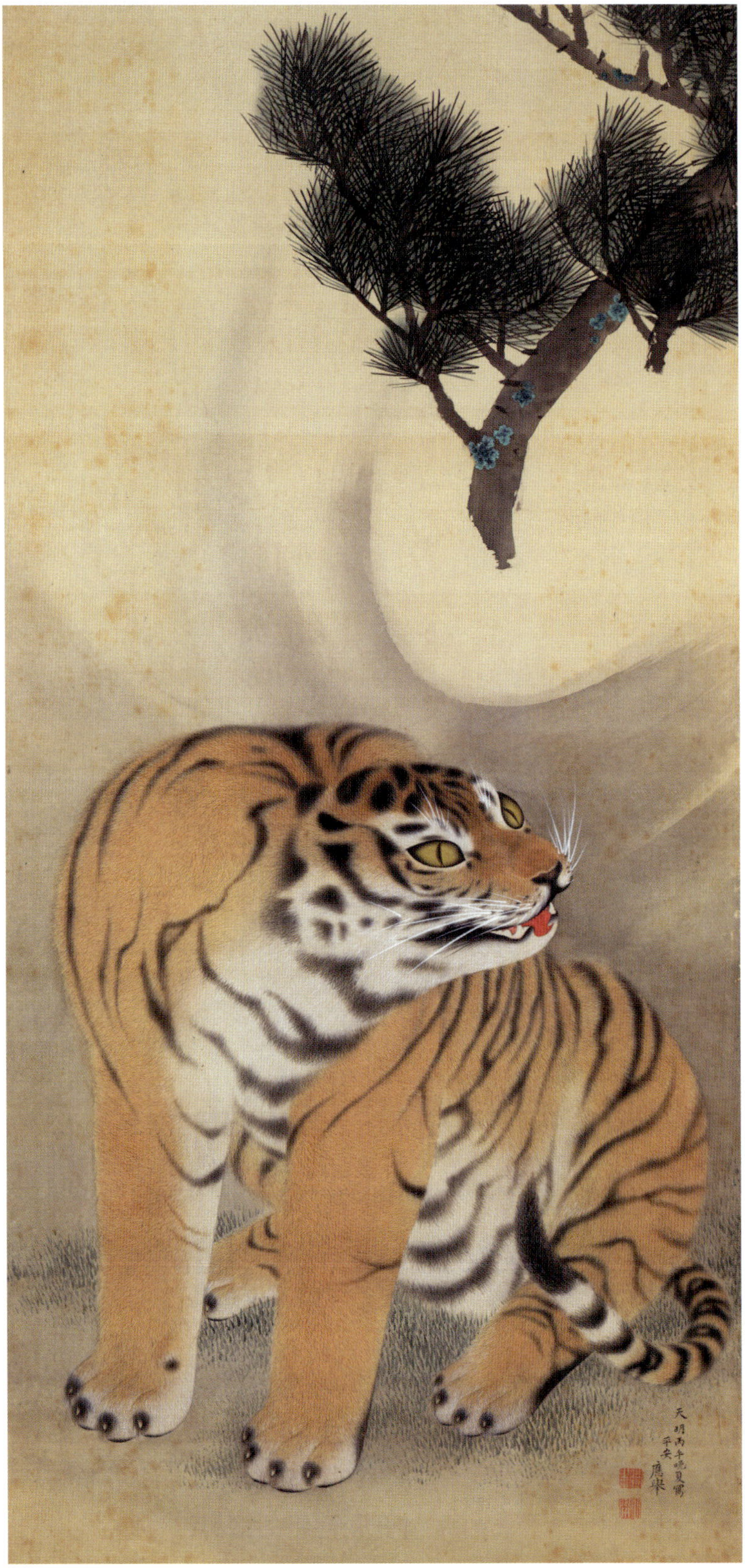

虎嘯生風図

円山応挙
天明6年（1786）
東京国立博物館

応挙は、ものの構造を把握した上で描写することの重要性を説くとともに、必要に応じて人形の使用も推奨した。この絵では立体感の表現は的確ながら、獰猛さに欠け、脚部の描写はこわばっていて、とても獲物を捕えられそうにない。この問題の解消には、十数年後の岸駒による挑戦まで待たねばならなかったのである。

Roar of Tiger Causing Wind

Maruyama Ōkyo
1786
Tokyo National Museum

Along with advocating for the importance of drawing things only after one has grasped their construction, Ōkyo also recommended using dolls when necessary. In this painting, while the representation of three-dimensionality is accurate, it lacks ferocity. The portrayal of the legs is stiff and gives no indication that this tiger could catch its prey. We would have to wait until Ganku took up this challenge about a dozen years later in order to resolve this issue.

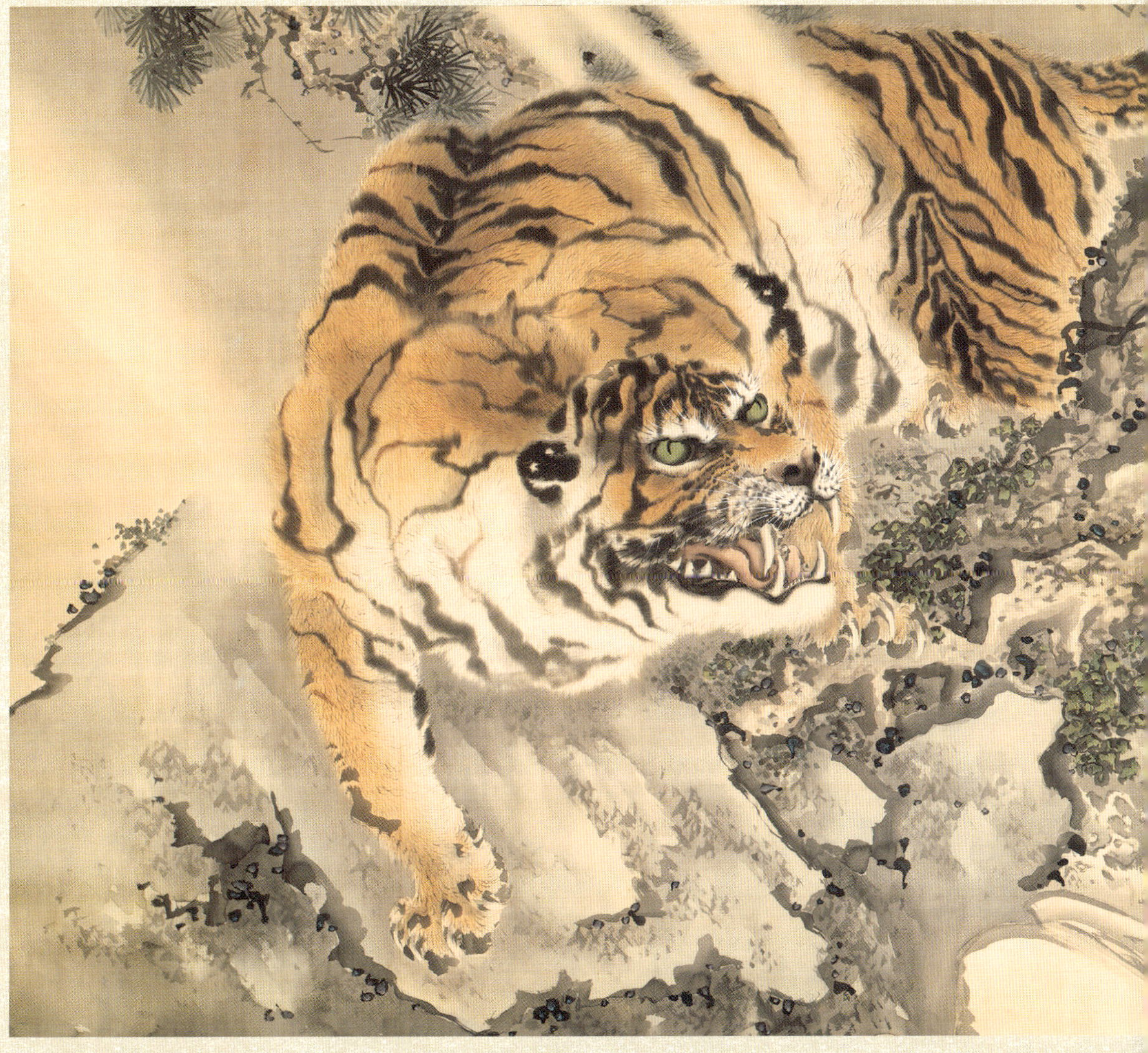

猛虎図

岸駒
江戸時代後期(18-19c)
本間美術館

虎の絵を得意とした岸駒の大作。脚の描写は、実際に入手した四脚の観察結果にもとづき、関節の動きにも留意した描写がなされているようだ。さらにこの大幅、画家は「実物大」をも意識していたようである。

Fierce Tiger

Ganku
18th–19th century
Homma Museum of Art

This is a masterpiece by Ganku, who was known for his tiger paintings. The depiction of the legs was a result of his having observed actual quadrupeds, and it seems that he accomplished a depiction that even took into consideration the movement of the joints. Moreover, its large size seems to be due to Ganku trying to emulate the "actual size" of the animal.

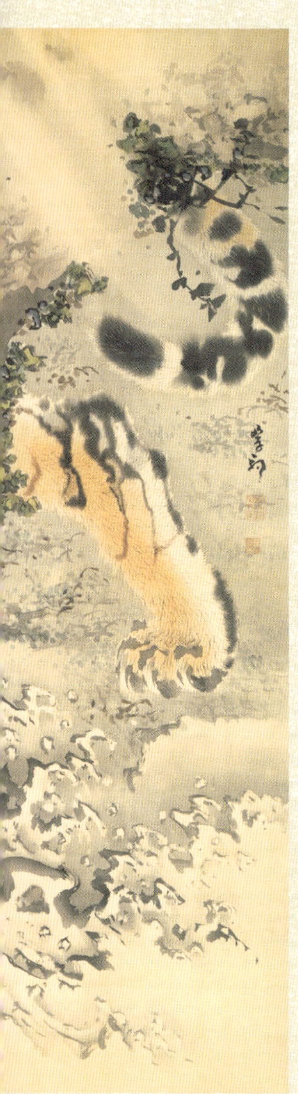

虎前脚後脚

岸駒旧蔵
江戸時代（18c）
富山市佐藤記念美術館

岸駒が中国商人から虎の頭骨を手に入れたのは1798年（寛政10）だったが、それに続けて入手した虎の四脚である。観察記録には「脚は四本指で五本爪、後脚の踵はなく、また前脚の左右は後脚よりずいぶん大きい。前脚の左右の膝下足に近く3、4寸のところに別の関節があって、屈伸でき自在に動く。執ったりつかんだりする力が出せるのは、こうした構造があるからだ」とある。頭蓋骨の寸法も細かく計測するなど、その姿勢は科学者そのものであろう。当時は解剖学の興隆期で、人物描写に際し骨の構造を把握することの重要性が応挙らによって唱えられていた。猫を手本にした従来の作風とは異なる、リアルな虎図誕生の裏には、このような秘密があったわけである。なお頭骨は、太平洋戦争前に男子出産祈願のため貸し出されて以来、行方不明という。

Forelimbs and Hindlegs of a Tiger

Collection of Ganku
18th century
Toyama city Satō Memorial Museum

Ganku obtained a tiger skull from Chinese merchants in 1798 (Kansei 10), and later also procured four tiger legs. In his observation records, it says: “There are four legs and five claws on its toes. There are no heels on its hind legs. Also, the left and right forelegs are much bigger than the hind legs. There is another joint on the left and right forelegs below the knee by about three or four *sun* (nine or twelve cm), and it bends and stretches freely. A body with this kind of construction demonstrates its power to catch and grab.” The approach of measuring the dimensions of the skull is close to that of a scientist. This was a period of development for the science of anatomy, and Ōkyo and his students advocated for the importance of grasping the construction of bones when drawing human bodies. This kind of teaching was behind the birth of realistic tiger paintings, which were so different from the traditional depictions of tigers that were modeled after regular cats. Also, since these were leant out to someone before the war in order to serve as a charm for the birth of a son, their current whereabouts are unknown.

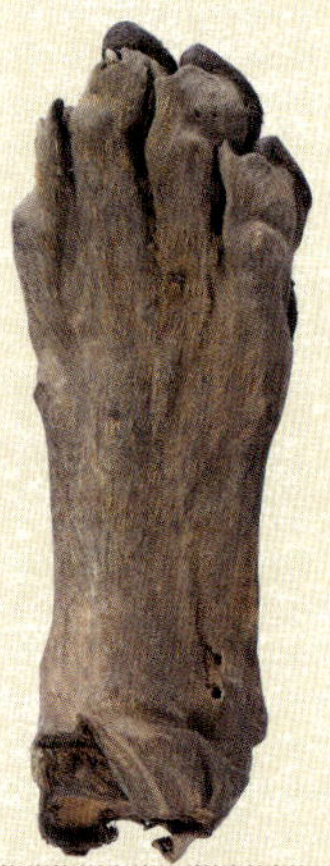

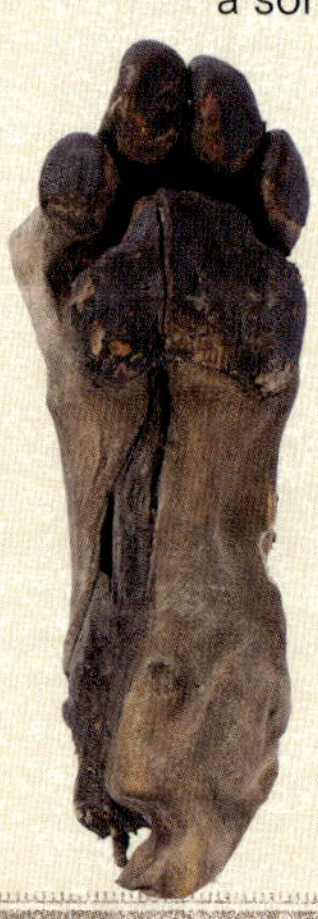

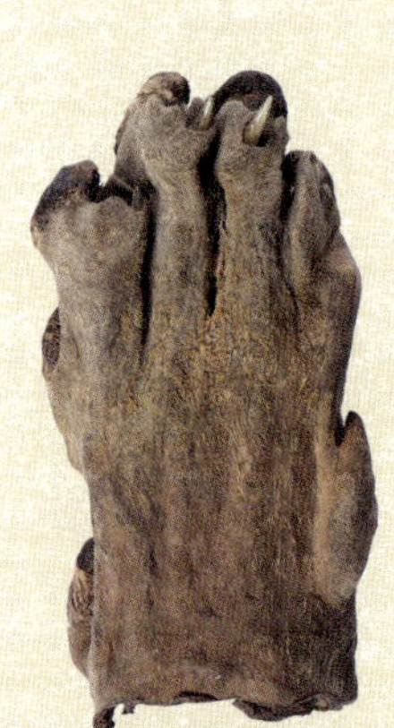

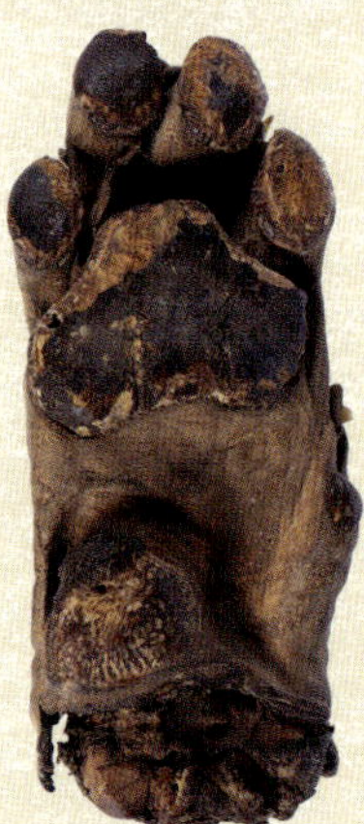

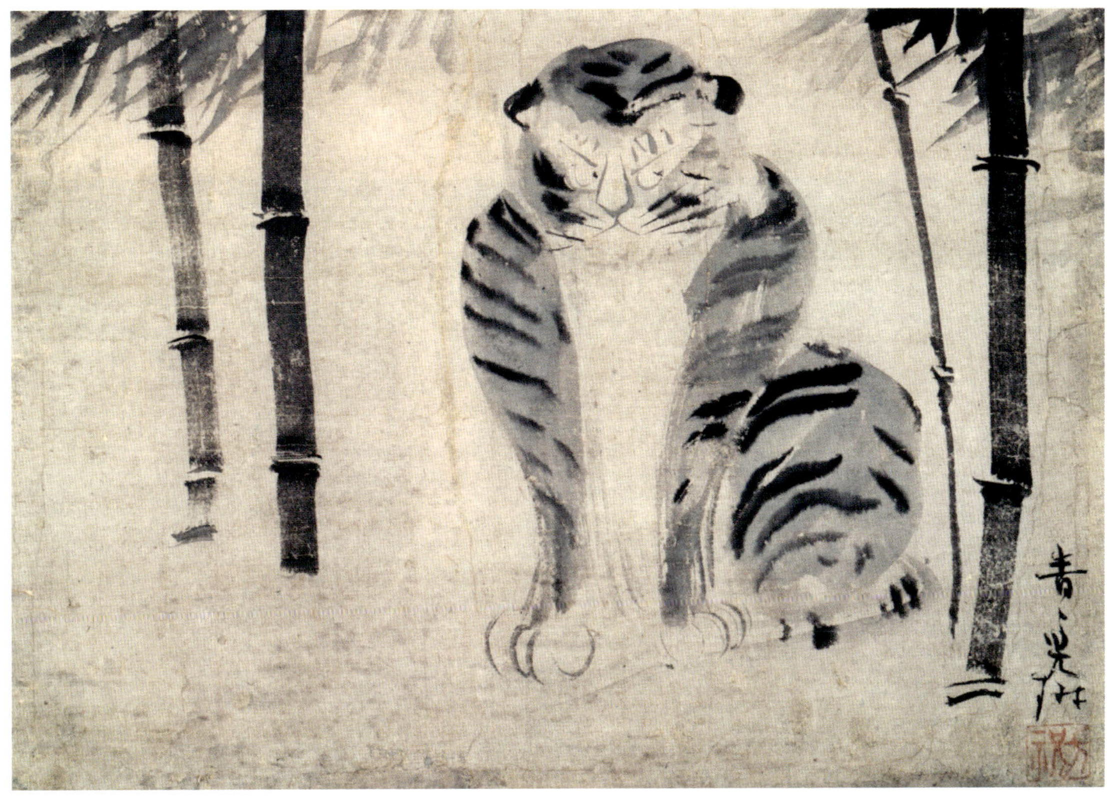

竹に虎図

尾形光琳
江戸時代(17c)
京都国立博物館

ご存じ京都国立博物館の人気キャラクター「とらりん」のモデル。「燕子花図屛風」や「紅白梅図屛風」の画家には、こんな剽軽な絵を描く洒脱な一面があった。わが国の虎の絵、とくに擬人化を思わせる表現では猫の雰囲気がついてまわる。猫からイメージを膨らませていった結果であろうか。

Bamboo and Tiger

Ogata Kōrin
17th century
Kyoto National Museum

This is the painting that was the model used for Torarin, the well-known mascot of the Kyoto National Museum. For the painter of *Irises* and *Red and White Plum Blossoms* to create such a humorous picture shows a sophisticated diversity in his work. In Japanese tiger paintings, especially in representations that have anthropomorphic qualities, there is often a catlike atmosphere. Doesn't the result here look like a big inflated cat?

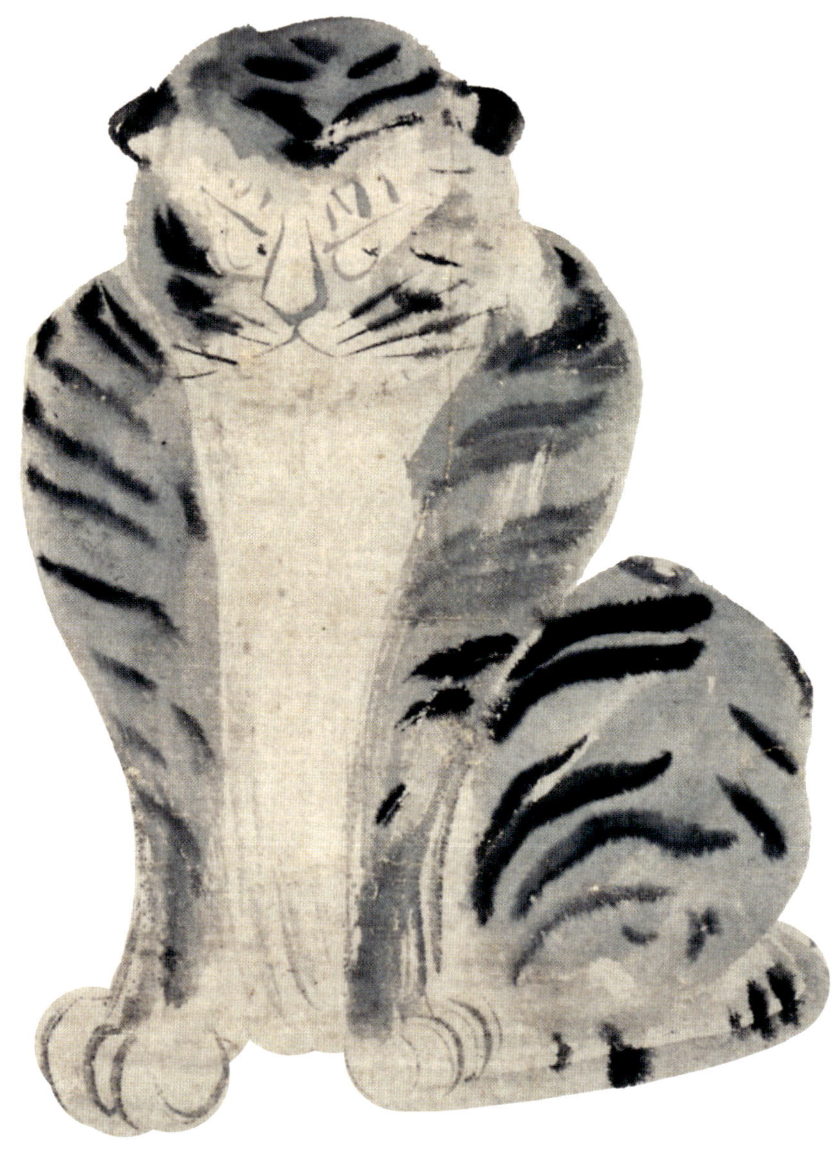

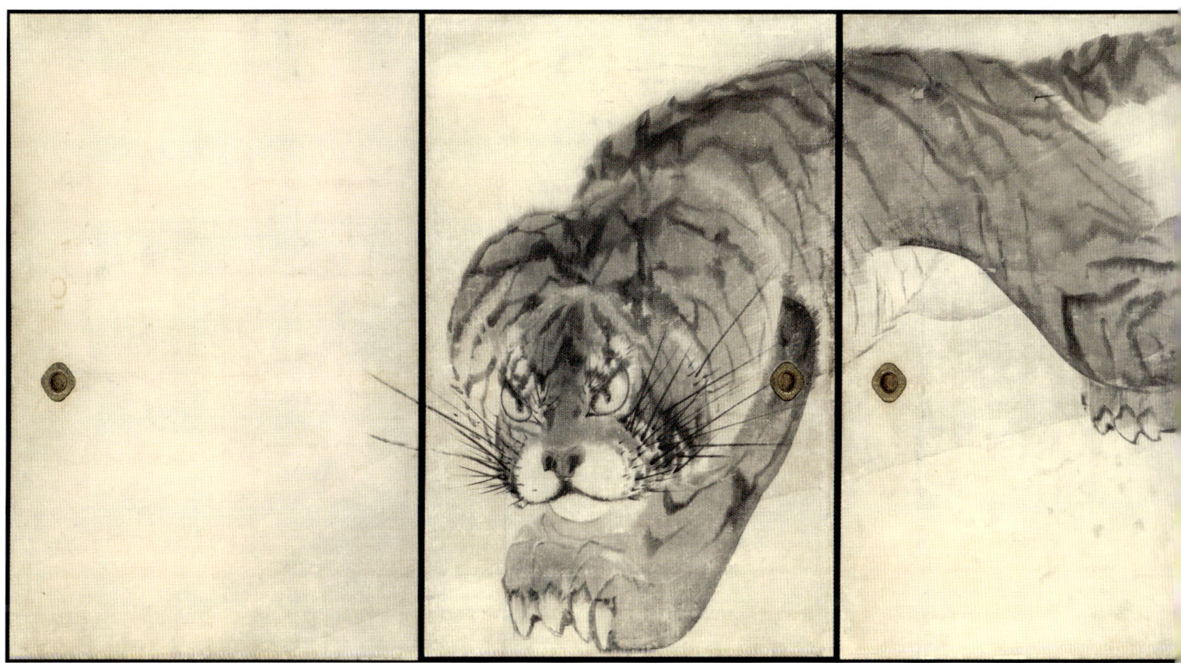

重要文化財

虎図襖

長沢芦雪
天明6年(1786)
和歌山・無量寺(串本応挙芦雪館)

1786年(天明6)10月、多忙な師の応挙に代わり南紀に向かった芦雪(1754～99)は、翌年2月までに諸寺院の障壁画を一気に制作して回った。本図はその代表作で、無量寺本堂の中央(室中之間)の障壁画である。奥の仏間にせり出す形で襖6面を使って、虎と龍が向かい合わせとなるが、巨大さのわりに虎の表情はあまりに可愛らしく猫にしか見えない。実は、虎図の裏面(顔面の真裏)には、猫が水中の魚を狙う情景が描かれている。そして虎に見られているのは鑑賞者。つまり、虎を見ている人間は、実のところ猫に狙われる小魚と何ら変わるところがないことを、この絵は教えているのだろうか。何とも機知に富んだ、芦雪ならではの作品である。

Important Cultural Property

Tiger Sliding Doors

Nagasawa Rosetsu
1786
Muryōji, Wakayama (Muryōji Kushimoto Okyo Rosetsukan)

In October of 1786 (Tenmei 6), Rosetsu (1754-99) went to Nanki in the stead of his teacher Ōkyo, who was busy. By February of next year, he had tirelessly completed wall paintings at various local temples. This painting is a representative work from this time, and it is from a wall painting in the central room of the main hall at Muryōji. The full image covers six sliding doors that protrude into the inner sanctum and depicts a tiger and a dragon opposite each other; however, despite the comparative hugeness of the work, the tiger just looks like a very cute cat. Actually, on the reverse of the tiger (right behind the face), there is a scene of a cat stalking a fish in the water. Also, what the huge tiger is fixated on is the viewer. In other words, isn't this picture telling us that there is no difference between the fish being hunted by the cat and the person the tiger is looking at? This work, full of clever playfulness, is characteristic of Rosetsu.

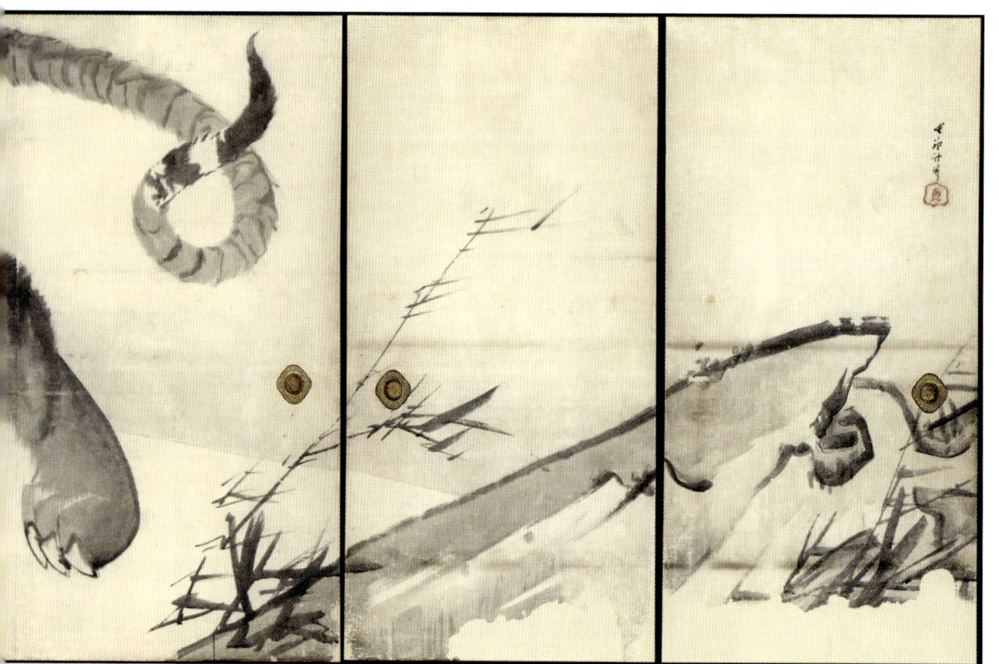

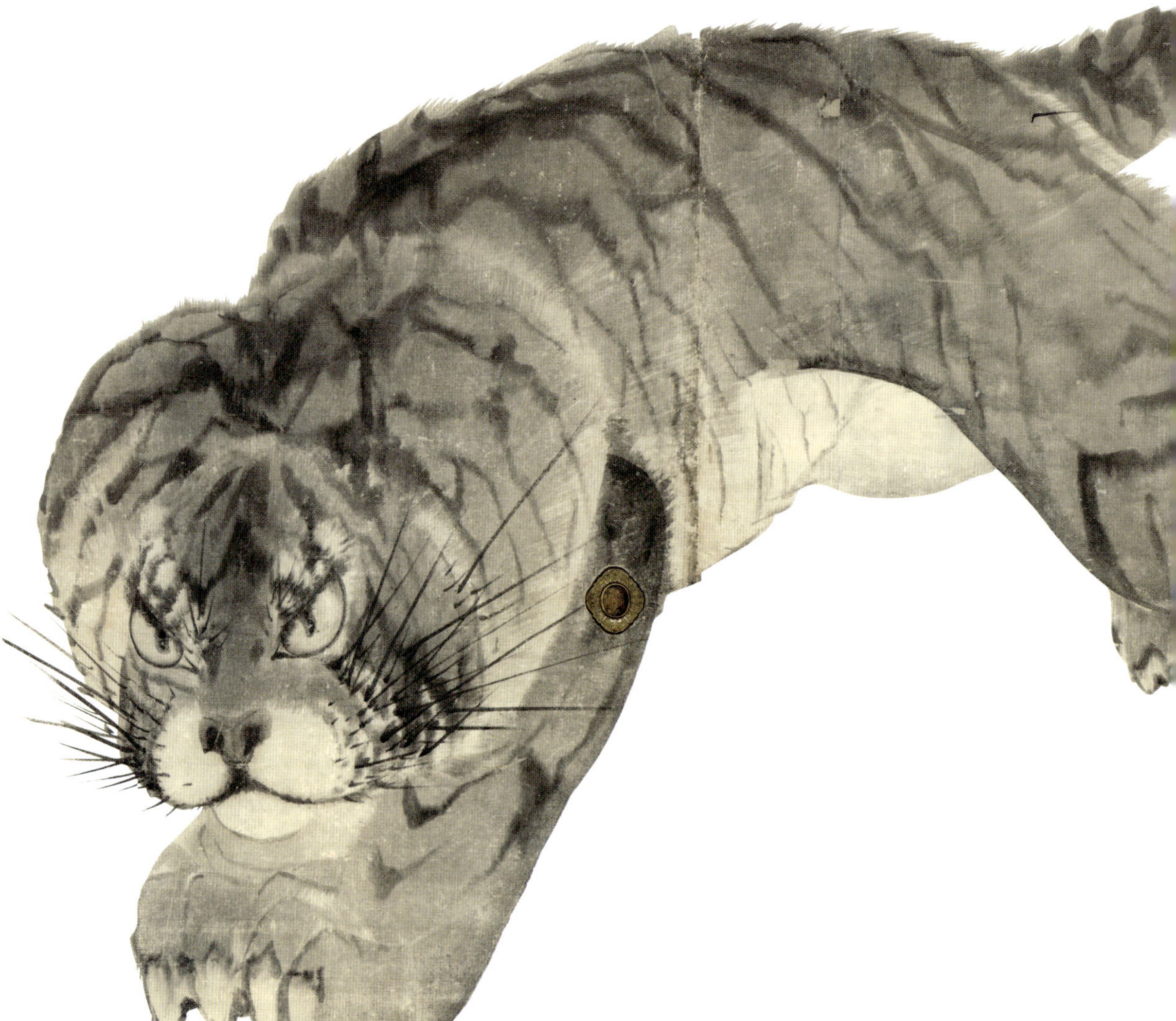

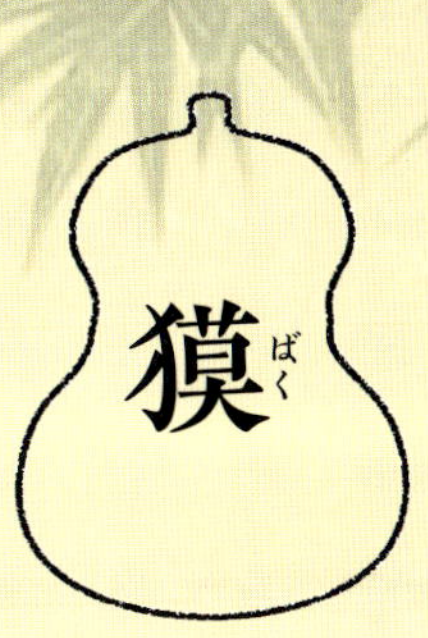

『本草綱目』によれば、貘（獏）は熊に似て頭は小さく脚は短い。黒白の駁文（まだらもよう）があり、毛は浅くて光沢がある。銅や鉄などを舐り食う、とある。また、鼻は象、目は犀、尾は牛、足は虎のようだという。さらに、尿は鉄を溶かして水にし、歯・骨は極めて堅く、刀や斧で打つと逆に打つ側が砕け落ちる。火にかけても焼けない、などと記される。その形を図しただけでも邪を避けることができ、唐代には獏を屏風に描き魔除けとすることが広く行われた。日本では、悪夢を食べてくれる動物とされるが、これは中国で獏の皮を敷いて寝ると邪気を払うとされたことに由来する。ちなみに、バクの日本初渡来は1903年（明治36）、大阪天王寺で開催された第5回内国勧業博覧会のとき。会場内に設けられた余興動物園で披露されたのだという。

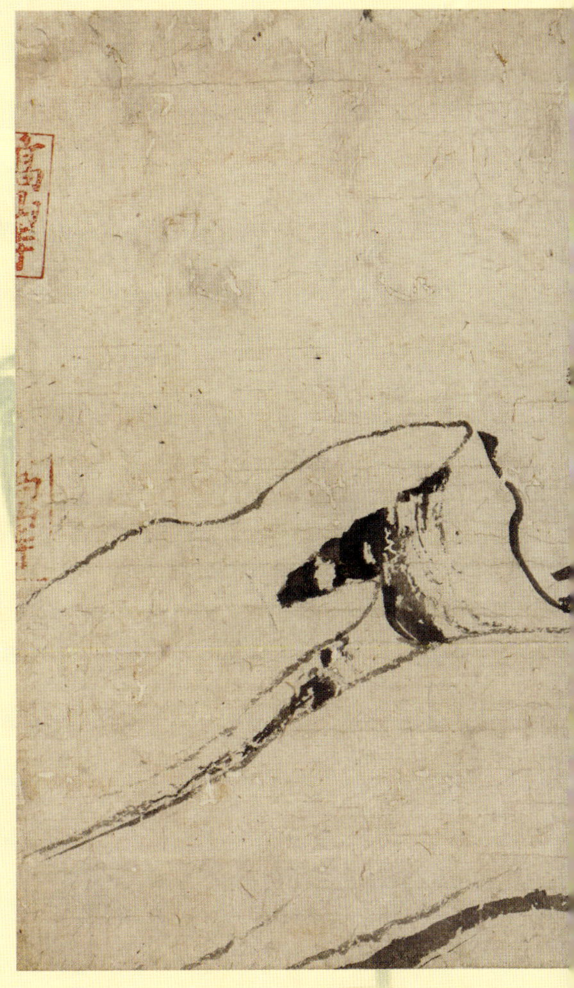

The *Baku* (Tapir)

According to the *Compendium of Materia Medica*, the *baku* is an animal with a small head and short legs that looks like a bear. It has a black and white spotted pattern (like that of a grey cod), and its fur is pale and lustrous. It licks its food, things like copper and iron. Also, its nose is that of an elephant, its eyes are that of a rhinoceros, its tail is that of a bull, and its legs are that of a tiger. Moreover, its urine melts iron, and its teeth and bones are extremely hard, such that when it is struck by swords or axes, the weapons will break apart. Even if it is exposed to fire, it will not be burnt. These are the types of descriptions recorded in the text. It was thought that even just drawing an image of this animal would ward off evil, and in the Tang dynasty, there were widely available folding screens with *baku* painted on them as a charm against evil spirits. In Japan, the *baku* is seen as a beast that eats nightmares, but this also has its origins in China, where laying out the hide of a *baku* and sleeping on it was believed to drive away vengeful ghosts. By the way, the first actual tapir was brought to Japan in 1903 (Meiji 36) to be displayed at the fifth domestic industrial exposition held at Tennōji in Osaka. It was apparently showcased at the zoo that had been set up within the fairgrounds.

獏木彫根付
江戸時代（18c）
メトロポリタン美術館

Crouching Baku Netsuke
18th century
The Metropolitan Museum of Art

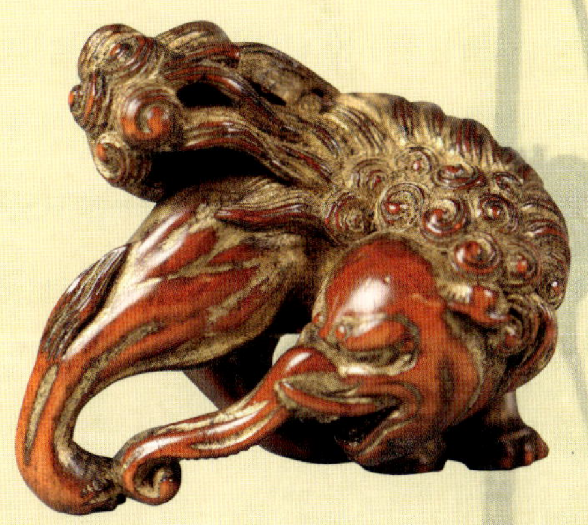

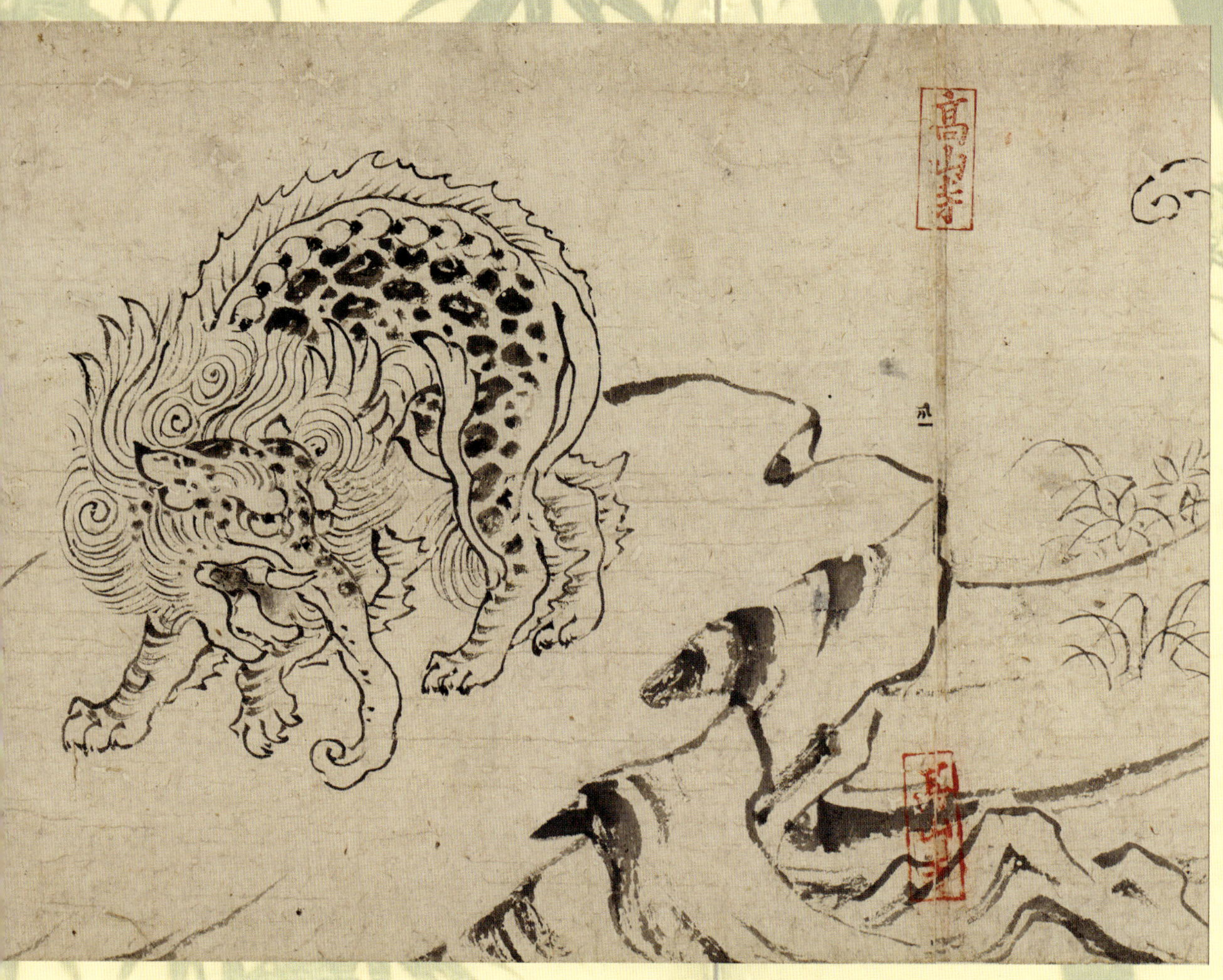

国宝

鳥獣人物戯画 乙巻（部分）

平安時代後期（12c）
京都・高山寺

甲乙丙丁の4巻からなる「鳥獣人物戯画」のうち、甲巻は擬人化された蛙や兎・猿などが登場するが、乙巻には霊獣といわれた獅子や麒麟・象・犀などから、馬や牛・鷹・犬・鶏・鷲と隼などが収録される。作者については、鳥羽僧正覚猷（1053～1140）の名が伝えられてきたが、確証は全くない。当時の密教図像との関連もうかがわれることから、絵の達者な僧侶の作と推測されている。

National Treasure

Scrolls of Frolicking Animals, Scroll Two (*Detail*)

12th century
Kōsanji, Kyoto

Within the four scrolls of *Frolicking Animals*, the first depicts anthropomorphized animals like frogs, rabbits and monkeys, but the second is a compilation of animals covering both sacred beasts, such as lions, *kirin*, elephants, and rhinoceroses, and everyday animals, such as horses and cattle, hawks, dogs, chickens, eagles and falcons. Regarding the author, the name of Kakuyū, the Bishop of Toba (1053-1140), has been passed down, but there is no conclusive evidence that it was really him. Since we can surmise that the painter had a link to contemporary esoteric Buddhist drawings, it is guessed that this was the work of a Buddhist priest who could draw.

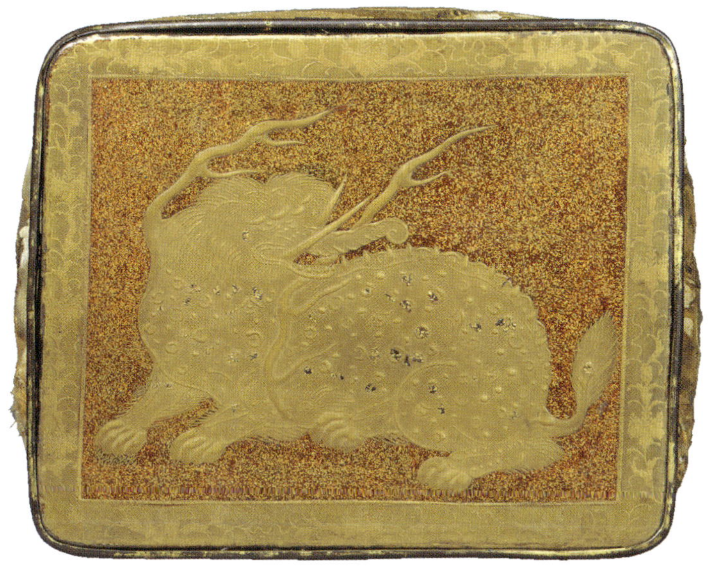

側面 Side

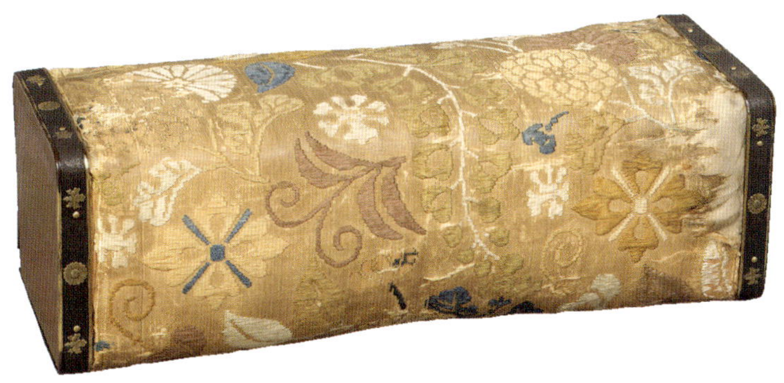

重要文化財

獏蒔絵枕

桃山時代(17c)
京都・高台寺

高台寺は豊臣秀吉の正室ねね(高台院・?～1624)の菩提寺。獏が悪夢を食べてくれると信じられた日本では、室町時代末以降、獏の図や文字は縁起物とされ、箱枕に絵を描いたり、獏の形をした「獏枕」が作られることもあった。枕は実用の具であったためか作例に恵まれず、これは数少ない貴重なもの。

Important Cultural Property

Baku Maki-e Lacquer Pillow

17th century
Kōdaiji, Kyoto

Kōdaiji was the family temple of Toyotomi Hideyoshi's principle wife, Kōdaiin (d.1624). In Japan, where it was believed that the *baku* would eat bad dreams, textual and pictorial representations of the *baku* were seen as lucky charms since the late Muromachi period; there were also box pillows with *baku* painted on them, as well as "*baku* pillows," themselves in the shape of a *baku*. Since pillows were made for practical use, we are not blessed with many surviving works, and this is one of the few precious extant works that we are lucky enough to have.

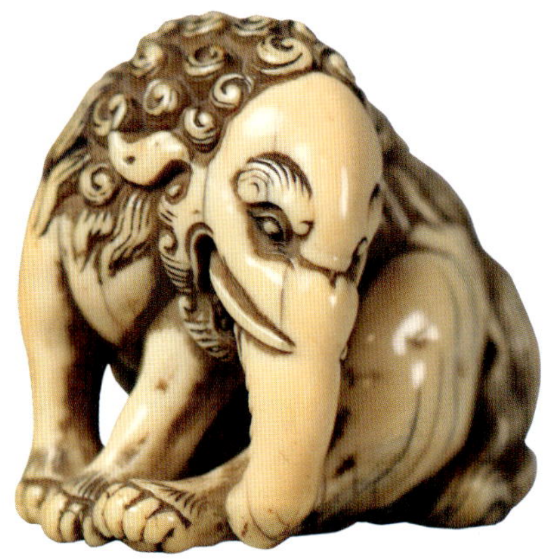

獏牙彫根付
江戸時代(19c)
メトロポリタン美術館

Netsuke of Seated Baku
19th century
The Metropolitan Museum of Art

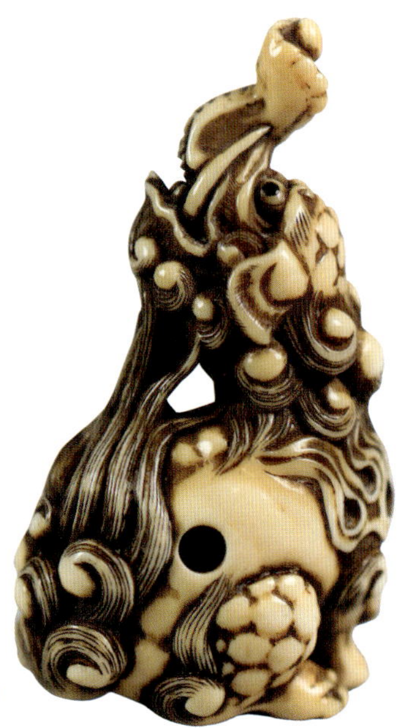

獏牙彫根付
江戸時代(18c)
メトロポリタン美術館

Netsuke of Seated Baku
18th century
The Metropolitan Museum of Art

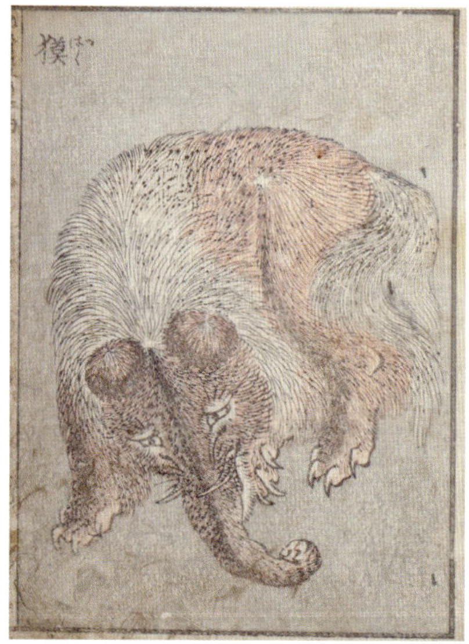

獏図(『北斎漫画』二編)
葛飾北斎
文化12年(1815)刊
メトロポリタン美術館

Baku (from Hokusai Manga, Volume Two)
Katsushika Hokusai
1815
The Metropolitan Museum of Art

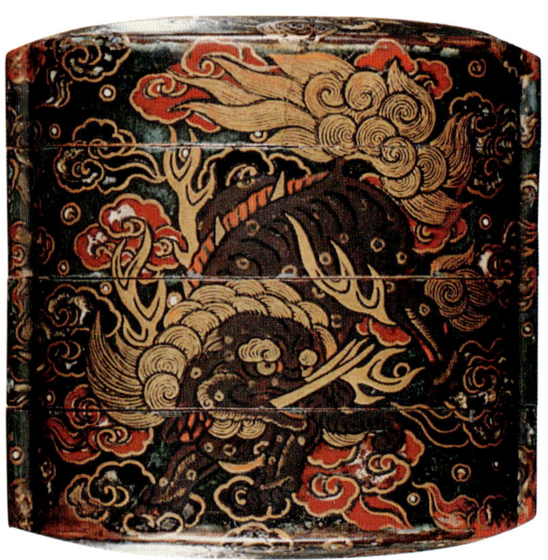

獏図蒔絵印籠
江戸時代(19c)
メトロポリタン美術館

Case (Inrō) with Design of Baku among Ruyi-Shaped Clouds
19th century
The Metropolitan Museum of Art

狻図杉戸

曾我蕭白
明和元年(1764)頃
三重・朝田寺

朝田寺の書院の廊下にある杉戸絵。4枚の杉戸(表裏8面)に、2面ずつを用いて着色の「狻図」(裏面は「旭日に杉図」)と「鳳凰図」(裏は「萩に兎図」)が描かれる。蕭白は、伊勢や播磨方面を交互に訪問し、長期滞在を繰り返しながら制作に従事したが、本図は再度の伊勢遊行時の作と考えられている。蕭白の持ち味を存分に発揮した、何とも奇怪な霊獣像である。

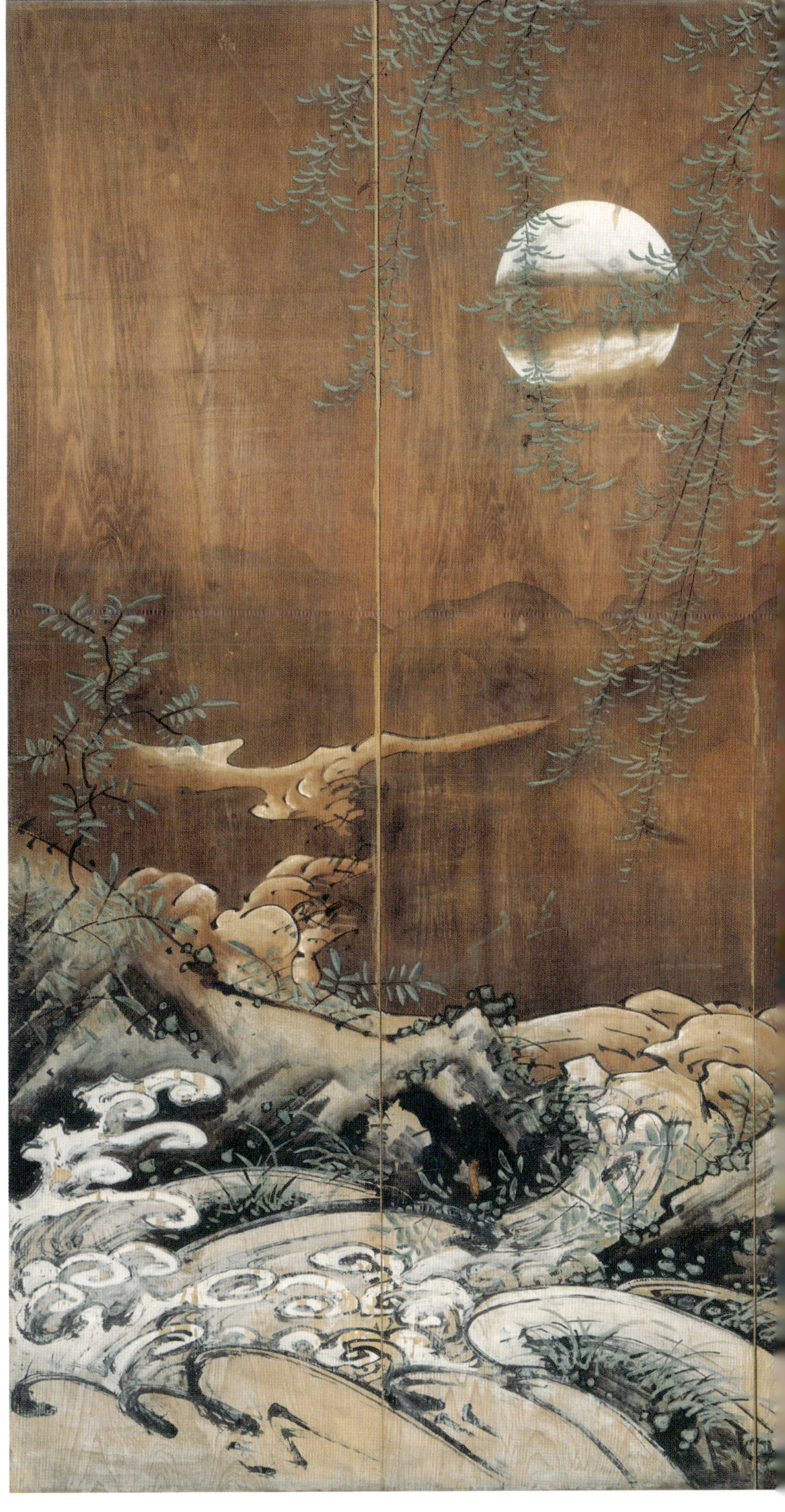

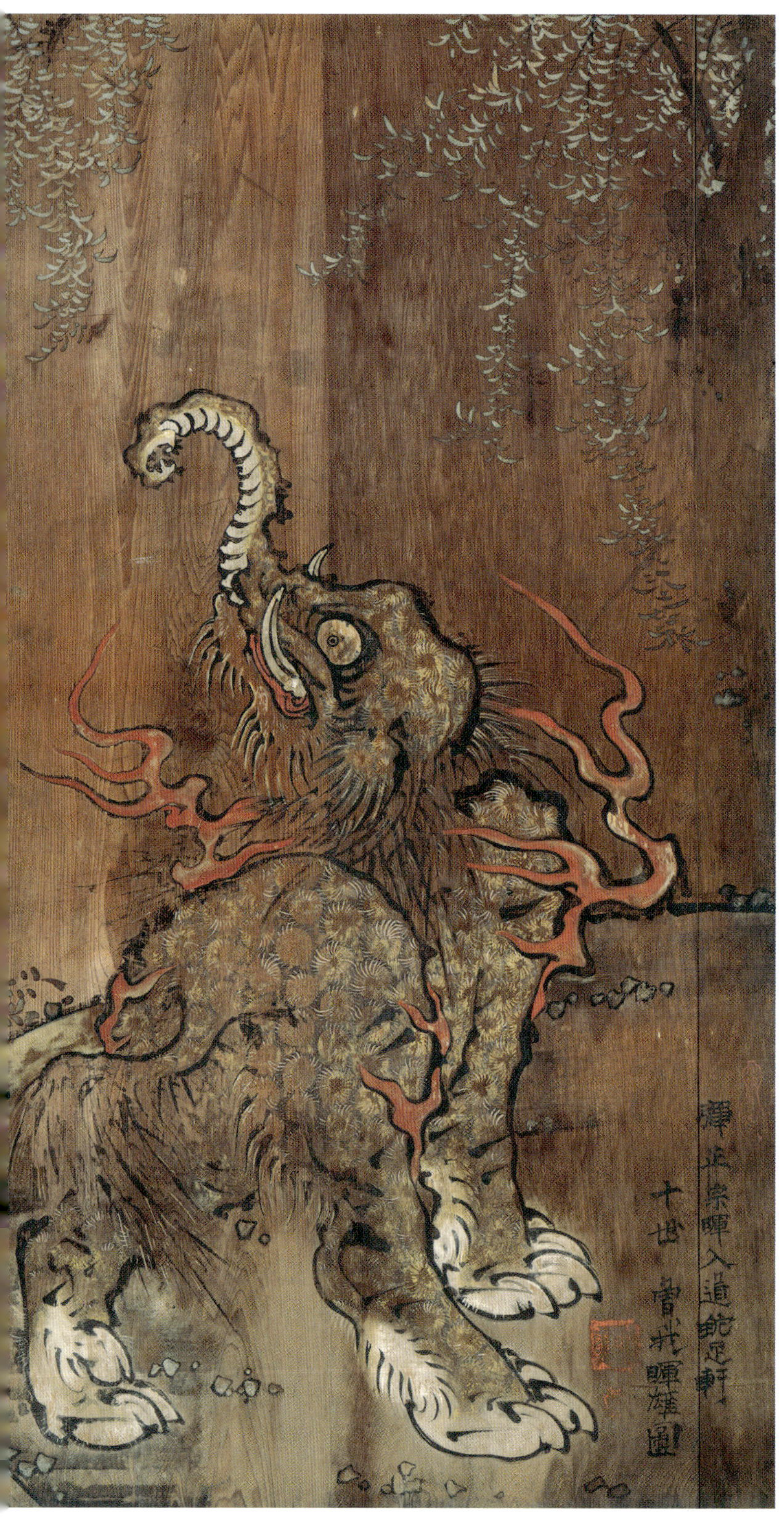

Baku Cedar Door

Soga Shōhaku
ca.1764
Chōdenji, Mie

These are painted cedar doors from the hallway near the head priest's study (*shoin*) at Chōdenji. There are four cedar door panels (eight sides front and back), and on one pair, the front painting is the *Baku* painted in color (the reverse is *Cedars and Rising Sun*) and on the other pair, the front painting is the *Phoenix* (the reverse is *Bush Clover and Hare*). Shōhaku visited both Ise and Harima, and he had been working through another a long-term stay, but it is thought that these paintings were done during his second Ise pilgrimage. This is a very bizarre image of a sacred beast, and it freely demonstrates the idiosyncratic nature of Shōhaku's style.

瑞獣の宝庫
日光東照宮の建築彫刻

A Treasure Trove of Auspicious Beasts:
The Architectural Sculptures at Nikkō Tōshōgū

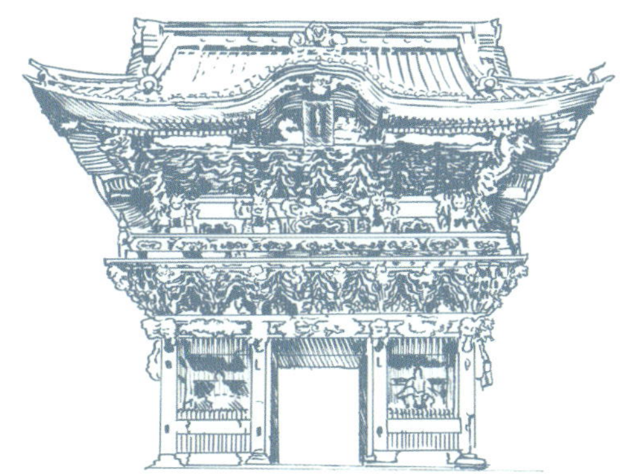
④ 陽明門　Yōmeimon Gate (main gate)

徳川家康（1543～1616）を祀る日光東照宮は、八州（日本全土）の鎮守たらんと願った家康の遺言により建立された。正遷宮は1617年（元和3）2代将軍秀忠の代だが、家康を敬慕してやまなかった3代将軍家光（1604～51）により、寛永の大造替と呼ばれる荘厳な社殿への大規模改造が行われ、1636年（寛永13）21回神忌に合わせ現在の建築群が完成した。本社（拝殿・石の間・本殿）はもとより、陽明門・唐門・廻廊・透塀など多くの社殿の各所に、植物や鳥類・仙人などとともに霊獣をはじめとする動物たちが彫り出されている。

Nikkō Tōshōgū was built according to the final wishes of the shogun Tokugawa Iyeyasu (1543-1616), who wanted to serve as the guardian Shinto deity for all of Japan. The spirit of Tōshō Daigongen was installed in 1617 (Genna 3) during the reign of the second Tokugawa shogun Hidetada, but it was the third shogun Iemitsu (1604-51), who deeply admired his grandfather, who oversaw the large-scale renovation of the magnificent shrine known as the "Great Reconstruction of the Kan'ei Era." The buildings that we have today were finally completed in 1636 (Kan'ei 13), coinciding with the twenty-first anniversary of the death of Ieyasu. The main building (the "front shrine" or "shrine with the stone room") and many locations within the shrine, such as the Yōmeimon (main gate), the Karamon Gate, the cloister, and the fence, had animals, especially auspicious ones, carved into the architecture, along with motifs like plants, birds and immortals from the very beginning.

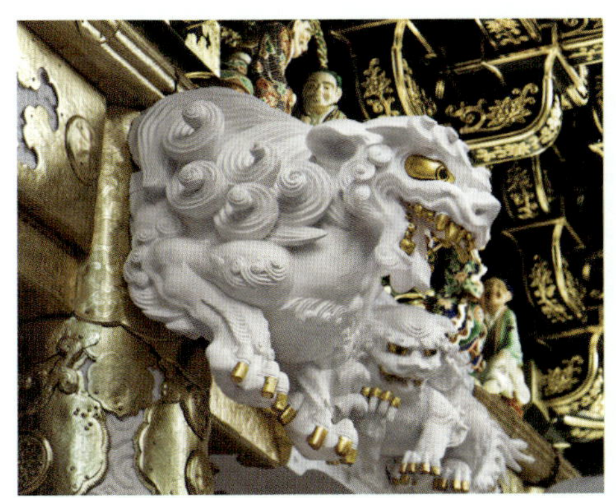
④ 獅子（陽明門） *Lion* (from Yōmeimon)

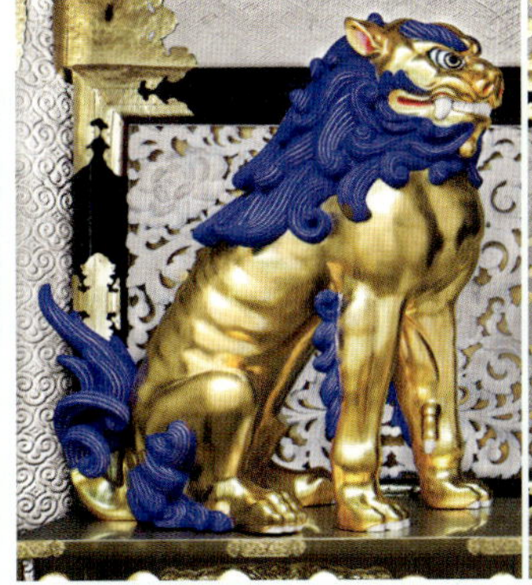
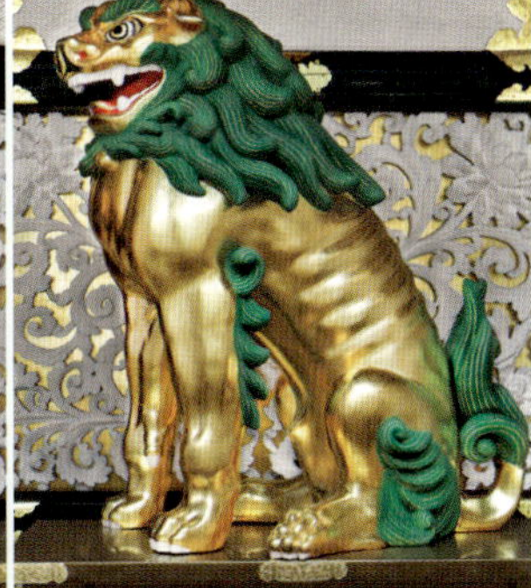
④ 唐獅子（陽明門） *Chinese Lions* (from Yōmeimon)

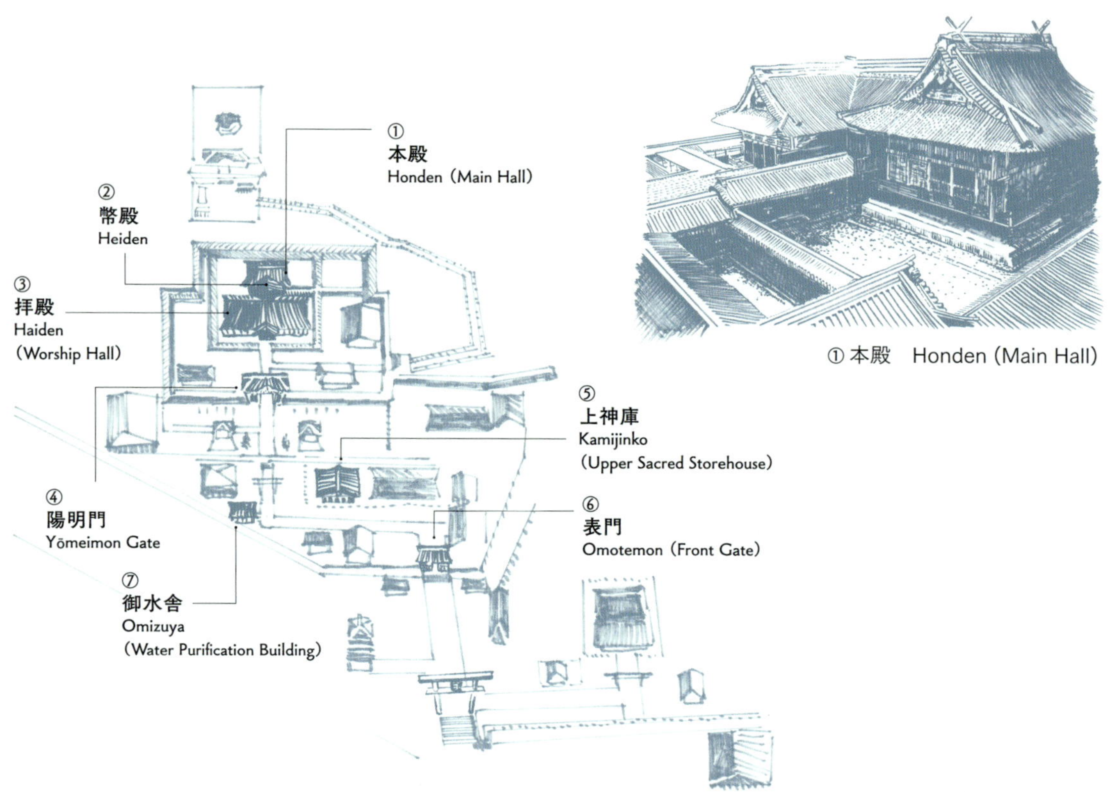

① 本殿　Honden (Main Hall)

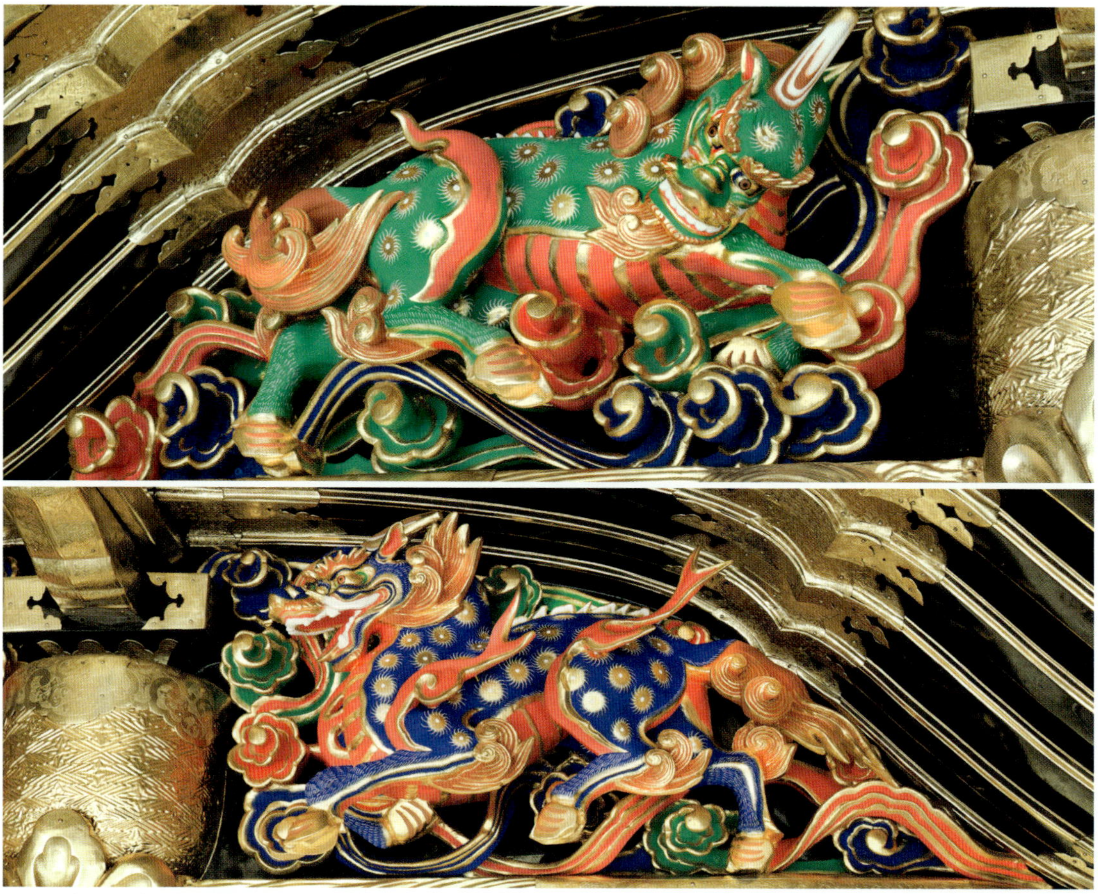

④ 麒麟(陽明門) *Kirin* (from Yōmeimon)

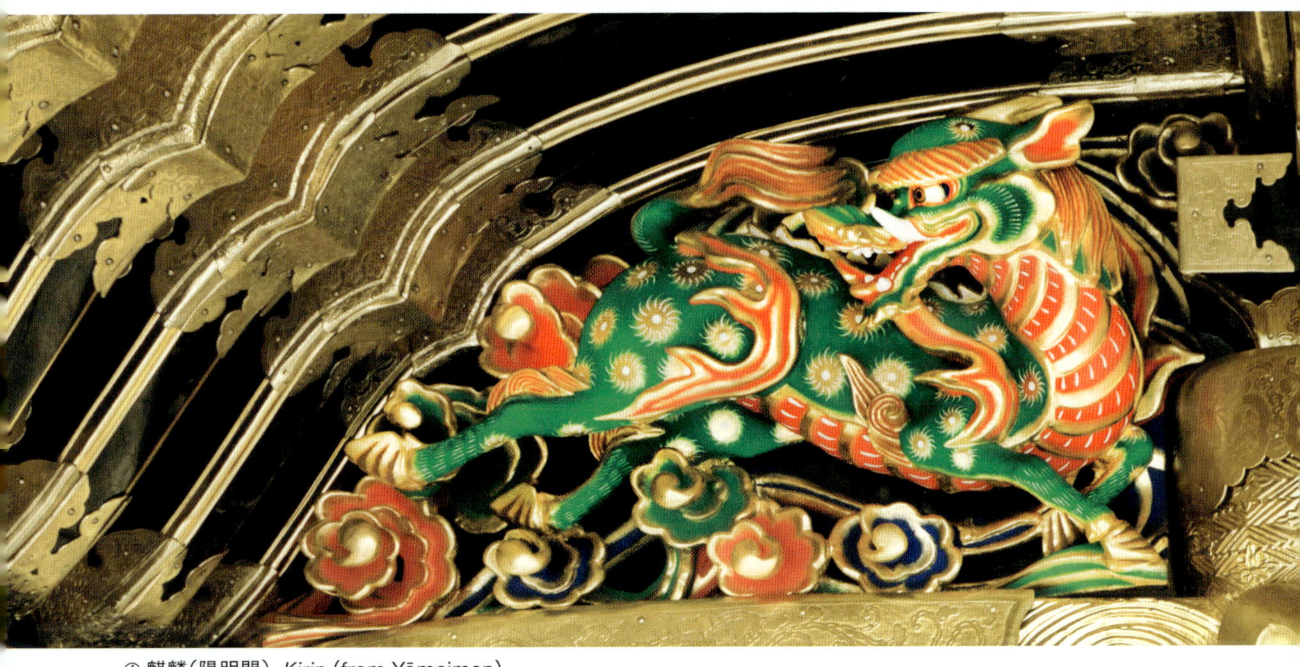

④ 麒麟（陽明門） *Kirin* (from Yōmeimon)

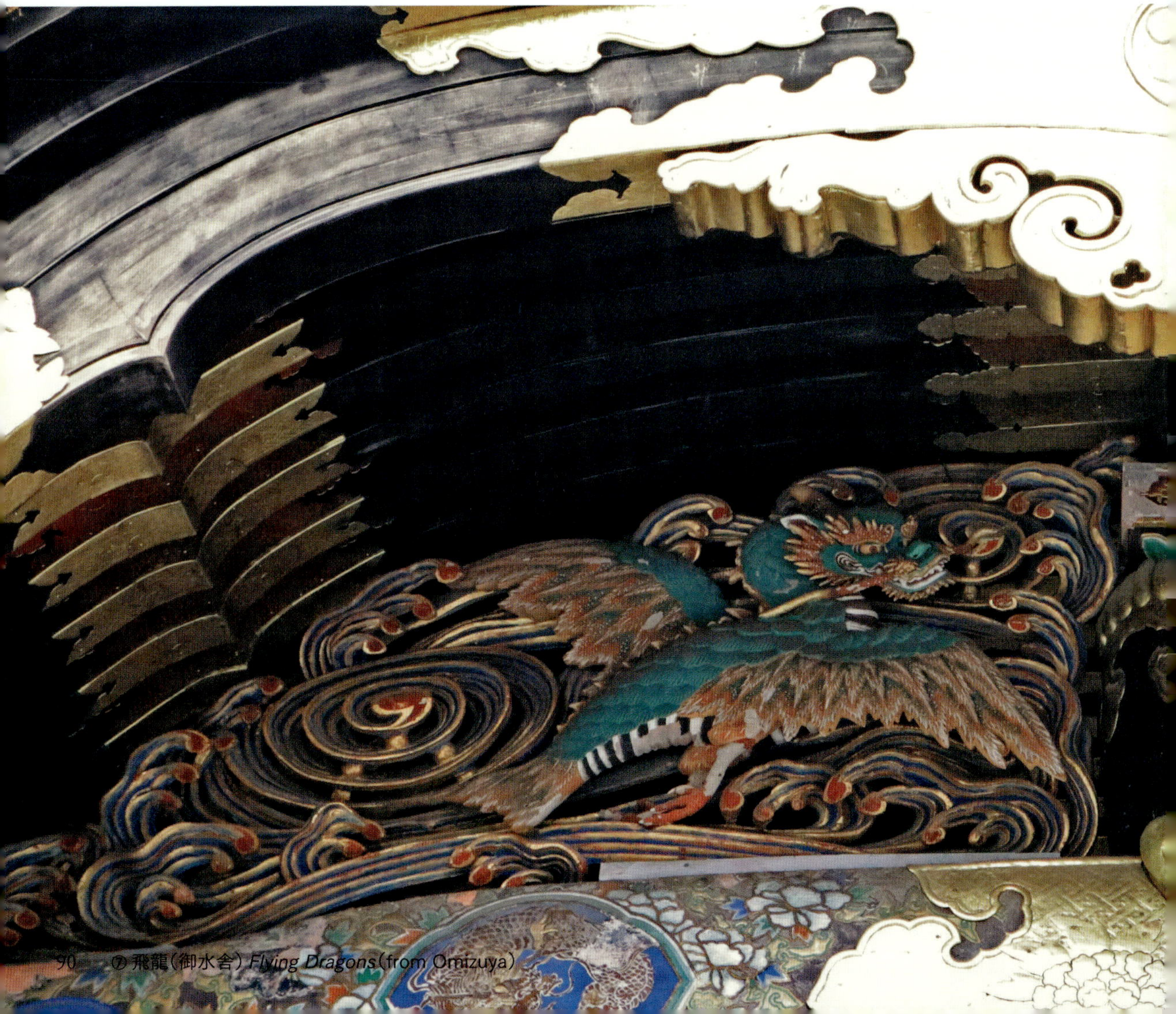

⑦ 飛龍（御水舎） *Flying Dragons*（from Omizuya）

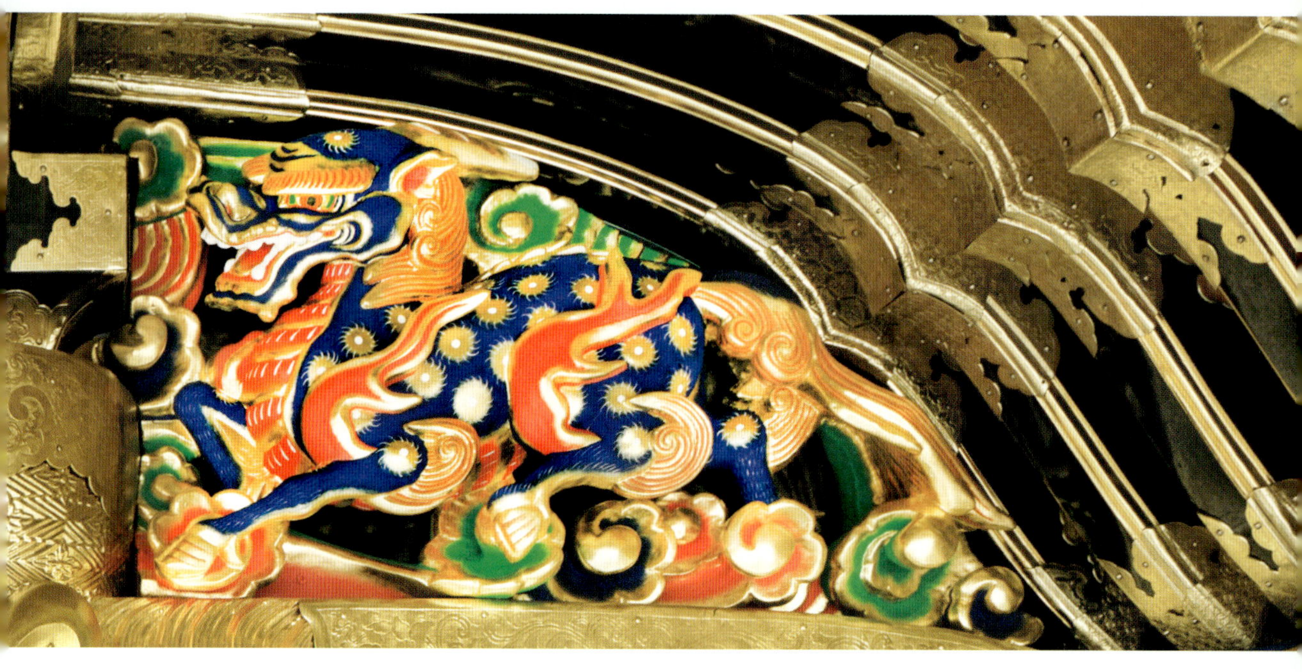

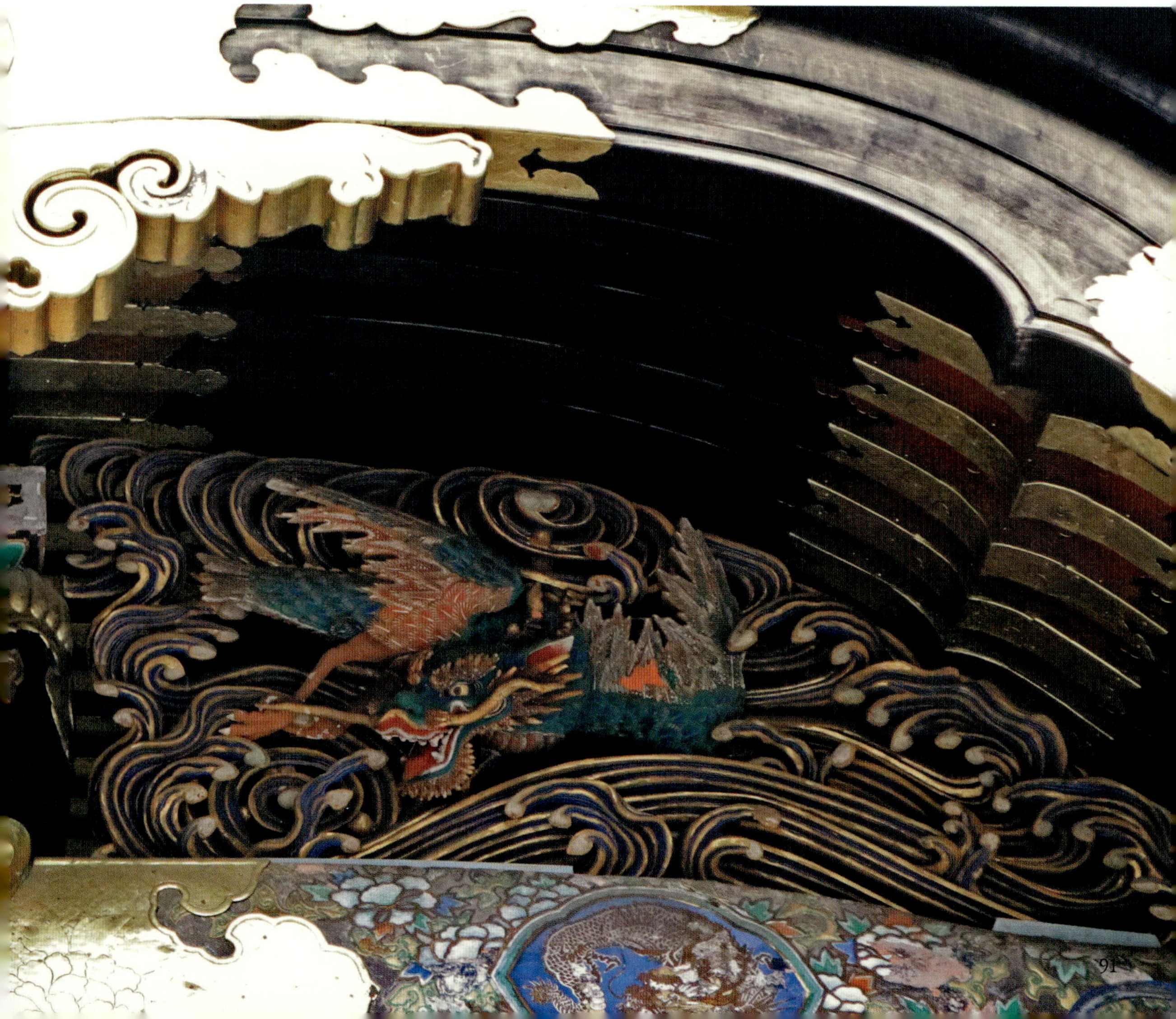

彫刻の総数は5173体とされ、うち508体は建物全体が極彩色の彫刻で覆われた陽明門に付属するという。それぞれに託された宗教的・思想的な意味に思いを巡らせつつ、その圧倒的な造形力に目を凝らしてもらいたい。

Supposedly, there are five thousand, one hundred and seventy-three sculptures in total, and five hundred and eight of those are the richly colored sculptures on just the Yōmeimon Gate. The overwhelming artistic virtuosity of the sculptures makes the viewer want to reflect on the religious and philosophical meanings embodied by each of them.

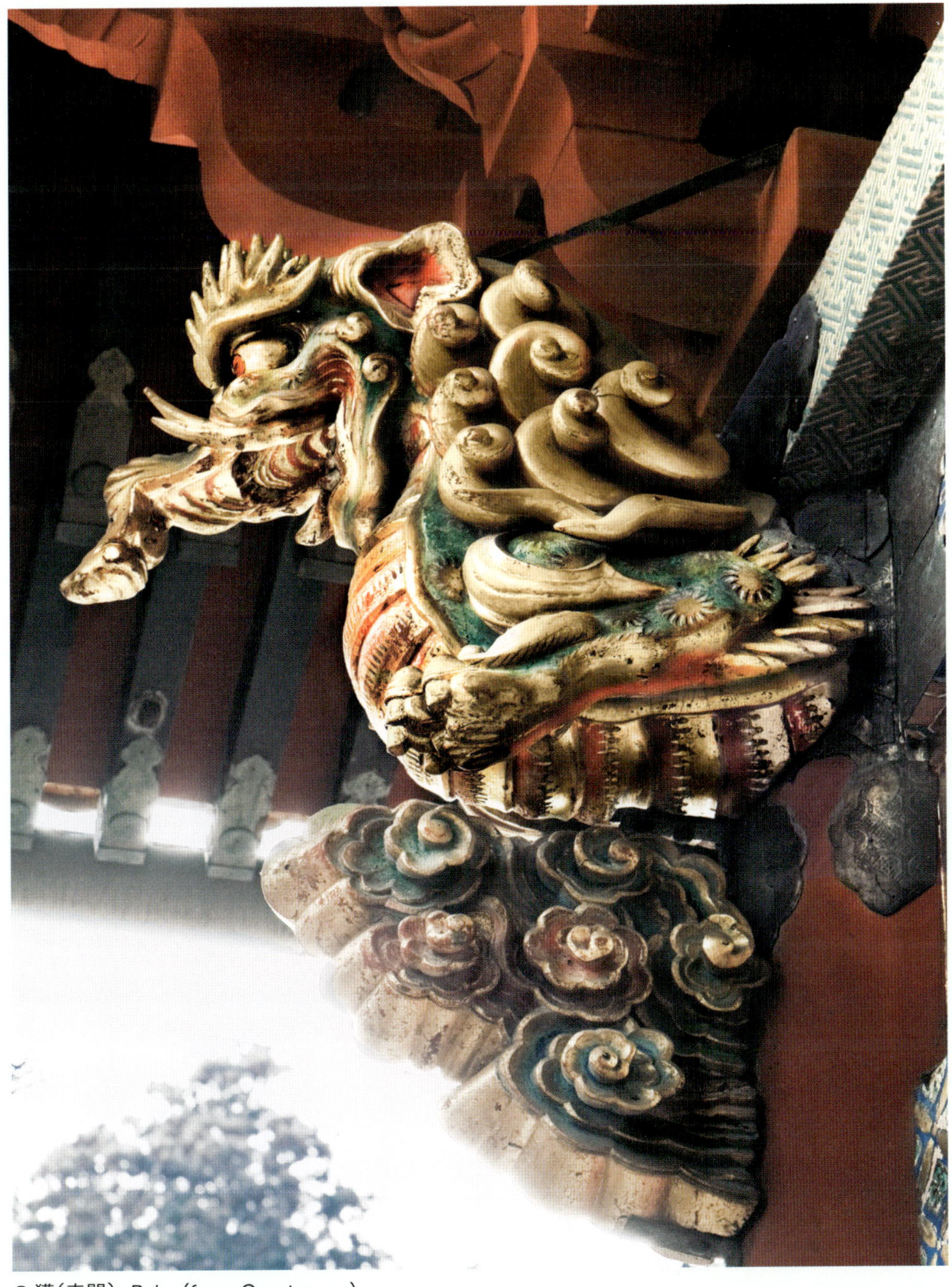

⑥ 貘(表門) *Baku* (from Omotemon)

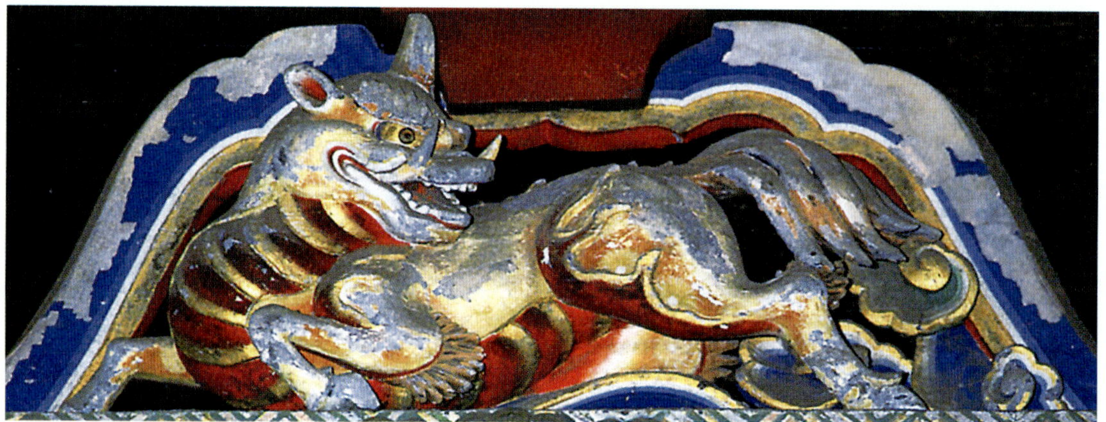
⑥ 麒麟（表門） *Kirin* (from Omotemon)

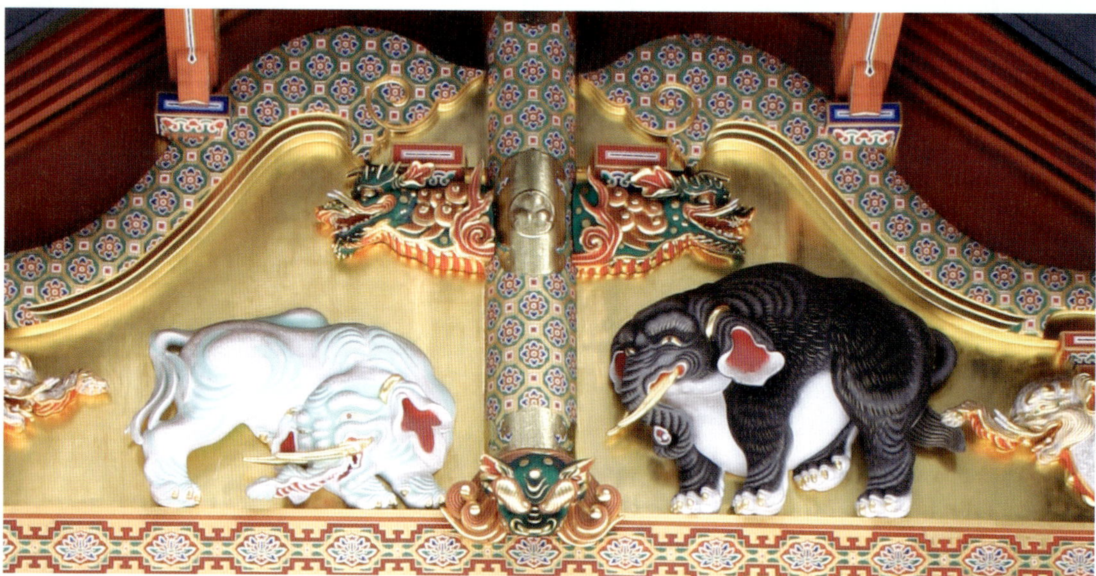
⑤ 象（上神庫） *Elephants* (from Kamijinko)

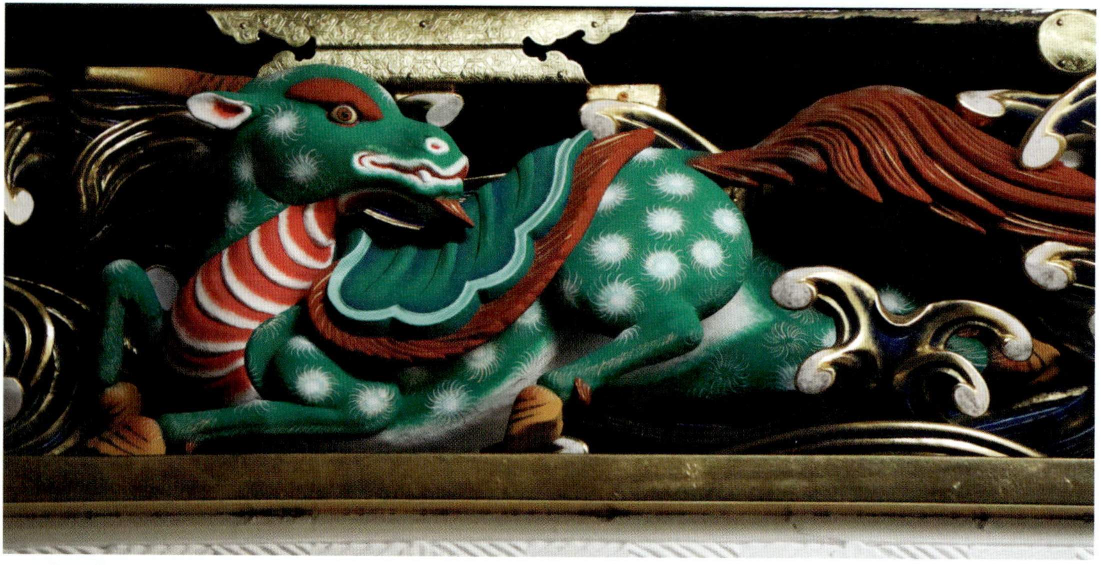
② 犀（幣殿） *Rhinoceros* (from Heiden)

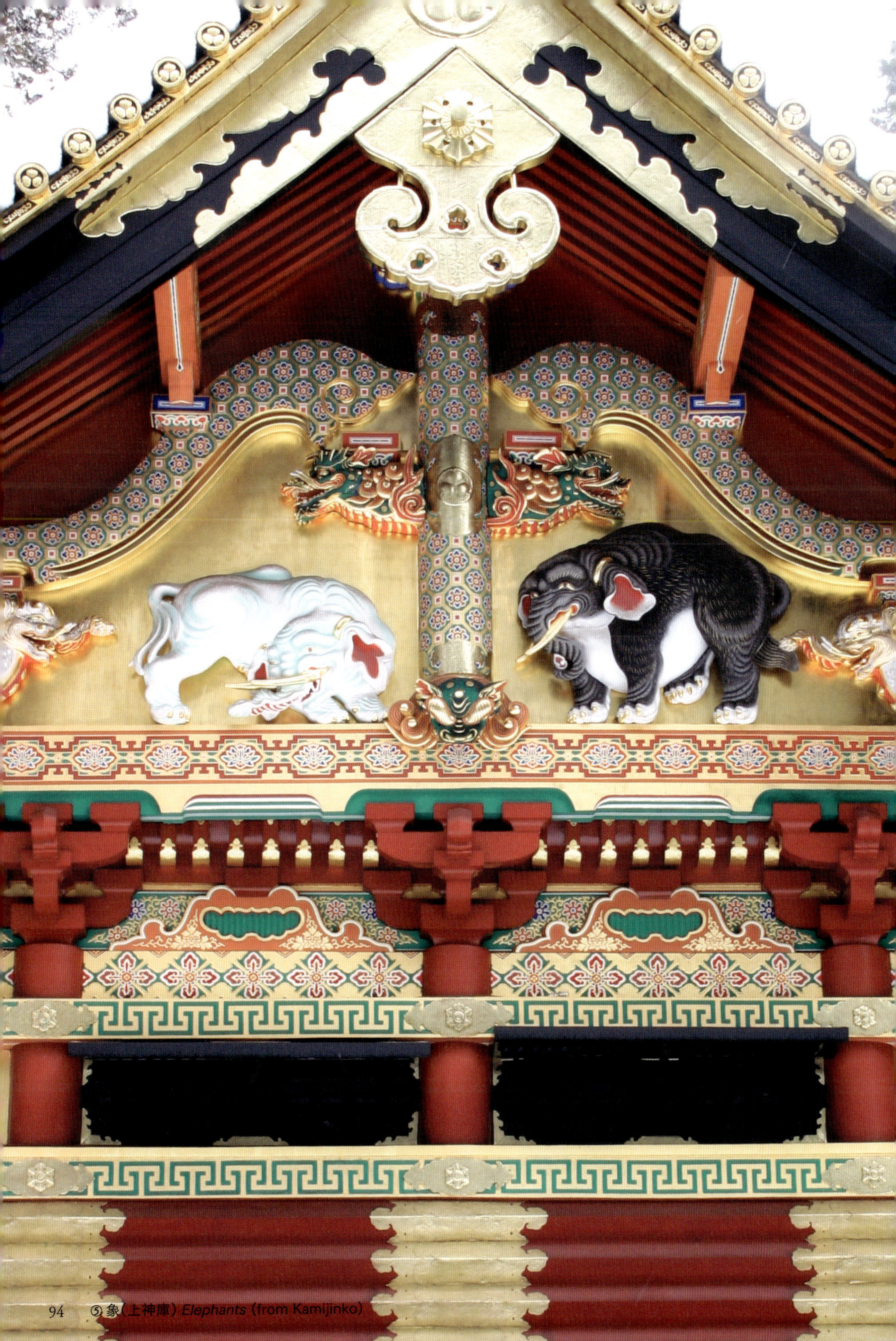

⑤ 象（上神庫）*Elephants* (from Kamijinko)

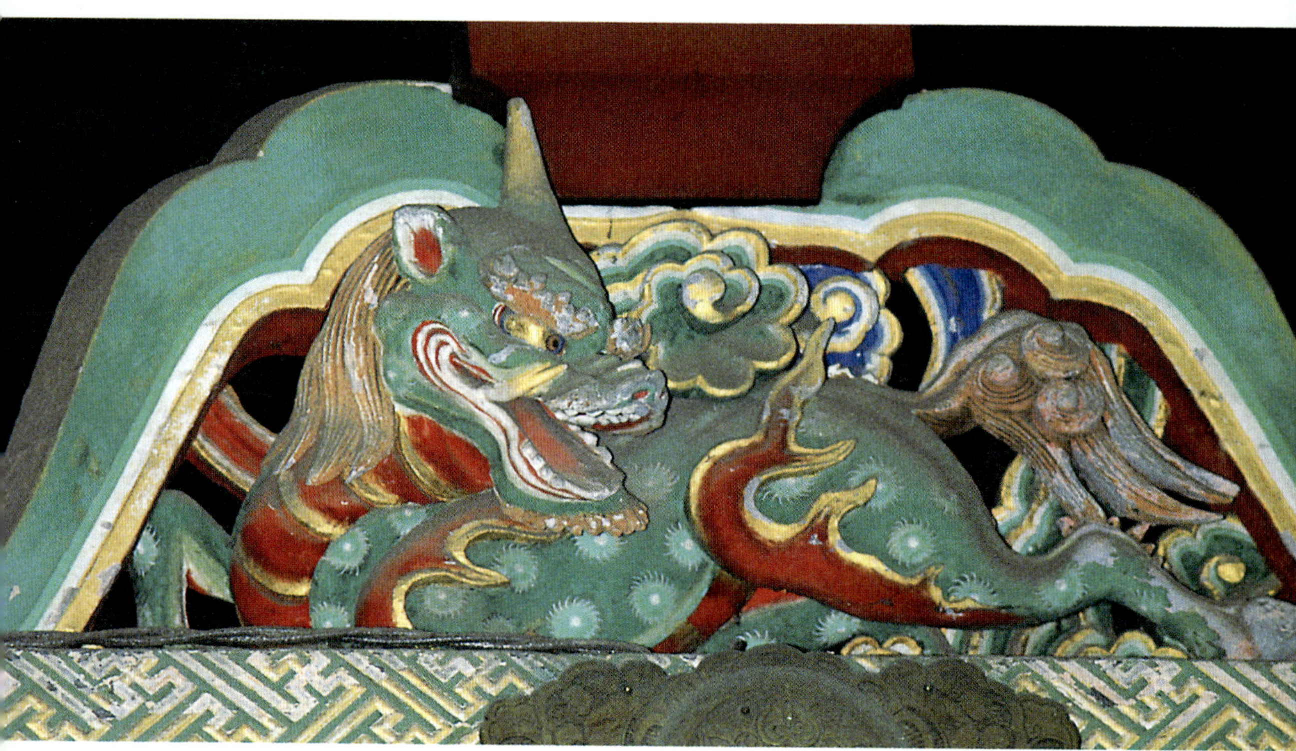
⑥ 麒麟（表門） *Kirin* (from Omotemon)

※88～95ページ掲載の彫刻はすべて国宝。
*All the sculptures featured in p. 88-95 are designated to National Treasure.

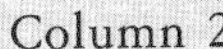

Column 2

リアリティと空想のはざま

ライオンと麒麟

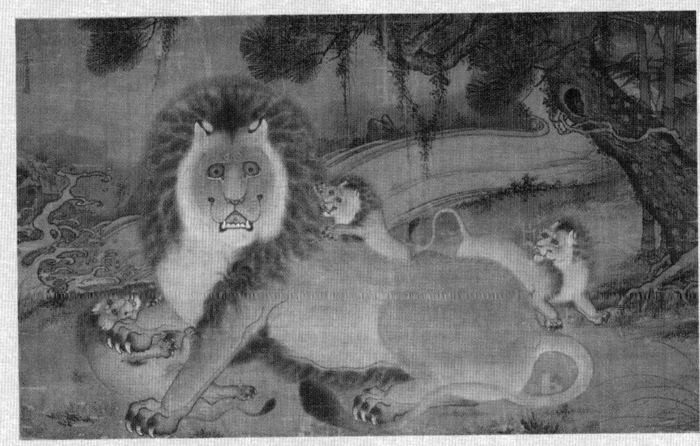

[1] 周全「獅子図軸」
Lions by Zhou Quan

日本人が古くから慣れ親しんできた異国の動物といえば、まず唐獅子(ライオン)があげられよう。釈迦の臨終の様子を描いた涅槃図には白象と対に大きく描かれ、また寺社に施された建築彫刻や障壁画などの絵画作品でも馴染み深いものだった。神社の鳥居脇などに置かれた狛犬(もとは「高麗犬」)も、朝鮮半島経由で入ってきた獅子イメージが転化した結果ともいう。

唐獅子の源流は、その名が示すとおり中国にある。『後漢書』西域伝に87年(章和元)安息国(イラン高原のパルティア王国)が献上したとあるのが、生身のライオンが中国にもたらされた最古の記録というが、存在自体は前漢時代からすでに知られていたらしい。時代は下って明時代。永楽帝の命により、1405年(永楽3)から1433年(宣徳8)にかけて7度もの「南海大遠征」を行った鄭和(1371～1434)の船団が訪れたのは、東南アジアからインド洋、ペルシャ湾・紅海の沿岸を経て、アフリカ東海岸にまで及んだ。ポルトガルやスペインはじめ西洋諸国が主導した「大航海時代」に80～90年も先んじて行われたものだが、その第4次遠征の際にペルシャ湾に面した忽魯謨斯(ホルムズ)の国王から使節が派遣され、明王朝あてに獅子や麒麟などが献上された(1415年)。さらに第5次遠征の際にも同国から獅子・金銭豹(レオポルド)・大西馬(アラビア馬)を、阿丹(アデン)国からは麒麟などを、木骨都束(モガディシオ)国からは花福鹿(シマウマ)と獅子を、卜剌哇(ブラワ)国からは千里駱駝(ラクダ)と駝鳥鶏(ダチョウ)などが献じられた(1420年)と記録されている。

それから半世紀後に活躍した画院画家(宮廷画家)周全が描いたのが「獅子図軸」[1]である。奔流を背にする獅子の姿には、南洋から朝貢の具(贈答品)としてもたらされた本物のライオンの余韻が色濃く残されている。ただし、子ライオンが父ライオンをそのまま縮小コピーしたようにたてがみを蓄えているところからすると、画家が目にしたのは成獣の雄ライオンだけだったと見える。さらに2世紀半が経過した頃に、沈南蘋(1683～1760～?)による「獅子戯児図」[2]が描

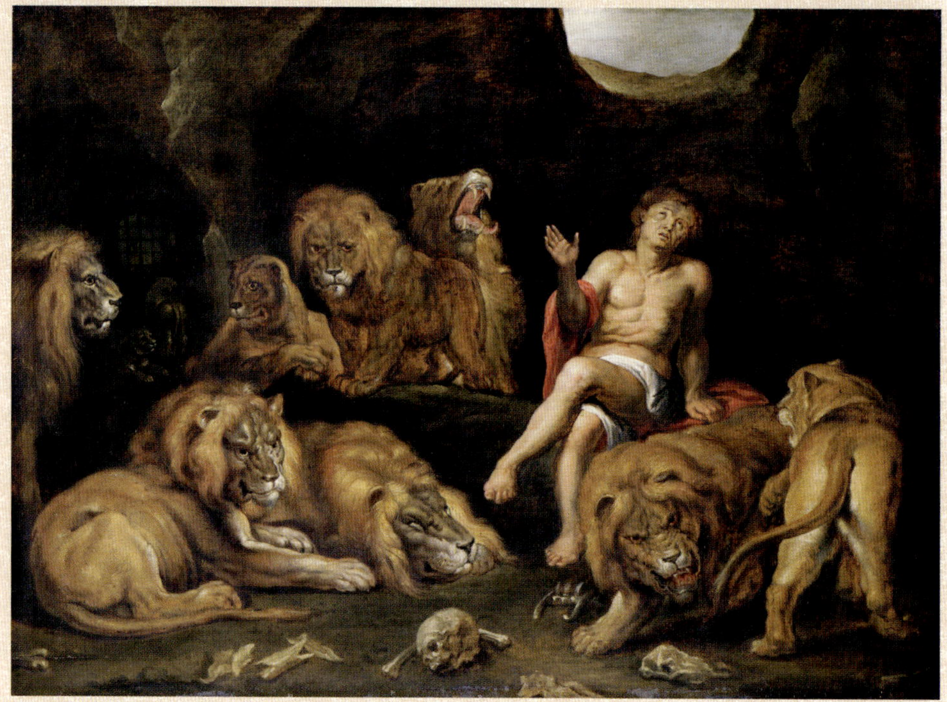

[6] ピーテル・パウル・ルーベンス「獅子の洞窟にいるダニエル」
Daniel in the Lions' Den by Peter Paul Rubens

Between Reality and Imagination:

Lions and *Kirin*

When considering strange creatures that have been familiar to the Japanese since ancient times, the first animal that comes to mind are so-called "Chinese lions" (J. *karajishi*). They are frequently depicted in so-called nirvana pictures that illustrate the death of the Buddha. Chinese lions are also found as sculptures and wall paintings in temples and shrines. Their shape is ubiquitous at *torii* gates of Shinto shrines. The common way that Chinese lions are rendered in Japan is derived from lion images on the Korean peninsula.

The Japanese term for the creatures, "Chinese lions," immediately clarifies their country of origin. The *Book of the Later Han* contains a record for the year 87 (Zhanghe 1) of a gift of a lion from the kingdom of Parthia in ancient Iran to China. Thus, we can assume that at least the existence of lions has been known in China since the Han dynasty. Let us fast forward to the Ming dynasty. By order of Emperor Yongle, under the command of Zheng He (1371-1434) a fleet of Chinese ships set out to distant lands roughly seven times between 1405 (Yongle 3) and 1433 (Xuande 8), traveling to Southeast Asia and from there on to the India Ocean and the Persian Gulf, and reaching as far as the east coast of Africa. These voyages preceded the Age of Discovery of the 1480s and 1490s, when Spanish and Portuguese ships explored the globe. The fourth Chinese expedition received an embassy from the kingdom of Ormuz that gifted lions and giraffes to the Ming court in 1415. The fifth voyage got more lions and leopards, as well as Arab horses, while Aden sent giraffes and other exotic animals. From Mogadishu, the Ming court received zebras and lions, while Bulawayo sent camels and ostriches in 1420.

Roughly half a century after, the Chinese court painter Zhou Quan created this painting.[1] The lions are positioned against the backdrop of a stream and the level of representational accuracy strongly reflects the presence of actual lions given to the Ming court. Be that as it may, the cubs are simply rendered as smaller versions of the male lion, indicating that the painter probably saw fully-grown lions only. Two and a half centuries after, the painter Shen Nanpin (1683-1760?) painted his own interpretation of a lion and its cubs. Nanpin hailed from Zhejiang Province and arrived in Japan in 1731 (Kyōhō 16). The eighth shogun, Tokugawa Yoshimune, had a thirst for antique Chinese paintings, which were difficult to acquire. As a substitute, he sent for Chinese painters to work in Japan. Although Shen Nanpin resided in Nagasaki less than two years, the influence of his

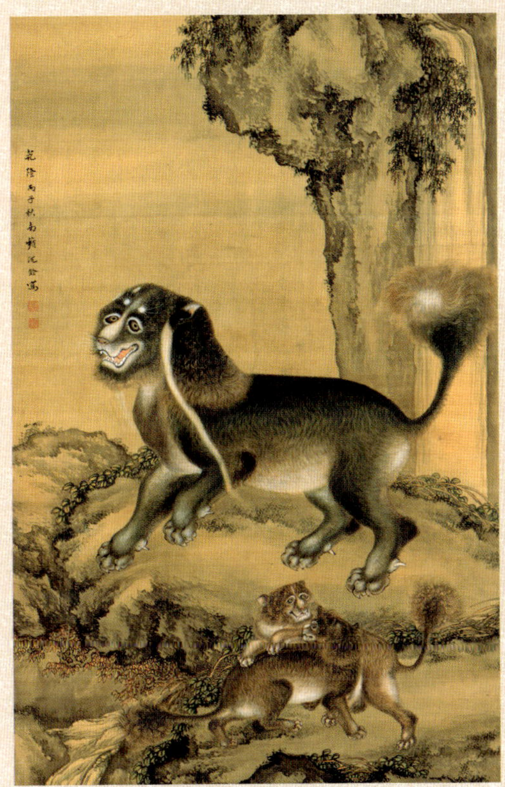

[2] 沈南蘋「獅子戯児図」
Lion and Cubs by Shen Nanpin

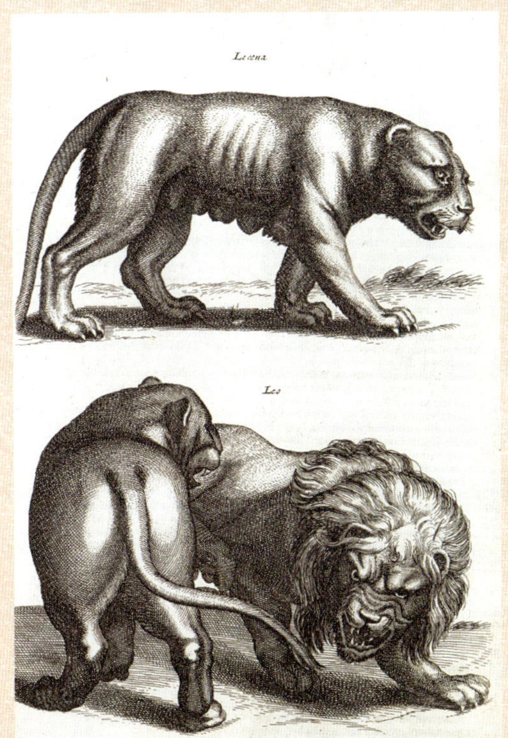

[3] ライオン図『ヨンストン動物図譜』より
Lions from *Historiae naturalis*

かれた。南蘋は中国・浙江省呉興の人で、1731年(享保16)に来日。中国の正統的な古画を求めた8代将軍吉宗に対し、その入手が困難だったための代替措置として派遣されたのであった。長崎滞在は2年に満たなかったが、その写生的で華やかな画風は江戸時代の画家たちに大きな影響を与えた。本図においては、宮廷画家が大画面に描き上げたライオンの片鱗こそ留めてはいるものの、たてがみや尾の形態は大きく変化してしまっていることがわかる。

南蘋が訪れた18世紀の日本は、出版文化が発展し情報化の時代を迎えつつあった。その流れが博物学という学問の流行を促すことになった経緯については、先に記したとおりである。その第一人者として知られる平賀源内(1728～79)が、家財・夜具までも売り払って購入したというオランダ渡りの分厚い本が『ヨンストン動物図譜』[3]である。オランダ商館長から4代将軍家綱に献上されながら、府庫に眠ったままだったのを、8代将軍吉宗が取り出して学者に翻訳させたことでも知られる本で、今の分類とは異なるものの哺乳類から魚類、鳥類、爬虫類、はては昆虫に至るまで総数250枚にも及ぶ銅版画が満載されていた。

源内と親しかった宋紫石(1715～86)は、源内入手後わずか2ヵ月にして「獅子図」[4]を描き上げ、そこに「この獅子図は平賀先生秘蔵の蛮獣譜(『ヨンストン動物図譜』のこと)に載せるもので、世の描くところとは違っている、思うに西洋人が写生したものだからであろう(此獅子図平賀先生秘蔵蛮獣譜中所載、与世之所画者異、蓋蛮人之写生云)」と記した。このライオンは、『解体新書』の挿図を手がけたことで知られる秋田蘭画の小田野直武(1749～80)や司馬江漢(1747～1818)ら洋風画家たちによって作品化され、さらに『紅毛雑話』(1787年刊)[5]という西洋事情の紹介書の挿図にもなり広く知られるところとなった。なお、同書のライオン図の源流をたどると、かのルーベンス(1577～1640)のデッサンや油絵[6]に行き着くとされるのだが、わが国の画人たちにはもちろん知る由もなかったことである。

vivid naturalistic style on Japanese artists of the Edo period was profound. The manes and tails in Shen Nanpin's picture of lions are drastically different from the snapshot-like large-format work done by Zhou Quan.

The eighteenth-century Japan that Shen Nanpin encountered upon his arrival witnessed a thriving publishing industry and expansive dissemination of knowledge. Natural history was a popular field of study. The foremost representative of that movement was Hiraga Gennai (1728-79) who, by selling household items and even his bedding, managed to acquire the sought-after encyclopedia *Historiae naturalis*, by Johannes Jonston.[3] The books came to Japan as a gift for the fourth shogun, Tokugawa Ietsuna, and had been forgotten until the eighth shogun Yoshimune unearthed them from storage. He ordered scholars to translate the books and reprint the roughly two hundred and fifty copperplate engravings that illustrate the different animals. Their categorization differs from today's science.

The painter Sō Shiseki (1715-86), created his own image of a lion[4] only two months after his friend Hiraga Gennai had acquired Johannes Jonston's encyclopedia. Shiseki added a note to his work stating: "This image of a lion is based on the encyclopedia of foreign beasts in the possession of Gennai called *Historiae naturalis*". Shiseki also notes that the image is different from our understanding, since its original was sketched from life by a foreign artist. The lion was also used as inspiration for paintings by Odano Naotake (1749-80), an artist known for his illustrations in *Kaitai shinsho* (*New Text on Anatomy*), and the Western-style painter Shiba Kōkan (1747-1818). It was also illustrated in the widely read *Kōmo zatsuwa* (*Miscellany of Westerners*), published in 1787. [5] The original source for the lion painting is said to have been a work[6] by Peter Paul Rubens (1577-1640), a history that Japanese artists were, of course, unaware of.

Images of lions did not only circulate in Edo and Japan's eastern regions. Also in Kyoto, the capital, painters rendered these exotic animals. Kishi Ganku (1749-1838), who worked in Kyoto, painted this work[7] in 1782 (Tenmei 2). Ganku painted Samson, a king in the Old Testament, as he is preventing a lion from charging at a lamb. Christian texts were banned in Japan at the time, so the iconography may have entered the country in the form of etchings in foreign books, a conjecture that is supported by the peculiar shading used in the painting. The lion, on the other hand, is painted in a rather weak manner. Maruyama Ōkyo's student Yoshimura Kōkei (1769-1836), an artist who like his teacher subscribed to naturalism,

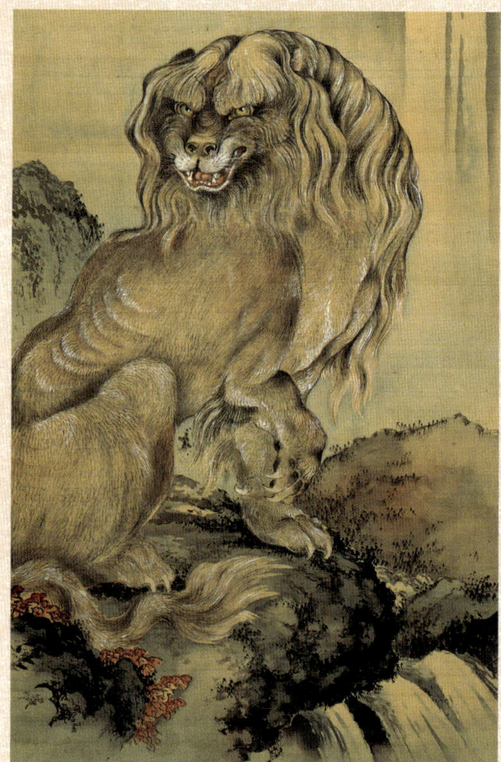

[4] 宋紫石「獅子図」部分
Lion by Sō Shiseki

ところで、ライオンのイメージは江戸・東国にとどまり、都には届かなかったものであろうか。「サムソンと獅子図」[7]は、京都で活躍した岸駒(1749〜1838)による1782年(天明2)の作。『旧約聖書』に登場する怪力の持ち主サムソンが、目の前に現れたライオンを子ヤギでも裂くように引き裂いた、という場面を描いたものである。おそらく舶載書(『旧約聖書』は禁教下のわが国にも入っていた)の銅版挿絵などに倣ったもので、どぎついまでの陰影表現が目を引く異色作なのだが、こと描かれたライオンに関して言えば、あまりにひ弱そうだ。また、写生に励んだ円山応挙の門人・吉村孝敬(1769〜1836)に1831年(天保2)作の「唐獅子図」[8]がある。子ライオンが親と同じたてがみを蓄え、鼻が奇妙に変形してしまっているのはまだしも、四脚の鋭い爪が失われ蹄のような代物と化してしまった事象をどう解釈すべきなのだろうか。ちなみに、生きたライオンが最初に日本にやってきたのは、1865年(慶応元)のことであった。

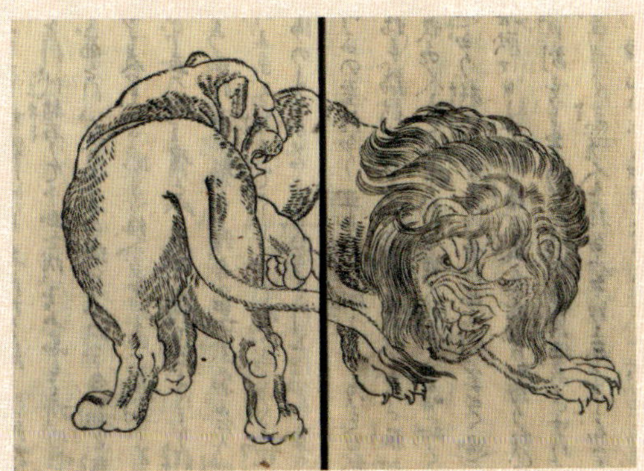

[5] ライオン図(『紅毛雑話』より)
Lions from *Miscellany of Westerners*

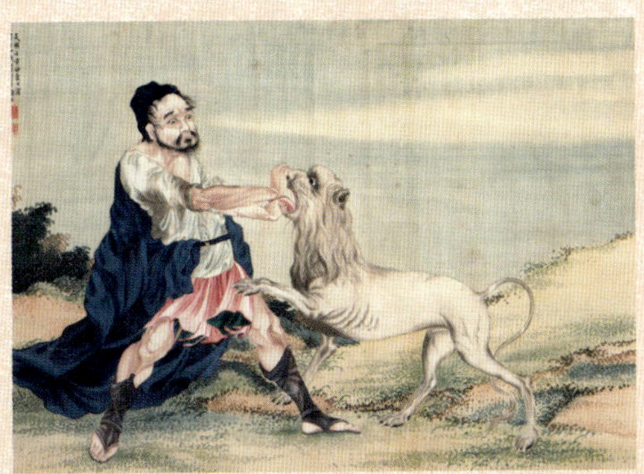

[7] 岸駒「サムソンと獅子図」
Samson and Lion by Ganku

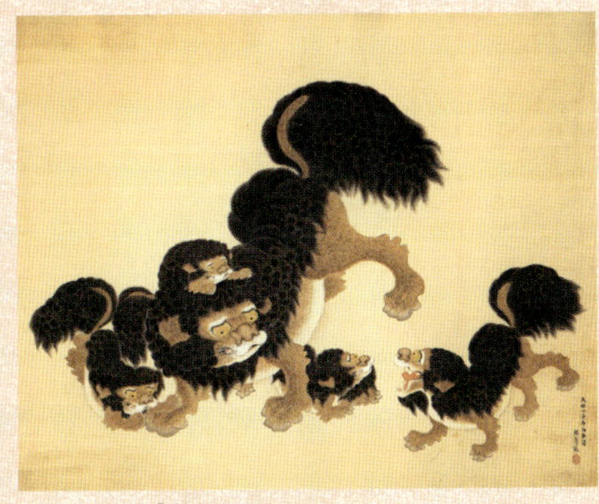

[8] 吉村孝敬「唐獅子図」
Chinese Lions by Yoshimura Kōkei

∽

中国における神話伝説上の霊獣で、鳳凰・亀・龍とともに「四霊」と称されてきた聖獣・麒麟。儒教における第一の徳目である仁徳を備えた一角をもつ「仁獣」で、360もの毛蟲(毛のある動物)の長とされる。情け深い動物で、肉食はおろか草などの植物すら食せず、歩行時も草の芽を踏まず、虫を踏みつけることもない。そして有徳の王者の治世には姿を見せるが、殺生を好む者が国を治めているときは姿を隠すと伝えられた霊獣である。体つきは麋(なれしか)に似て、牛の尾、そして一角を持ち、さらに蹄は馬のような単蹄ということであった。角の端に肉があるのは仁の顕(あらわ)れ、すなわち何物も傷つけることのないようにとの配慮からだという。

鳳凰とともに瑞祥の代表として重んじられ造形化されていったのだが、時代の経過とともに形態的にも大きく変化し、体軀が鱗文で覆われるとともに、本来の一角が双角に、単蹄が偶蹄で表わされるようになっていったという。そのような

painted a lion in 1831 (Tenpō 2).[8] The cubs have the same fur and peculiar nose as the larger lion, and claws that resemble hooves. How is one to read these interpretations of a lion's physique? Granted, the first living lion was brought to Japan only in 1865 (Keiō 1).

∽

The auspicious creatures of Chinese mythology—phoenixes, turtles, and dragons—are often listed together with *kirin* as the so-called "Four Sacred Beasts." In Confucianism, the first virtue is benevolence and is symbolized by the one-horned creature *jinjū*, which is considered the highest-ranking of the three hundred and sixty animals. Its body resembles that of a moose with the tail of an ox, a single horn, and the hoofs of a horse. Since its horns are coated with thin flesh, it behaves so as to not hurt anything—a sign of benevolence.

Giraffes or *kirin*, together with phoenixes, symbolize good omens and were depicted often. With the passing of time, their renderings changed dramatically. Their bodies once were covered in scales with two horns adorning the heads. Their ungulate feet were often depicted as even-toed. With these misconceptions in mind, in 1414 the aforementioned overseas expedition under Zheng He brought back a living giraffe to the Ming court as a gift from Bengal. The emperor was greatly pleased and, given giraffes' auspicious symbolism in Chinese mythology, his delight was not surprising. To mark the occasion, painters were summoned to depict the animal and a member of the Hanlin Academy wrote an appropriate laudation. On that occasion, the ruler of Bengal sent a giraffe he had acquired from Africa, but as noted earlier other giraffes were gifted to the Ming court on later occasions.

The name "giraffe" originates from an ancient Arabian word meaning "running fast." In Japan, the first giraffe arrived five hundred years after the Ming court witnessed the animal. In 1907, Ueno Zoo acquired a specimen and initially referred to it by its mythical name, *kirin*. The name was given by the director of the zoo, Ishikawa Chiyomatsu. Following this precedent, giraffes came to be referred to as *kirin* in Japanese. The reason for Ishikawa's choice lies in the animal's country of origin and the Somali word *giri*, designating long-necked herbivores. Because the word was so close to the ancient term *kirin*, it came to be used as the Japanese word for giraffe. However, when looking at Shen Nanpin's rendering of a giraffe [10], the visual parallels between a *kirin* and a giraffe are not at all obvious. As we can see, the Japanese

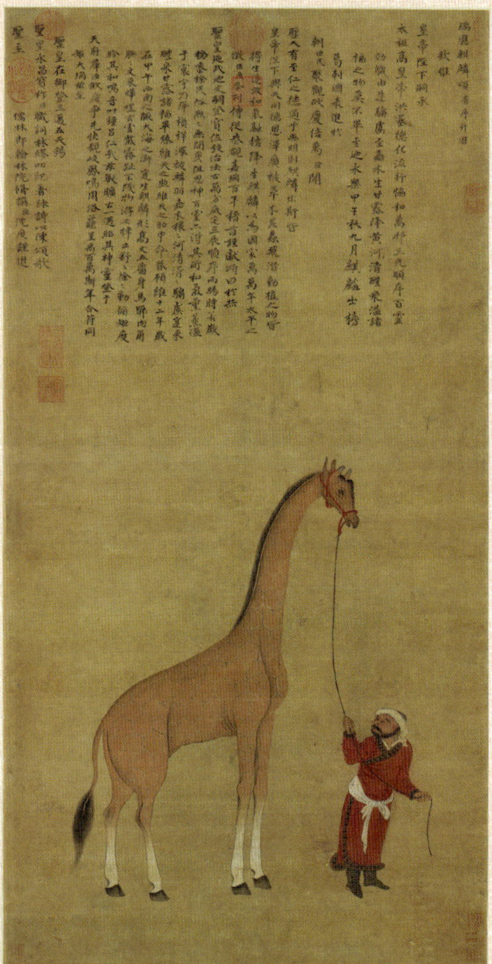

[9] 明人「瑞応麒麟図(画麒麟沈度頌)」
The Lucky Kirin by Ming dynasty painter

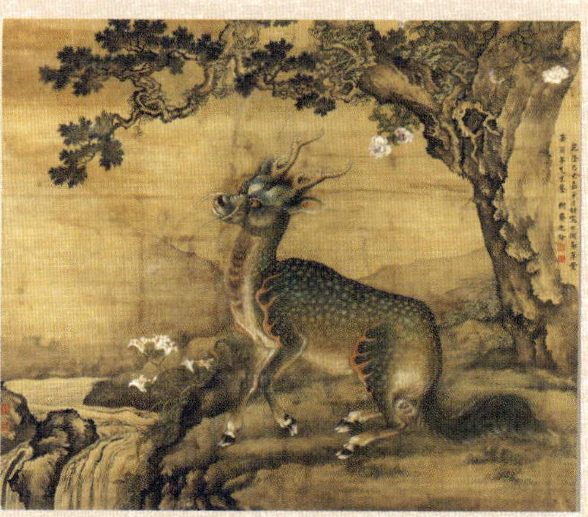

[10] 沈南蘋「麒麟図」
Kirin by Shen Nanpin

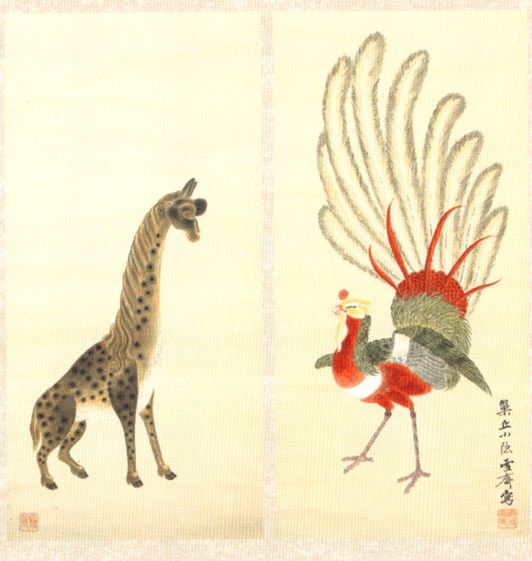

[12] 増山雪斎「麒麟・鳳凰図」
Kirin and Pheonix
by Mashiyama Sessai

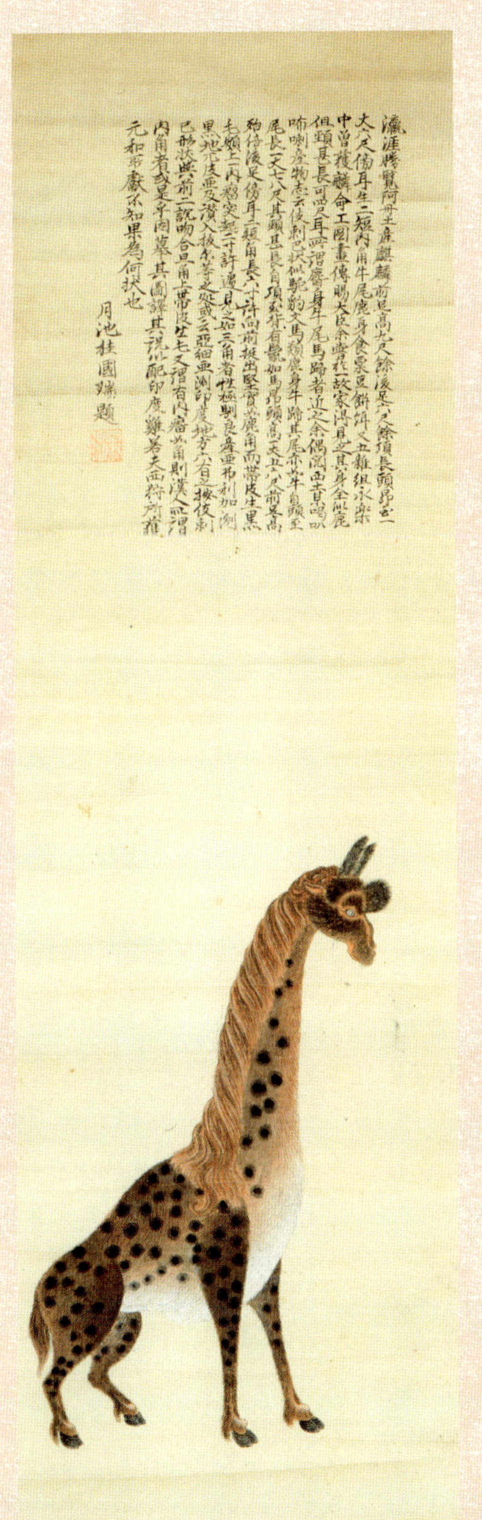

[11] 桂川甫周「麒麟図」
Kirin (Giraffe) by Katsuragawa Hoshū

状況下、先に紹介したように鄭和による4回目の大遠征が契機となり、1414年（永楽12）榜葛剌（ベンガル）国の使節が生きたままのキリンを明王朝に献上した。皇帝は大いに喜んだというが、聖王の治世に現れるとされる「麒麟」であれば当然だったろう。慶事を記念して、その姿を絵師に描かせ、翰林院の役人に顕彰文を書かせている。この時はアフリカから買い入れたキリンが送られたようだが、先述のようにキリンの贈答はこれ以後、頻繁に行われていったようである。

なお、キリンは「速く走るもの」を意味する古代アラビア由来の「ジラフ」と呼称するのが一般的である。日本での初登場は明国の事例に遅れること500年、1907年（明治40）上野動物園においてであったが、その時の呼称は「キリン」であった。名付け親は動物学者で当時の同園館長・石川千代松とのことだが、それに倣ってここではジラフを日本人に馴染みのキリンと表記しよう。そもそも、キリンが「麒麟」と認識されるに至った背景として、現地語（ソマリ語）で首の長い草食動物を意味する「ギリン」が、麒麟の発音に近かったためと言われるが、朝貢品として贈り、贈られる側双方の思惑が一致した結果でもあったろう。しかし、沈南蘋が手がけた「麒麟図」[10]を見ると、先述の獅子図とライオンとの関係とは異なり、キリンの気配は微塵も感じられない。先の事

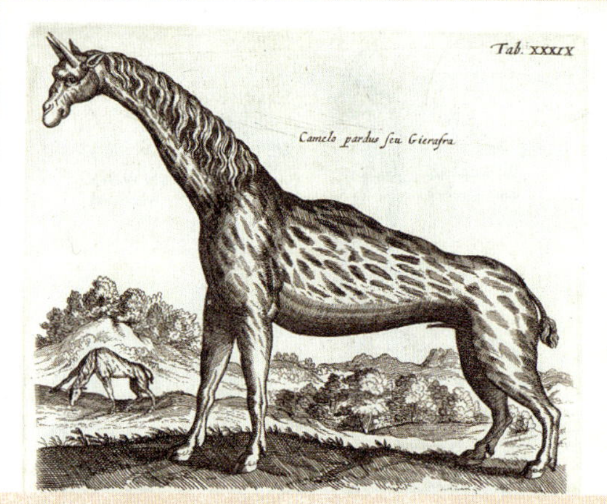

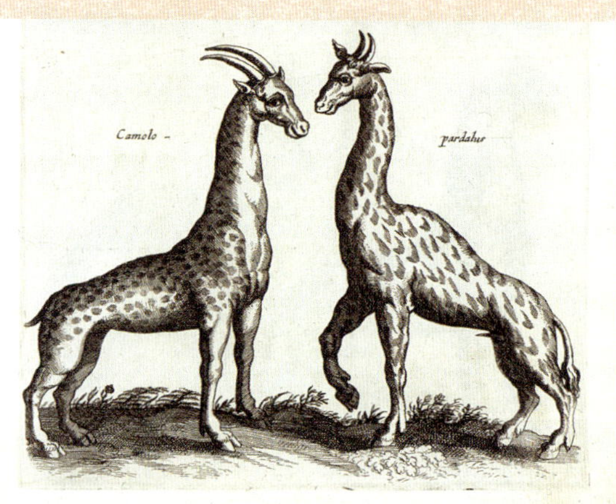

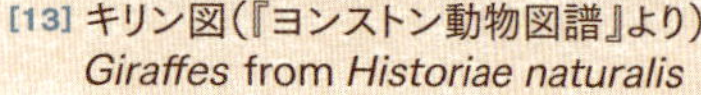

[13] キリン図(『ヨンストン動物図譜』より)
Giraffes from *Historiae naturalis*

件が契機となって、キリンが「麒麟」にとって変わることはなかったのである。なお、中国ではキリンを麒麟ではなく「長頸鹿」と呼称する。

日本でも長らく、麒麟は麒麟のままに社寺の建築彫刻や絵画・工芸など様々な分野で造形化され続けてきた。そのような中、キリンを絵入りで記録した最初の人物が、幕府の蘭医・桂川甫周(1751～1809)であった。図上の賛には、先の鄭和の南海大遠征の記録『瀛涯勝覧』などを引用しつつ、蘭書「喝叭唏喇(現ケープタウン辺り)産物志」の「伎剌巴(ギラハ＝ジラフ)」の記述と比較することにより、麒麟とキリンを同定。同書に掲載の図を模写し、その概要を記したという。

甫周の写した麒麟図[11]は、蘭学を好み甫周とも交流のあった伊勢長島藩主・増山雪斎(1754～1819)により鳳凰図と対の作品[12]として残されることになった。さらに、甫周と並ぶ優れた蘭学者の大槻玄沢(1757～1827)は、『ヨンストン動物図譜』掲載の銅版画[13]との比較から、麒麟を「疑拉法(ジラフ)」と同定。麒麟は王者の美徳に応じて出現するものではなく、異国に常時存在するものとして中国の瑞獣説を否定したのである。ただし、この一事をもって一般の麒麟イメージがキリンに変わることはなかったようだ。霊獣としての麒麟は、麒麟のまま変わることなく現在も生き続けているのである。

word for giraffe is not simply an adaptation of the mythical meaning. What is more, in Chinese giraffes are called "long-necked deer."

For the longest time, in Japan *kirin* were depicted as mythical creatures in sculptures, paintings, and other artworks. The first Japanese to render a *kirin* in the shape of a giraffe was the physician Katsuragawa Hoshū (1751-1809). In the inscription above the painting, he quotes the record of Zheng He's voyages, *Yingya shenglan* (*Overall Survey of the Ocean's Shores*; J. *Eigai shōran*), saying: "a creature from Kahala" (the area of today's Cape Town). We further learn that he identified the giraffe as a *kirin*, and that he copied the illustration of the book as is.

The giraffe[11] that Hoshū copied entered the collection of Mashiyama Sessai (1754-1819), the lord of Ise Nagashima Domain, as a diptych together with an image of a phoenix.[12] Another esteemed scholar of Dutch learning, Ōtsuki Gentaku (1757-1827), also identified giraffes as *kirin* on the basis of *Historiae naturalis*.[13] He determined that *kirin* were not beings of benevolence as in ancient Chinese mythology, but in fact actual creatures living in a faraway land. However, the general, mythical perception of *kirin* did not change. Even today, *kirin* survive as auspicious beings.

麒麟紋章
（一品武官麒麟補子）

明時代後期（17c後半）
メトロポリタン美術館

Rank Badge with Kirin

Ming dynasty, Late 17th century
The Metropolitan Museum of Art

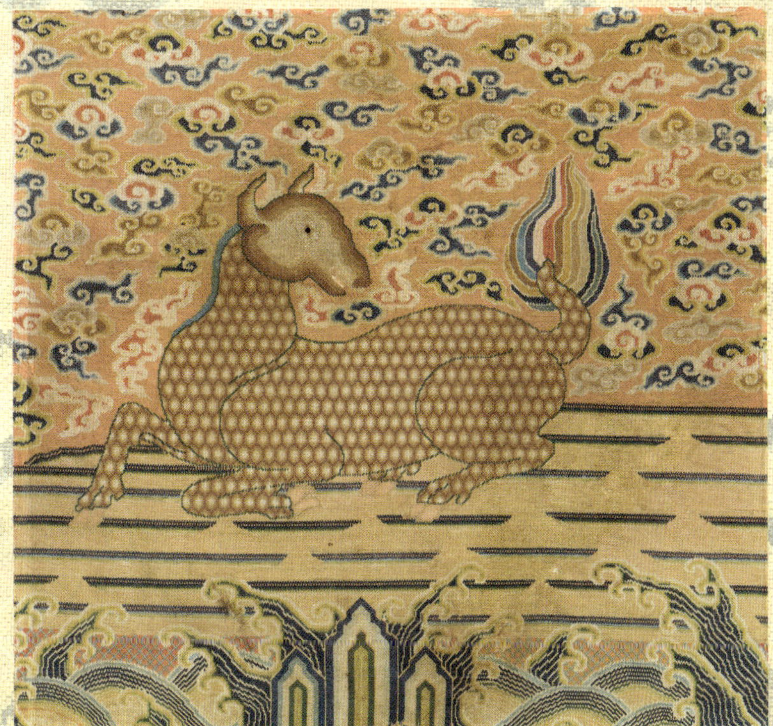

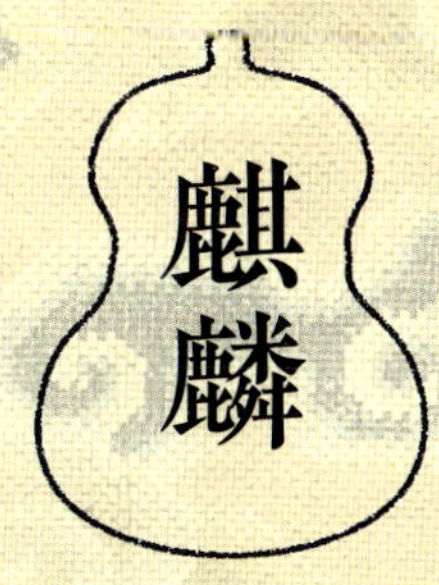

中国における神話伝説上の霊獣で、鳳凰・亀・龍とともに「四霊」と称されてきた聖獣・麒麟。儒教における第一の徳目である仁徳を備えた「仁獣」で、360もの毛蟲（毛のある動物）の長とされる。情け深い動物で、肉食はおろか草などの植物すら食せず、歩行時も草の芽を踏まず、虫を踏みつけることもない。そして有徳の王者の治世には姿を見せるが、殺生を好む者が国を治めているときは姿を隠すと伝えられた霊獣である。体つきは麋に似て、牛の尾、そして一角を持ち、さらに蹄は馬のような単蹄ということであった。角の端に肉があるのは仁の現れ、すなわち何も傷つけることのないようにとの配慮からだという。鳳凰とともに祥瑞の代表として重んじられ造形化されていったのだが、時代の経過とともに形態的にも大きく変化し、体軀が鱗文で覆われるとともに、本来の一角が双角に、単蹄が偶蹄で表わされるようになっていったという。

The *Kirin* (Giraffe)

This is a sacred beast that comes from Chinese myths and legends and is part of the "Four Sacred Beasts," together with the phoenix, turtle, and dragon. In Confucianism, it is known as a virtuous beast that is imbued with the first virtue, benevolence. It has one horn, and it is the lord of three hundred and sixty types of furry creatures. It is a deeply compassionate animal, and it does not eat grass or plants, let alone meat; when it walks, it does not step on seedlings or bugs at all. It is also said that this sacred beast will appear during the reign of a virtuous monarch, but will hide itself when the country is governed by someone who delights in the destruction of life. Its body is like a European deer, and its tail is that of a bull; also, it has one horn, and its hooves are solid like that of a horse. The flesh at the edge of the horn is a manifestation of its benevolence; that is to say, it is born from a desire not to hurt anything. Along with the phoenix, the *kirin* (C. *qilin*) has come to be esteemed as a representative of good omens (such as being a beast that the heavens send down to our world in praise of a ruler, like an emperor or sovereign, who presides over the land with a virtuous reign where there is widespread peace), but as time passed, its physical appearance also drastically changed, and in addition to its physique ending up covered in scales, the original single horn became a pair of horns, and the solid hooves became cloven.

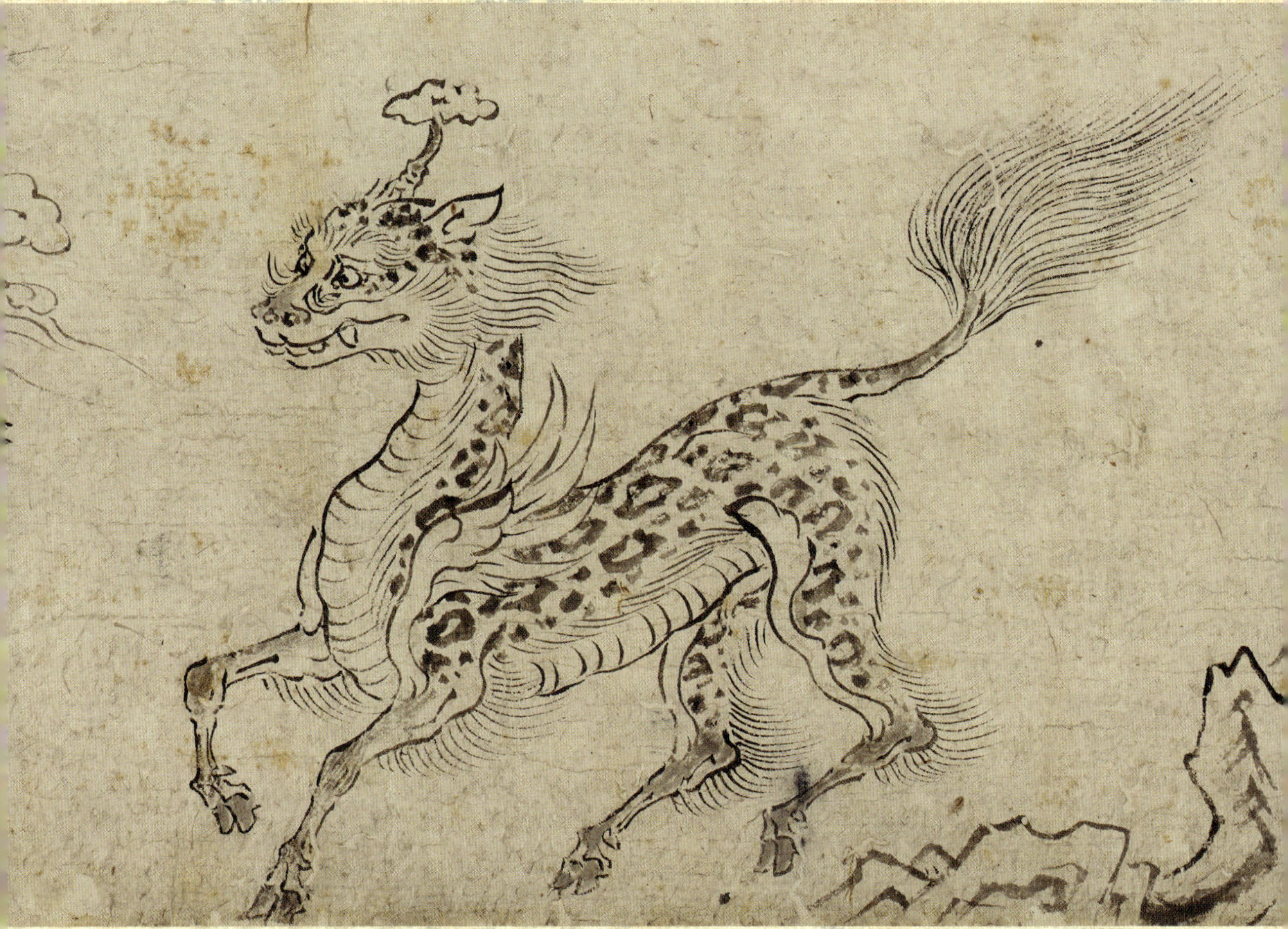

国宝
鳥獣人物戯画 乙巻（部分）
平安時代後期（12c）
京都・高山寺

National Treasure
Scrolls of Frolicking Animals, Scroll Two *(Detail)*
12th century
Kōsanji, Kyoto

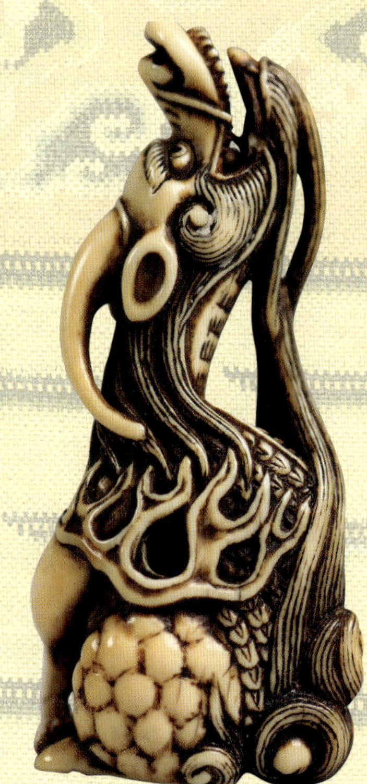

麒麟牙彫根付
江戸時代（18c）
メトロポリタン美術館

Netsuke of Kirin
18th century
The Metropolitan Museum of Art

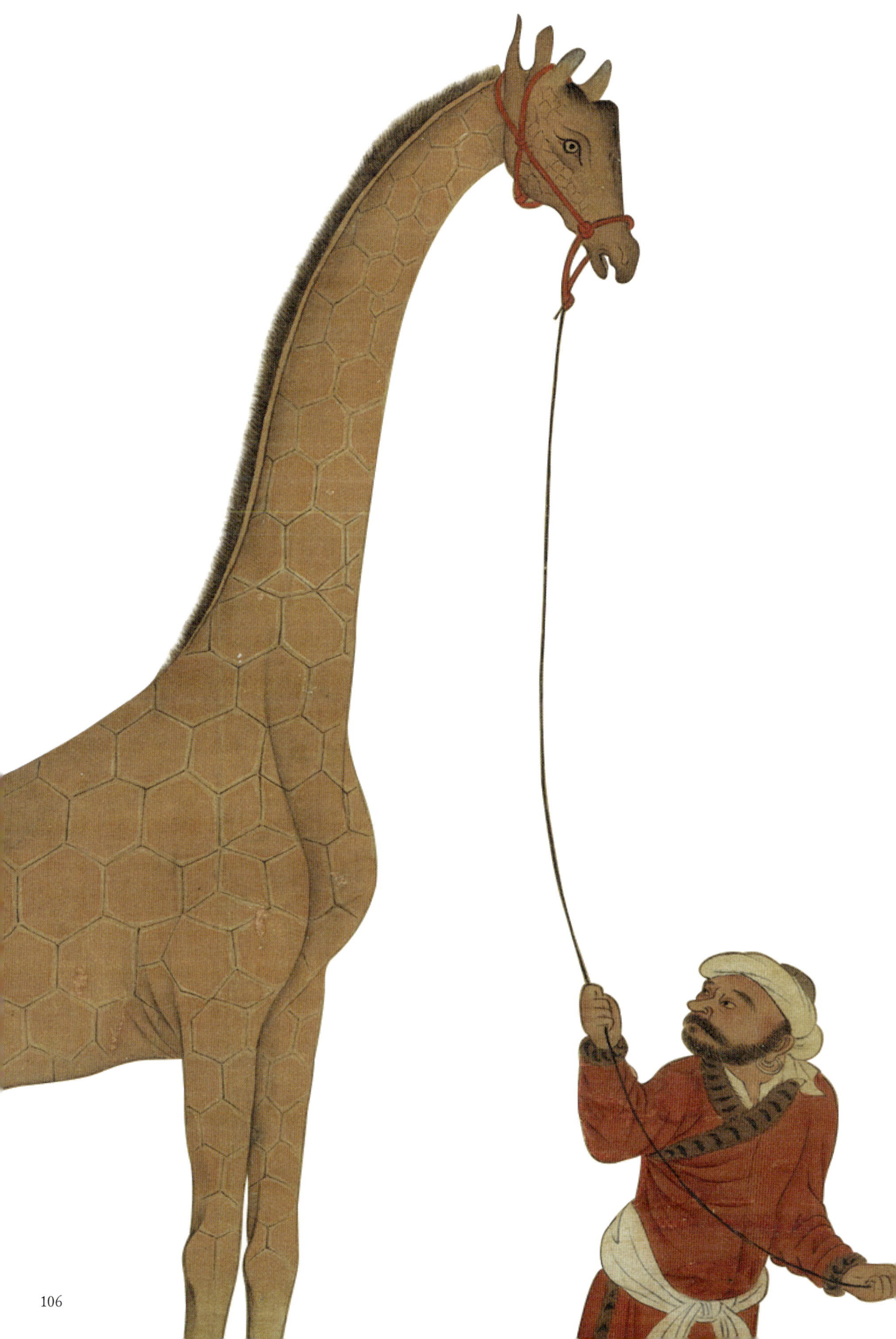

瑞応麒麟図（画麒麟沈度頌）

明人
中国・永楽12年（1414）頃
台北・國立故宮博物院

明の皇帝・永楽帝の命で鄭和（1371～1434）が行った南海大遠征のうち4回目の遠征が契機となり、1414年（永楽12）榜葛剌（ベンガル）の使節が生きたままのキリンを献上した。皇帝は大いに喜んだというが、聖王の治世に現れるとされる「麒麟」であれば当然だったろう。キリンが「麒麟」と認識されるに至った背景として、現地語の音が麒麟の発音に近かったためとの説もあるが、煎じ詰めれば政治的な駆け引きの結果との見解が当を得ているようだ。リアルなキリンの姿を写生的に描いた本図の図上には、この慶事を寿ぎ翰林院の沈度（1357～1434）による「瑞応麒麟頌」が記されている。しかしこれを契機として、キリンが「麒麟」にとって変わることはなかったようである。

The Lucky Kirin

(Kirin Painting with Inscription by Shen Du)

Ming dynasty painter
Ming dynasty, ca. 1414
National Palace Museum, Taipei

Zheng He (1371-1434) made several major expeditions to Southeast Asia during the reign of the Ming Yongle Emperor, and while he was on his fourth expedition in 1414 (Yongle 12), the Bengali envoy presented him with a still living *kirin* (which was actually a giraffe). It is said that the Emperor was overjoyed, but if it had indeed been the "*kirin*" of legend that appeared during the reign of a worthy monarch, it would have probably been justified. As an explanation for how the real life giraffe had come to be understood as the legendary "*kirin*," there is a theory that it was due to the pronunciation of giraffe in its home country being close to the pronunciation of *kirin*, but in my opinion it seems that if you boil it down, this was most likely the result of a political strategy. In this image, the shape of the giraffe is realistically rendered, and on the top of the image is written "In Praise of the Lucky *kirin*"; this inscription celebrating the auspicious event was brushed by Shen Du (1357-1434) of the Imperial Academy. However, it seems that they did not take this as an opportunity to replace the conception of a *kirin* with that of a giraffe, even with this realistic image of the animal.

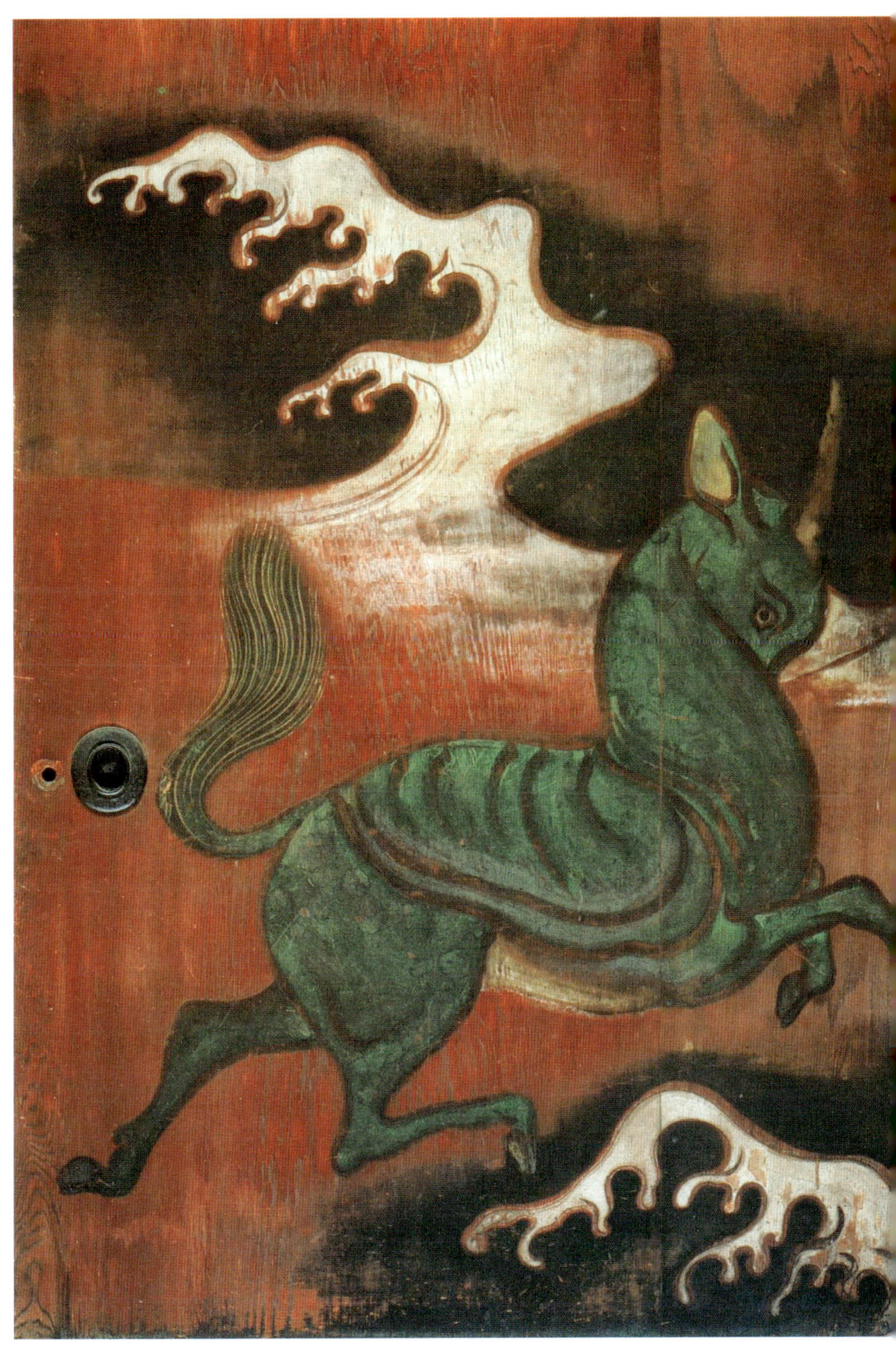

重要文化財

波に麒麟図杉戸（水犀図）

俵屋宗達
元和7年（1621）以降
京都・養源院

養源院は戦国武将・浅井長政（1545～73）の菩提寺。俵屋宗達による本作は、寺伝では麒（雄）と麟（雌）の番とされている（文化庁の指定名称は水犀とされる）。長女だった淀殿が創建し、火災後には三女で2代将軍秀忠夫人となった江（崇源院）らにより伏見城の遺構を移して1621年（元和7）再建された。玄関を入るとまず目に入るこれら霊獣たちを杉戸に描いたのは俵屋宗達である。

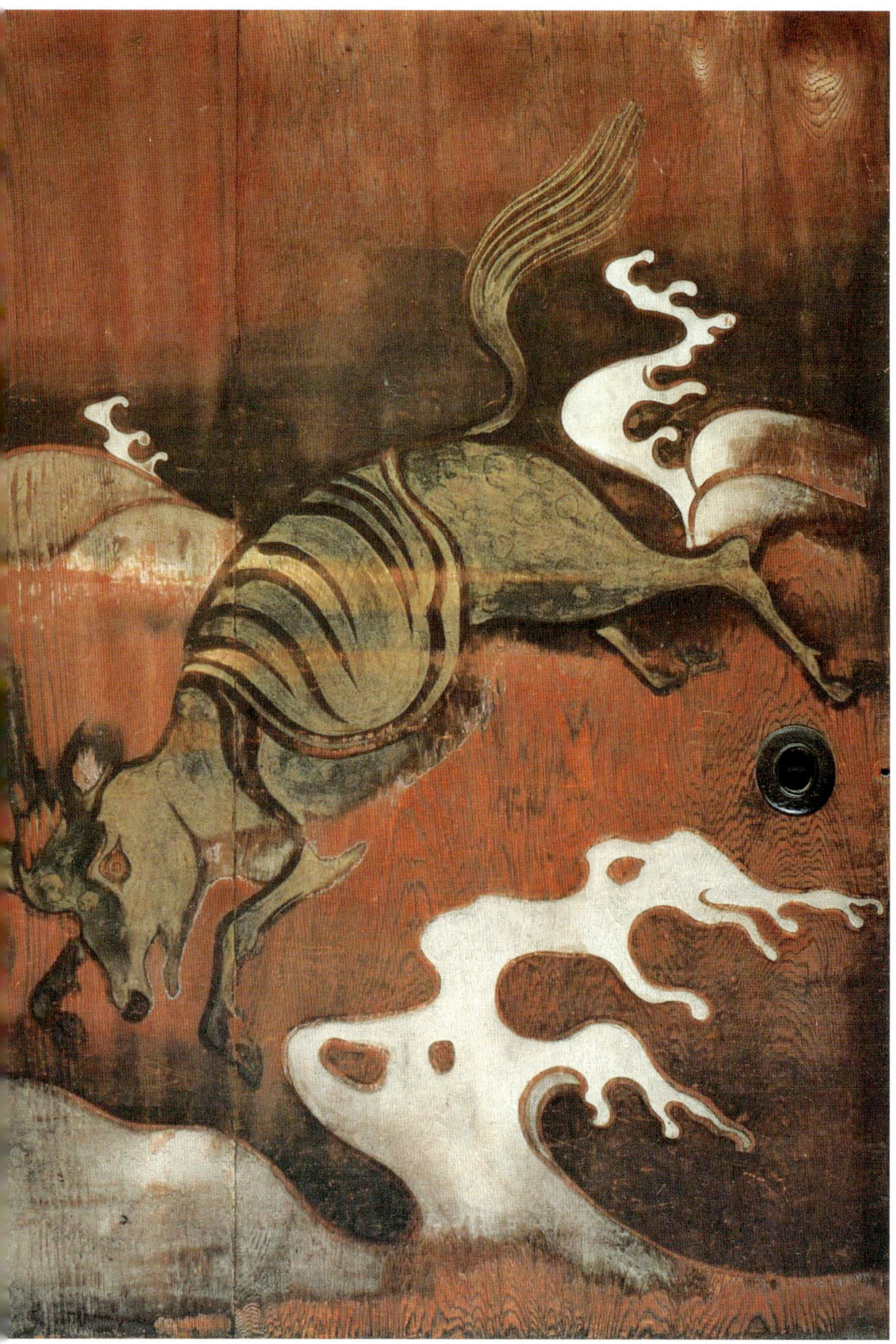

Important Cultural Property

Waves and Kirin (Water Rhinoceros) Cedar Doors

Tawaraya Sōtatsu
After 1621
Yōgen'in, Kyoto

Yōgen'in was the family temple of Asai Nagamasa (1545-73), a military commander during Japan's Warring States period. His eldest daughter Yodo-dono established the temple, and in 1621 (Genna 7) his third daughter Gō (Sūgen'in), the wife of the second shogun Hidetada, transferred the remains of Fushimi Castle and rebuilt the temple after the original had been lost in a fire. When you enter the vestibule, the first thing that you see is these sacred beasts that have been painted on the doors by Tawaraya Sōtatsu.

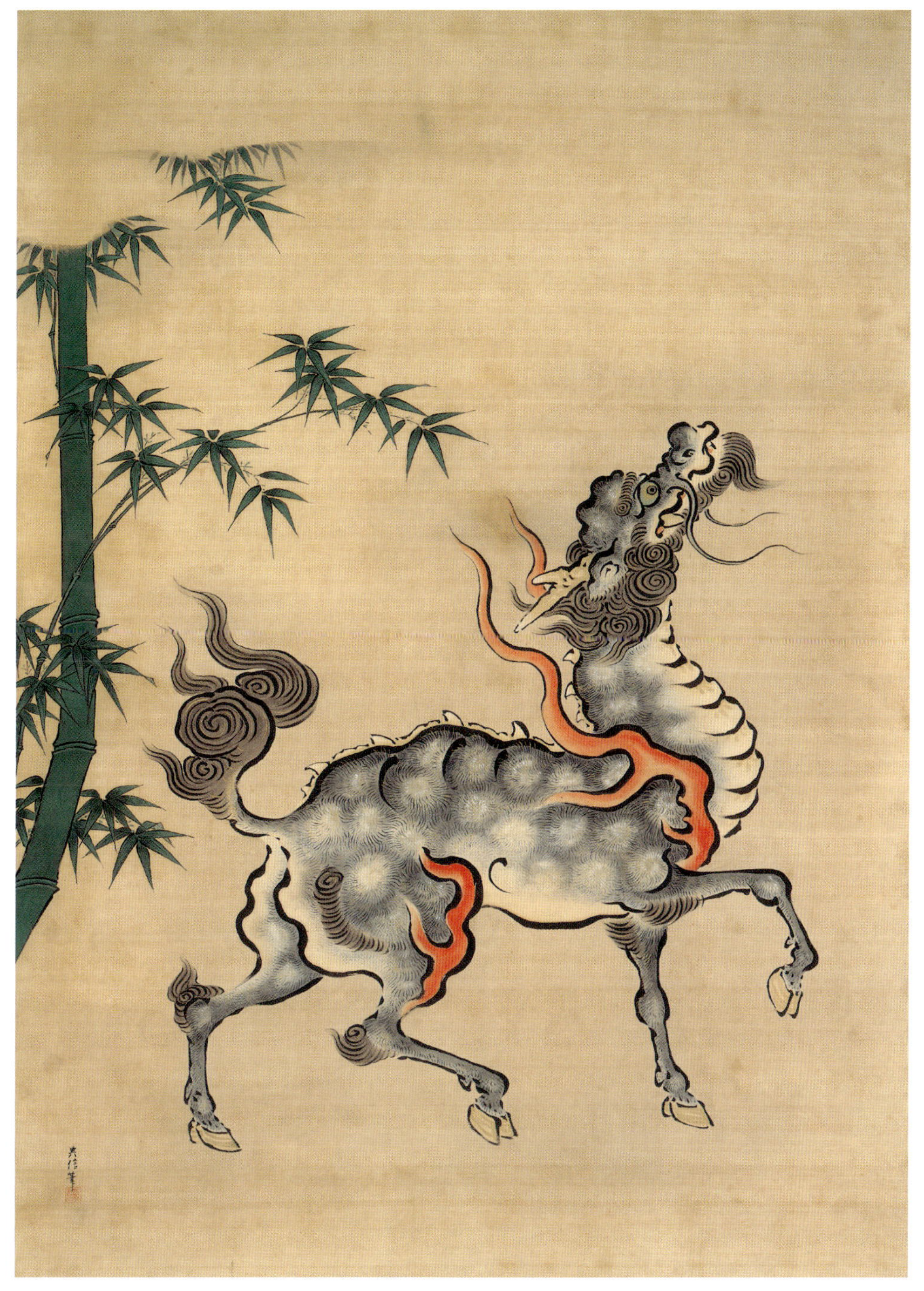

麒麟・鳳凰図

狩野典信
江戸時代（18c）
兵庫・白鶴美術館

狩野典信（1730～90）は、幕府に仕えた奥絵師４家のうちの木挽町狩野家当主。10代将軍家治に絵を教えるなどし、田沼意次の屋敷の一角を拝領。木挽町に移り住んだため、以降この家は木挽町狩野と称されるようになり、宗家の中橋狩野家に代わり狩野派の中心を担うことになった。本図は、鳳凰と麒麟を対に描いた大幅であり、格式の高い祝儀などに用いられたものであろう。狩野派では、江戸時代を通じて伝統的な画風を守り続けたのである。

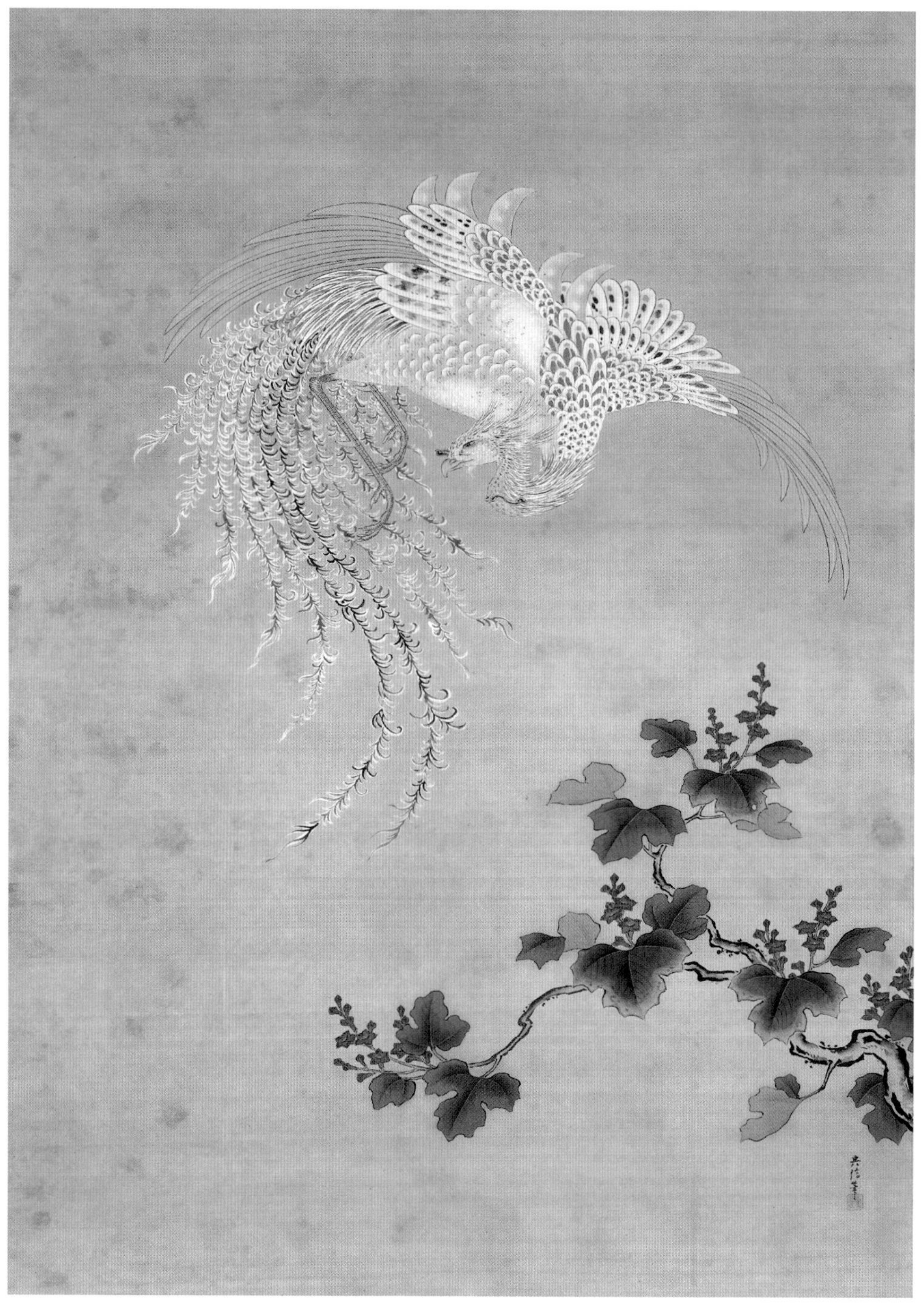

Kirin and Phoenix

Kano Michinobu
18th century
Hakutsuru Fine Art Museum, Hyogo

Kano Michinobu (1730-90) was the head of the Kobikichō Kano, one of the four houses that served the shogunate as "inner painters." He taught painting to the tenth shogun Ieharu, and he received part of the estate of Tanuma Okitsugu for his residence. This painting is a large-scale work that depicts a *kirin* and phoenix as a pair, and it was probably used for very formal celebrations. The Kano School continued to preserve a traditional style of painting throughout the Edo period.

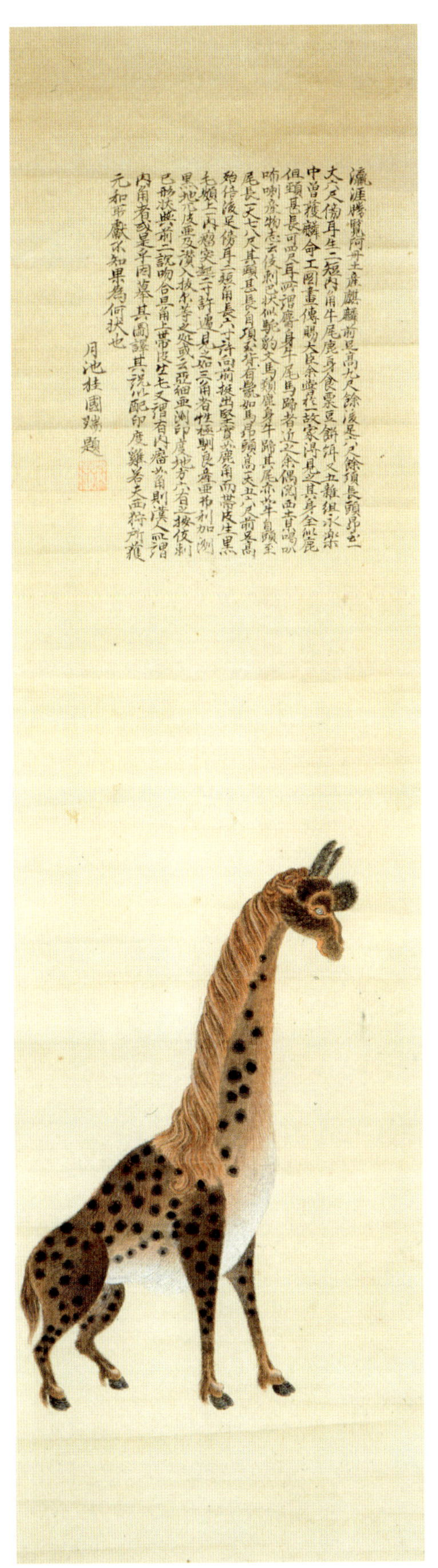

麒麟図

桂川甫周
江戸時代後期(18c)

幕府の蘭医・桂川甫周(1751～1809)が、実在のキリンを紹介した絵。賛には、鄭和の南海大遠征の記録『瀛涯(えいがい)勝覧(しょうらん)』などを引用しつつ、蘭書「喝叭咘喇(カハブラ)*産物志」の「伎剌巴(ギラハ)(＝ジラフ)」の記述と比較して、麒麟とキリンを同定。同書の挿絵を模写し、その概要を記した、とある。この蘭書は未特定だが、1775年(安永4)に来日した日本動植物の学名の名付け親となったツュンベリー(ツンベルク、1743～1828)編纂のものだったかもしれない。彼は来日前の1772年からアフリカ南端の喜望峰周辺で植物等を調査・採集し、帰国後『喜望峰植物誌』などを出版した。日本滞在は1年余りだが、1776年(安永5)にオランダ商館長とともに江戸参府した際に甫周らと親交を重ね、多くの情報や文物のやりとりをしたことが知られている。

＊現在のケープタウン周辺

Kirin (*Giraffe*)

Katsuragawa Hoshū
18th century

This is a picture of an actual giraffe that was introduced by shogunal doctor and scholar of Western studies Katsuragawa Hoshū (1751-1809). The inscription compares quotes from texts like the record of Zheng He's major expeditions to Southeast Asia in the *Overall Survey of the Ocean's Shores* to the descriptions of the "girafa (giraffe)" from Western books, and it identifies the giraffe and *kirin* as the same creature. It also says that he copied the illustration from that book, and recorded the synopsis. The owner of the book is unspecified, but it was probably the property of Carl Peter Thunberg (1743-1828), who came to Japan in 1775 (An'ei 4) and would become the father of giving Japanese plants and animals their scientific names. From 1772, before he went to Japan, he visited the southern tip of Africa around the Cape of Good Hope (near modern day Cape Town), and examined and collected the plants there, later publishing works such as *Flora Capensis* after he returned to his home country. He stayed in Japan for just over a year, but when he went to visit Edo in 1776 (An'ei 5) together with the delegation of Dutch merchants, he built up a friendship with Hoshū and his associates, and it is known that there was a lively exchange of information and cultural products between them.

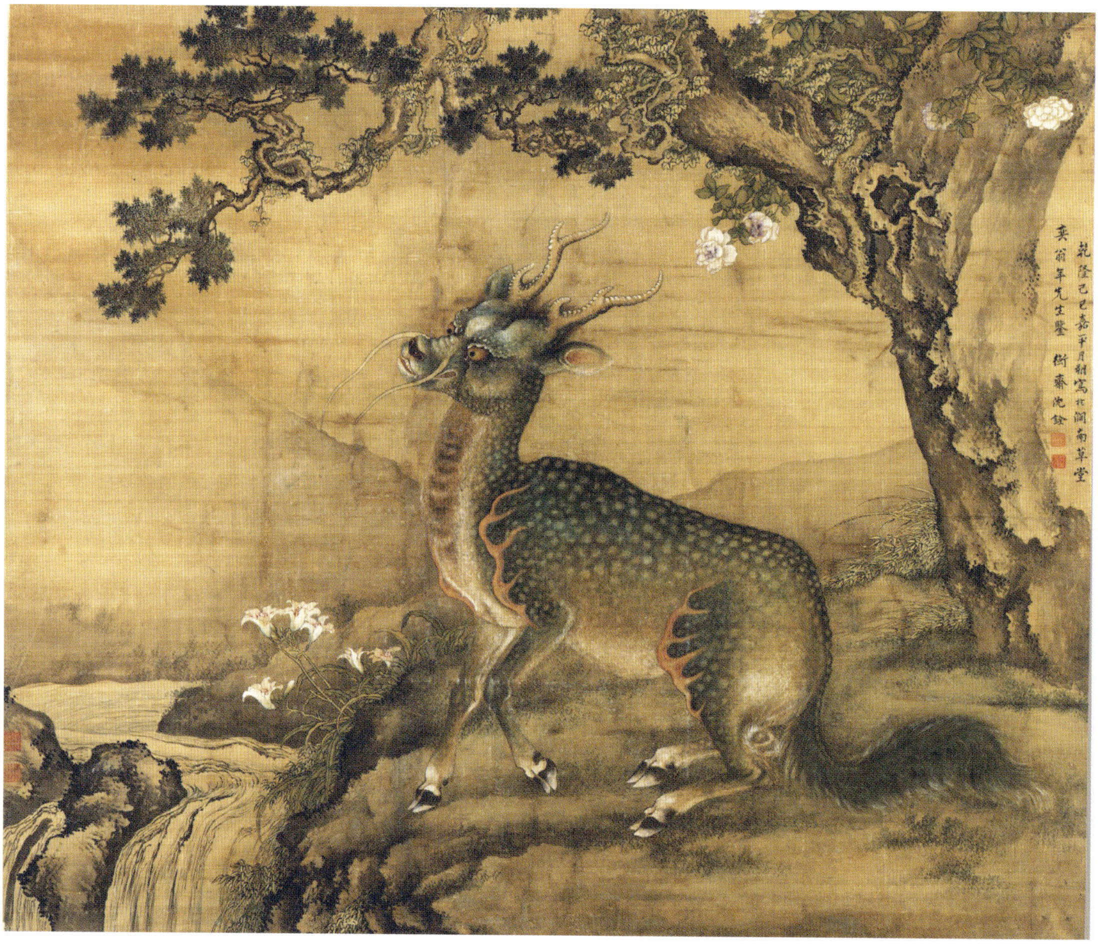

麒麟図

沈南蘋
中国・乾隆14年（1749）
長崎歴史文化博物館

Kirin

Shen Nanpin
Qing dynasty, 1749
Nagasaki Museum of History and Culture

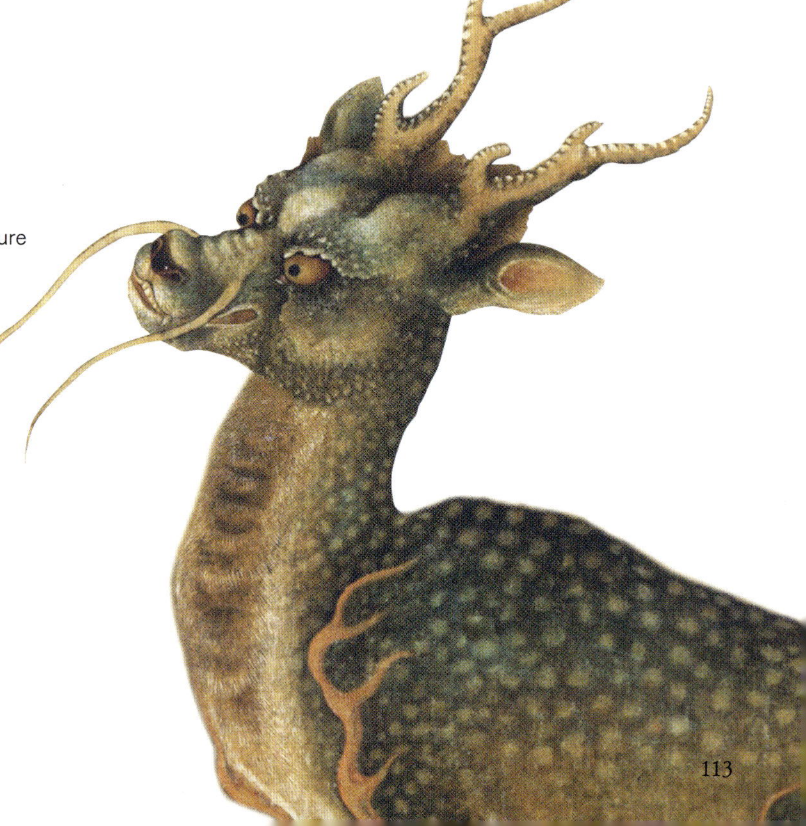

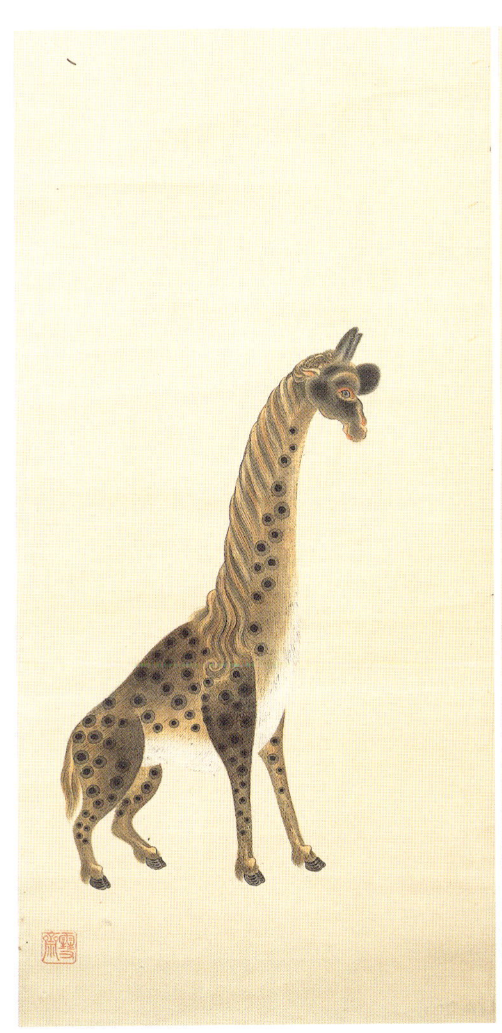

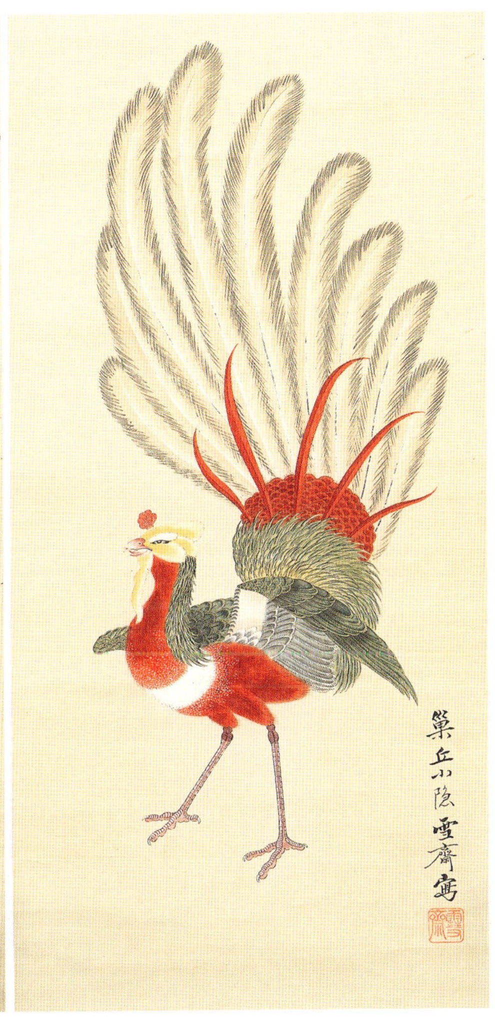

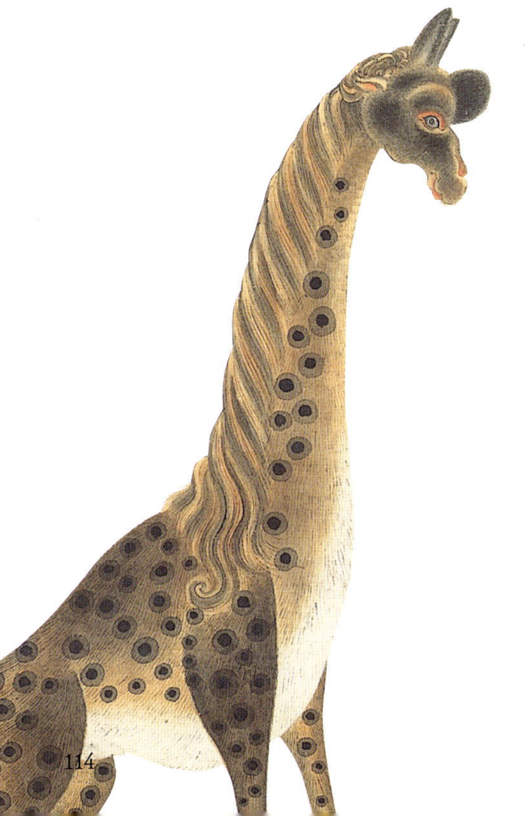

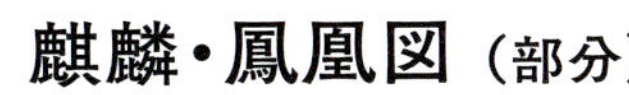

麒麟・鳳凰図（部分）

増山雪斎
江戸時代（18-19c）

桂川甫周の写したキリン図にならったキリンと鳳凰とを取り合わせた作品。筆者・増山雪斎（1754～1819）は、伊勢国長島藩主。さまざまな昆虫の図を集めた「虫豸帖」（東京国立博物館蔵）の筆者としても知られる博物学好きの大名で、甫周とも交流があった。

Kirin and Phoenix (*detail*)

Mashiyama Sessai (Masakata)
18th-19th century

This is a work that combines a phoenix and a *kirin*, based on the picture of a giraffe that Katsuragawa Hoshū had copied. The artist, Mashiyama Masakata (1754-1819), was the daimyo of Nagashima, Ise Province. He was an associate of Hoshū, and he shared his passion for natural history. Masakata was also known as the author of the *Chūchijō*, a collection of drawings of various insects (Tokyo National Museum).

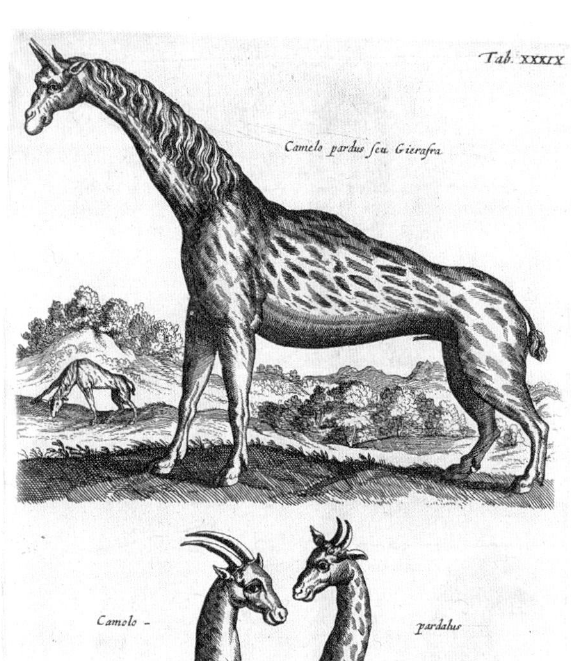

キリン図
（『ヨンストン動物図譜』より）

ヤン・ヨンストン
1660年
仙台市博物館

蘭学者の大槻玄沢（1757～1827）は、本図の観察をもとに、麒麟は「疑拉法（ジラフ）」であると同定した。麒麟はジラフであり、異国に常時存在するものとして中国の瑞獣説を否定したのである。

Giraffes (*from Historiae naturalis*)

Johannes Jonston
1660
Sendai City Museum

The scholar of Western studies Ōtsuki Gentaku (1757-1827) realized that the *kirin* was a “giraffe” as a result of this work. It stated that the *kirin* was a giraffe, and it repudiated the idea that it was an auspicious beast from China, emphasizing that it had always existed in foreign countries.

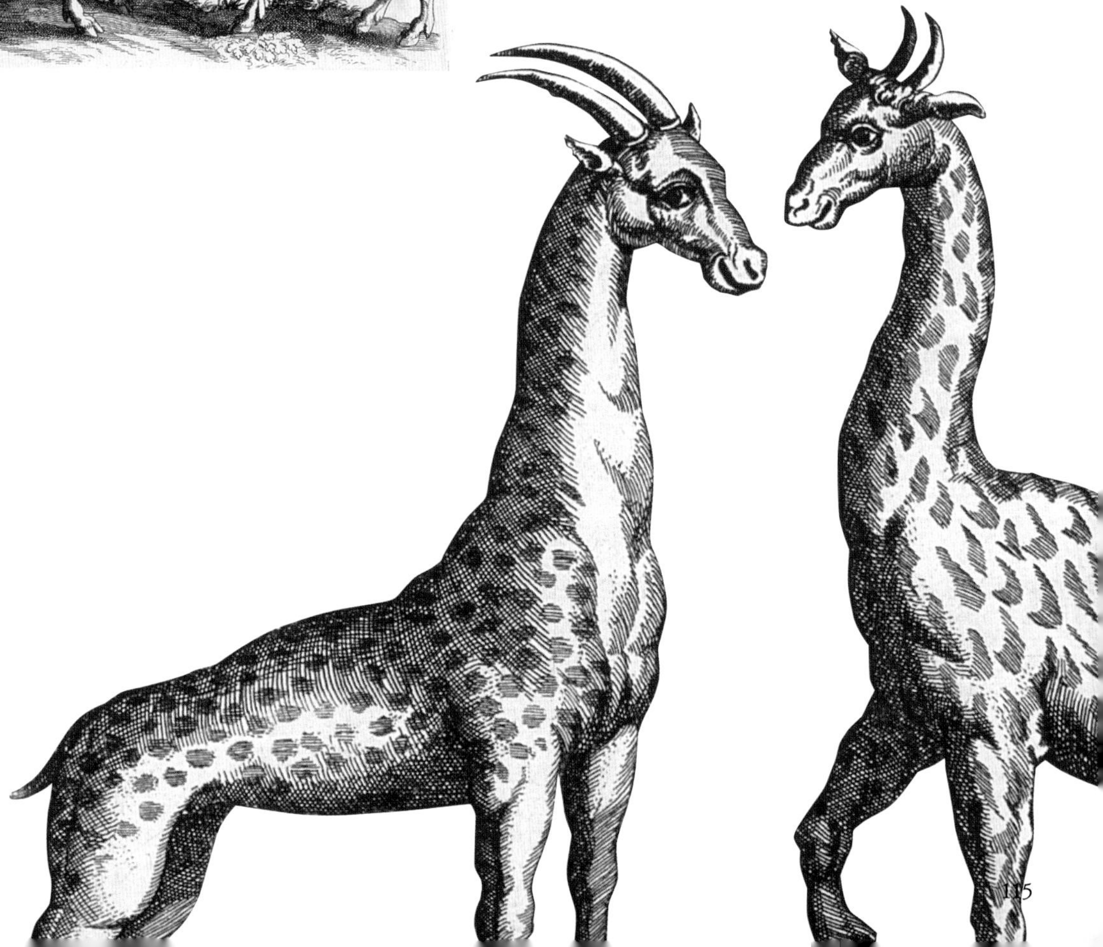

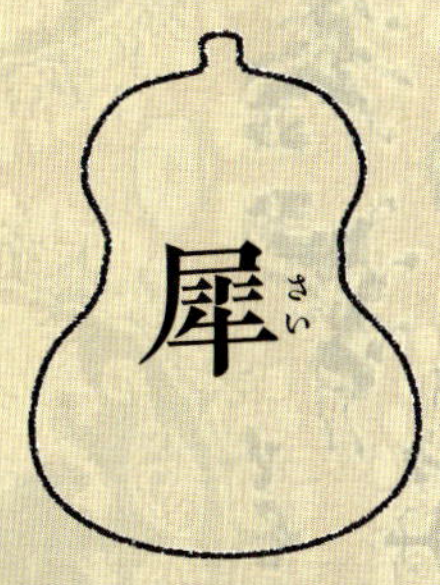

犀

明代の『本草綱目』には、犀は「水牛に似て首は豬のよう、腹は太く、脚は短く象に似て3つの蹄があり、色は黒、舌上に刺があって、好んで棘刺を食う。また、犀には山犀・水犀・兕犀の3種があり、山犀は山林にいて一般に入手しやすいが、水犀は水中を出入りするので捕えにくい。いずれも二角があって、鼻角が長く額角は短い。水犀は皮に珠甲があるが、山犀にはない。兕犀（沙犀とも）は犀の牝のことで、一角が頂にあるだけ」、とある。中国では、犀の角を解毒剤や毒味の道具として珍重し、角の粉末は辟邪の効能があるとされた。日本でも存在自体は舶載品を通じて知られていたようで、古くは正倉院宝物の鏡背にその姿を留めている。とくに水犀は、波濤の上を駆ける甲羅を背にした一角獣として、ちょうど甲羅を付けた麒麟のような姿で「鳥獣人物戯画・乙巻」や社寺の装飾彫刻などに登場する。一方、全身が鎧に包まれたようなインドサイも蘭書『ヨンストン動物図譜』を通じて石川大浪や谷文晁らが正確な模写を残している。

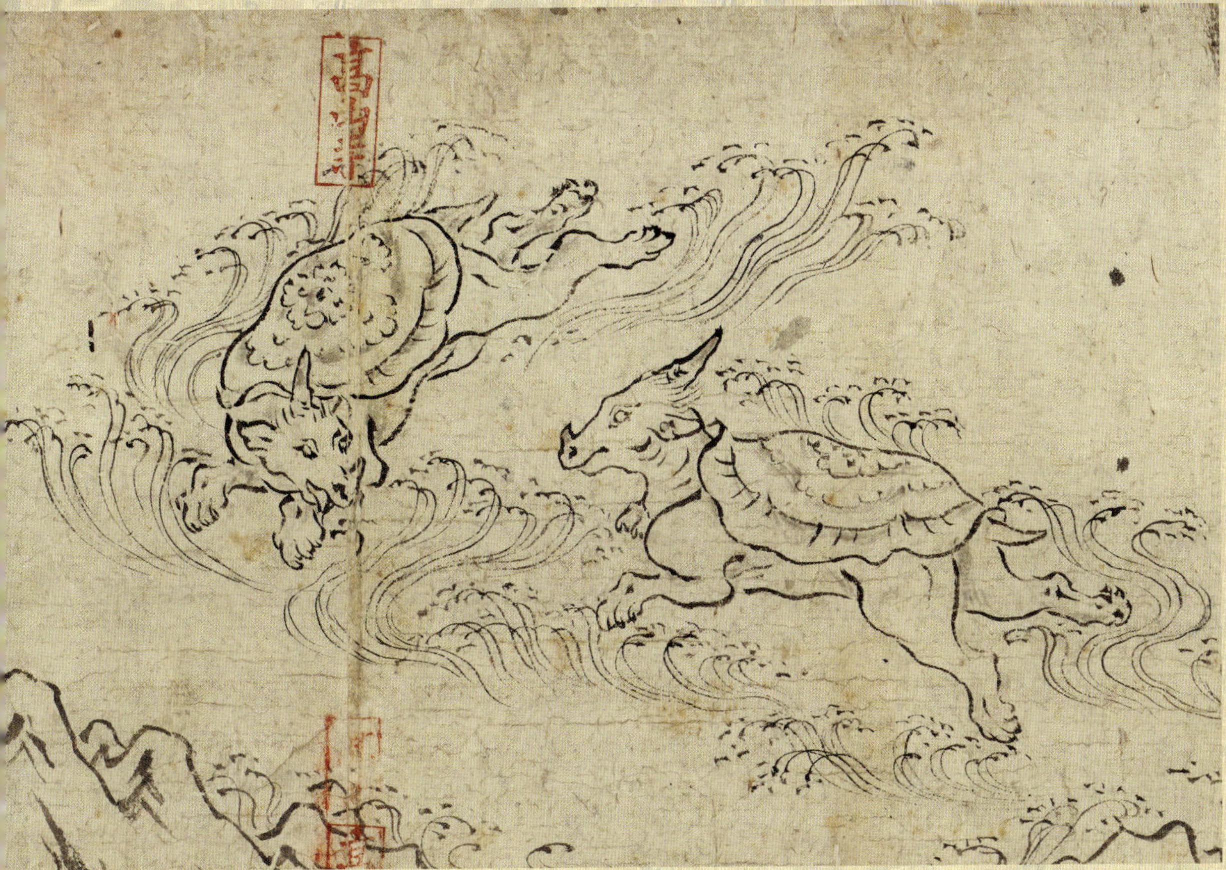

国宝
鳥獣人物戯画 乙巻（部分）
平安時代後期（12c）
京都・高山寺

National Treasure
Scrolls of Frolicking Animals, Scroll Two (*Detail*)
12th century
Kōsanji, Kyoto

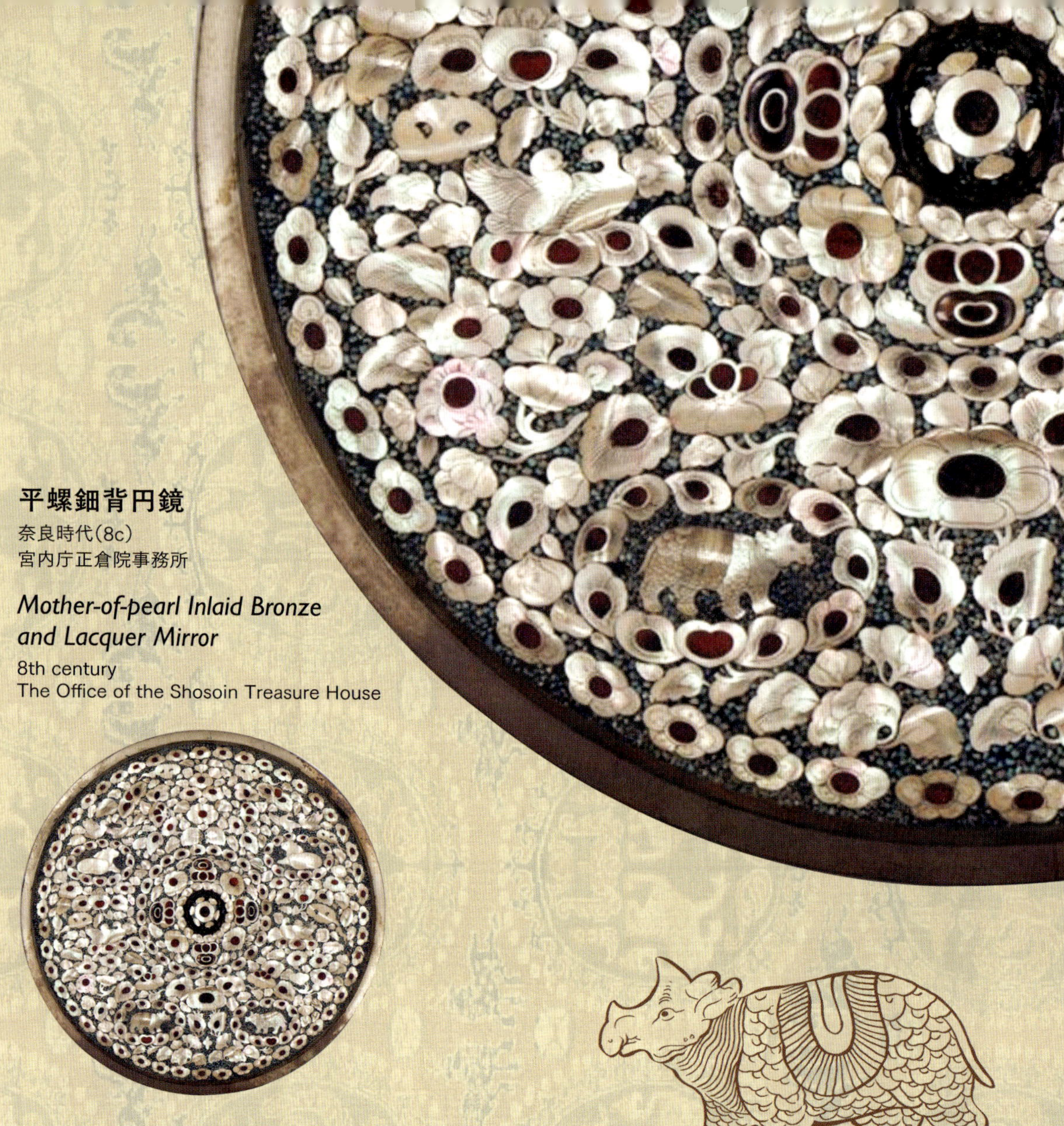

平螺鈿背円鏡
奈良時代(8c)
宮内庁正倉院事務所

Mother-of-pearl Inlaid Bronze and Lacquer Mirror
8th century
The Office of the Shosoin Treasure House

The Rhinoceros

In the Ming dynasty encyclopedia *Compendium of Materia Medica*, the following is said about the rhinoceros: "It resembles a water buffalo, and its neck is that of a hog; its belly is flat, its legs are short and resemble those of an elephant, and it has tripartite hooves. It is black in color, there are spines on top of its tongue, and it happily eats thorny shrubs. Also, within the species of rhinoceros, there are three kinds – the mountain rhinoceros, the water rhinoceros, and the female rhinoceros. The mountain rhinoceros lives in mountain forests and is generally easy to get, but since the water rhinoceros goes in and out of the water, it is hard to catch. Both of these have two horns; the horn on the nose is long, and the horn on the forehead is short. The water rhinoceros has a bumpy armor-like hide, but the mountain rhinoceros does not. The female rhinoceros (also known as the sand rhinoceros) is the female of the species, and it has just one horn on its crown." In China, rhinoceros horn is prized as an antidote and means to check for poisons, and it is thought that finely ground rhinoceros horn is effective for warding off evil. Even in Japan, the existence of these animals was known via import goods, and long ago the horns appeared in the records of the Shōsōin treasury. This is especially the case with the water rhinoceros; since it was a horned beast that could gallop over the waves with a shell on its back, it looks like a *kirin* with a shell in works such as Scroll Two of *Scrolls of Frolicking Animals* and decorative sculptures in temples and shrines. On the other hand, the accurate copies that Ishikawa Tairō and Tani Bunchō made from the Western book the Jonston *Historiae naturalis* depicting the Indian rhinoceros, whose whole body looks like it is wrapped in armor, still exist today.

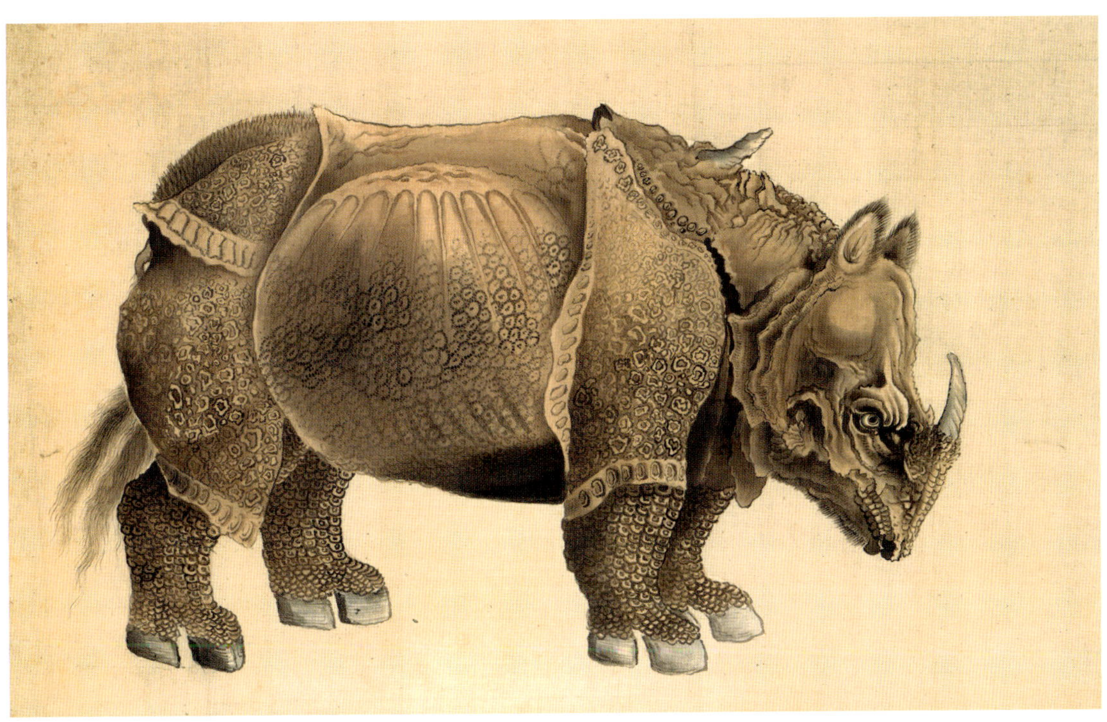

犀図

谷文晁
江戸時代(18c)

『ヨンストン動物図譜』収録の銅版画のサイ図を、毛筆で忠実に拡大模写したもの。文晁は同工の作を寛政2年(1790)11月に描いたことが知られており、本図もその頃の作と考えられる。文晁が「泰西画法」の師と仰いだ旗本・石川大浪(1762～1817)の研究ぶりはさらに徹底していて、犀皮の拓本まで図画に残した。実像を手繰り寄せようとする彼らの行為の源泉は、ひとえに尽きせぬ知に対する好奇心だったと言えよう。

Rhinoceros

Tani Bunchō
18th century

This is an enlarged and faithfully drawn copy of the image of the rhinoceros from the collection of copperplate engravings in the *Historiae naturalis.* Tani Bunchō was doing that kind of work in November 1790 (Ansei 2), and it is thought that this work is also from that around that time. Shogunal vassal Ishikawa Tairō (1762-1817), whom Bunchō looked up to as his mentor in Western studies, was doing a thorough study, and there is even a rubbing of a rhinoceros hide that remains in his drawings. You could say that their interest in working from real images was due entirely to their everlasting thirst for knowledge.

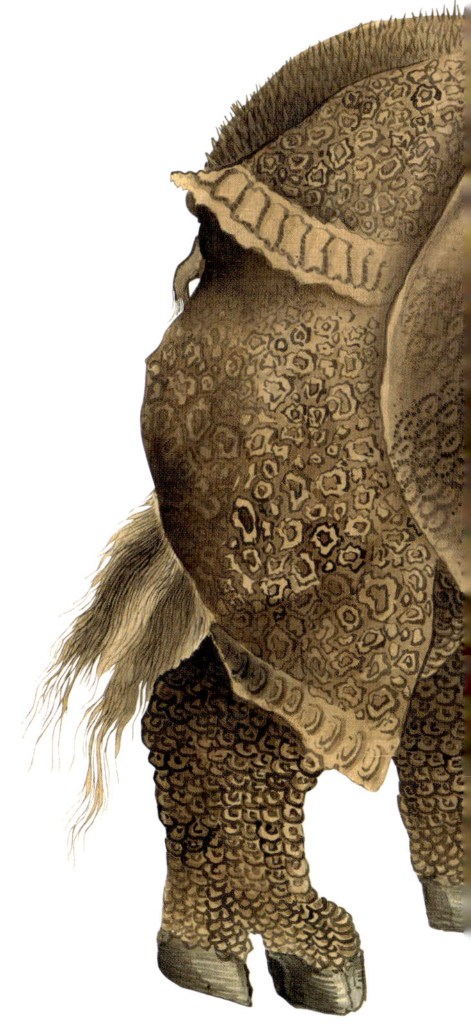

犀図（『ヨンストン動物図譜』より）

ヤン・ヨンストン
1660年
仙台市博物館

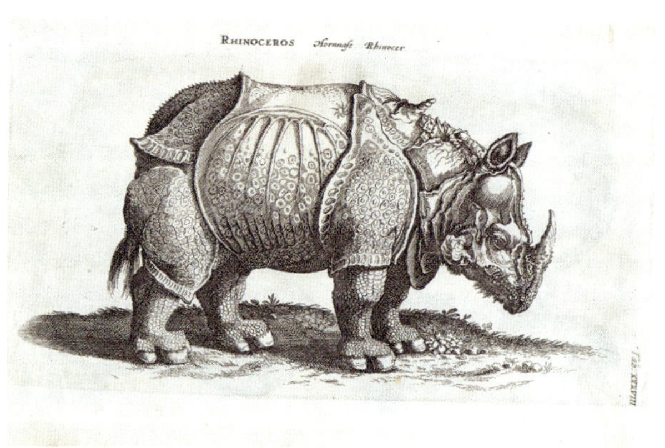

1515年5月、ポルトガル国王マヌエル1世に贈られたインドサイが、インドからリスボンに到着。鎧を着たようなインドサイの簡略なスケッチと解説をもとにしたアルブレヒト・デューラーの木版画（1515年作）は、『ヨンストン動物図譜』ほか多くの図鑑に銅版画で転載され、18世紀に至るまで強固なイメージを保った。なお、先のサイは同年12月ローマ教皇へ贈られる途中、嵐に遭い船とともに沈んでしまったという。気の毒な最期であった。

Rhinoceros

(from Historiae naturalis)

Johannes Jonston
1660
Sendai City Museum

The Indian rhinoceros gifted to King Manuel I of Portugal arrived in Lisbon from India in May of 1515. Albrecht Durer's woodblock print (1515) was based on descriptions and a brief sketch of the rhinoceros that looked like it was wearing armor. In addition to the Jonston *Historiae naturalis*, the image was reprinted as a copper-plate engraving in many other illustrated field guides, and by the eighteenth century, it was a well-established image. However, in December of the same year, while that rhinoceros was still on its way to be given to the Pope, it met with an unfortunate end when it got caught in a storm and sank along with the boat it was on.

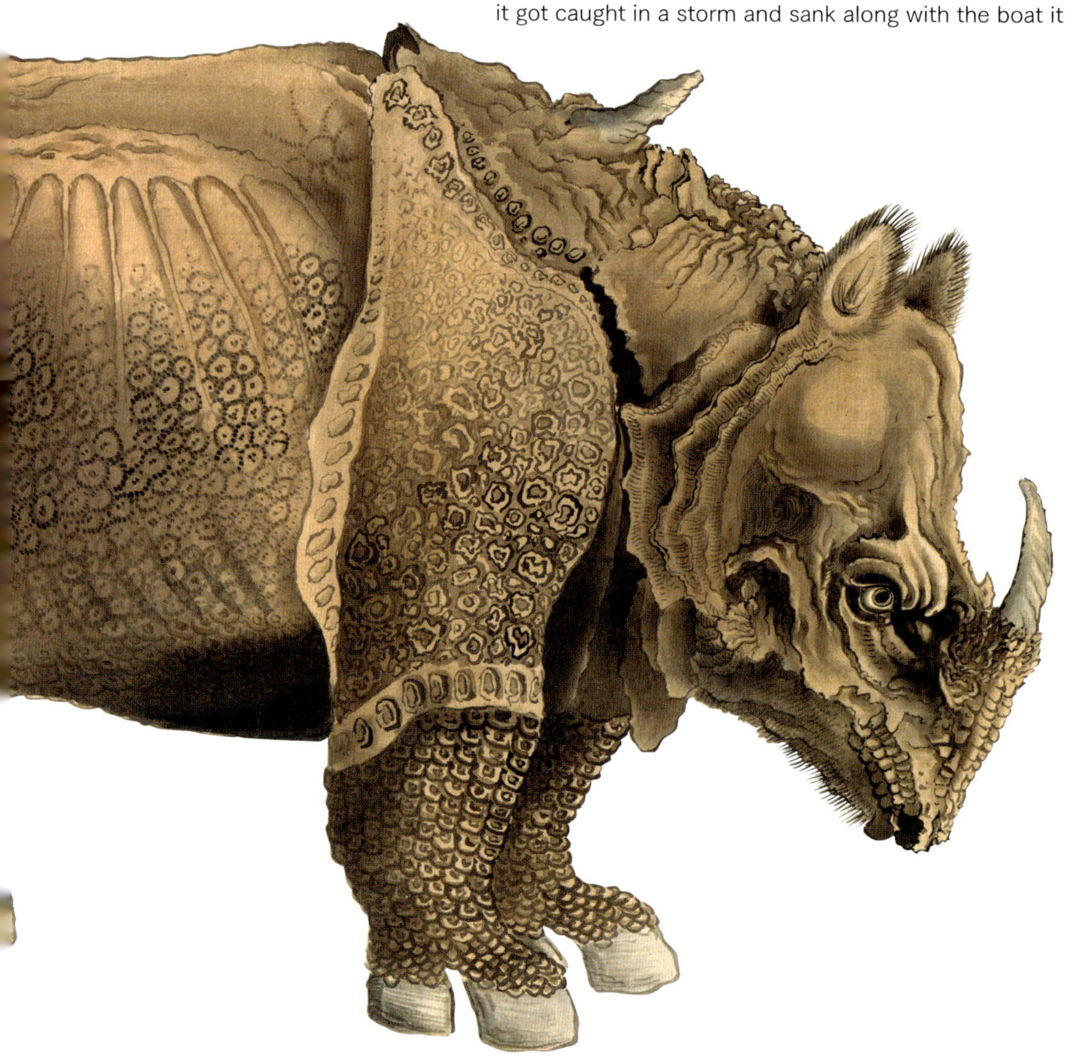

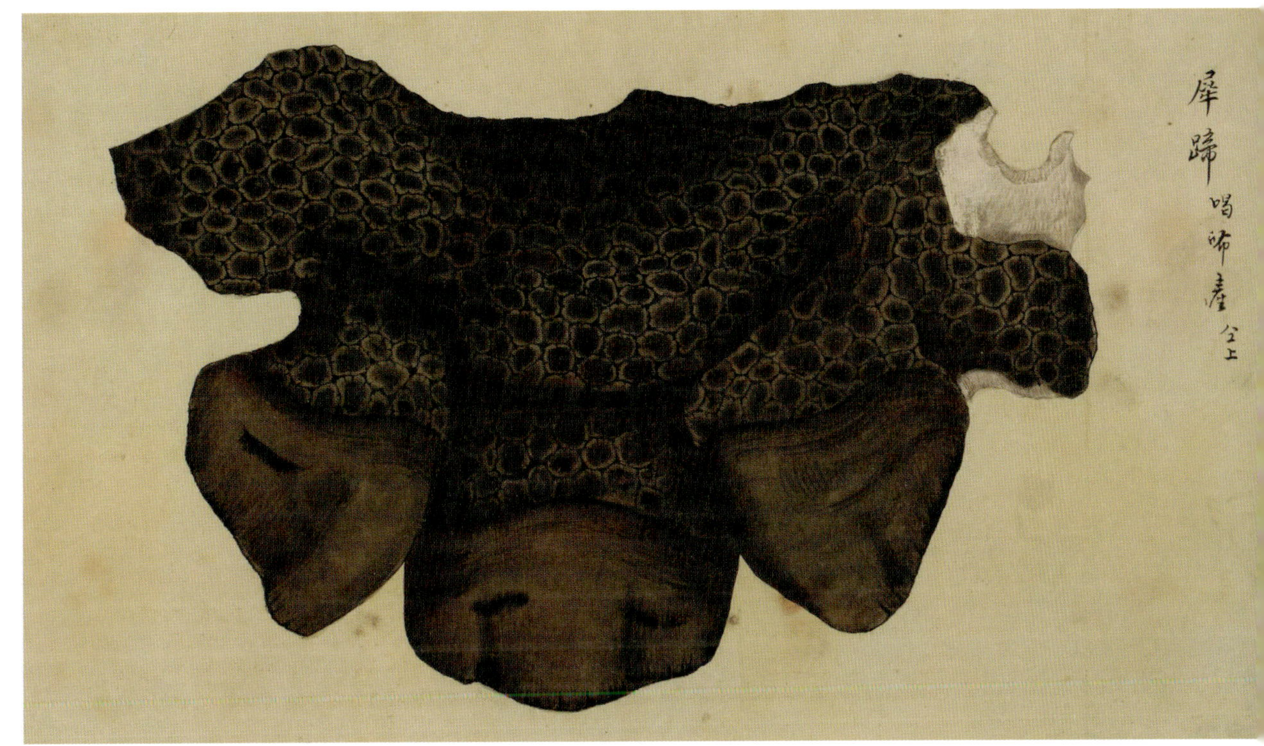

外国産動物図巻
（犀蹄・犀尾）

桂川甫周
江戸時代後期（18c末〜19c初め）
早稲田大学図書館

薩摩藩８代藩主・島津重豪（1745〜1833）が所有していた動物標本類。海亀（玳瑁）や大トカゲのほか、フウチョウやサイチョウの頭部、犀蹄・犀尾なども描かれている。

Foreign Animals Scroll
(*Rhinoceros Hoof and Tail*)

Katsuragawa Hoshū
Late 18th–early 19th century
Waseda University Library

This is a taxonomic catalogue of animals that was in the possession of Shimazu Shigehide (1745-1833), the eighth daimyo of the Satsuma Domain. There are portrayals of sea turtles (*Eretmochelys imbricata*) and monitor lizards, as well as the skull of a bird-of-paradise and a rhinoceros hornbill, in addition to the hoof and tail of a rhinoceros.

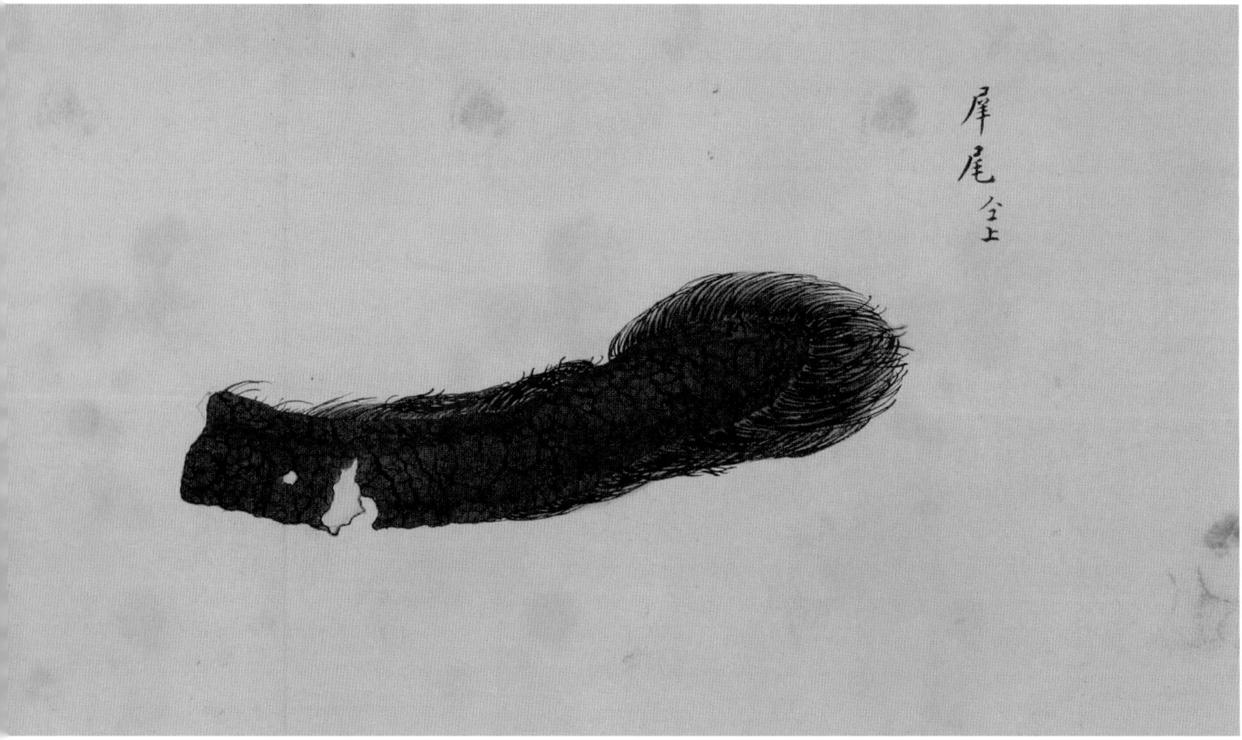

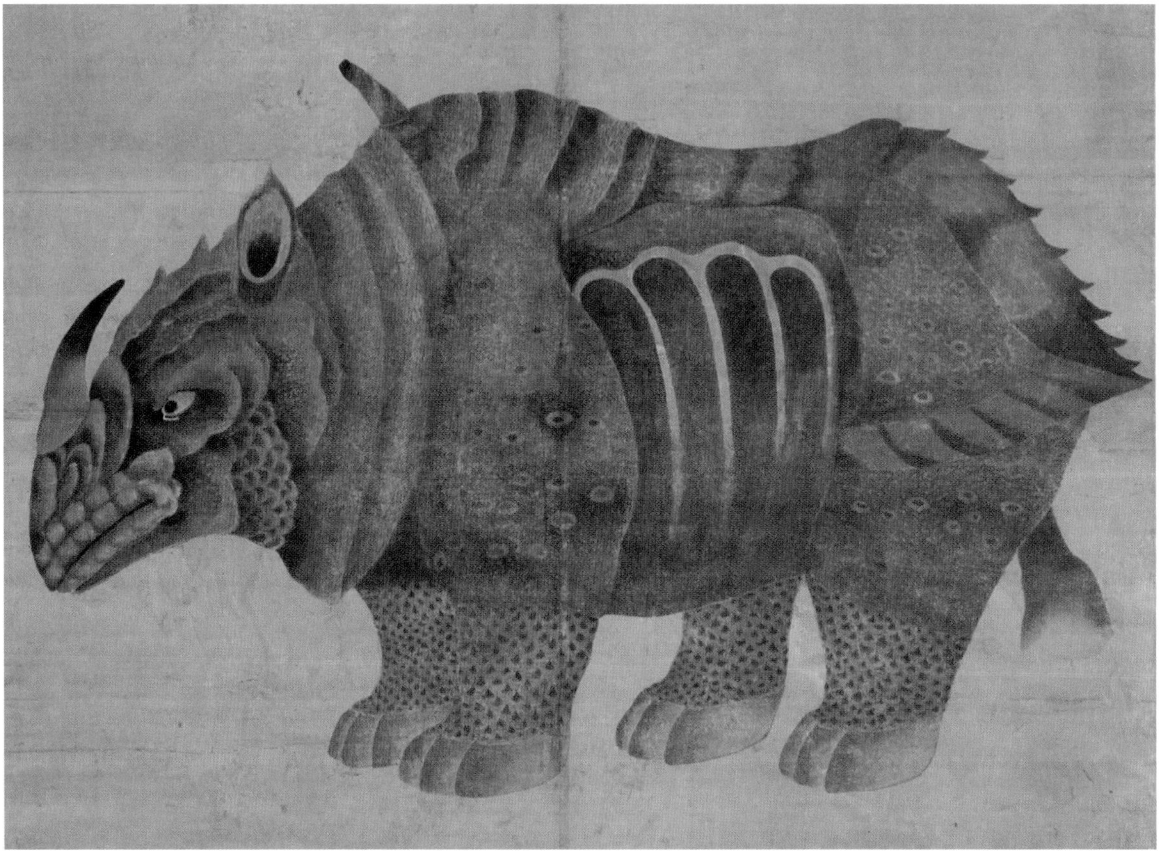

犀図(部分)
江戸時代(18c)
神戸市立博物館

Rhinoceros *(detail)*
18th century
Kobe City Museum

白澤・唐木図杉戸

狩野派
寛永13年（1636）
栃木・日光東照宮

Bai Ze and Exotic Trees Cedar Doors

Kano School
1636
Nikko Toshogu Shrine, Tochigi

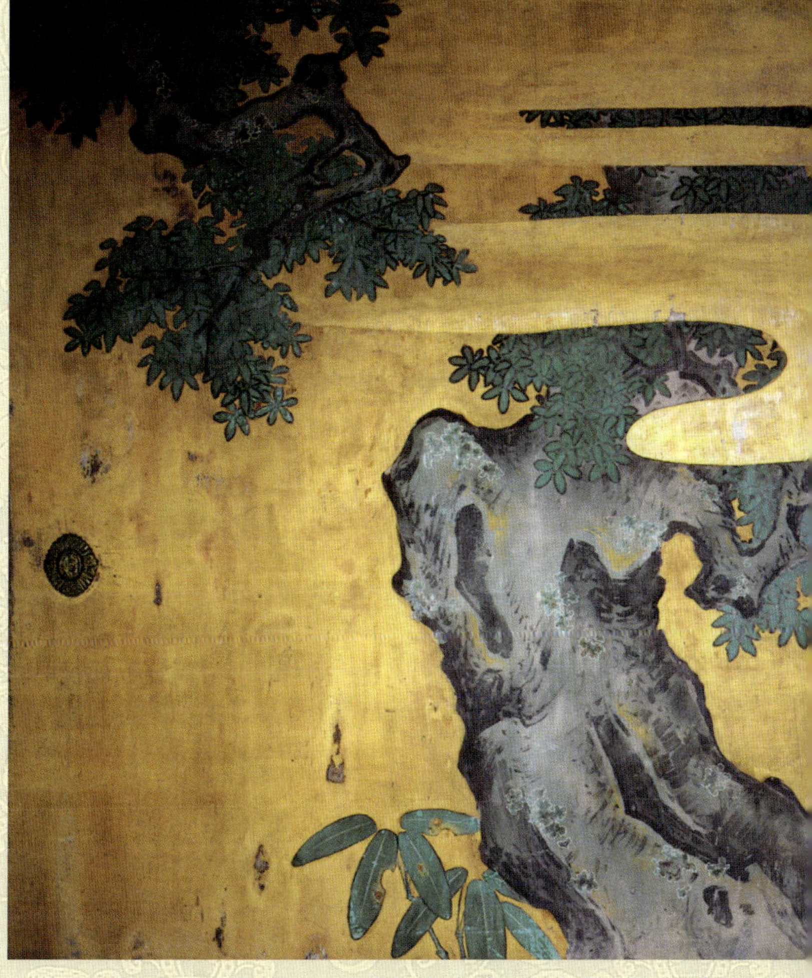

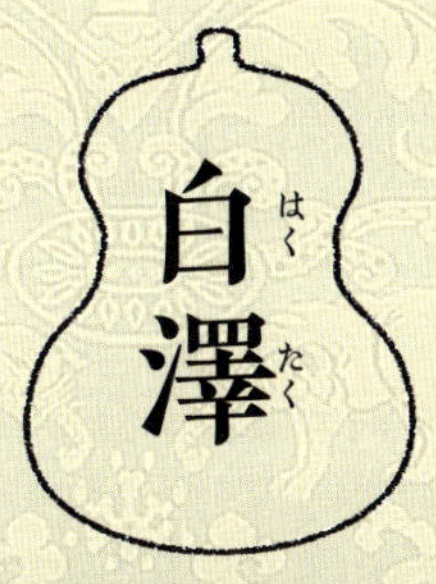

明代の絵入り百科事典『三才図会』によれば、「東望山（江西省）に沢獣がいる。一名を白沢。よく言語をあやつる。王者が有徳で、その徳が明照幽遠なときは姿を現わす。昔、黄帝が巡狩して東海に至ったとき、この獣の忠言によって世のために害を除いた」とある。深山にすむという中国の想像上の霊獣で、6つの角と体の各所に9つの眼を持ち、人語を解すという。麒麟や鳳凰同様、徳のある為政者の時に出現し、病魔を防ぐ力があると信じられていた。江戸時代には、旅をする際に白澤の絵を懐中に入れておくと災難に遭わないと信じられ、またコレラ除けの護符としても用いられた。

The *Bai Ze*

According to the *Collected Illustrations of the Three Realms*: “There is a marsh beast in Jiangxi Province. One name for it is the *bai ze* (J. *hakutaku*). It has a good command of language. It will appear when there is a just ruler and his benevolence brings light to the realm. Long ago, when Huangdi made an imperial visit to the east, he was able to ward off evil by following the advice of this beast.” This is a beast from Chinese legend that supposedly lives deep in the mountains, has six horns and nine eyes on various parts of its body, and understands human speech. Like the *kirin* and phoenix, it appears during the reign of a virtuous ruler, and it is believed to have the power to prevent diseases and misfortune. Travelers during the Edo period would leave an image of the *bai ze* in their pockets, believing that this was a way to avoid meeting with misfortune; it was also believed to be a talisman against cholera.

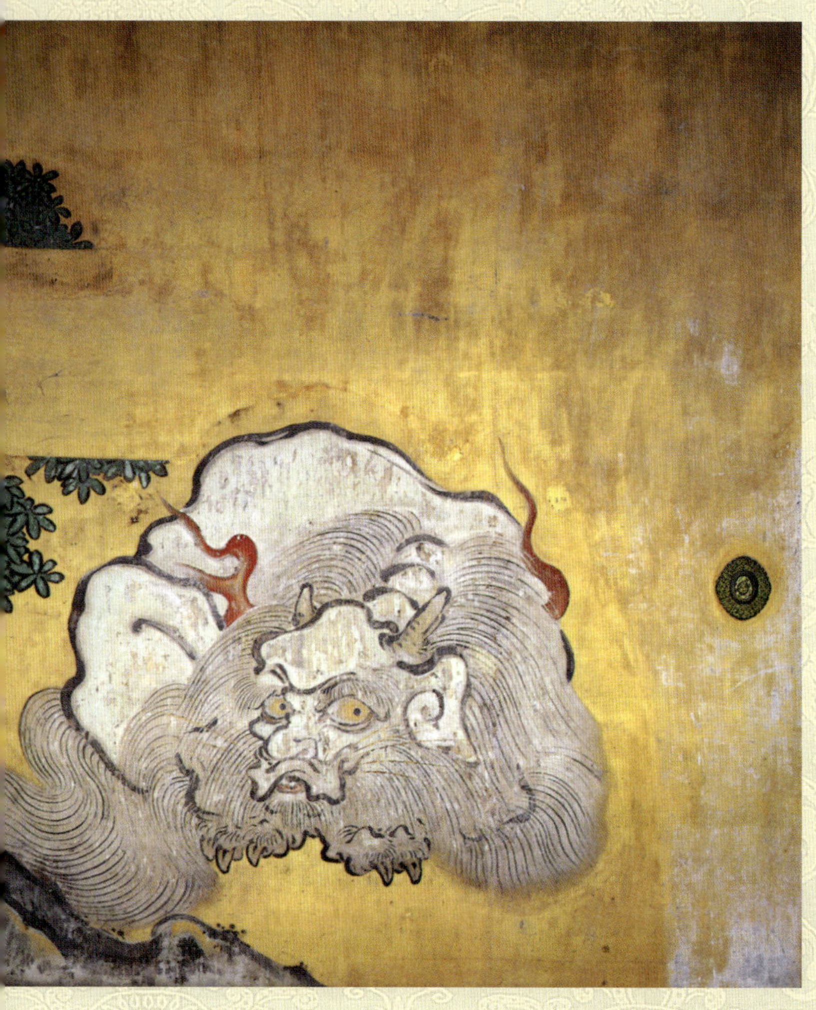

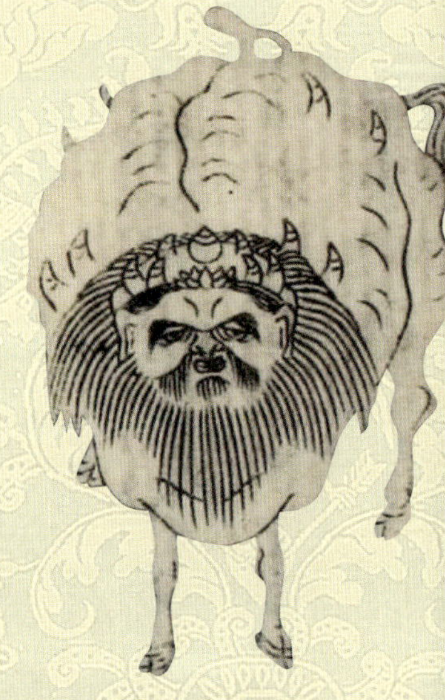

『旅行用心集』

八隅蘆庵
文化7年(1810)刊
国立国会図書館

白澤は病魔を防ぐということから転じて、その絵を持っていれば道中の災難や病気を免れると信じられ、江戸時代の旅には欠かせない護符(お守り)であった。コレラ流行の際にも白澤の絵が売り出されたという。

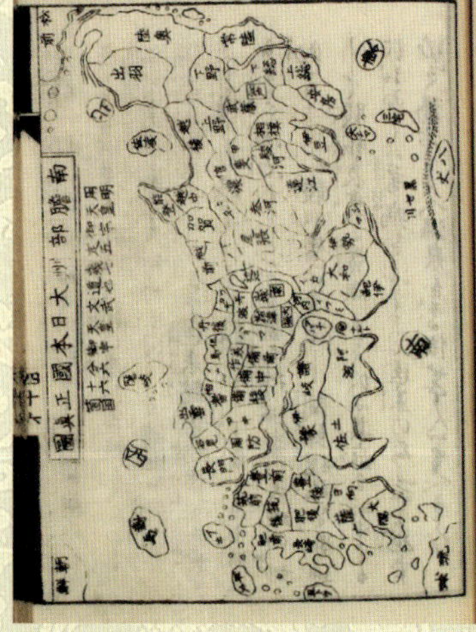

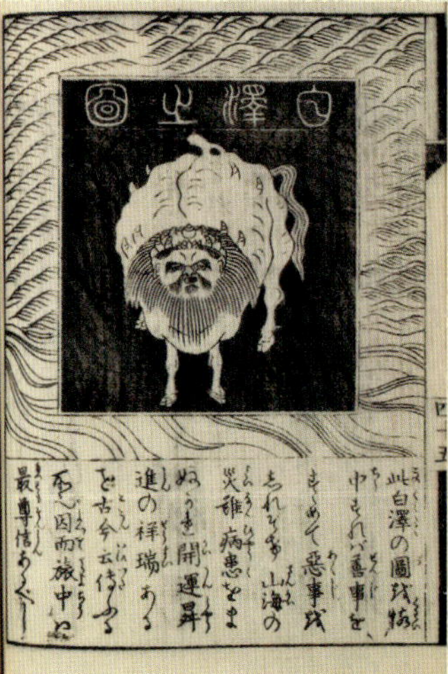

Precautions for Travelers

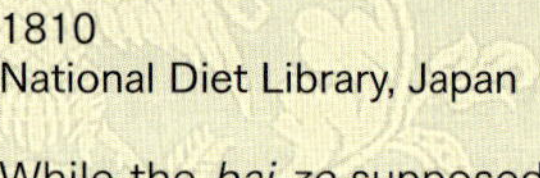

Yasumi Loan
1810
National Diet Library, Japan

While the *bai ze* supposedly warded off illness, it was also believed that those who carried images of the creature could avoid calamity and disease while on the road. These pictures were indispensable talismans for Edo period travelers, and depictions of the *bai ze* were also popular during cholera outbreaks.

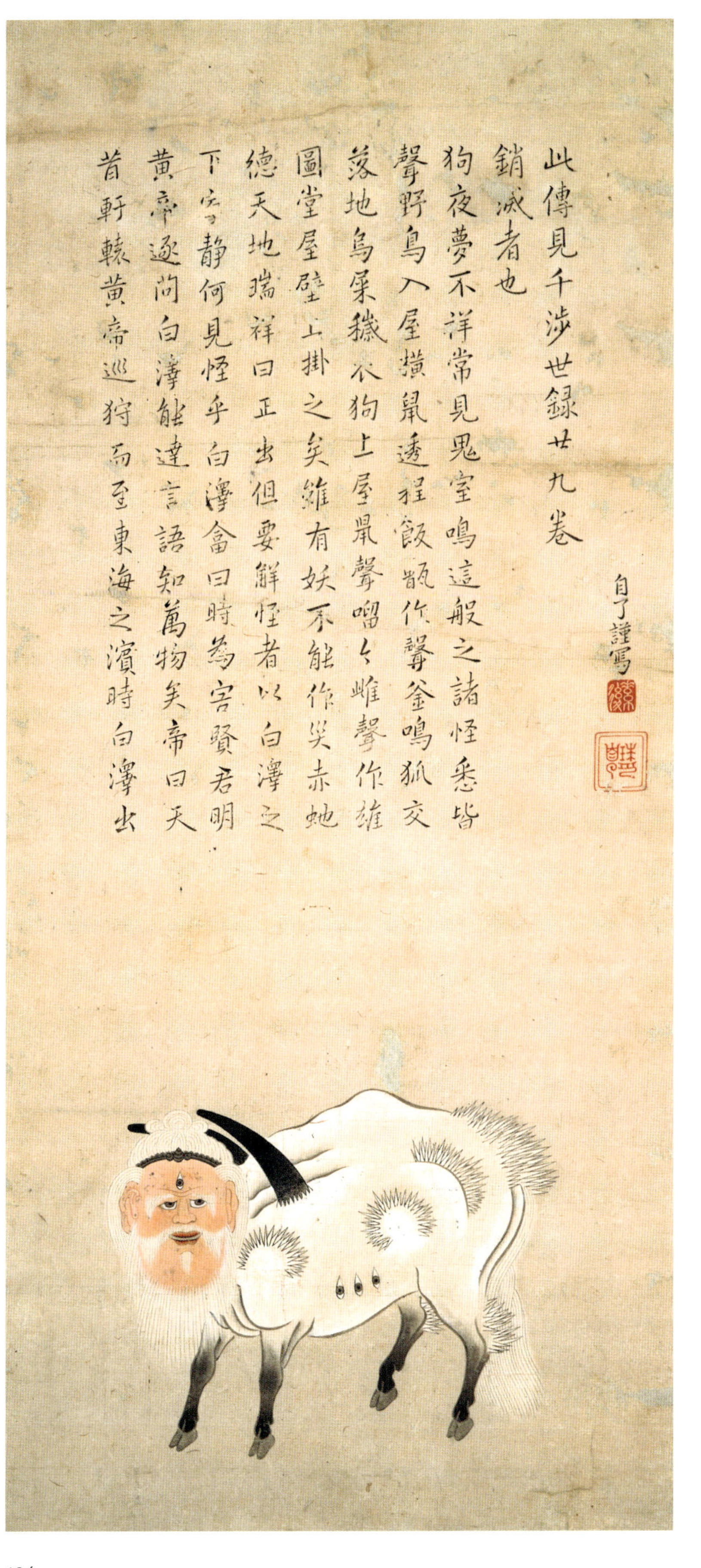

白澤之図

城間清豊
17世紀
沖縄美ら島財団

城間清豊(ぐすくませいほう)（1614～44）は、琉球の絵師で、唐名は欽可聖。琉球最古の絵師と言われ、口と耳が不自由であったと伝えられる。清豊の作品のほとんどは、太平洋戦争末期の沖縄戦で焼失し、本図は唯一の現存作品とされる。先の首里城火災（2019）でも、幸いに難を逃れた。

Bai Ze

Gusukuma Seihō
17th century
Okinawa
Churashima Foundation

Gusukuma Seihō (1614-44) was a painter from Ryūkyū, and his Chinese-style name was Qin Kesheng. He is said to be the oldest painter from Ryūkyū; it is also reported that he had hearing and speaking impairments. Most of Seihō's works were destroyed in the Battle of Okinawa at the end of the Pacific War, and this painting is thought to be the only extant work. Fortunately, it escaped harm during the 2019 Shuri Castle fire.

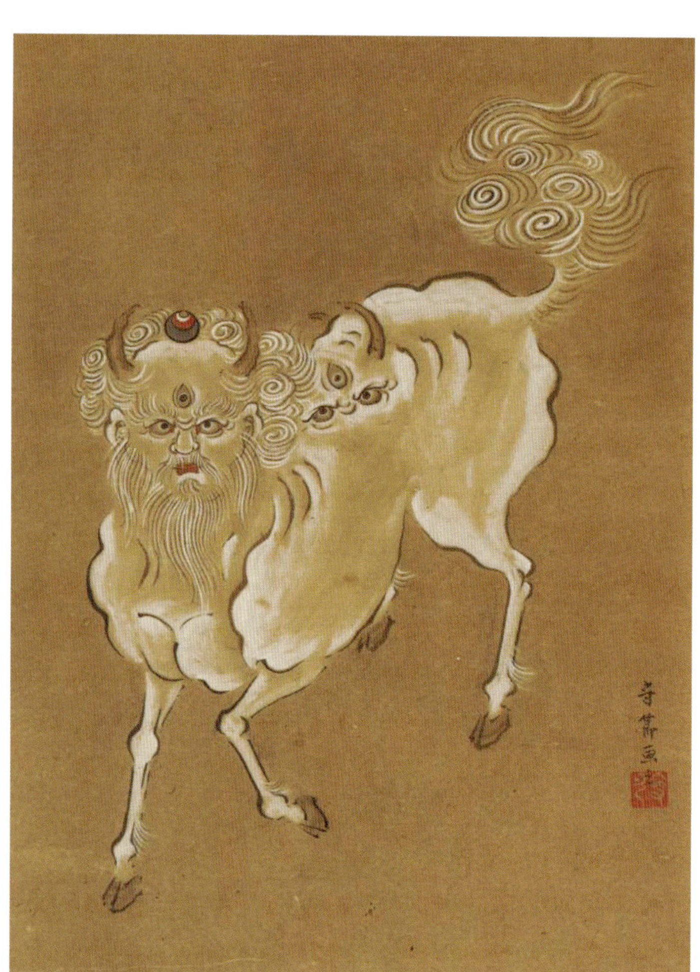

白澤図（部分）
守節
江戸時代（18c）
国際日本文化研究センター

Bai Ze *(detail)*
Shusetsu
18th century
International Research Center
for Japanese Studies

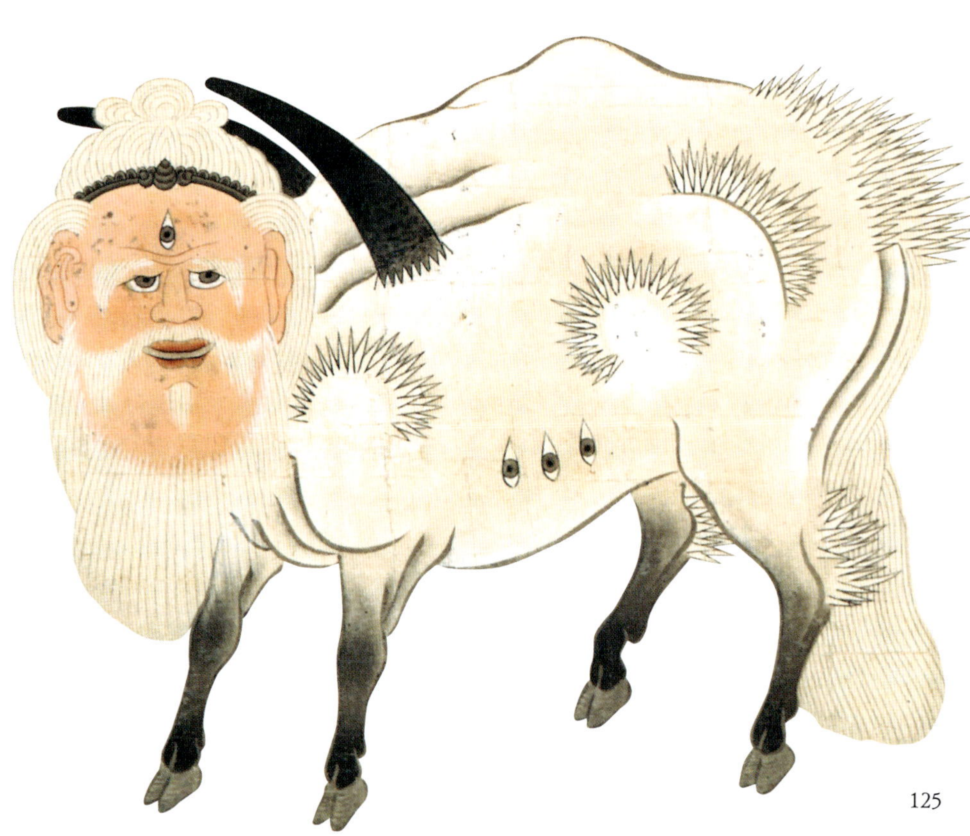

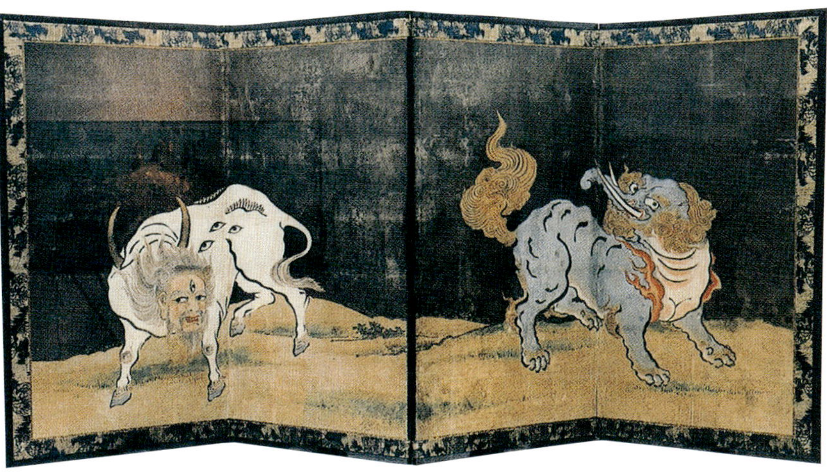

白澤図（枕屏風）

江戸時代後期（19c）
岐阜・内藤記念くすり博物館

白澤は病魔を防ぐ力があると信じられたことから、寝る際に風よけのために用いられる枕屏風に描かれた。

Bai Ze (Bedside Screen)

19th century
The Naito Museum of Pharmaceutical Science and Industry, Gifu

Since it was believed that the *bai ze* had the power to prevent illnesses, this bedside screen was painted to be used as a windbreak for when people slept.

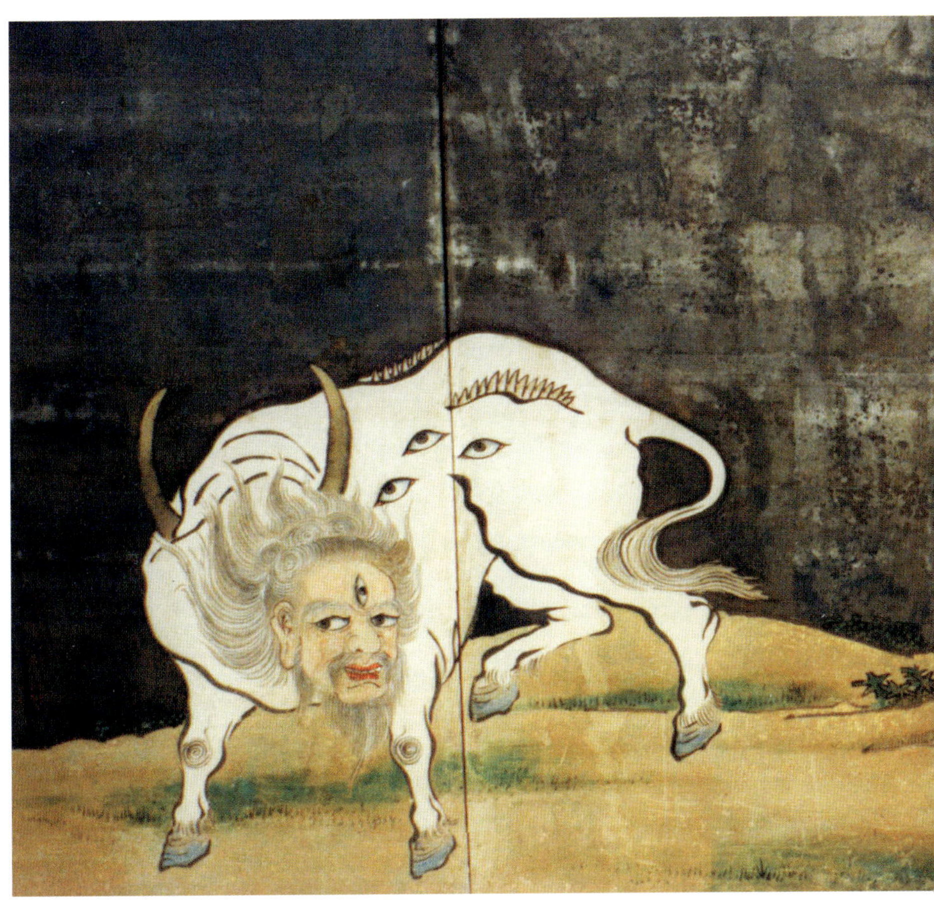

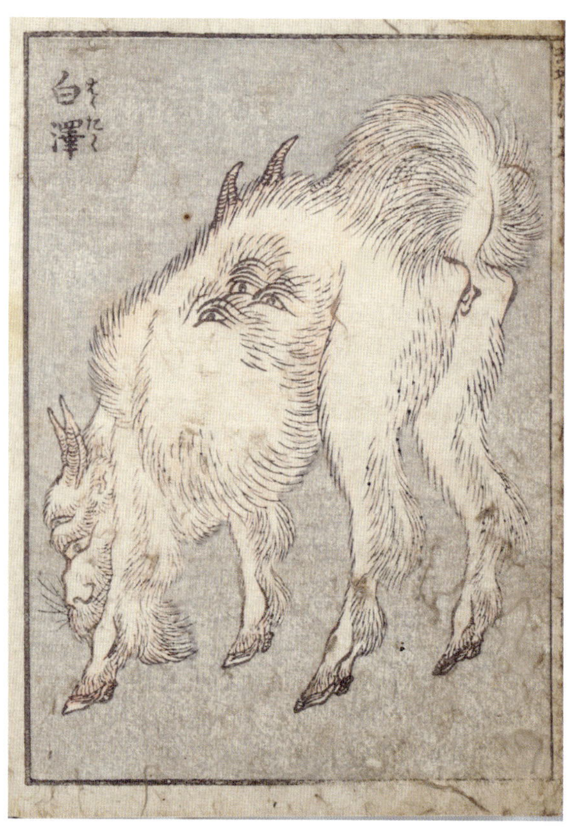

白澤図

（『北斎漫画』二編より）

葛飾北斎画
文化12年（1815）刊
メトロポリタン美術館

Bai Ze

(*from Hokusai Manga, Volume Two*)

Katsushika Hokusai
1815
The Metropolitan Museum of Art

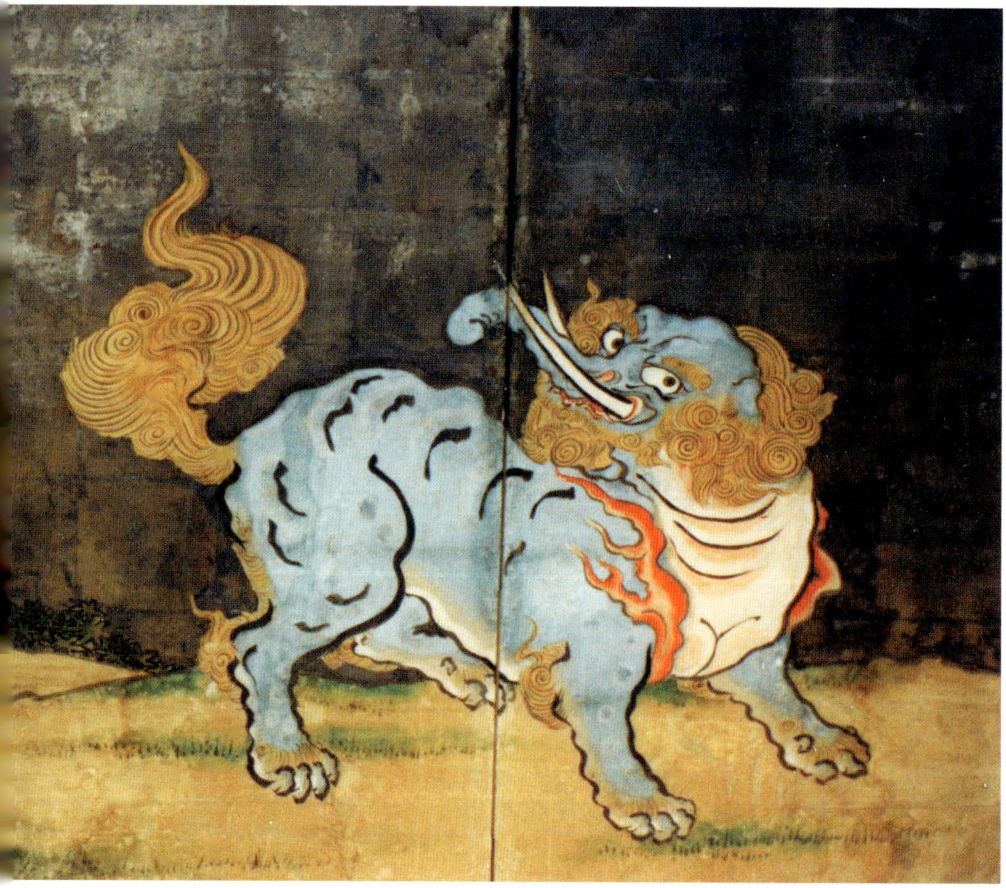

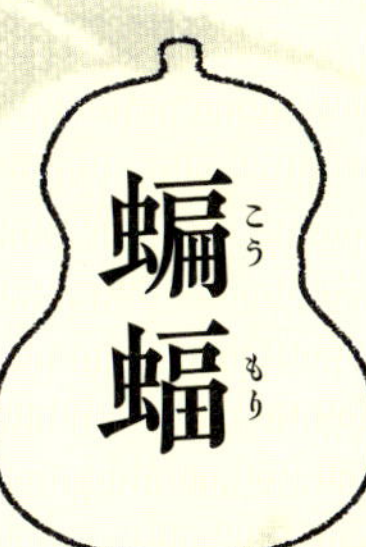

中国では、蝙蝠の「蝠」が「福」と音が通ずるところから、コウモリを幸福の象徴とみなす。とくに5匹の蝙蝠を描いた図案は「五福」と呼ばれ、長寿・富・高位・健康・子孫繁栄の象徴として喜ばれた。蝙蝠はまた、「変福（福に転じる）」とも音を同じくするため、とくに明・清時代に図様が流行、日本にも江戸時代に伝来した。蝙蝠自体も長命のための霊薬と信じられ、糞までが夜盲症や視力回復の薬に用いられたという。

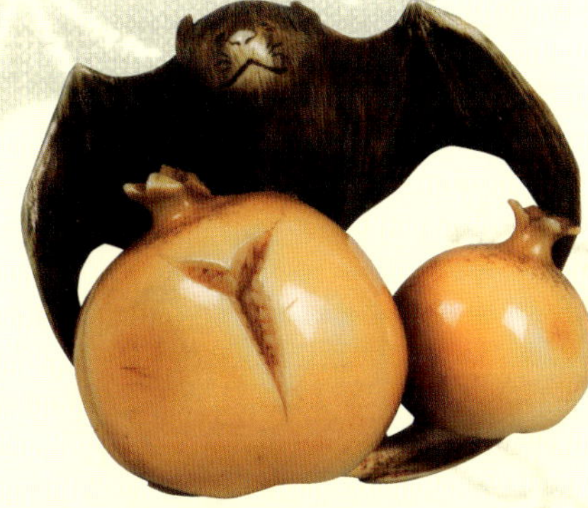

蝙蝠牙彫根付
江戸時代（19c）
メトロポリタン美術館

Netsuke of Bat and Pomegranate
19th century
The Metropolitan Museum of Art

The Bat

In China, since the second character of the word for "bat" is homophonous with the character for "good luck," the bat is seen as a symbol of good fortune. The design of five bats is called the "Five Lucks," and it is enjoyed as a symbol of long life, wealth, high status, health, and the perpetuation of one's family line. Since the word "bat" also sounds similar to the word "changing for the better," this design was especially popular in the Ming and Qing dynasties, and it also came to Japan during the Edo period. The actual bat itself was also believed to be a miracle medicine for long life, and even its excrement was used in medicines for night blindness and vision improvement.

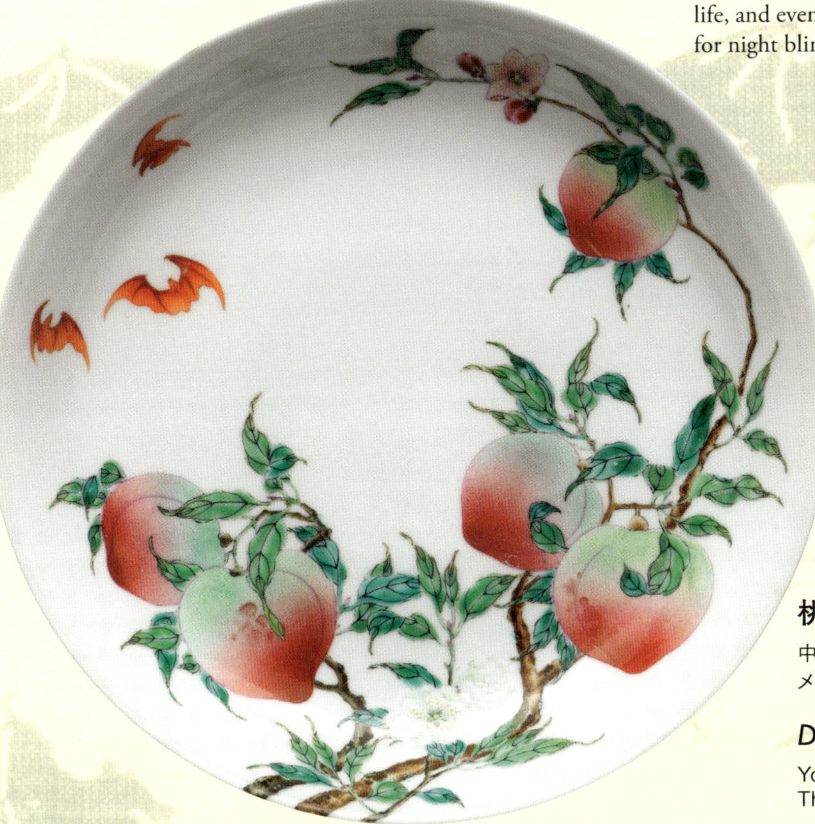

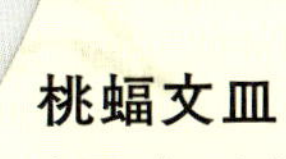

桃蝠文皿
中国・雍正年間（18c）
メトロポリタン美術館

Dish with Peaches and Bats
Yongzheng era, 18th century
The Metropolitan Museum of Art

納涼美人図

歌川豊国
江戸時代（18c後半～19c初め）
群馬県立近代美術館
戸方庵井上コレクション

白い振袖姿の町娘が、夕涼みにそぞろ歩く風情である。赤い襦袢とともに足下まで透け見えるのがいかにも涼しげ。風に揺れる葉を揺らす柳の下には蝙蝠が2匹飛び、夕暮れの時刻を告げる。

Woman Enjoying the Evening Cool

Utagawa Toyokuni
Late 18th century–early 19th century
Kohoan Inoue Collection, The Museum of Modern Art, Gunma

A town girl wearing a white long-sleeved kimono seems to be taking a stroll in the evening cool. Including the red undershirt, her outfit it is almaost transparent down to her feet, and it looks very refreshing in the summer heat. Two bats fly below the willow that has its leaves rustling in the breeze, and they indicate the twilight hour.

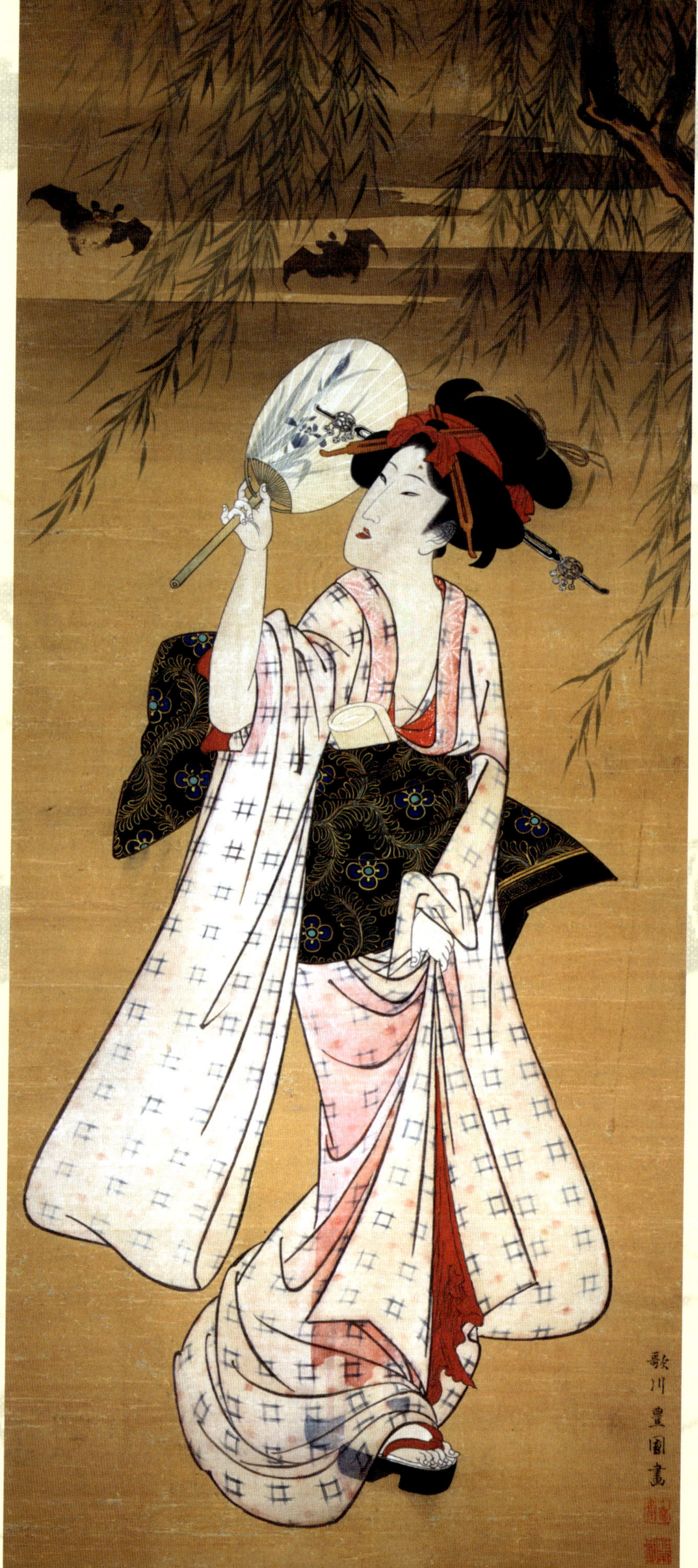

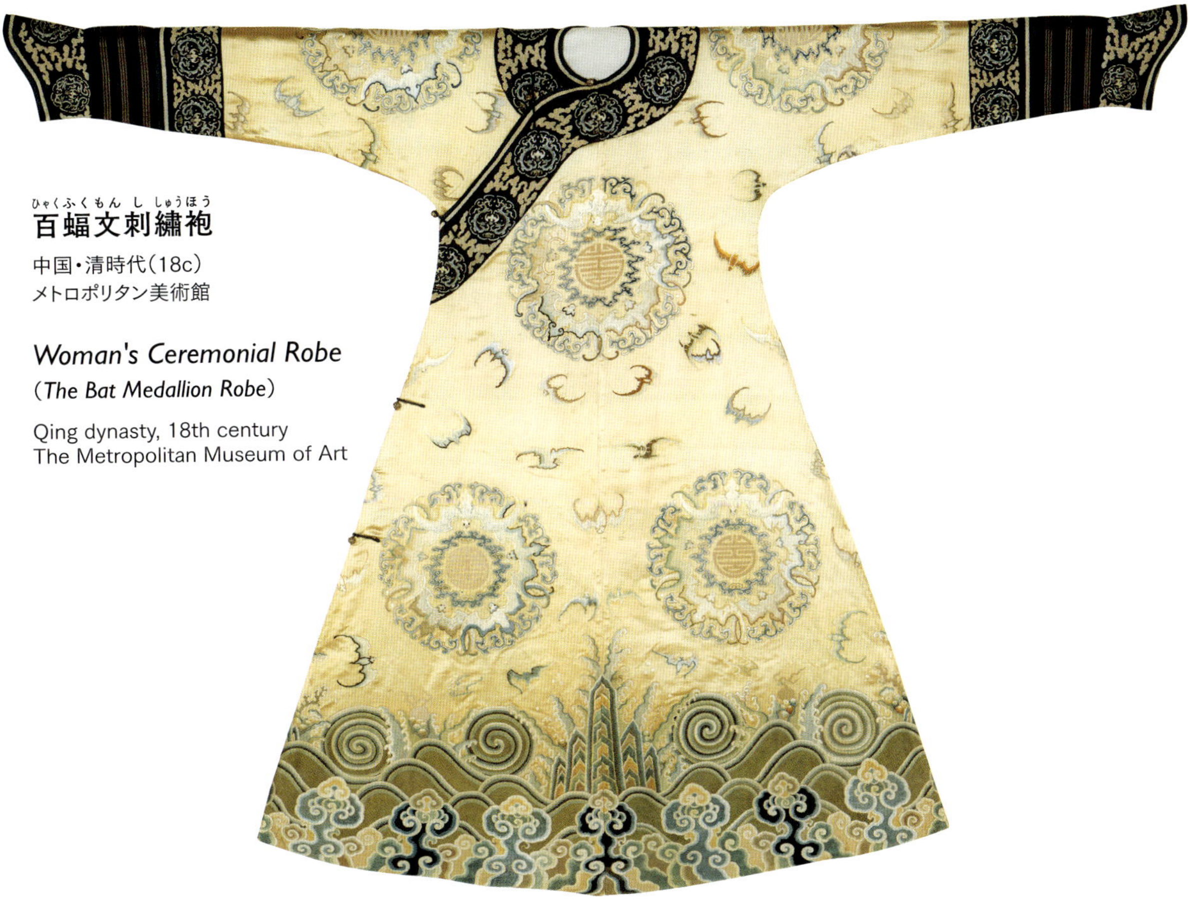

百蝠文刺繡袍

中国・清時代（18c）
メトロポリタン美術館

Woman's Ceremonial Robe
（*The Bat Medallion Robe*）

Qing dynasty, 18th century
The Metropolitan Museum of Art

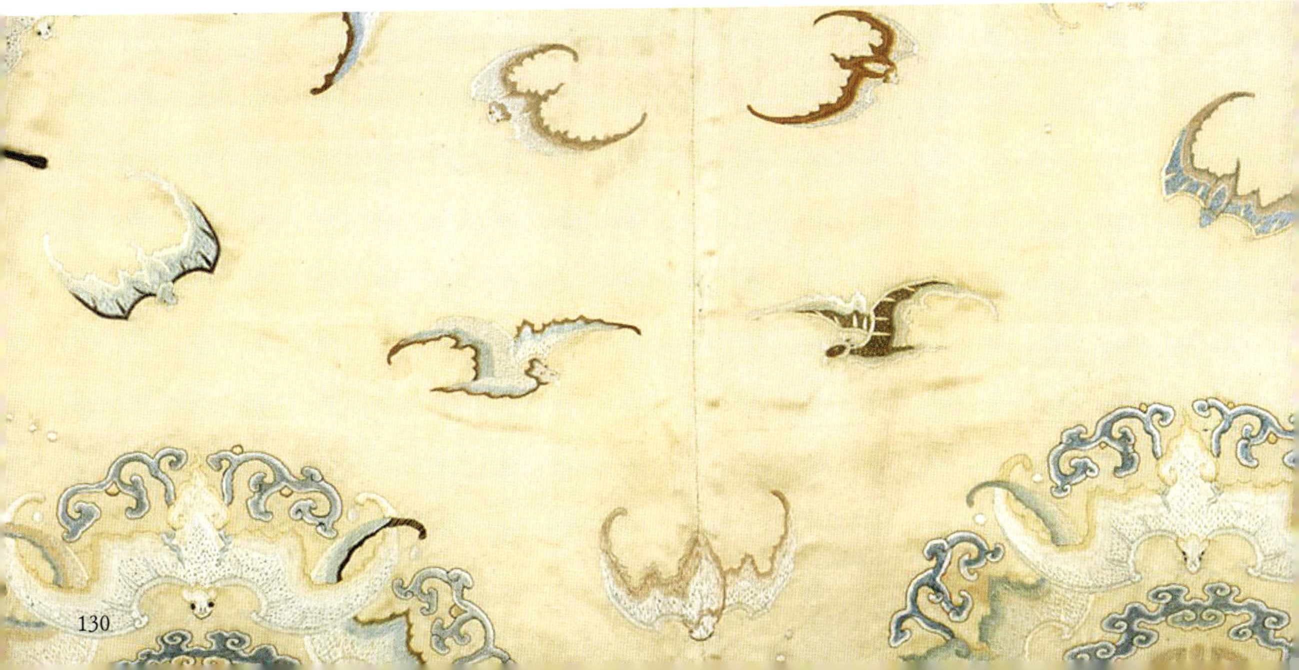

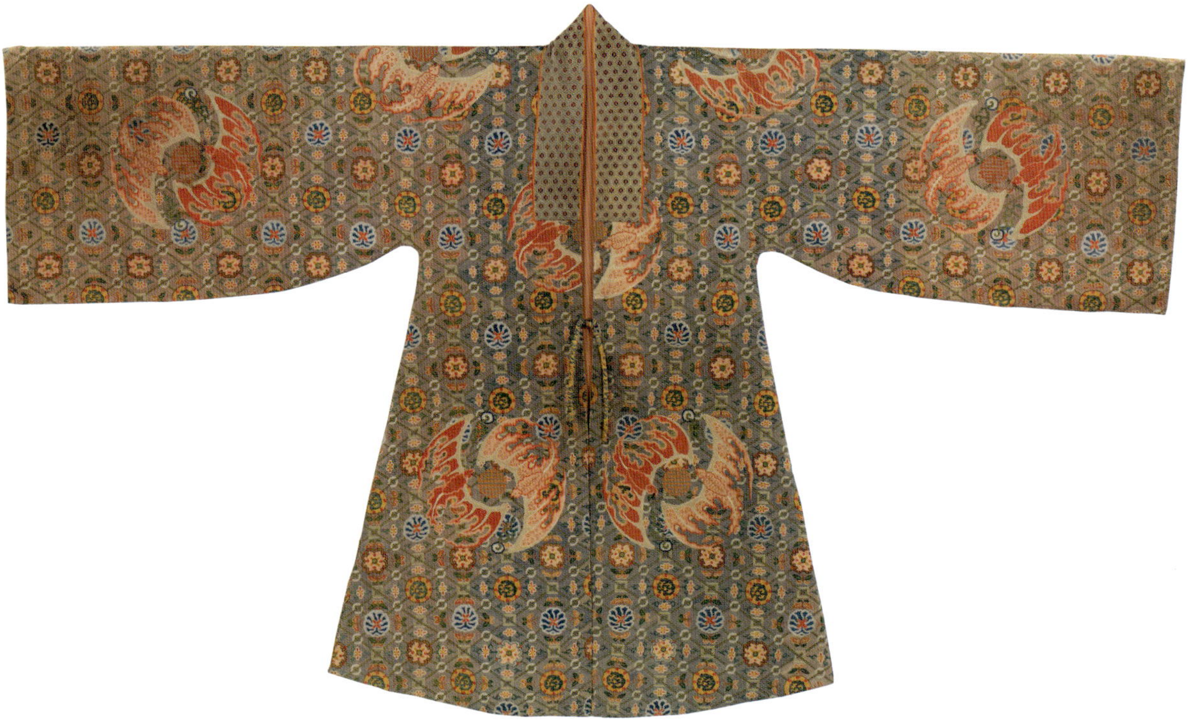

蝙蝠文紗刺繡袍（へんぷくもんしゃししゅうほう）

中国・清時代（18c）
メトロポリタン美術館

Theatrical Robe for a Male Role

Qing dynasty, 18th century
The Metropolitan Museum of Art

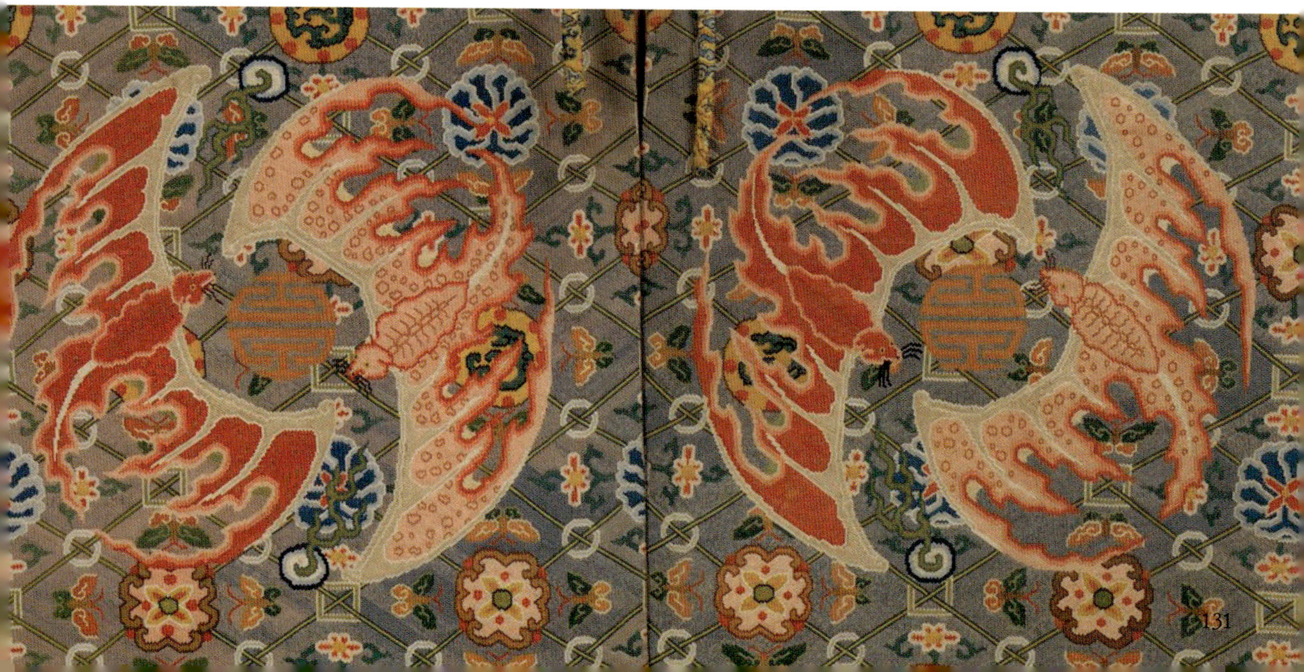

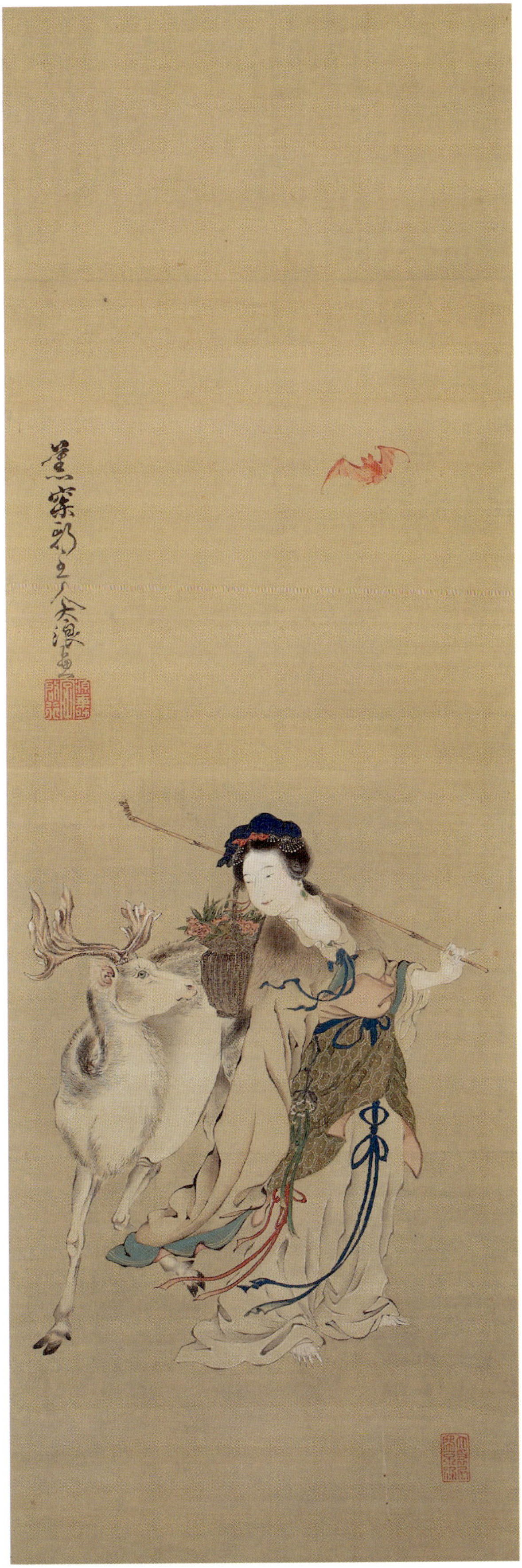

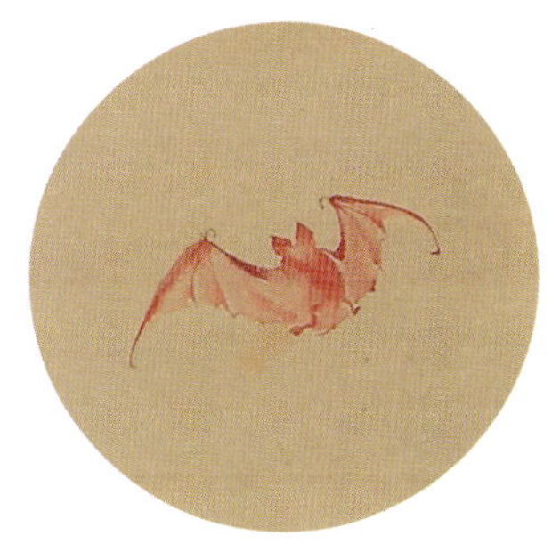

麻姑仙人図

石川大浪
江戸時代（18c後半～19c初め）
歸空庵コレクション

麻姑は、中国の神話に登場する若く美しい仙女。鳥のように長い爪を持ち、西王母の誕生祝いに霊芝で造った美酒を贈ったという。長寿の象徴でもあった。本図は、麻姑の頭上に赤い蝙蝠、かたわらには鹿を配し、「福禄」と音を通じさせることでさらに吉祥性を高めている。石川大浪（1765–1817）は幕府旗本で、大槻玄沢ら蘭学者らと親交しつつ洋風画を手がけた。号の大浪はアフリカ南端の喜望峰付近の山名に由来する。一見伝統的な描法に見える本図ではあるが、特殊な角の表現からして、鹿は鹿でも当時蘭学者の間で話題になっていたヘラジカのイメージが反映されているようだ。

The Immortal Ma Gu

Ishikawa Tairō
Late 18th–early 19th century
Kikūan Collection

Ma Gu is a beautiful immortal woman that appears in Chinese myths. It is said that she has long nails like the talons of a bird, and that at the birthday celebration of the Queen Mother of the West, she gave her a fine wine made from *lingzhi* mushrooms. She was also a symbol of longevity. In this image, there is a red bat (the second character of which can be read as “*fuku*”) above Ma Gu’s head, and a deer (the character of which can also be pronounced as “*roku*”) standing next to her; thus, this is a rebus picture which implies the pronunciation of “happiness and luck (*fukuroku*),” making this an even more auspiciousness depiction. Ishikawa Tairō (1765-1817) was a shogunal vassal, and while maintaining close friendships with Ōtsuki Gentaku and other scholars of Western studies, he also did Western style paintings. His sobriquet “Great Wave” is based on the name of a mountain near the Cape of Good Hope. At first glance this work seems like a traditional painting, but the horns of the deer look like they have been influenced by depictions of the horns of moose, which was a topic often discussed between scholars of Western studies at the time.

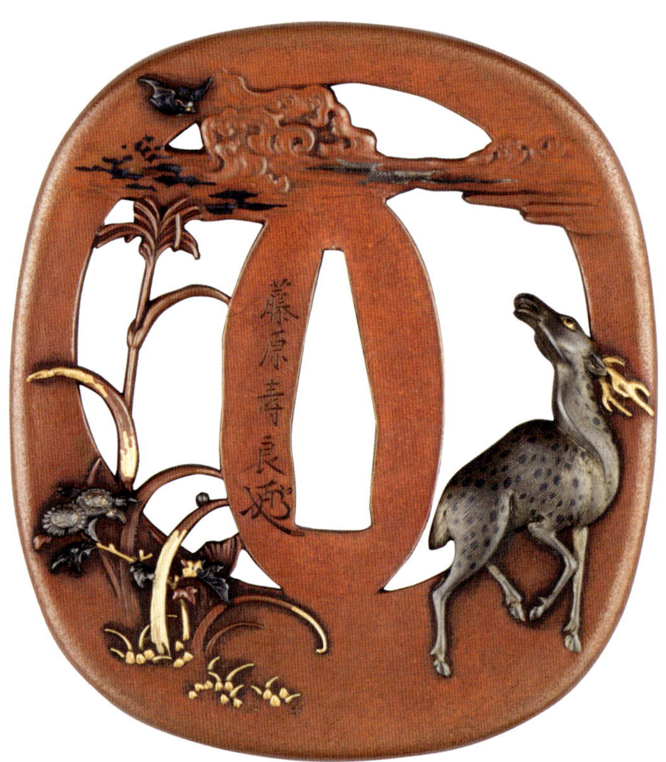

鹿図鐔

江戸時代(19c)
メトロポリタン美術館

Deer Tsuba (*Sword Guard*)

19th century
The Metropolitan Museum of Art

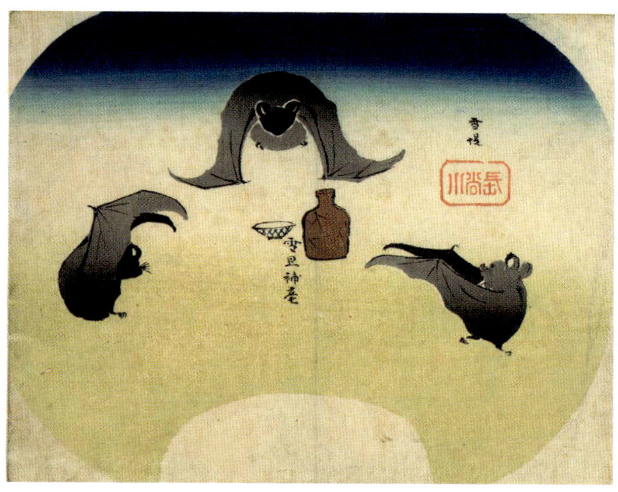

蝙蝠図(団扇絵判)

長谷川雪旦・雪堤
江戸時代(19c)
東京国立博物館

徳利と切子の杯を中央に、蝙蝠が座敷遊びに興じる様子を描いた父子合作の団扇絵。3匹の蝙蝠は、両手を上げたり伏せたり前に出したりと、思い思いのポーズに興じているように見える。江戸時代以来流行した藤八拳(狐拳)や虫拳、虎拳、そして石拳(じゃんけん)などの三すくみ拳をしているようである。

Bats (*Fan Painting*)

Hasegawa Settan and Settei
19th century
Tokyo National Museum

This is a fan painting that is a father and son collaboration depicting a central sake bottle and a faceted sake cup around which bats are making merry. Three bats are amusing themselves in different poses with one raising both wings in the air, one lying down, and one reaching forward. The game *tōhachiken* (or *kitsuneken*) was a game that was popular since the Edo period, and it was a type of rock-paper-scissors game in which the three hand poses were a bug, a tiger, and a rock.

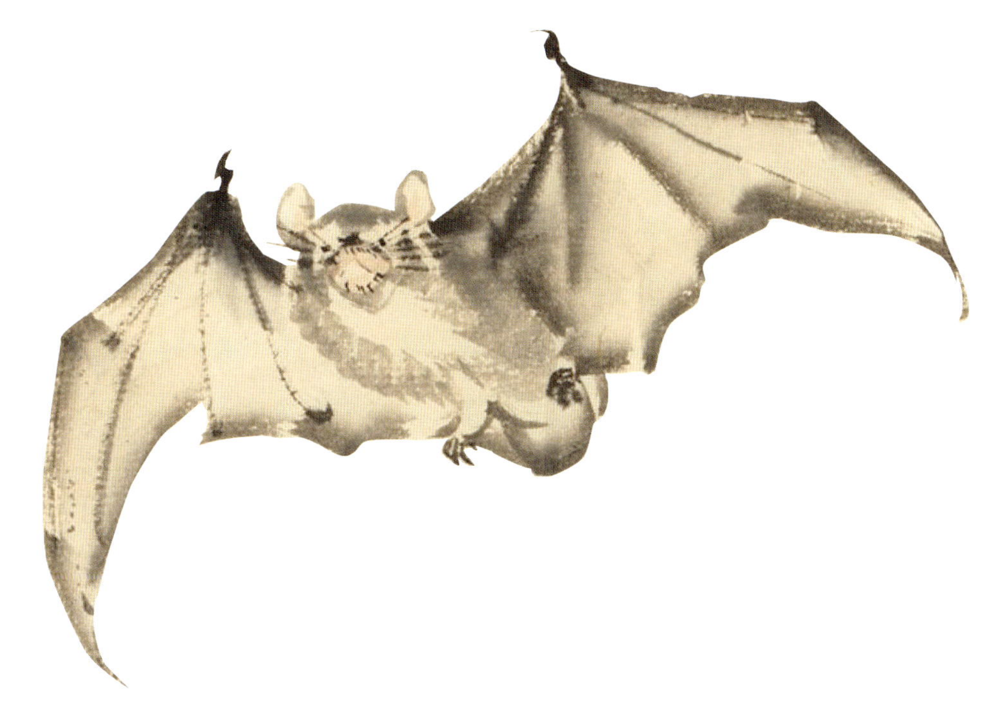

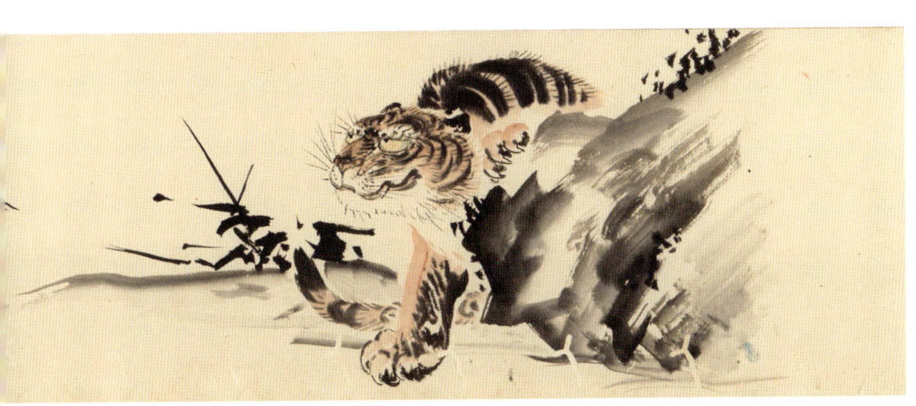

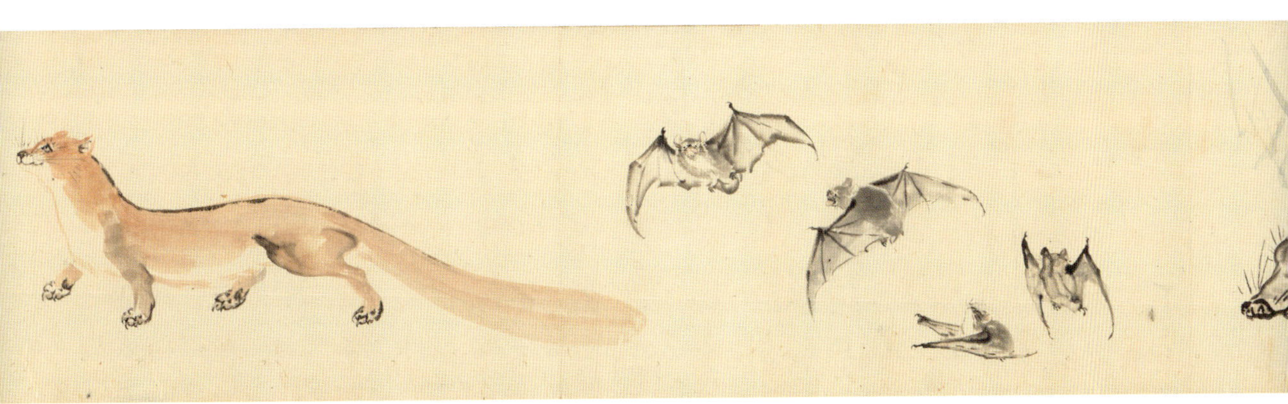

鳥獣画巻

河鍋暁斎
江戸時代末期（19c 後半）
メトロポリタン美術館

Sketches of Birds and Animals

Kawanabe Kyōsai
Late 19th century, before 1870
The Metropolitan Museum of Art

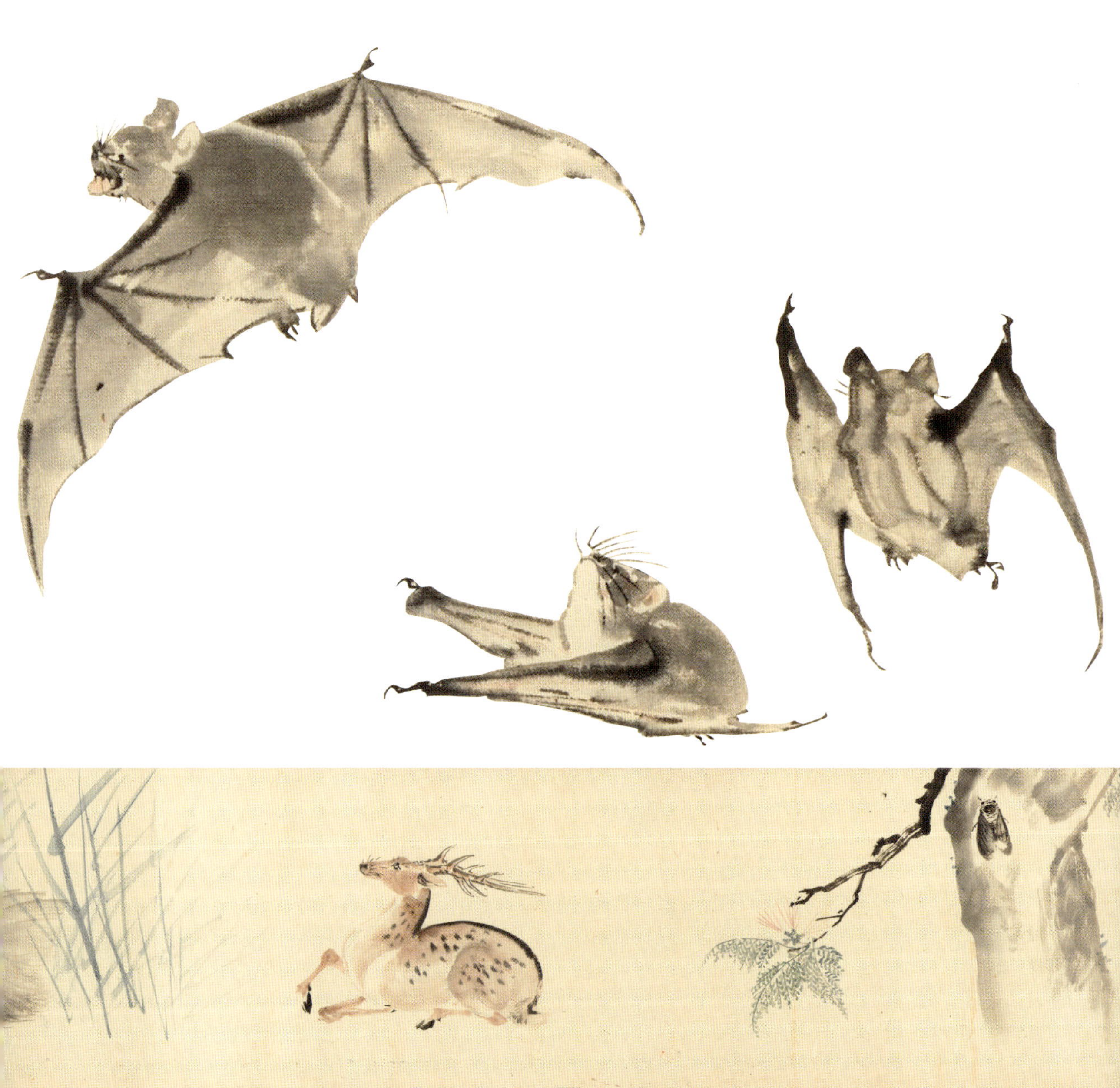

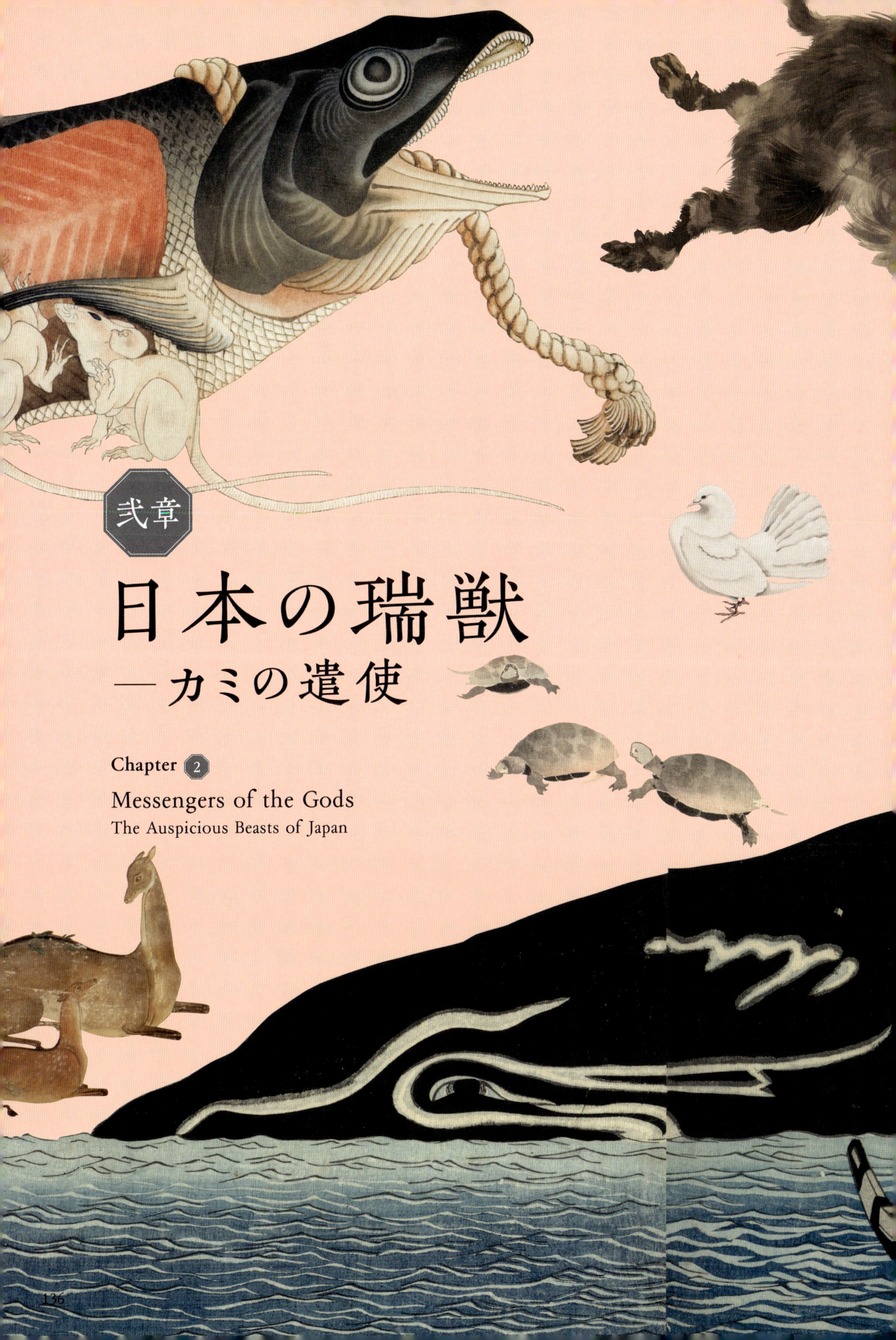

弐章

日本の瑞獣
―カミの遣使

Chapter 2

Messengers of the Gods

The Auspicious Beasts of Japan

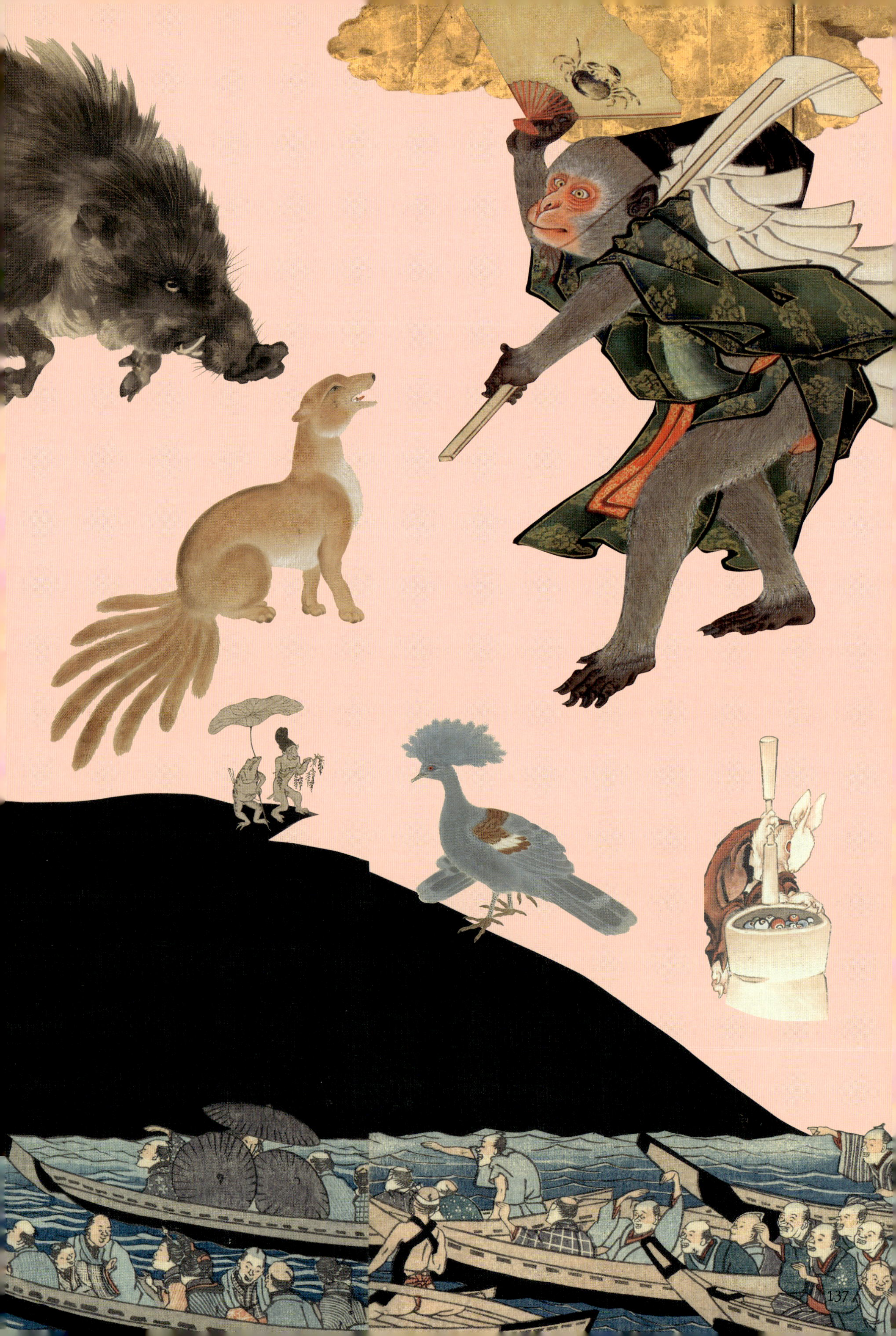

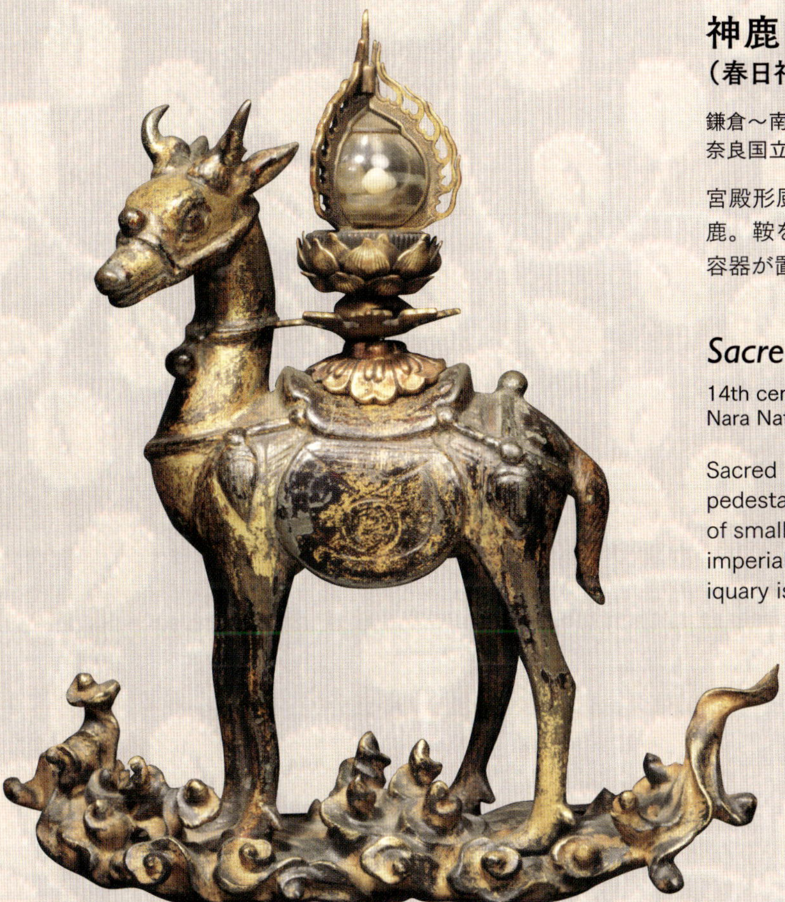

神鹿
（春日神鹿舎利厨子安置）

鎌倉～南北朝時代（14c）
奈良国立博物館

宮殿形厨子に安置された飛雲座に立つ神鹿。鞍をのせた背には、火焔宝珠形舎利容器が置かれている。宝珠は水晶製。

Sacred Deer

14th century
Nara National Museum

Sacred deer like this one placed on a pedestal of clouds would have been part of small shrines used by members of the imperial court. A crystal containing a reliquary is placed on the animal's back.

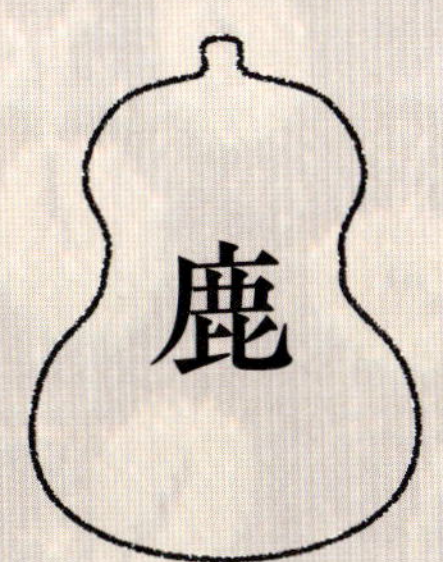

鹿は長寿の象徴とされ、また発音が「禄」に通じる吉祥動物でもあった。日本では、奈良・春日大社の神の使い。社伝によれば、神社の創始にあたり祭神として迎えた常陸国鹿島神宮の武甕槌神が白い鹿に乗って春日山に来訪したことにより、この地の鹿は神使として崇められるようになったという。中国古来の道教に説く寿老人は、日本では七福神にも数えられ、牡鹿を従えている姿で描かれた図像は正月の床間を飾るにふさわしいめでたいものである。

The Deer

Deer are symbols of long life, Since the Japanese pronunciation of the Chinese character for "deer" (*roku*) is homophonous with the word for "fortune," deer are seen as auspicious beings. At Kasuga Shrine in Nara, deer are worshipped as divine messengers. According to the shrine's mythical origins, Takemigazuchi, a deity of Kashima Shrine in Hitachi Province, arrived at Mount Kasuga mounted on a white deer. For that reason, the deer of that area are regarded as messengers of the gods. Jurōjin, the deity of long life in ancient Chinese Taoism, is worshipped as one of the Seven Gods of Good Fortune in Japan. Paintings of Jurōjin paired with a deer are often hung at traditional Japanese homes around New Year's.

重要文化財

春日鹿曼荼羅

鎌倉時代(14c)
奈良国立博物館

神鹿が雲に乗って春日の地に飛来する姿を表現する。鞍上には神木の榊が立てられ、枝先には春日社の若宮と本社第一殿から四殿までの祭神の本地仏が描かれている。図の上下には、霞のたな引く春日野に浮かぶ御蓋山と春日山、鹿が群れ遊ぶ一の鳥居周辺の景観を描き、生き生きとした現実感を与えている。

Important Cultural Property

Kasuga Mandala

14th century
Nara National Museum

The image depicts a sacred deer riding atop a cloud towards Kasuga. From the saddle, a sacred sakaki tree is growing whose branches carry renderings of the Buddhist avatars of the deities enshrined at Kasuga. Between the mist surrounding the central image on the top and bottom, the viewer glimpses the area of the shrine with Mount Mikasa and Mount Kasuga in the distance. The scene is populated with groups of deer around the shrine gate. The painting is striking in its life-likeness.

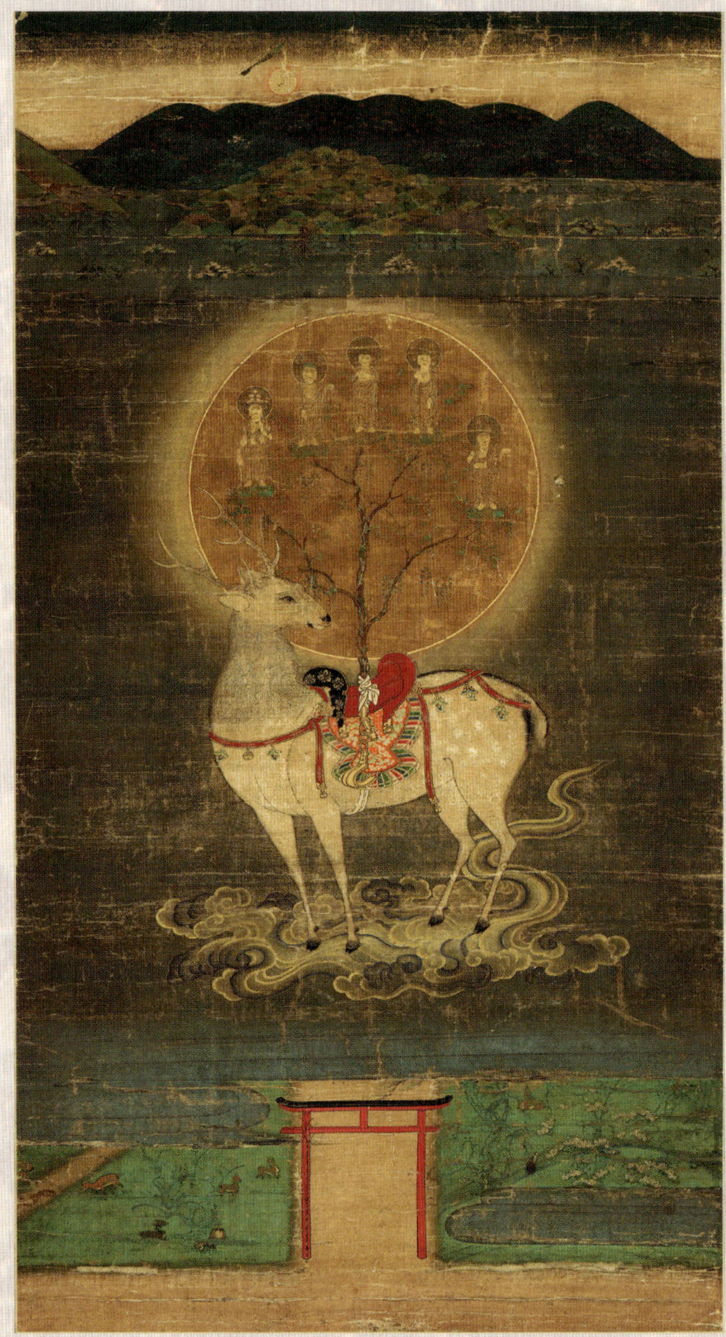

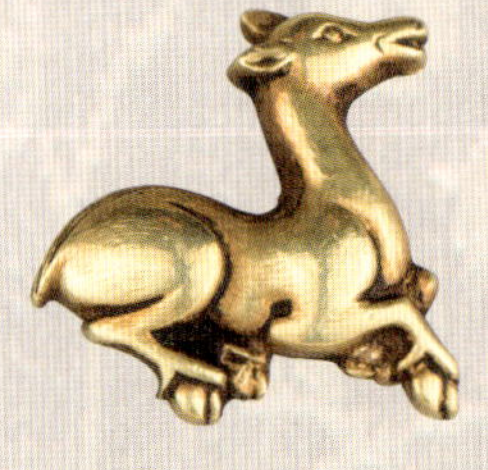

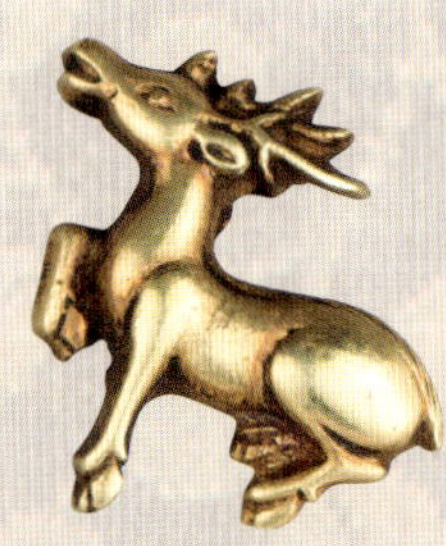

鹿図目貫

江戸時代(18c)
メトロポリタン美術館

Pair of Deer Menuki

(*Sword-grip Ornaments*)

18th century
The Metropolitan Museum of Art

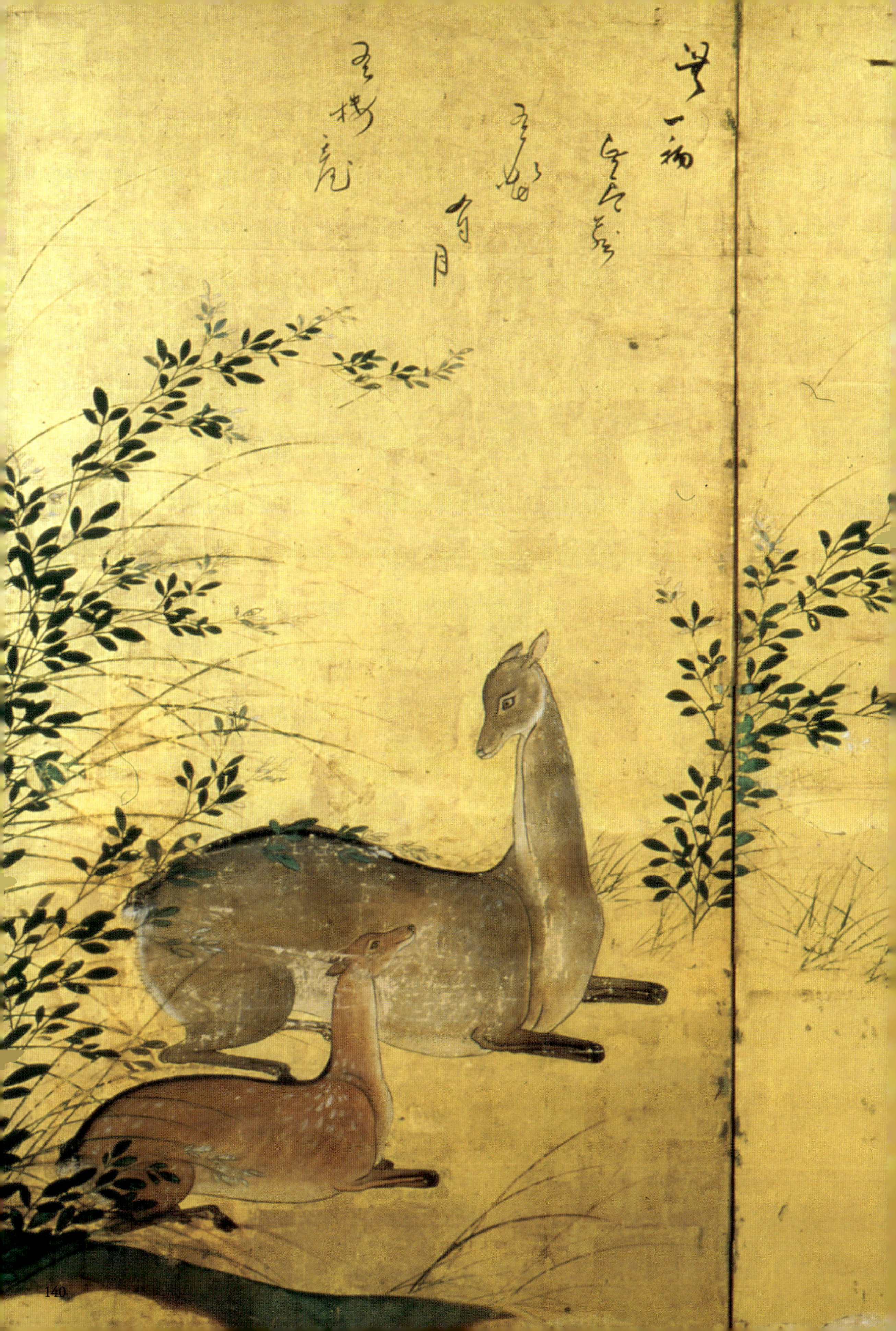

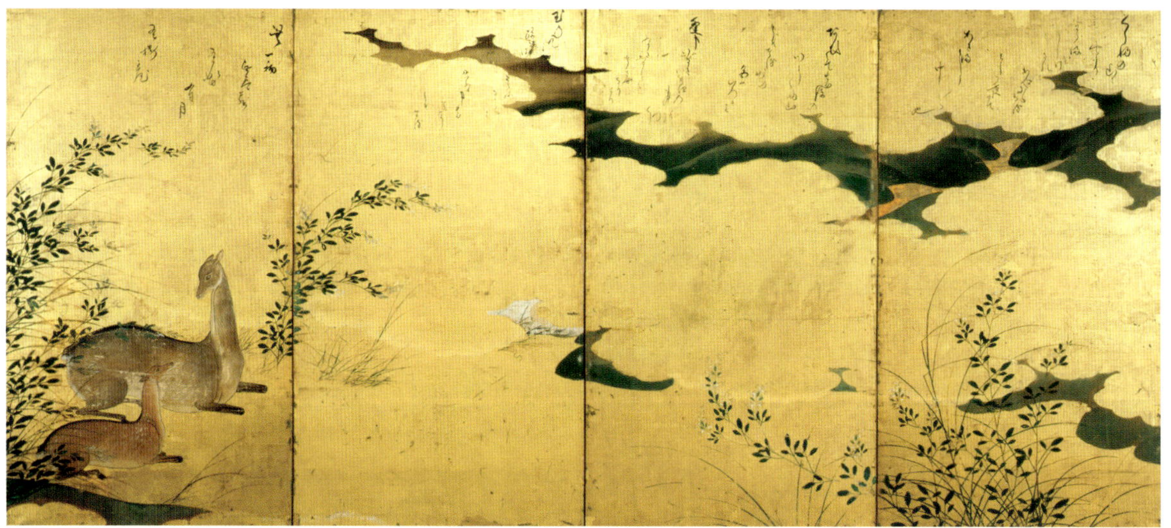

重要美術品

萩に鹿図屏風(左隻)

伝 狩野左京筆、伊達政宗書
寛永5年(1628)
仙台市博物館

現在屏風に改装されているが、もとは1628年(寛永5)に完成した伊達政宗(1567〜1636)晩年の居城・若林城の襖絵だったと推測される。萩が咲き乱れる光景は、若林城の所在した宮城野の地にふさわしい主題であった。

Important Work of Art

Deer and Clover Folding Screen (*Left screen*)

Attributed to Kano Sakyō, Inscribed by Date Masamune
1628
Sendai City Museum

Although the painting is now mounted on a folding screen, it was probably conceived as the decoration of a sliding-door at Wakabayashi Castle, the late residence of Date Masamune (1567-1636). The castle was completed in 1628 (Kan'ei 5). The deer are placed amid a field of swaying clover which represents Miyagino, the area around Wakabayashi Castle.

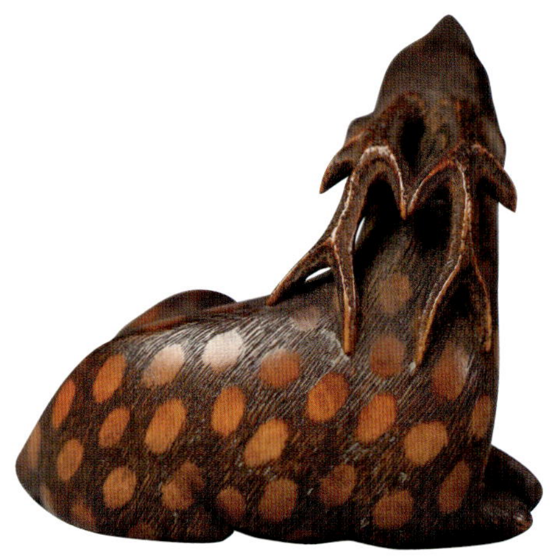

鹿木彫根付

江戸時代(19c)
メトロポリタン美術館

Netsuke of Deer

19th century
The Metropolitan Museum of Art

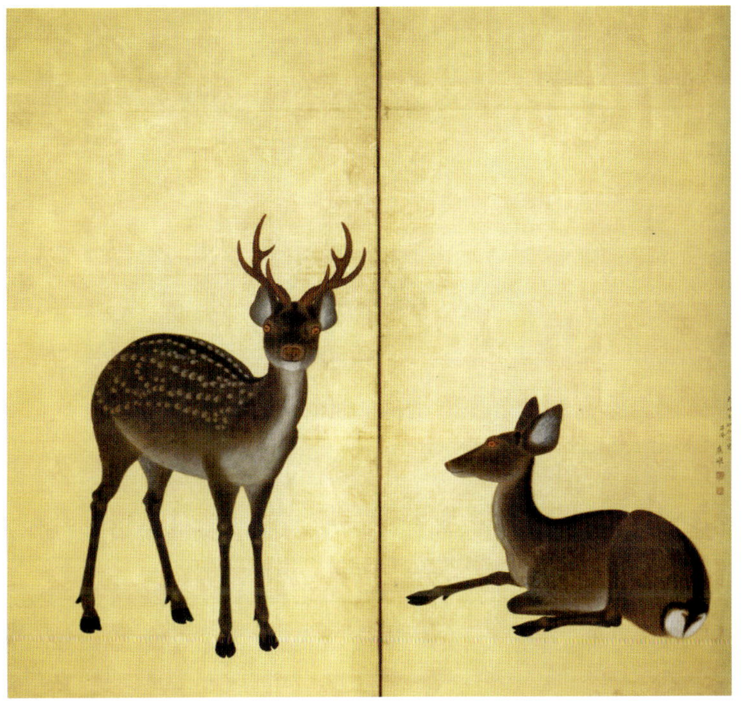

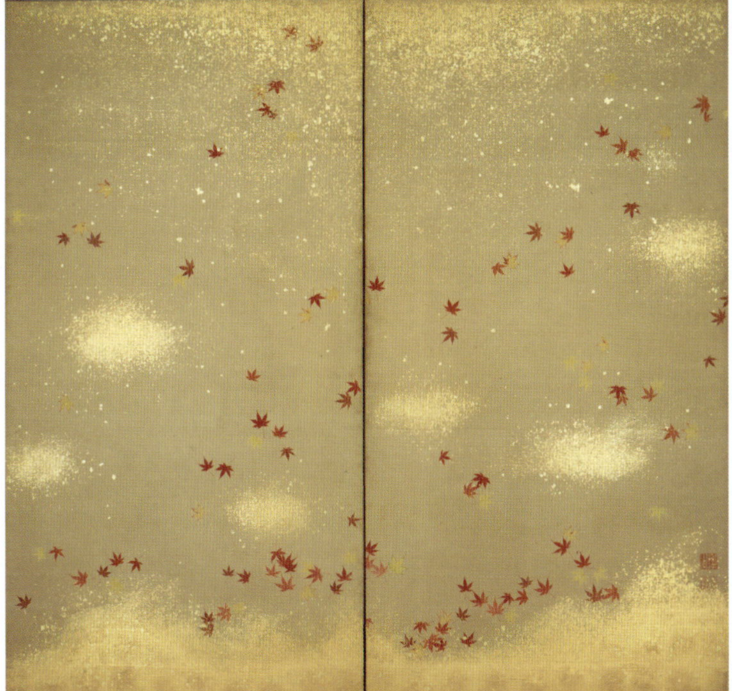

双鹿図屏風

円山応挙
天明3年(1783)
京都国立博物館

正面向きと横向きの雌雄2頭の鹿を金地画面に描く。あるべき地面や背景など周囲の環境を感じさせるものは一切省かれ、鹿の体軀そのものが際立つ。とくに左の雄鹿の表現に、見る者は奥行を感じさせられる。短縮法により画面に空間が生み出されているのである。屏風の背面には、紅葉の散り行く様子が描かれ、表裏で「紅葉に鹿」となる。何とも粋な趣向だ。

Pair of Deer Folding Screen

Maruyama Ōkyo
1783
Kyoto National Museum

Two deer are placed against a ground of gold leaf. One is looking in our direction and the other gazes into the distance. Any defining elements in the foreground and background have been deleted, and only the deer's bodies remain the focus of the painting. The posture of the left deer in particular creates a sense of depth in the composition, and the foreshortening of its body helps define the picture's spatiality. The reverse side of the screen carries an image of colored leaves, creating a delicate autumnal scenery in combination with the front.

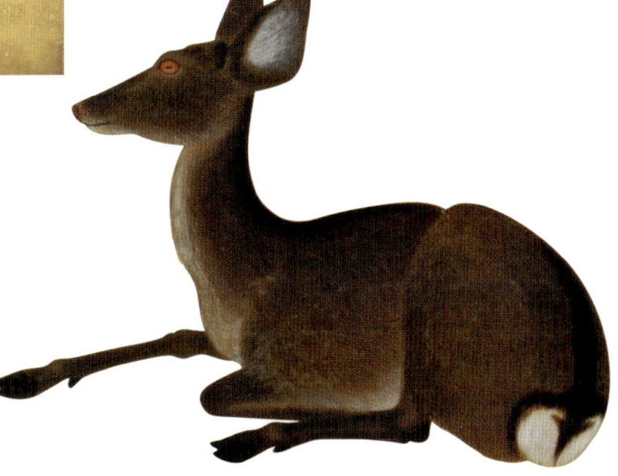

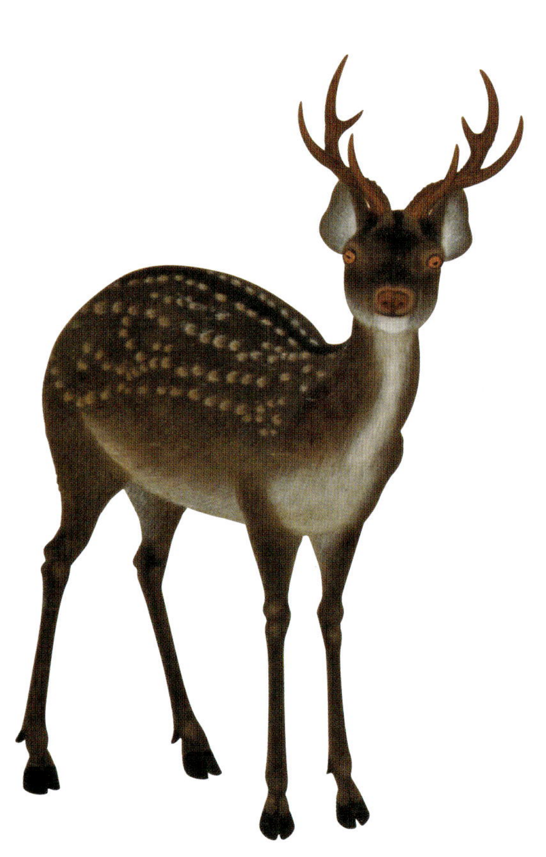

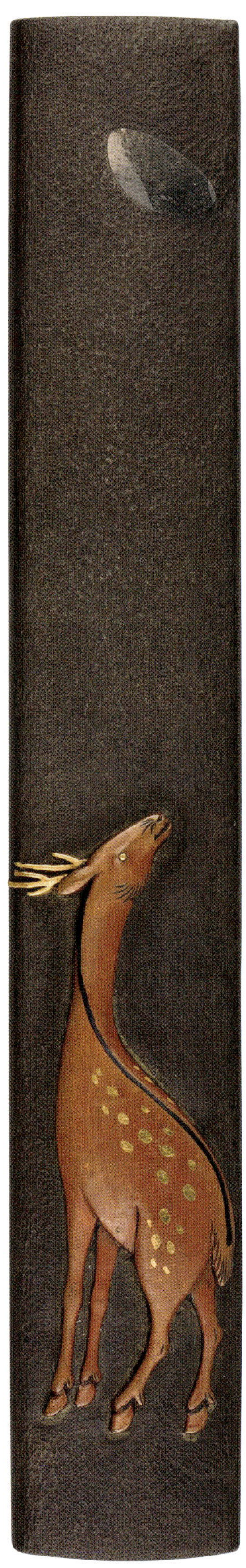

鹿図小柄

江戸時代（19c）
メトロポリタン美術館

***Deer Kozuka* (*Knife Handle*)**

Edo period, 19th century
The Metropolitan Museum of Art

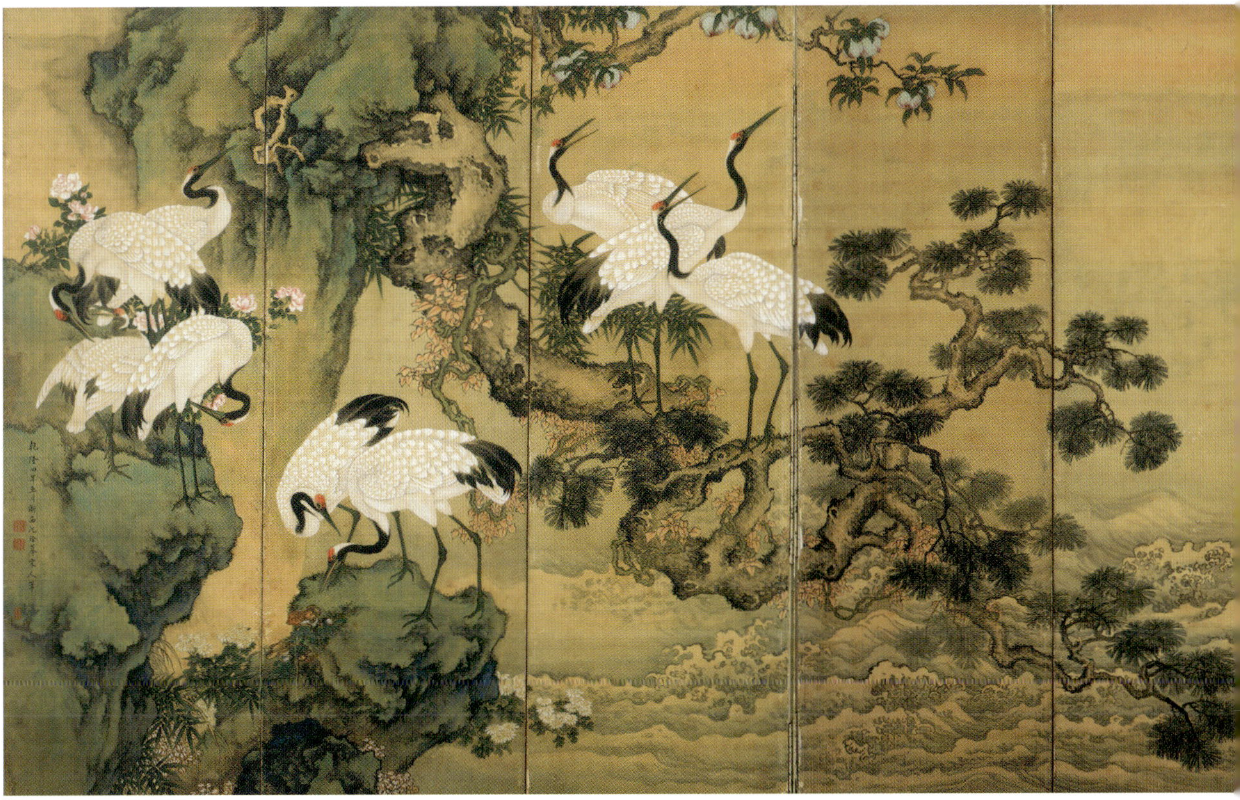

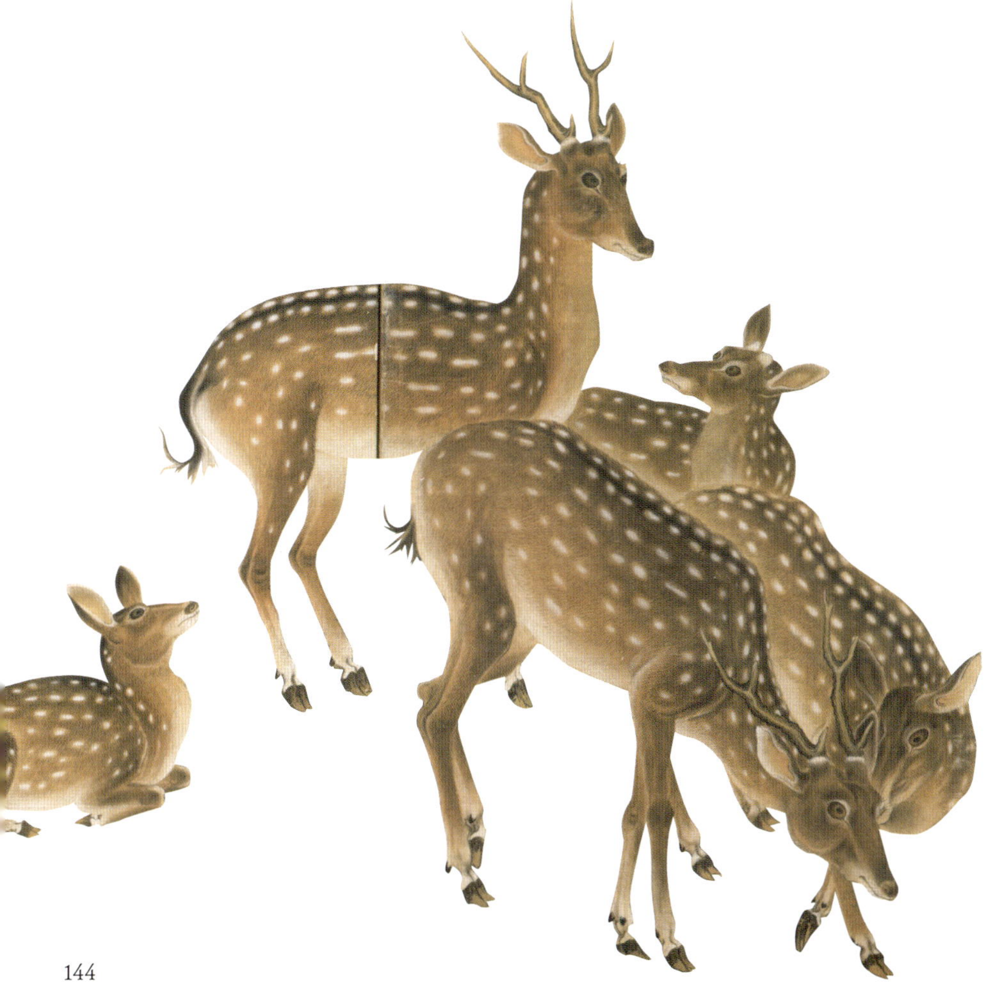

鹿鶴図屏風

沈南蘋
中国・乾隆4年(1739)
東京国立博物館

1731年(享保16)に来日した沈南蘋(1683～1760～?)の長崎滞在は2年に満たなかったが、その写生的で華やかな画風は江戸時代の画家たちに大きな影響を与えた。本図は屏風形式であることから、帰国後の南蘋が幕府の注文を受けて描いたものと考えられている。中国で鹿は、給与や褒美を意味する「禄」と音通するため、吉祥の動物とされた。

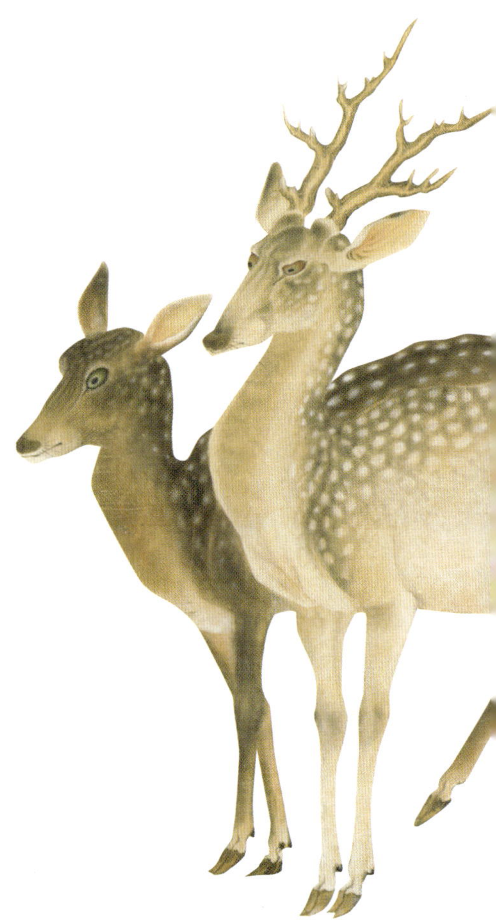

Deer and Cranes Folding Screens

Shen Nanpin
Qing dynasty, 1739
Tokyo National Museum

Shen Nanpin (1683-1760?) arrived in Japan in 1731 (Kyōhō 16) and stayed in Nagasaki a little less than two years. His naturalistic, sumptuous paintings had a big influence on Edo period painters. This pair of screens was made on order for the shogunate after Shen Nanpin had returned home to China. In China, deer are considered animals of good fortune.

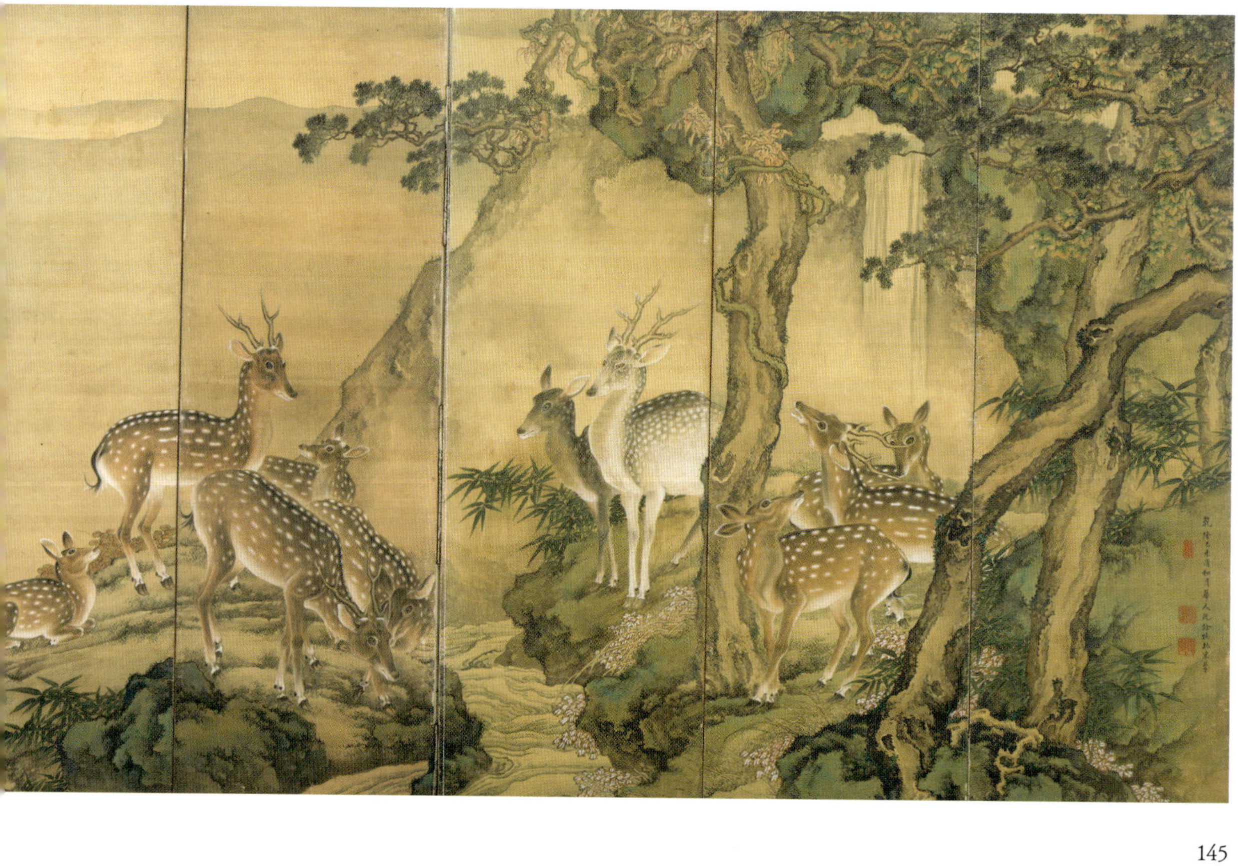

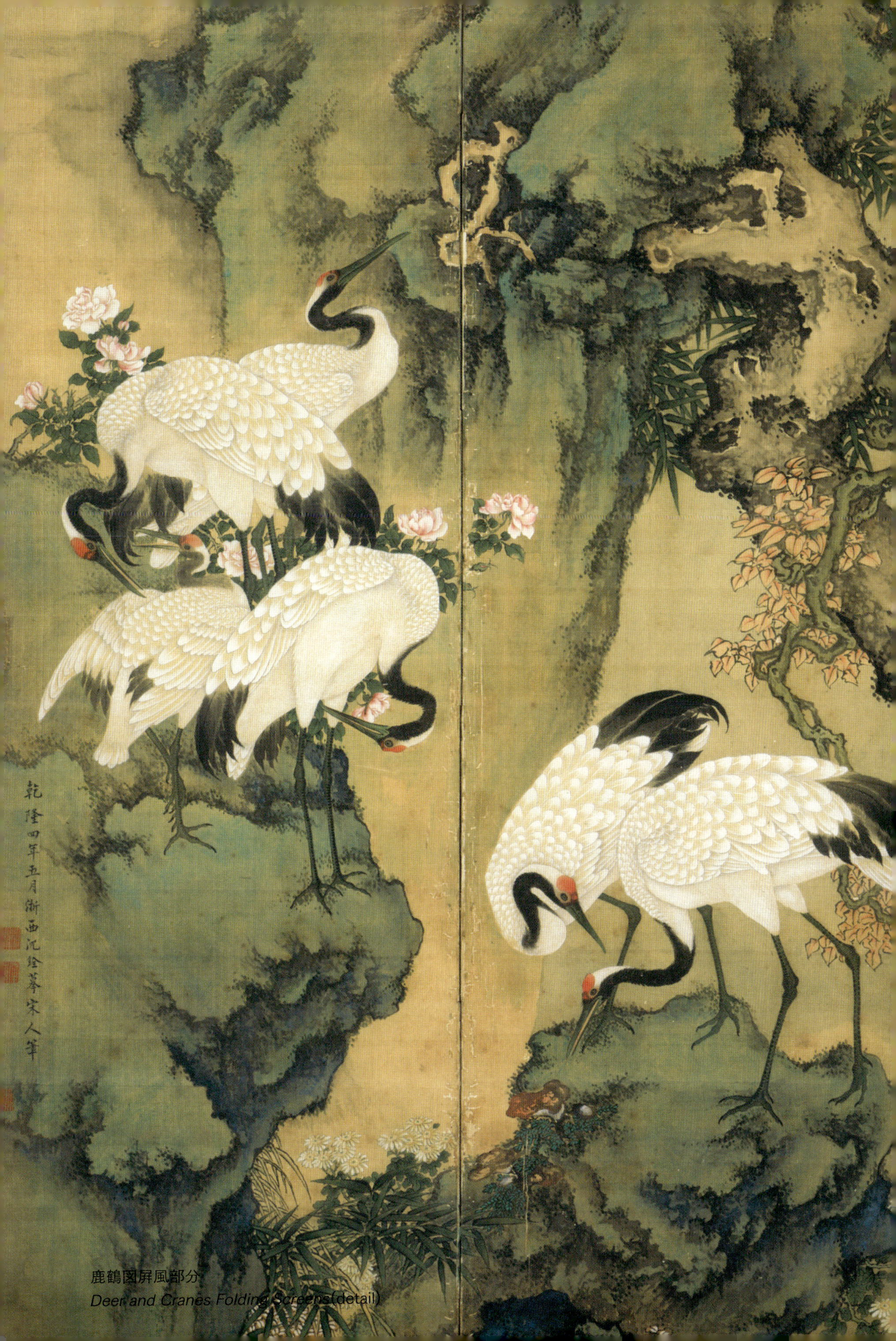

鹿鶴図屏風部分
Deer and Cranes Folding Screens(detail)

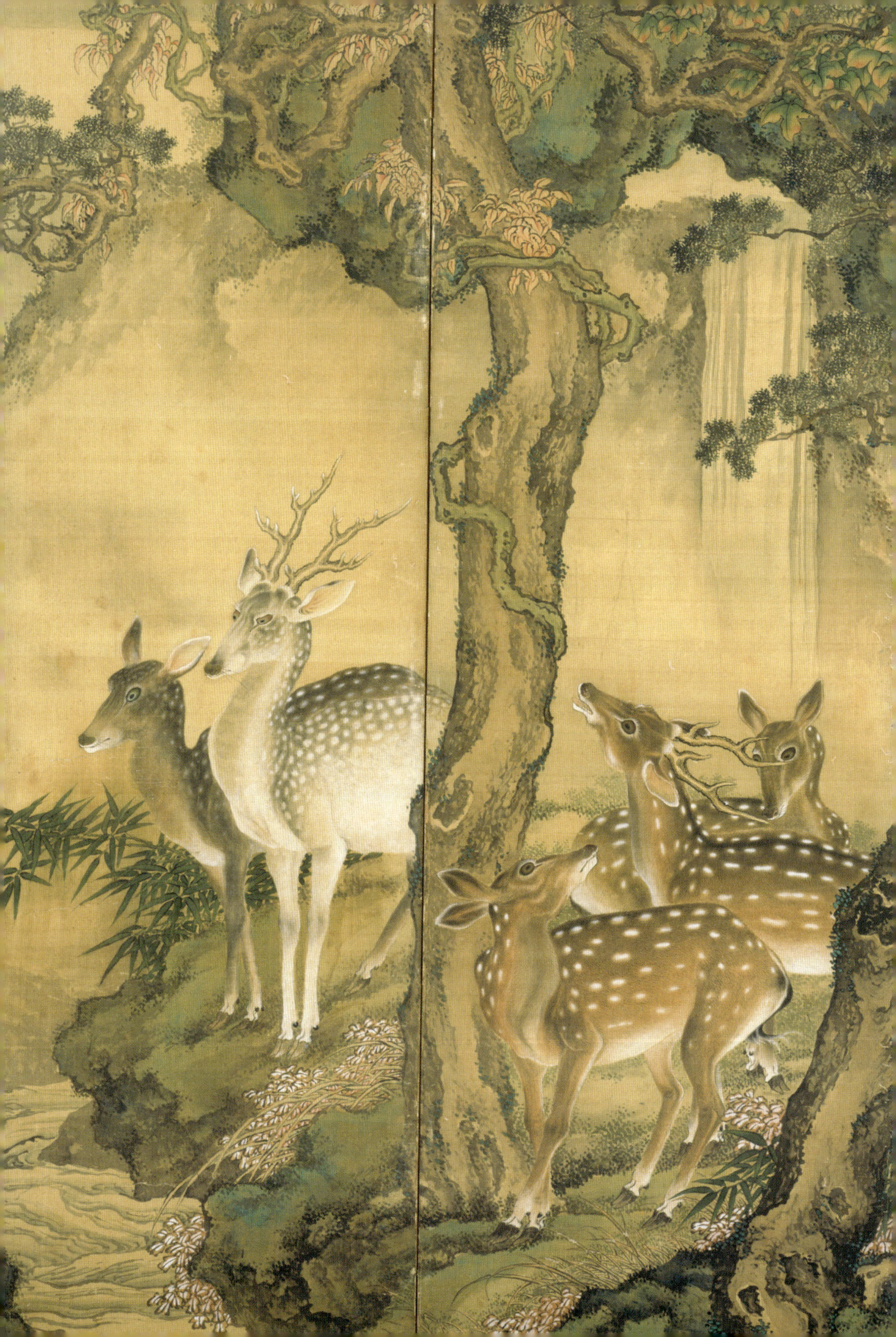

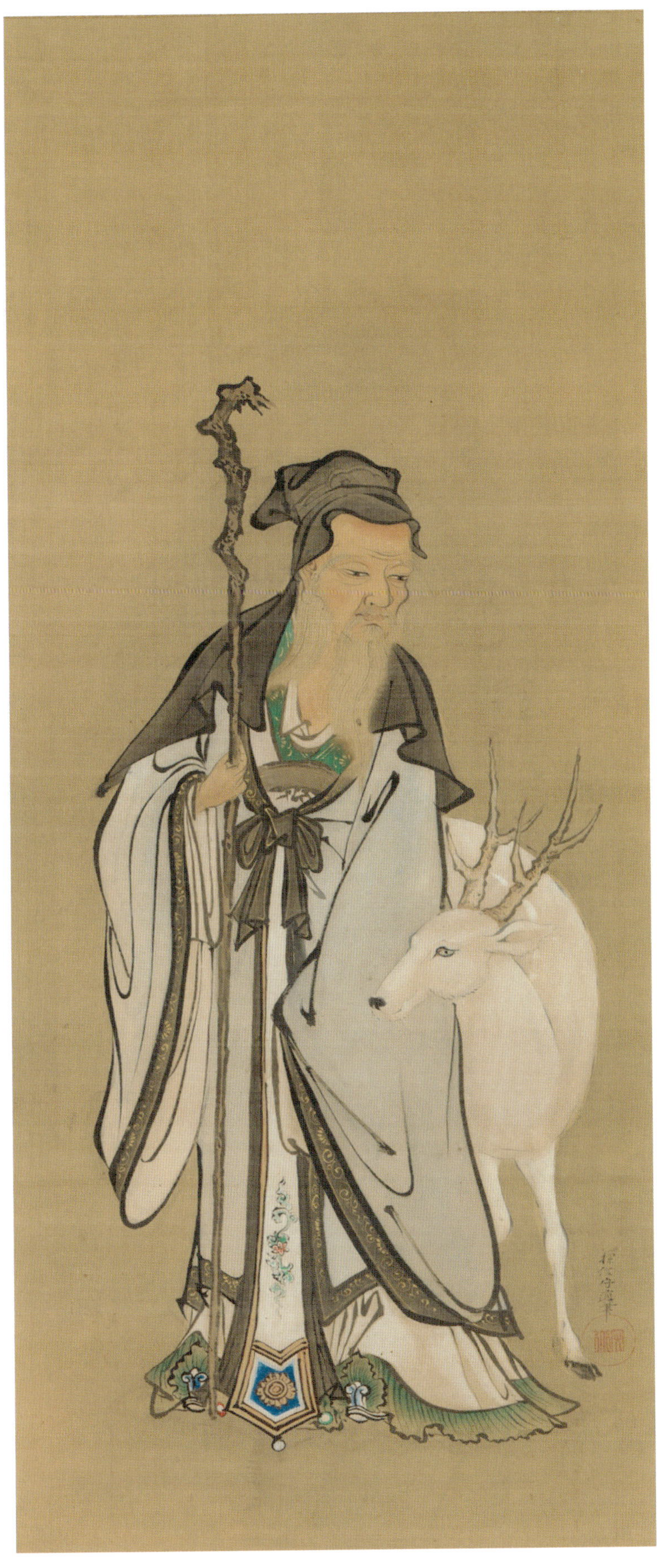

寿老人図

狩野探信
江戸時代(17〜18c)
メトロポリタン美術館

狩野探幽の長男・探信(1653〜1718)の作。寿老人は道教の神仙で、南極星の化身とされる。日本では七福神として、長頭短身の姿で表現される場合が多く、福禄寿と同一神とされる場合もある。不死の霊薬を含んだ瓢箪を帯び、長寿のシンボルである牡鹿を従える姿で表わされる。

Jurōjin

Kano Tanshin
17th-18th century
The Metropolitan Museum of Art

This is a work by Kano Tan'yū's oldest son, Tanshin (1653-1718). Jurōjin is a Taoist immortal, and is also considered to be an incarnation of the Southern Polar Star. In Japan, as one of the Seven Lucky Gods, there are many cases where he is portrayed as a man with dolichocephaly (an unusually elongated head), and there are also cases where he is conflated with the god Fukurokuju, the god of happiness, prosperity and long life. He is portrayed wearing a calabash filled with the elixir of immortality, and accompanied by a male deer, which symbolizes long life.

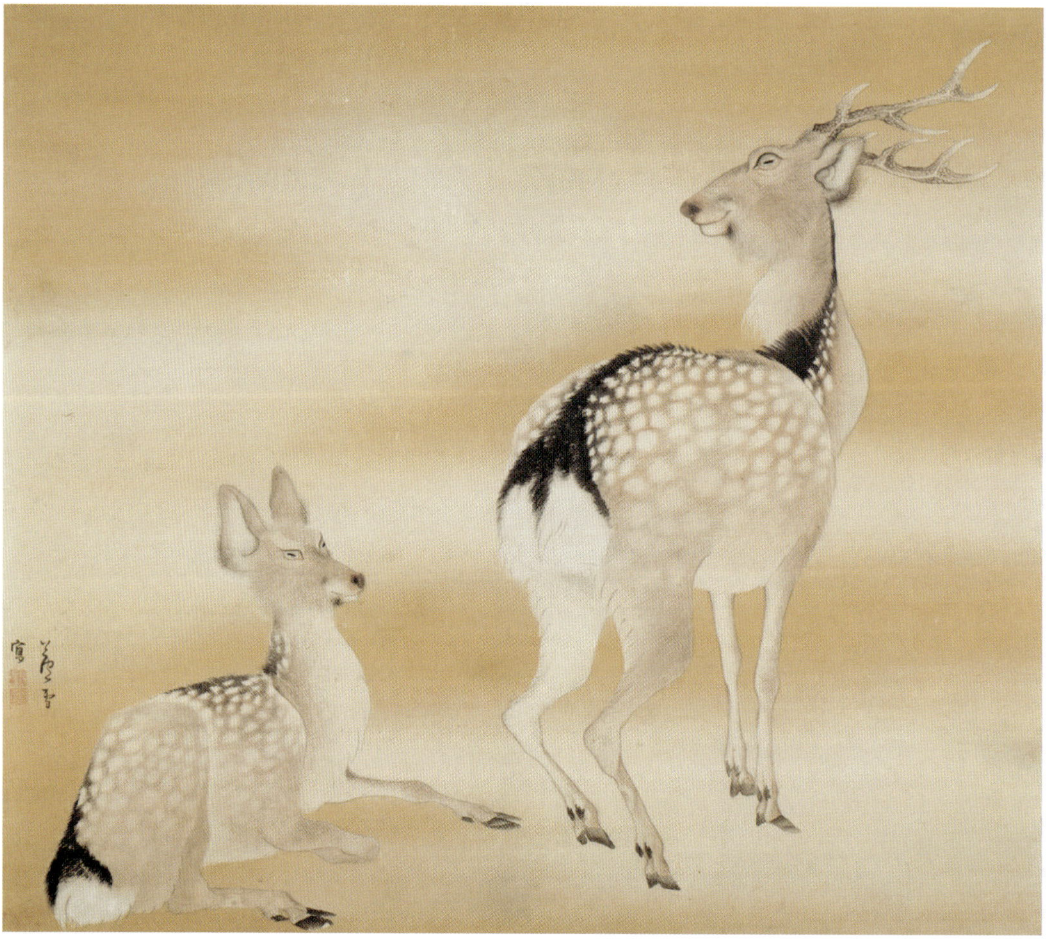

双鹿図

長沢芦雪
江戸時代(18c)
京都国立博物館

Pair of Deer

18th century
Nagasawa Rosetsu
Kyoto National Museum

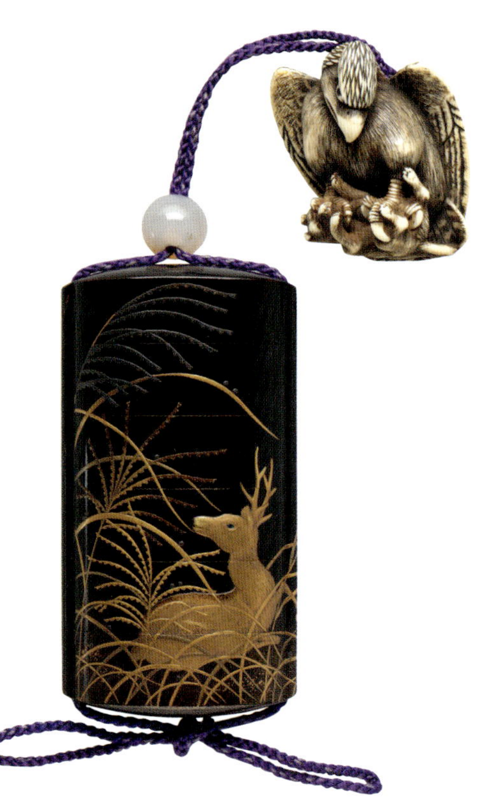

秋草鹿蒔絵印籠

江戸時代(19c)
メトロポリタン美術館

Inrō (*Case*)
with Design of Eulalia Grass and Deer

19th century
The Metropolitan Museum of Art

猿

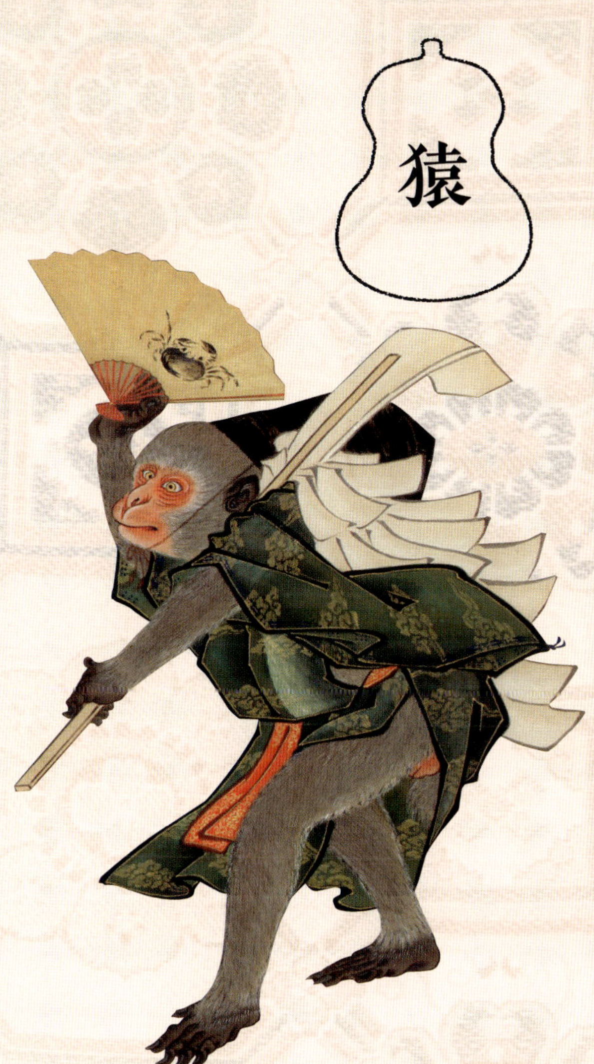

比叡山の麓に鎮座する日吉大社（祭神は大山咋神）では猿を神使として崇める。神猿と呼ばれた猿は、やがて厄を「去る」魔除けの象徴としても信仰された。また、猿が馬を守護するとの俗信から、厩につなぎ、あるいはその中で舞わせ馬の安全を祈願した。猿曳、猿飼などとも呼ばれた猿回しはその名残りで、すでに鎌倉時代から職業化していたという。江戸にも猿曳がいて、季節ごとに城中や諸藩邸内の厩を祈祷して回った。また、日光東照宮の神厩舎の有名な猿の彫刻も、この信仰に由来する。

The Monkey

At Hiyoshi Shrine at the foot of Mount Hiei, monkeys are venerated as divine messengers. The shrine's main deity of worship is Ōyamakui. The so-called *masaru*, sacred apes, are symbolic of misfortune since the character for "monkey" in Japanese is homophonous with the word for "to leave." But monkeys are also worshipped as protectors of stables and the horses in them. Traces of that veneration can be found in the monkey trainers now called *sarumawashi*, but formerly known as *saruhiki* and *sarukai*. The profession has been around since at least the Kamakura period. In the Edo period, *saruhiki* thrived and toured castles and the homes of provincial lords at New Year's to pray for the safety of horse stables. The famous wood carvings of three monkeys at Nikkō also originated within that belief.

日吉山王本地仏曼荼羅図

鎌倉時代（14c）
東京国立博物館

滋賀・延暦寺の鎮守神である日吉山王権現の神使の猿たちが、正面の階段あたりに3匹描かれている。異時同図法的に、供え物をして去っていく時間の経過を表現したものとも考えられている。日吉大社の境内には猿塚があり、神使として大切にされてきた歴史を伝えている。

Hie Sannō Mandala

14th century
Tokyo National Museum

The protective deity of Enryakuji in Shiga Prefecture is attended by monkeys, and the mandala contains three images of the animal. Using a technique of traditional Japanese painting where different scenes are depicted in one image, the work appears to illustrate the practice of votive offerings. The premises of Hiyoshi Shrine contain a so-called monkey mound, highlighting their important role as divine messengers.

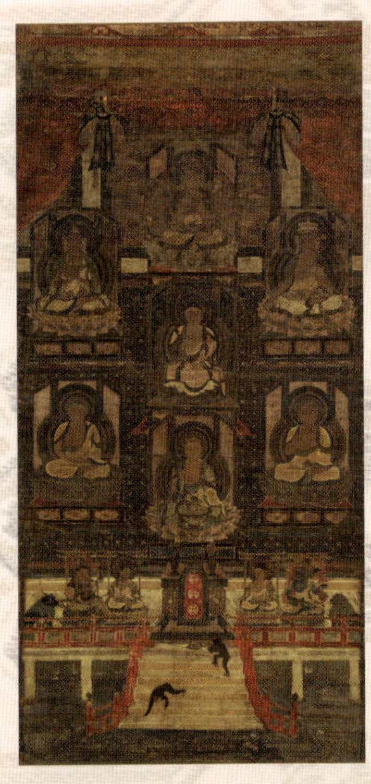

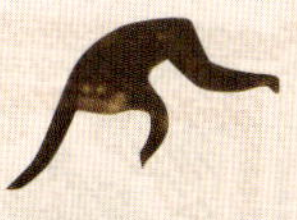

旭日猿図

鳥山石燕
江戸時代(18c)
熊本県立美術館

正月の門付けに回る猿が御幣を担ぎ、金扇をかかげる。旭日や松も添えられ、吉祥性が高まっている。筆者の鳥山石燕(1712〜88)は喜多川歌麿の師としても知られる狩野派の絵師で『画図百鬼夜行』の出版でも有名。

Monkey and the Rising Sun

Toriyama Sekien
18th century
Kumamoto Prefectural Museum of Art

The painting shows a monkey wielding a fan and carrying a *gohei*, a staff with paper streamers that would be placed at the gate of someone's property during New Year's. Paired with the rising sun and a pine tree, the monkey symbolizes wishes for good fortune in the New Year. The painter, Toriyama Sekien (1712-88), is famous as the teacher of Kitagawa Utamaro and for his book of supernatural beings, *Hyakki yagyō*.

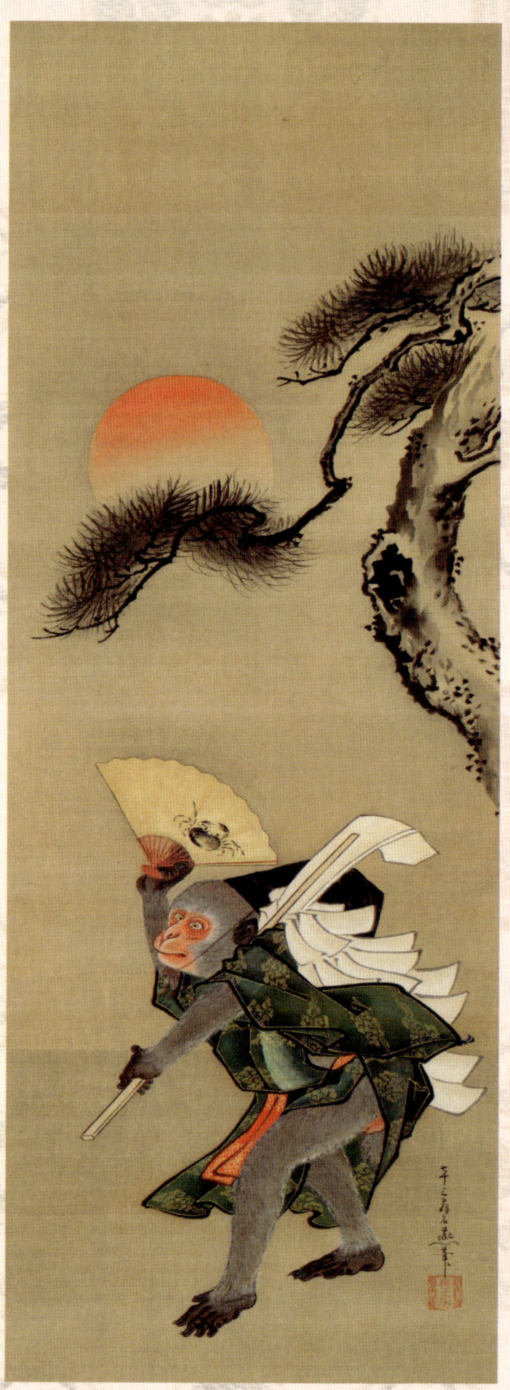

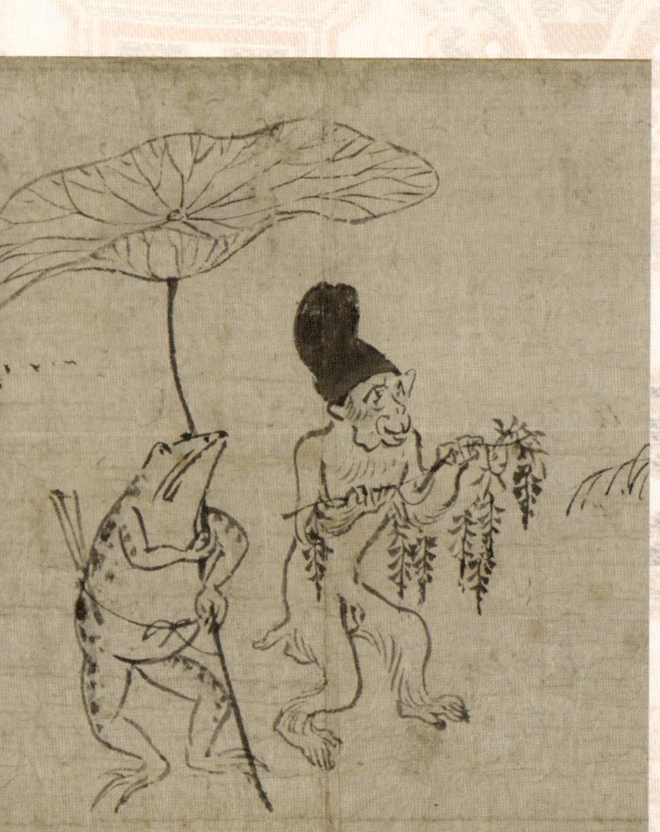

重要文化財

鳥獣人物戯画 断簡

平安時代(12c)
東京国立博物館

Important Cultural Property

Scrolls of Frolicking Animals
(Handscroll Fragment)

12th century
Tokyo National Museum

重要文化財

巌樹遊猿図屏風

式部輝忠
室町時代(16c)
京都国立博物館

式部輝忠(生没年不詳)は、16世紀中頃に駿河や相模など東国で活躍したと推測される室町後期の画家。鎌倉の祥啓や伊豆を出自とする狩野派に連なる画家から学んだものと考えられている。中国北宋時代の易元吉などが得意とした聚猿図などに倣ったものだろうが、猿が所狭しと描かれる本図は、百猿図とも言えるような作品。擬人化された猿の表情が目をひく。

Important Cultural Property

Monkeys on Trees and Rocks

Shikibu Terutada
16th century
Kyoto National Museum

Shikibu Terutada (dates unknown) is thought to have worked during the mid-16th century in Suruga and Sagami, areas in the eastern regions of Japan. It is assumed that he either studied painting with Keison in Kamakura or among the Kano school that originated in Izu. He may have also had access to paintings by the Northern Song artist Yi Yuanji, who excelled in depicting monkeys. Paintings like this screen are referred to as "images of a hundred (many) monkeys." The animals' expressions are almost human, making this an intriguing work of art.

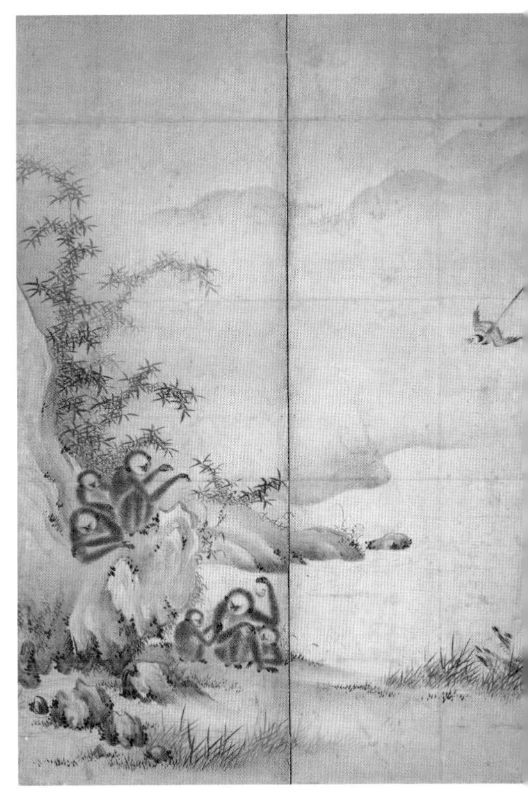

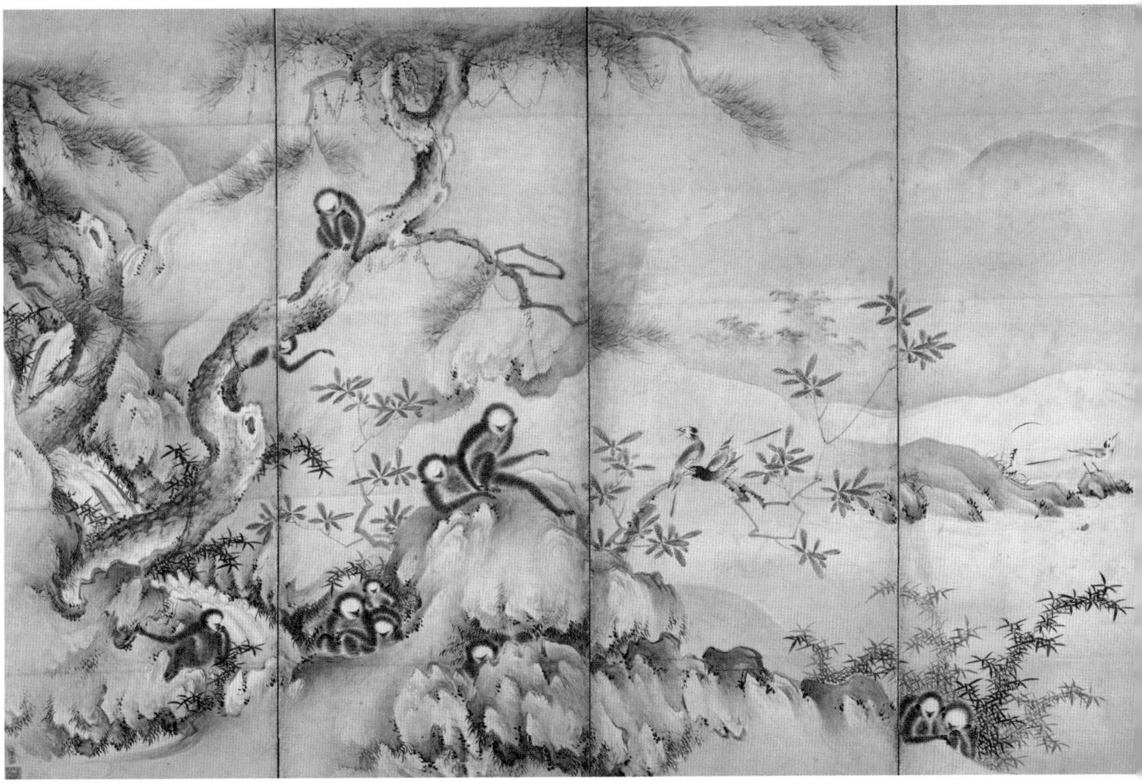

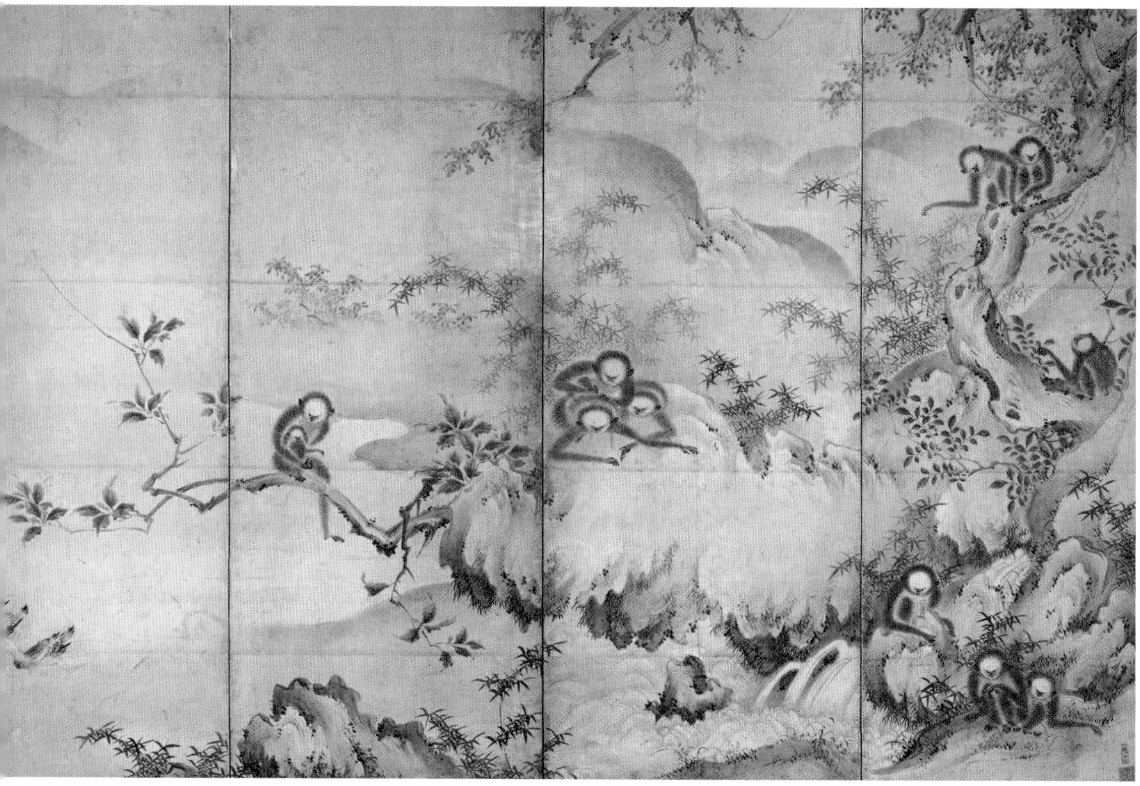

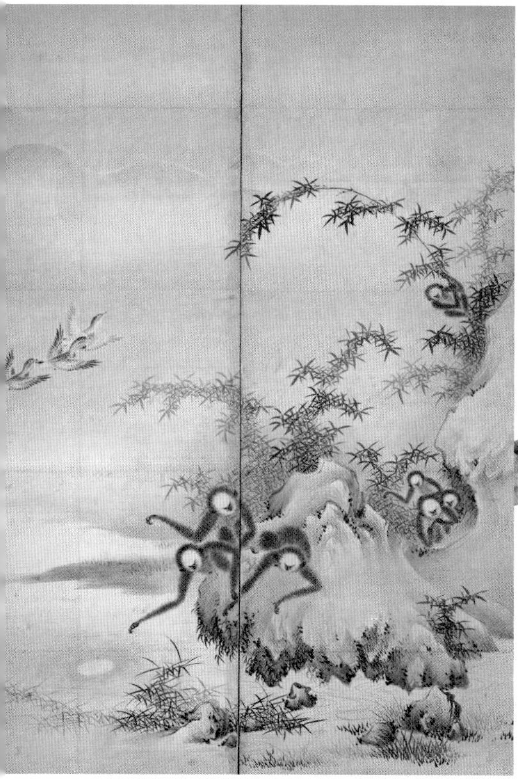

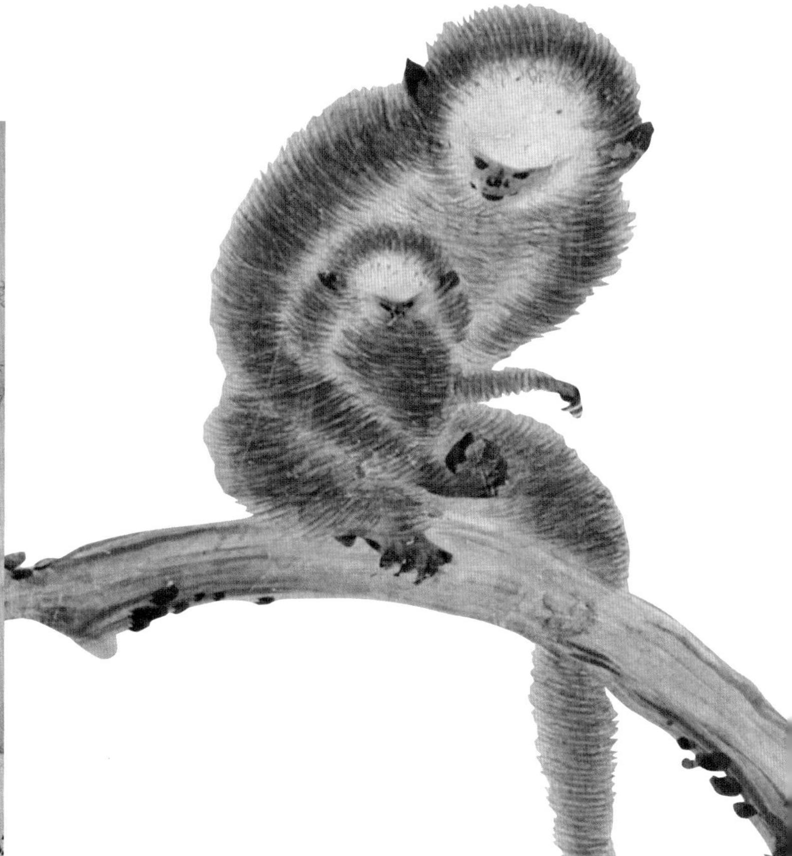

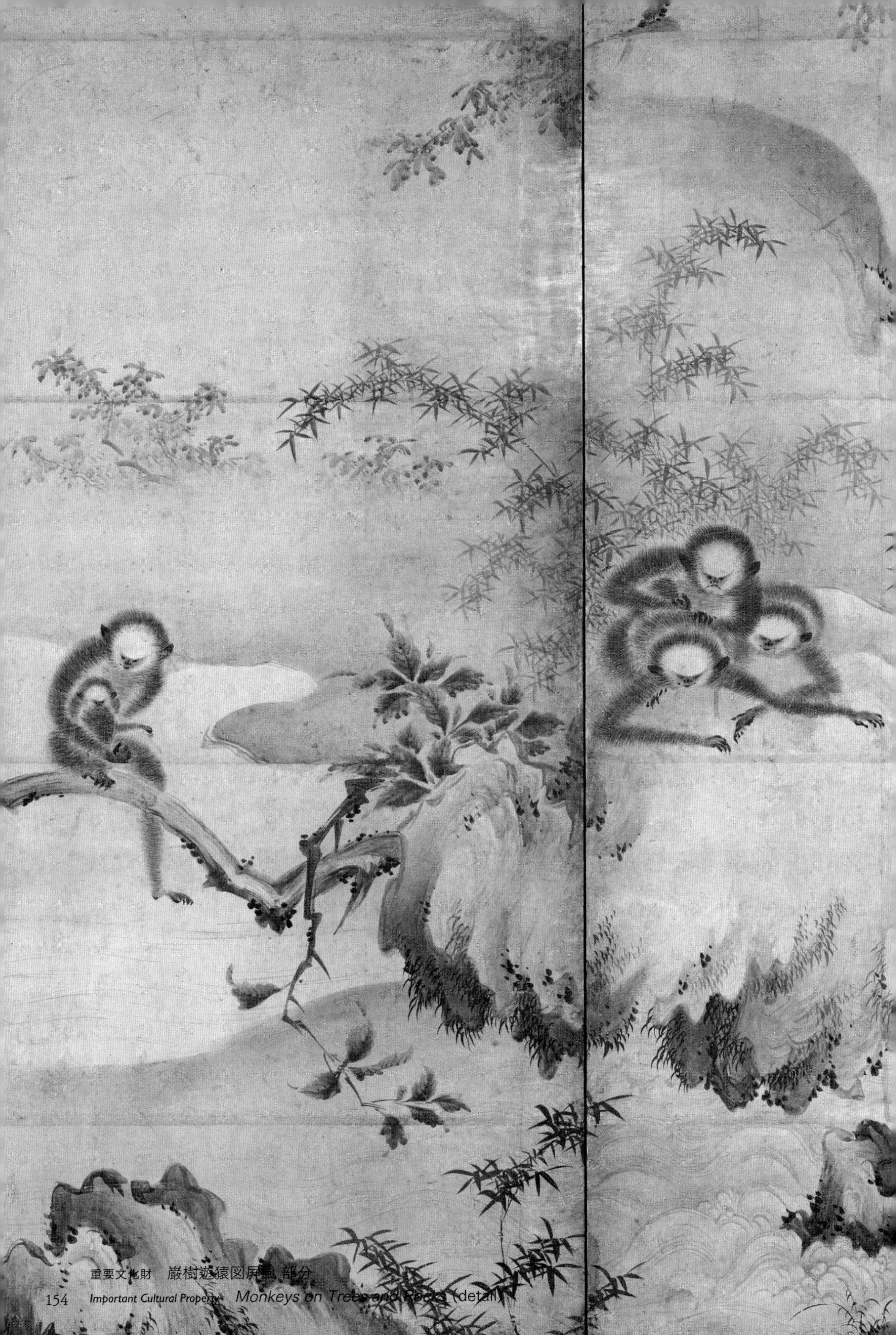

重要文化財　巌樹遊猿図屏風 部分
Important Cultural Property　*Monkeys on Trees and Rocks* (detail)

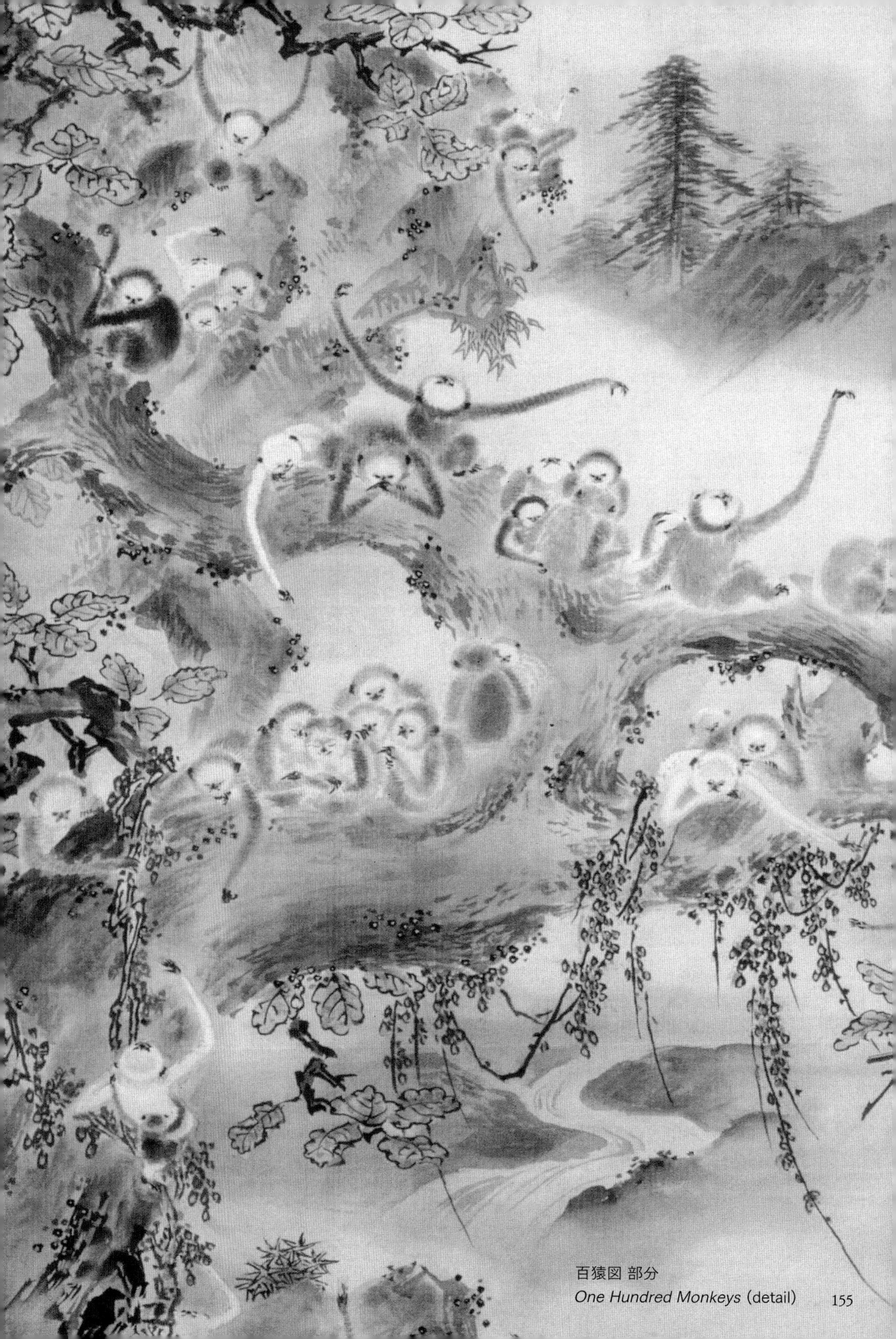

百猿図 部分
One Hundred Monkeys (detail)

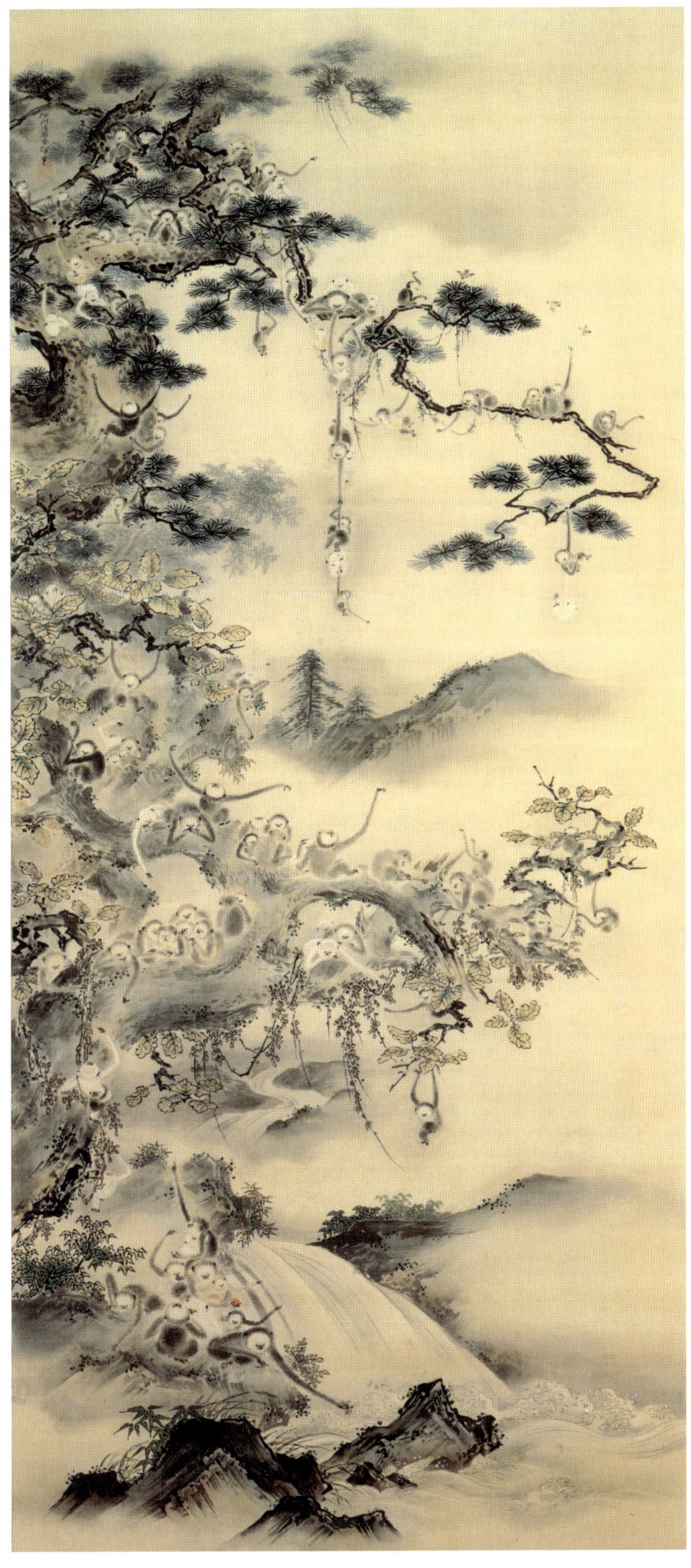

百猿図

狩野栄信
享和2〜文化13年（1802〜16）
静岡県立美術館

描かれるのは100匹の猿。長寿を寿ぎ延年を祈願する算賀の席などに飾られたものだろう。筆者の狩野栄信（1775〜1828）は、幕府お抱えの奥絵師の筆頭格である木挽町狩野家の当主。

One Hundred Monkeys

Kano Eishin
1802-16
Shizuoka Prefectural
Museum of Art

The work literally shows one hundred monkeys. A painting such as this can be imagined decorating the seat of honor during a celebration of long life. The painter, Kano Eishin (1775-1828), was the head of the Kobikichō Kano atelier, which served the shogunate.

封侯図

森周峰・狙仙・徹山・雄仙
文化11年(1814)

周峰(1738～1823)が蜂を、弟の猿描き名人・狙仙(1747?～1821)が猿を、それぞれの実子徹山(1775～1841)・雄仙(1780～1851)が蜘蛛の巣と藤を描いた合作。蜂と猿は領地を与えられて諸侯に列する「封侯」に音が通ずることから中国では吉祥の画題とされ、蜘蛛は別名(喜蛛または喜子)に「喜」が含まれることからめでたい画題であった。多くの種入り豆果の藤は、子孫繁栄などを表すと考えられ、本図は吉祥性が増幅されている。親子兄弟そろって、森派繁栄の願いが幾重にも託された欲張りな内容と言える。

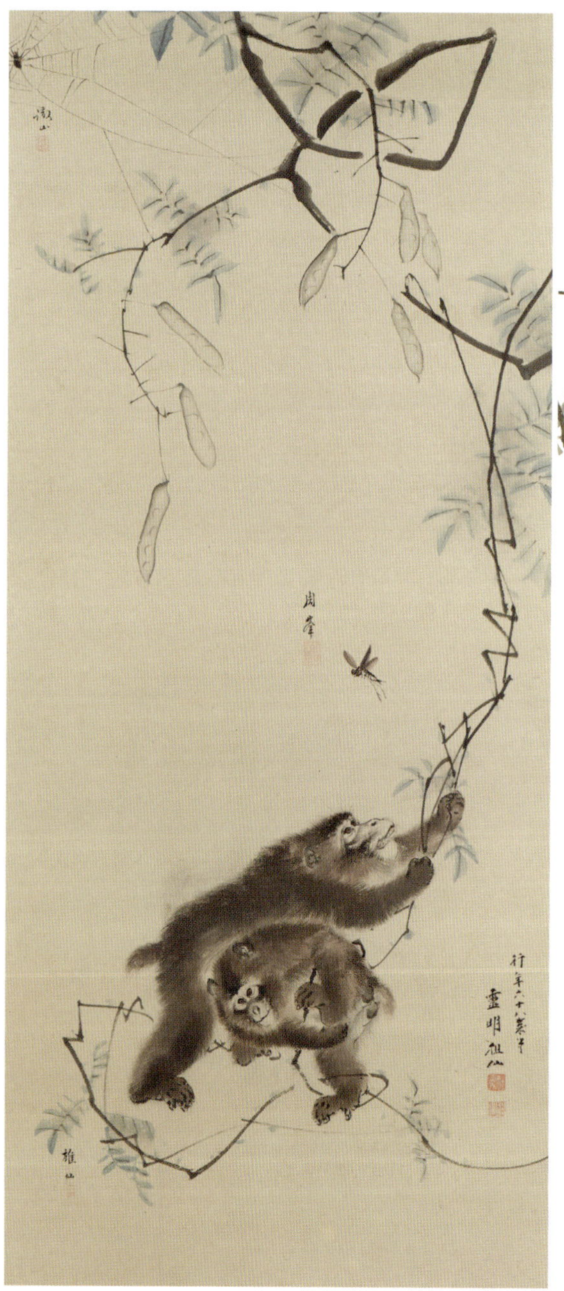

Monkeys and a Bee

Mori Shūhō, Sosen, Tetsuzan,
and Yūsen
1814

The bee was painted by Mori Shūhō (1738-1823) while his younger brother, the famous painter Mori Sosen (1747?-1821) produced the monkeys. His sons, Tetsuzan (1775-1841) and Yūsen (1780-1851), together added the spider web and the wisteria. As explained earlier, bees and monkeys in combination stand for "feudal enfeoffment," thus conveying benevolent meaning. Spiders in Japan are associated with joy, whereas the many legumes produced by wisterias stand for fecundity. All in all, the painting is a manifestation of auspicious meaning. The collaboration between different generations of the Mori family in producing the work might also represent a wish for prosperity for their clan.

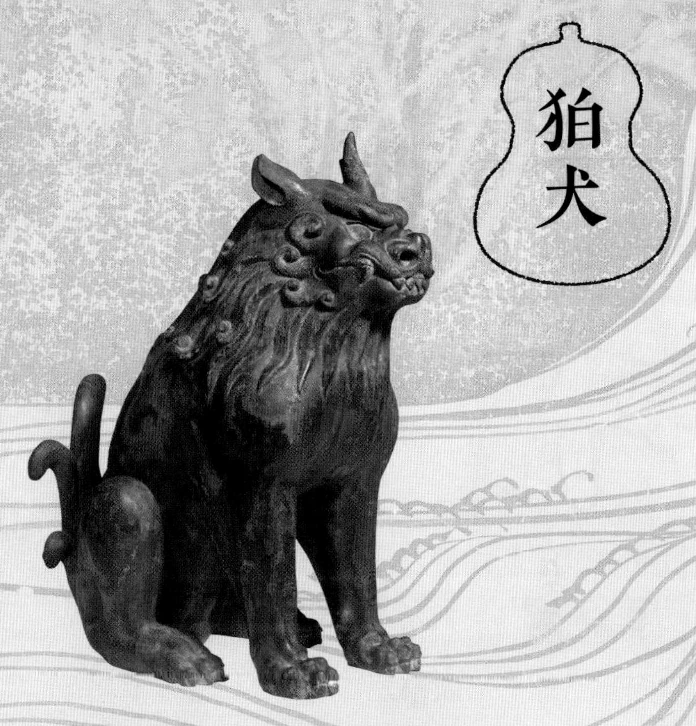

狛犬

神社の社殿前などに置かれ、日本人にとっては馴染み深い動物だが、その起源についてはよく分かっていない。当初は、インドや中国で仏菩薩のかたわらに置かれた守護獣ライオンを象ったものだったが、平安時代になると獅子と狛犬とがセットで用いられるようになったらしい。一般には口を開く阿形と閉じる吽形とが対となっているが、厳密には阿形は獅子で、吽形の方が狛犬であるという。狛犬は一角を備えているため、中国の瑞獣である「兕(じ)」や「獬豸(かいち)」「天鹿」などと同一視されることもある。古くは宮中の調度品として用いられたが、時代が下るとともに拝殿の床上から拝殿前、さらには鳥居の側へと屋外に置かれるようになり、素材も木製から石製へと変化していった。同じく時代の経過とともに、獅子と狛犬とは混同され、ほとんど見分けがつかない形状を示している場合も多い。邪気を払い聖域を守る鎮獣として、また仏法護持の守護獣と位置づけられている。

重要文化財
狛犬(吽形)
鎌倉時代 (13c)
奈良国立博物館

Important Cultural Property
Guardian Dog
(um-gyo style)
13th century
Nara National Museum

The Guardian Dog

Sculptures of guardian dogs can be found at the gates of shrines, making these animals familiar sights for people in Japan. Their origins, however, are unclear. Lions can be found as protectors of bodhisattvas in Indian and Chinese Buddhist iconography. In the Heian period, Chinese lions and guardian dogs seem to have started appearing in pairs, often with one having the mouth open saying "aum" and the other closed voicing "um." Strictly speaking, Chinese lions are rendered with their mouths open, while guardian dogs are shown with closed mouths. Guardian dogs carry one horn on their heads and for that reason are likened in China to auspicious beings, such as *xiezhi* and heavenly deer. In ancient times, guardian dogs were used as parts of palace furnishings, but with time they were placed in front of beds and halls of worship. Guardian dogs positioned at *torii* gates of shrines were initially made of wood and later stone. With their change in use, the iconographies of Chinese lions and guardian dogs were merged together and they are often indistinguishable from one another. They protect sacred spaces by warding off evil and safeguarding the Buddhist faith.

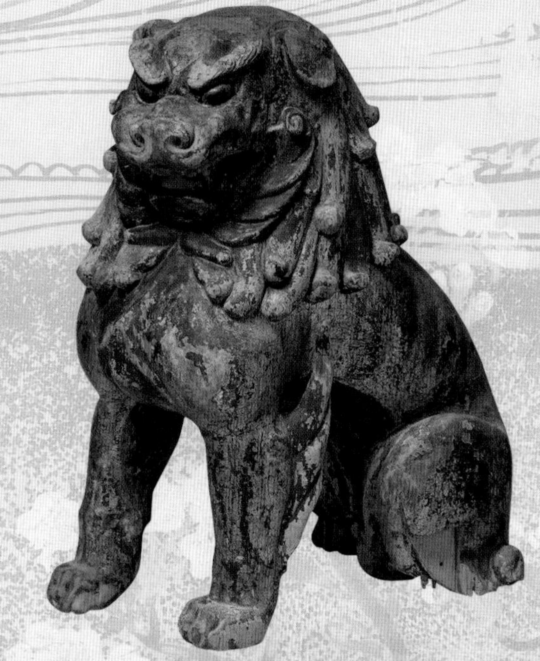

狛犬
鎌倉時代(13c半ば)
メトロポリタン美術館

Guardian Dog
Mid-13th century
The Metropolitan Museum of Art

高野四所明神像

室町時代(16c)
メトロポリタン美術館

高野四所明神とは、高野山の麓にある丹生都比売神社の祭神で、高野の地主神である高野(狩場)明神と丹生明神、それに鎌倉時代に加えられた気比明神と厳島明神のこと。正面の階上には、阿吽の獅子と狛犬とが対坐している。階段下の白黒二匹の犬は、高野明神の連れで、空海を高野山に案内したとされる。

Kōya Shisho Myōjin

16th century
The Metropolitan Museum of Art

Kōya Shisho Myōjin is a group of deities worshipped at Niutsu Hime Shrine at the foot of Mount Kōya. The group combines the main Shinto deities of Mount Kōya, Kōya Myōjin and Niu Myōjin, as well as Kehi Myōjin and Itsukushima Myōjin who were added during the Kamakura period. At the top of the stairs, a Chinese lion and a guardian dog face each other, forming the syllables "aum" and "um" with their mouths. At the bottom of the stairs, a black and a white dog are shown who, according to legend, accompanied Kōya Myōjin and led the monk Kūkai to the site of Mount Kōya where he founded a temple.

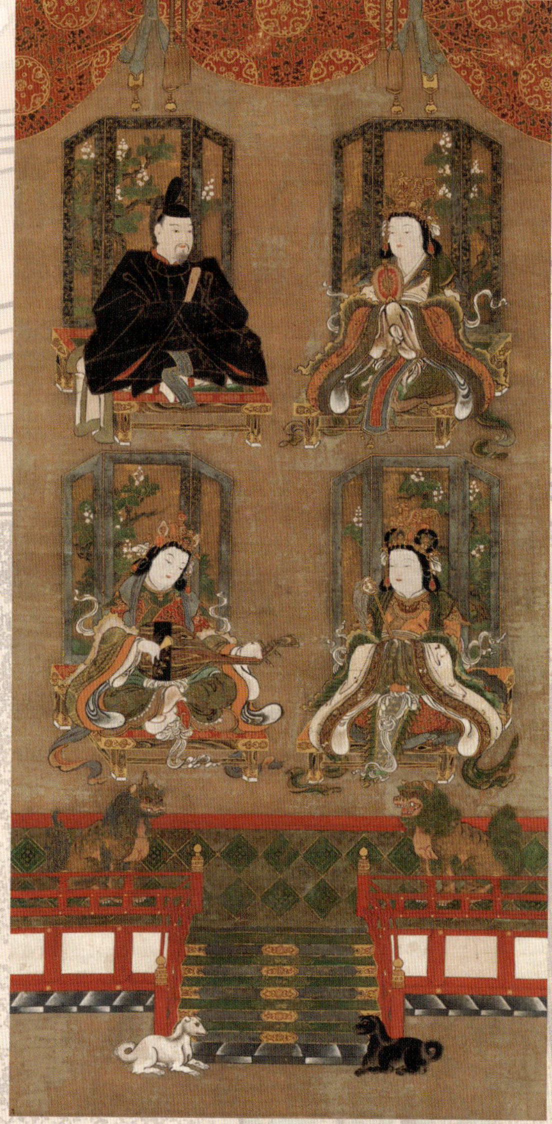

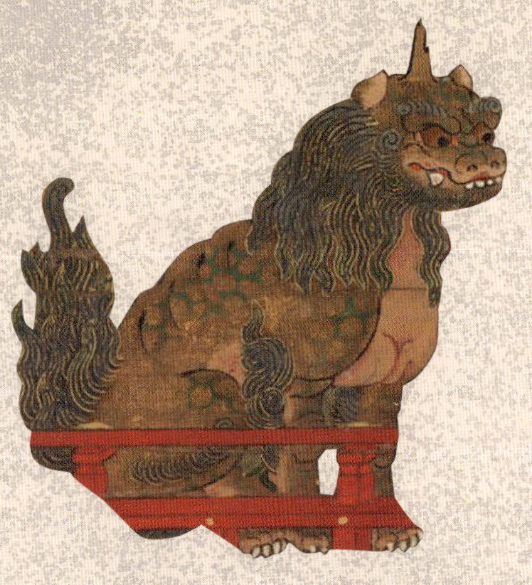

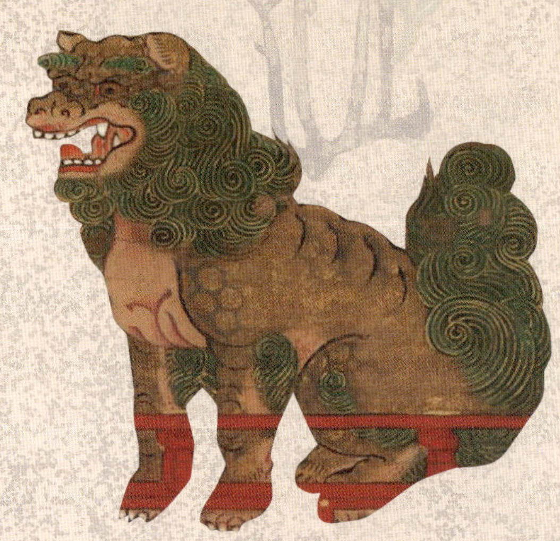

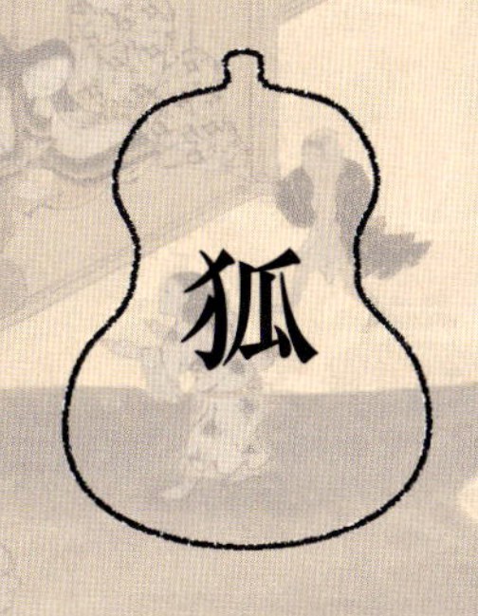

狐は、日本で古くから穀物神として信仰された豊穣神・稲荷の神使。京都・伏見稲荷大社を中心に全国に広がる稲荷信仰においては、この狐を尊崇する。また、富の象徴とされる密教の秘神・茶枳尼天（だきに）が中世以来、稲荷神と同一視されたことにより、茶枳尼天を白虎と同一視する信仰もうまれた。

The Fox

Foxes have been worshiped in Japan since ancient times as part of the cult of grain and rice deities. The Fushimi Inari Shrine in Kyoto is the center for the veneration of Inari, the rice deity. There, foxes are revered as symbols for abundance. During the medieval period, the Inari deity had become the avatar of Dakini (J. Dakiniten), a female spirit in esoteric Buddhism. For that reason, Dakini is often shown with a white tiger.

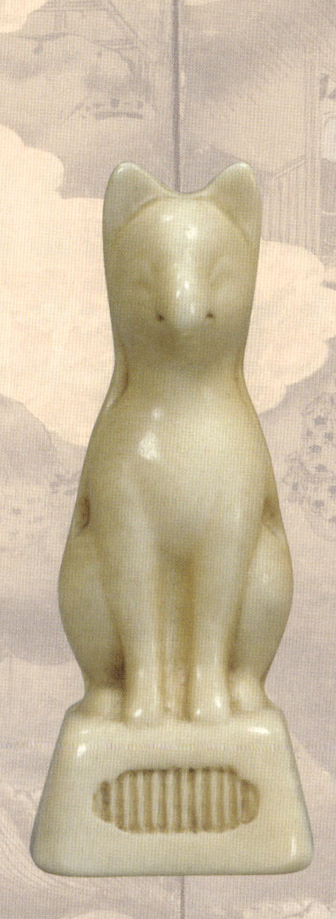

狐牙彫根付
江戸時代(19c)
東京国立博物館

Netsuke of Fox
19th century
Tokyo National Museum

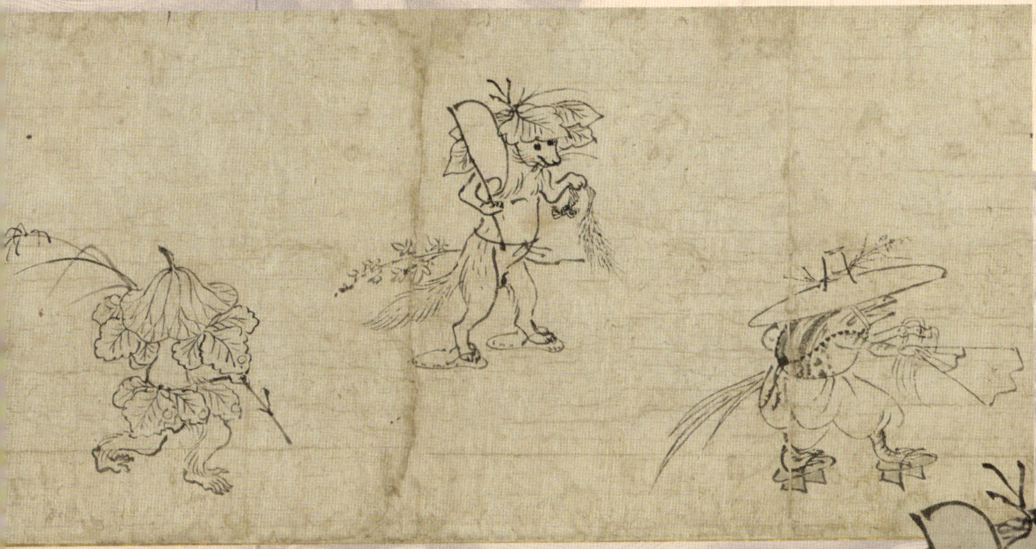

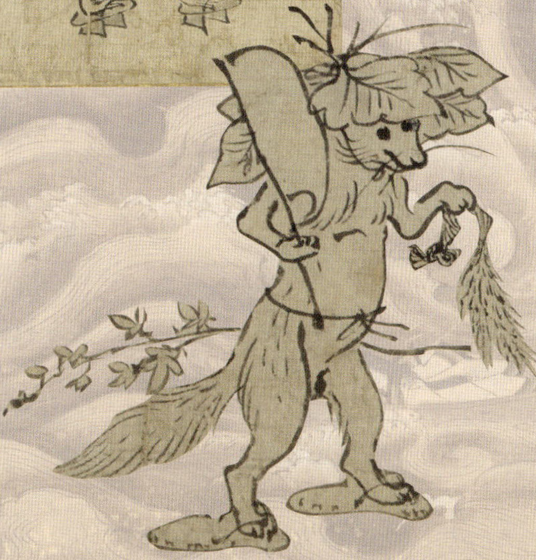

重要文化財
鳥獣人物戯画断簡
平安時代(12c)
東京国立博物館

Important Cultural Property
Scrolls of Frolicking Animals (*Handscroll Fragment*)
12th century
Tokyo National Museum

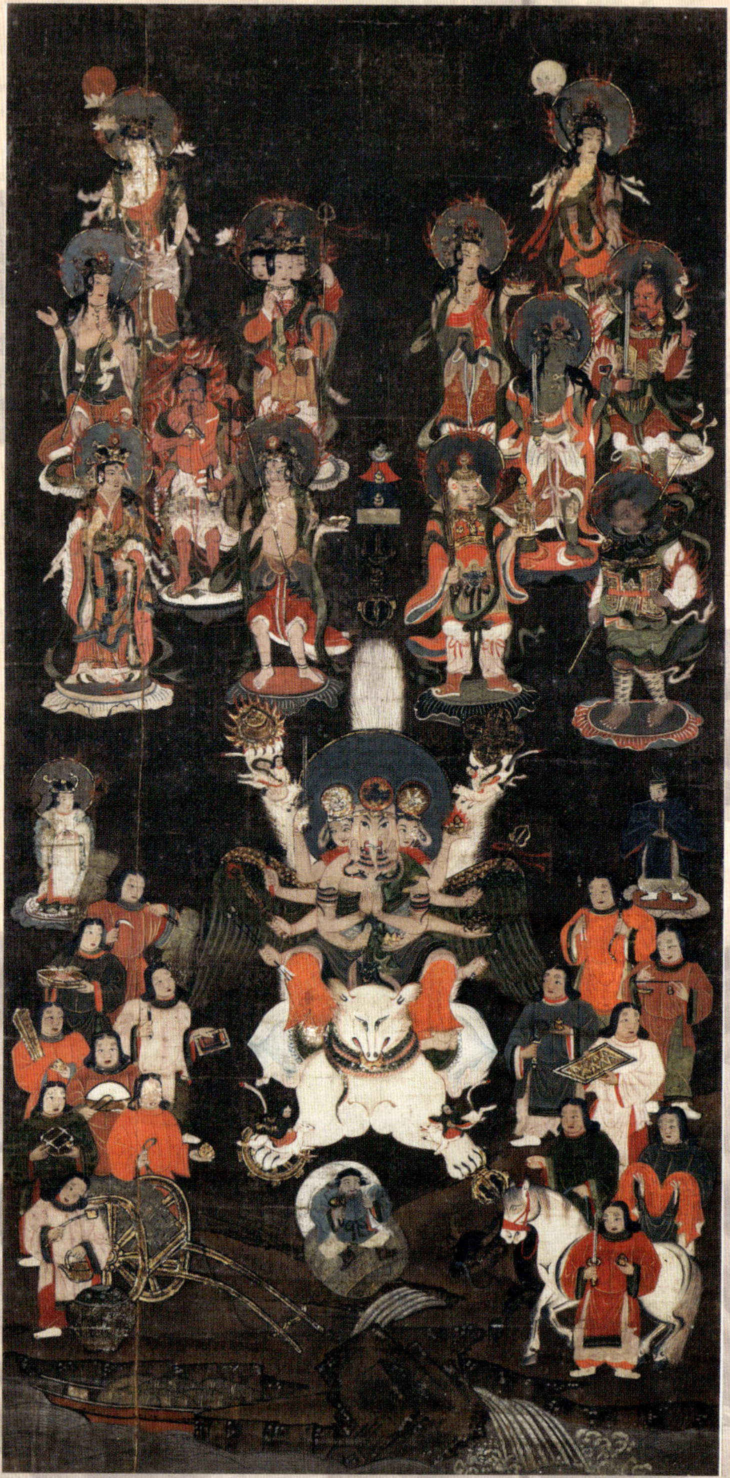

荼枳尼天曼荼羅図

室町時代(16c)
東京国立博物館

荼枳尼は梵語ダーキニーの音訳。古代インドでは裸身で虚空を駆け、人肉を食う魔女だったが、仏教に取り入れられてからは羅刹女の類として扱われた。大黒天の眷属とされ、6か月前に人の死を予見するという。やがて日本の稲荷信仰と習合し、白狐に乗る天女の姿で表現された。狐の精とされ、稲荷権現、飯綱権現とも同一視される。剣や宝珠・稲束・鎌などを持物とする。本図は、画面中央に3面12臂の荼枳尼天を大きく描き、周囲には牛や馬、十六童子などが配される。

Dakini Mandala

16th century
Tokyo National Museum

In ancient India, Dakini was thought of as a naked female demon flying around and feasting on human flesh. Eventually, she was enveloped into the Buddhist canon as a *rakshasi*, a man-eating being, before being viewed as an attendant of Mahakala (J. Daikokuten), a Buddhist deity that in Japan is one of the Seven Gods of Good Fortune. Eventually, Dakini came to be associated with the Inari cult and was depicted as a heavenly maiden riding a white fox. She was thought to represent the spirit of foxes. For that reason, she is also considered a manifestation of Inari and foxes. Among her accoutrements are a sword, jewels, a sheaf of rice, and a sickle. This image shows a large three-faced, twelve-armed Dakini flanked by sixteen attendants, an oxen, and a white horse.

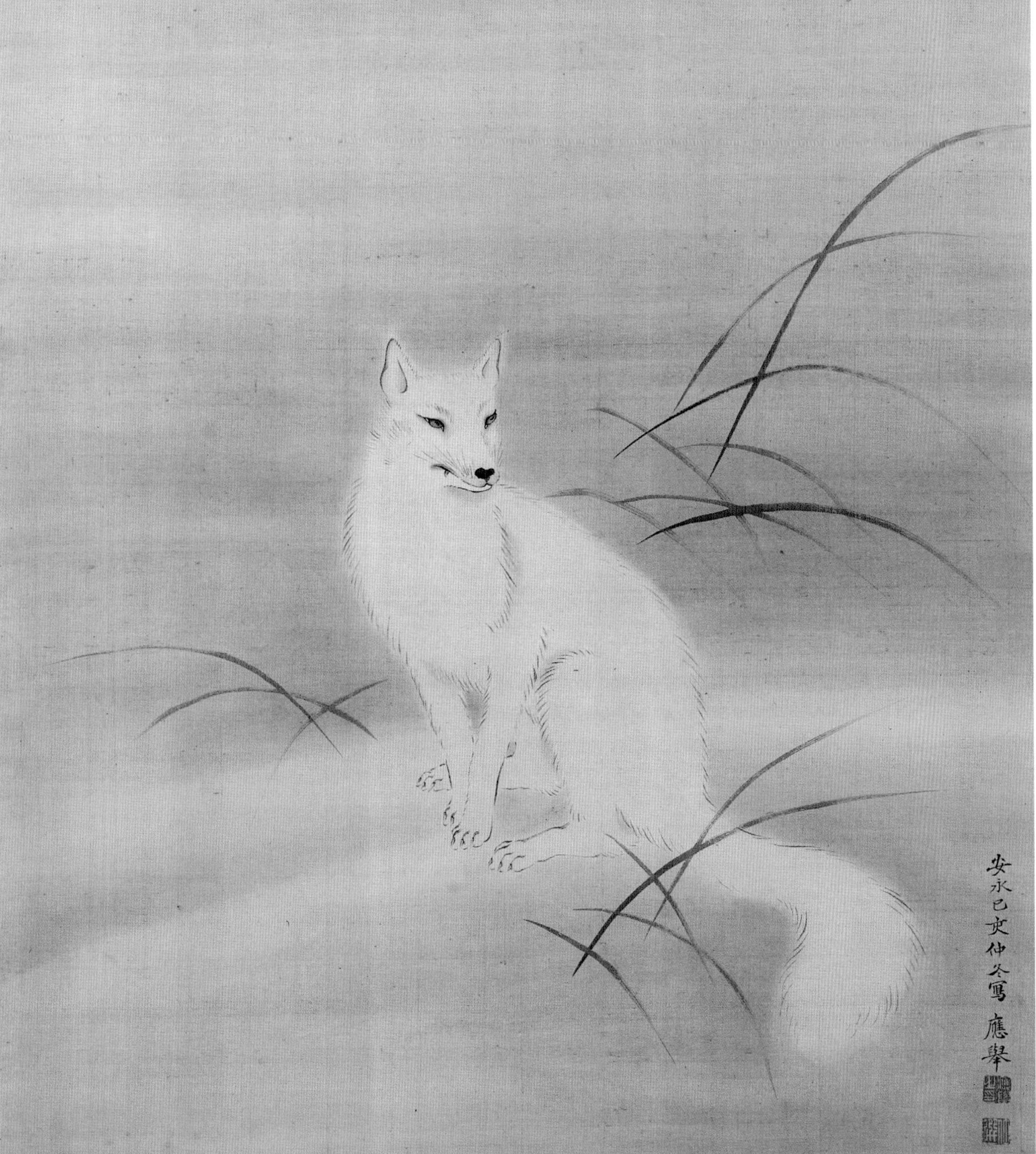
安永己亥仲冬寫 應擧

白狐図

円山応挙
安永8年(1779)

白狐は九尾狐や玄狐とともに「延喜式」で「上瑞」に位置づけられる。本来、白い動物は吉兆として尊崇されてきたのだが、本図にはむしろもの悲しさが漂うことから浄瑠璃「葛の葉」に登場する葛の葉狐のイメージの投影を見る識者もいる。この話は、人間の夫と狐の妻という異類婚姻譚。狩人に追われているところを、安倍保名に助けられた和泉国信太の森の白狐が、人間の女に化けて結婚する。夫婦は一子をもうけたが、やがて正体が知れて古巣に帰ることに。そのときに詠んだ歌が「恋しくば尋ね来て見よ 和泉なる 信太の森の うらみ葛の葉」。確かに、愛児に後ろ髪を引かれるような哀しみの姿を思わせる。

White Fox

Maruyama Ōkyo
1779

Along with with nine-tailed foxes and apparition foxes, white foxes belong to the most elevated category of auspicious beings. Since old days, white animals were revered as harbingers of good omens. This painting may also refer to the puppet theater play *Kuzunoha*, where a laborer encounters the projection of a fox against an arrowroot leaf (*kuzu no ha*). The tale, as many others like it, features a marriage between a man and a fox. Abe no Yasuna rescued a white fox from hunters in the woods of Shinoda in Izumi Province. The fox later appeared to him in the shape of a woman, whom he married. Although she bore him a child, the fox soon disappeared by uttering the poem: "If you love me, visit me in the woods of Shinoda, under an arrowroot leaf." Truly, this image seems filled with the sadness of longing for the fox's child.

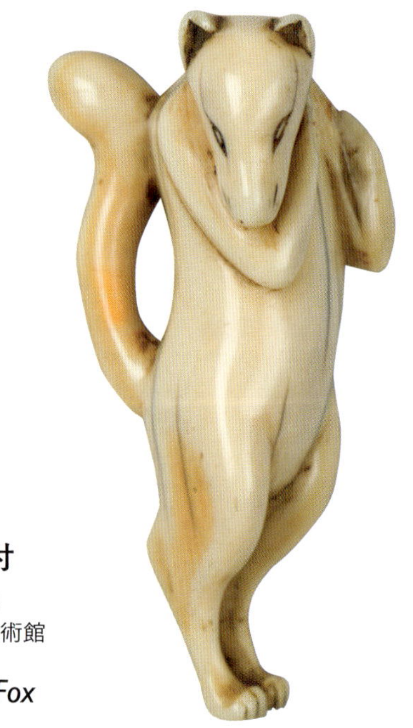

狐牙彫根付

江戸時代(19c)
メトロポリタン美術館

Netsuke of Fox

19th century
The Metropolitan Museum of Art

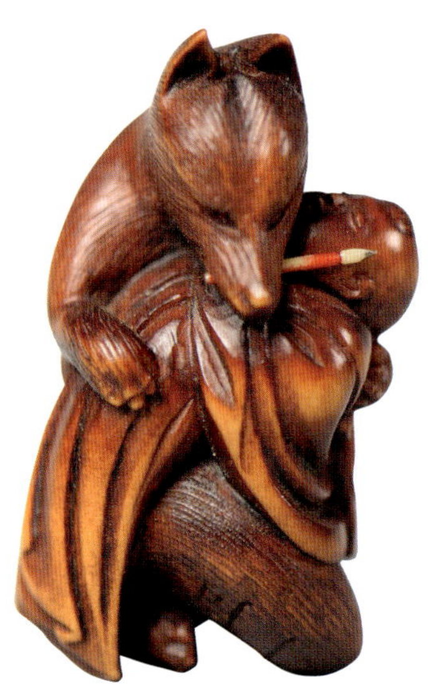

葛の葉狐木彫根付

江戸時代(19c)
メトロポリタン美術館

Netsuke of Fox Holding Baby from the Kabuki Play "Shinoda Zuma, Kuzunoha"

19th century
The Metropolitan Museum of Art

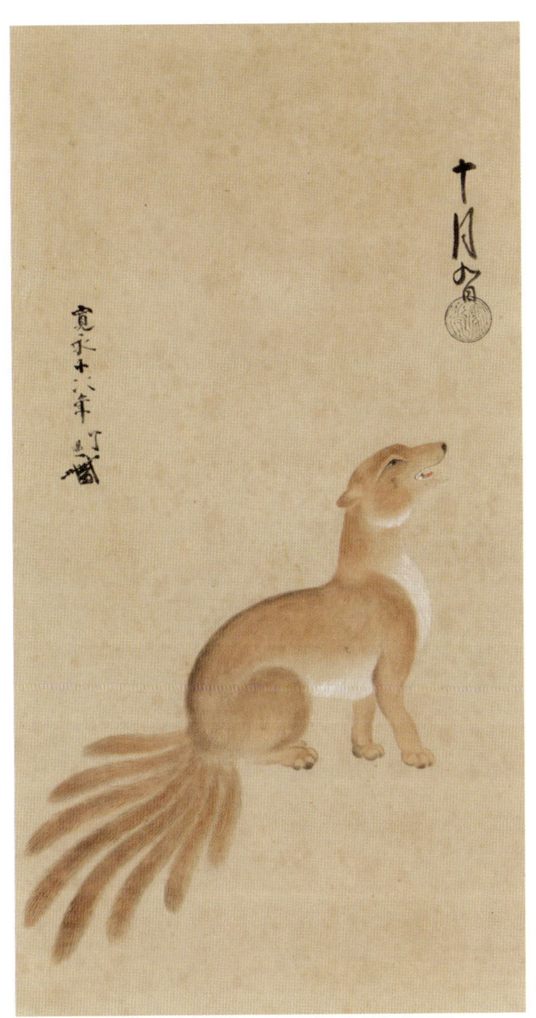

Eight-tailed Fox

Kano Tanyū
1637

The handscroll *Twelve Sacred Beasts* (Seika-do Bunko Art Museum) contains three multi-tailed animals, illustrating how such creatures were thought to possess spiritual powers. This painting was created by order of the third shogun, Tokugawa Iemitsu (1604-51), by his painter-in-waiting, Kano Tan'yū (1602-74), after the shogun had witnessed an eight-tailed fox in a dream. The upper part of the work bears an inscription by Iemitsu himself, dating to the ninth day of the tenth month. It also bears the year Kan'ei 14 inscribed by the founder of the temple Kan'eiji, Tenkai (d. 1643). The work was likely kept at the Tōshōgu Shrine on the premises of Edo Castle.

八尾狐図

狩野探幽
寛永14年(1637)

「十二霊獣図巻」(静嘉堂文庫美術館)にも3種登場するように、尾が複数ある動物は霊力のシンボルだったようだ。本図は、3代将軍徳川家光(1604～51)の霊夢に現れた八尾の狐を、御用絵師の狩野探幽(1602～74)に命じて描かせたもの。絵の上部には家光自筆の「十月九日」の日付、寛永寺の開山・天海(?～1643)による「寛永十四年」の年記が記される。江戸城内の紅葉山東照宮に収められていた可能性が高い。

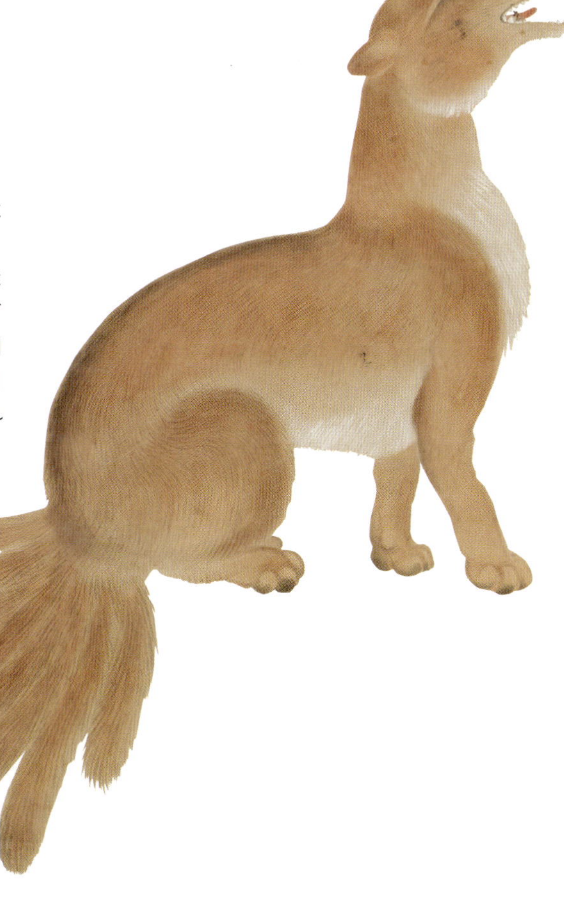

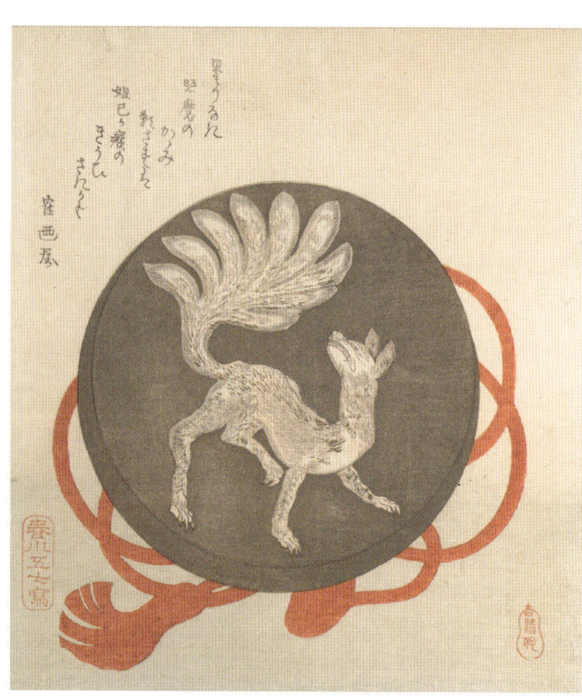

九尾狐文鏡図

春川五七
江戸時代(19c)
メトロポリタン美術館

Mirror With the Design of a Nine-tailed Fox

Harukawa Goshichi
19th century
The Metropolitan Museum of Art

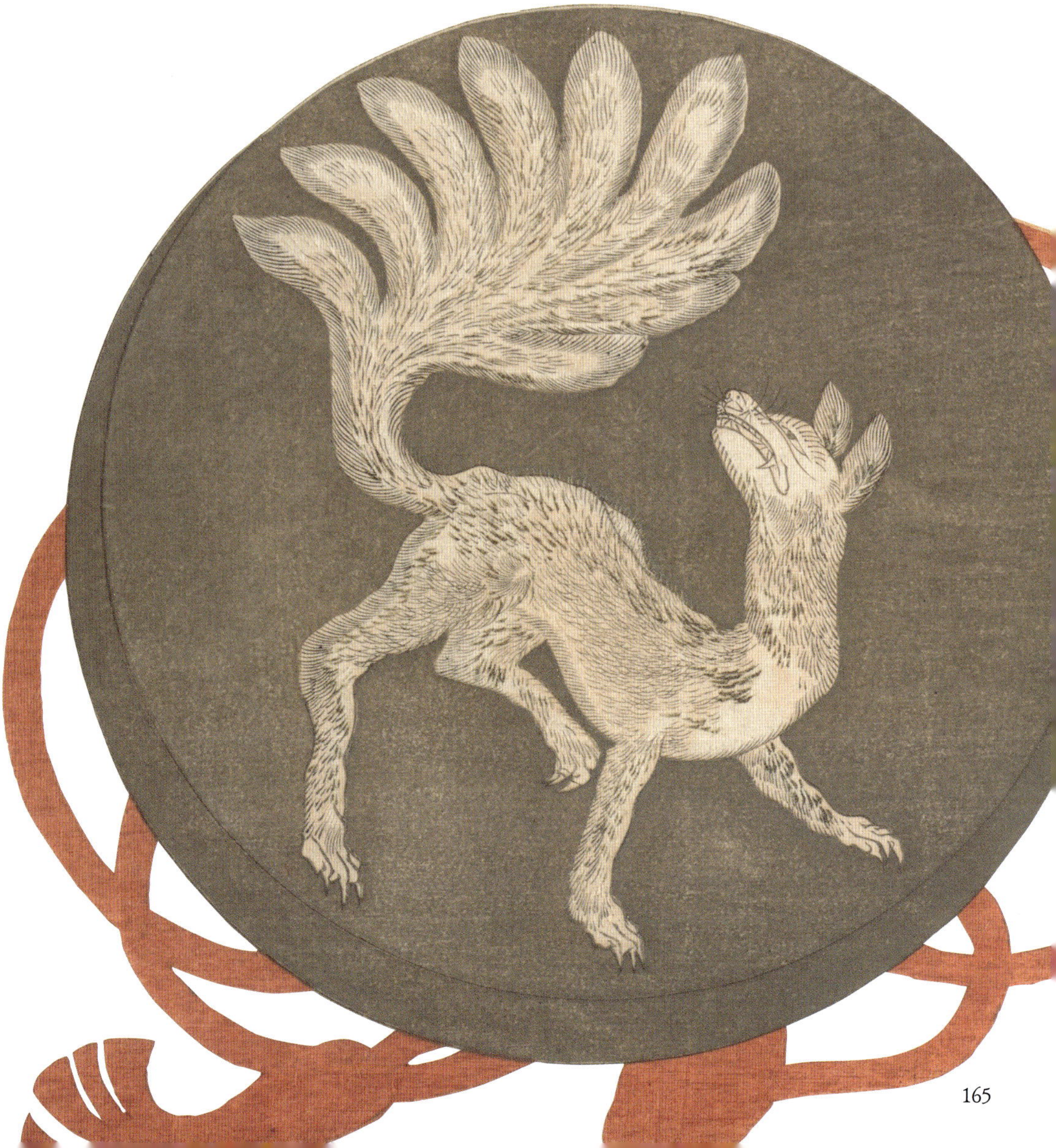

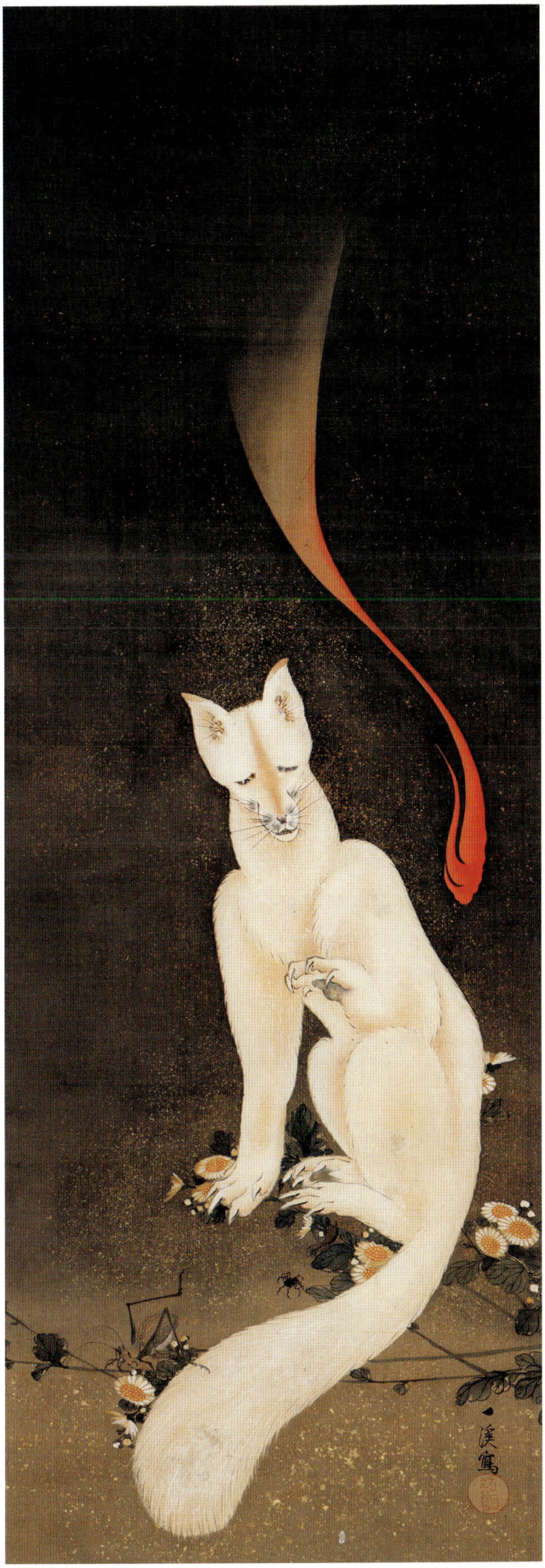

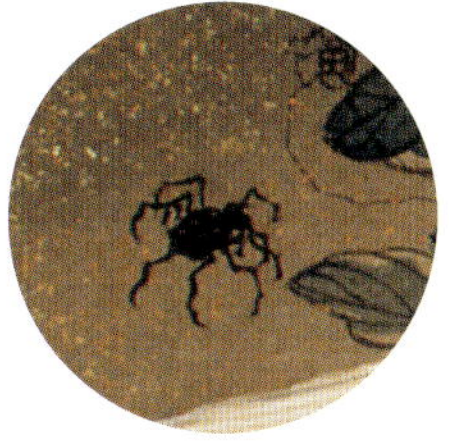

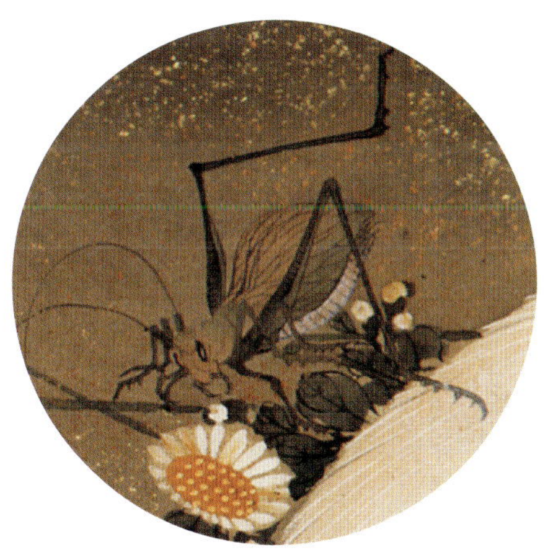

白狐図

吉川一渓
江戸時代（18c後半～19c初め）
摘水軒記念文化振興財団

吉川一渓（1763～1837）は名古屋で活躍した狩野派の画家。狐火とともに描かれた白狐の足下には、踏みしだかれた秋草。そしてよく見ると、そこには虫たちの姿が描かれている。狐火を使って虫をおびき寄せる猟法と見える。画家はこの表現に、どのような意味を託そうとしたのだろうか。

White Fox

Yoshikawa Ikkei
Late 18th century-early 19th century
Tekisuiken Memorial Foundation of Culture

Yoshikawa Ikkei (1763-1837) was a painter affiliated with the Nagoya-based atelier of the Kano school. The image includes the characteristic flame that is said to accompany foxes; its paws are stepping on autumn grasses. Upon closer looking, we also notice the shapes of small insects that are attracted by the fox's flame. What is the painter trying to say?

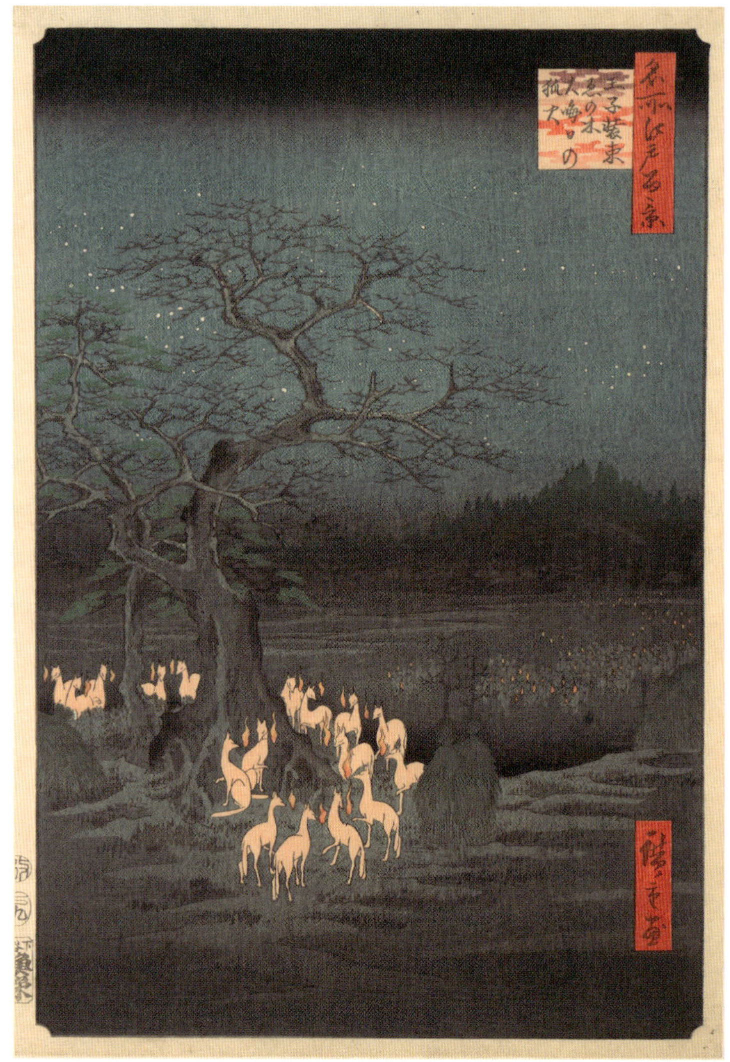

名所江戸百景
王子装束ゑの木
大晦日の狐火

歌川広重
安政4年(1857)
メトロポリタン美術館

王子稲荷神社には、大晦日の晩に関東中から集まった狐が、榎の大木の下で装束を整えた上で参詣したという伝承がある。本図は、その情景を描いた錦絵。榎に集まる狐の一群を前景に、画面後方には狐火を点した狐の群れが森の中の神社へと進んでゆく。夜空にかすかに瞬く星と地上の狐火とが呼応し、暗夜の夢幻的な世界が広がっている。なお、先の榎は道路拡張工事にともない切り倒されてしまったが、その付近に装束稲荷神社が建立されている。

Shozokuenoki Tree at Oji: Fox–fires on New Year's Eve

Utagawa Hiroshige
1857
The Metropolitan Museum of Art

It is said that, on New Year's Eve, foxes from around the Kantō region come together at Ōji Inari Shrine and pay reverence to a large hackberry tree. This print depicts that moment. A group of foxes is shown in the foreground, while a lot more are noticeable by their flames as they are approaching the shrine from the dark woods. The stars in the sky echo the light of the foxes, tainting the world in an eerie glow. The hackberry tree depicted here was cut down in the wake of a road expansion, but the shrine was reconstructed at a nearby site.

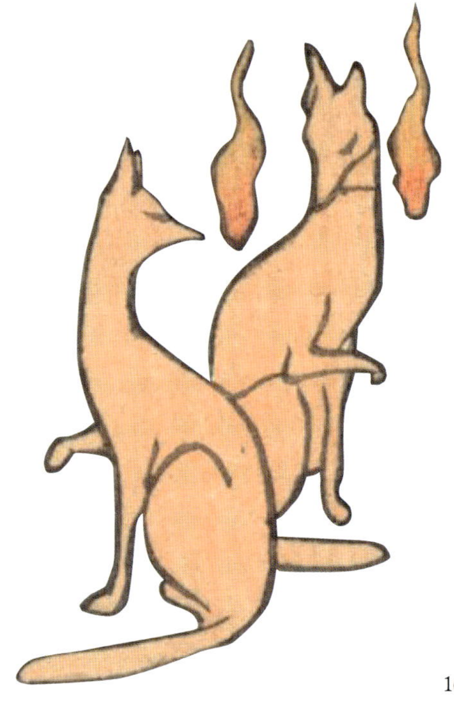

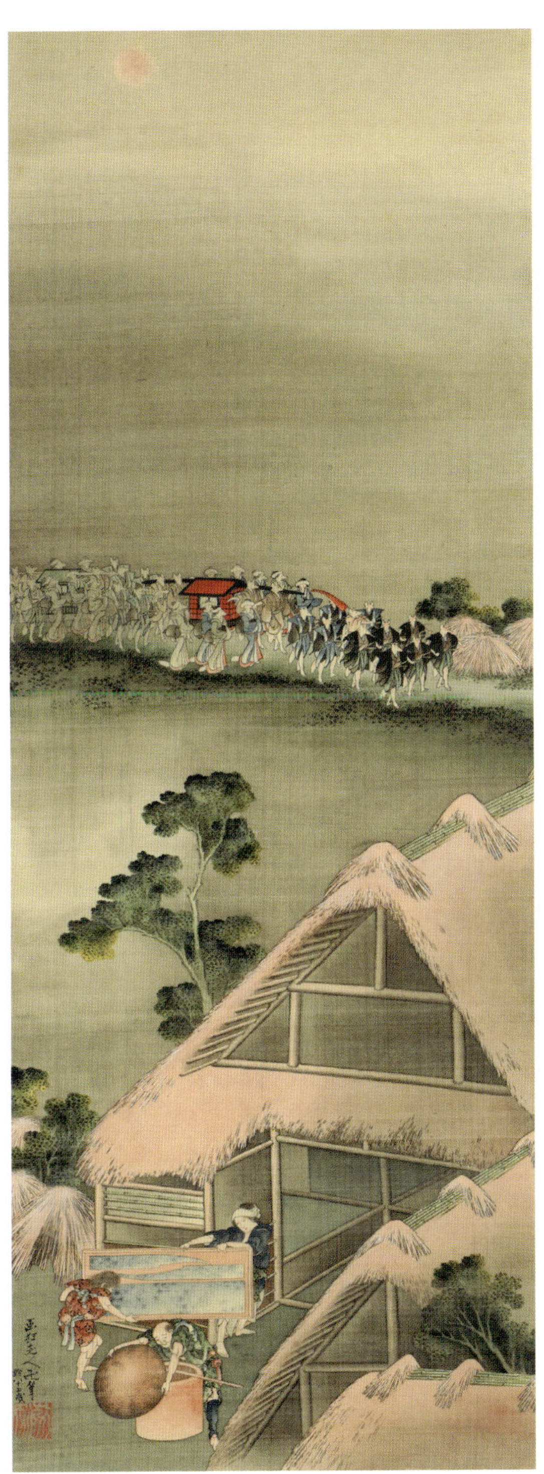

狐の嫁入図

葛飾北斎
天保15年（弘化元、1844）
島根県立美術館（永田コレクション）

陽が照りながら小雨の降る現象「狐の嫁入」を描く。前景のにわか雨に慌てる現実的な情景と、中景に描かれた幻想的な嫁入り行列の対照が見どころ。

Fox Wedding

Katsushika Hokusai
1844
Nagata Collection, Shimane Prefectural Museum

Although the sun shines rain is falling in this painting of a fox wedding. The scenery in the foreground is disrupted by rain, while the wondrous fox procession is advancing in sunlight.

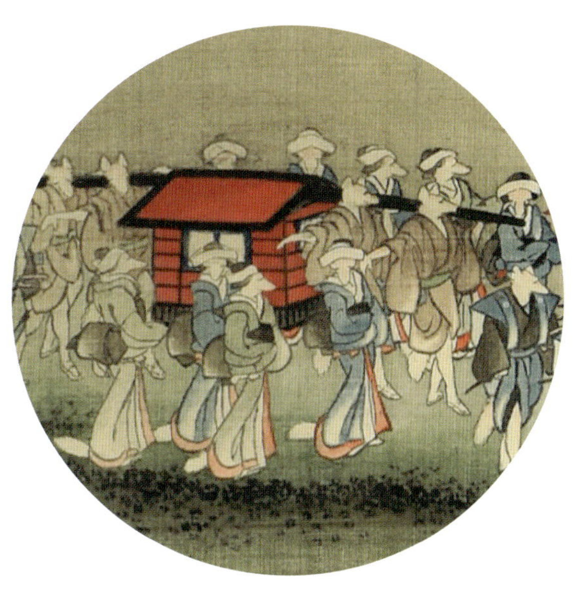

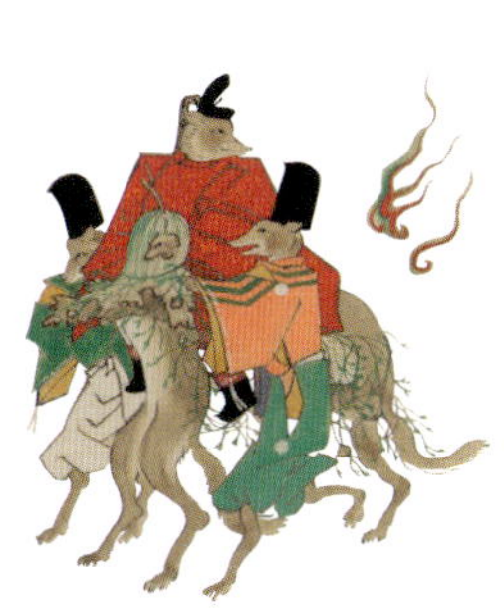

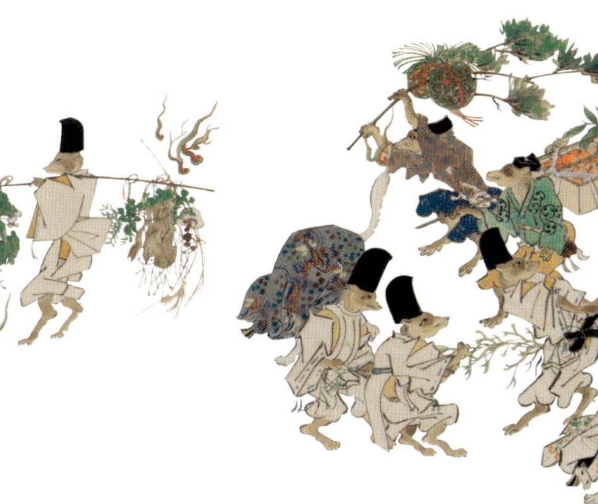

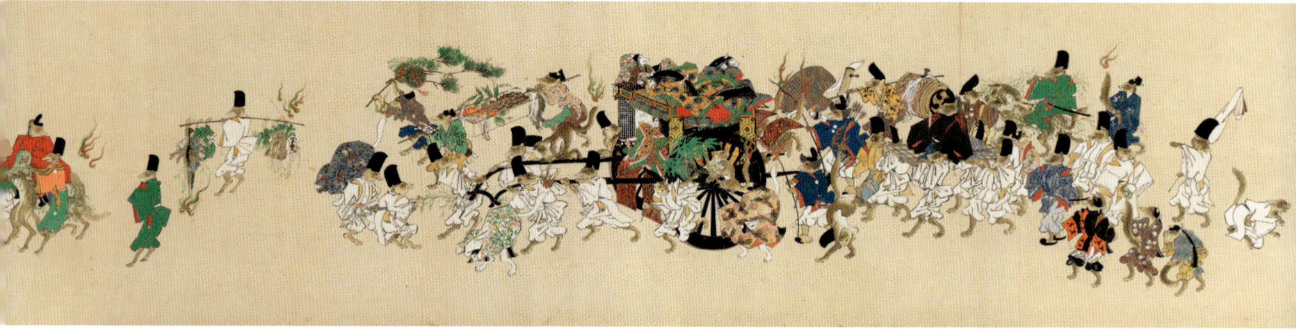

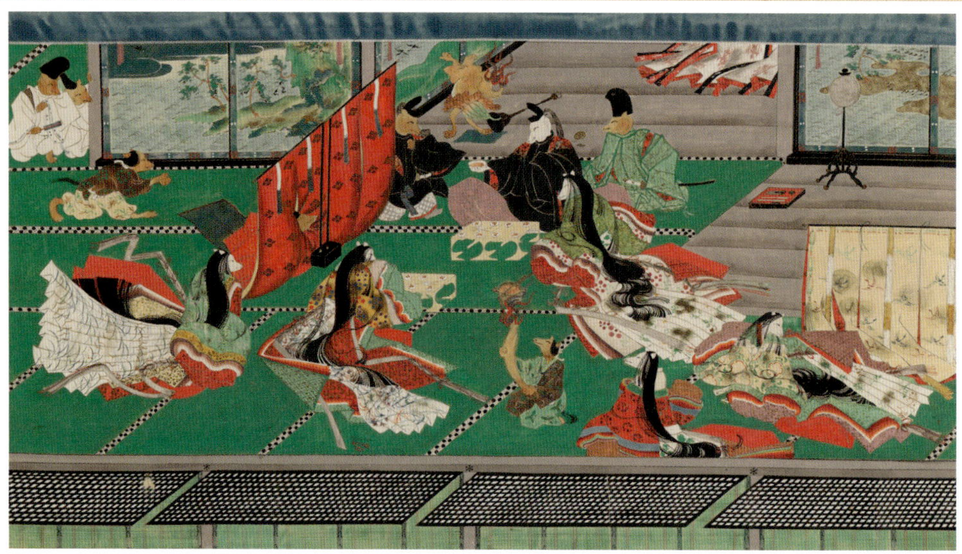

婚怪草紙絵巻

浮田一蕙
安政4年(1858)頃
メトロポリタン美術館

狐と人間との異類婚姻譚を題材とするが、幕末の公武合体策による、皇女和宮の徳川家茂への降嫁に対する風刺画と考えられてきた作品。浮田一蕙(1795〜1859)は、幕末に活躍した復古大和絵派の画家で、尊皇攘夷運動に奔走。安政の大獄で捕えられ入獄し、出獄後間もなく没した。

Konkai zōshi (*Tale of a Strange Marriage*)

Ukita Ikkei
ca. 1858
The Metropolitan Museum of Art

The scroll depicts the tale of a marriage between a fox and a human being. It was made towards the end of the Edo period and is thought to have been among the dowry of Princess Chikako when she married the shogun Tokugawa Iemochi. The painter, Ukita Ikkei (1795-1859), part of the *yamato-e* revival during the late Edo period, was engaged in the anti-Western movement at the time. As a royalist, he was imprisoned during the shogunate's crackdown on pro-emperor intellectuals, the so-called Ansei Purge. He died soon after his release.

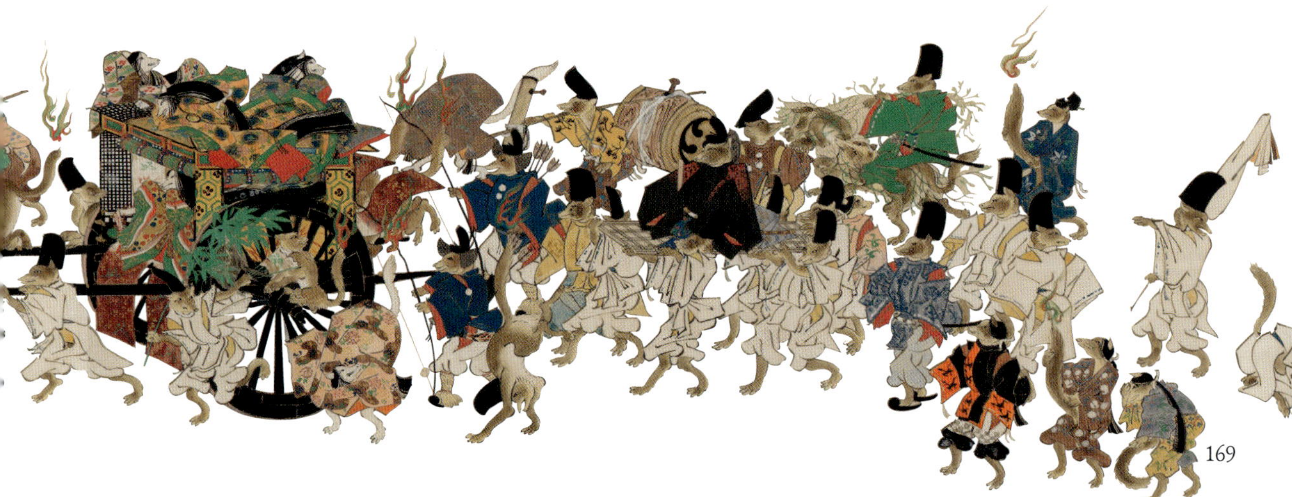

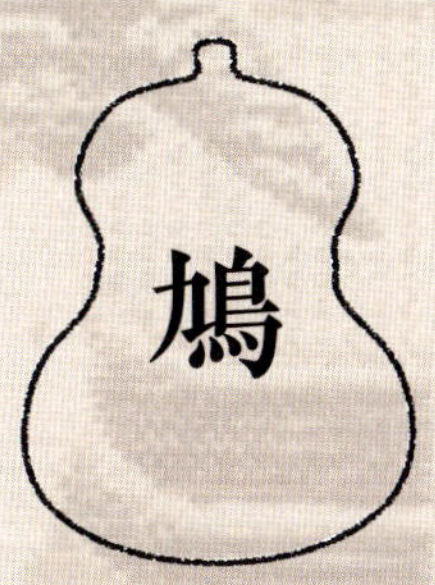

鳩は八幡神の使いとされ、八幡宮では古くから鳩を霊鳥として崇めてきた。八幡神の総社は、平安時代前期の清和天皇の時代に、宇佐八幡の神を山城の男山（鳩ヶ峰）に遷した石清水八幡宮だが、源義家がここで元服したこともあり、源氏をはじめとする武家の信仰を集めた。

The Pigeon

Pigeons are thought of as attendants of the deity Hachiman. Since ancient times, pigeons have been venerated as sacred birds at Hachiman shrines. At the time of Emperor Seiwa, the deity Usa Hachiman was transferred to the Iwashimizu Hachimangu Shrine at Otokoyama (also called Hatogamine, or "Pigeon Peak") in Yamashiro. Beginning with the coming-of-age ceremony of Minamoto no Yoshiie that was performed there, the shrine became a center of warrior pilgrimages.

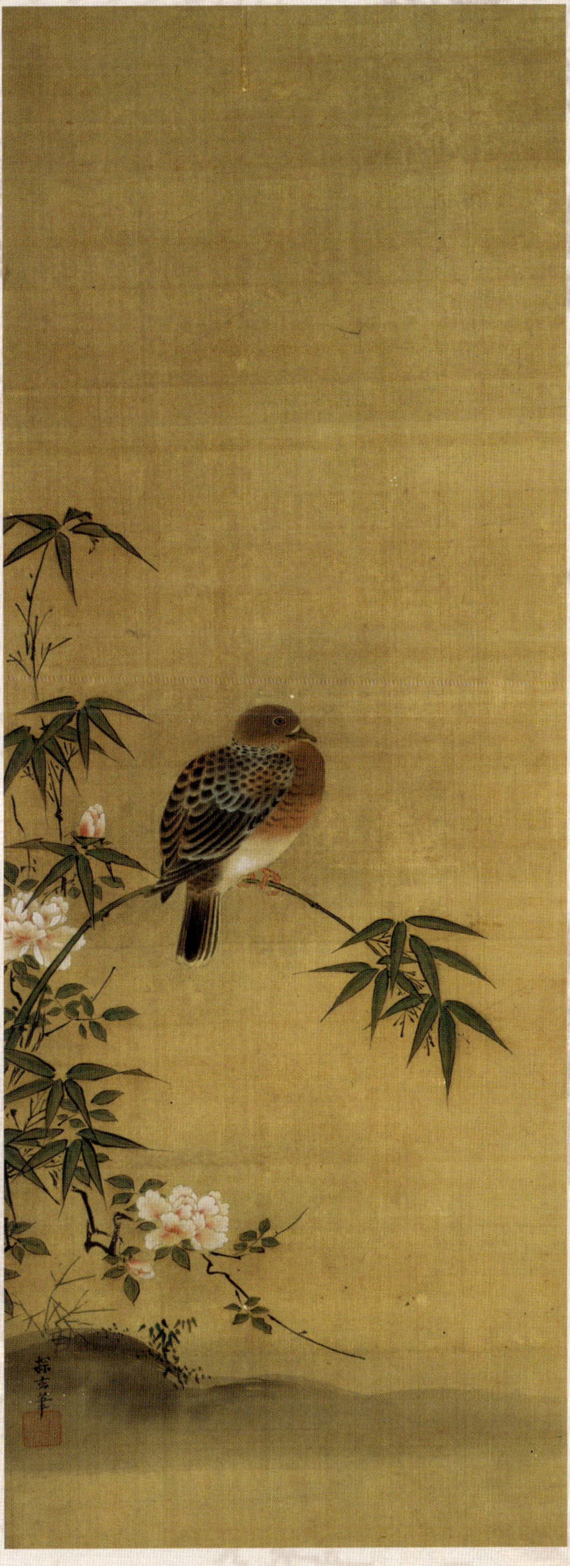

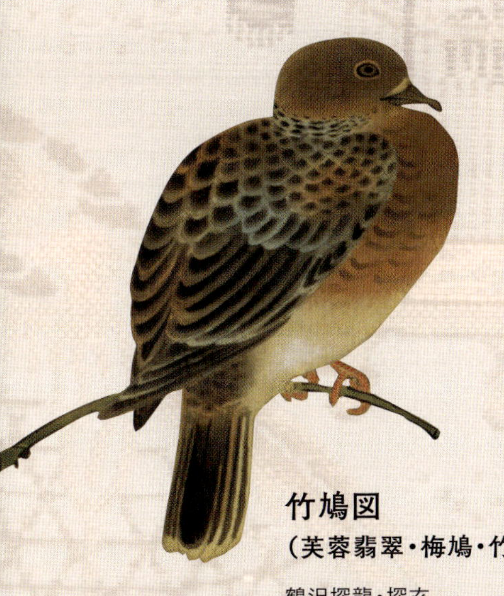

竹鳩図
（芙蓉翡翠・梅鳩・竹鳩図のうち）

鶴沢探龍・探玄
江戸時代（19c）
東京国立博物館

Pigeon and Bamboo (*part of a triptych*)

Tsurusawa Tanryū and Tangen
19th century
Tokyo National Museum

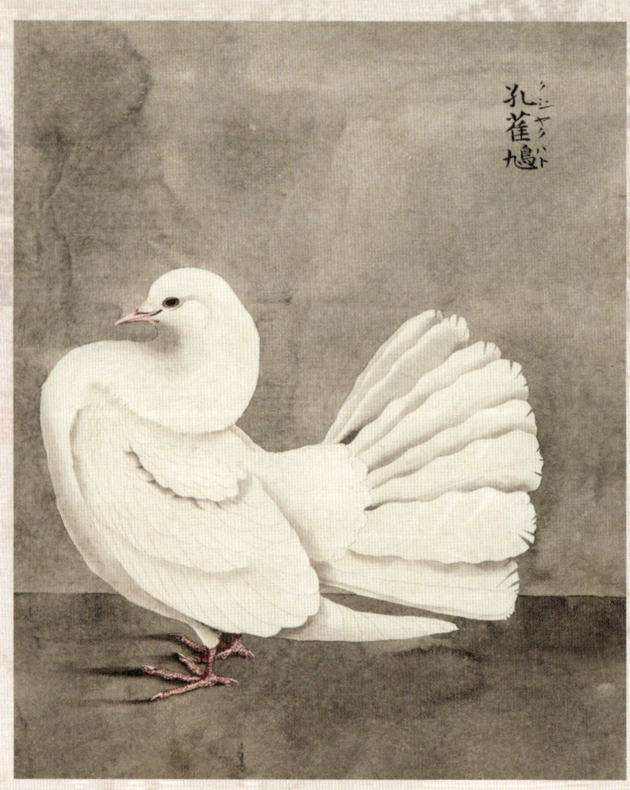

県指定文化財

孔雀鳩図（左）、**銀鳩図**（下）
（『佐竹曙山写生帖』より）

佐竹曙山
安永7年（1778）頃
秋田市立千秋美術館

Prefectural Cultural Property

***Fantail Pigeon** (left), **Ring dove** (lower)*
(from Satake Shozan shaseijō)

Satake Shozan
ca. 1778
Akita Senshu Museum of Art

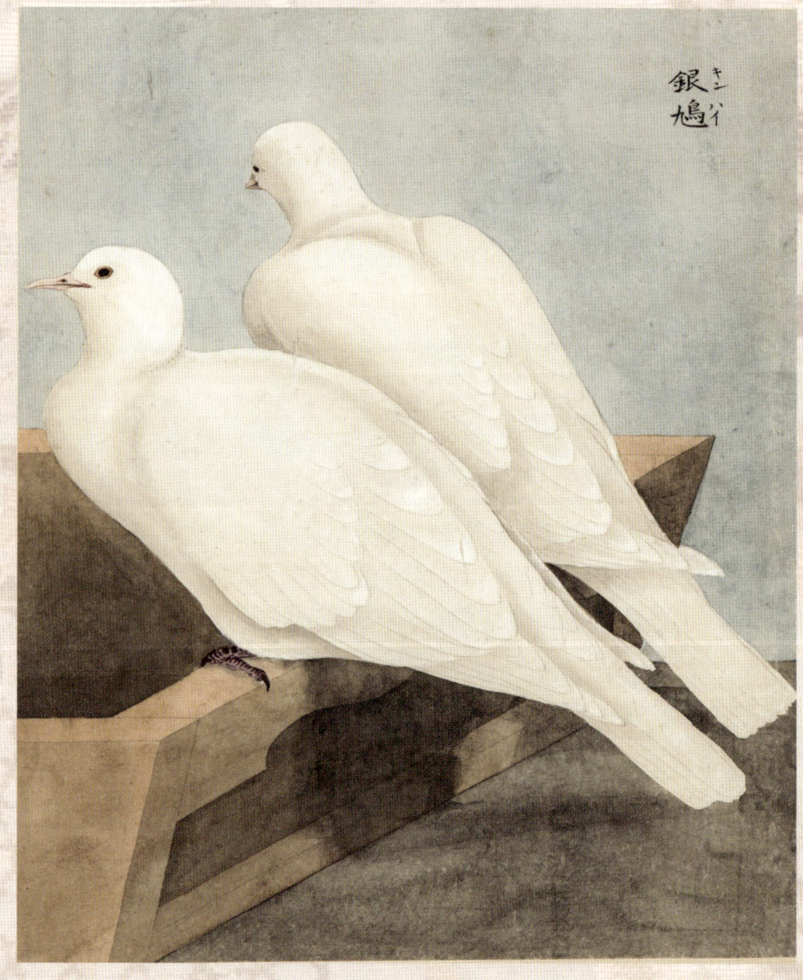

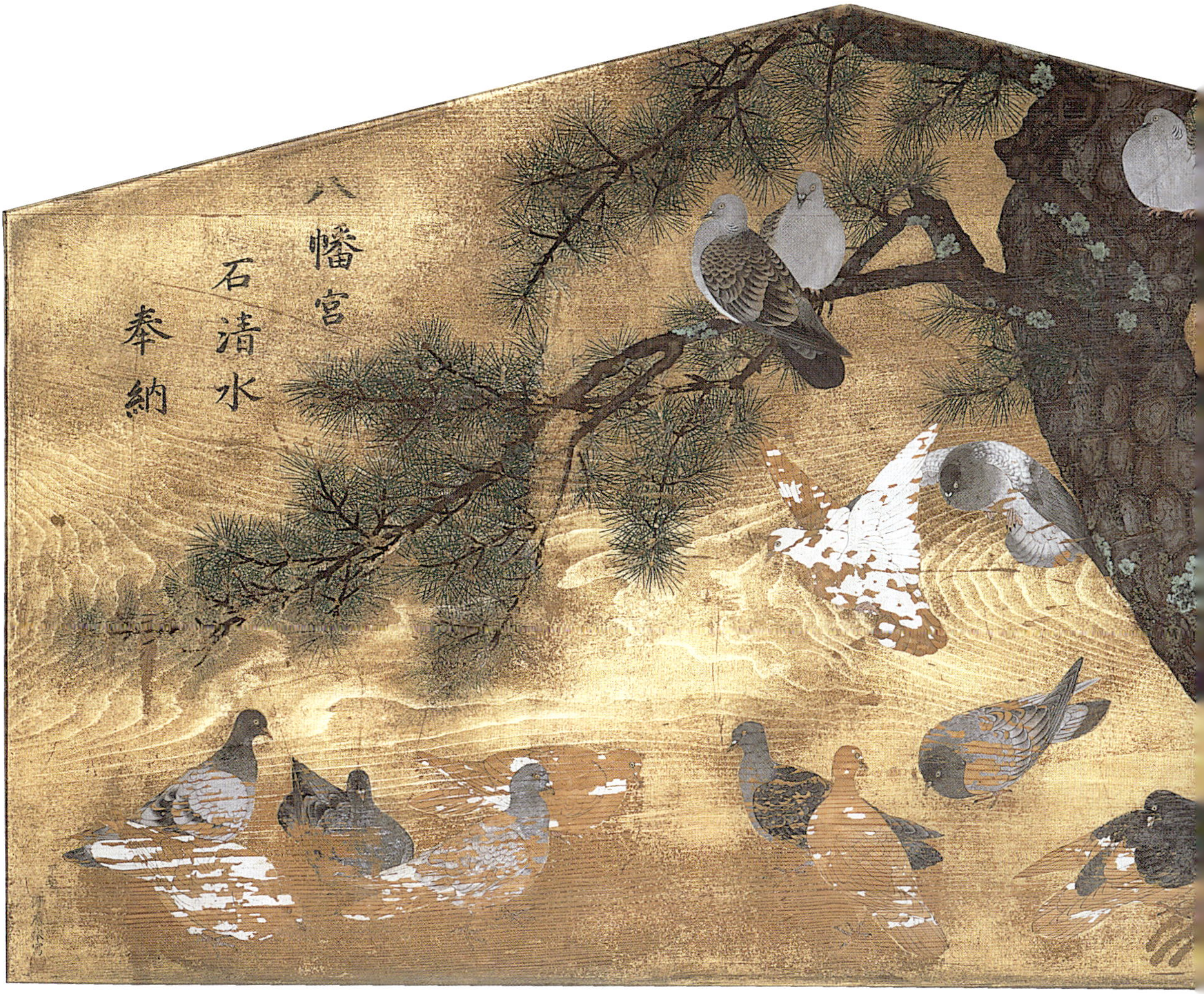

松鳩図絵馬

円山応挙
天明6年(1786)
京都・石清水八幡宮

八幡神の使いとされる鳩を老松とともに描く。多彩な羽毛をもつ幾種類もの鳩がていねいに描き分けられており、鳥類図鑑の趣さえある。画面右側に墨書された奉納銘からは、異国の文物に限りない憧れをいだいた蘭癖(蘭学マニア)大名の一人・島津重豪(1745～1833)により、1787年(天明7)正月に奉納された絵馬と知れる。琉球との交易を通じて薩摩藩は異国の情報や文物に恵まれており、とくに重豪については後年、シーボルトから直に鳥の剥製方法を伝授されたとのエピソードも伝えられている。このような蘭癖をも納得させる描写力が、応挙の写生には備えられていたわけである。

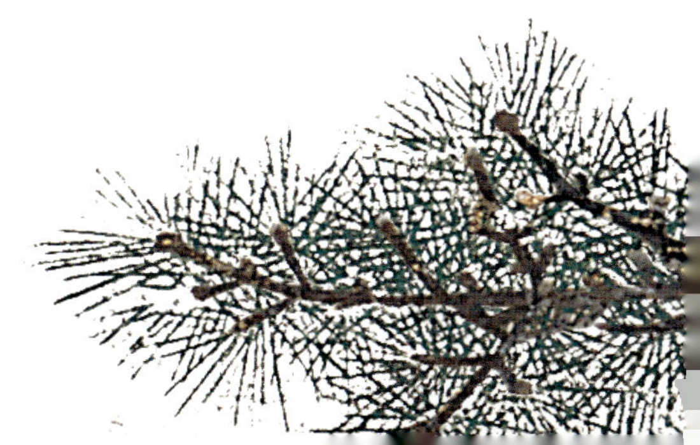

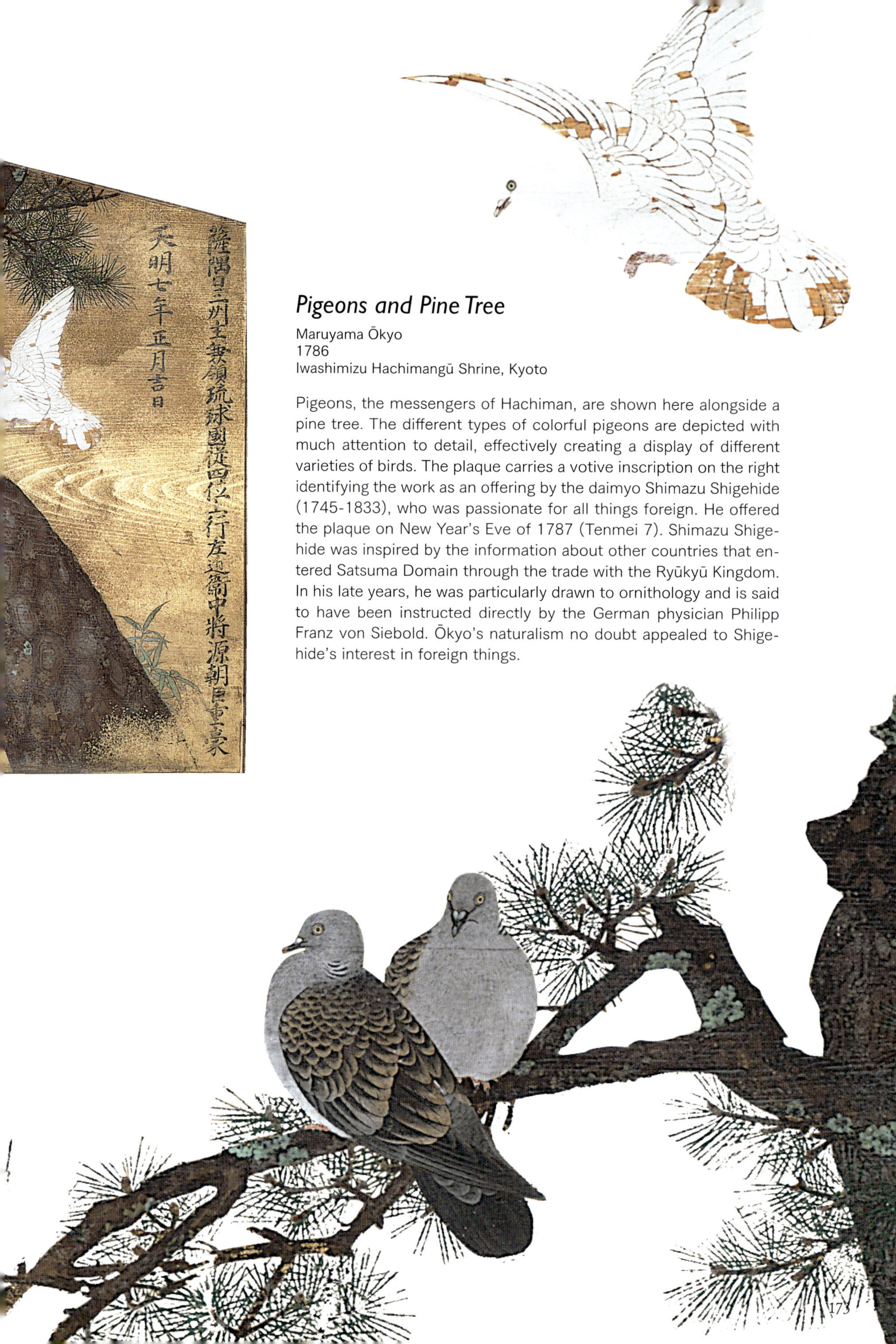

Pigeons and Pine Tree

Maruyama Ōkyo
1786
Iwashimizu Hachimangū Shrine, Kyoto

Pigeons, the messengers of Hachiman, are shown here alongside a pine tree. The different types of colorful pigeons are depicted with much attention to detail, effectively creating a display of different varieties of birds. The plaque carries a votive inscription on the right identifying the work as an offering by the daimyo Shimazu Shigehide (1745-1833), who was passionate for all things foreign. He offered the plaque on New Year's Eve of 1787 (Tenmei 7). Shimazu Shigehide was inspired by the information about other countries that entered Satsuma Domain through the trade with the Ryūkyū Kingdom. In his late years, he was particularly drawn to ornithology and is said to have been instructed directly by the German physician Philipp Franz von Siebold. Ōkyo's naturalism no doubt appealed to Shigehide's interest in foreign things.

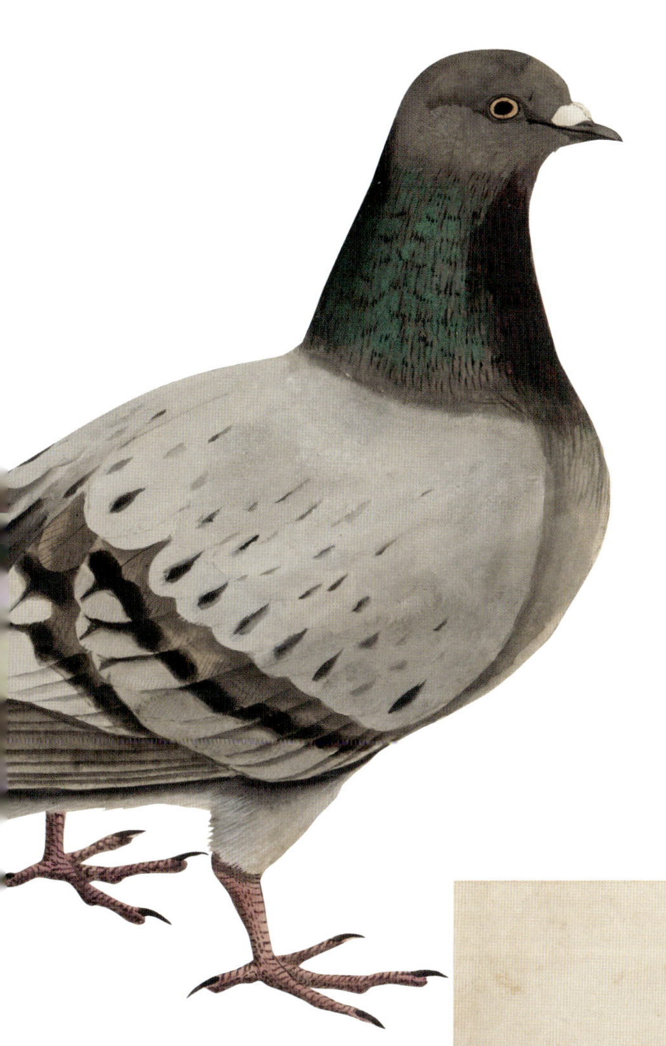

県指定文化財

鴿図

(『佐竹曙山写生帖』より)

佐竹曙山
安永7年(1778)頃
秋田市立千秋美術館

Prefectural Cultural Property

Pigeon

(from Satake Shozan shaseijō)

Satake Shozan
ca. 1778
Akita Senshu Museum of Art

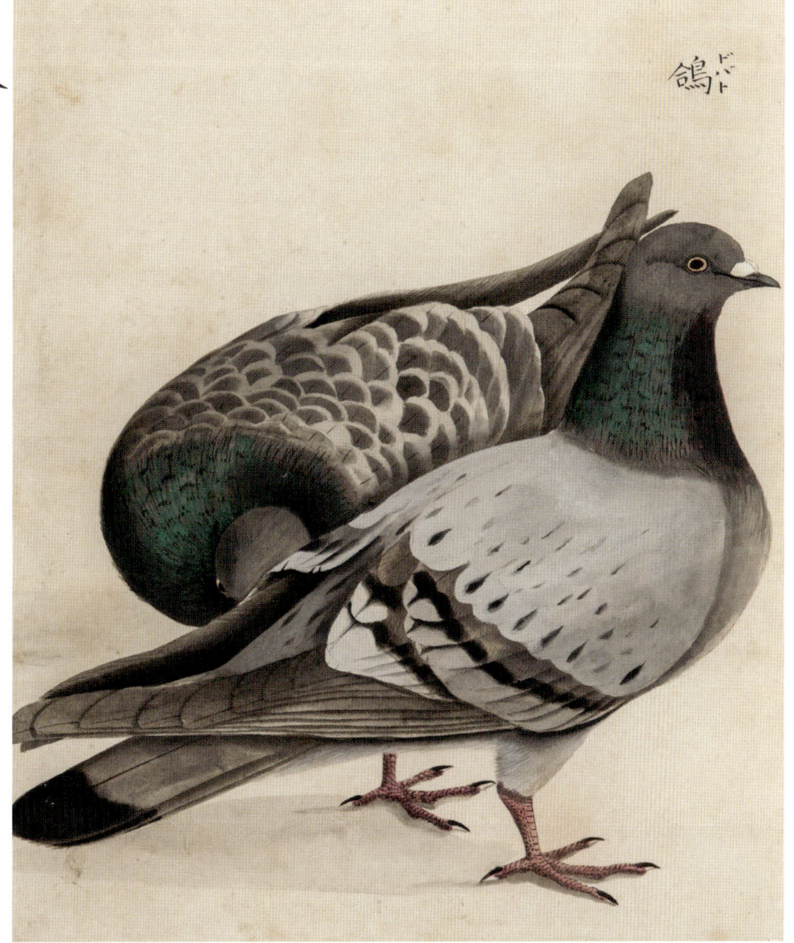

かんむり鳩図

山路探定
天明8年(1788)
仙台市博物館

長崎に舶載されたインドネシア産の鳥「かんむり鳩」を描く。筆者の山路探定(1728～93)は、薩摩藩のお抱え絵師。薩摩藩主・島津重豪から仙台藩主・伊達重村(1742～96)に贈られたものと考えられる。博物学マニアの大名同士における、情報のやりとりの一端を教えてくれる。

Crowned Pigeon

Yamaji Tanjō
1788
Sendai City Museum

The image depicts a type of pigeon native to Indonesia, a so-called crowned pigeon. The painter, Yamaji Tanjō (1728-93), was in the service of Satsuma Domain. The birds are said to have been a gift from the lord of Sendai Domain, Date Shigemura (1742-96) to the lord of Satsuma, Shimazu Shigehide. Both daimyo were natural history enthusiasts and the work illustrates their exchange of information.

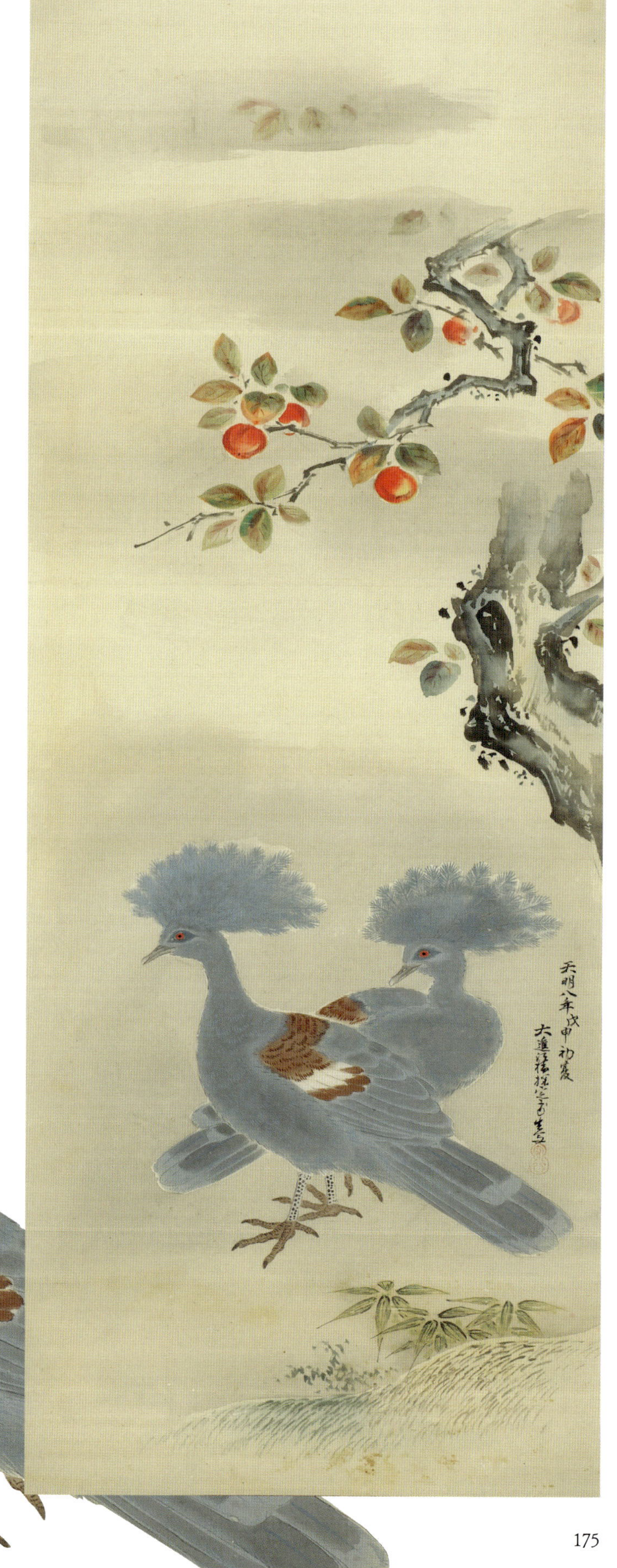

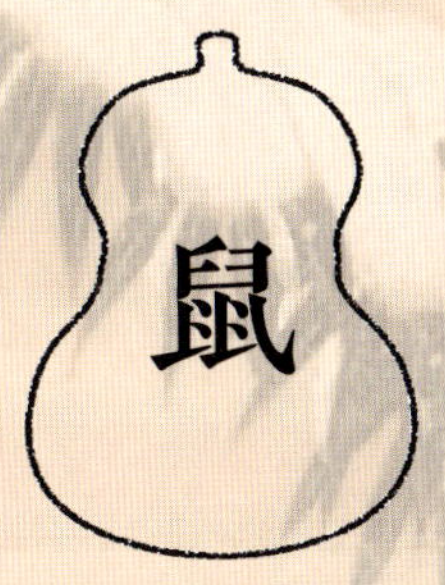

『古事記』には、大穴牟遅神（大国主神）が須佐之男命の放った野火に囲まれた時、現れた鼠に地下の空洞を教えてもらって難を逃れた、という話がある。一方、大黒天はインド仏教に由来する台所の守護神。大国主神は、その名や俵をかつぐ姿が大黒天と似ていることから次第に混同され、やがて大国主神の命を救った鼠が大黒天の使いと考えられるようになったという。七福神の一つである大黒天の使者であることから、鼠自体も福をもたらす存在とされた。また、ねずみ算という語があるように多産であることから、子孫繁栄や豊穣のシンボルともなった。

The Mouse

Japan's ancient chronicle, the *Kojiki*, contains a passage discussing how the deity Ōnamuchi, when engulfed in a fire laid by Susanoo no Mikoto, was taught an escape route by a mouse. The deity Daikokuten, on the other hand, finds its origins in Indian Buddhism as a protector of kitchens. Ōnamuchi, thought of as the protector of the realm, is often shown with a rice bundle, leading to an association with Daikokuten's iconography. As a result, both deities were often confused and combined. In the process, the mice linked with Ōnamuchi became a symbol for Daikokuten as well. As messengers of Daikokuten, one of the Seven Gods of Good Fortune, mice also came to signify luck. Their many offspring made them symbols for easy childbirth and a prosperous lineage.

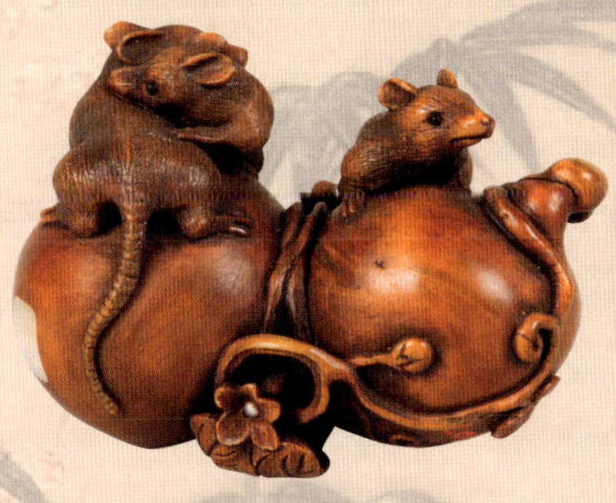

瓢箪に鼠木彫根付
江戸時代(19c)
メトロポリタン美術館

Netsuke of Gourd and Mice
19th century
The Metropolitan Museum of Art

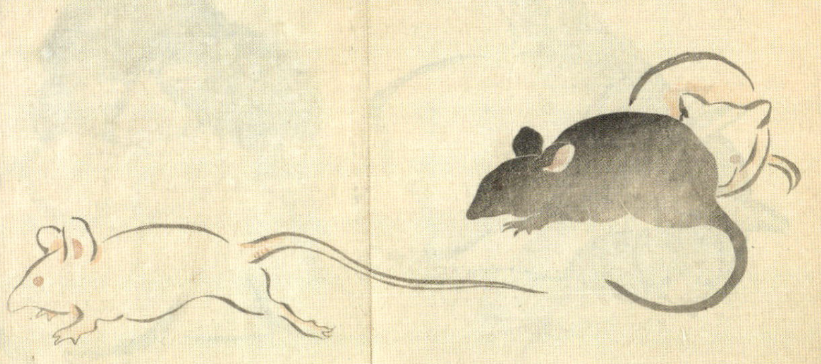

鼠図（『光琳画譜』より）
中村芳中
文政9年(1826)以降
メトロポリタン美術館

Mice from Kōrin Painting Manual
After 1826 (reprinted posthumously)
Nakamura Hōchū
The Metropolitan Museum of Art

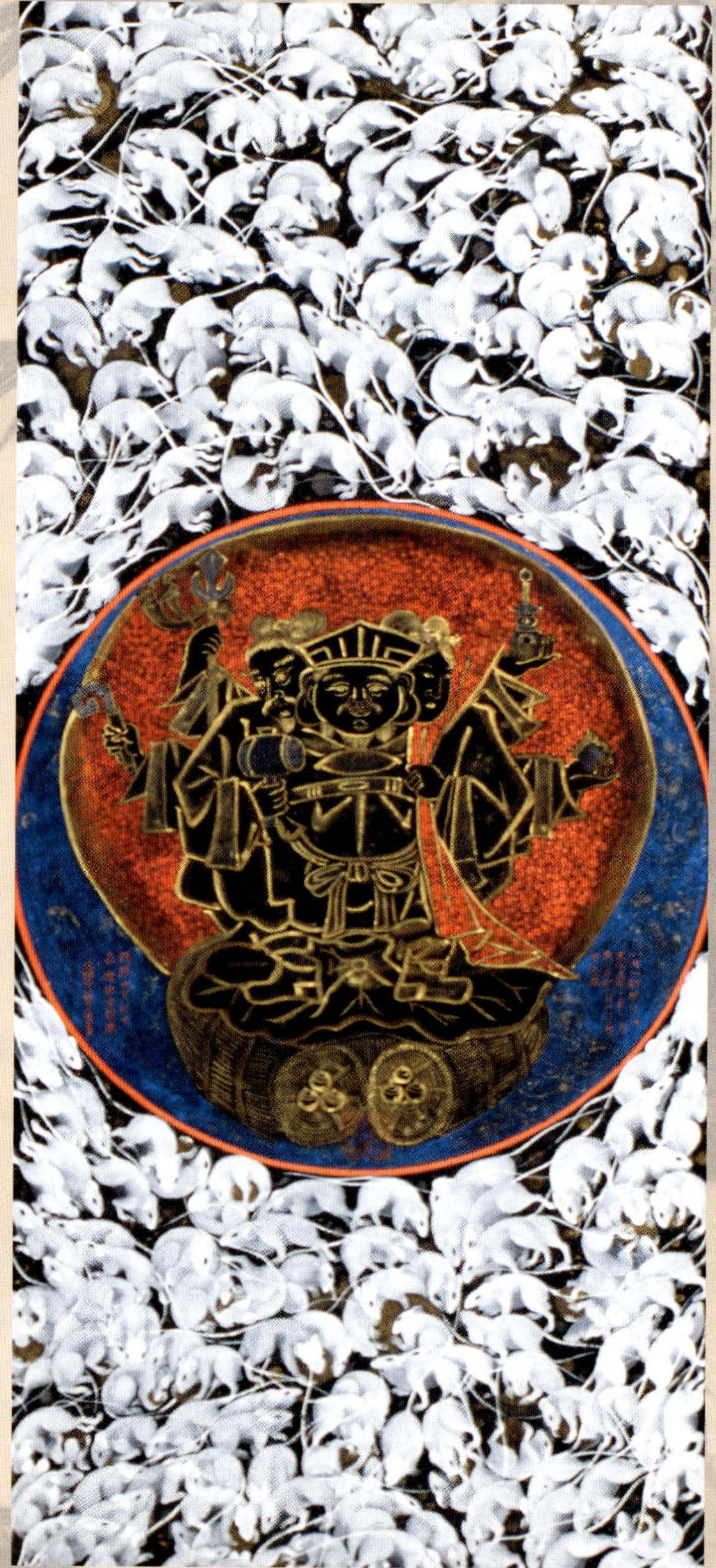

三面大黒天画像

真田幸貫・谷文晁
天保6年(1835)
長野・真田宝物館

画面中央・大黒天の筆者は、信州松代藩8代藩主・真田幸貫(1791～1852)である。1832年(天保3)11月23日から3年後の閏7月17日まで毎日一枚ずつ欠かさずこの尊像を描いたことが朱書されており、晴れて1000枚に達した満願の日に合わせて完成させた本格的作品が本図であると知れる。注目すべきは谷文晁(1763～1840)による、周囲を埋め尽くさんばかりの白鼠の数々。大黒天の使いとしての豊穣のイメージを、かくも極端なまでに表現した例は稀だろう。

Three-faced Daikokuten

Sanada Yukitsura and Tani Bunchō
1835
The Sanada Treasures Museum, Nagano

The image of Daikokuten at the center was painted by the eighth lord of Matsushiro Domain, Sanada Yukitsura (1791-1852). According to his vermillion inscription, Yukitsura began painting an image of Daikokuten in 1832 and continued to do so every day for a full three years. This painting is the culmination of his effort that yielded roughly one thousand pieces. Daikokuten is surrounded by an avalanche of white mice painted by Tani Bunchō (1763-1840). As attendants to Daikokuten, mice were symbols of abundance. However, peculiar depictions like this painting are rare.

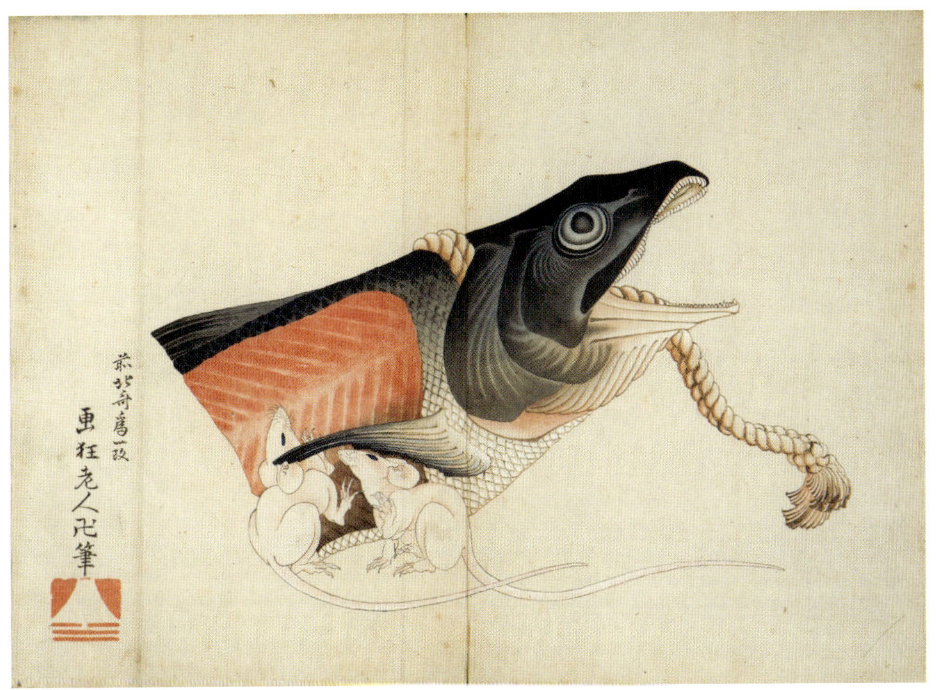

塩鮭と白鼠
(「肉筆画帖」より)

葛飾北斎
天保5～15年(1834～44)頃
北斎館

北斎の肉筆画帖に収録された10図のうちの一図。右頁同様、塩鮭と白鼠をセットで描く。これも恵比須・大黒の見立てと考えると、新春などの祝祭の場を飾るにふさわしい内容だと言えるだろう。

Salted Salmon and White Mice (*from An Album of Paintings*)

Katsushika Hokusai
1834-44
The Hokusai-kan Museum

This image is part of an album of ten paintings by Hokusai. Like in the work by Hakyō and his descendants, Hokusai paired white mice with a salmon. The two creatures are symbols of the lucky gods Ebisu and Daikokuten, thus representing the wish for good fortune in the New Year.

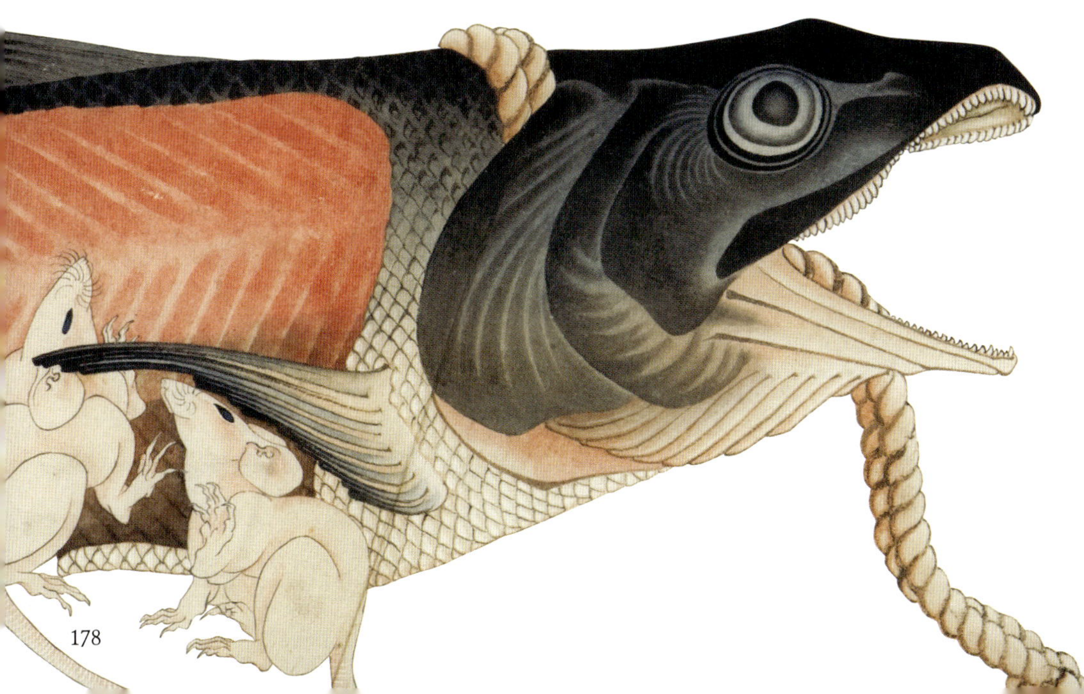

鮭図

蠣崎波響・東東洋・東寅
文化11年(1814)

蠣崎波響(1764～1826)と東洋父子による合作。波響は、松前藩12代藩主松前資広の五男で、蠣崎家の嗣となり、やがて藩の家老をつとめた。絵は建部凌岱や宋紫石、さらに円山応挙に学んだ。1807年(文化4)に松前から梁川(福島県)に転封され、しばらく同地にあったのである。1814年(文化11)京都から郷里に帰る途中、東洋(1755～1839)は息子東寅(1793～1853)とともに波響を訪問した。その際に、波響が塩鮭、東寅が鮎、そして東洋は白鼠を描き添えている。奥州や蝦夷地では、鮭を恵比須に見立てる風習があったという。してみると、白鼠を大黒に見立て、恵比須・大黒と洒落たものかもしれない。

Salmon

Kakizaki Hakyō, Azuma Tōyō, Azuma Tōin
1814

This work was made by Kakizaki Hakyō (1764-1826) in collaboration with his son, Tōyō (1755-1839). Hakyō was the fifth son of the lord of Matsumae Domain and eventually became a chief retainer of the domain. He studied painting with a number of artists, among them Takabe Ayatari, Sō Shiseki, and Maruyama Ōkyo. In 1814 (Bunka 11), he left his residence in Kyoto to return to his native domain. Along the way Hakyō was joined by his son Tōyō and his grandson Tōin (1793-1853). On that occasion, the three made this painting together: Hakyō drew the salmon, Tōyō the ayu, and Tōin the white mouse. In northern Japan and Hokkaidō, salmon were thought to embody the lucky god Ebisu. Since white mice represent Daikokuten, this painting pairs the two deities by way of their symbols.

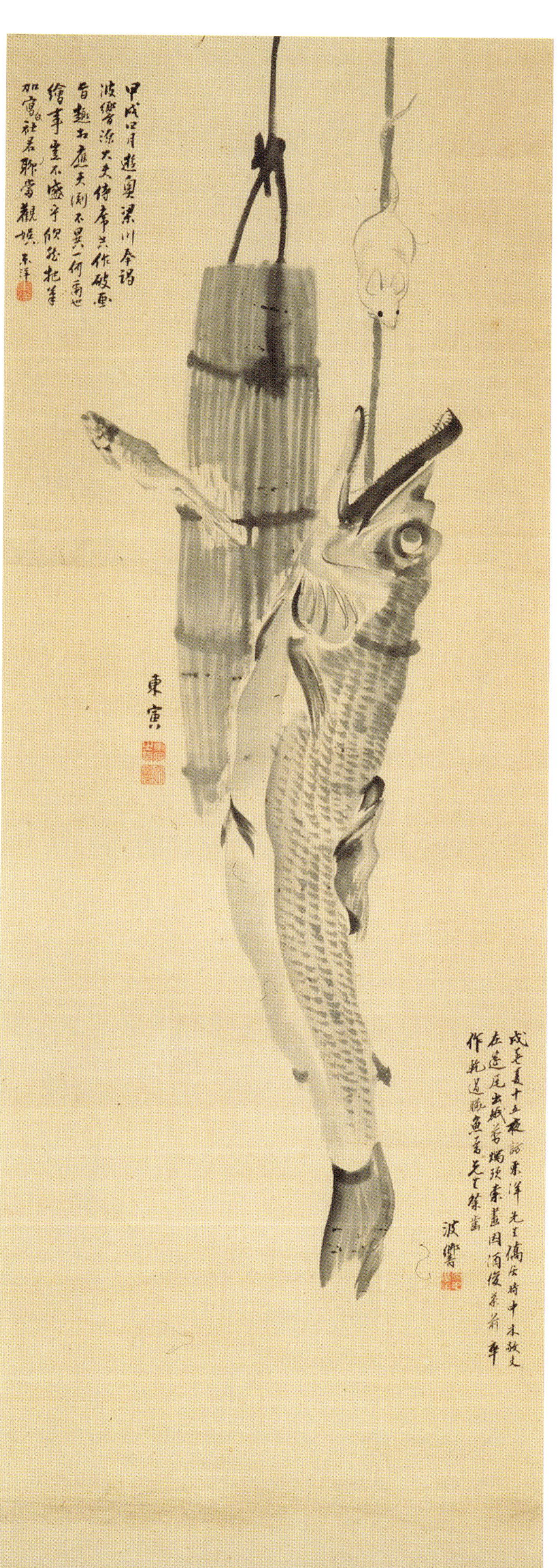

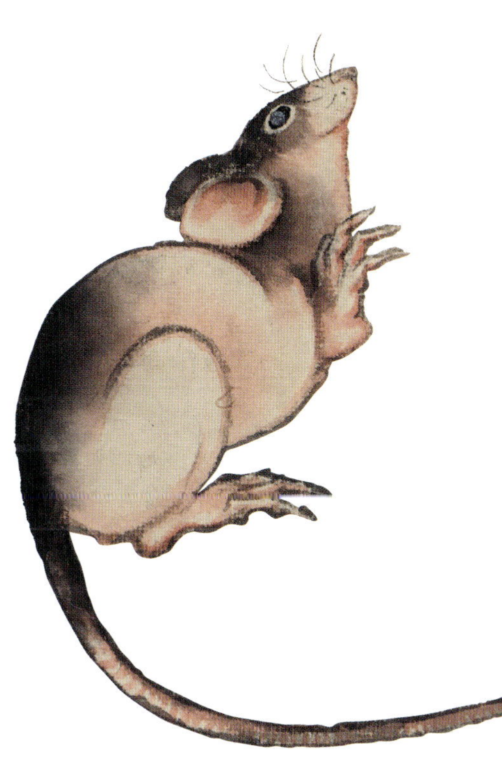

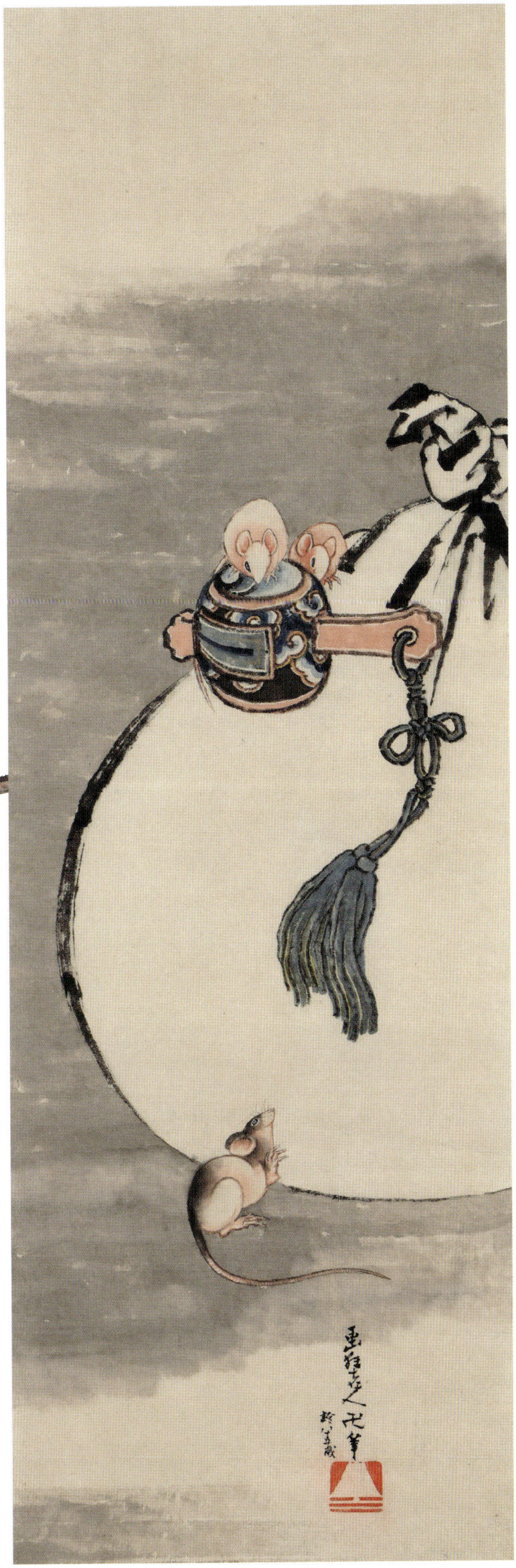

鼠と小槌図

葛飾北斎
天保15年（1844）
島根県立美術館（永田コレクション）

大黒天の持ち物である打出小槌と大きな布袋、そこに3匹の鼠が加わる。願いをかなえる小槌に乗る白鼠が大黒天の使いとすれば、それを下から見上げる斑模様の鼠は何を意味するのだろうか。

Mice and Mallet

Katsushika Hokusai
1844
Shimane Art Museum (Nagata Collection)

The painting pairs a mallet with a cloth bag, two items usually carried by Daikokuten, alongside three mice. The rodents have climbed on top of the mallet—a wish-granting symbol. What is Hokusai trying to tell us by placing a lonesome mouse at the foot of the bag?

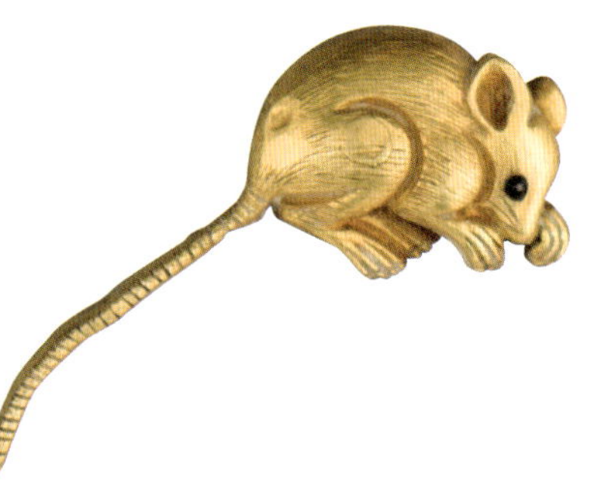

鼠図目貫

江戸時代(18c)
メトロポリタン美術館

Pair of Mice Menuki
(*Sword-grip Ornaments*)

18th century
The Metropolitan Museum of Art

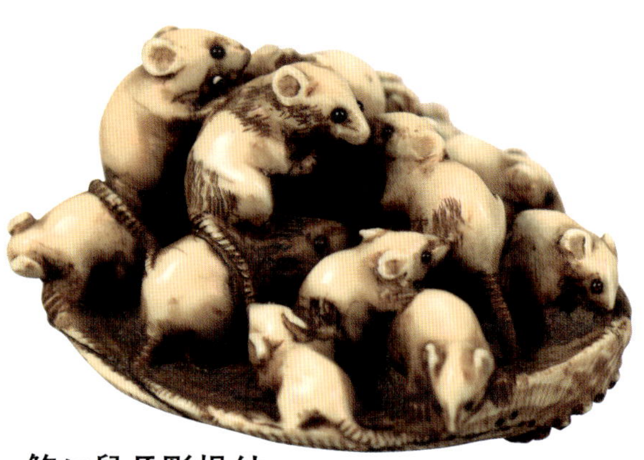

鮑に鼠牙彫根付

江戸時代(19c)
メトロポリタン美術館

Netsuke of a Group of Rats Nestled in an Abalone Shell

Late 19th century
The Metropolitan Museum of Art

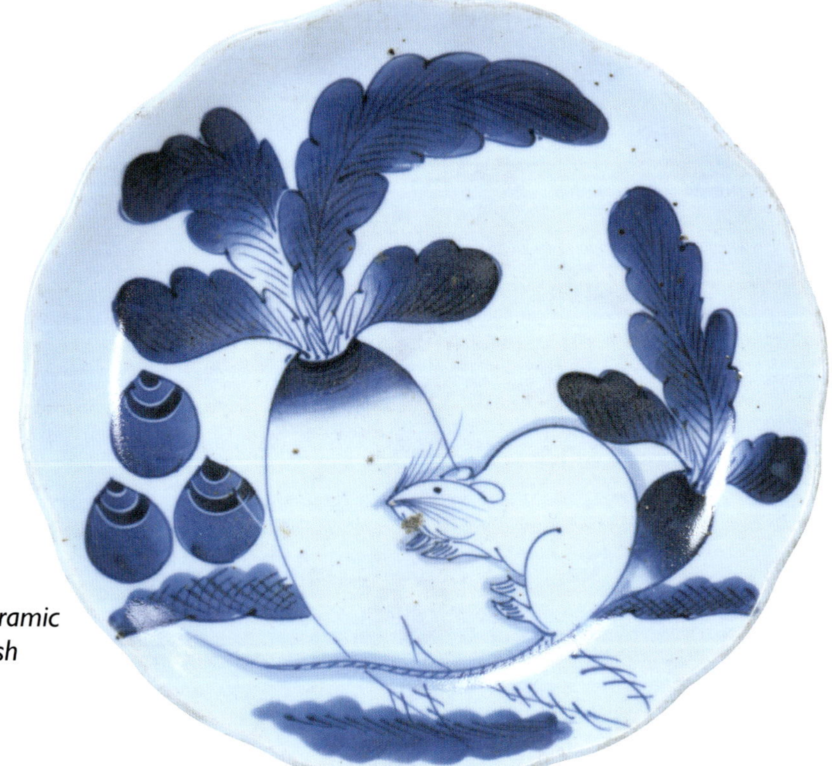

染付大根鼠図輪花皿

伊万里焼
江戸時代(19c)
東京国立博物館

Blue-and-White Imari Ware Ceramic Dish with a Mouse and a Radish

19th century
Tokyo National Museum

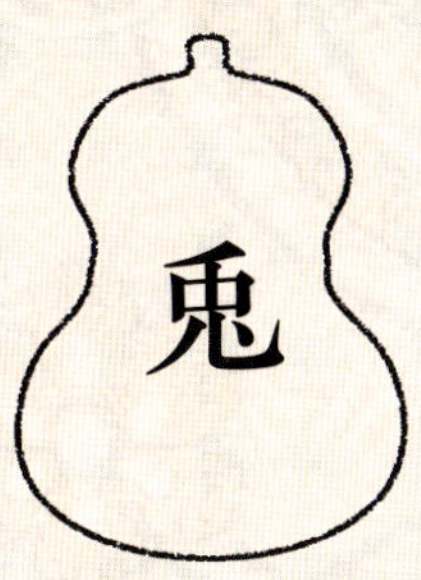

古代中国の古制を踏襲したわが国の『延喜式』では、赤兎を「上瑞」とし王者の徳が盛んであれば現れるという。それに対し白兎は「中瑞」、月の精で寿命は千年と記される。こちらは、王が老人を敬えば現れるという。日本においてはむしろ、鰐鮫にだまされ毛を剝がれた兎を大国主神が助けた、という『古事記』の「因幡の白兎」が有名だろう。これにもとづき、大国主神を祀る神社では、兎を神使として崇めている。月のなかで餅をつく、との俗信は中国伝来。また繁殖力が旺盛なことから、多産の象徴とも見なされた。一方、波の上をはねる兎をモチーフとした「波兎」は、謡曲『竹生島』にもとづく。琵琶湖の夜の湖面の波に月光が射し、ちょうど兎が水面をはねているように見えると謡った一節に因むという。波とともに表現されることから、火防の兎として造形化される場合も少なくなかった。

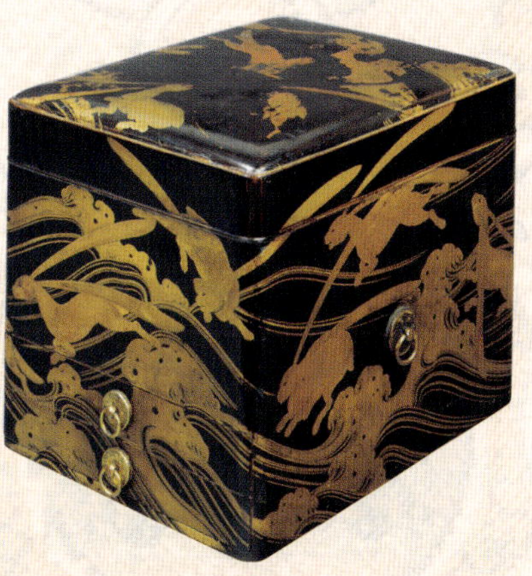

波兎蒔絵旅櫛笥
江戸時代（17c）
東京国立博物館

Lacquer Travel Chest with Motif of Rabbits and Waves
17th century
Tokyo National Museum

The Rabbit

The Japanese book of laws and customs, *Engishiki*, follows ancient Chinese legal conventions. Among the section entitled "great omens," the book lists red rabbits as the supreme manifestation of virtue. White rabbits, on the other hand, are included in the "median omens" section and were thought to have been embodiments of the moon's purity and symbols of long life. In Japan, rabbits are also understood through a story in the ancient chronicle *Kojiki*. There, a rabbit is seen fearlessly helping the god Ōkuninushi. For that reason, rabbits are venerated at Ōkuninushi shrines as divine attendants to the deity. The folkloristic understanding of white rabbits living inside the moon and making *mochi* rice cakes originated in China. Due to their fertility, rabbits are also symbolic of fecundity. Often, rabbits are depicted riding on top of wave crests, an iconography that originated in the Noh theater play *Chikubushima*. The play immortalized the glistening of moonlight on the waves of Lake Biwa, a sight that was likened to rabbits—creatures of the moon—surfing on the water. As a result of that association, rabbits are often considered guardians against fire.

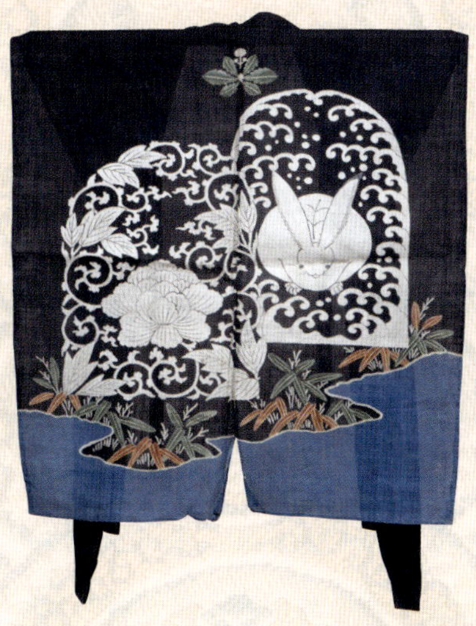

黒麻地波兎牡丹唐草州浜笹文肩衣
江戸時代（19c）
東京国立博物館

Sleeveless Robe with Motif of Rabbit and Waves
19th century
Tokyo National Museum

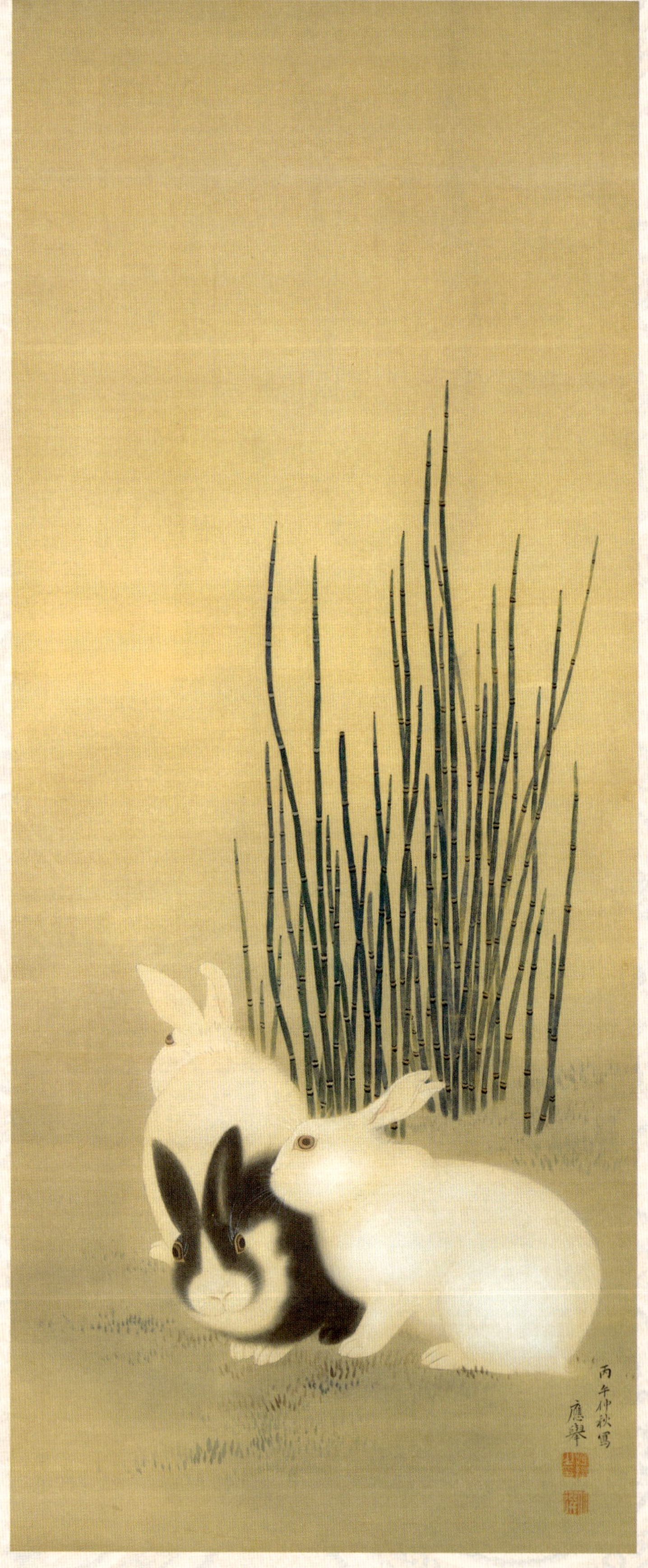

木賊兎図

円山応挙
天明6年(1786)
静岡県立美術館

正面に横、そして後ろ向きの３羽の兎を、木賊と組み合わせて描いた作品。若い頃から応挙は、対象をさまざまな角度から描き分けることを提唱していた。謡曲「木賊」からの連想により、鑑賞者には画面の外にある月をイメージすることが期待されたのだろう。落款から、描かれた時期がまさに仲秋(旧暦８月)だったと知れる。

Rabbits and Horsetail Reeds

Maruyama Ōkyo
1786
Shizuoka Prefectural Museum of Art

The painting brings together three rabbits and horsetail reeds. From a young age, Ōkyo had a habit of organizing his compositions through skillfully angling his subjects. The image takes inspiration from the Noh theater piece *Tokusa*, but it omits the moon lauded in the play. Ōkyo's signature discloses that the work was made on the fifteenth day of the eighth month, the time of autumn in the lunar calendar.

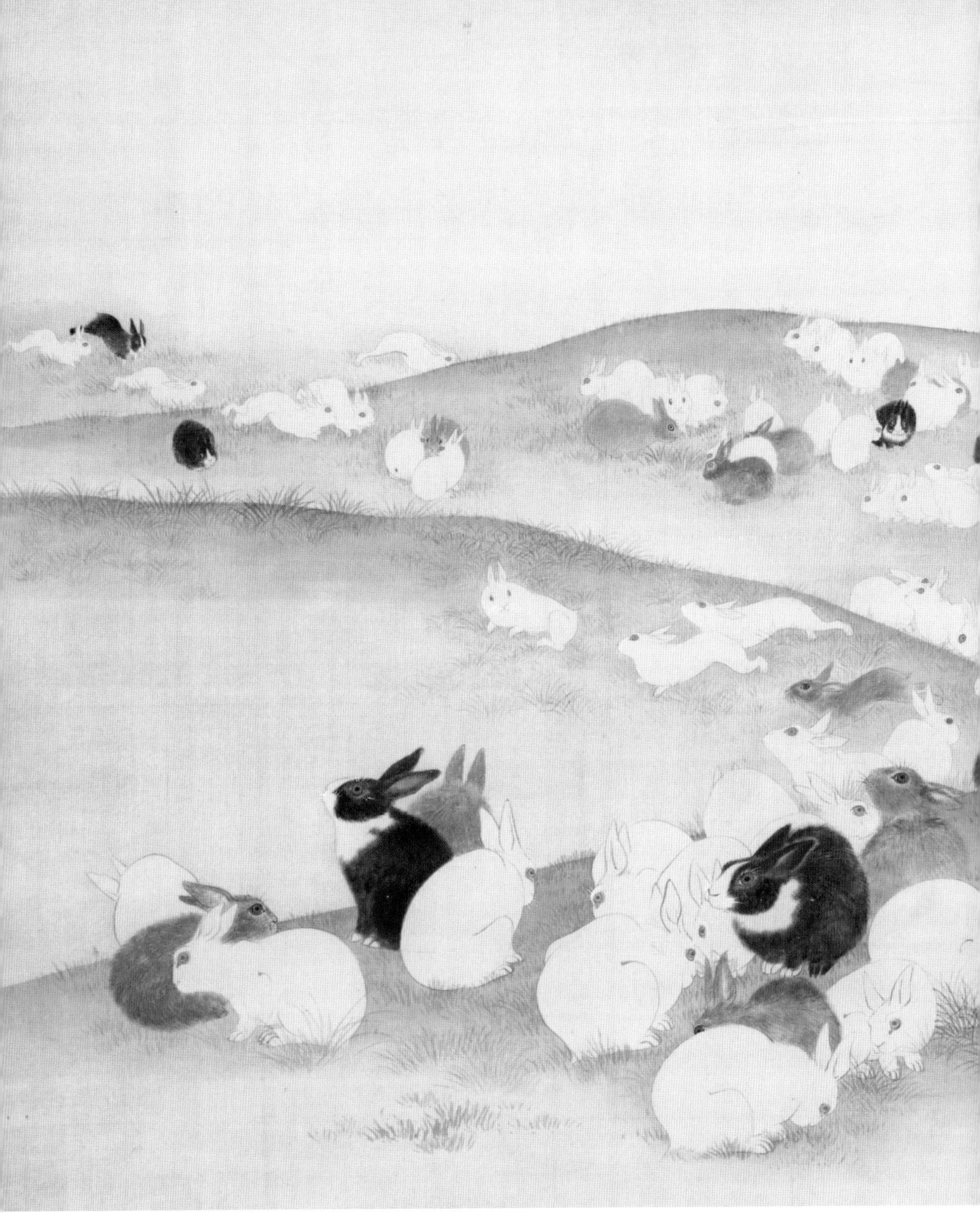

百兎図
円山応挙
天明4年（1784）

画面を埋め尽くすように描かれた、おびただしい数の兎たち。応挙得意の兎の組合せが各所に見出せる。子孫繁栄を願っての作に違いない。

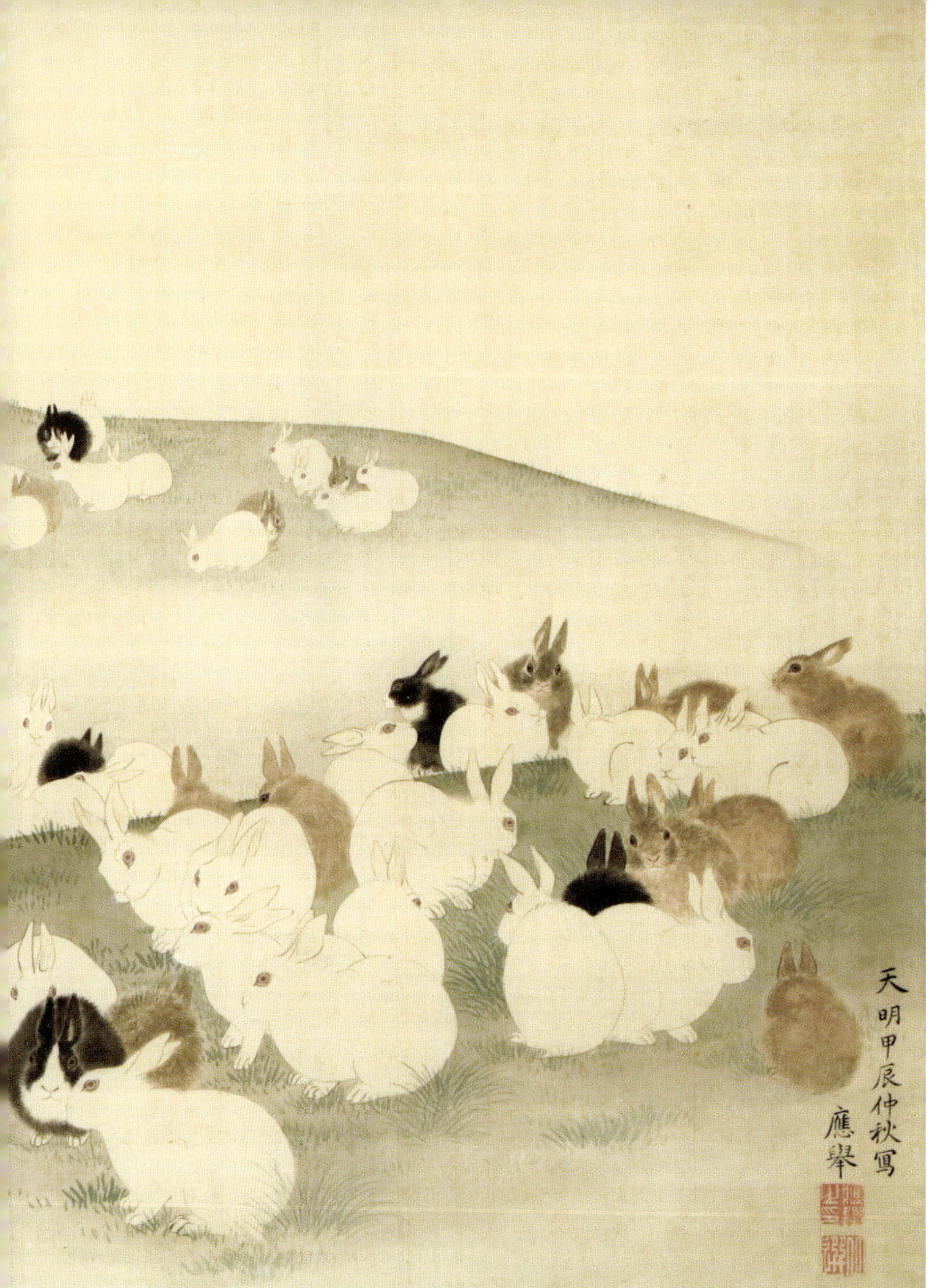

One Hundred Rabbits

Maruyama Ōkyo
1784

The image is filled to the brim with rabbits painted in Ōkyo's signature style. The work no doubt reflects a wish for abundant offspring.

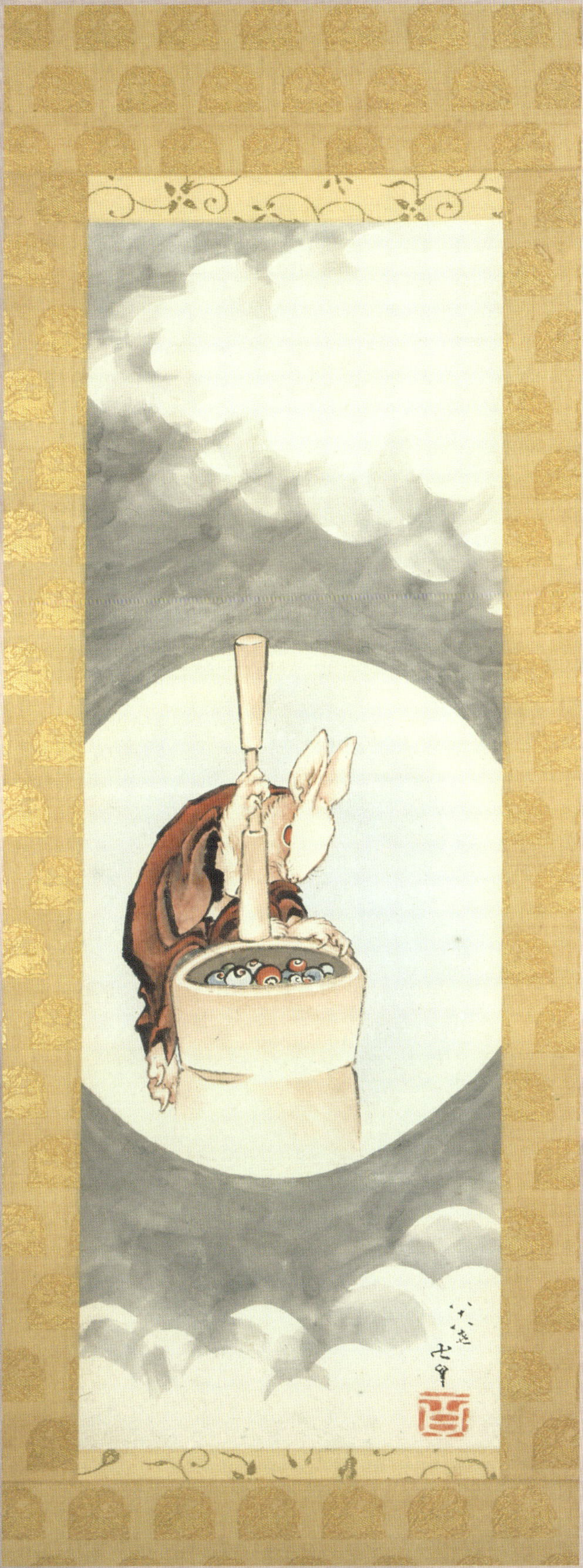

宝珠を搗く月兎

葛飾北斎
江戸時代後期（19c前半）

月のなかで兎が搗くのは、餅ではなく宝珠である。外隈（そとぐま）の技法で表わされた満月を上下から挟む雲の表現がリアルだ。白兎が着る赤い上衣から、ある人物の還暦を祝っての作かとも想像される。表具裂にも花兎金襴を用いている。

Moon Rabbit Pounding Wish-granting Jewels

Katsushika Hokusai
Early 19th century

This rabbit is not pounding mochi but wish-granting jewels. By accentuating the moon with contours of ink, the celestial body appears as if encircled by clouds in a real night sky. The red garments worn by the rabbit might indicate that the painting was made for someone celebrating their sixtieth birthday.

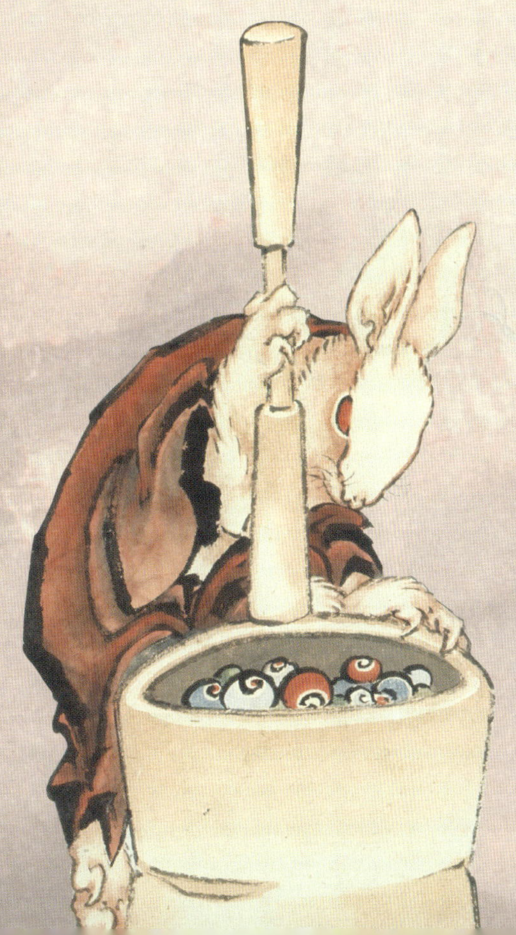

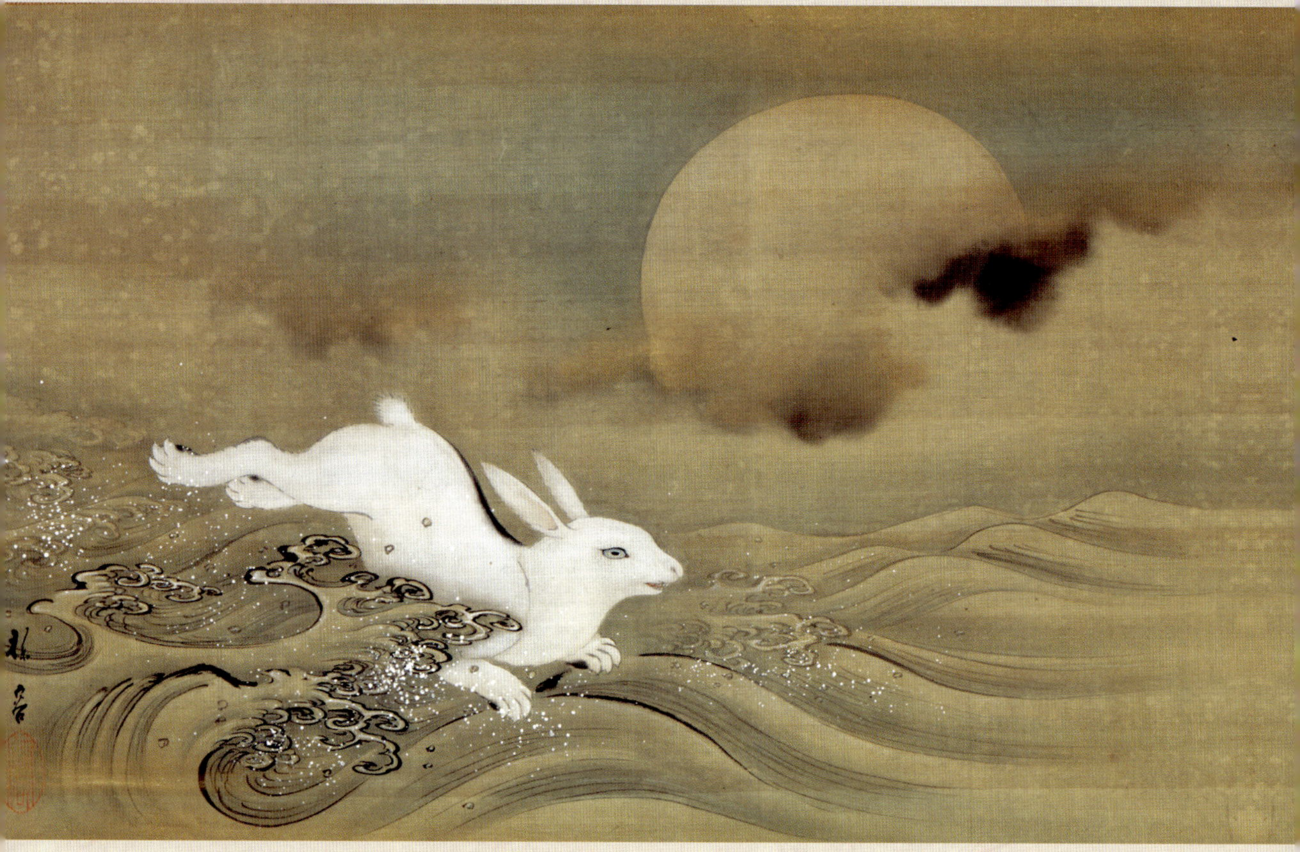

浪兎図

沖探容
江戸時代後期(19c前半)

Rabbit and Waves

Oki Tanyō
Early 19th century

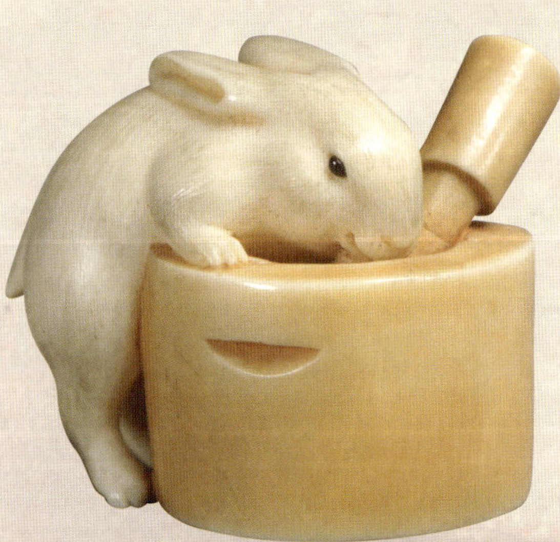

臼兎(うすうさぎ)牙彫根付

江戸時代(18c)
東京国立博物館

Netsuke of a Rabbit Pounding Mochi

18th century
Tokyo National Museum

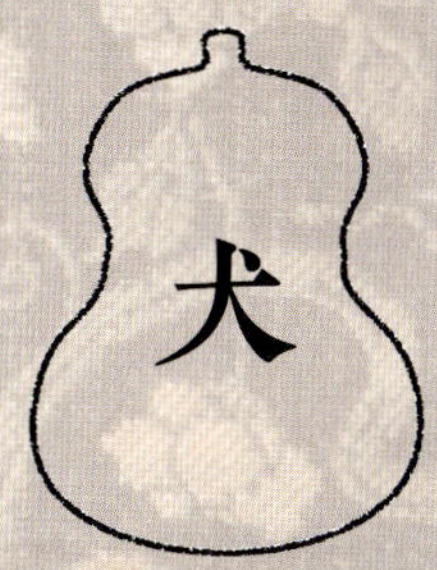

犬は多産で、産が軽いとされたことから、安産や子孫繁栄の象徴となった。室町時代以降、公家や武家の間に伏せた犬の形を模した一対の小箱(「宿直犬」・「犬筥」)が、安産のまじないや小児の魔除けとして普及し、婚礼道具に取り入れられた。これを踏襲するかたちで江戸時代には、犬の形に似せた張子細工の人形「犬張子」が出産のお守りとして庶民の間に広まり、嫁入り道具の一つになった。

The Dog

With their many offspring dogs were considered giving easy birth, making them symbols for fecundity and a thriving lineage. Since the Muromachi period, small boxes in the shape of dogs presented at weddings were popular among nobles and warriors alike as charms for easy childbirth and the protection of offspring. On the basis of this tradition, papier mâché toys in the shape of dogs were developed as part of dowries in the Edo period to protect women and children during childbirth.

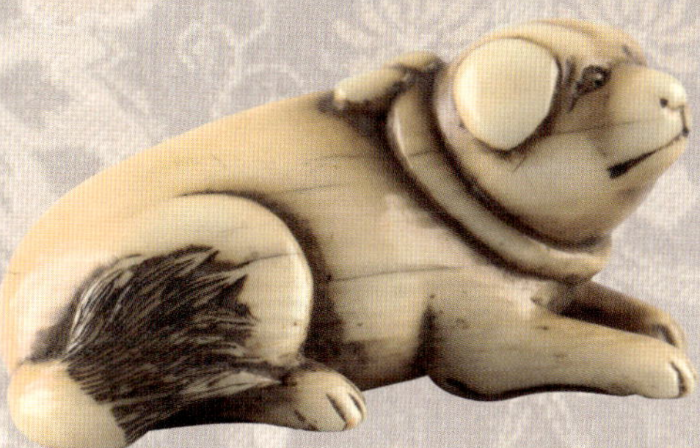

子犬牙彫根付
江戸時代(18c)
メトロポリタン美術館

Netsuke of Puppy
18th century
The Metropolitan Museum of Art

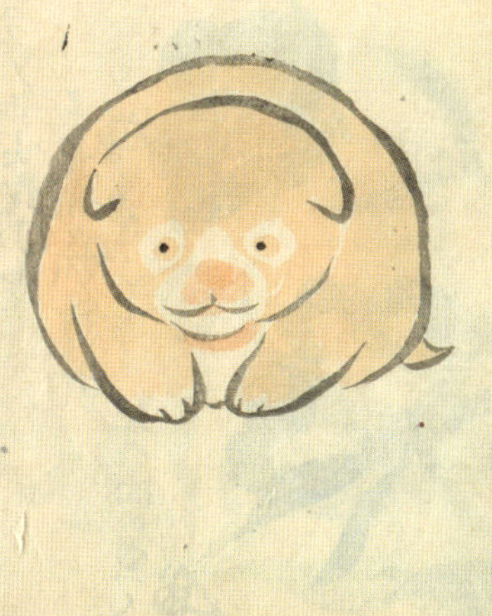

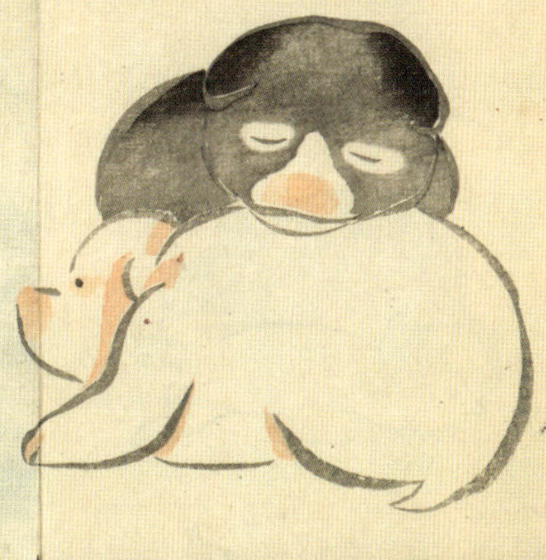

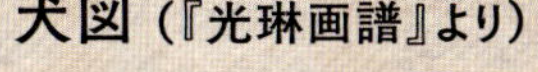

犬図(『光琳画譜』より)
中村芳中
文政9年(1826)以降
メトロポリタン美術館

***Dogs** (from Kōrin Painting Manual)*
After 1826 (reprinted posthumously)
Nakamura Hōchū
The Metropolitan Museum of Art

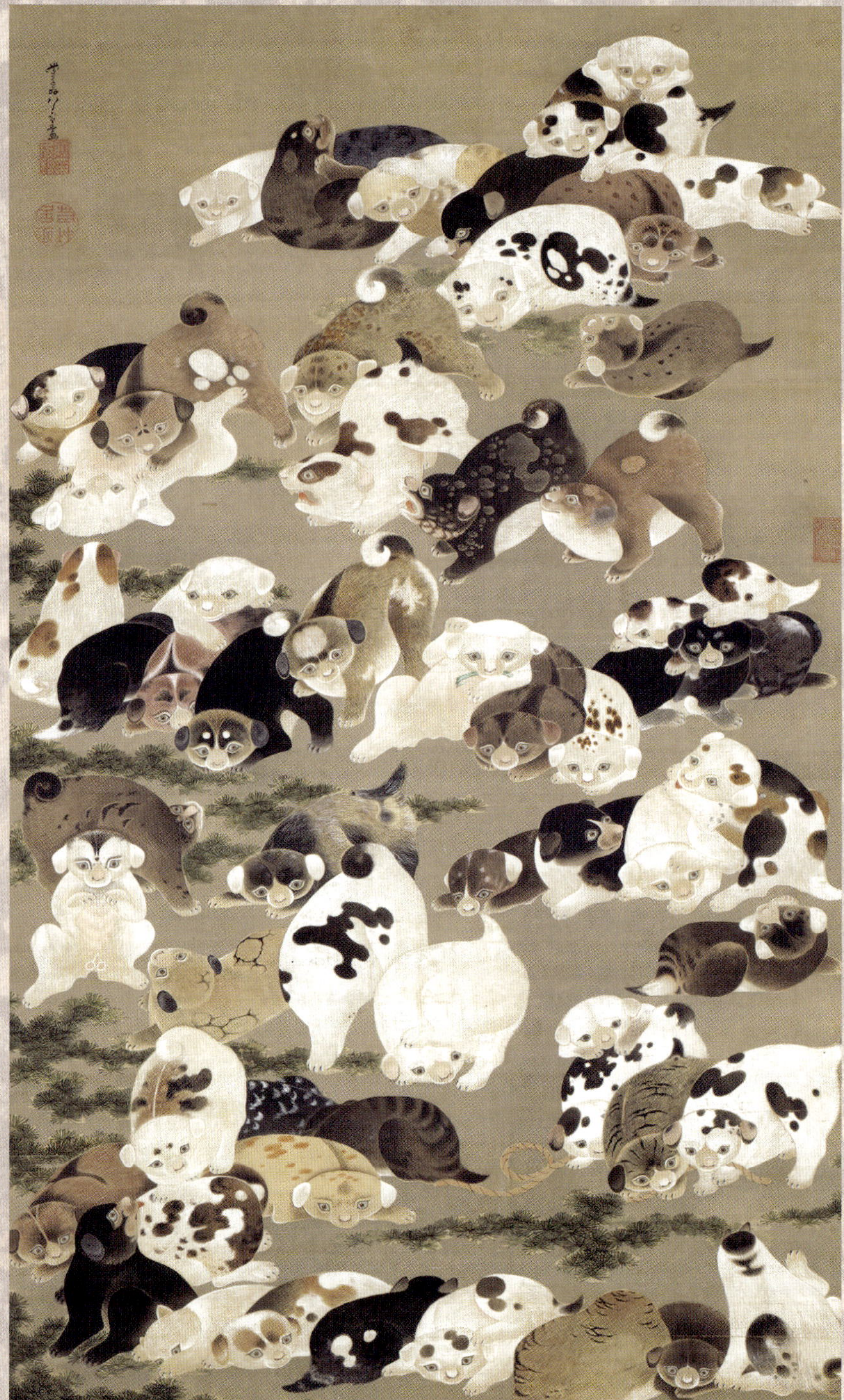

百犬図

伊藤若冲
寛政12年(1800)
京都国立博物館

蛇行しつつ画面を埋め尽くすように配される、おびただしい数の子犬たち。子孫繁栄を願う吉祥画に違いないが、子犬同士の重なりと毛斑とがつくり出す独特の文様が、見る者を幻惑の世界に誘う。

One Hundred Dogs

Itō Jakuchū
1800
Kyoto National Museum

Jakuchū filled this image with a meandering arrangement of dogs. This image, too, was probably commissioned as a plea for abundant children. However, the individual character of Jakuchū's overflowing image and the attention given to the fur of each individual animal invite the viewer into a world of wonder.

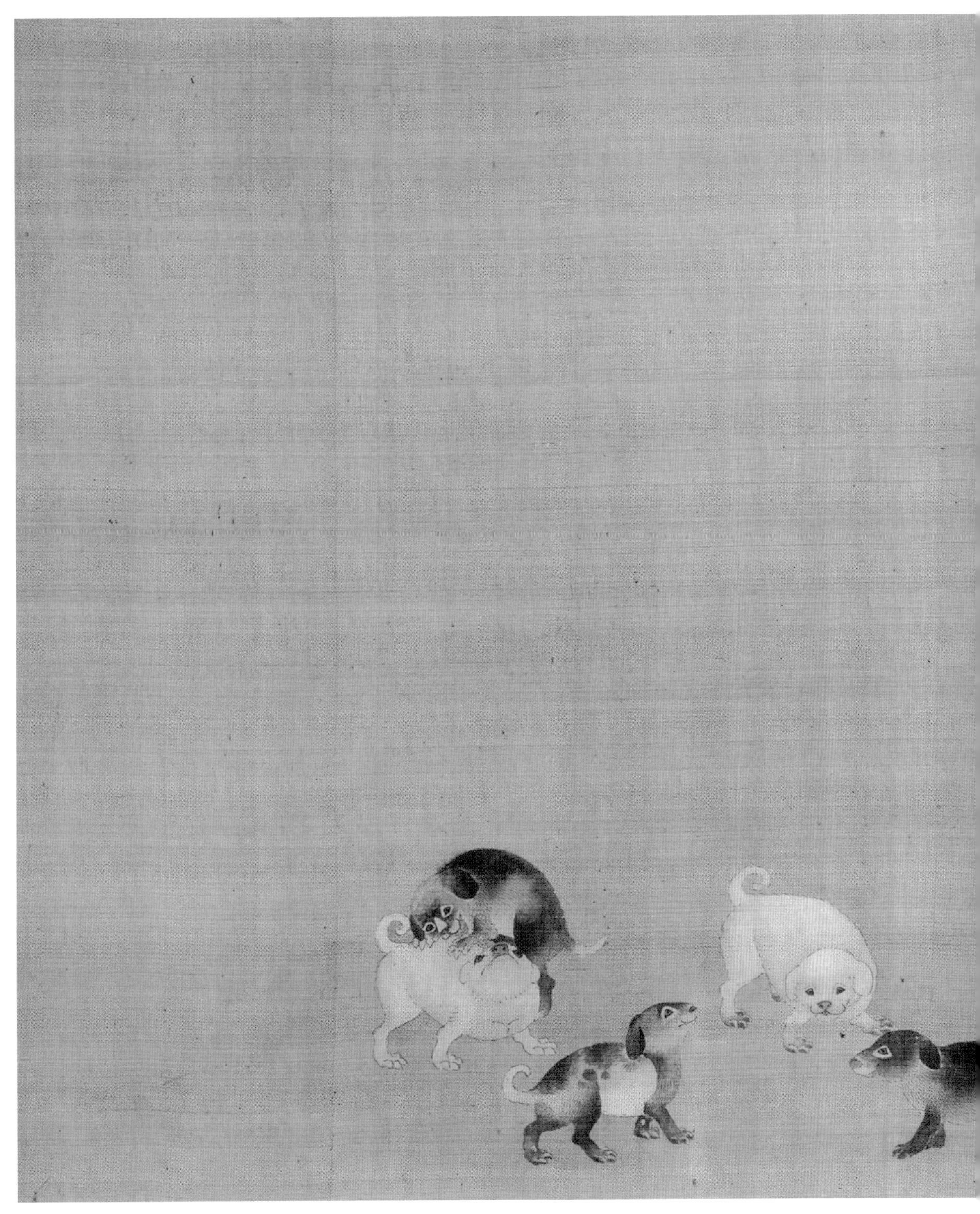

親子犬図

狩野永良
江戸時代(18c)
静岡県立美術館

狩野永良(1741〜71)は、わずか31歳で夭逝してしまった6代目の京狩野家当主。黒・白それぞれの親犬から産まれた5匹の子犬の色具合が楽しい。平穏な情景から、一族の子孫繁栄の願いも垣間見える。

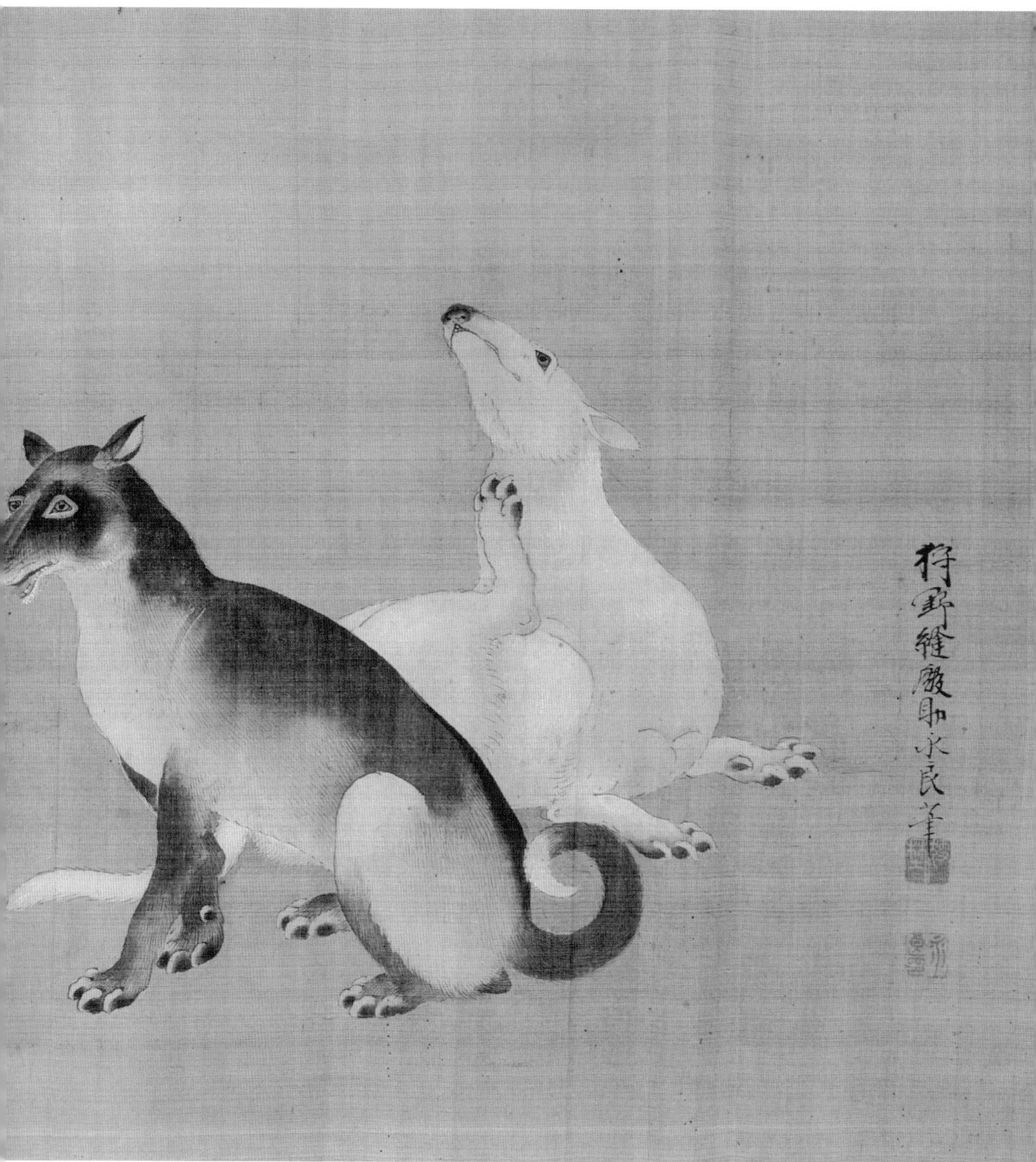

Dogs and Puppies

Kano Eiryō
18th century
Shizuoka Prefectural Museum of Art

Kano Eiryō (1741-71), the sixth head of the Kyoto Kano school, was only thirty-one years old when he died. The black and white dogs are watching over their five offspring who are frolicking at their feet. The peaceful nature of paintings like this reflected the wish for a prospering family.

朝顔狗子図杉戸

円山応挙
天明4年（1784）
東京国立博物館

日本最古の眼病治療院として知られた尾張国海部郡・明眼院の書院障壁画だったもの。一時期、眼を患った応挙が世話になり、回復後に御礼の意味で描いたものという。書院は現在、東京国立博物館内に移築され、応挙館と呼ばれている。本図は杉戸に朝顔の咲くかたわらで戯れる5匹の子犬を描く。応挙とその門人たちには、かわいい子犬を描いた作が多い。安産や子孫繁栄を象徴する主題でもあり、注文も多かったことだろう。

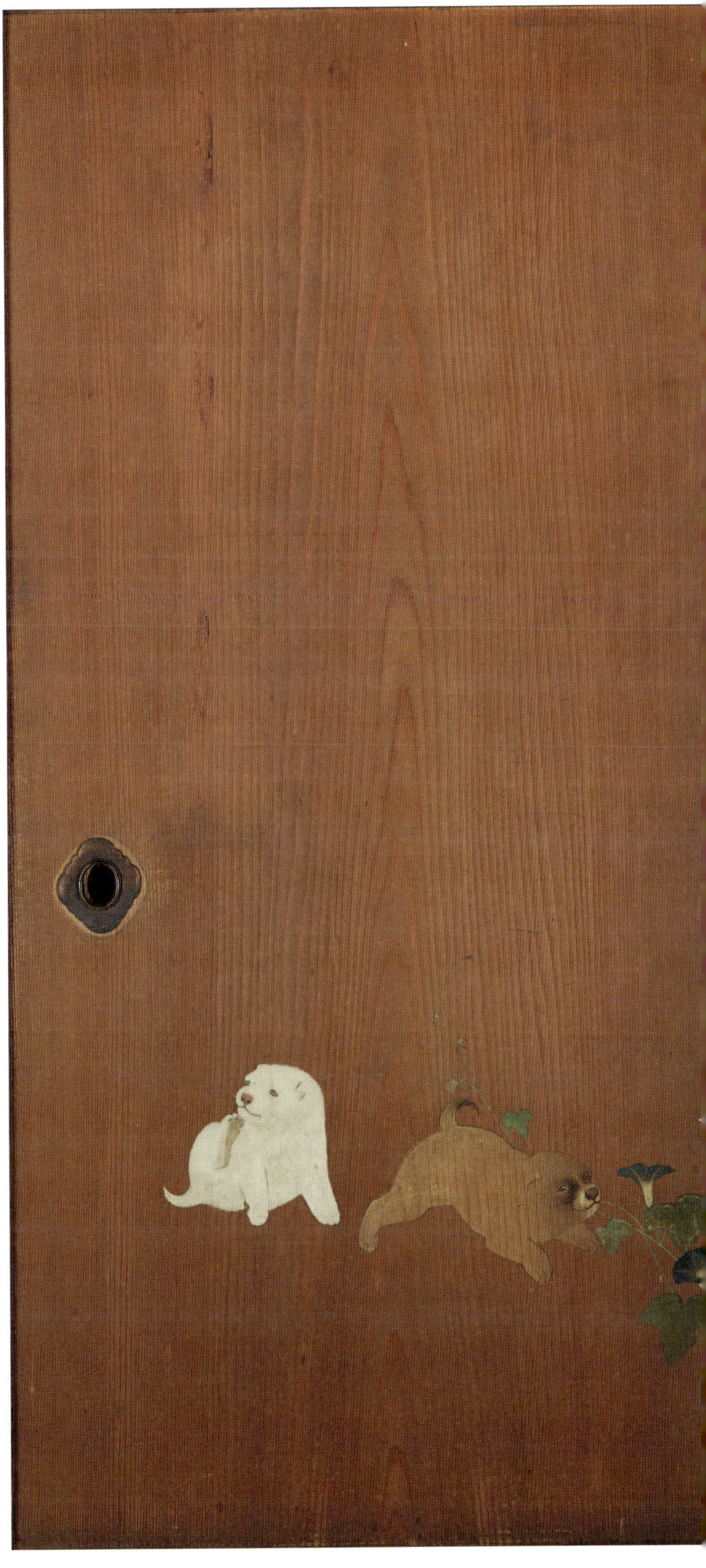

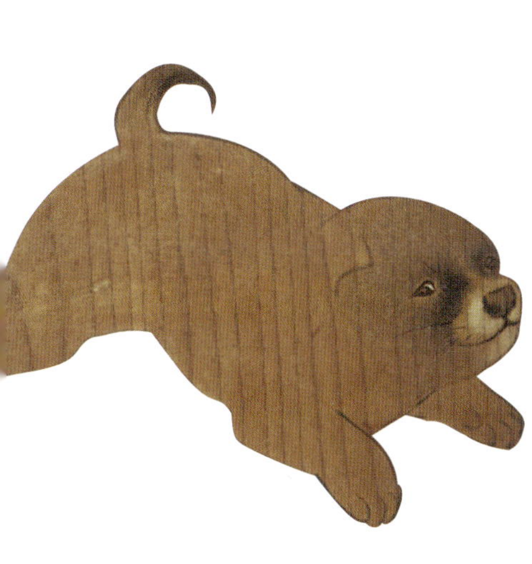

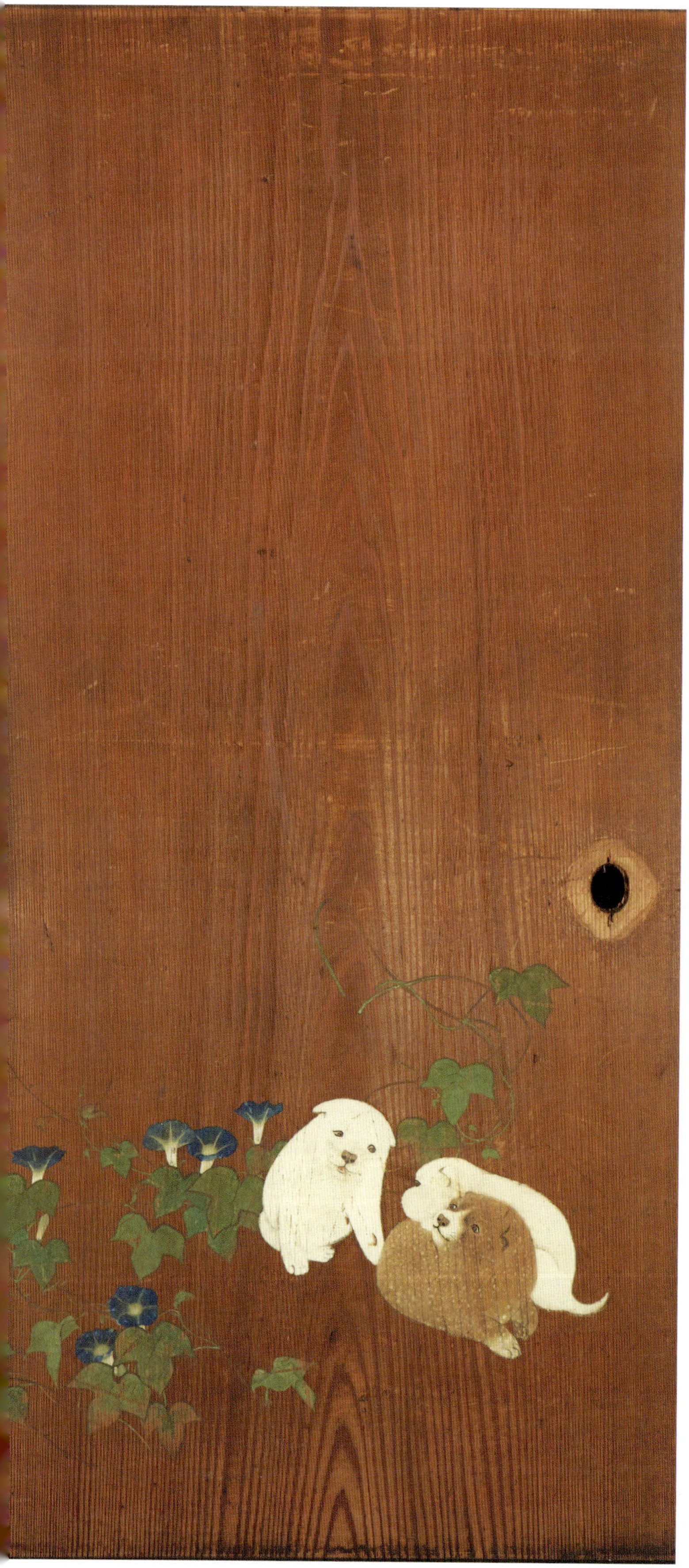

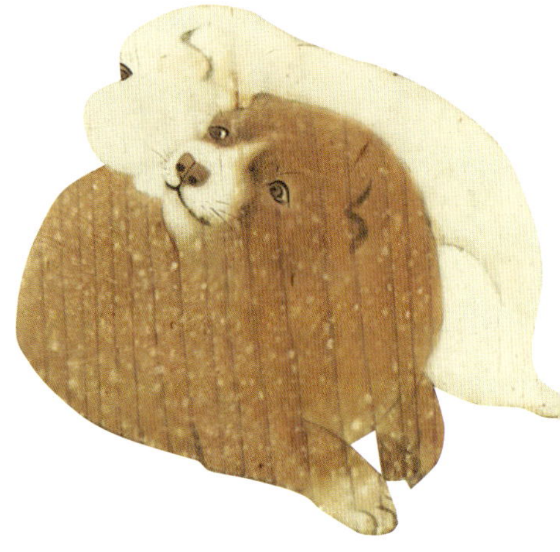

Puppies and Morning Glories

Maruyama Ōkyo
1784
Tokyo National Museum

These sliding doors were part of the oldest ophthalmological hospital, the Myōgen'in in Owari Province. The hospital treated Ōkyo for an ailment of the eyes, and as a token of his gratitude he made these paintings. Part of the facility has been moved to the premises of the Tokyo National Museum, where the building is now called the "Ōkyo House." The image shown here depicts five puppies beneath flowering morning glories on sliding doors made of plain cypress wood. Ōkyo and his pupils painted a great number of puppies, reflecting their symbolism as harbingers of easy childbirth and fecundity.

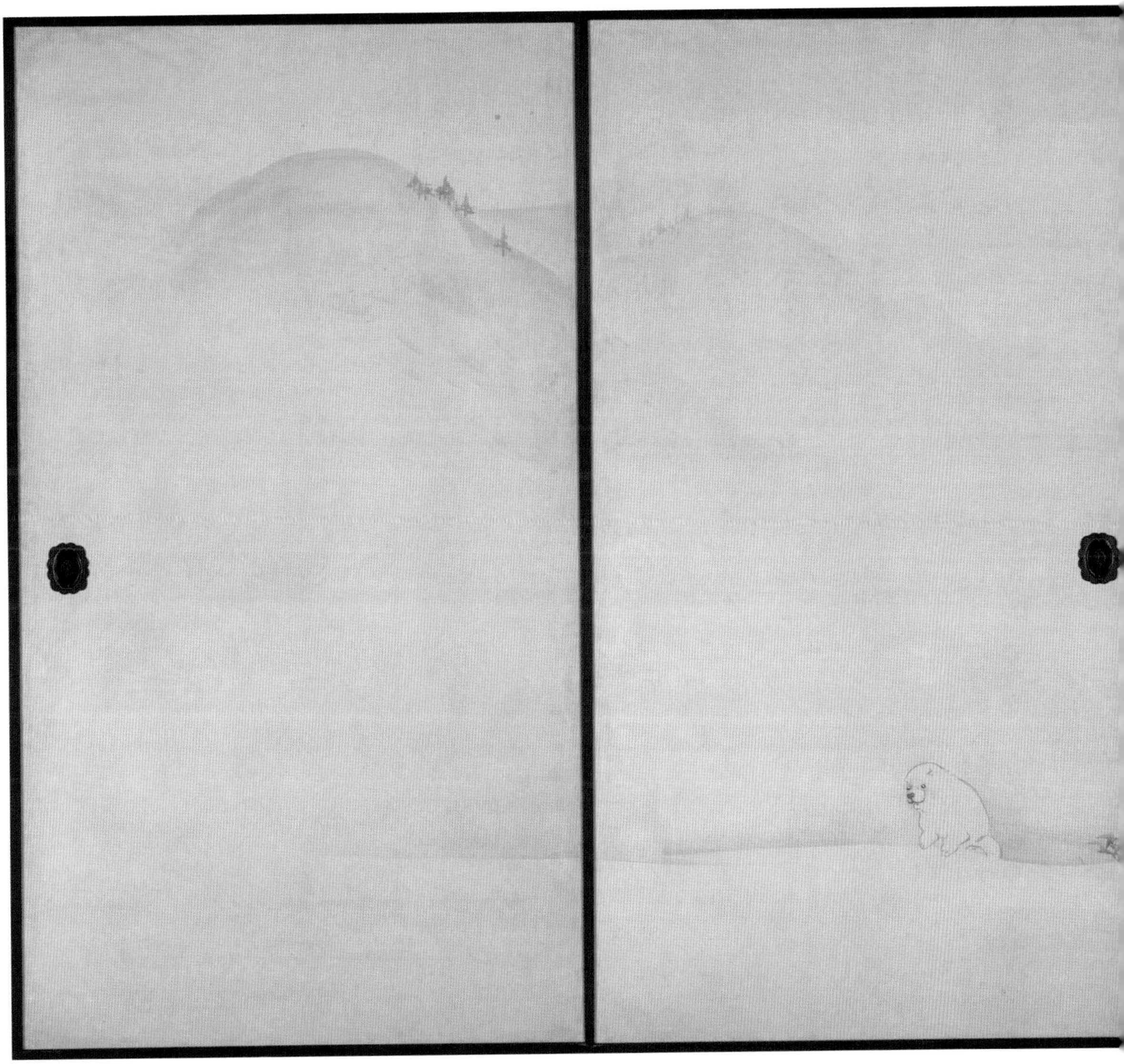

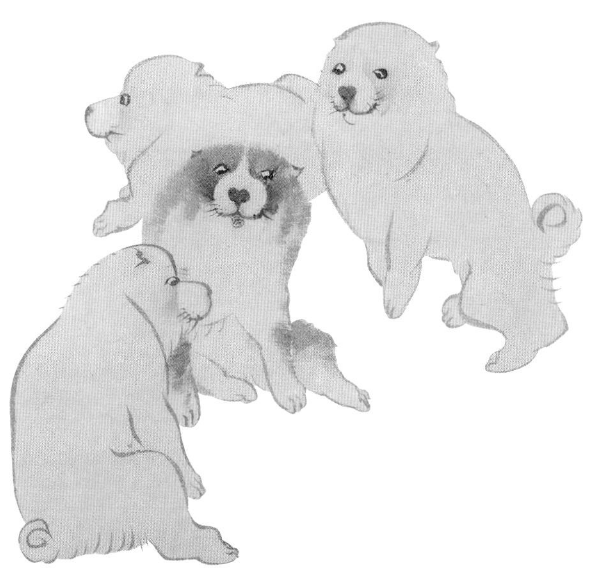

雪狗子図襖

長沢芦雪
寛政4～11年（1792～99）
メトロポリタン美術館

Puppies in the Snow

Nagasawa Rosetsu
1792–99
The Metropolitan Museum of Art

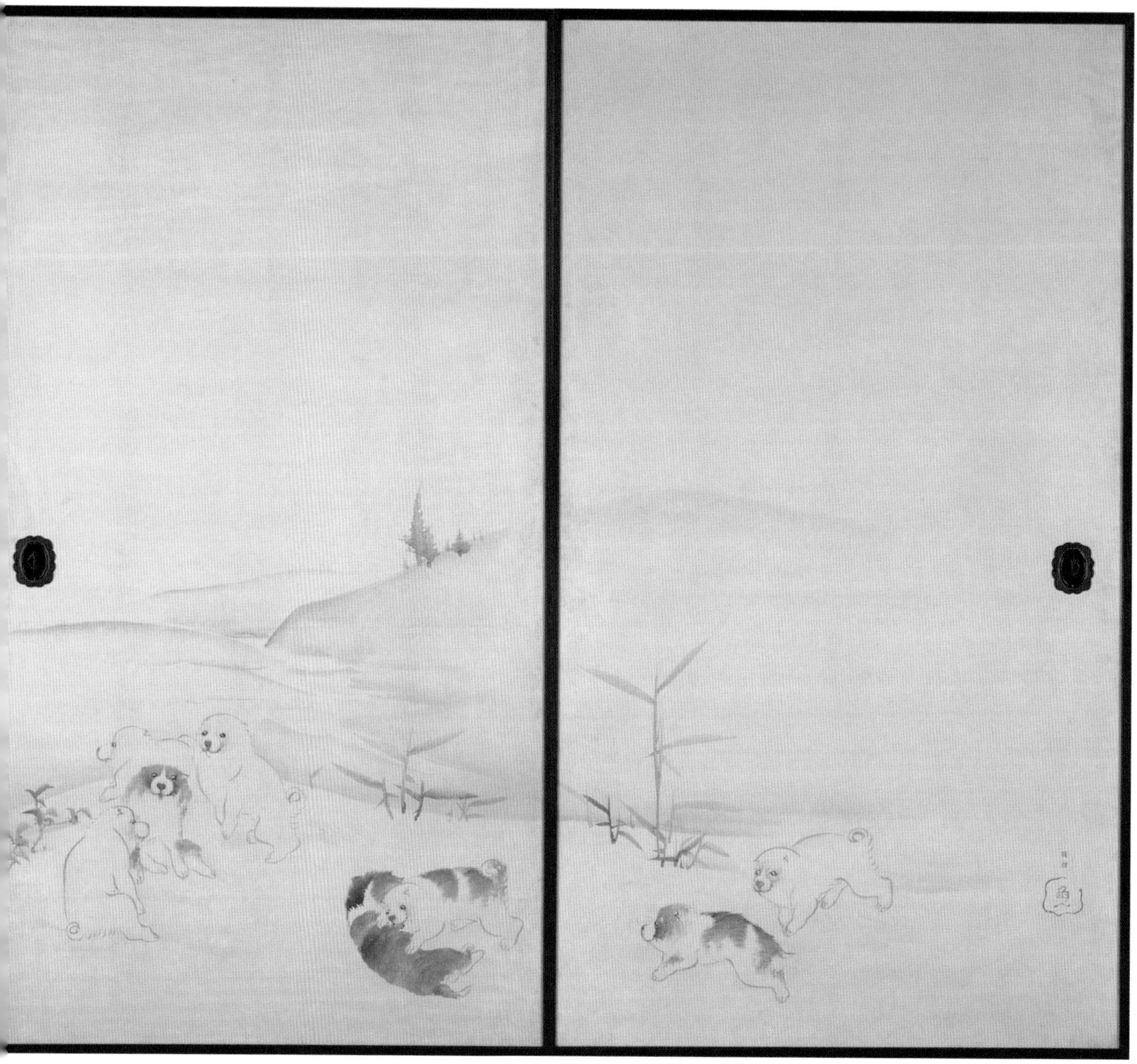

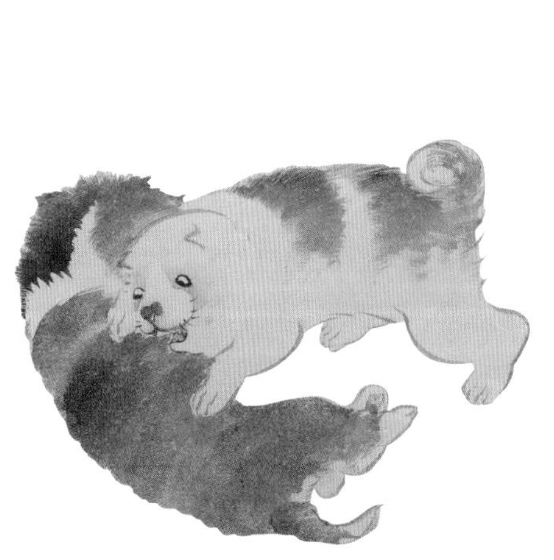

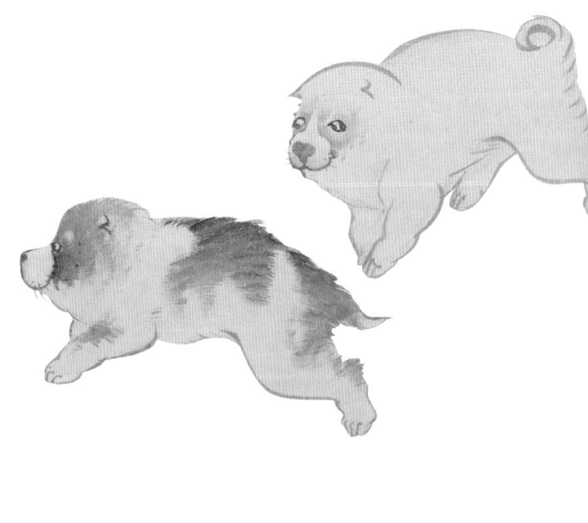

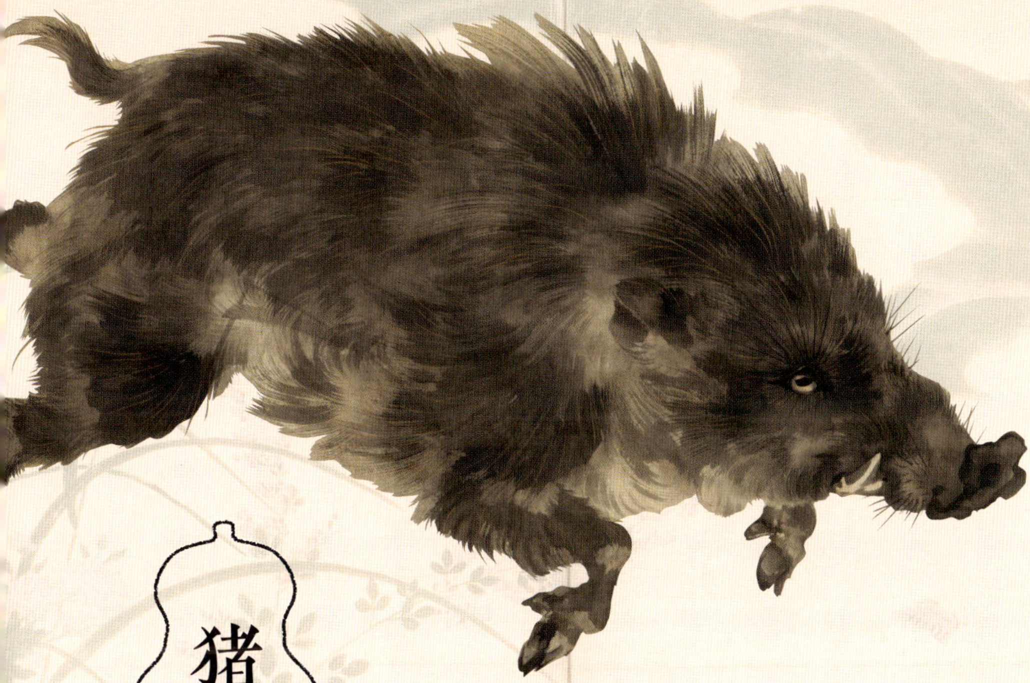

猪

野山を駆けまわる猪は、様々な神仏の乗り物とされた。陽炎を神格化した仏教の守護神である摩利支天は、忿怒形の福徳神で、弁才天・大黒天とともに蓄財の神として信仰された。そのままでは速すぎて人の目には見えないため、猪に乗せて図像化するようになったのだという。一方、身を伏せた猪の姿は「臥猪」と称され、天下泰平を表す語「撫綏」に通じる吉祥画として描かれてきた。円山応挙が伏した猪を描いたものの、老翁から病気の猪であると指摘され、ますます写生に励んだとの逸話（曲亭馬琴『著作堂一夕話』）は、この主題の流行を踏まえての話だったと言える。また、猪は多産なため子孫繁栄の象徴ともされた。

The Wild Boar

Boars roaming the wilderness are considered to carry Buddhas and Shinto deities on their backs. Marici (J. Marishiten), the guardian deity thought to be an embodiment of heat, symbolizes fortune and virtue. It is often worshipped alongside Sarasvati (J. Benzaiten) and Daikokuten. Marici is frequently depicted as riding a boar and galloping at a speed that is too far for mortals' eyes to see. The crouching postures of boars are often associated with peace and prosperity in the realm. Ōkyo chose to depict an aged boar, seemingly struck by illness. The moving work is a rendering of the famous tale *Chosakudō issekiwa* by Kyokutei Bakin. Boars were also considered symbols of fecundity.

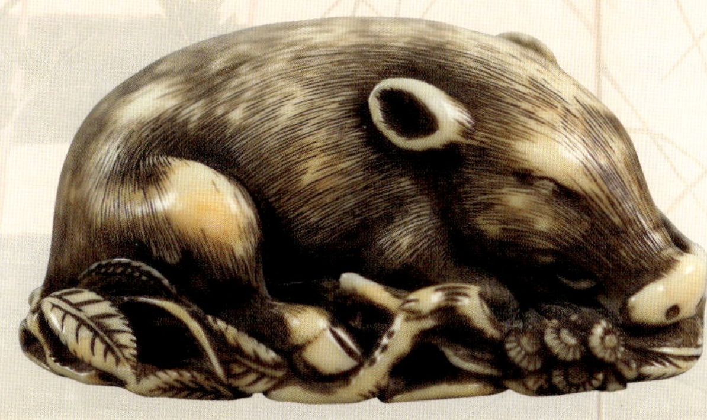

猪牙彫根付
江戸時代（18c末〜19c初め）
メトロポリタン美術館

Boar Netsuke
Late 18th–early 19th century
The Metropolitan Museum of Art

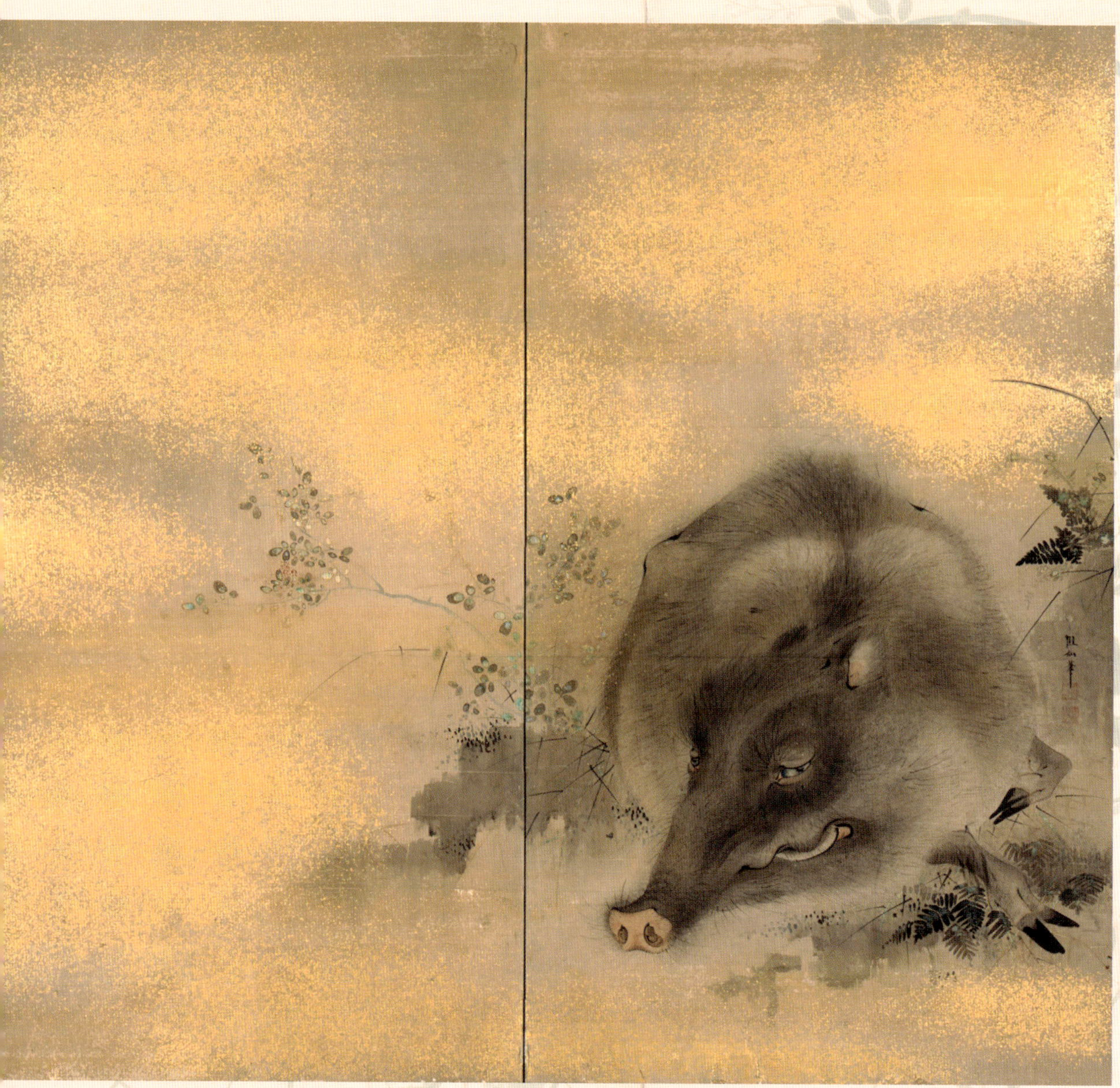

猪図

森狙仙
文化4年(1807)以前
株式会社　千總

「臥猪図」の代表的作例。伝来は不明ながら、大名家など貴顕からの注文品だったものと推測される。

Boar

Mori Sosen
Before 1807
Chiso Co.Ltd.

This image is one of the prime depictions of a crouching boar. Its original owner and circumstances are unknown, but it may have been commissioned by a daimyo or person of similar high rank.

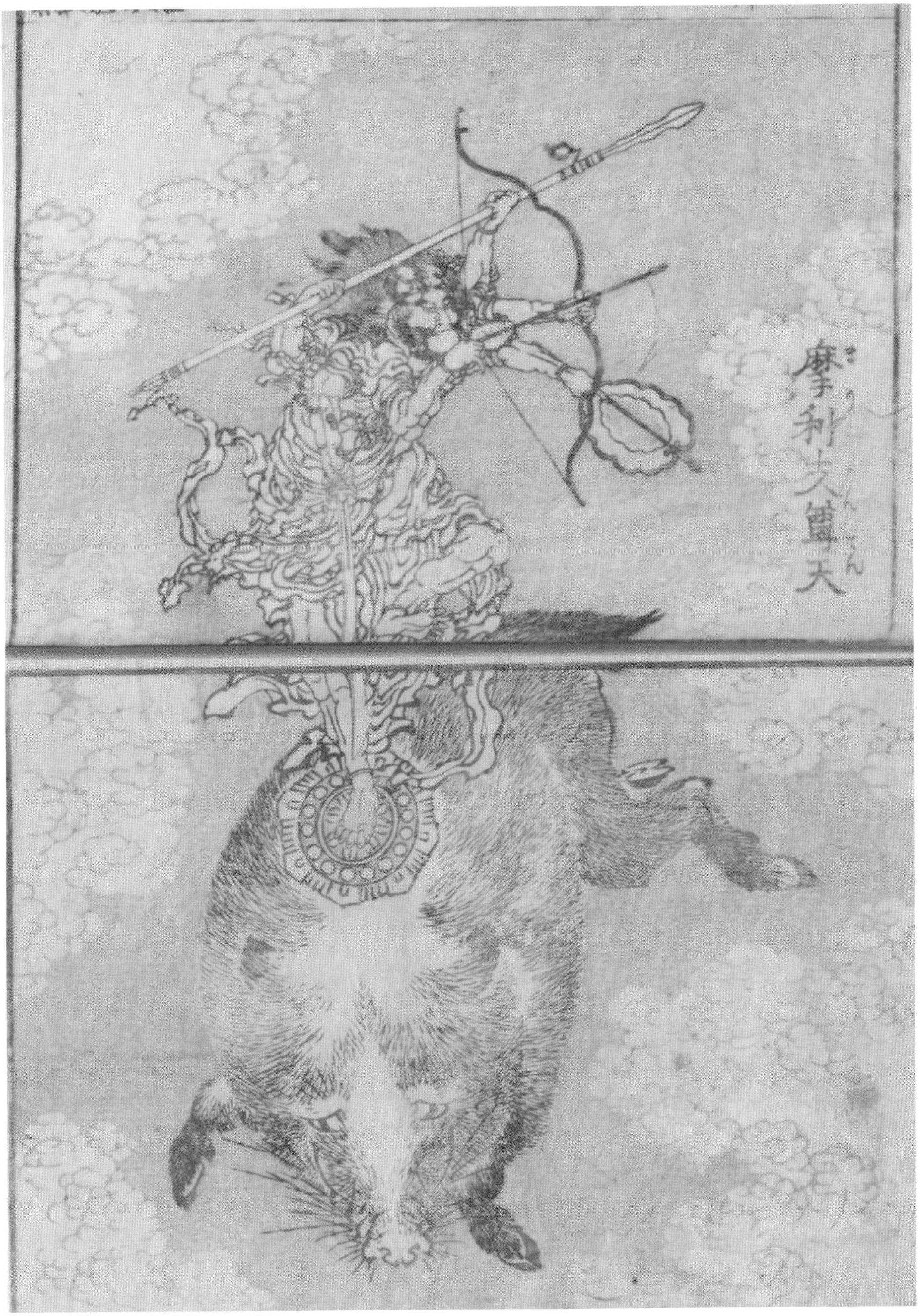

摩利支天像（『北斎漫画』六編より）

葛飾北斎
文化14年（1817）刊
メトロポリタン美術館

Marici (*from Hokusai manga, Volume Six*)

Katsushika Hokusai
1817
The Metropolitan Museum of Art

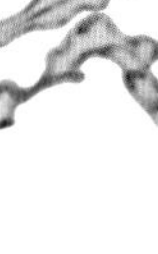

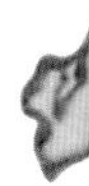

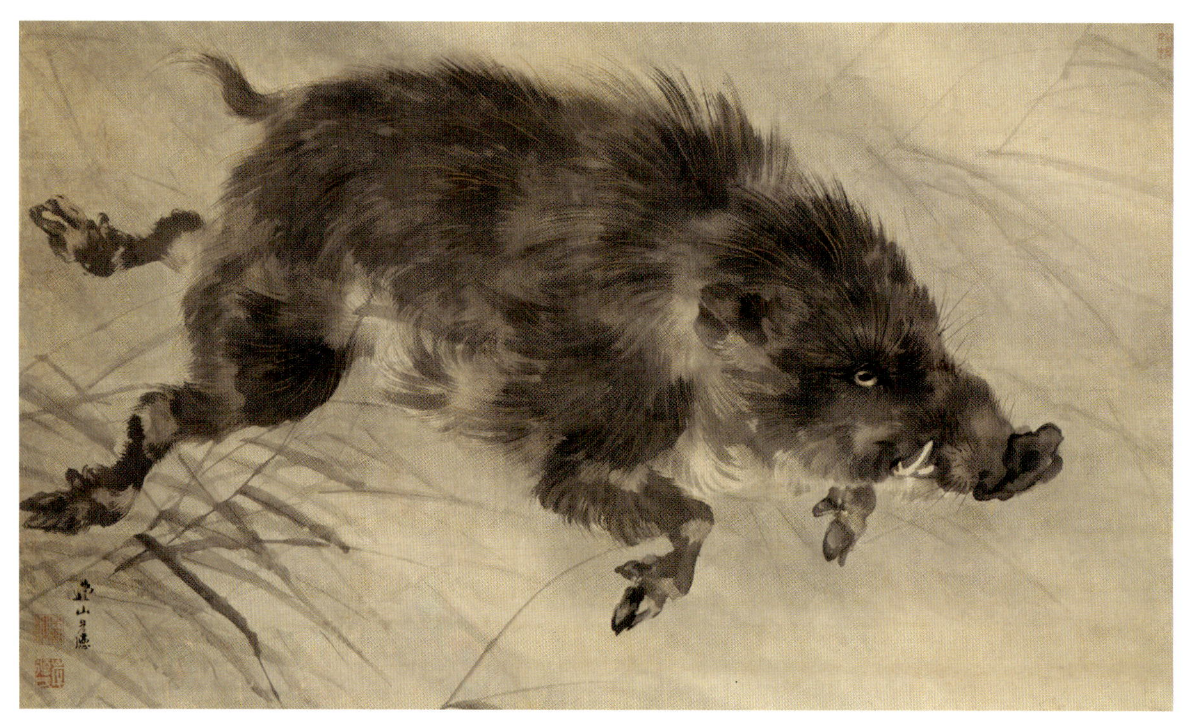

猪図

岸連山(1804〜59)
江戸時代（19c）
東京国立博物館

「猪突猛進」という言葉どおりに、勢いよく駆ける猪を画面いっぱいに描く。岸連山(1804〜59)は、岸駒の孫娘の婿となり、岸派の3代目を継いだ京都の画家。

Boar

Kishi Renzan
19th century
Tokyo National Museum

The Japanese term for "rushing recklessly," literally "advancing like a boar," illustrates the force embodied by these animals. Kishi Renzan (1804-59) was the third head of the Kyoto-based Kishi school. He married the granddaughter of the famous painter Kishi Ganku.

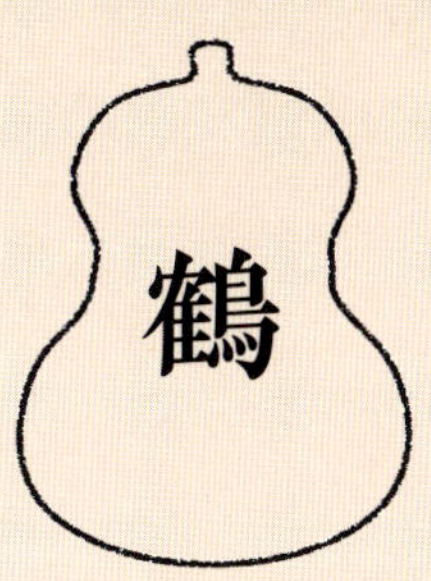

神仙思想にもとづき、古代中国では仙人の乗り物、また不老長寿の象徴とされた。その思想が日本に入ってきたのは平安初期頃とされ、日本でも1000年の寿命を保つ瑞鳥と捉えられた。また、同じく長寿と信じられた亀と組合わされることで、吉祥性はさらに増幅した。

The Crane

According to ancient Chinese folklore, immortals and sages are riding on cranes. For that reason, cranes were seen as symbols of longevity. This belief came to Japan as early as the beginning of the Heian period, and cranes have been venerated in this way for a thousand years. They are often depicted with turtles as two symbols of good fortune.

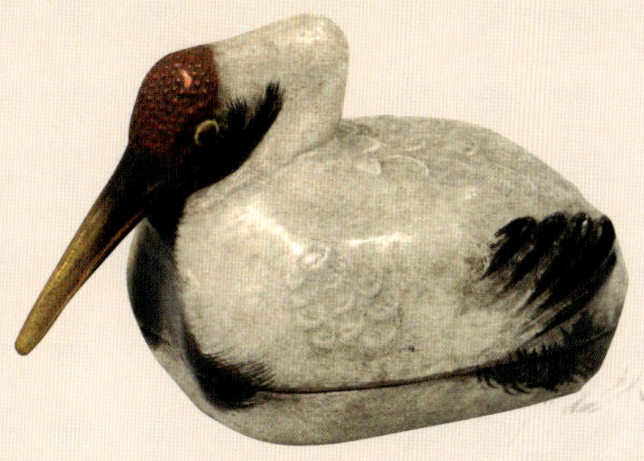

鶴形漆筥
江戸時代(19c)
メトロポリタン美術館

Box in the Shape of Young Crane
19th century
The Metropolitan Museum of Art

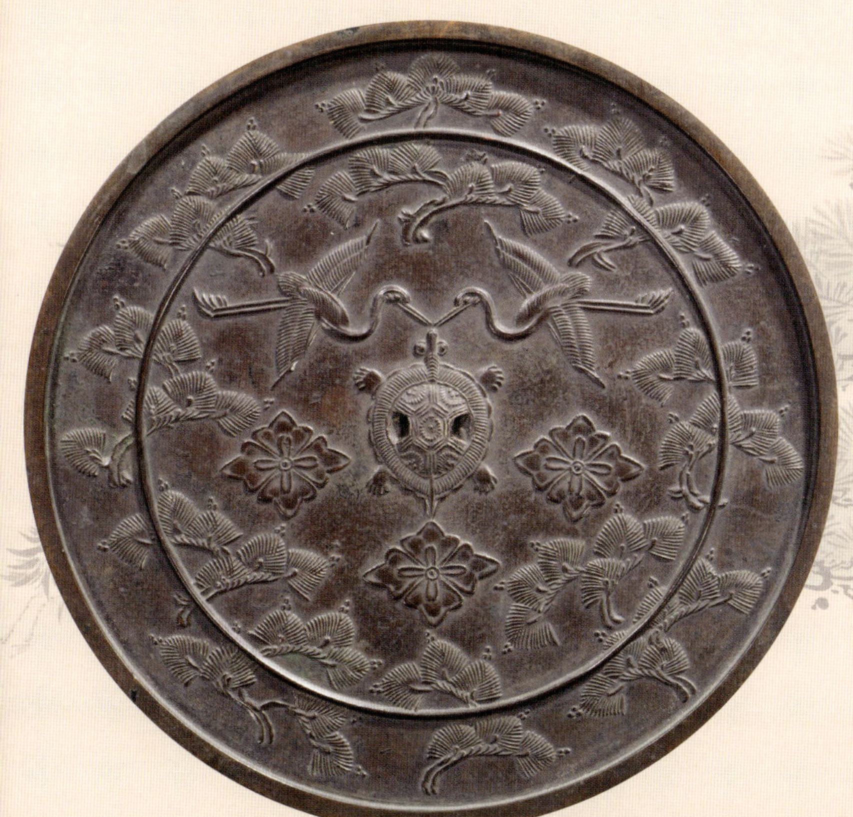

花菱松双鶴鏡
室町時代(15c)
東京国立博物館

Mirror with Motif of Cranes and Flowers in the Shape of a Diamond
15th century
Tokyo National Museum

松梅孤鶴図

伊藤若冲
江戸時代（18c）
東京国立博物館

若冲による墨画の鶴図は、一筆書きで卵型の体軀を表現する。その技は、もはや名人芸の域に達している。

Pine, Plum Tree, and Crane

Itō Jakuchū
18th century
Tokyo National Museum

Jakuchū's paintings of cranes frequently render the birds' bodies in egg-shaped circles done in a single brushstroke—a stroke of genius.

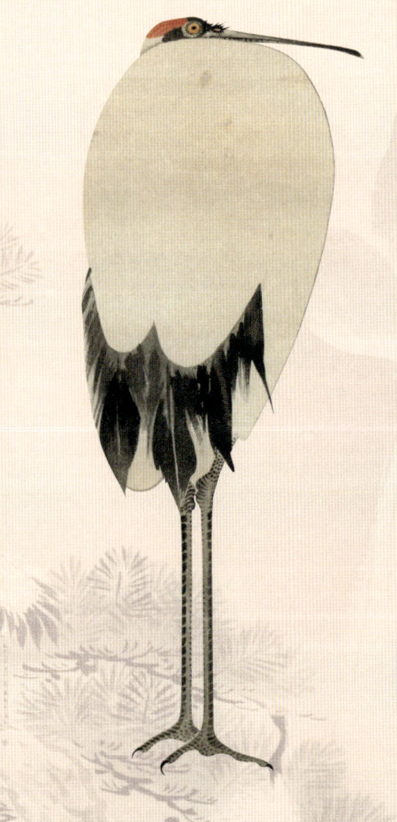

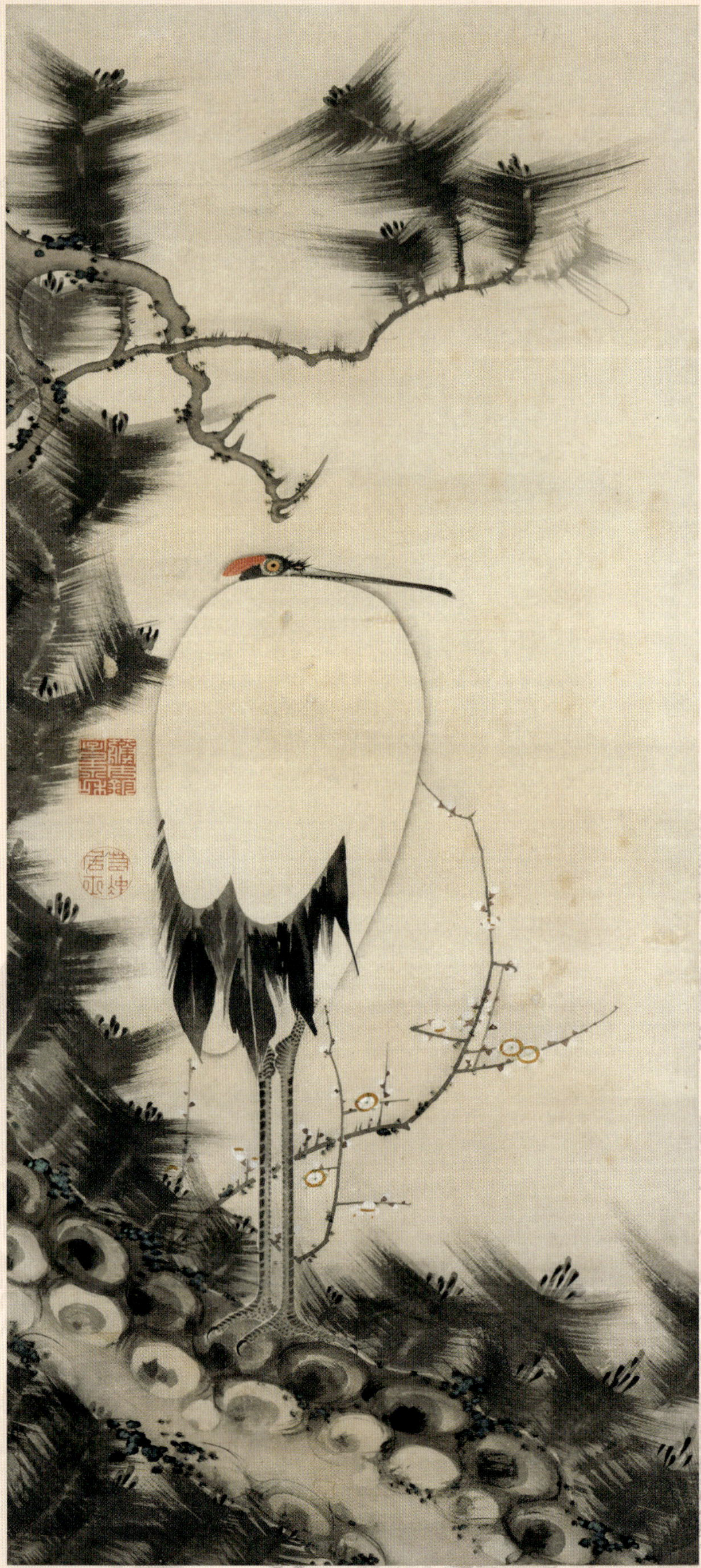

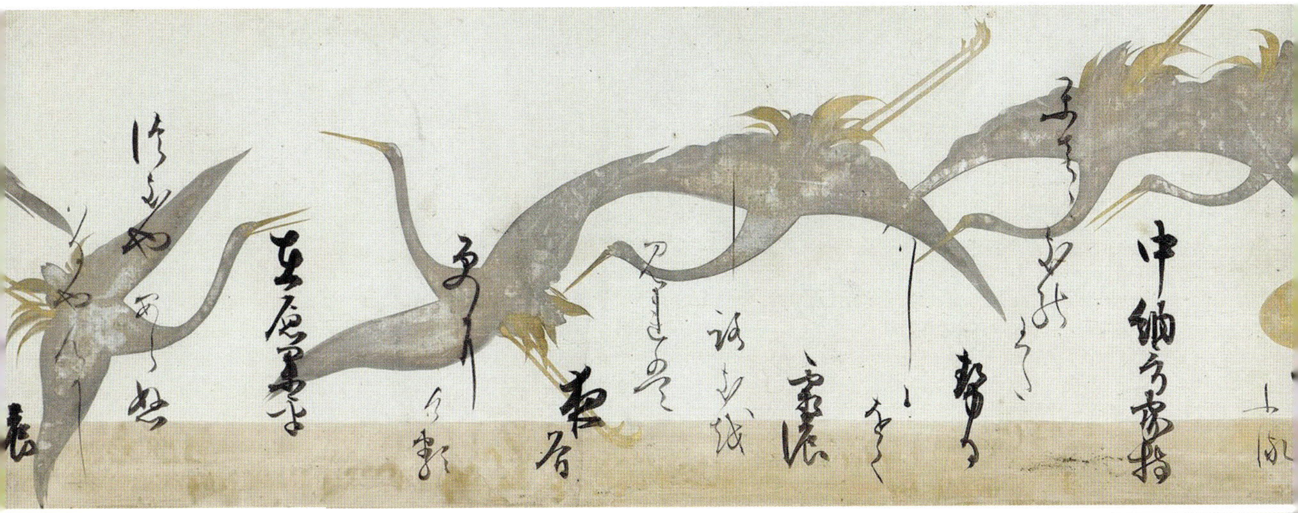

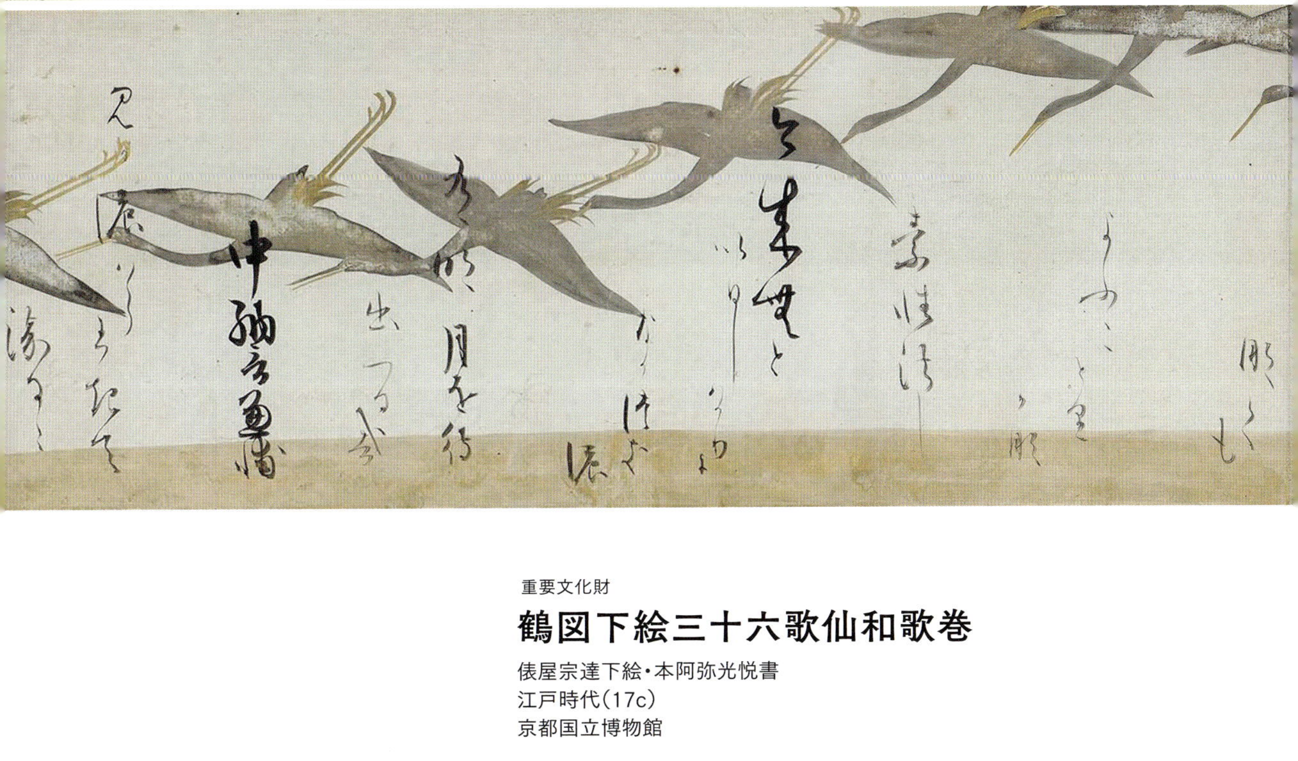

重要文化財

鶴図下絵三十六歌仙和歌巻

俵屋宗達下絵・本阿弥光悦書
江戸時代(17c)
京都国立博物館

俵屋宗達(活躍期1602〜1635年頃)が金・銀泥を駆使して、飛翔しまた羽を休めて寄りつどう鶴の群れをリズミカルな筆致のもとに描き出す。料紙装飾という位置づけながら、本阿弥光悦(1558〜1637)の書に従属するでもなく、両者見事なコラボレーションを見せる。

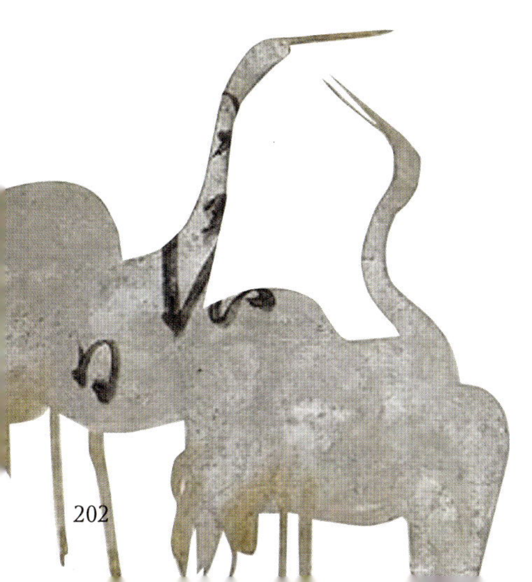

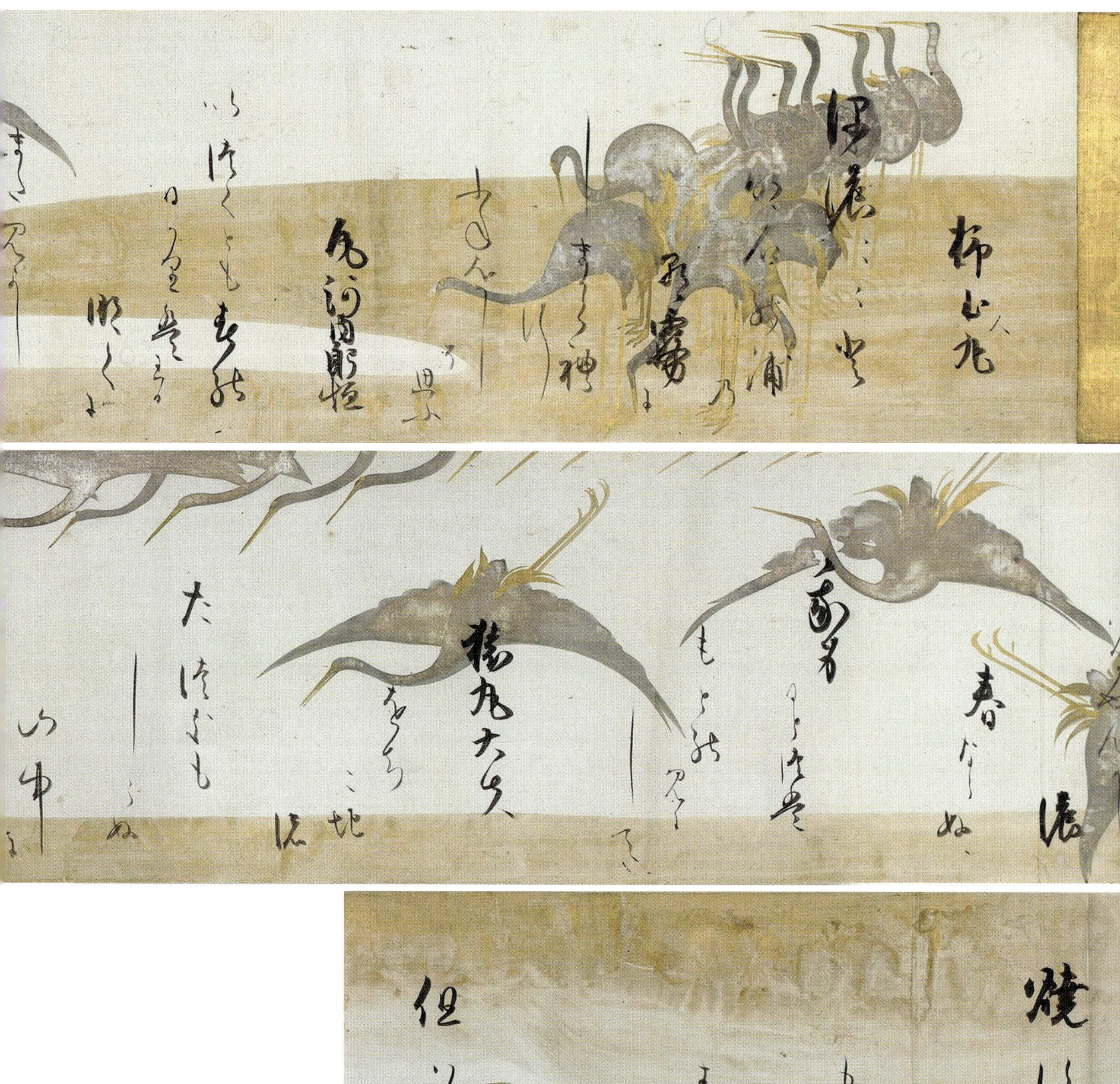

Important Cultural Property

Poetic Anthology Thirty-Six Poet Immortals, with Design of Cranes

Painting by Tawaraya Sōtatsu,
Caligraphy by Hon'ami Kōetsu
17th century
Kyoto National Museum

Tawaraya Sōtatsu (act. ca. 1602-35) added rhythmical images of flying and resting cranes in gold and silver pigment. On top of that paper décor, Hon'ami Kōetsu added the poems in his characteristic calligraphy, resulting in a masterful collaboration between the two artists.

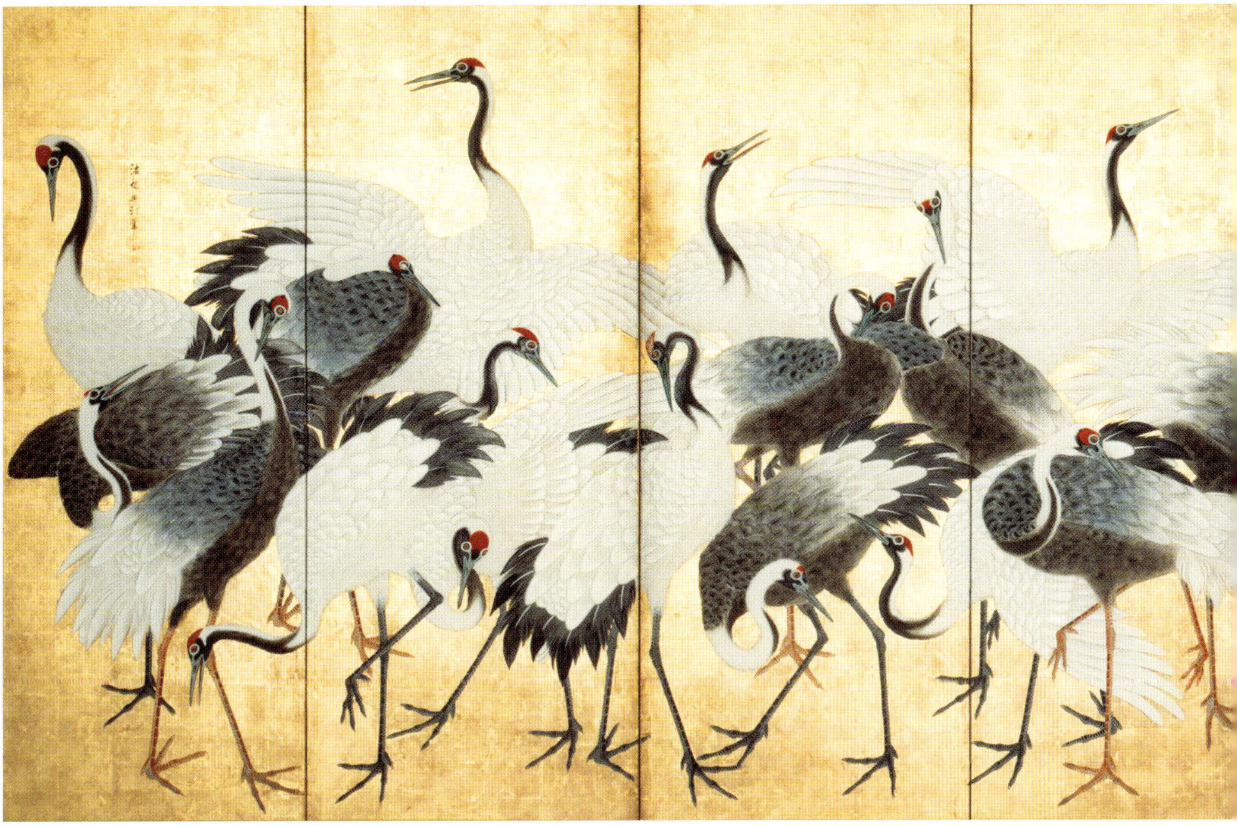

群鶴図屏風

石田幽汀
江戸時代中期（18c）
静岡県立美術館

円山応挙が一時師事した石田幽汀（1721～86）の作。タンチョウやナベヅル、マナヅルのほか、数種の鶴が画面を埋め尽くすように描かれる。

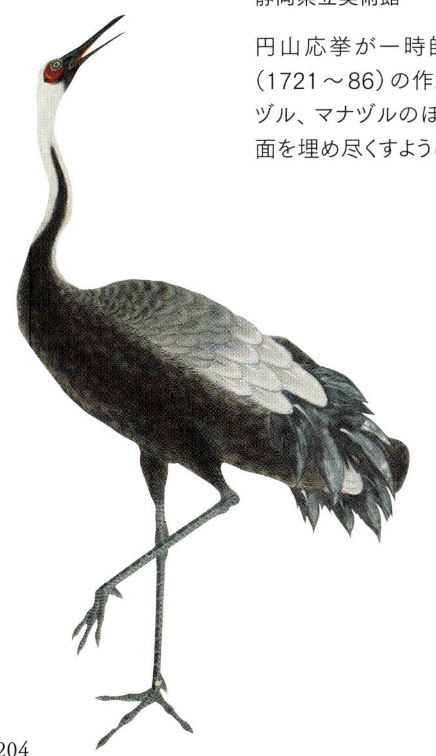

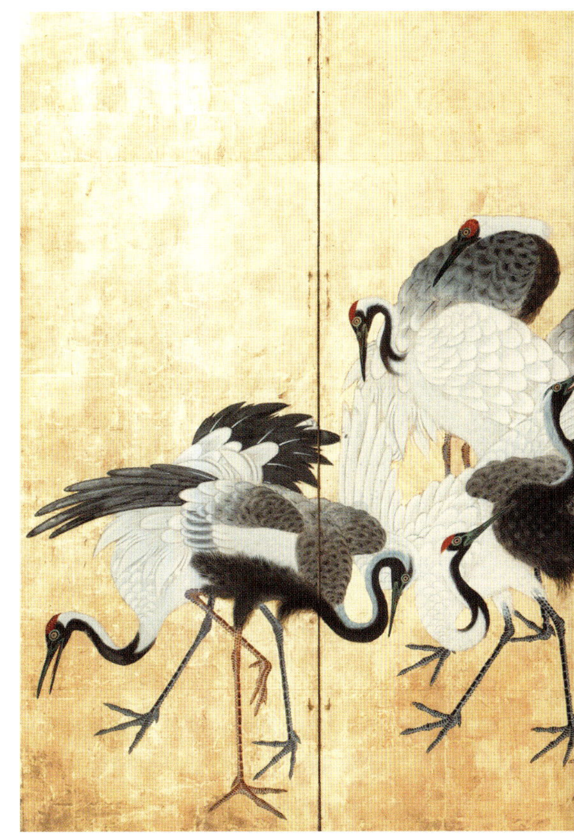

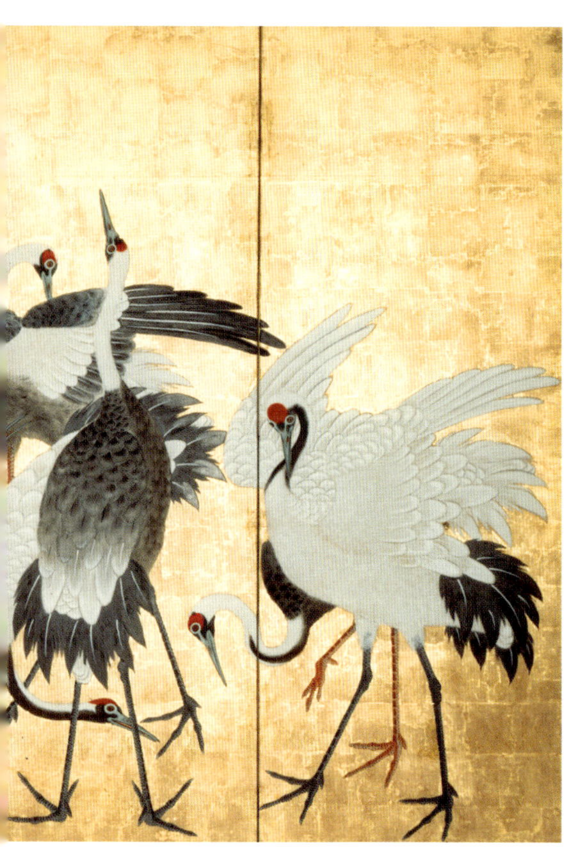

Cranes

Ishida Yūtei
Mid-18th century
Shizuoka Prefectural Museum of Art

Ishida Yūtei (1721-86), who studied with Maruyama Ōkyo, created these screens depicting a variety of crane species.

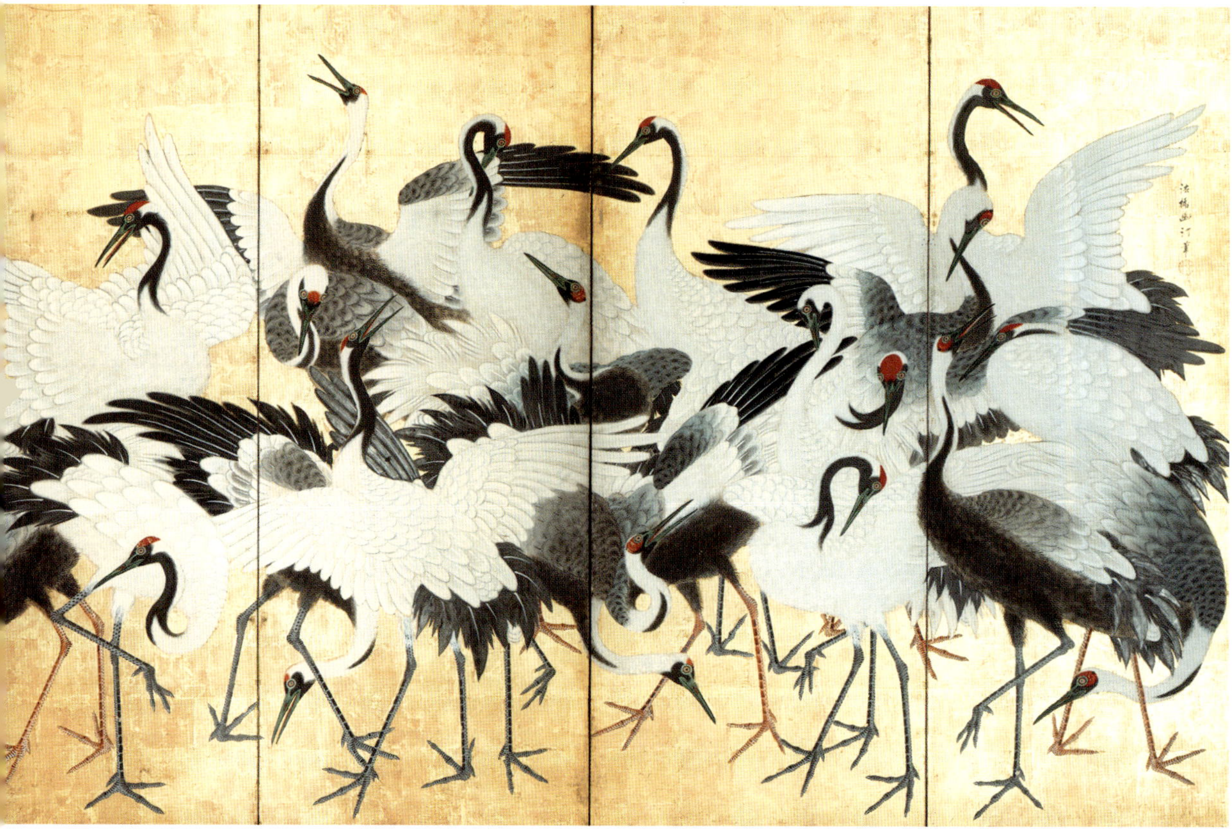

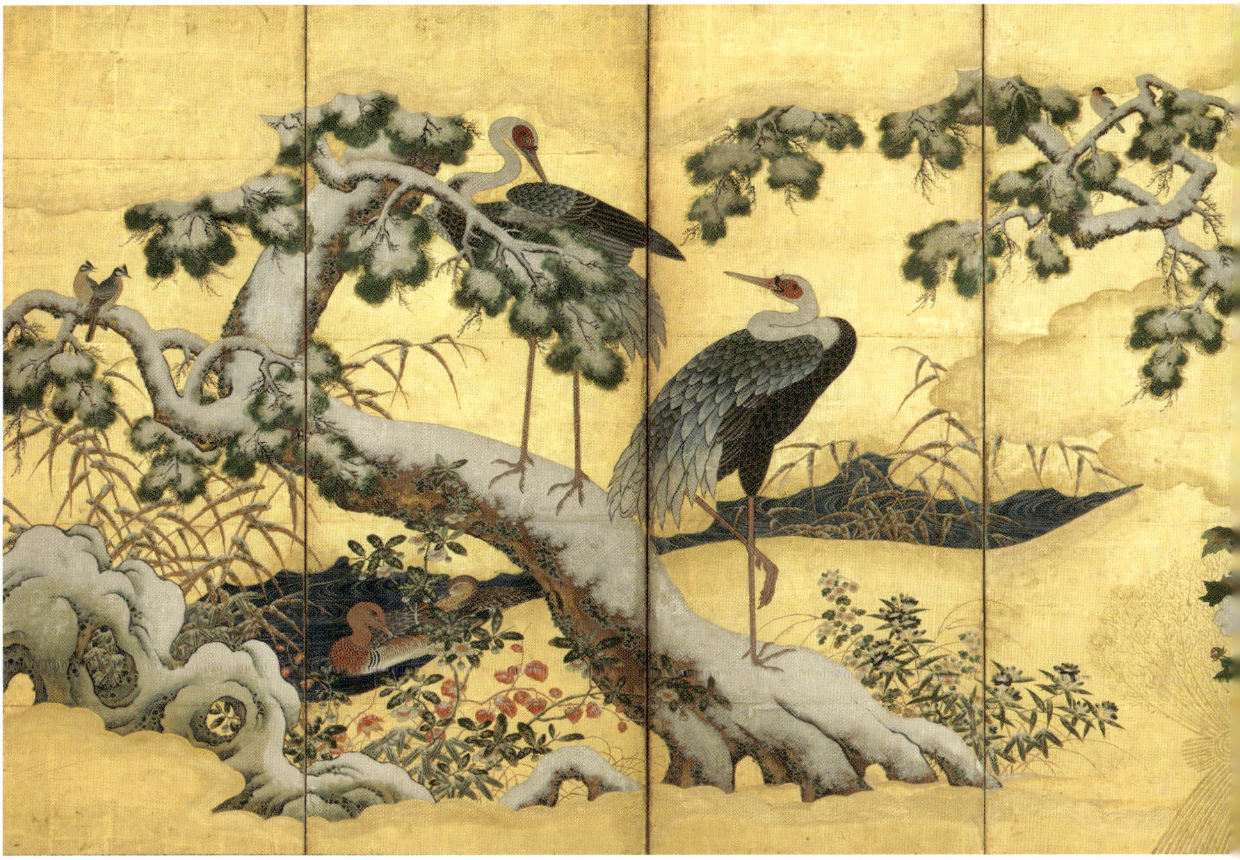

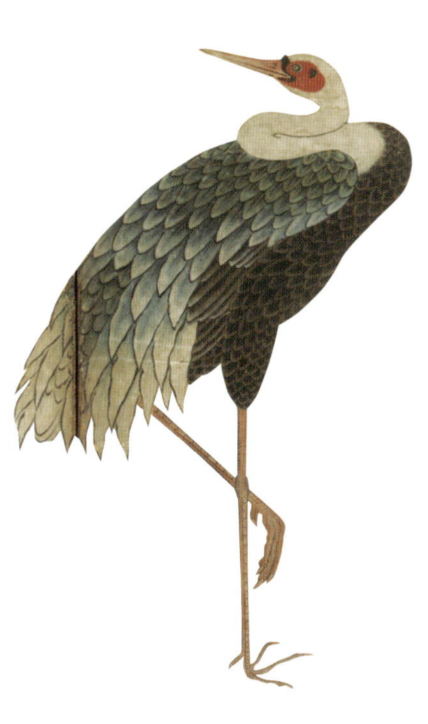

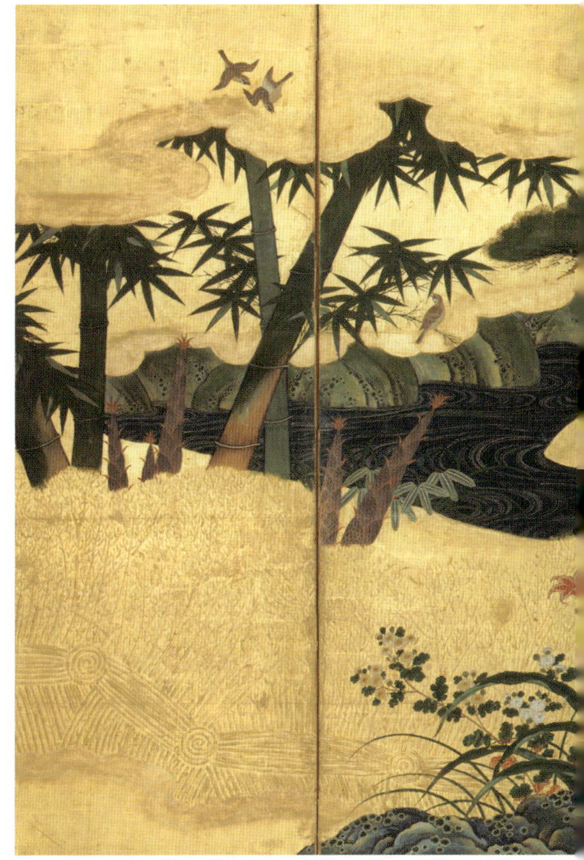

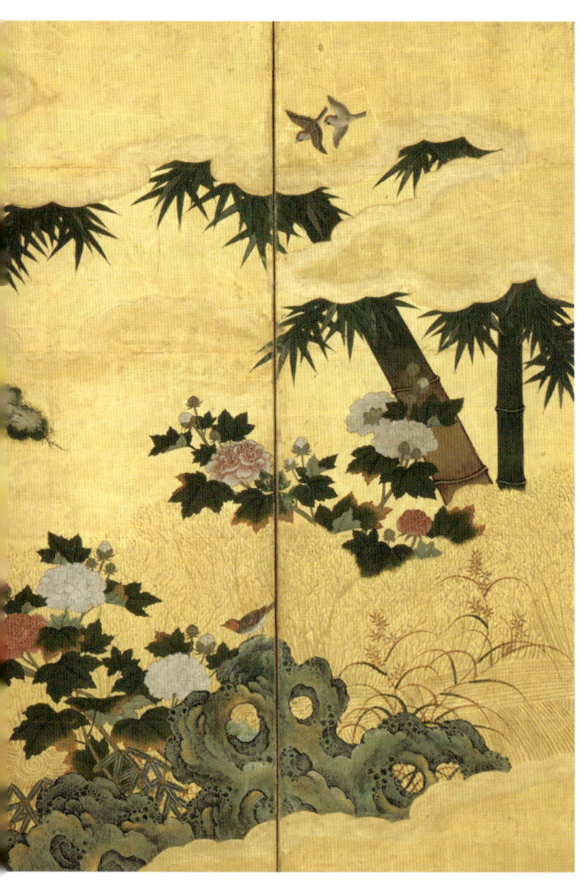

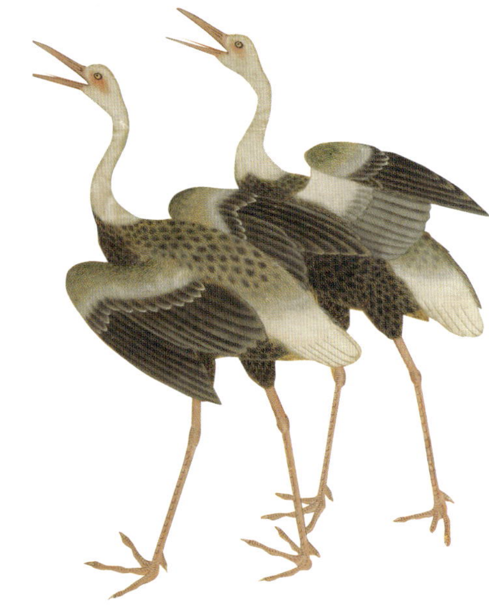

四季花鳥図屏風

桃山時代（16c後半）
メトロポリタン美術館

Birds and Flowers of the Four Seasons

Late 16th century
The Metropolitan Museum of Art

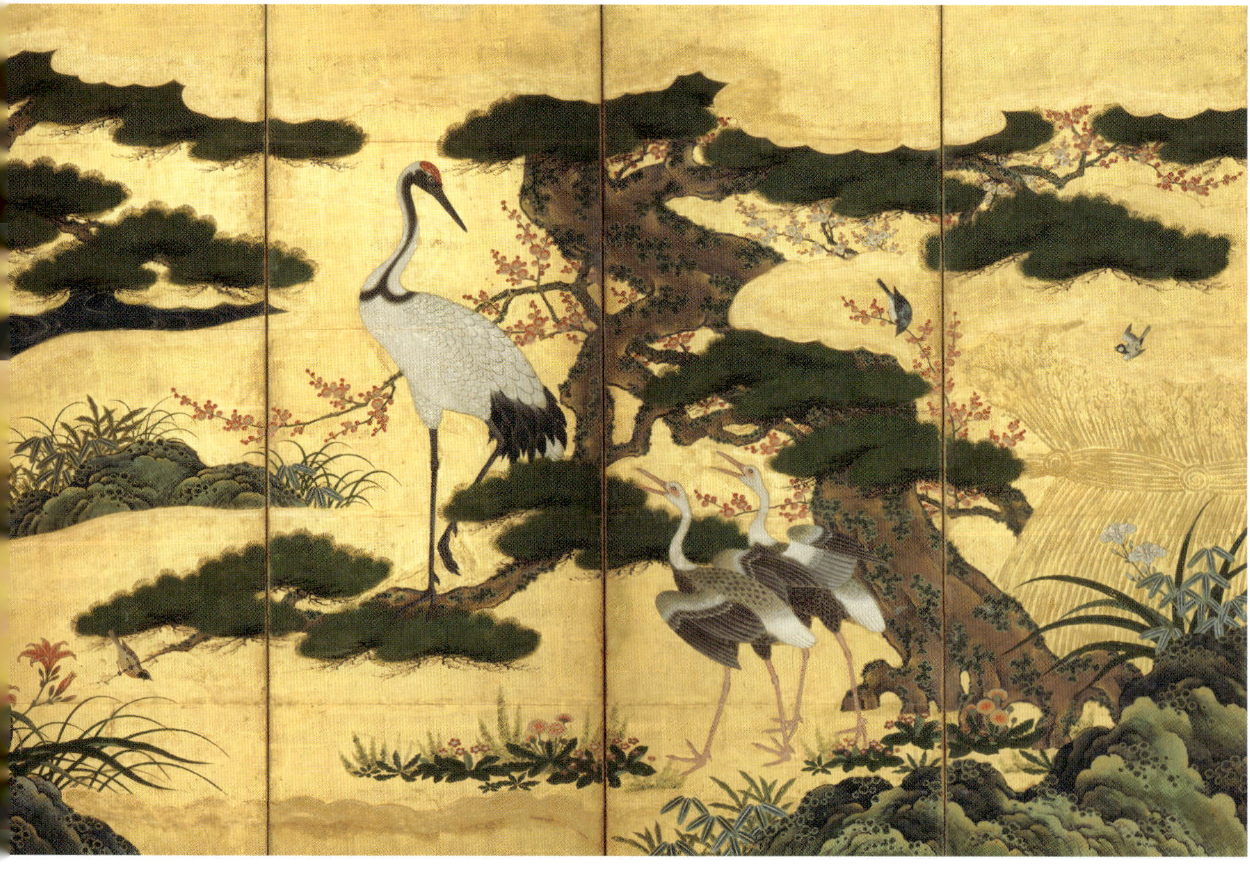

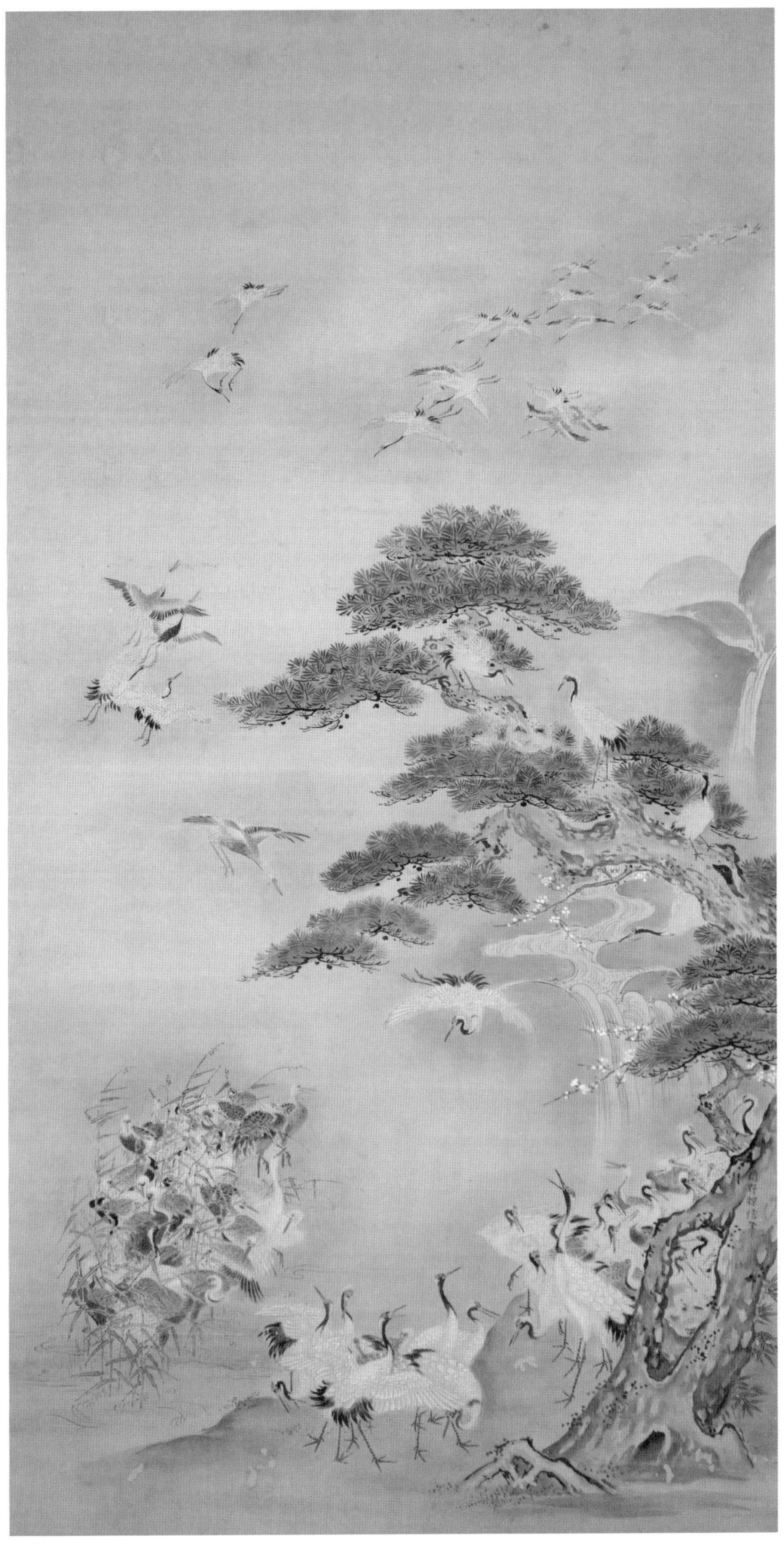

群鶴図

狩野探信
江戸時代(17〜18c)
メトロポリタン美術館

Flock of Cranes

Kano Tanshin (Morimasa)
17th–18th century
The Metropolitan Museum of Art

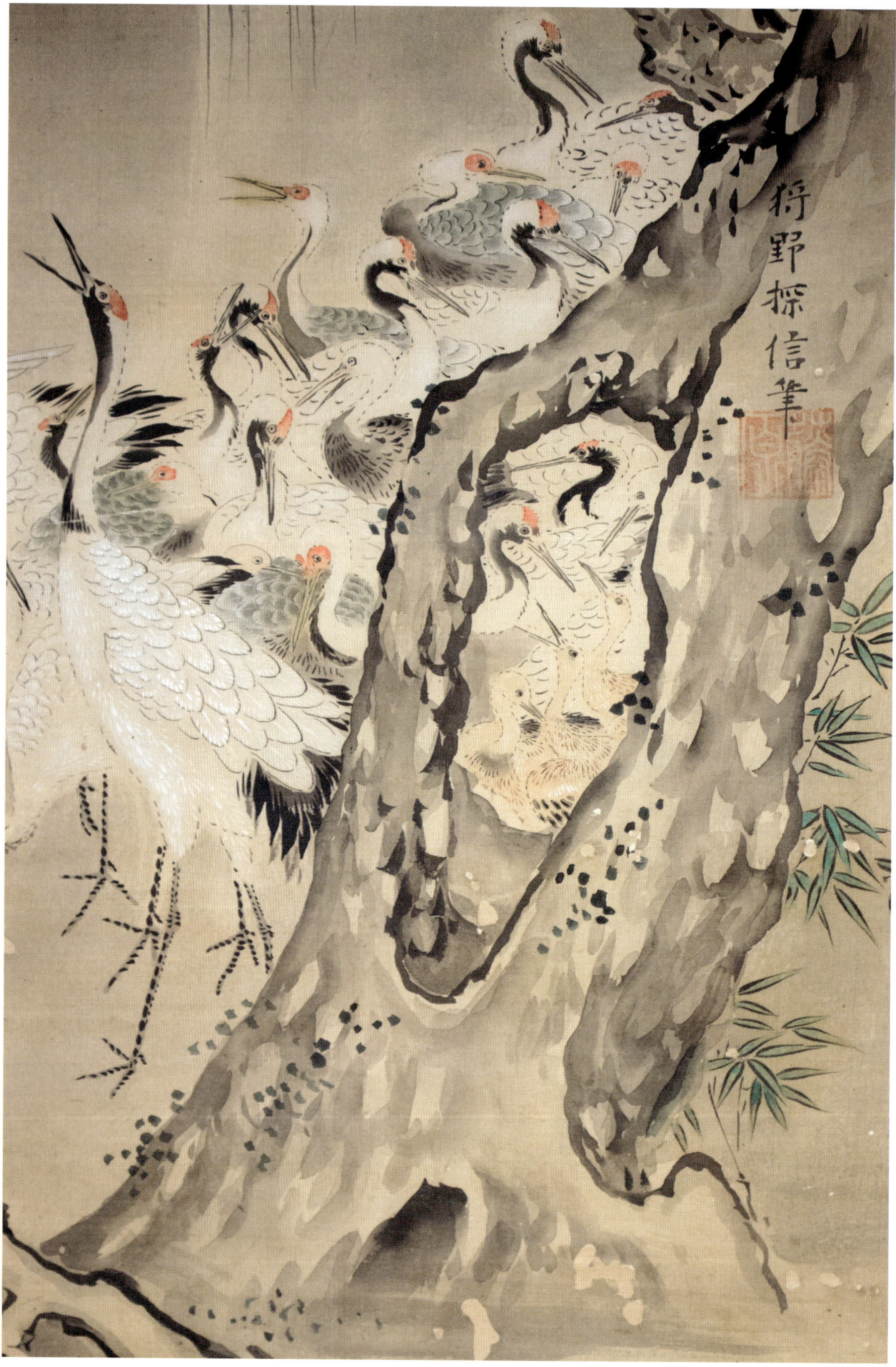
狩野探信筆

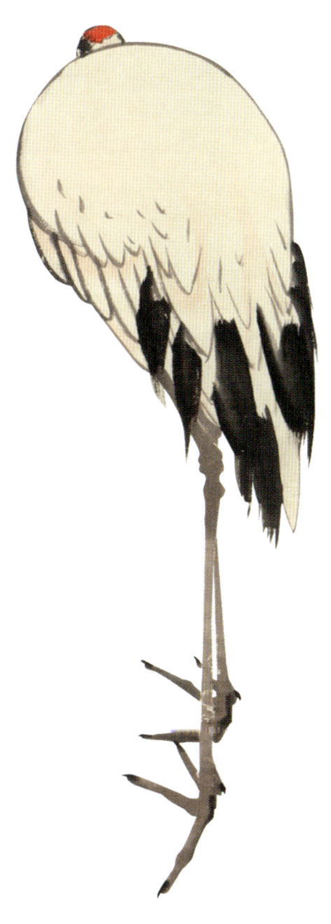

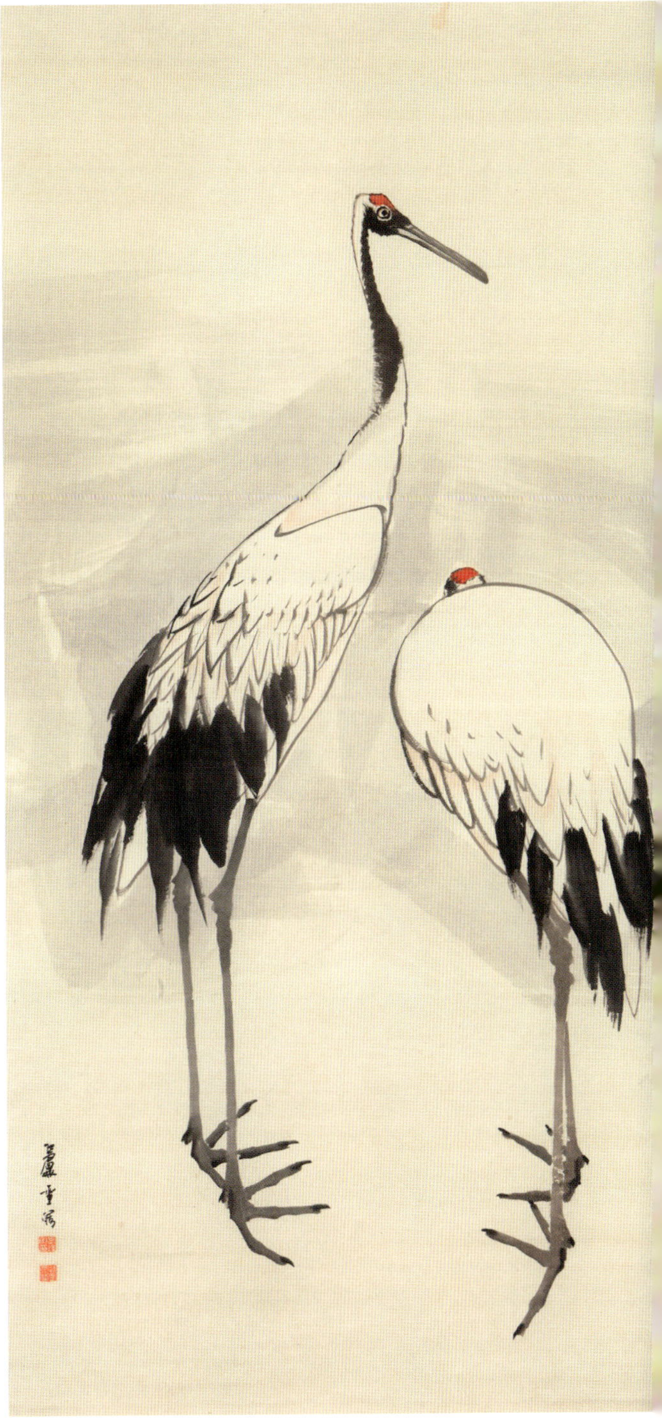

鶴図

長沢芦雪
江戸時代（1780年代後半）
メトロポリタン美術館

Cranes

Nagasawa Rosetsu
Late 1780s
The Metropolitan Museum of Art

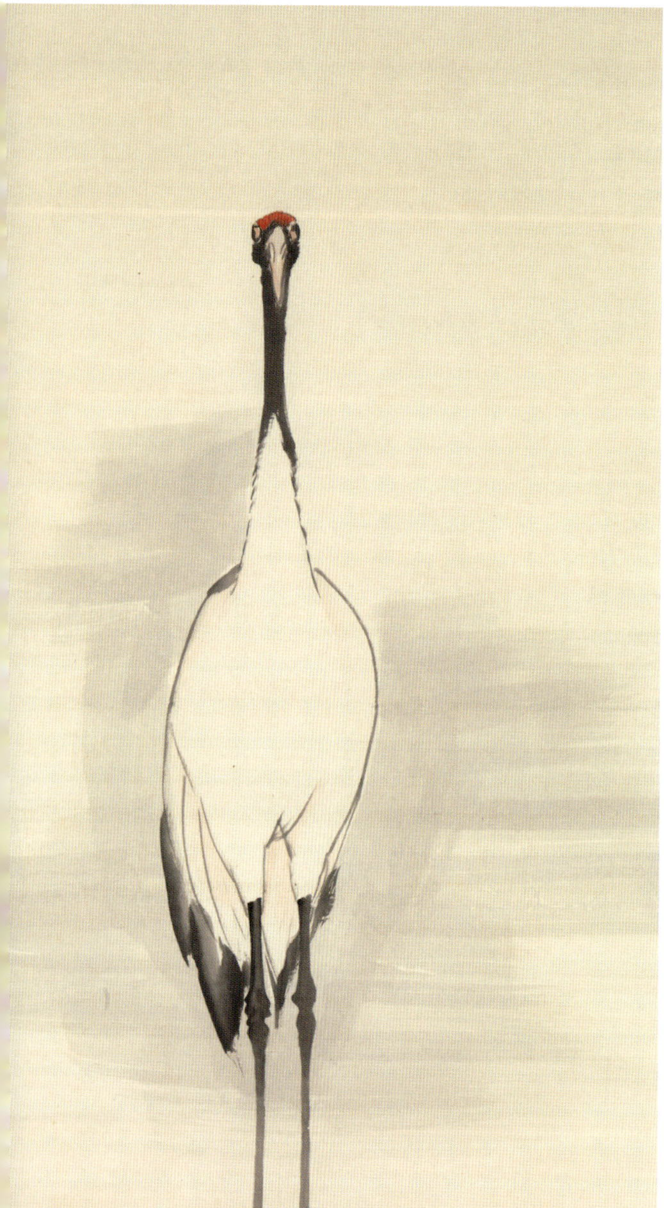

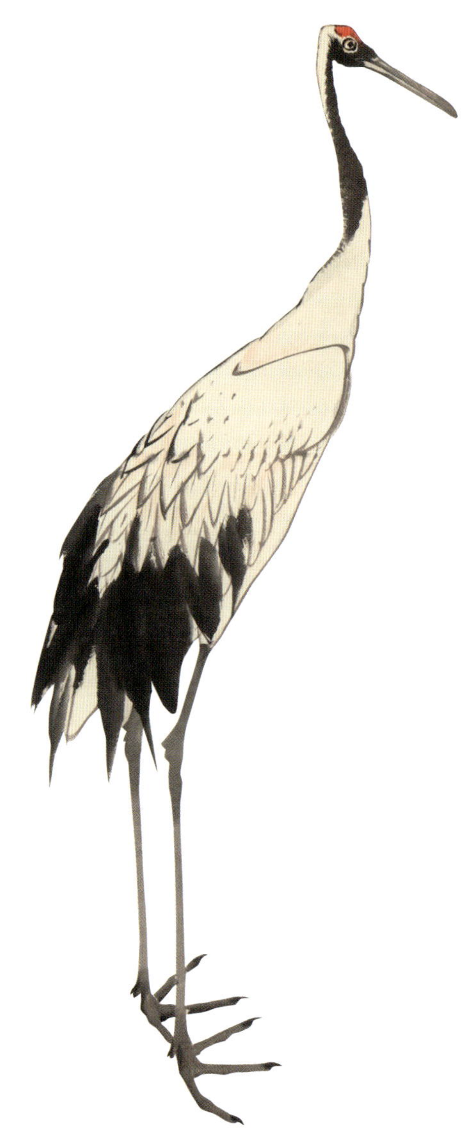

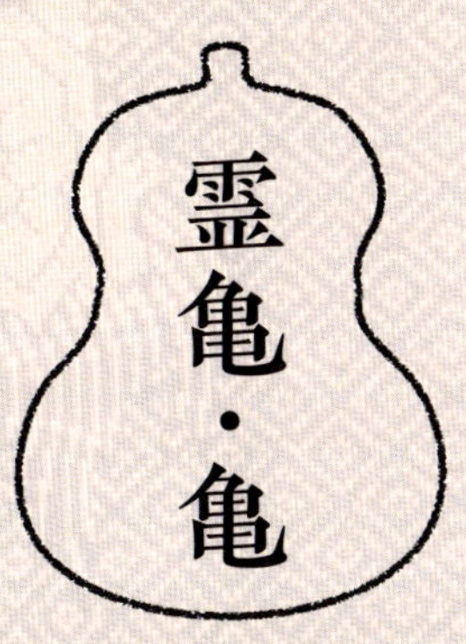

古代中国では甲蟲（甲や殻を負う動物）360種の長で、齢百千年に達すると、五色を備え、大小自在に変化できる神亀になる、とある。神亀は『延喜式』においても「大瑞」に挙げられ、五色鮮明で存亡を知り、吉凶を明らかにするとされた。その出現により日本でもたびたび改元が繰り返されたことが知られている。また、腹甲を用いて占う亀卜も行われた。もっとも馴染みのあるのは、「鶴は千年、亀は万年」と称されるように、鶴とともに長寿の象徴とされたことであろう。高砂の翁・媼とともに描かれることも多かった。亀の背に緑藻類が生えたものを、中国では緑毛亀と呼んだ。日本では蓑亀と呼ばれ、とくに長寿の瑞祥として喜ばれた。

The Turtle

Among the three hundred and sixty kinds of shelled creatures recognized in ancient China, the long-living, self-protecting turtle was considered the highest-ranking of them all. *Engishiki* includes divine tortoises in the “great omens” category. The text describes the creatures as knowledgeable of life and death, and lays out how turtles are able to foretell someone’s fortunes. In Japan, the sighting of a turtle occasionally instigated the change of era names to mark that omen. Like in China, divinations performed with turtle shells were also conducted in Japan. The most persistent interpretation of tortoises in Japan is encompassed by the saying “cranes live a thousand years, turtles live ten thousand.” Together with cranes, turtles are symbols of everlasting life. These animals are often depicted alongside the old man and woman featured in the Noh theater play *Takasago*. Turtles with moss growing on their backs are commonly called “green-haired tortoises” in China. In Japan, such moss-covered turtles are also seen as auspicious omens and symbols of long life.

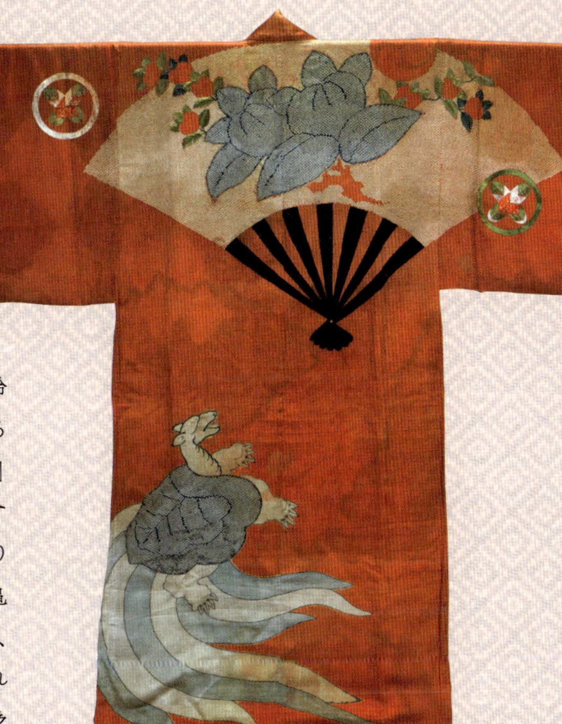

紅綸子地
末広亀文夜着

江戸時代（19c）
東京国立博物館

夜着は江戸時代の寝具。寝ているあいだに悪夢をみないよう、吉祥模様を表したものが多い。

Night Gown with a Turtle Pattern

19th century
Tokyo National Museum

Such kimono were worn as night gowns during the Edo period. In order to inspire pleasant dreams, the garments were often decorated with auspicious motifs.

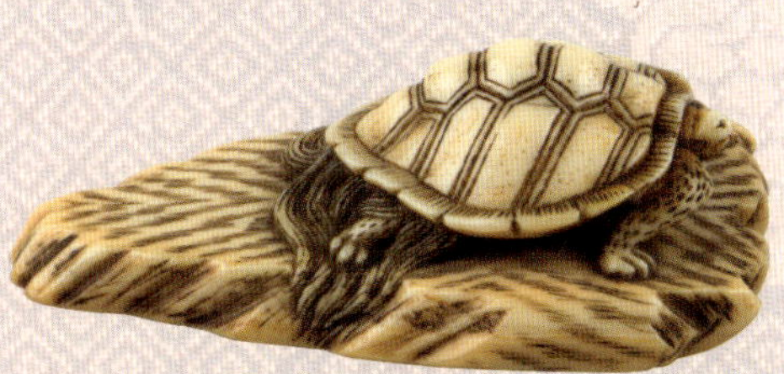

岩上亀牙彫根付

江戸時代（19c）
メトロポリタン美術館

Netsuke of Turtle Crawling over a Rock

19th century
The Metropolitan Museum of Art

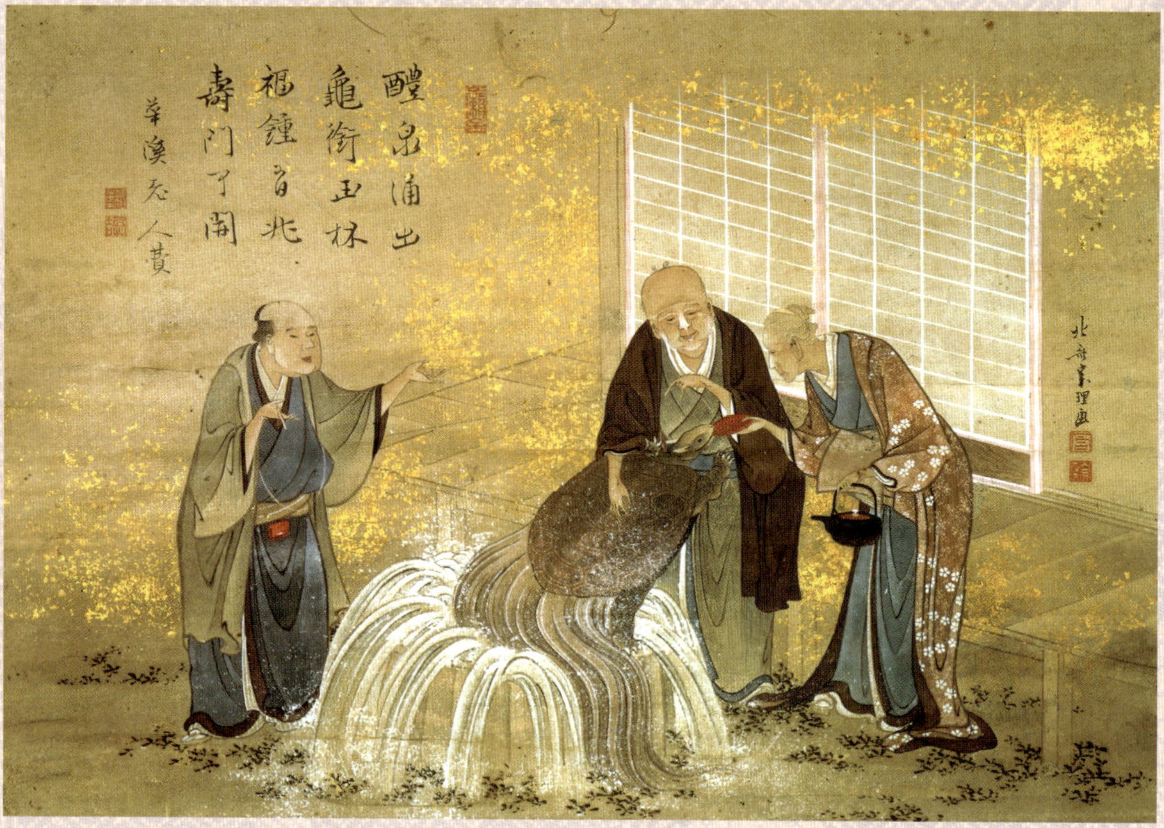

瑞亀図

葛飾北斎
寛政8年(1796)頃
奈良県立美術館

老夫婦の長寿を祝うように、こんこんと湧き出る清水から瑞亀が姿を現す。その亀を老夫が抱え、老妻が盃で酒を飲ませている。見守る左端の男は、これを称えて柏手を打つ。長寿の祝いにふさわしい情景である。

Auspicious Tortoise

Katsushika Hokusai
18th century
Nara Prefectural Museum of Art

As an elderly couple is celebrating their long lives, an auspicious turtle is emerging from a fresh-water well. The couple embrace the animal and welcome it by giving it alcohol. The man to the left is rejoicing at the scene by clapping his hands. This painting was likely made to celebrate someone's advanced age.

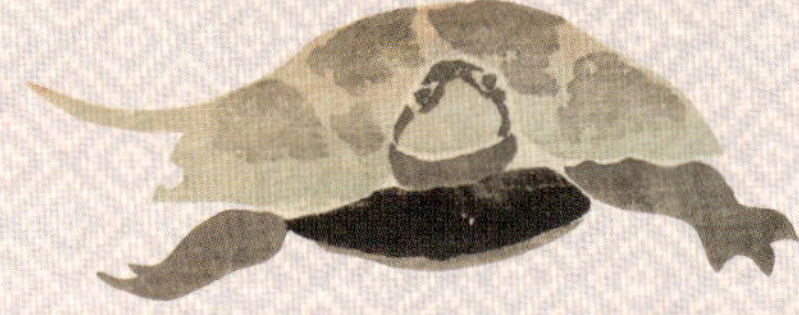

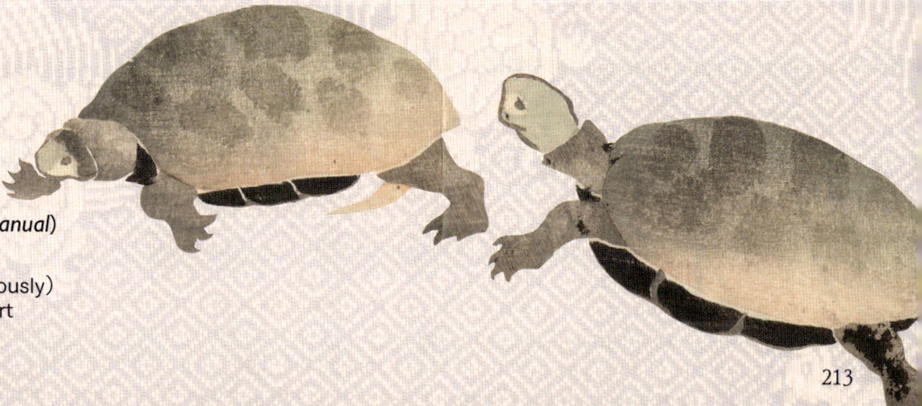

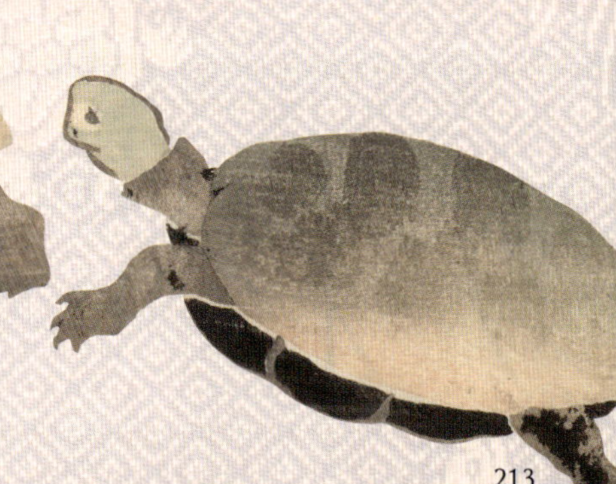

亀図（『光琳画譜』より）

中村芳中
文政9年(1826)以降
メトロポリタン美術館

Turtles (*from Kōrin Painting Manual*)

Nakamura Hōchū
After 1826 (reprinted posthumously)
The Metropolitan Museum of Art

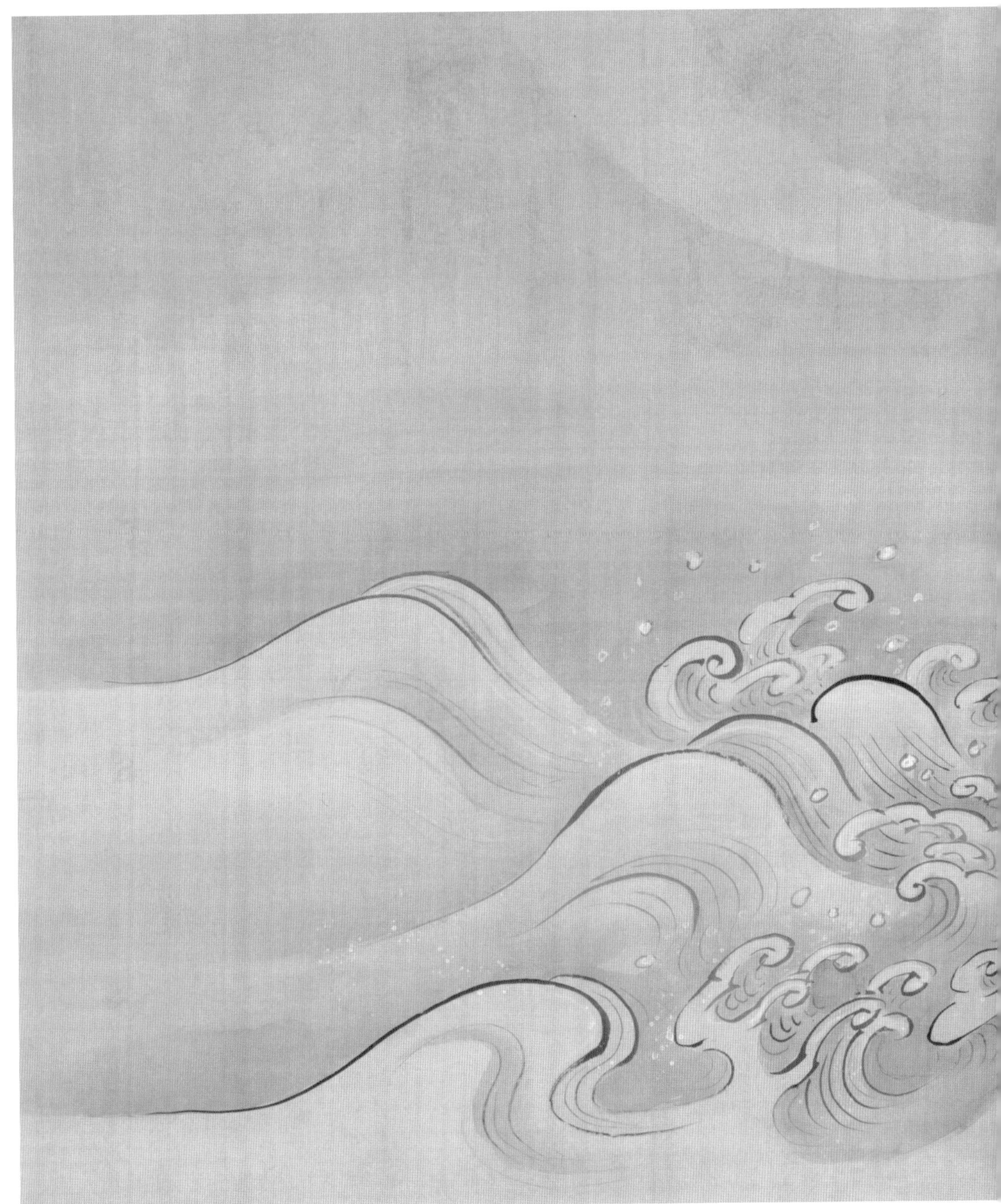

瑞亀図

狩野常信
江戸時代(17c)
福岡市美術館

海上に姿を現した蓑亀が天空に向けて霊気を発する。狩野常信(1636～1713)は幕府奥絵師4家のうちの木挽町狩野家の当主で、狩野探幽の甥に当たる画人。

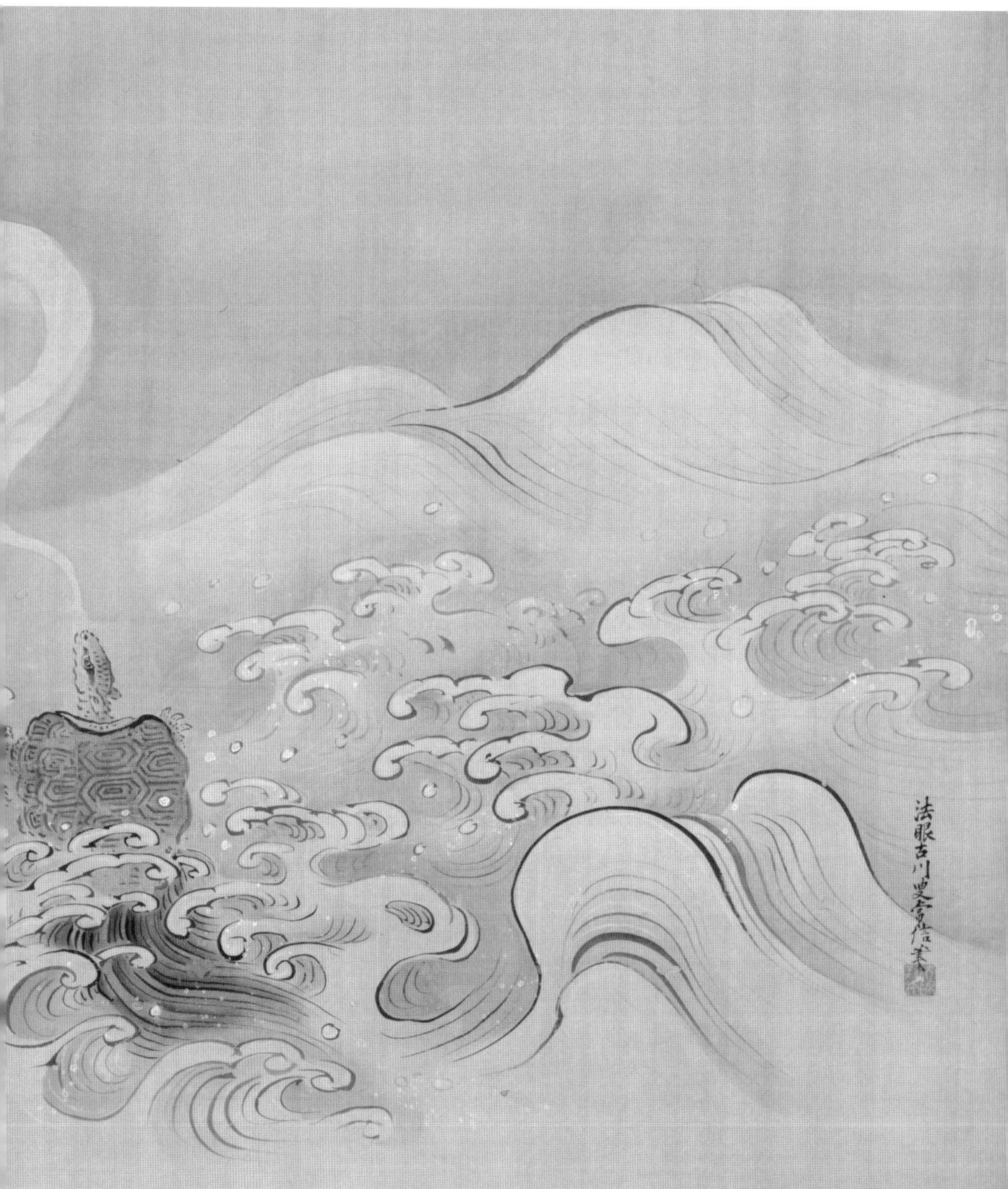

Auspicious Tortoise

Kano Tsunenobu
17th century
Fukuoka Art Museum

A moss-tailed turtle is emerging from the sea and is emitting spiritual force towards the heavens. The painter, Kano Tsunenobu (1636-1713), was the head of the Edo-based Kobikichō atelier that served the shogunate as painters-in-waiting. Tsunenobu was a nephew of the famous Kano Tan'yū.

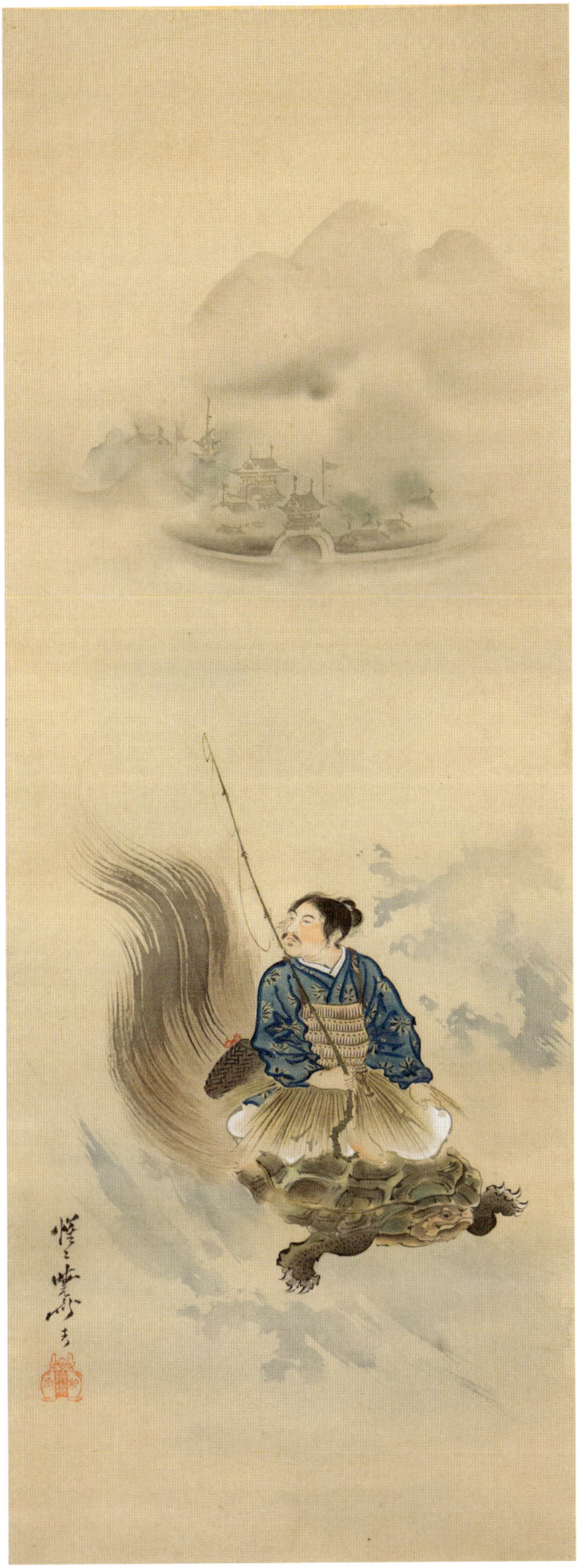

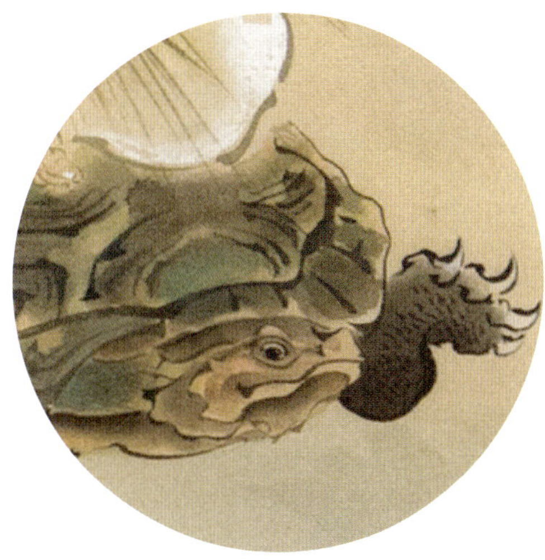

浦島太郎騎亀図

河鍋暁斎
明治時代（1888年以降）
メトロポリタン美術館

Urashima Tarō Riding on a Tortoise

Kawanabe Kyōsai
After 1888
The Metropolitan Museum of Art

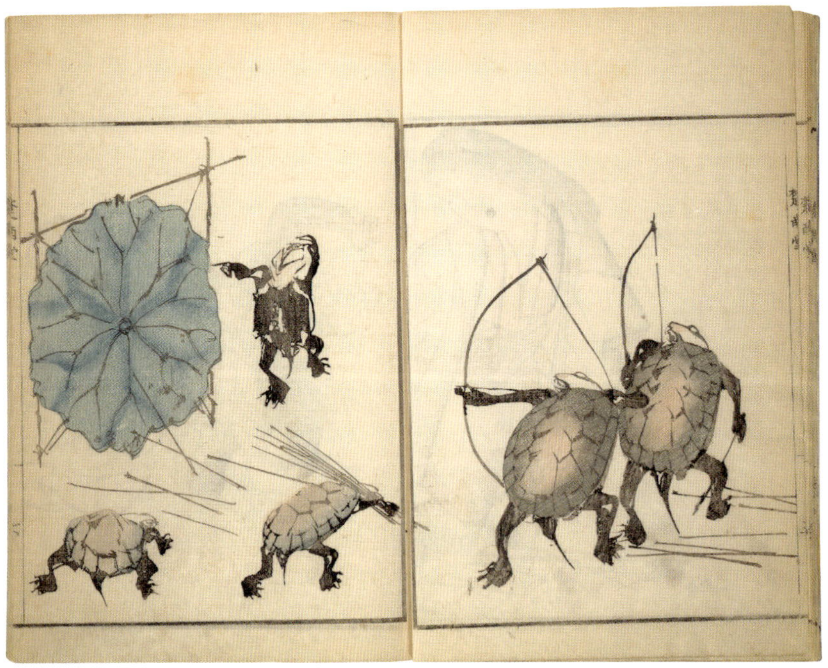

亀図（『楚南画譜』より）

大西椿年
天保5年（1834）
メトロポリタン美術館

Turtles (*from Sōnan Picture Album*)

Ōnishi Chinnen
1834
The Metropolitan Museum of Art

亀図（『光琳画譜』より）

中村芳中
文政9年（1826）以降
メトロポリタン美術館

Turtles (*from Kōrin Painting Manual*)

Nakamura Hōchū
After 1826 (reprinted posthumously)
The Metropolitan Museum of Art

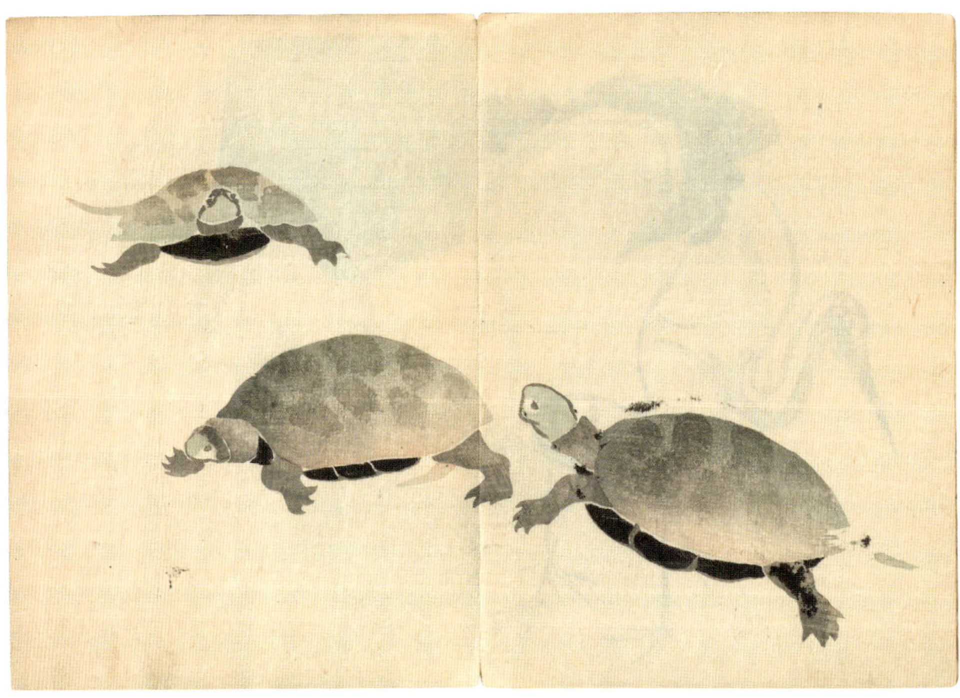

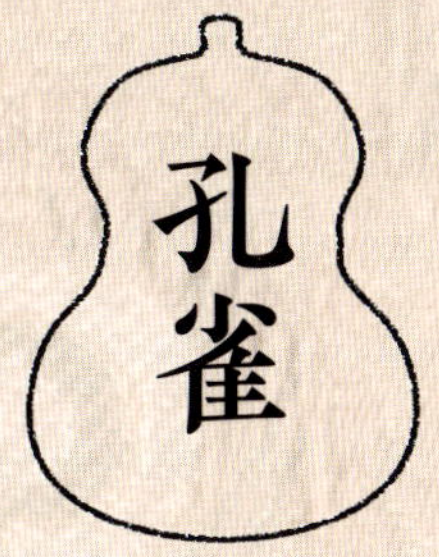

孔雀は蛇を喰う習性から、インドでは悪を払う聖鳥とみなされたが、中国では色彩豊かな衣服を身につけた人を見れば必ず啄みに来る嫉妬深い鳥と考えられていた。日本では美しい霊鳥として、ほぼ全面的な称賛の対象だった。文献から知られる初渡来は、598年(推古天皇6)に新羅王から献上されたもの。ついで647年(大化3)にも新羅から、さらに847年(承和14)には遣唐使僧が持ち帰った。1408年(応永15)若狭国に漂着した南蛮船は象や馬とともに孔雀を舶載。江戸時代の寛永年間に至ると、孔雀の見世物が流行し、江戸後期になると浅草や両国に孔雀を鑑賞しながら茶を楽しむ趣向の「孔雀茶屋」「鹿茶屋」と呼ばれる施設ができて大盛況となった。その姿の美しさから、日本では古くから花鳥画の題材として盛んに描写され続けた。なお、孔雀が西洋に知られたのは、天正遣欧使節がローマ教皇に贈った絵画に描かれていたことがきっかけという。そのイメージは、イタリアの博物学者により「日本孔雀」と紹介され、やがて『ヨンストン動物図譜』にも掲載されるに至った。

The Peacock

Since peacocks have a habit of eating snakes, they have long been revered in India as divine birds that crush evil. In China, their colorful plumage was likened to a person wearing emphatically gorgeous attire. For that reason, the birds were also seen as jealous creatures. The Japanese belief considered peacocks to be heavenly birds that were praised and admired. According to records, the first peacock arrived in Japan as a gift from the kingdom of Silla on the Korean peninsula in 598. A peacock was again brought to Japan from Silla in 647, and an embassy to Tang China in 847 returned with another specimen. A vessel from Southeast Asia is reported to have been set off course and drifted towards Wakasa Province in 1408. The ship carried elephants and horses, and also peacocks. During the Kan'ei era of the Edo period, peacocks became a popular urban spectacle, and during the late Edo period people could watch peacocks while enjoying a cup of tea at the Kujaku Tea House and the Shika Tea House. The beautiful appearance of these birds made them a reoccurring subject in Japanese paintings. It was the Japanese who introduced peacocks to Europe through a painting given to the pope by the Tenshō embassy in the 1580s. The bird in the image became known among Italian scientists as a "Japanese peacock." Ironically, the picture made its way into Johannes Jonston's *Historiae naturalis*, which was imported to Japan during the Edo period.

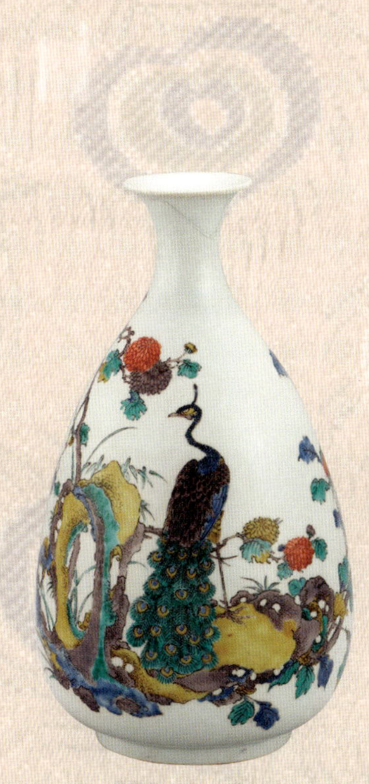

色絵孔雀牡丹太湖石図瓶
江戸時代(17c中葉)
九州国立博物館

Vase with Design of a Peacock and Peonies
Mid-17th century
Kyushu National Museum

国宝

孔雀明王像

平安時代後期（12c半ば）
東京国立博物館

孔雀明王は、密教において一切の煩悩をほろぼし安楽を得させる孔雀経法の本尊として祀られ、人界における様々な災悪を祓うものとして尊崇された。明王でありながら温和な菩薩の表情で、孔雀の背に坐す4臂の姿。明王と孔雀を画面いっぱいに大きく正面向きに表す構図は空海ゆかりの図像の系譜を引くとも考えられている。胸前に掲げた吉祥果を、一般的な円形から安産に関わる柘榴形に変更していることから、皇室の御産にまつわる祈祷に用いられた可能性も指摘されている。

National Treasure

Mahamayuri

(J. Kujaku Myōō)

Mid-12th century
Tokyo National Museum

A deity venerated in esoteric Buddhism, Mahamayuri is known to destroy worldly desires and pacify the mind. The deity is worshipped as a savior from evil and calamities. Mahamayuri is commonly depicted with the gentle face typically found in bodhisattvas, an iconography that dates back to the monk Kūkai. The auspicious fruit the deity is holding in front of their chest is depicted here in the shape of a pomegranate. Works like these were likely commissioned for and worshipped by the imperial court.

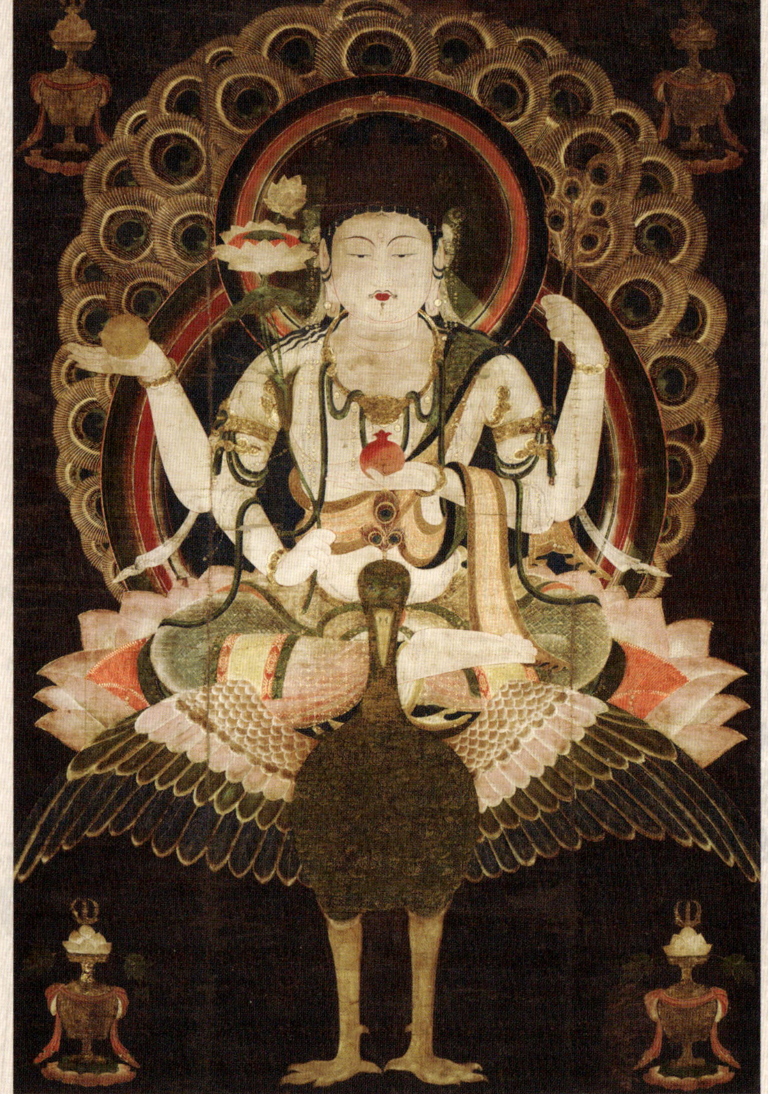

重要文化財

鳳凰文戧金経箱（京都・高山寺伝来）

元時代（14c）
奈良国立博物館

Important Cultural Property

Sutra Box with Design of Phoenixes

(originally in the collection of Kōsanji, Kyoto)

Yuan dynasty, 14th century
Nara National Museum

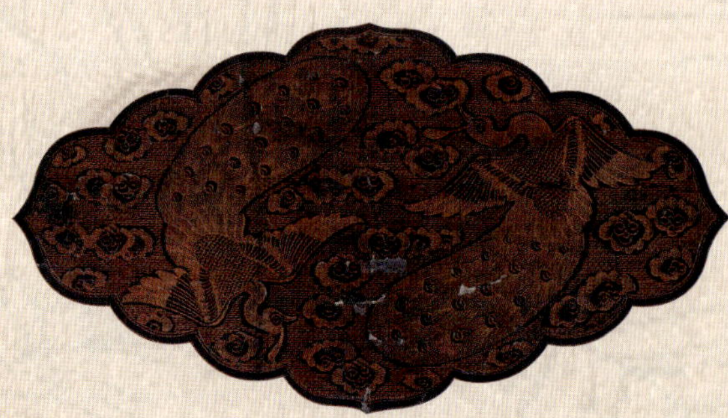

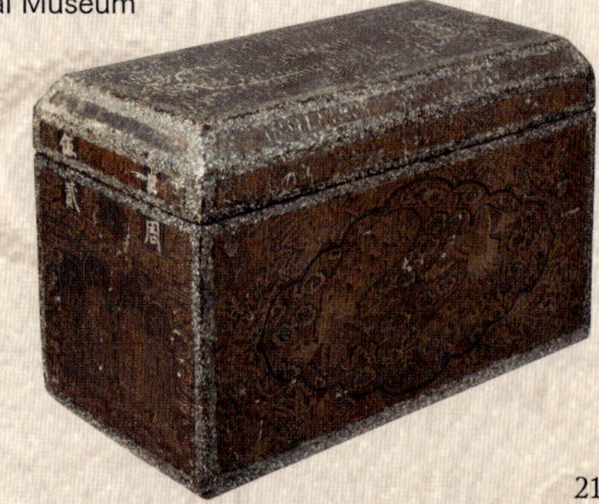

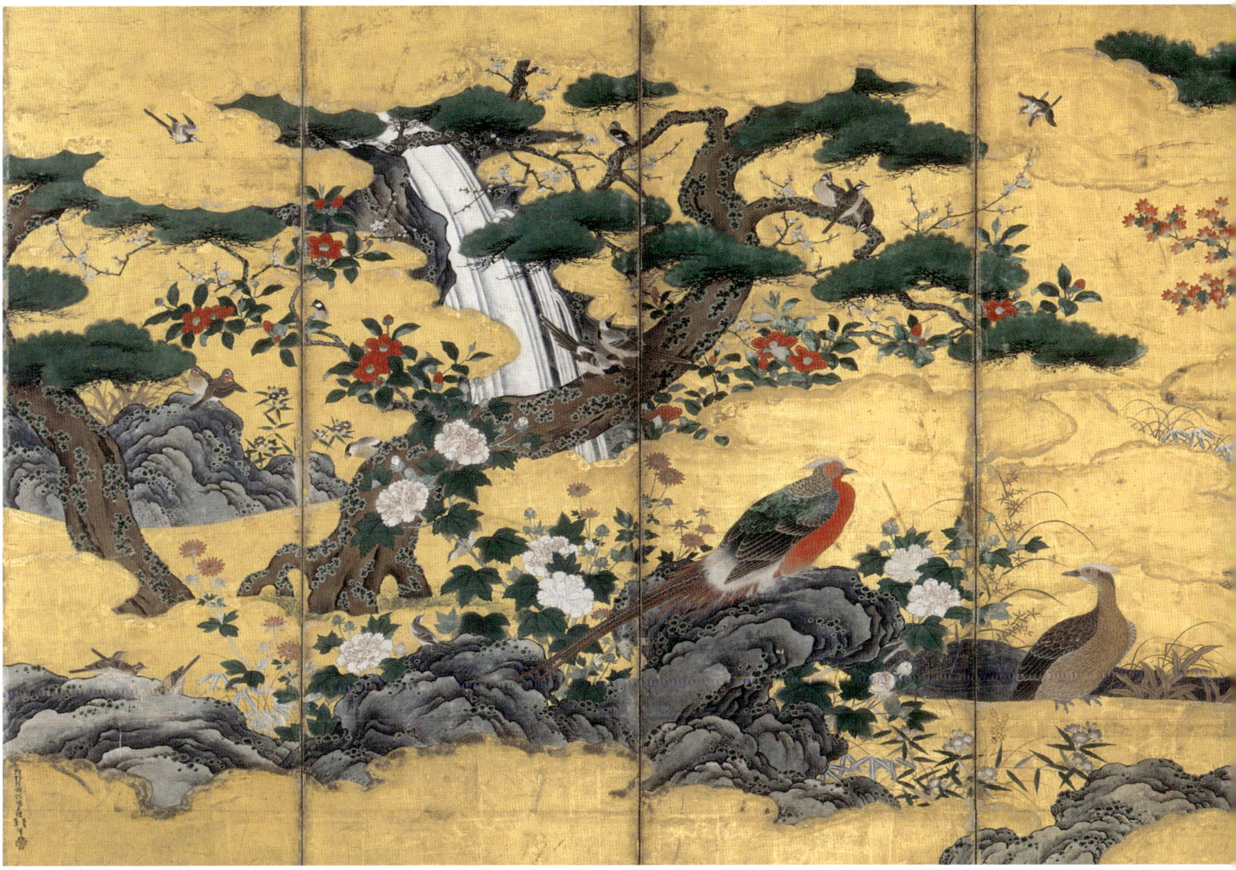

重要文化財

四季花鳥図屏風

狩野元信
天文19年（1550）
兵庫・白鶴美術館

狩野派の基礎を確立した狩野元信（1476?～1559）による、やまと絵学習の成果を教える大画面の金碧画。土佐派のお株を奪ってしまったかのような豪華さと、漢画の堅固で構築的な空間構成をあわせ持つ。本図は、奈良・興福寺の僧侶の求めで制作されたというが、元信の金屏風は中国でも人気で、盛んに輸出されていた。

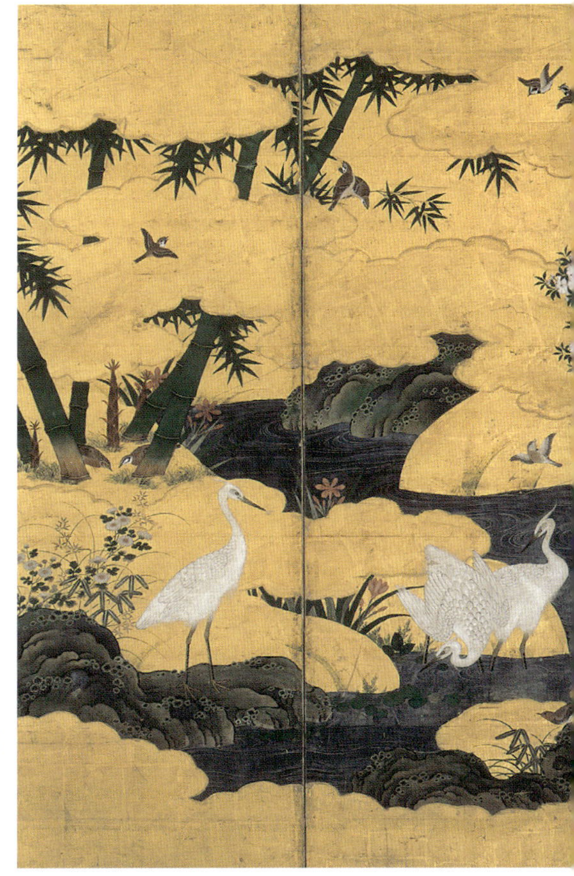

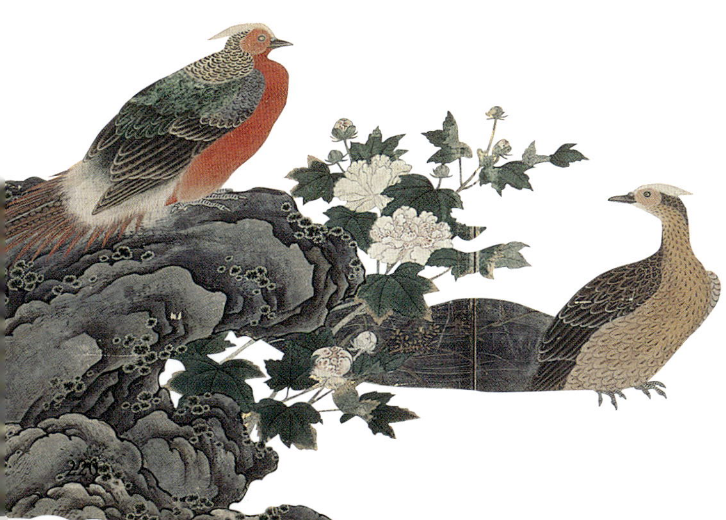

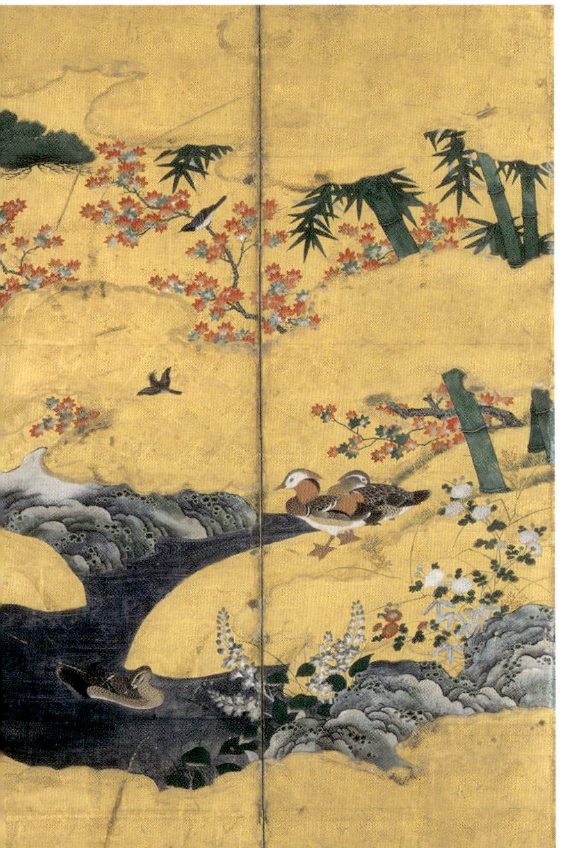

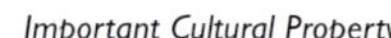

Important Cultural Property

Birds and Flowers of the Four Seasons

Kano Motonobu
1550
Hakutsuru Fine Art Museum, Hyogo

This painting encapsulates the mastery of the traditional Japanese painting mode by the founder of the Kano school, Kano Motonobu (1476?-1559). Originally a prerogative of the Tosa school, Motonobu fused the traditional Japanese mode with the strict compositional rules of Chinese-style painting. The screen paintings were originally made for Kōfukuji in Nara, but similar gilded screens by Motonobu were also desired in China and exported there.

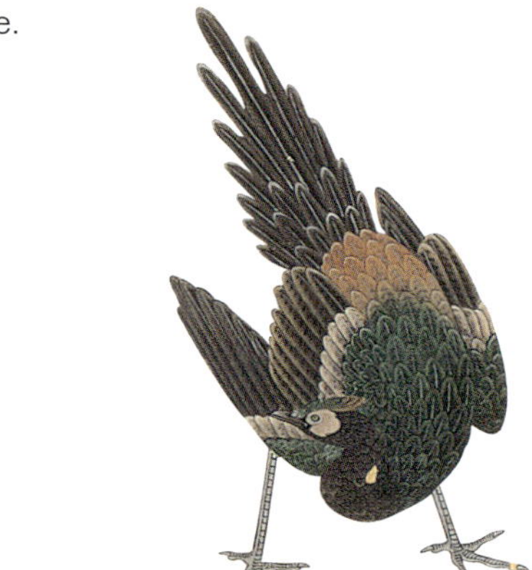

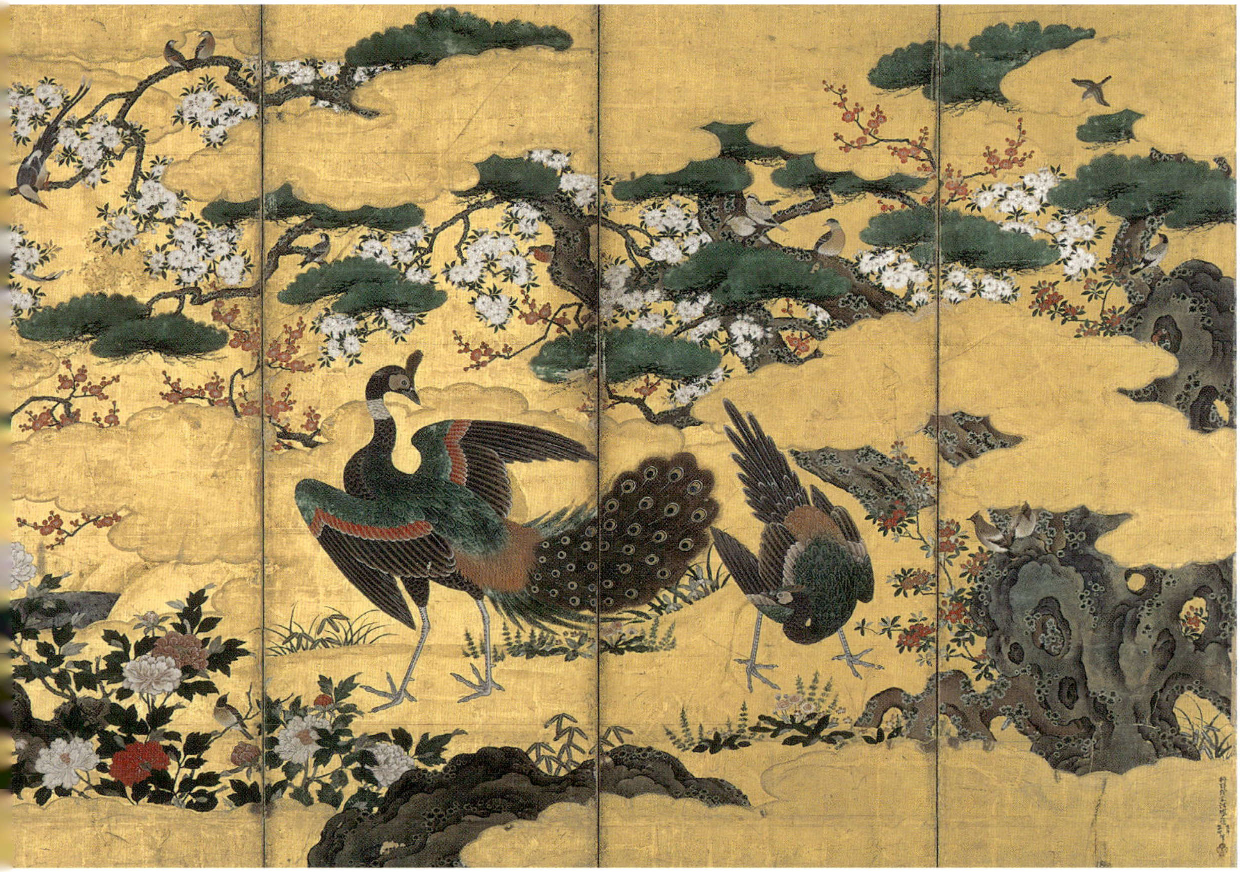

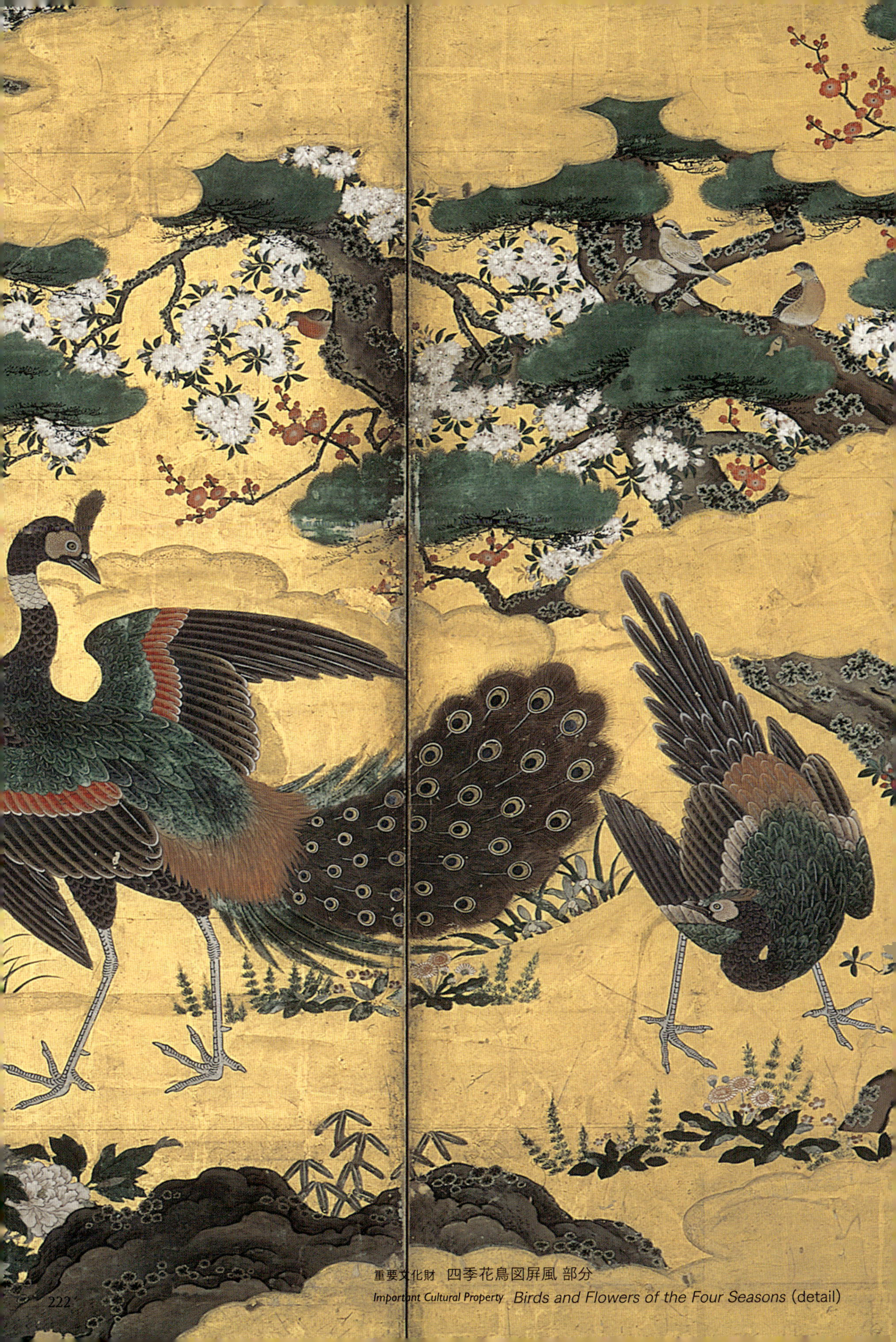

重要文化財　四季花鳥図屛風 部分
Important Cultural Property *Birds and Flowers of the Four Seasons* (detail)

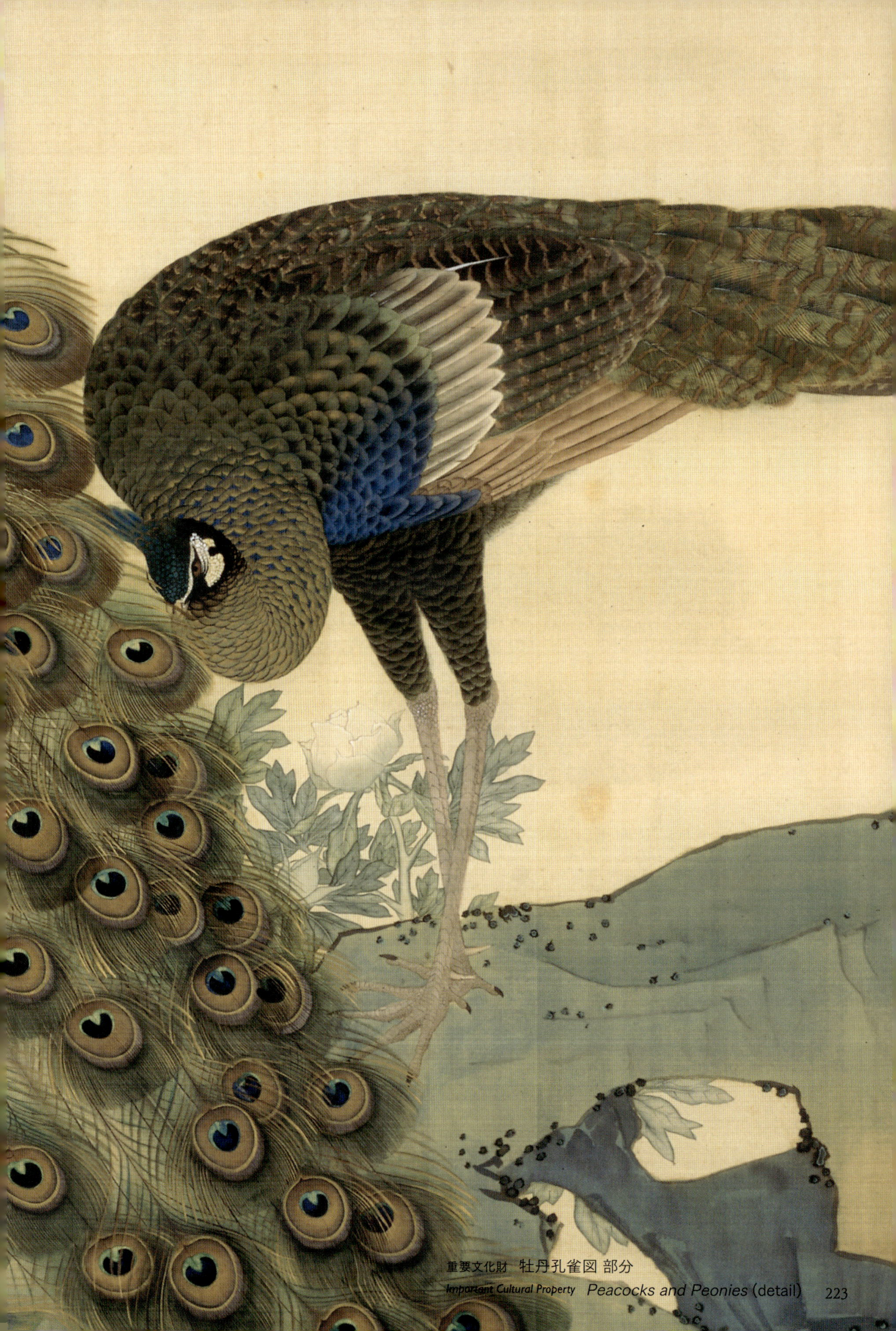

重要文化財　牡丹孔雀図 部分
Important Cultural Property *Peacocks and Peonies* (detail)

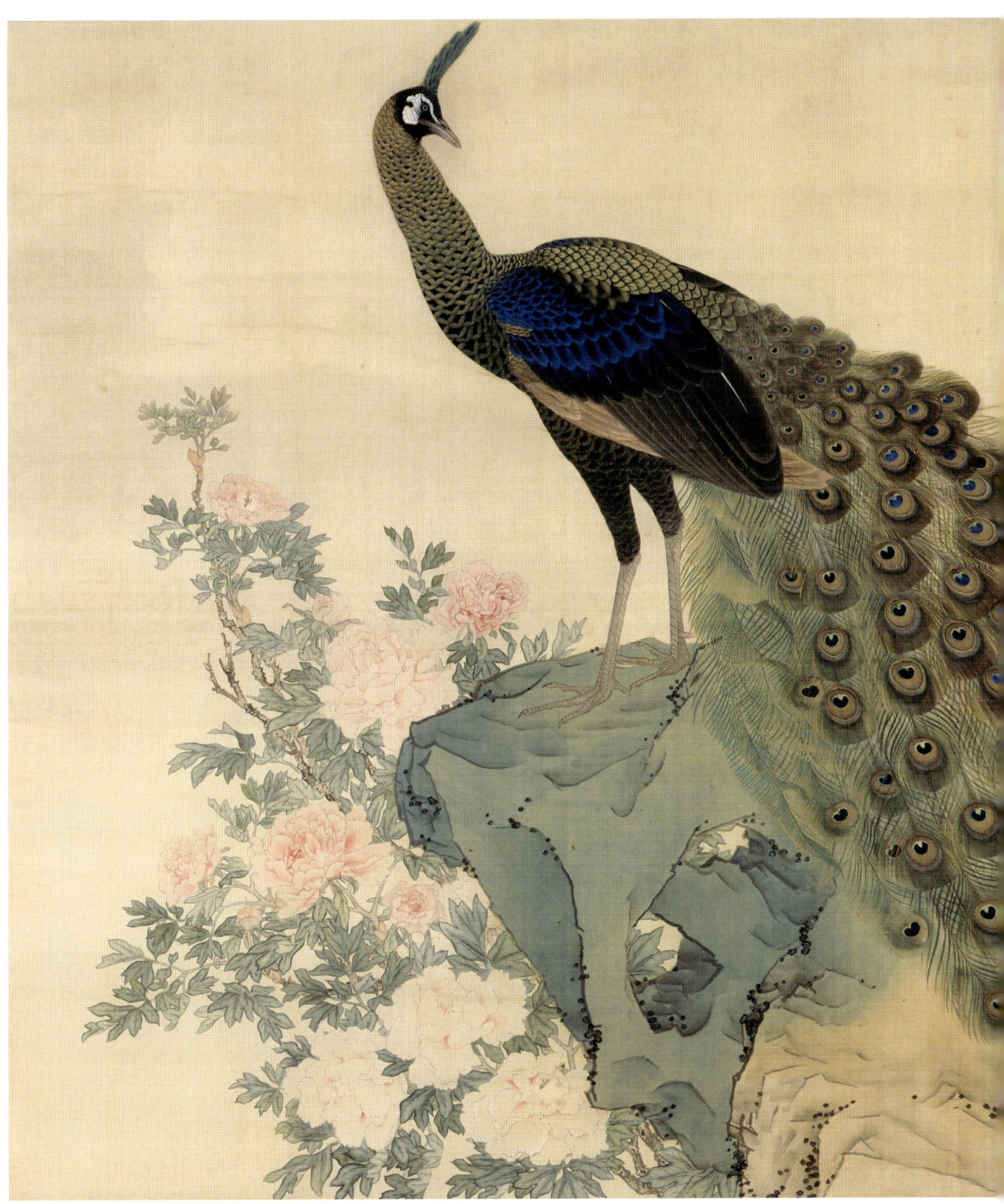

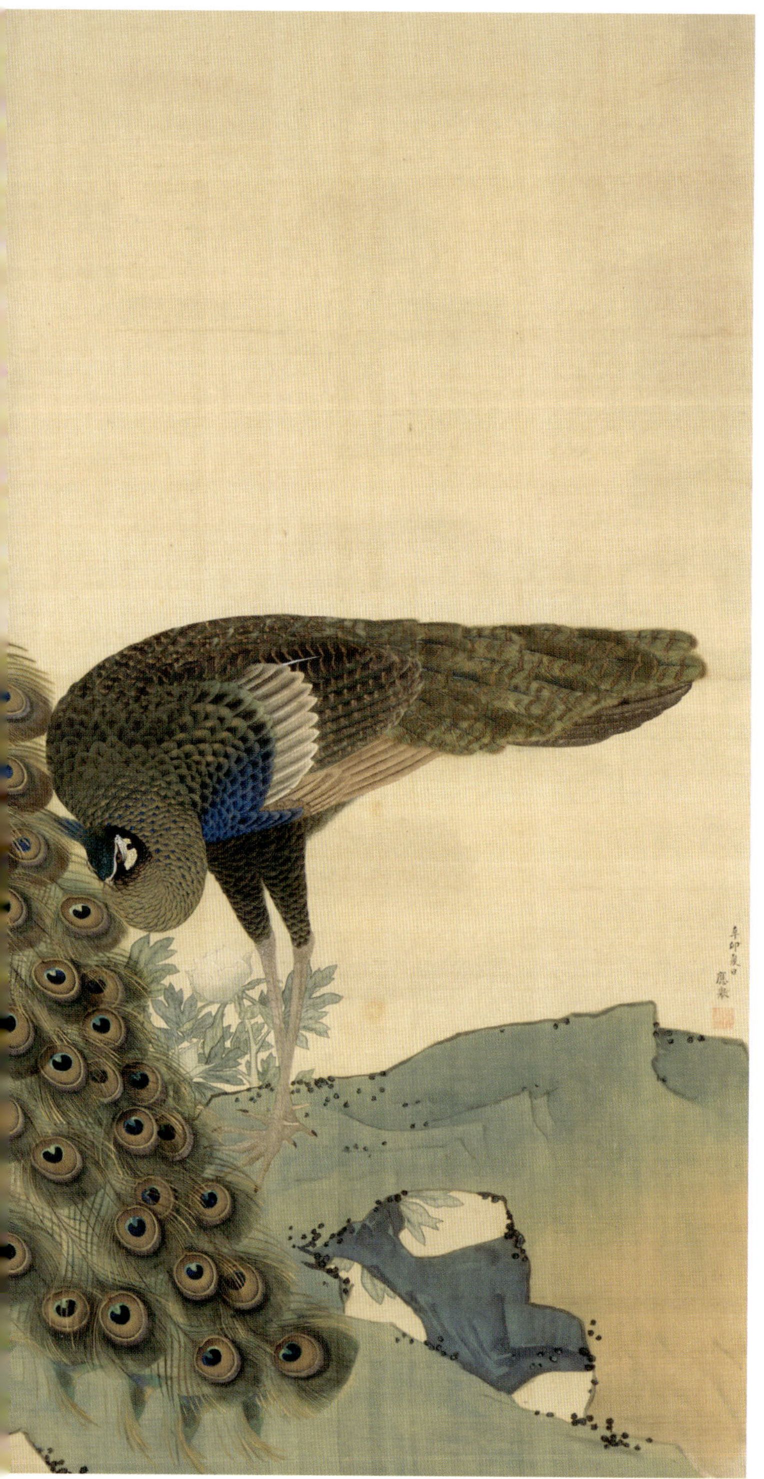

重要文化財

牡丹孔雀図

円山応挙
明和8年(1771)
京都・相国寺

太湖石の上にたたずむ雌雄の孔雀を、大輪の牡丹とともに描く。用いられた上質な絵の具のうち、とくに群青・緑青と金泥との対照が効果的で、装飾性と写実性とが見事に融合した作品である。孔雀の頭部から首、胸にかけての量感表現が見事だが、これは墨の諧調で立体感をつくり出した上に岩絵の具を薄く載せることで実現させたもの。応挙の円満院時代、すなわち絵画表現の試行を繰り返した画風形成期を代表する傑作で、長沢芦雪が雌孔雀を除いてほぼ同図様の作品化を図るなど、円山四条派画家たちの手本となった。滋賀・円満院旧蔵。

Important Cultural Property

Peacocks and Peonies

Maruyama Ōkyo
1771
Shōkokuji, Kyoto

Perched on a rock next to blossoming peonies, we encounter a male and a female peacock. The naturalistic yet decorative painting is done in sumptuous pigments including azurite, malachite, and gold that form a delicate unison. The bodies of the peacocks are rendered in great detail and the careful harmony of different gradations of ink, along with faint mineral pigments, imbues the birds with a strong sense of plasticity. The work is considered a representative masterpiece of Ōkyo's formative period, a time when he was working on commissions from the temple Enman'in. The painting became a template for other artists in Ōkyo's orbit, and his pupil Nagasawa Rosetsu made his own version of it. The work was once owned by Enman'in in Shiga Prefecture.

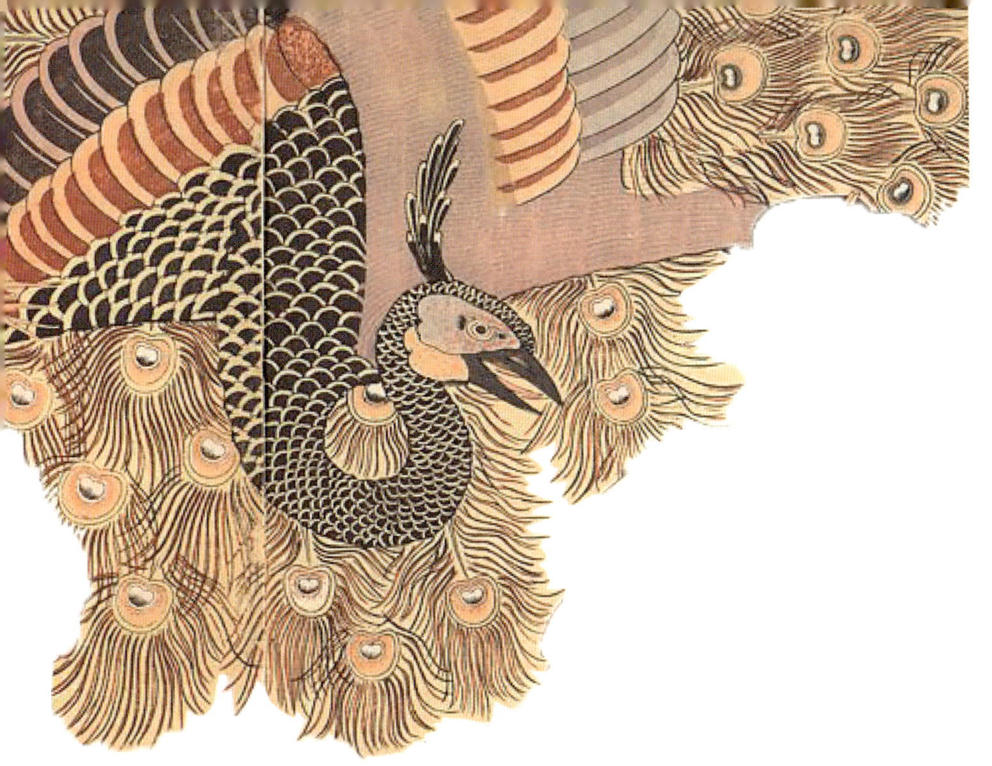

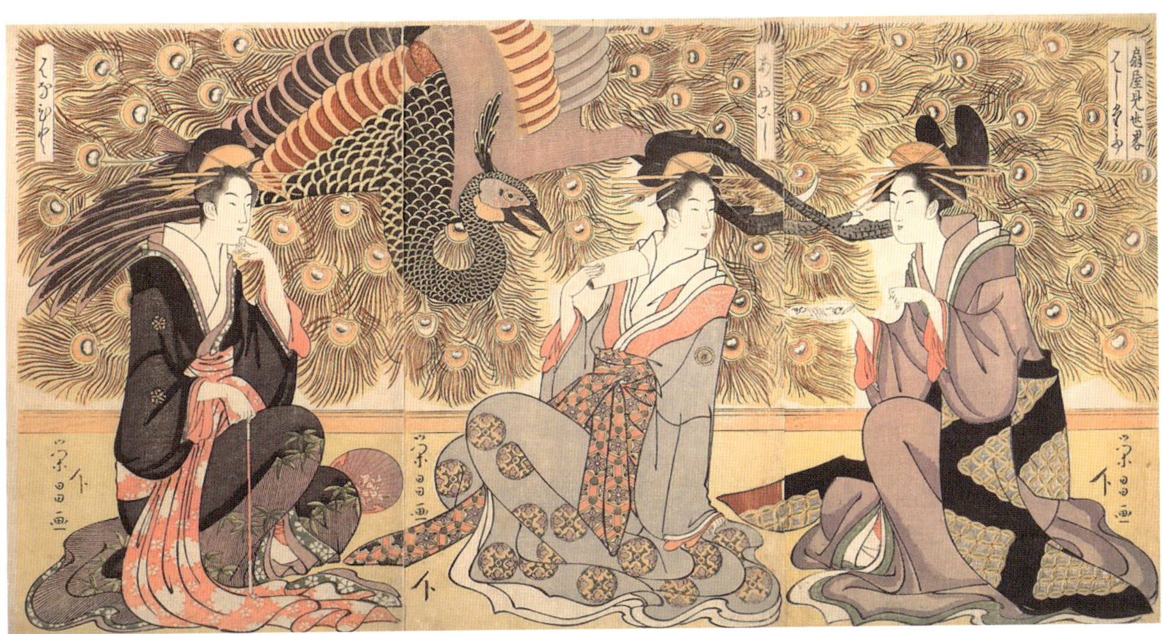

扇屋見世畧
鳥高斎栄昌
寛政5～11年（1793～99）
メトロポリタン美術館

Interior of the House called Ōgiya
Chōkōsai Eishō
1793-99
The Metropolitan Museum of Art

「孔雀茶屋」
(『摂津名所図会』(東生郡 二)より)

秋里籬島
寛政10年(1798)刊
国立国会図書館

大田南畝(蜀山人)は、その随筆『芦の若葉』において、1801年(享和元)に四天王寺参詣の帰途に孔雀茶屋に立ち寄り、金鶏や灰鶴・孔雀・羊を見たと記す。また、当時の見世物流行の様子は、伴蒿蹊の『閑田耕筆』(1801年刊)にも、「年毎に洛北今宮(神社)の御旅所、四条河原の納涼などに出る奇獣異鳥の類さまざまなり。浪華はまして是を売買もの多しとぞ。…水豹(アザラシ)…がらん鳥(ペリカン)…豪猪…駝鳥…求歓鳥…からくん鳥(シチメンチョウ)、…海山の広き、国々の多き、さまざまの物出るかし。」と記述されている。

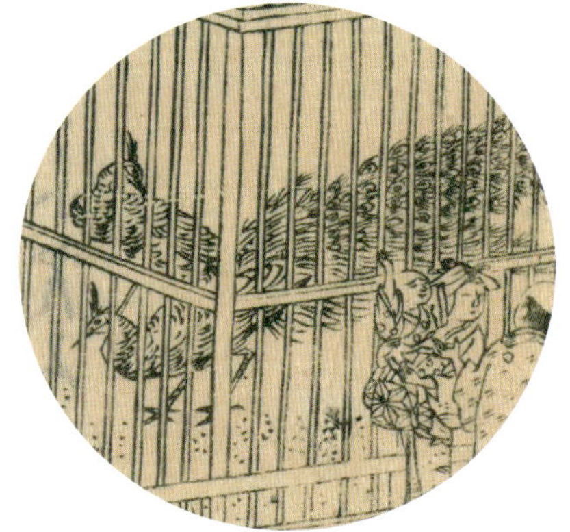

Kujaku (Peacock) Tea House,
(*from Settsu meisho zue*)

Akisato Ritō
Published in 1798
National Diet Library, Japan

Ōta Nanpo wrote in his novella *Ashi no wakana* that he marveled at golden pheasants, cranes, peacocks, and goats when visiting the Kujaku Tea House in 1801 upon returning from a pilgrimage to Shitennōji. In his book *Kanden kōhitsu* of the same year, Ban Kōkei records popular items of the time. It contains the following passage: “At the inn near Kyoto’s Imamiya Shrine and a restaurant at Shijō Kawara, one can see all kinds of rare beasts and birds. In Osaka, however, one can even buy them! There are seals, pelicans, porcupines, ostriches, mynah birds, and turkeys—all together there are myriads of creatures!”

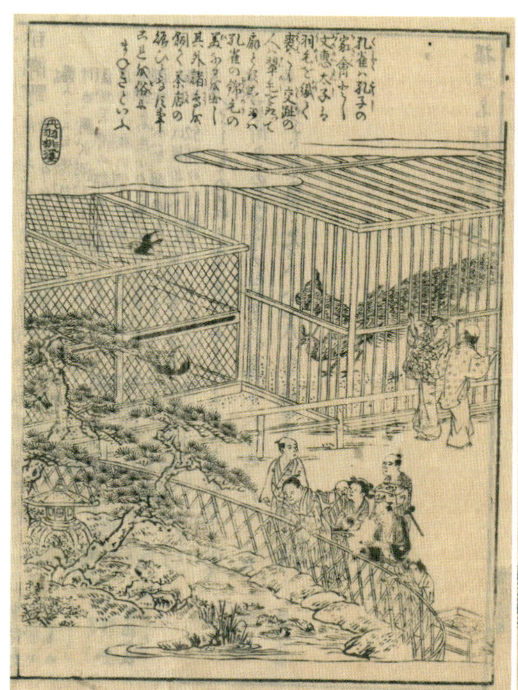

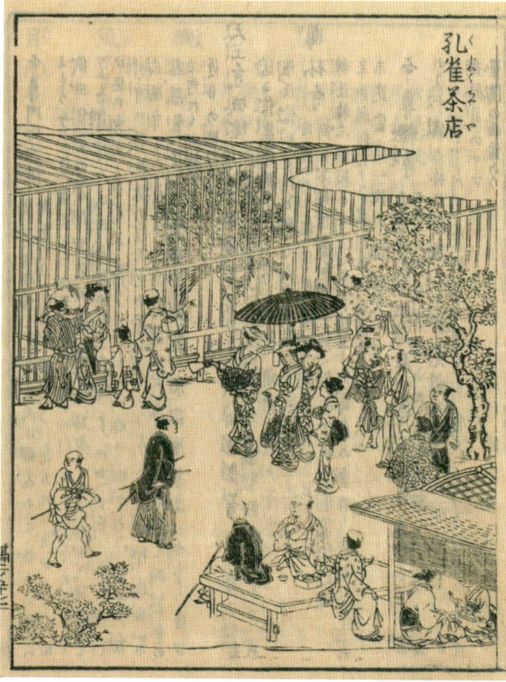

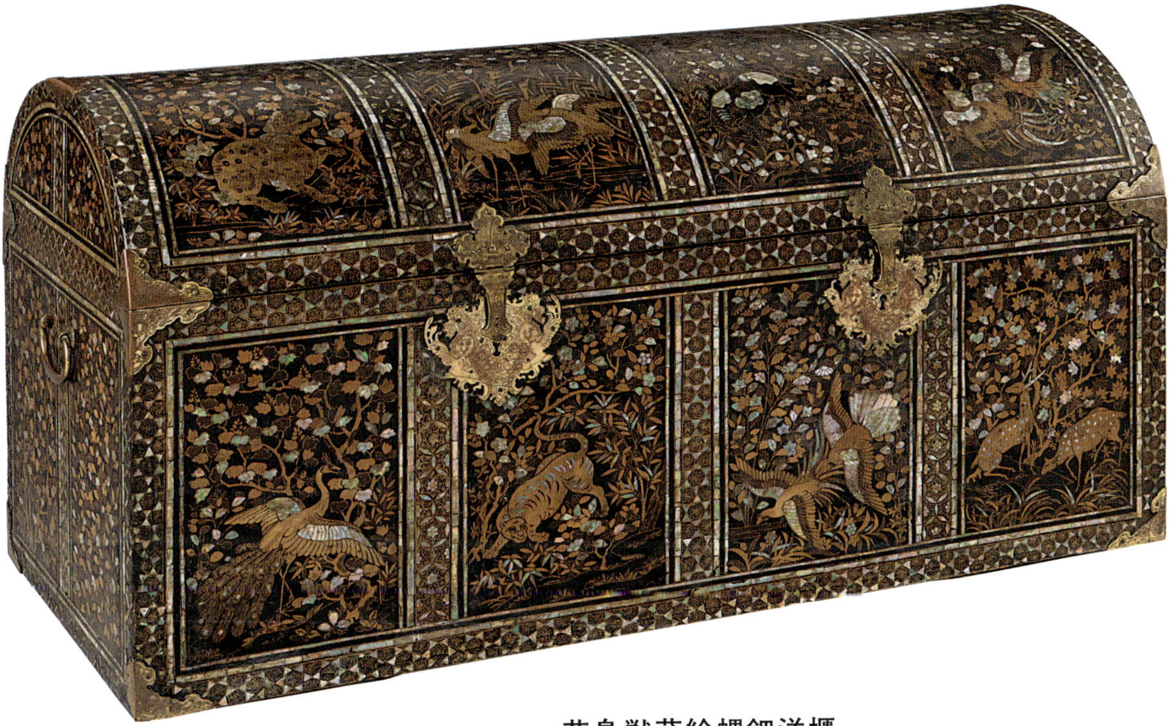

花鳥獣蒔絵螺鈿洋櫃

桃山時代末期〜江戸時代初期（16c末〜17c初め）
メトロポリタン美術館

Nanban Coffer with Animals and Landscapes

Late 16th–early 17th century
The Metropolitan Museum of Art

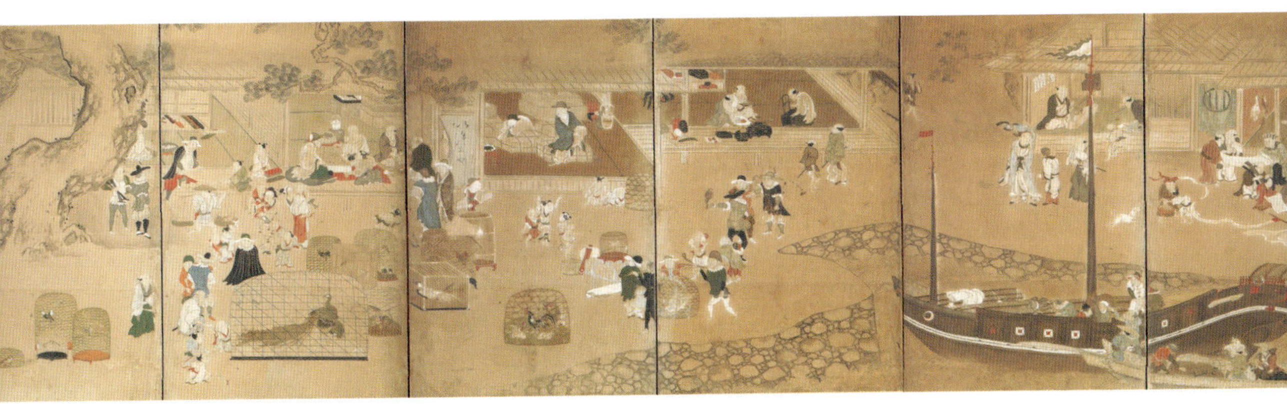

異国人交易図屏風

江戸時代中期（18c）
メトロポリタン美術館

Foreign Merchants in Japanese Trade Port

18th century
The Metropolitan Museum of Art

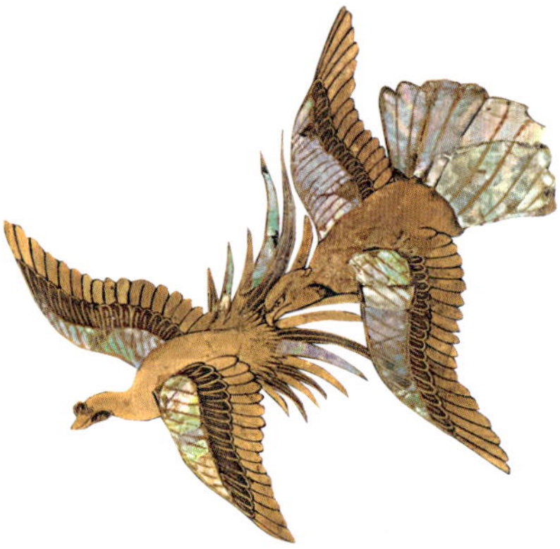

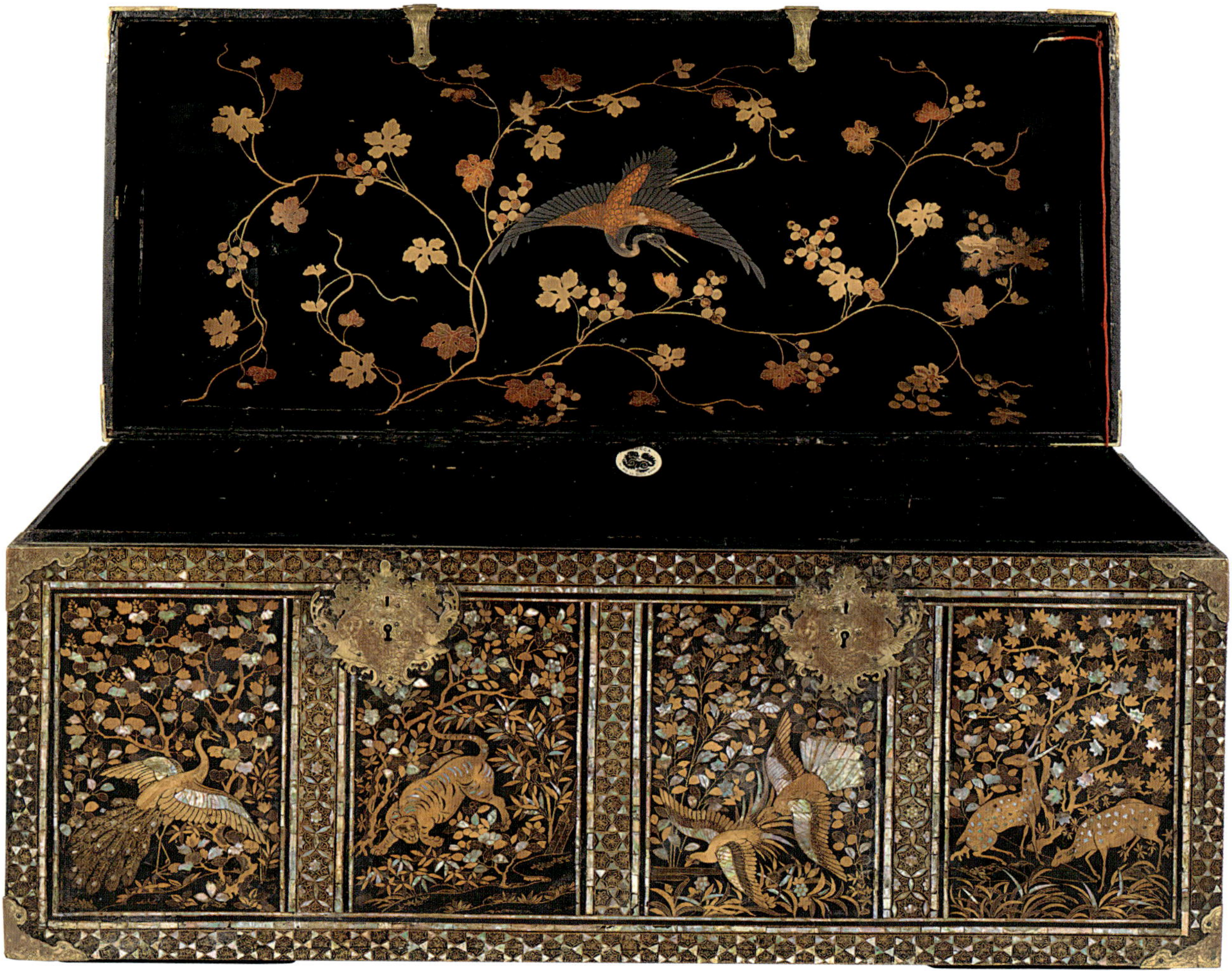

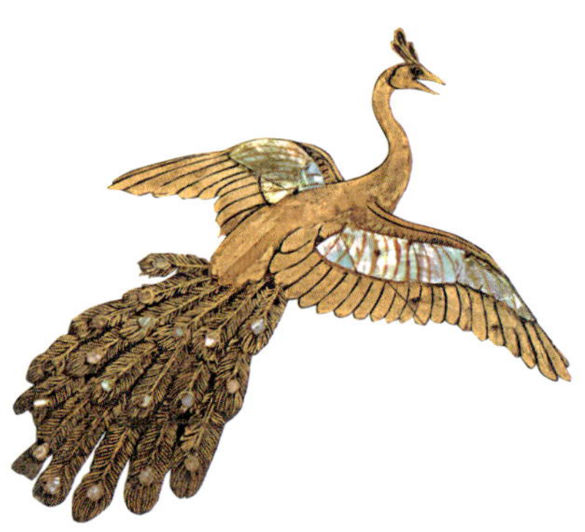

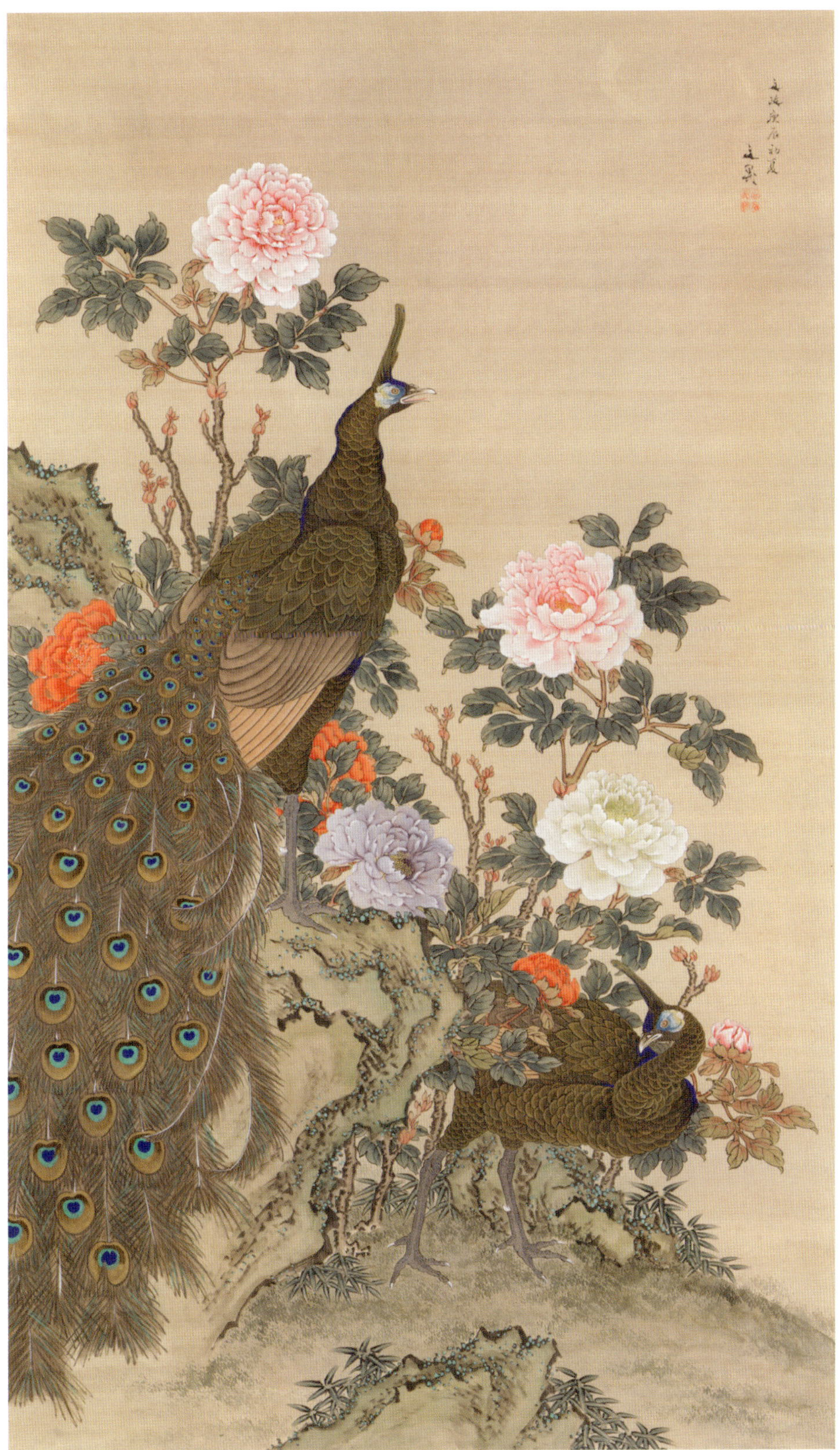

牡丹に孔雀図

谷文晁
文政3年（1820）
メトロポリタン美術館

Peacocks and Peonies

Tani Bunchō
Edo period, 1820
The Metropolitan Museum of Art

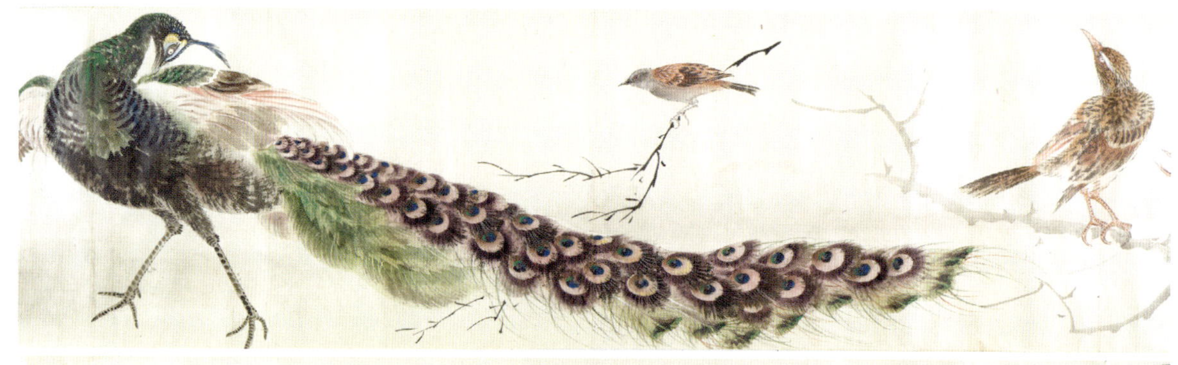

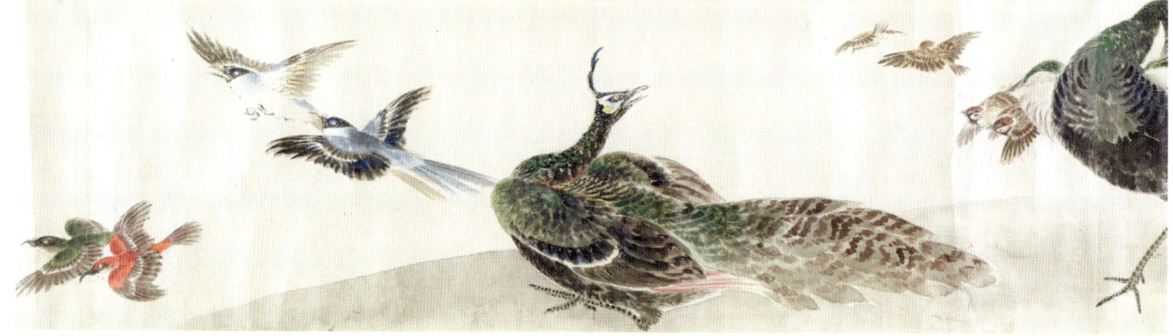

鳥類写生図巻

岡本秋暉
江戸時代(19c)
東京国立博物館

岡本秋暉(1807～62)は小田原藩に仕えた絵師で、渡辺崋山らと親交した。とくに、孔雀の絵を得意としたことで知られる。

Birds Painted from Life Scroll

Okamoto Shūki
19th century
Tokyo National Museum

Okamoto Shūki (1807-62) was a painter that worked for the Odawara Domain, and was friendly with Watanabe Kazan. Shūki was considered especially talented at painting peacocks.

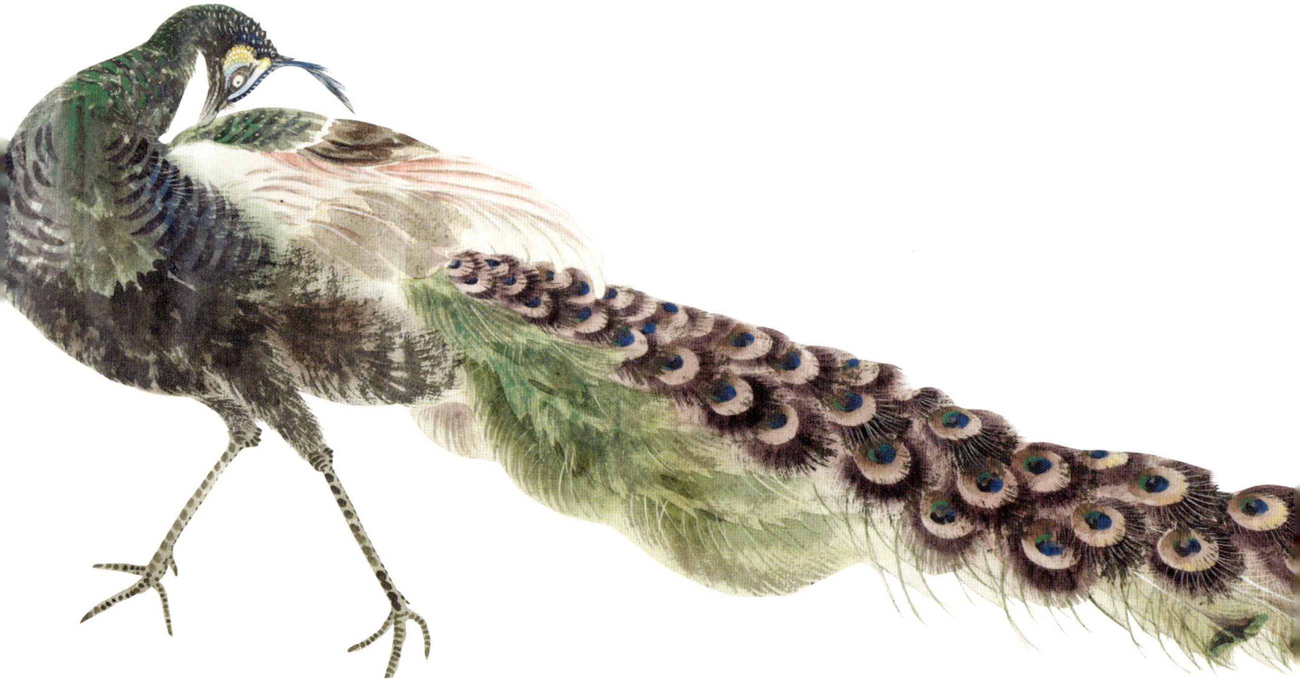

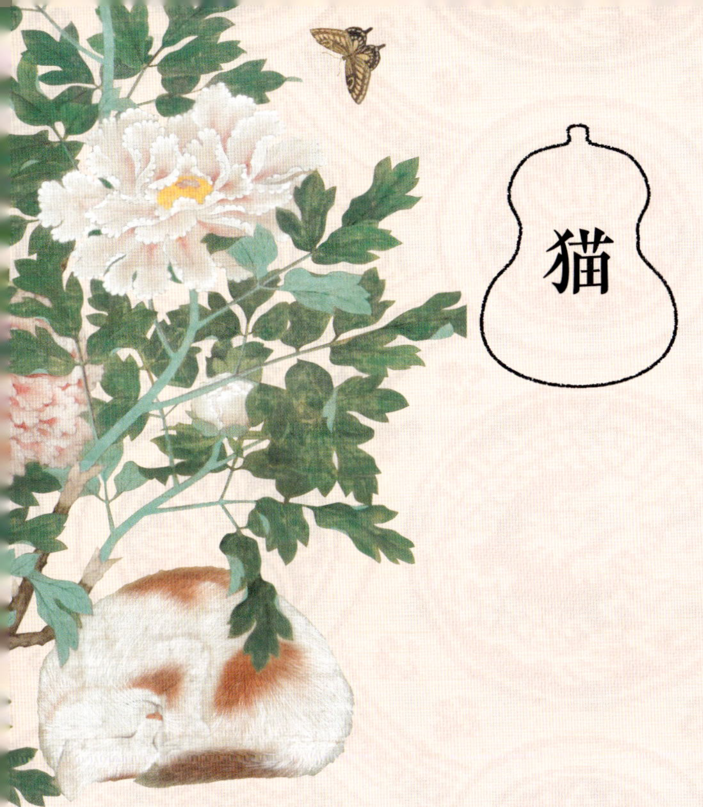

猫

猫は、仏典を鼠の害から守るため仏教とともに日本に入ってきたとされ、平安時代には宮廷でも飼われるようになっていった。また、片足を上げ人を招くようなポーズをとった招き猫が、古くから商売繁盛のお守りとして流行した。猫が顔を洗えば、すぐ客が来るという中国伝来の俗信にもとづくものらしい。江戸の豪徳寺には、寺で飼っていた猫が彦根藩主・井伊直孝の一行を招き入れたのが縁で、井伊家の菩提寺となり栄えたという縁起が伝えられ、招き猫発祥の地として知られる。また、猫は中国での発音māoが「耄(mào)」(80～90歳ぐらいの老齢)に通ずることから、同じく「耋(dié)」(70～80歳ぐらいの老年)と通ずる蝶(dié)とともに長寿を表すとされ、日本でも画題として描きつがれた。

The Cat

It is said that cats were brought to Japan to protect Buddhist scriptures from damage by mice. As early as the Heian period we find evidence of cats as pets among the aristocracy. The well-known *manekineko* that beckon customers to enter stores or restaurants have been around as protectors of businesses for a long time. The belief embodied by *manekineko* that customers will enter if a cat starts cleaning its face originated in China. It is said that a cat led the daimyo of Hikone Domain, Ii Naotaka, to the Edo temple Gōtokuji which he subsequently made his family's mortuary temple. The story embodies the auspicious meaning of cats in Japan. In Chinese, the word for "cat" is *mao*, a word that is homophonous with the term for "age eighty to ninety," in the same way as *die* ("butterfly") means "age seventy to eighty." This association of cats with long life also made its way into Japanese paintings.

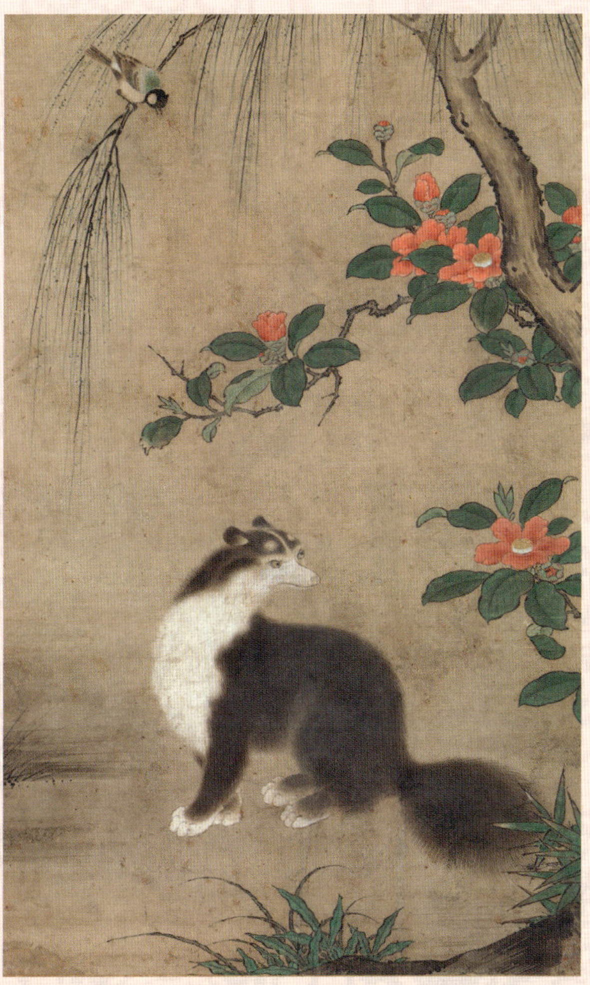

麝香猫図(じゃこうねこ)
右都御史(狩野玉楽か)
室町時代(16c 後半)
メトロポリタン美術館

Musk Cat
Uto Gyoshi (Kano Gyokuraku?)
Late 16th century
The Metropolitan Museum of Art

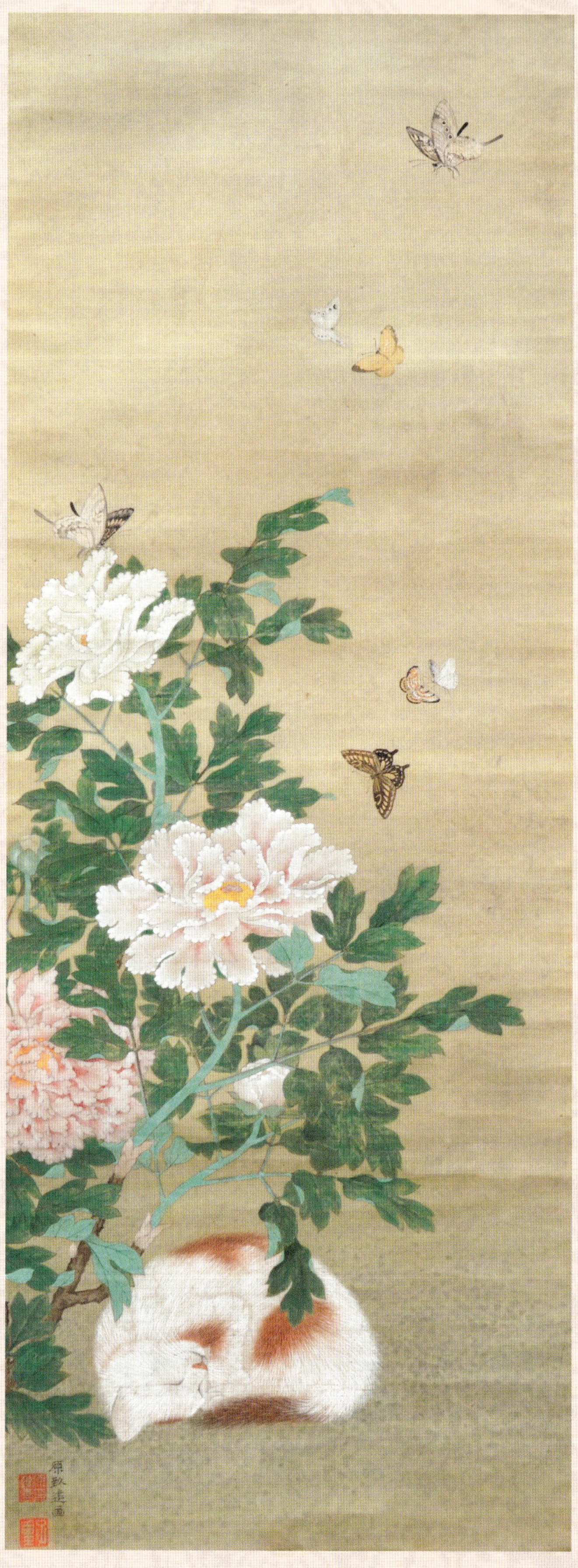

牡丹に猫図

原在中
江戸時代（18c後半～19c前半）
仙台市博物館

中国語の猫（mão）・耄（mào）、蝶（dié）・耋（dié）の音通から長寿を表す画題。あるいは蝶（ちょう）と猫（みょう）とで「長命」の語呂合わせも成り立つだろう。年齢を重ねた長寿を寿ぐ「算賀」という儀礼があるが、猫はそのような祝儀にふさわしい画題だったといえる。

Cat and Peonies

Hara Zaichū
Late 18th century-early 19th century
Sendai City Museum

The painting illustrates the association of cats and butterflies with long life. Just like in Chinese, the Japanese phonetic readings for “cat” and “butterfly” together spell out the word for “long life.” Paintings like this one would have been appropriate for longevity celebrations.

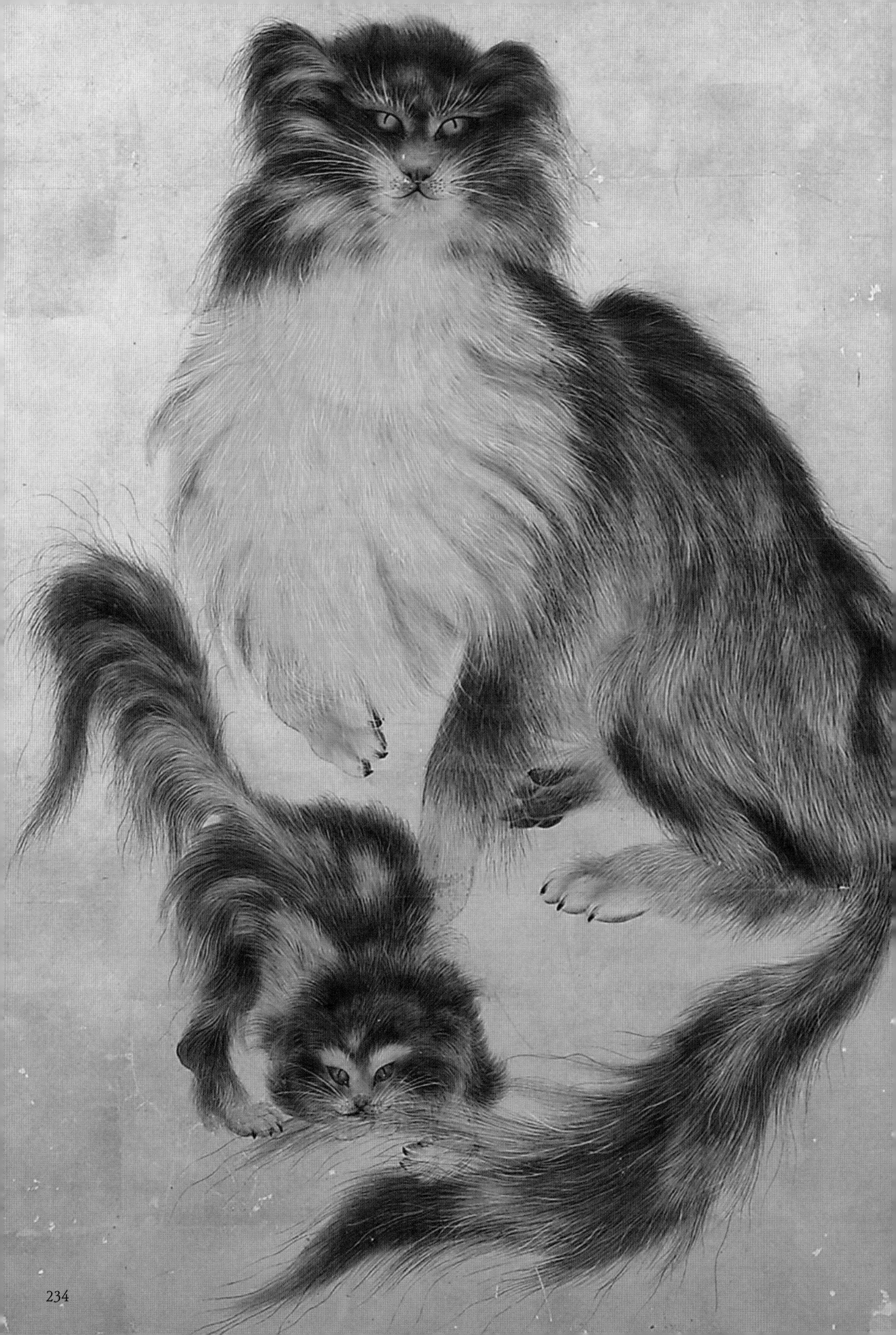

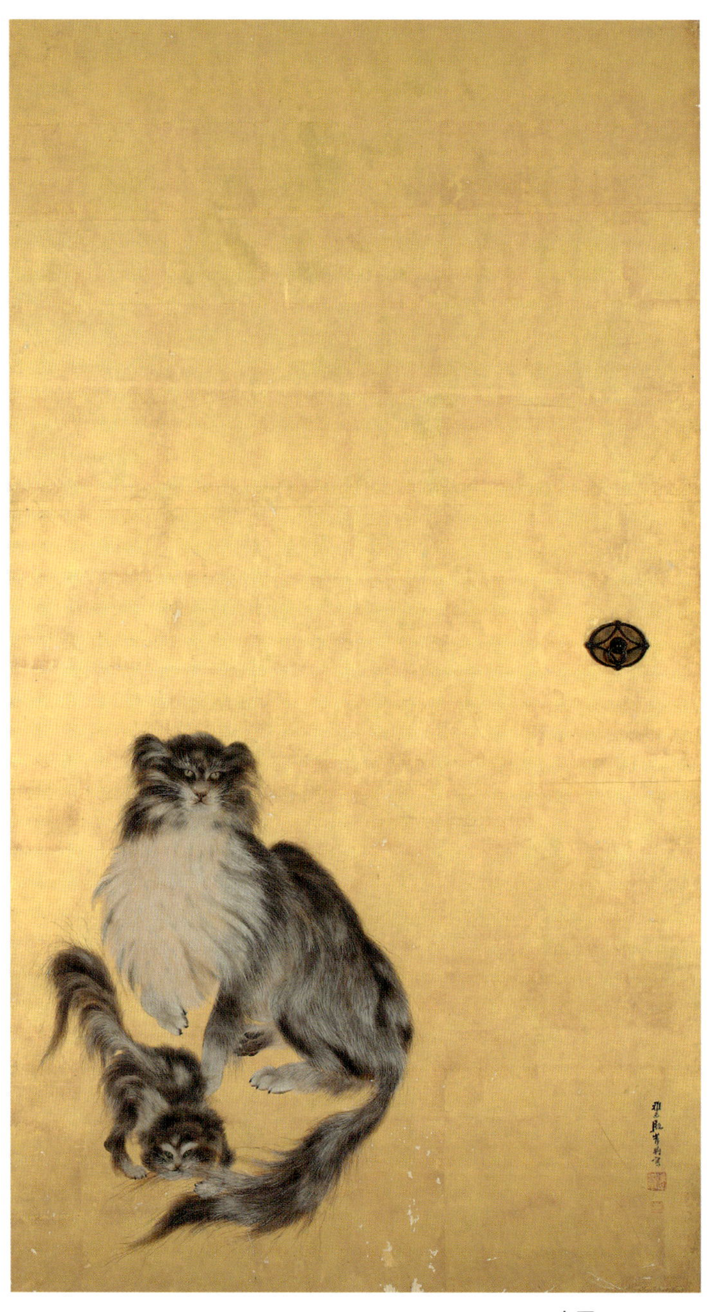

全図　overview

霊猫図

岸駒
天明3年（1784）〜文化5年（1808）
富山市郷土博物館

霊猫とは麝香猫のこと。岸駒は虎の絵を得意としたが、毛描きの妙技は本図にも生かされている。京都・金光院の伝来とされ、画面右上の金具の存在から、もとは引き戸として利用されたらしい。

Civet

Ganku
1784-1808
Toyama Municipal Folk Museum

This is a civet, also known as a *toddycat*. *Ganku* was a gifted tiger painter, but his exquisite skill in depicting fur is also used to great effect here. This work is thought to have been passed down at Konkōin in Kyoto, and judging from the presence of a metal pull on the upper right of the image, it seems that this work was originally a sliding door.

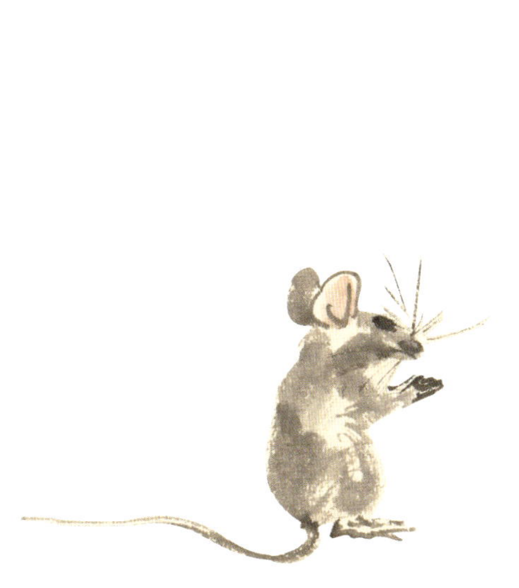

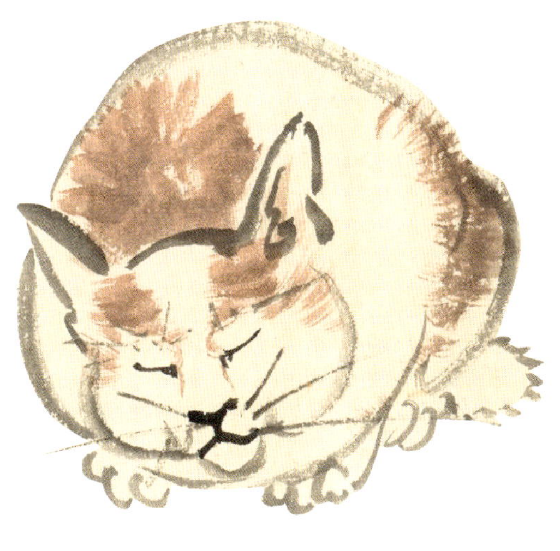

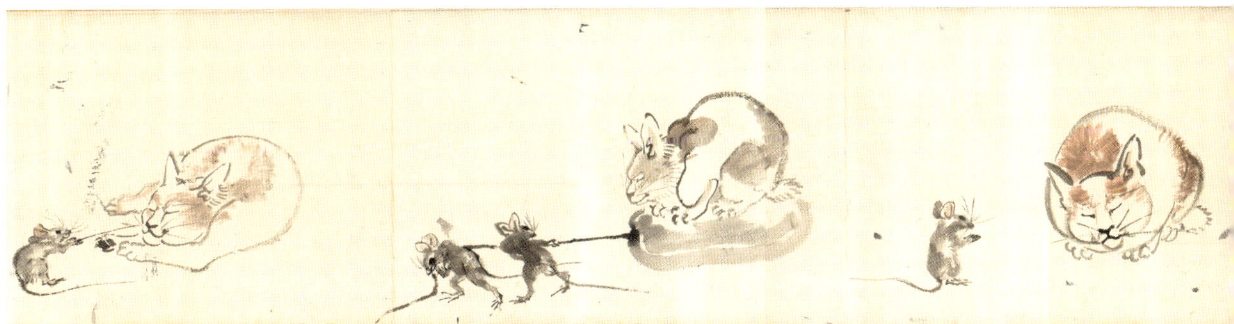

群獣人物図巻　部分

河鍋暁斎
江戸時代(19c)
メトロポリタン美術館

Cats and Mice (*from Frolicking Figures and Animals*)

Kawanabe Kyōsai
19th century
The Metropolitan Museum of Art

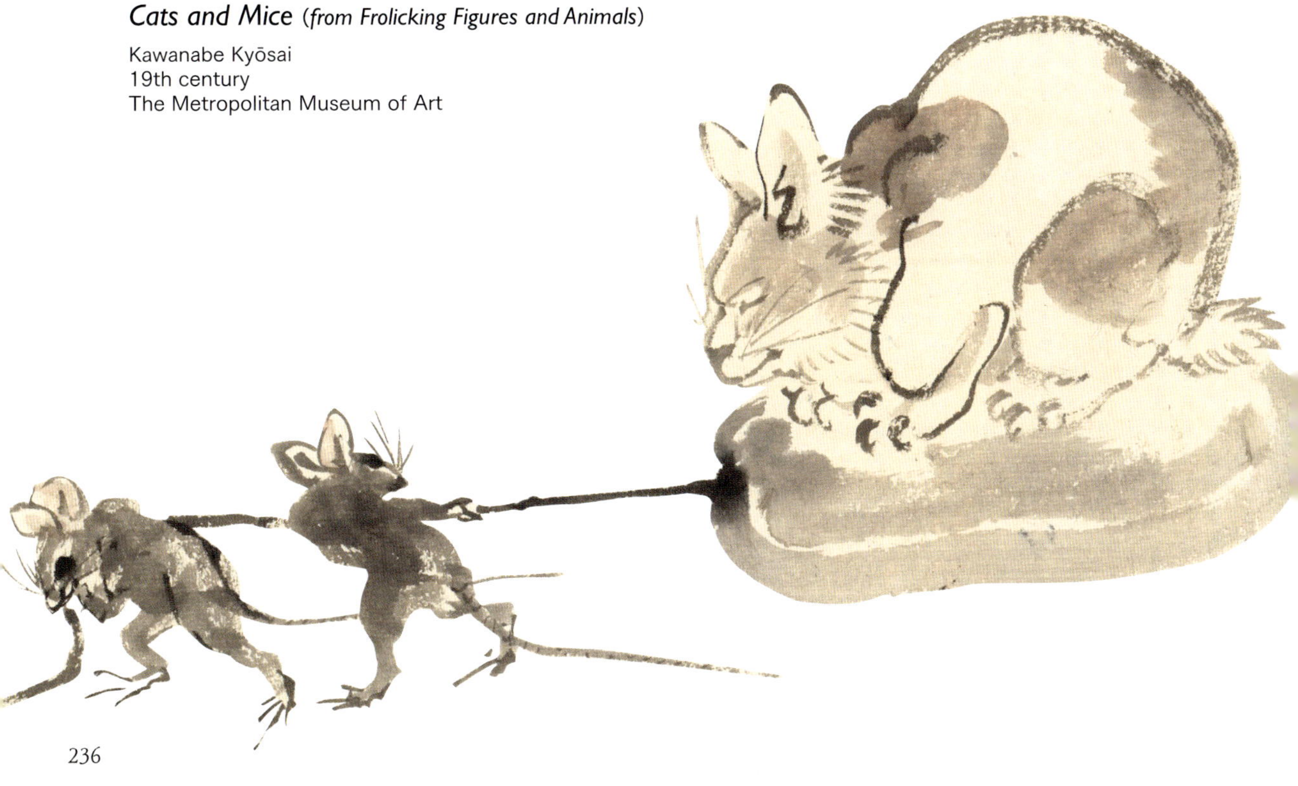

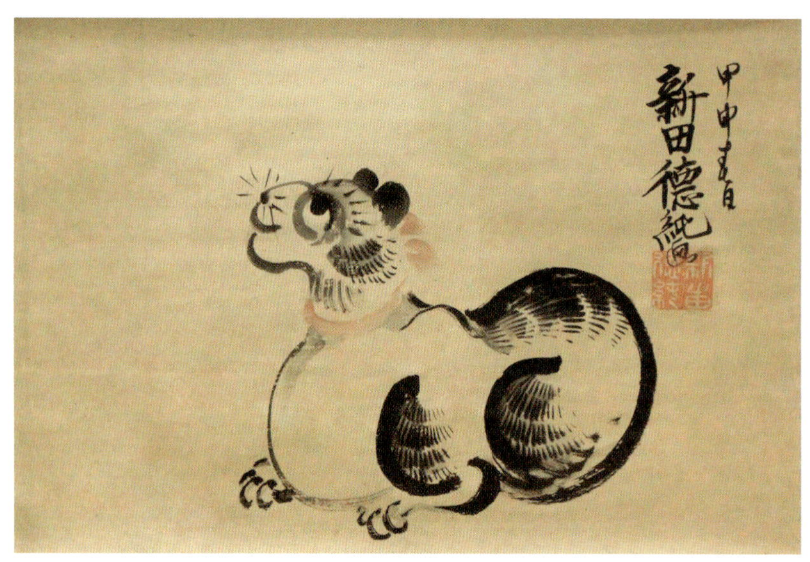

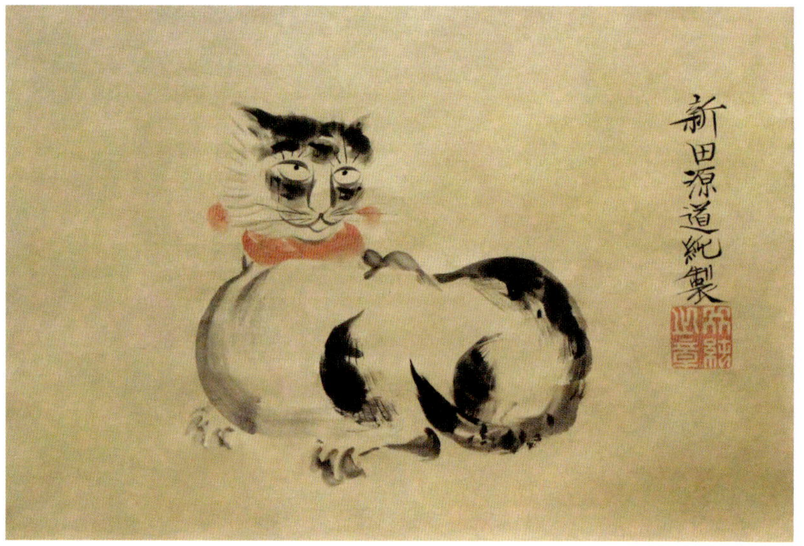

新田猫図

(上)岩松徳純・(下)岩松道純
江戸時代(19c)
太田市立新田荘歴史資料館

上野国新田郡(群馬県太田市)に屋敷を構えた旗本・新田岩松氏は、江戸住まいを免除される代わりに、大名に準じて参勤交代のある「交代寄合」格だった。歴代当主のうち、江戸後期から明治期にかけての4代(温純・徳純・道純・俊純)が描いた猫絵を「新田猫」と称している。わずか120石という微禄を補う意味もあったが、直筆の猫絵は養蚕の盛んな地域において鼠害除けの護符として絶大な効果を期待され、武州や信州など周辺諸地域からの需要も多かったという。

Nitta Cats

Above: Iwamatsu Yoshizumi, Below: Iwamatsu Michizumi
19th century
Ōta Municipal Nittanoshou History Museum

The Nitta Iwamatsu were shogunal retainers whose residence was in Nitta, Kōzuke Province (Ōta, Gunma Prefecture), and they were required to participate in the *sankin kōtai* required attendance system like the other daimyo, and keep a residence in Edo. In successive generations, the four heads of the domain from the late Edo period to the Meiji period (Atsuzumi, Yoshizumi, Michizumi, and Toshizumi), drew pictures of cats, and these were known as "Nitta Cats." This was perhaps to compensate for their small stipend of just one hundred and twenty *koku*, but cat pictures done in their own hand were thought to be tremendously effective as talismans to repel damage from rats and mice, which was a major concern in an area where sericulture flourished; there were also many requests for these from the surrounding regions, like Musashi and Shinano Provinces.

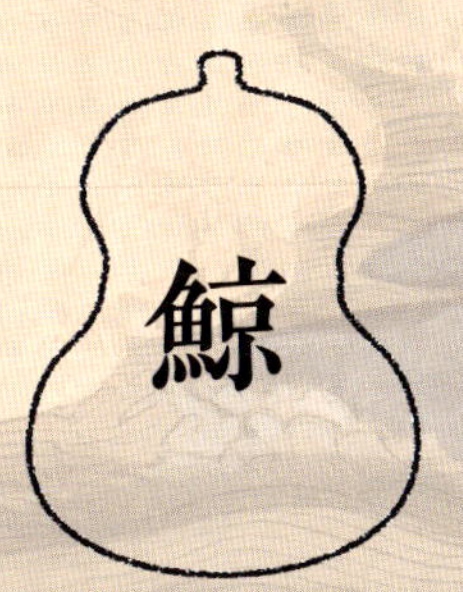

日本では古くから勇魚（いさな）と呼んで魚とみなし、その巨大な体軀から畏敬の念をもって迎えられてきた。回遊性のある鯨が紀伊半島や土佐の沿岸に現れるのは陰暦正月頃だったため、当地では「鯨の神詣で」などと呼び神聖視したという。また、その出現が豊漁をもたらすとの考えから、「えびす」と称し漁業神とされることもあった。旭日とともに鯨が水面に大きな背を見せ、潮を吹く様子をとらえた作や、「鯨寄れば七浦潤す（賑わう）」といわれた賑わいを錦絵に表現したものなど、鯨漁の繁栄の様子は水産業者ならずとも吉祥画として受け止められたのではなかろうか。

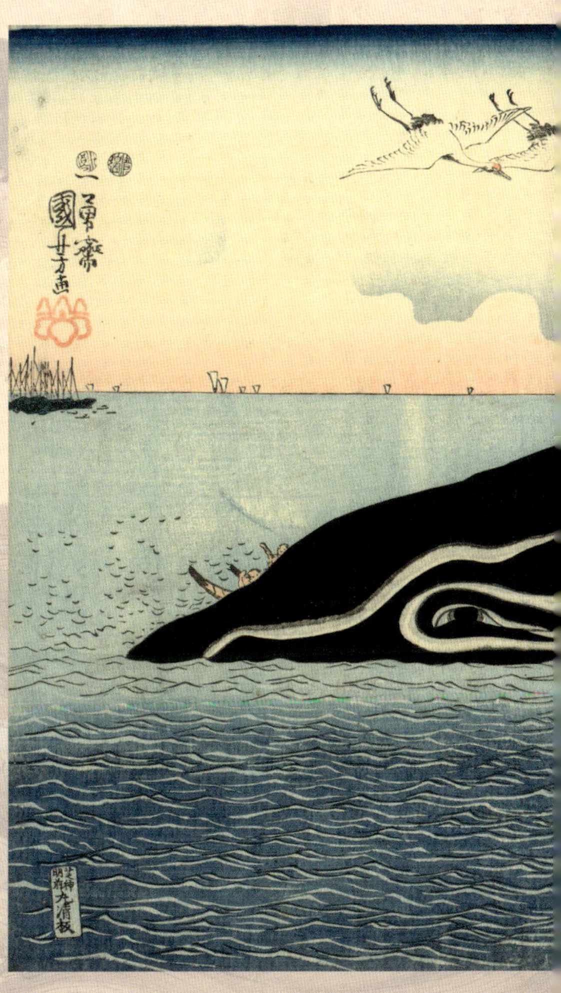

The Whale

The old Japanese name for whales, *isana*, literally means "heroic fish," a designation that encapsulates the respect for these majestic creatures of the sea. Schools of whales often appeared around the lunar New Year in the areas of the Kii Peninsula and the Tosa shore. The sight led people in Japan to read this spectacle through a religious lens: as a New Year's pilgrimage of whales. The abundance of whales and fishermen hunting them also encouraged an association of Ebisu, the god of wealth, with fish. Prints depicting whales with their large backs surfacing from beneath the water became popular emblems of good fortune.

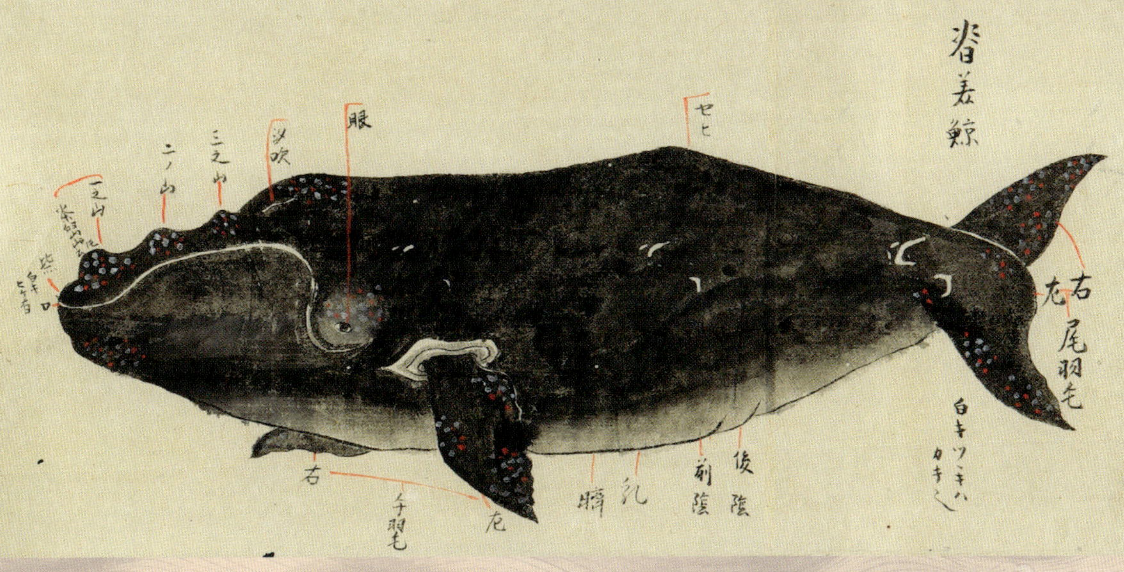

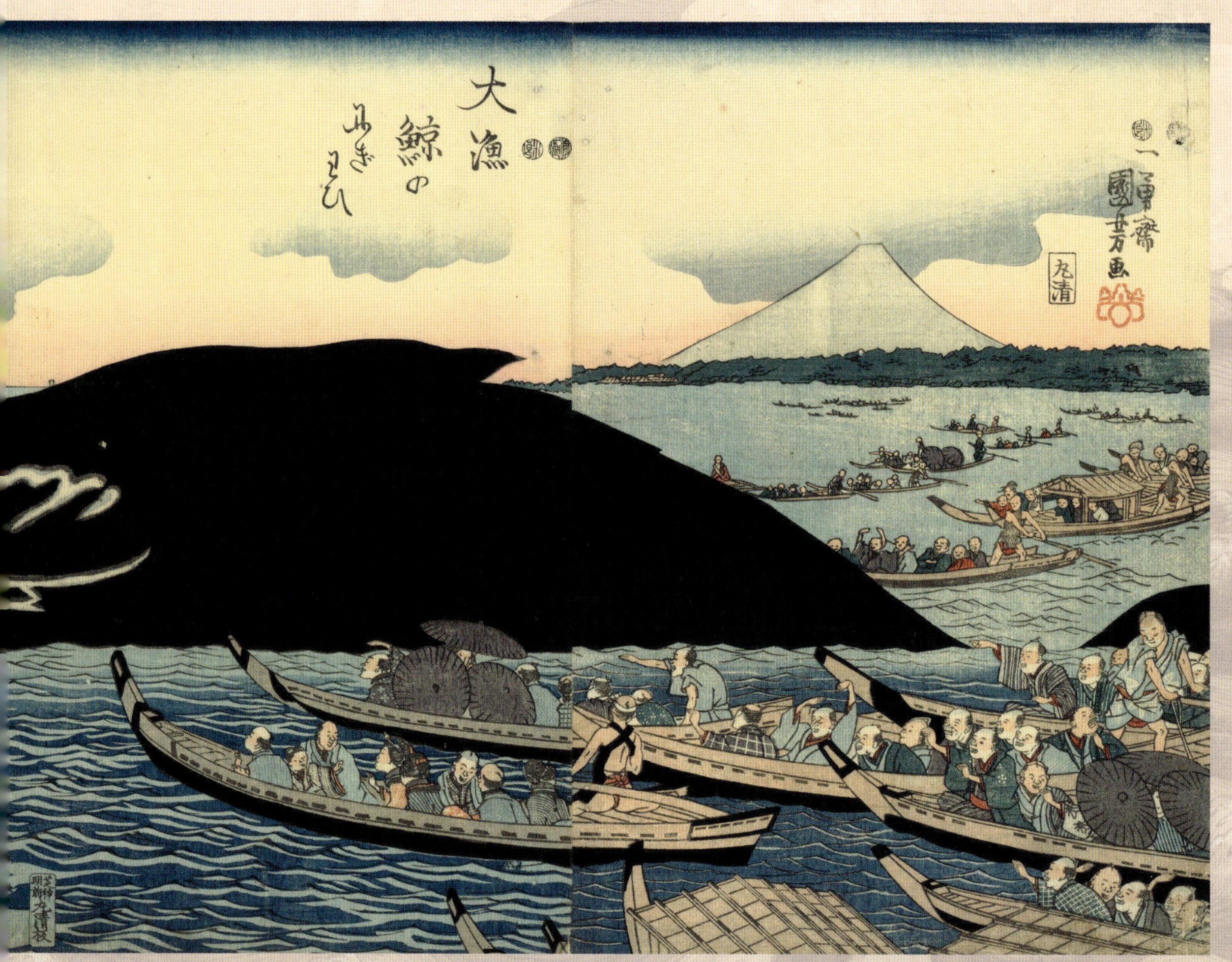

大漁鯨のにぎわひ

歌川国芳
嘉永4年(1851)
ギャラリー紅屋

かつては、「鯨寄れば七浦潤す(賑わう)」「一匹の鯨に七浦賑う」などといわれ、鯨は富の象徴だった。遠くに富士を望み、空には鶴が舞う。人々は小船に乗って大きな鯨を見物するため集まっている。1851年(嘉永4)4月、荏原郡大井村(今の品川区内)の海岸に、長さ3間余(約6m)の鯨が漂着し、その後、浅草奥山で見世物となった。この絵は、その時の鯨を描いたものとみられている。

Great Whale Spectacle

Utagawa Kuniyoshi
1851
GALLERY BENIYA

In the past, the sight of a single whale was seen as an auspicious omen. For that reason, whales were considered symbols of wealth. In this image, Mount Fuji can be seen in the distance and cranes are flying in the sky as large numbers of people in small boats crowd around an enormous whale. In the fourth month of 1851 (Kaiei 4), a whale of about six meters in length was washed ashore at the town of Ōi. The creature was carried to Edo and put on display in Asakusa. This triptych of prints was made around the same time.

六鯨図并捕鯨具 部分

天保15年(1844)
三重県総合博物館

Rokugeizu narabini hogeigu (*detail*)
(*Six Pictures of Whales and Tools for Hunting Them*)

1844
Mie Prefectural Museum

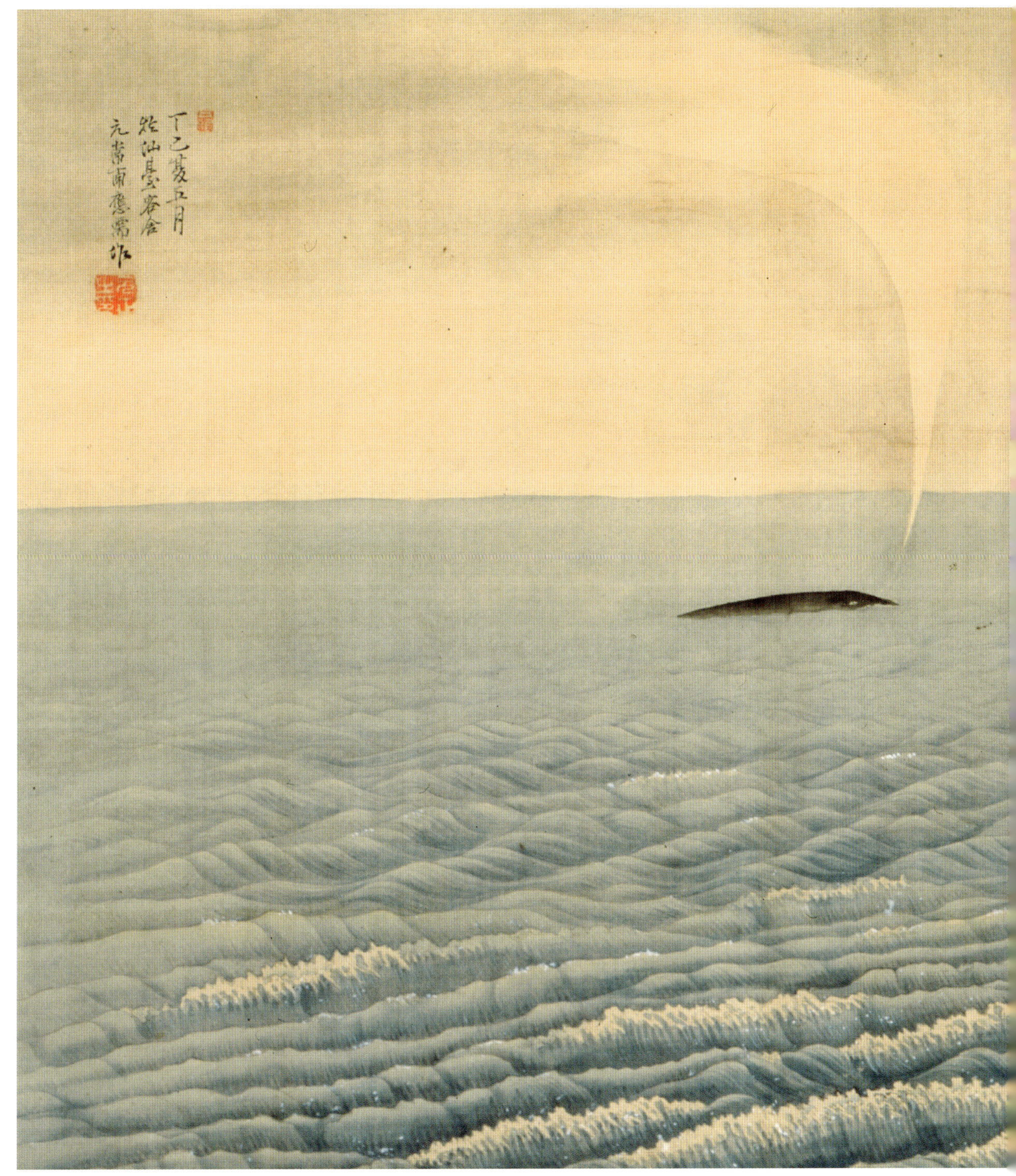

旭潮鯨波図

根元常南
寛政9年(1797)

根元常南は菅井梅関の師。関東や南東北を遊歴しながら、あくの強い画風の絵を描いた。本図に描かれるのは、鯨の背中だけが浮かぶ大海原とわずかに姿をあらわした旭日のみ。鯨が、豊漁や商売繁盛などの願いを託されたモチーフだったことがわかる。

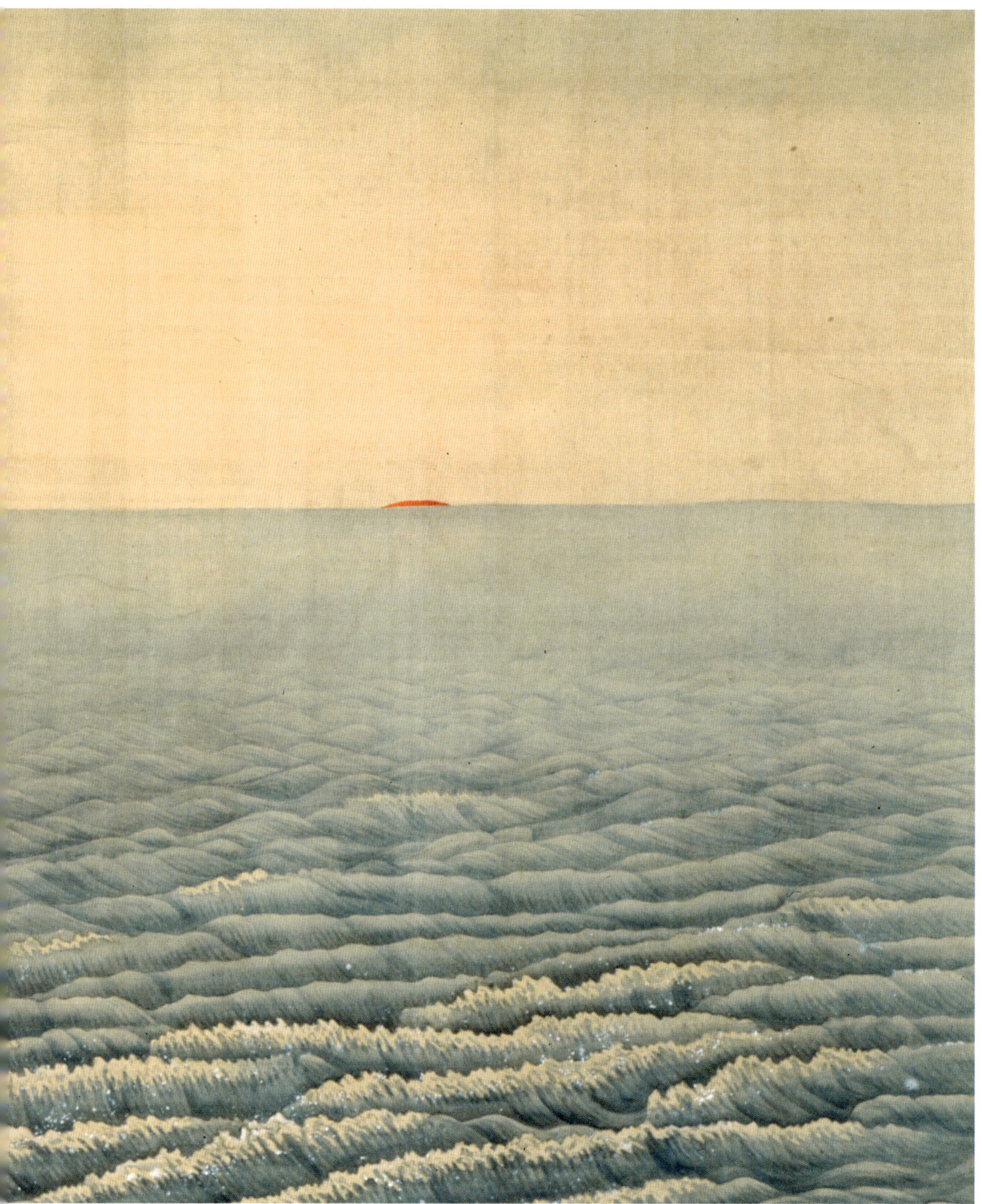

Whale Against the Rising Sun

Nemoto Jōnan
1797

Nemoto Jōnan was a teacher of the painter Sugai Baikan. While traveling around the Kantō and southern Tōhoku regions, Jōnan created a number of idiosyncratic pictures. This image shown here depicts the back of a whale emerging from the water against the rising sun. Whales were thought of as symbols of wealth, and images such as this might have been commissioned by a merchant.

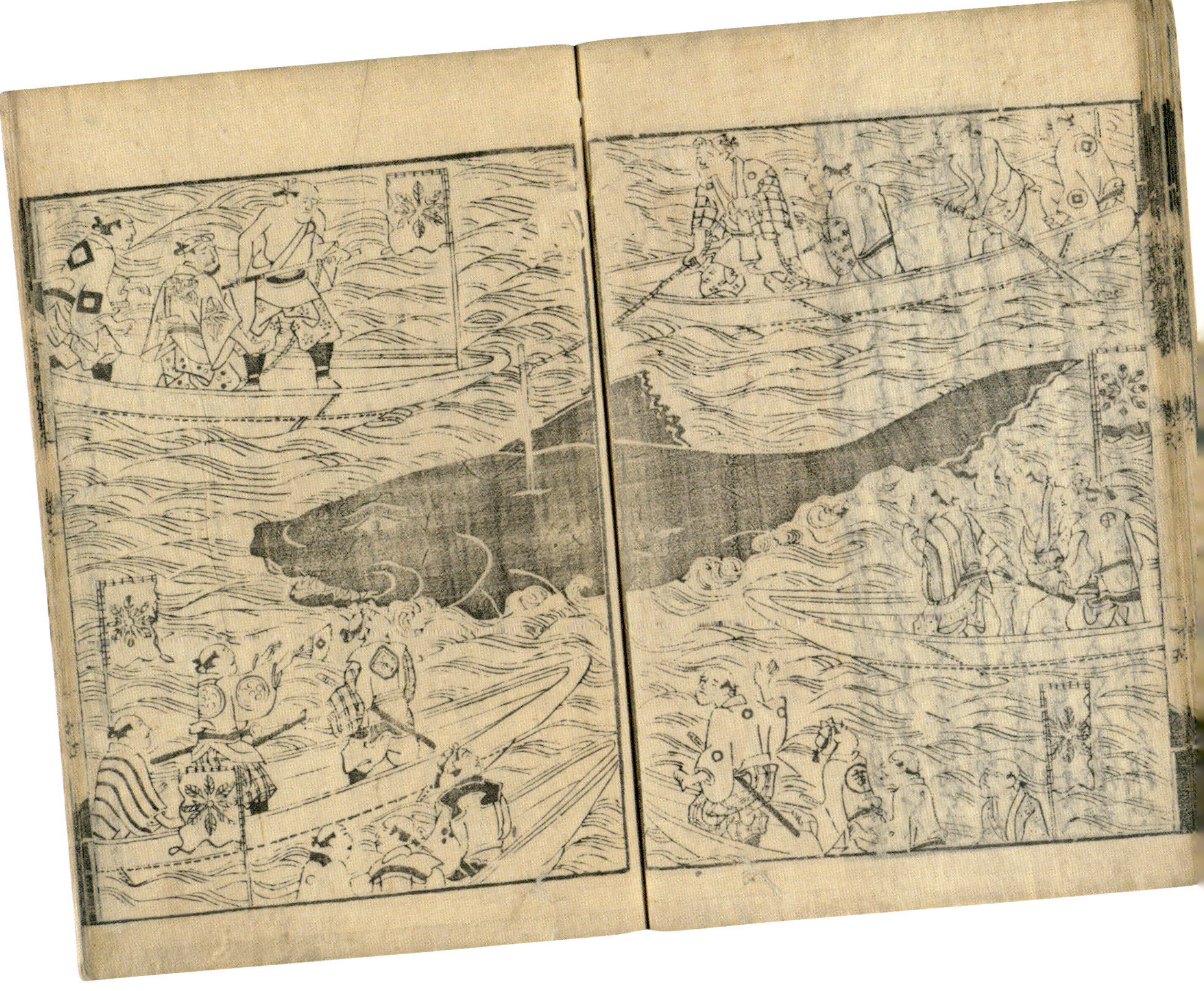

『日本永代蔵』

井原西鶴
貞享5年(1688)刊
国立国会図書館

井原西鶴(1642?〜93)作の浮世草子で、町人物の代表作のひとつ。巻二には「天狗ハ家名の風車／紀伊国に隠れなき鯨ゑびす、横手ふしの小哥の出所」の項で、多くの富をもたらした紀州における捕鯨の様子が描写される。

Nippon eitai kura

(Repository of an Eternal Japan)

Ihara Saikaku
Published in 1688
National Diet Library, Japan

Ihara Saikaku (1642?-93) composed this illustrated novella about the lives of towns-people of his time. In the second volume, the book shows the capturing of a whale in Kii Province, and interprets the event as an omen of great wealth and prosperity for the region.

『頭書 増補訓蒙図彙』

中村惕斎（1629〜1702）編、下河辺拾水画
寛政元年（1789）刊
国立国会図書館

Kashiragaki zōho kinmō zui

(*Illustrated Instructional Encyclopedia, with Foreword*)

Edited by Nakamura Tekisai, Illustrated by Shimokōbe Shūsui
Published in 1789
National Diet Library, Japan

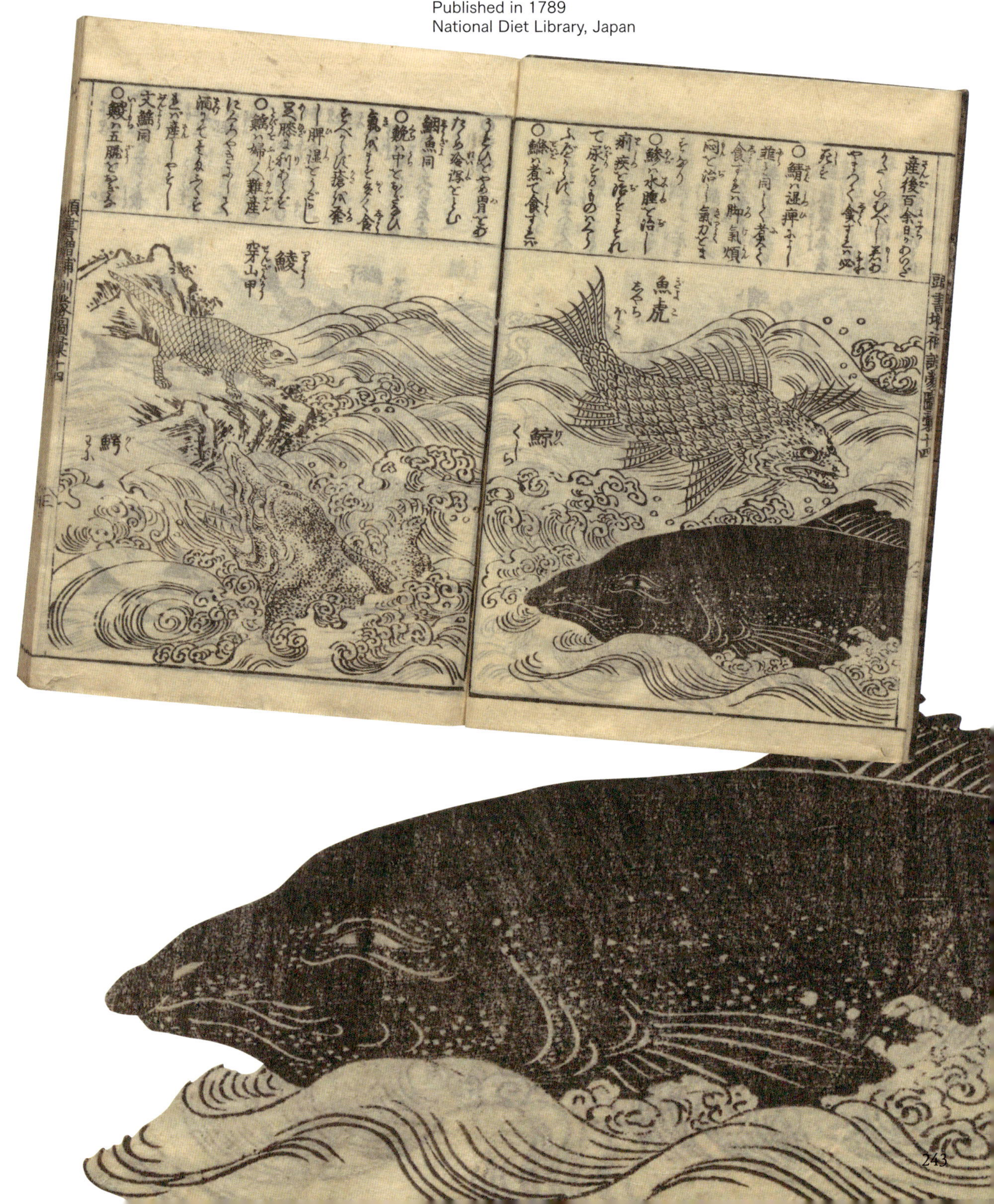

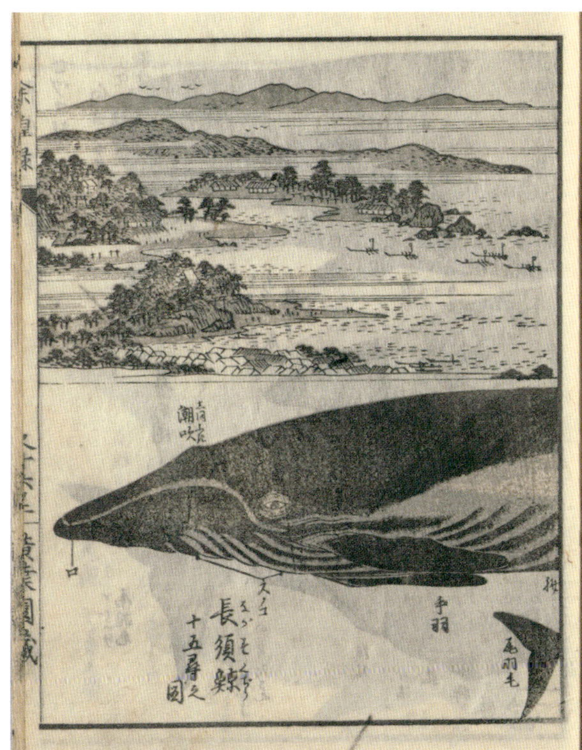

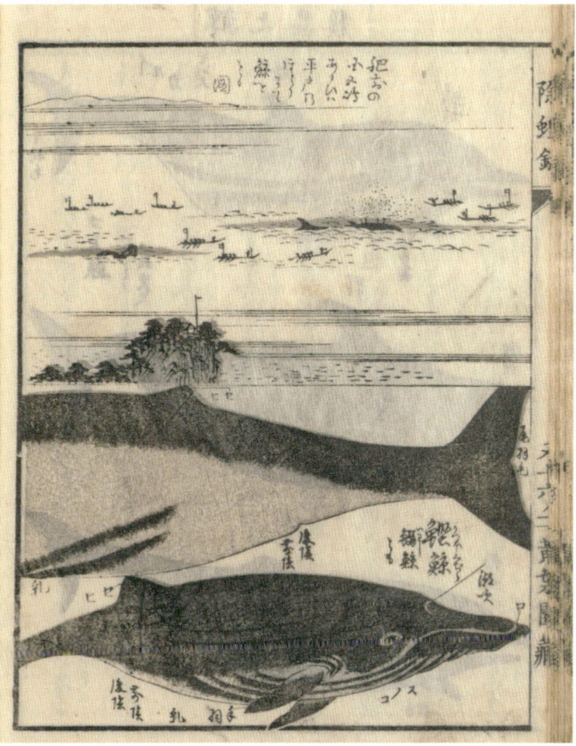

『除蝗録』(じょこうろく)

大蔵永常
文政9年(1826)刊
国立国会図書館

凶作の大きな原因とされる稲の害虫ウンカの駆除法として、鯨油を水田に流すことの効用を説く。長谷川雪旦の挿絵により、「鯨之品類」として、イルカ、コト鯨、長須鯨、鰹鯨(鰯鯨)、マツコ鯨(真甲鯨)、座頭鯨、背美鯨、シャチ、児鯨(小鯨)、大魚喰といった諸種の鯨類を紹介する。1844年(弘化元)には、『除蝗録後編』も刊行された。

Jokōroku

(*Record to Rid Yourself of Grasshoppers*)

Ōkura Nagatsune
Published in 1826
National Diet Library, Japan

One method to prevent insects from damaging rice crops was to mix whale oil into the rice paddies' water. The illustrations of the book by Hasegawa Settan makes clear which sea creatures were considered part of the whale family: dolphins, gray whales, fin whales, sei whales, sperm whales, humpback whales, North Pacific right whales, and orcas. The book was republished in its second edition in 1844 (Kōka 1).

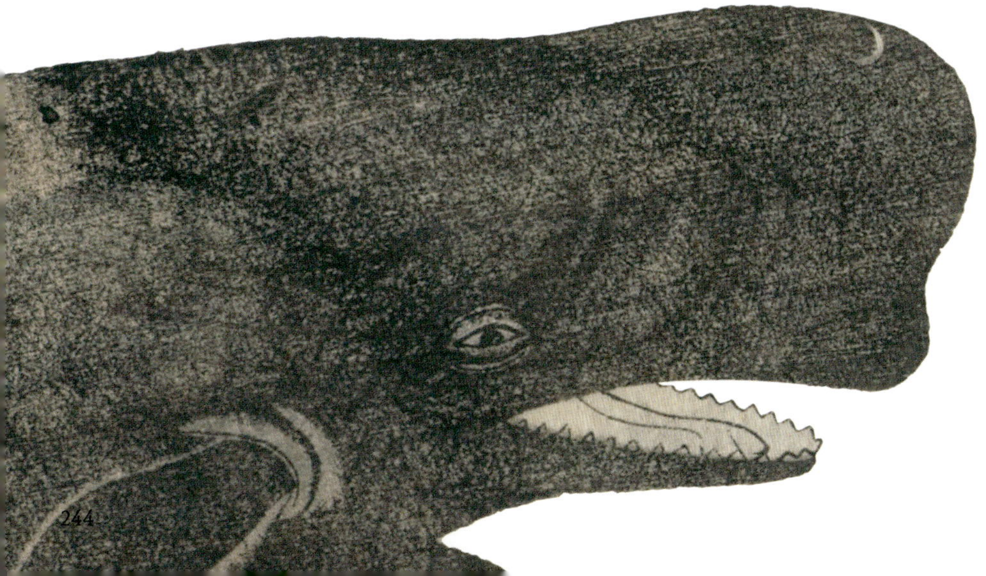

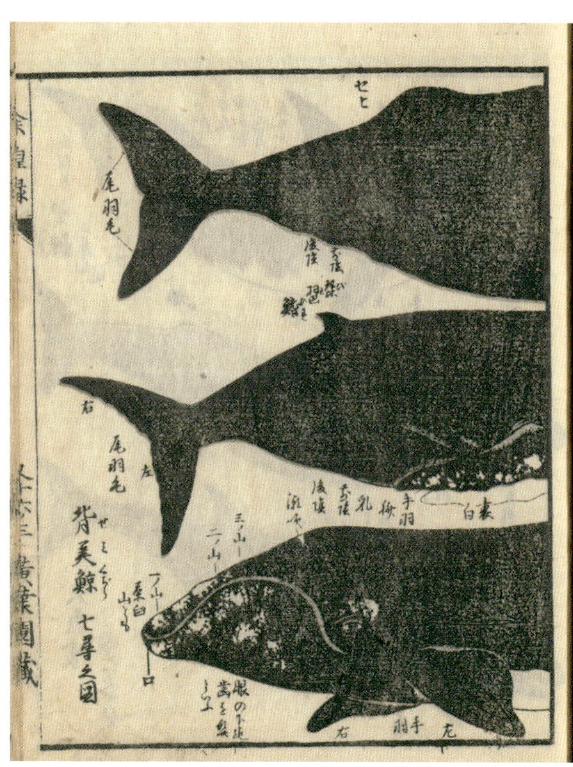

尾羽毛
右
尾羽毛
左
手羽
背美鯨　七尋之図
口
右
手羽
左

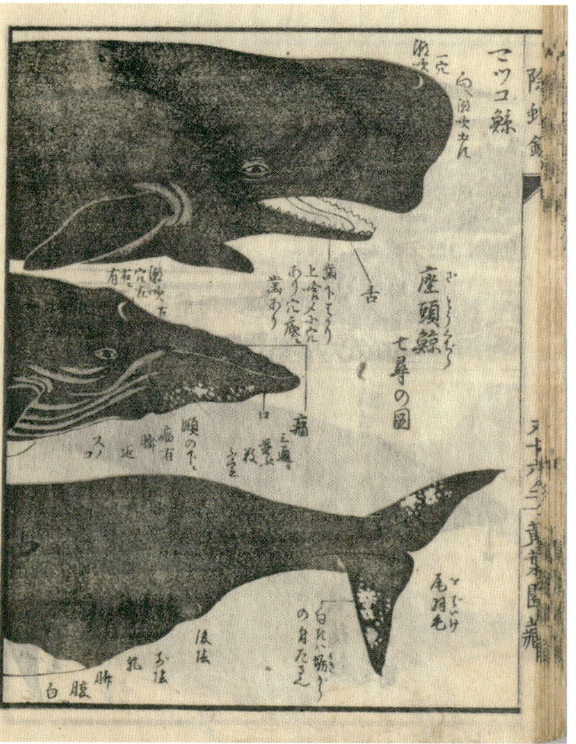

マツコ鯨
舌
座頭鯨　七尋の図
口
尾羽毛
腹
白

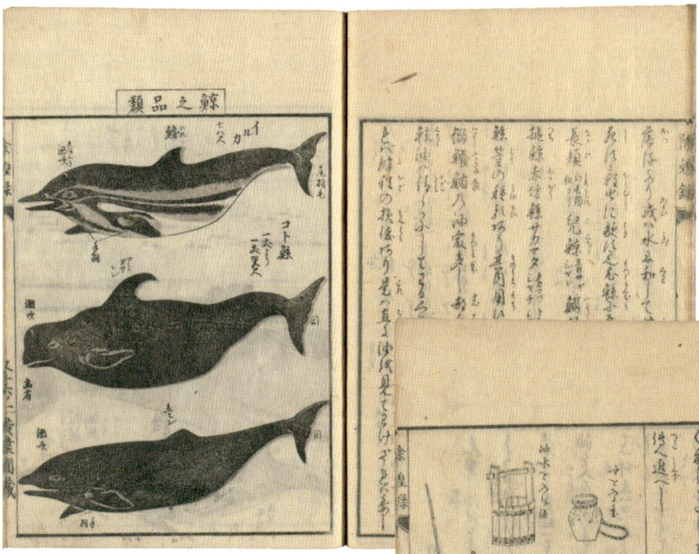

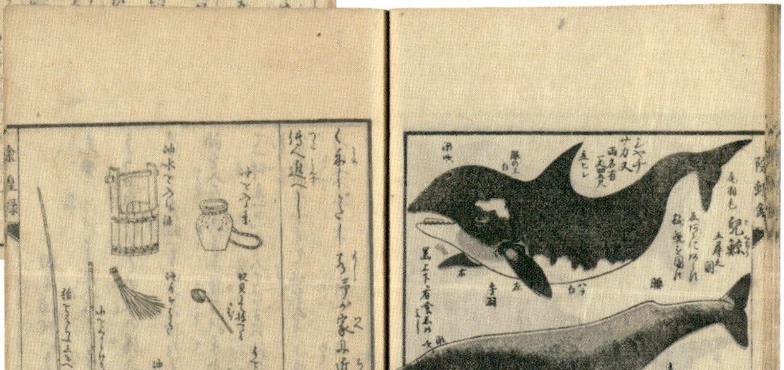

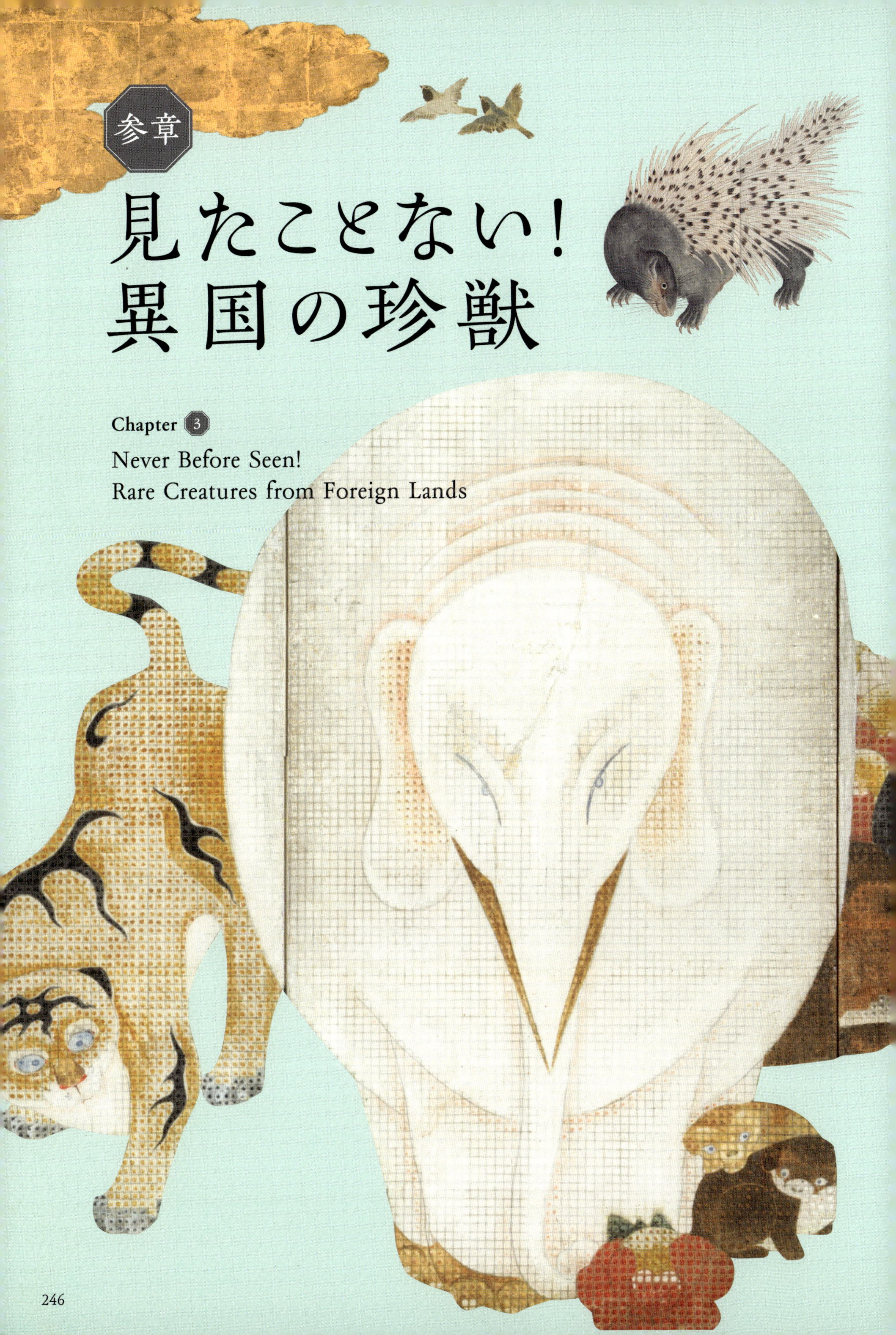

参章

見たことない！異国の珍獣

Chapter 3

Never Before Seen!
Rare Creatures from Foreign Lands

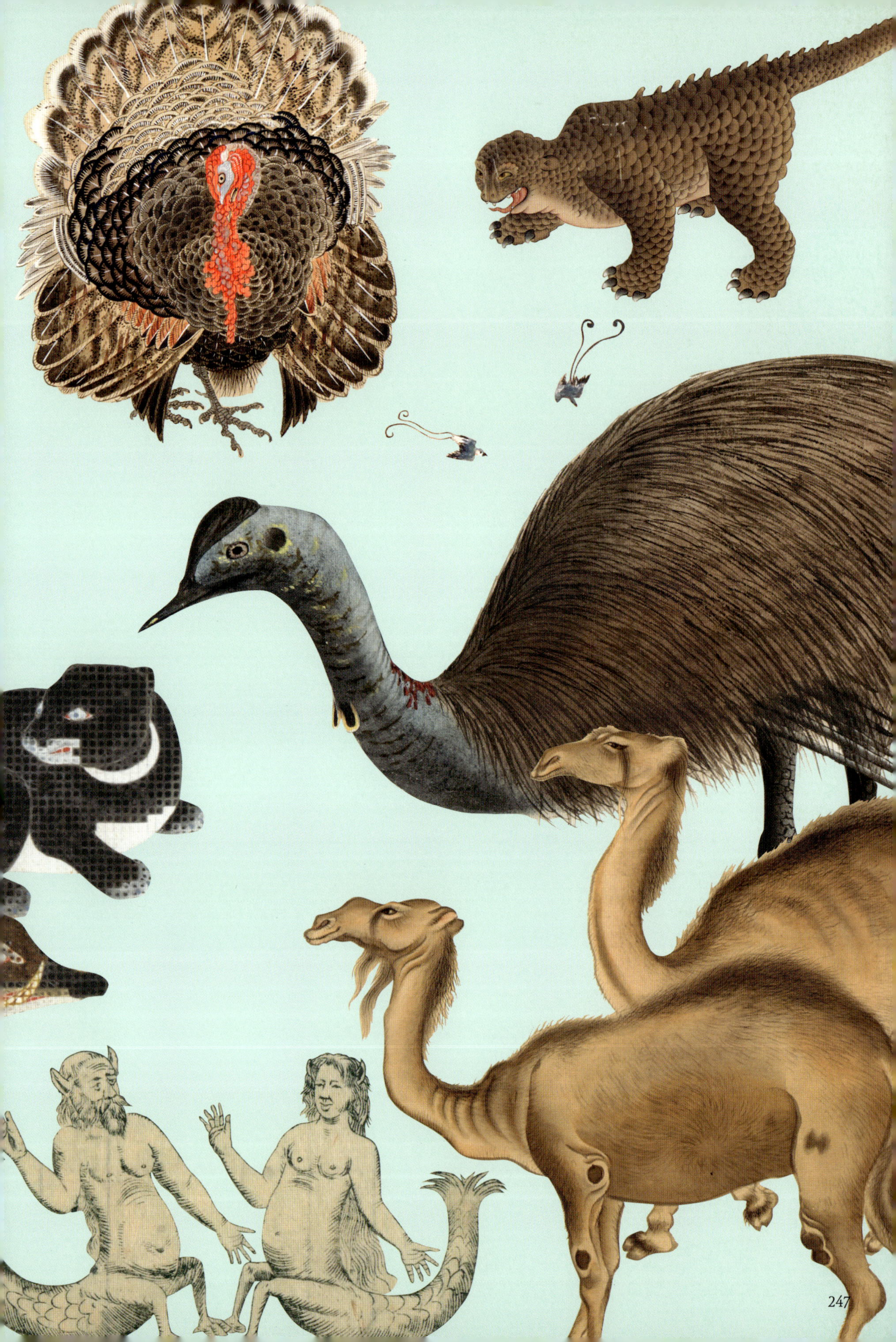

象

白象は、鳳凰や麒麟・龍などと同じ「大瑞」に位置づけられる。仏教では普賢菩薩の乗る獣でもあったことから、日本でも古来親しまれてきた。実際の生きた象は1408年（応永15）以来たびたび渡来し、足利将軍家や豊臣秀吉、徳川家康といった時の最高権力者に贈られた。とくに大きな話題となったのが、8代将軍徳川吉宗の要請に応え、1728年（享保13）にもたらされた時である。

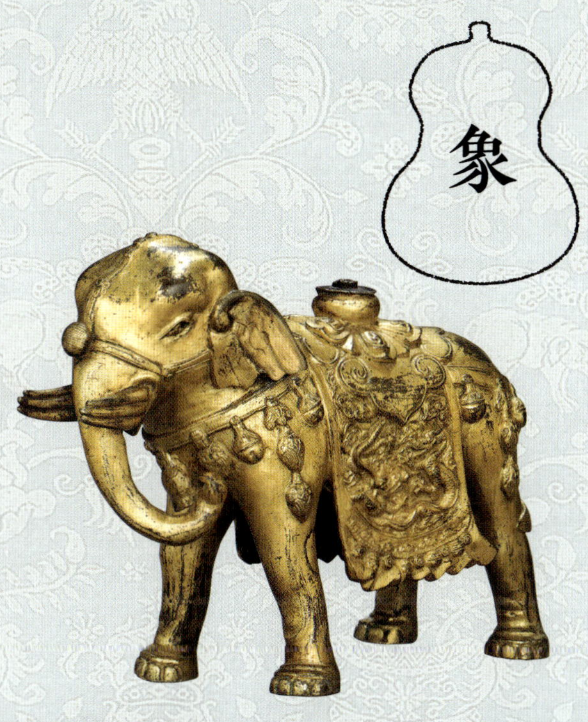

象の鳥獣座
（普賢菩薩騎象像部分）

中国・遼時代（10c頃）
クリーブランド美術館

Caparisoned Elephant

Liao dynasty, ca. 10th century
The Cleveland Museum of Art

The Elephant

Like the phoenix, *kirin* and dragon, the white elephant is also considered to be an auspicious beast. Since it was the steed of Samantabhadra (J. Fugen Bosatsu) in Buddhist lore, even Japan has been aware of its existence for centuries. Real live elephants had often been imported to Japan since 1408 (Ōei 15), and they were given as gifts to the most powerful men ruling the country, such as the Ashikaga shoguns, Toyotomi Hideyoshi, and Tokugawa Ieyasu. The elephant that was brought in 1728 (Kyōhō 13) at the request of Tokugawa Yoshimune, the eighth Tokugawa shogun, became an especially popular topic of conversation.

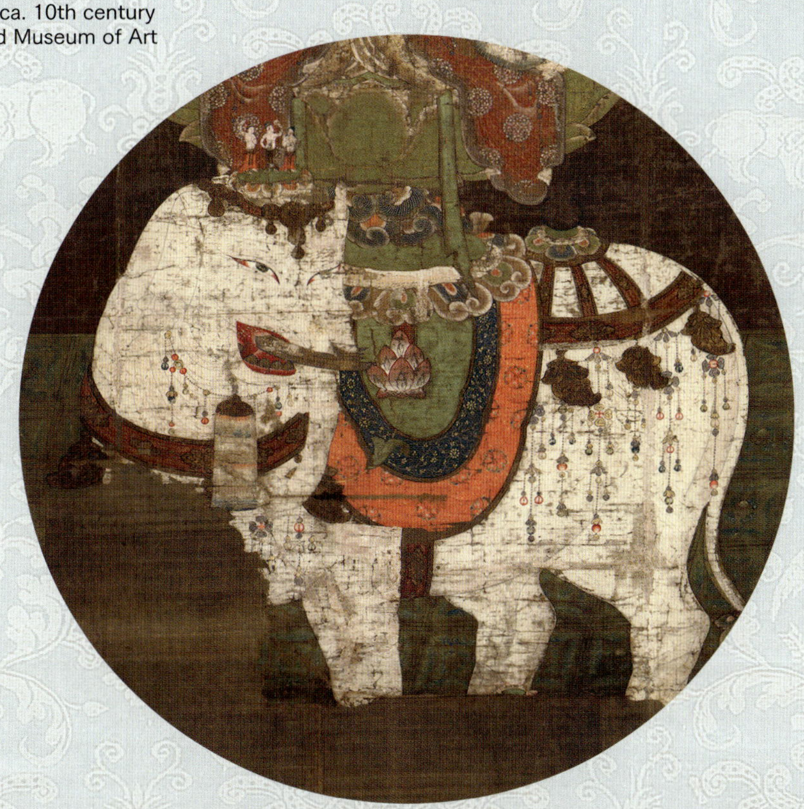

国宝

普賢菩薩像

平安時代(12c中頃)
東京国立博物館

普賢菩薩が6牙の白象の背に乗り、光を発し花を降らせながら法華経信者の前へと歩み寄る情景を描く。法華経は女人即成、すなわち一旦男身に変ずることなく女身のままで成仏できると説くため、女性に支持された。

National Treasure

Samantabhadra

Mid 12th century
Tokyo National Museum

In this scene, Samantabhadra is drawn astride the back of a white elephant with six tusks, and he approaches *Lotus Sutra* devotees amid a shower of glowing blossoms. The *Lotus Sutra* preaches the immediate salvation of women – that is, the idea that women can immediately transform into enlightened Buddhas without taking a male body for even for a moment. As a result, it was popular with women.

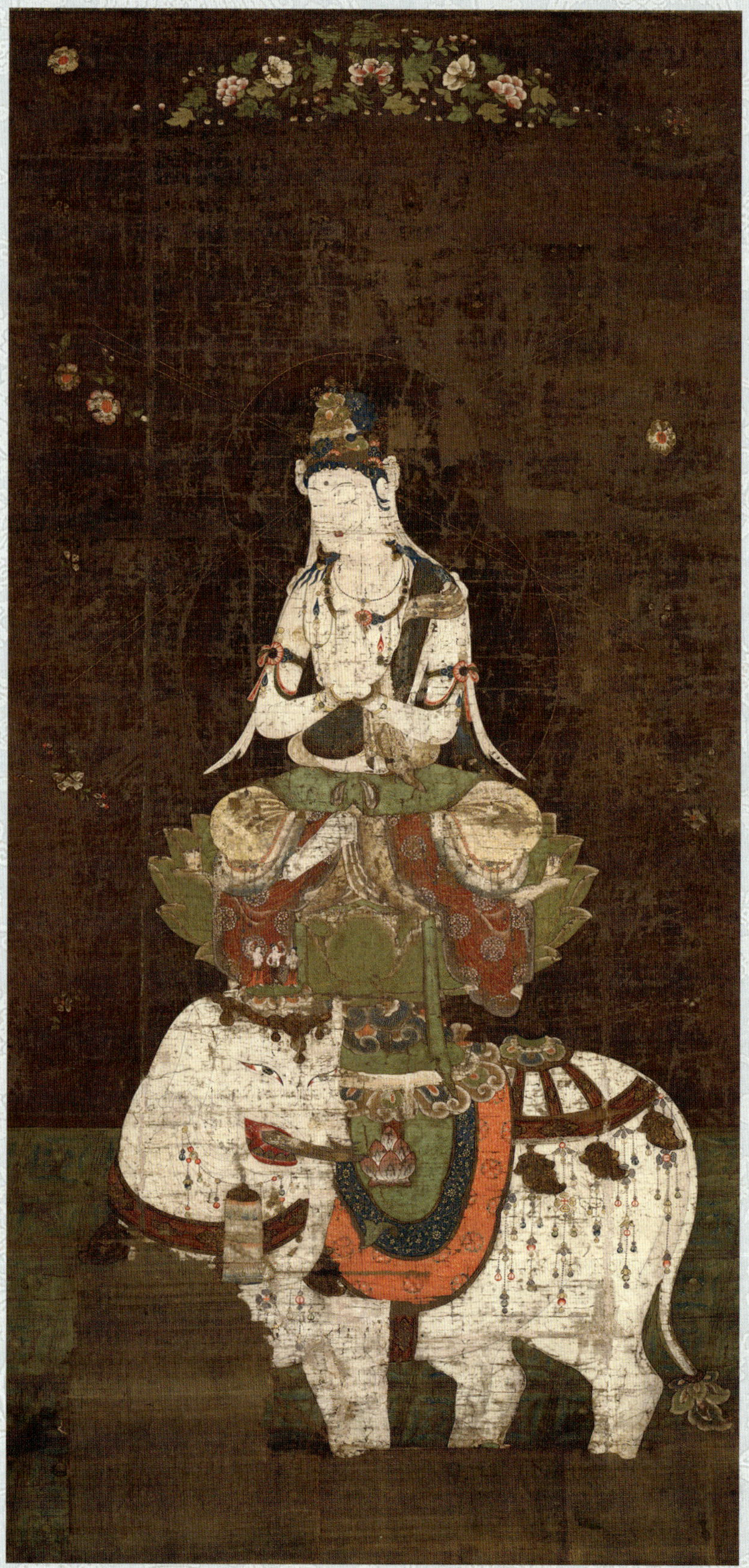

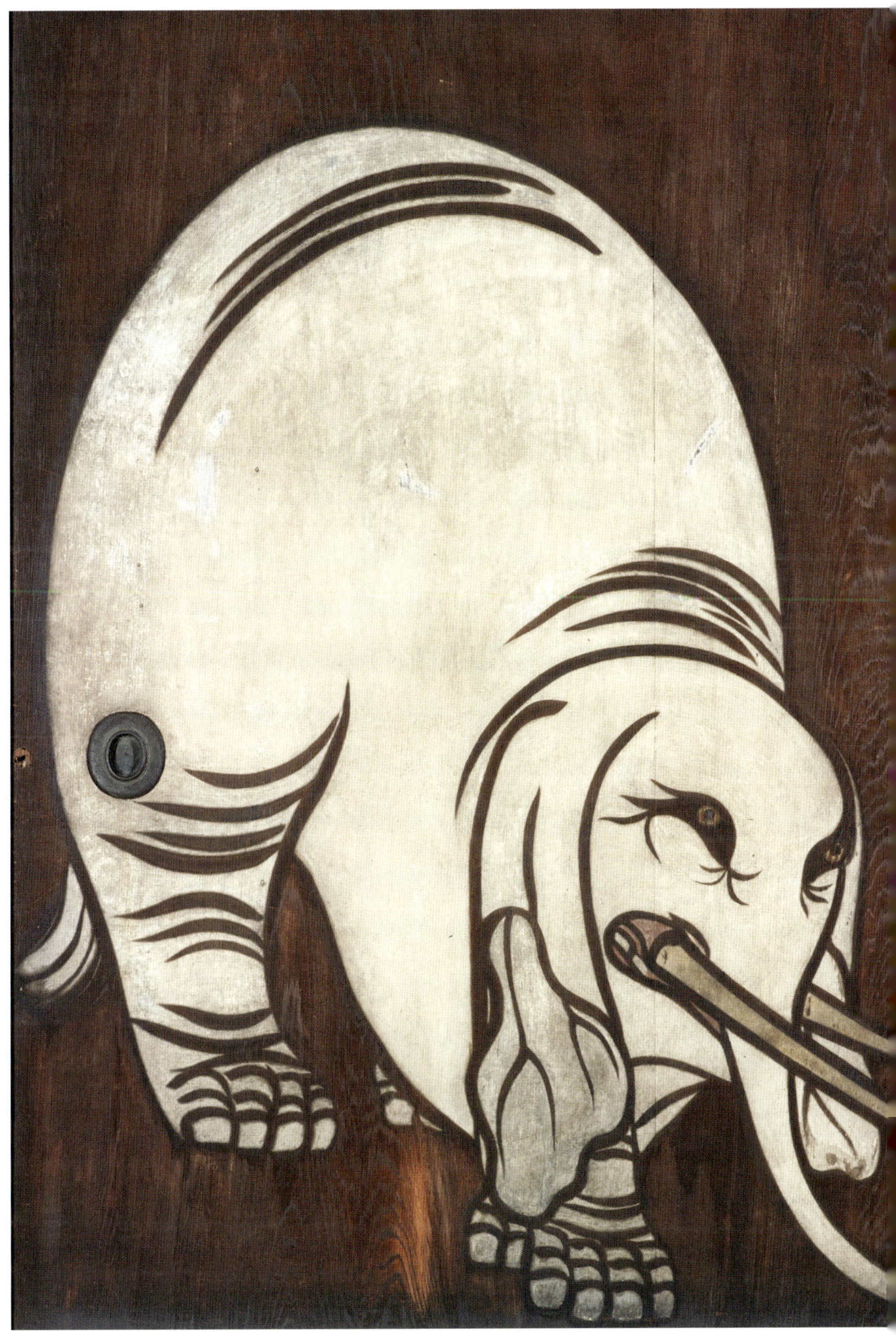

重要文化財

白象図杉戸

俵屋宗達
元和7年(1621)以降
京都・養源院

「唐獅子図杉戸」(p.31)と対をなす白象図。獅子は文殊菩薩の乗る獣、白象は普賢菩薩の乗獣で、いずれも釈迦如来の脇侍であることから、釈迦三尊が建築意匠を通して想起される構成になっている。

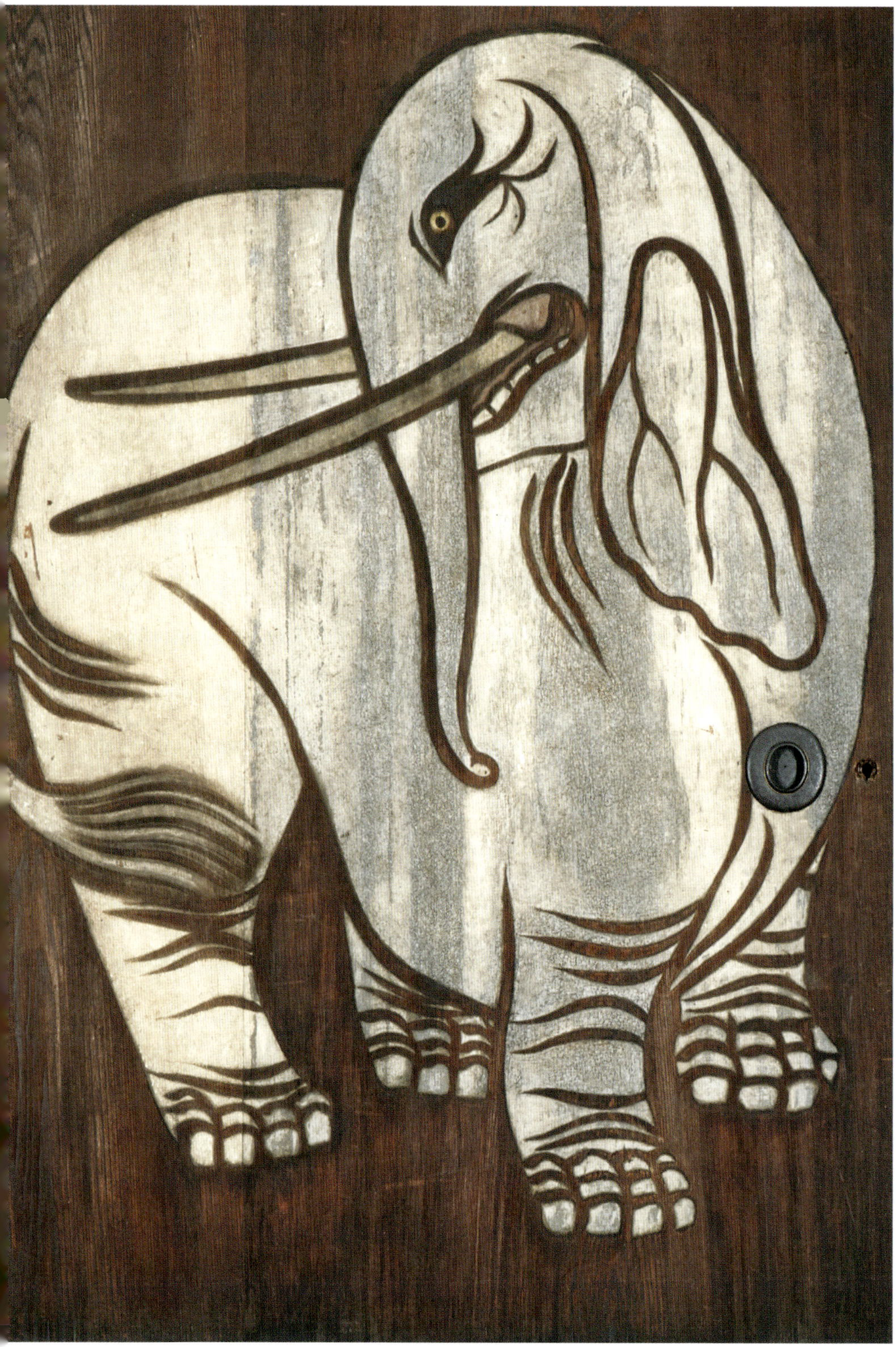

Important Cultural Property

White Elephant Cedar Doors

Tawaraya Sōtatsu
After 1621
Yōgen'in, Kyoto

This a painting of a white elephant that is meant to form a pair with *Chinese Lions Cedar Doors* (p.31). The lion is the steed of Manjushri (J. Monju Bosatsu), and the white elephant is the steed of Samantabhadra, and since they both flank Shakyamuni (J. Shaka Nyorai) in Shaka Triads, the architectural design here evokes the construction of a Shaka Triad.

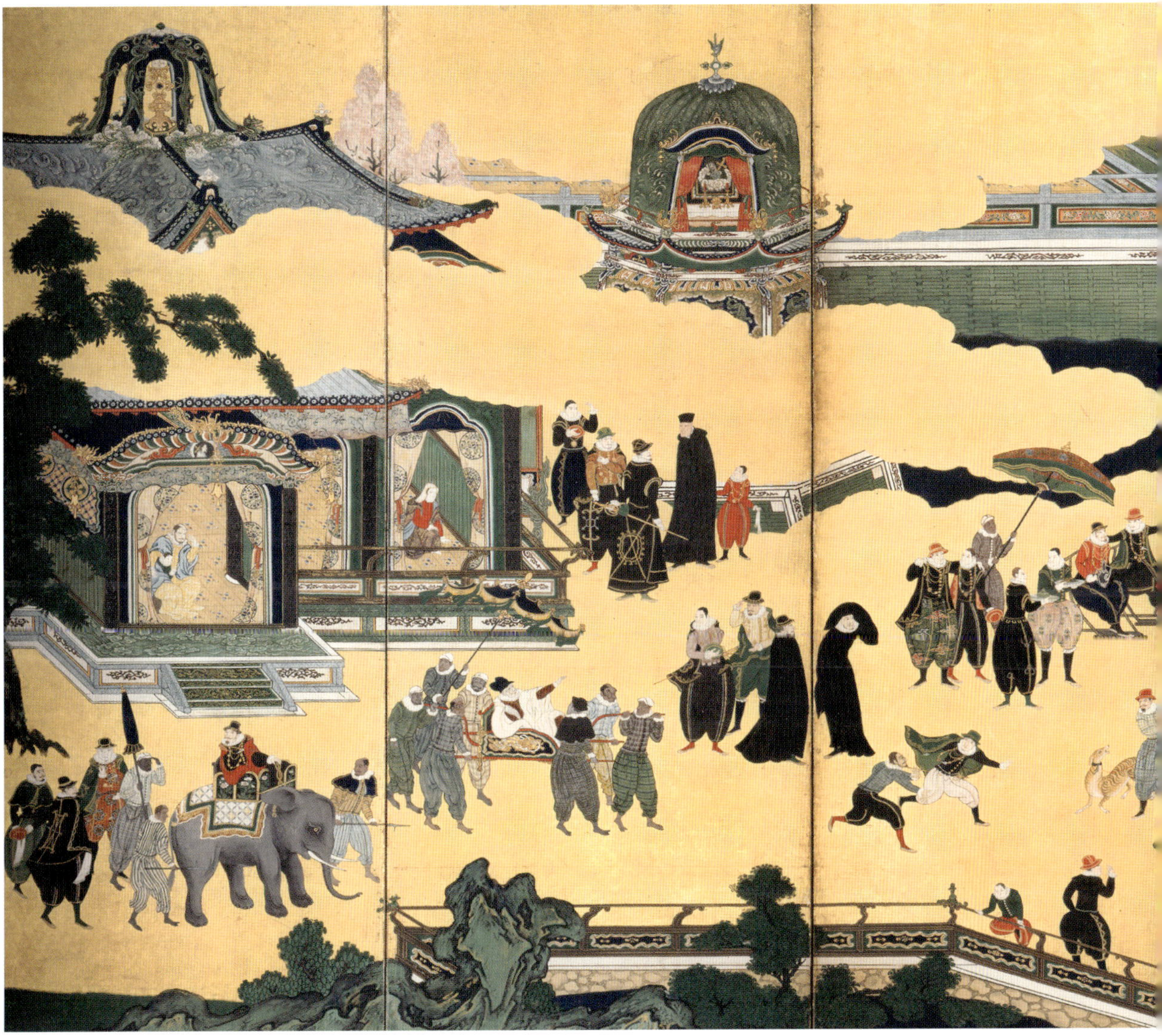

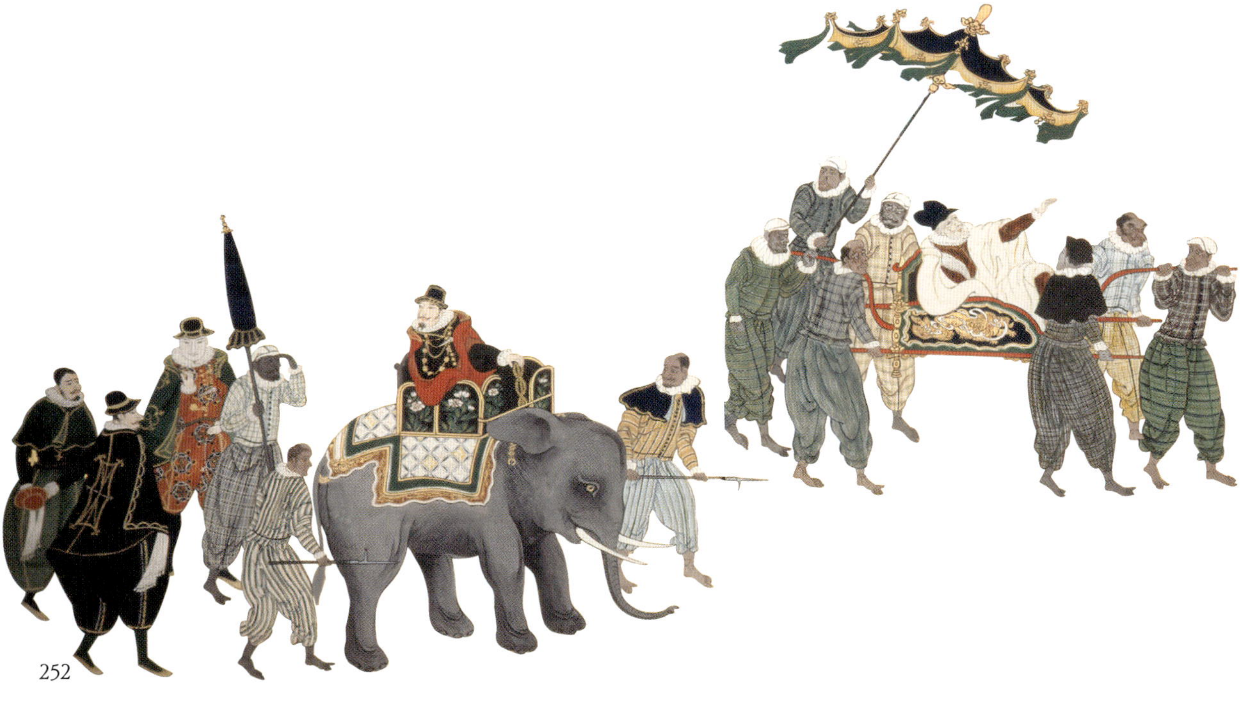

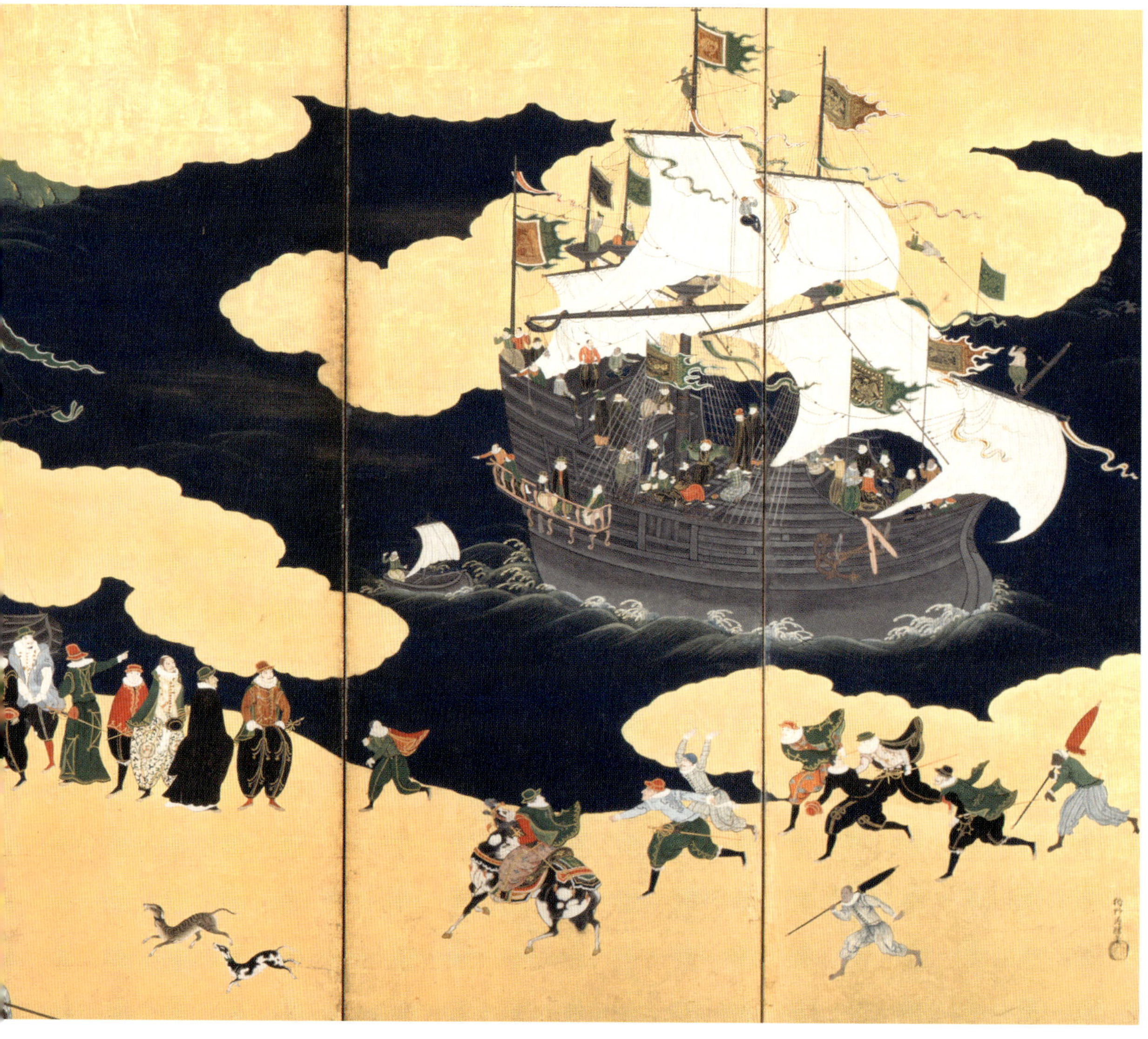

重要文化財

南蛮屏風

狩野内膳
桃山時代(16c末～17c初め)
神戸市立博物館

マニラ総督が1597年(慶長2)に秀吉に贈った黒象は、豊臣家お抱えの狩野内膳(1570～1616)が描いた南蛮屏風に登場する。象を先導するように輿に乗る秀吉らしき人物の姿も見える。描かれた象は、従来の仏画などに登場するものと比べ格段にリアルだ。類品がいくつも制作されており、人気の図様だったと知れる。ちなみに、同一画面に描かれるアラビア馬は、1591年(天正19)イエズス会巡察師ヴァリニャーノが、インド副王使節の名目で聚楽第を訪問した際に、外国製の輿(パランキーン)とともに秀吉に献上したもの。

Important Cultural Property

Nanban (*Southern Barbarian*) *Screen*

Kano Naizen
Late 16th century-early 17th century
Kobe City Museum

The black elephant that the governor of Manila gave to Hideyoshi in 1597 (Keichō 2) appears in the Southern Barbarian screen painted by the Toyotomi clan's personal artist Kano Naizen (1570-1616). We can also see a figure resembling Toyotomi Hideyoshi riding a litter in advance of the elephant. Comparing the elephant here to previous depictions of elephants, such as those in Buddhist paintings, this one looks dramatically more real. It is known that this was a popular subject, and that many similar works were produced. Incidentally, the Arabian horse also portrayed in this work is the same horse that Jesuit missionary Alessandro Valignano presented to Hideyoshi on behalf of the Indian ambassador, in addition to a foreign style palanquin, when he visited Jurakudai in 1591 (Tenshō 19).

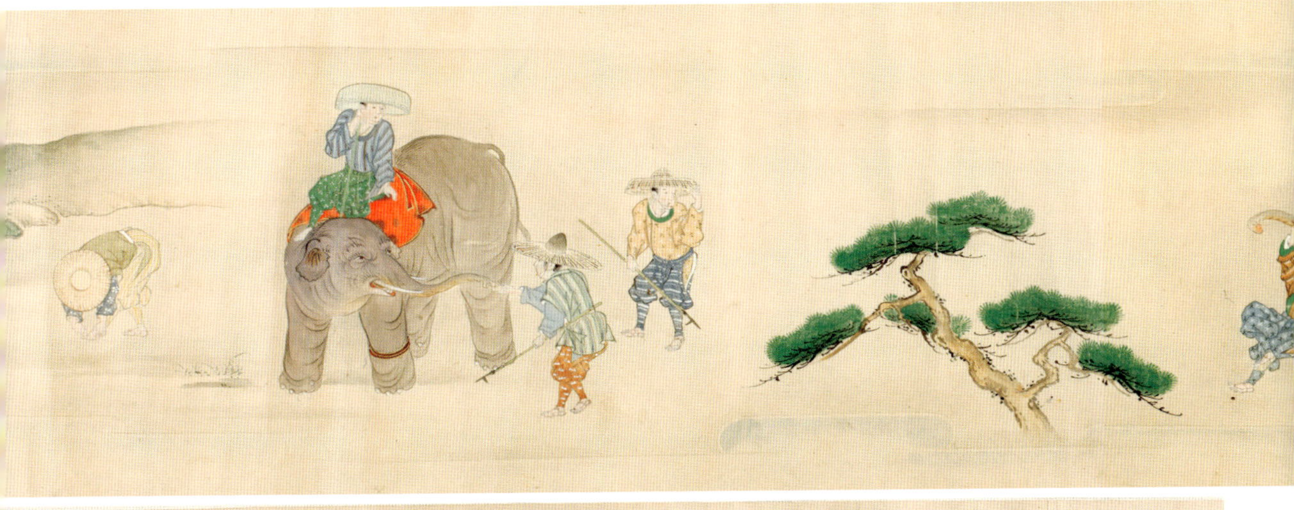

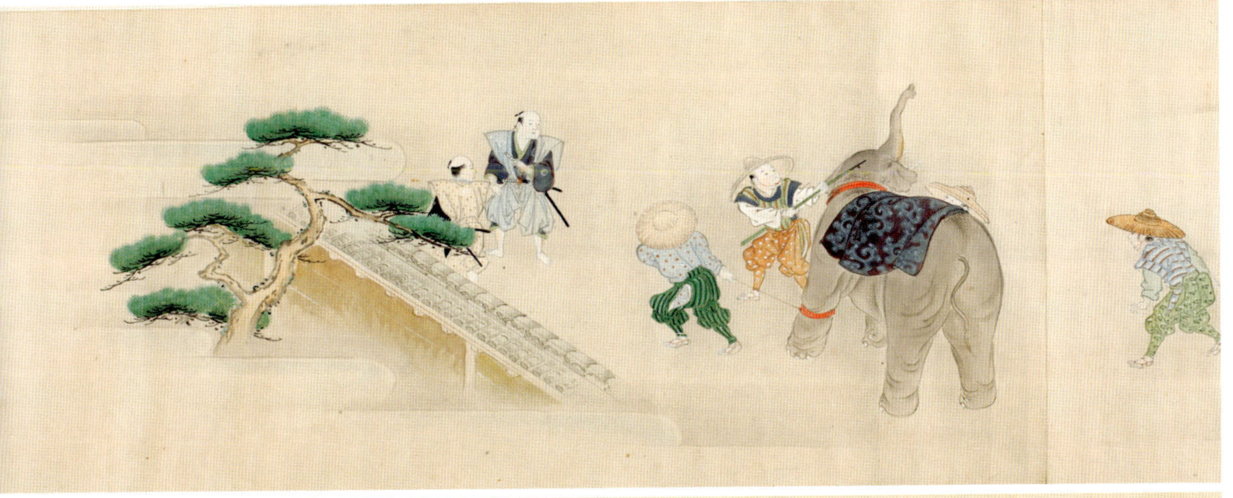

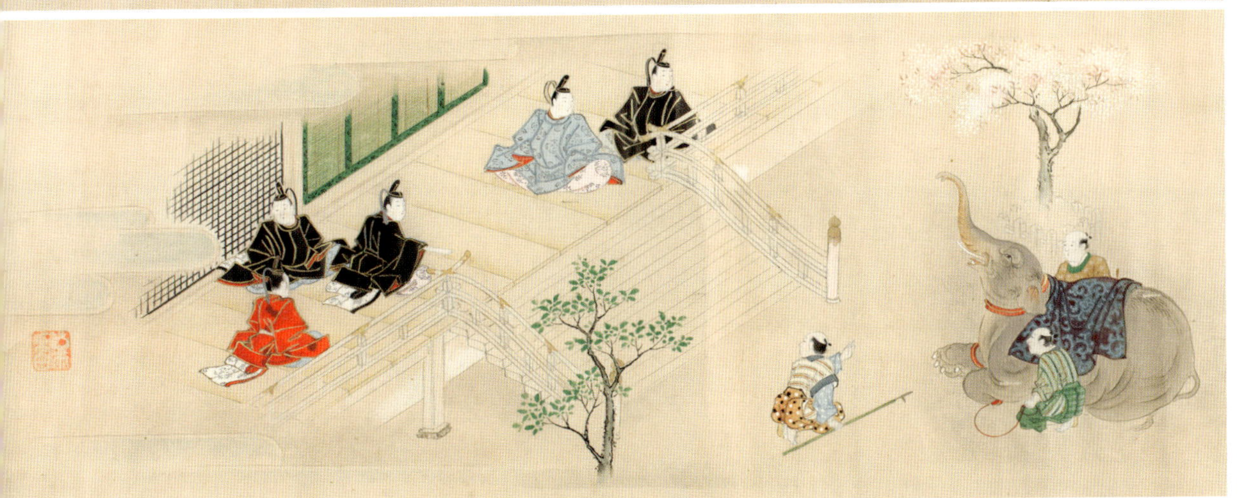

象之絵巻物

尾形探香
江戸時代中期(19c半ば)
関西大学図書館

1728年(享保13)にやってきた象が、京都の御所で天皇らに謁見する情景を描いたもの。象の行く先々では多くの規制があった。象が騒がしさを嫌うことから、見物は家のなかに限定、鐘・太鼓などの鳴り物も禁止。時の鐘や火災を知らせる半鐘も、象の滞留中は鳴らさないという徹底ぶりだった。河渡りや峠越えなど長途の旅ゆえの多くの苦労があったようだ。京都では、御所内で中御門天皇らが上覧することになり、「広南従四位白象」という位まで下賜された。お目見えの際に象は膝をついて敬礼したという。

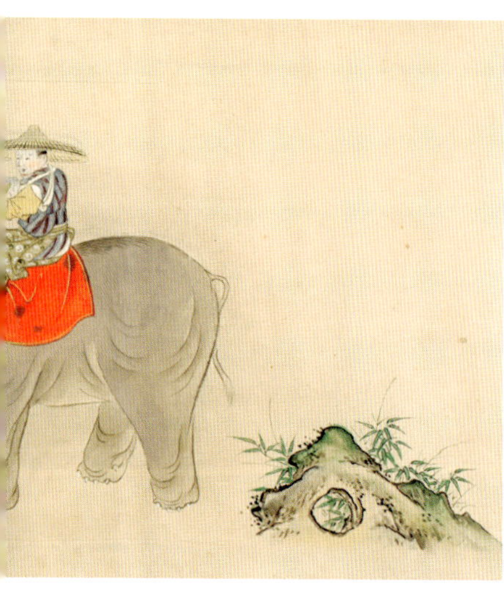

Elephant Scroll

Ogata Tankō
Mid 19th century
Kansai University Library

This is a portrayal of the scene at the Imperial Palace in Kyoto where the Emperor granted an audience to the elephant that was brought to Japan in 1728 (Kyōhō 13). Strict regulations were implemented wherever the elephant went. Since the elephant hated noise, people were only allowed to view the animal from inside their homes, and musical instruments like bells and drums were forbidden. While the elephant was touring the city, the prohibition on loud noises was so thoroughly enforced that even the clock chimes and fire alarm warning bells were silenced. It seems that many pains were taken on the long journey, involving areas such as river crossings and mountain passes. In Kyoto, Emperor Nakamikado met the elephant within the Imperial Palace grounds, and bestowed upon it the title of "Nguyễn Fourth Rank White Elephant." It is said that when they met, the elephant bent its knee in supplication.

象のかわら版

享保14年（1729）
関西大学図書館

1728年（享保13）、清国の商人により交趾国から長崎に雌雄2頭の象がもたらされた。上陸3カ月後、雌象は長崎で病死し残された雄象だけが翌年3月、江戸に向け2カ月以上におよぶ陸路の旅に出て、国内の注目を集めた社会現象となった。

Elephant Broadside

1729
Kansai University Library

In 1728 (Kyōhō 13), a male and female pair of elephants were brought from Jiaozhi to Nagasaki by Qing merchants. Three months after they made landfall, the female elephant died from an illness in Nagasaki, and in March of the following year, the remaining male elephant took the two-month overland journey towards Edo, and it became a social phenomenon that garnered attention from all over Japan.

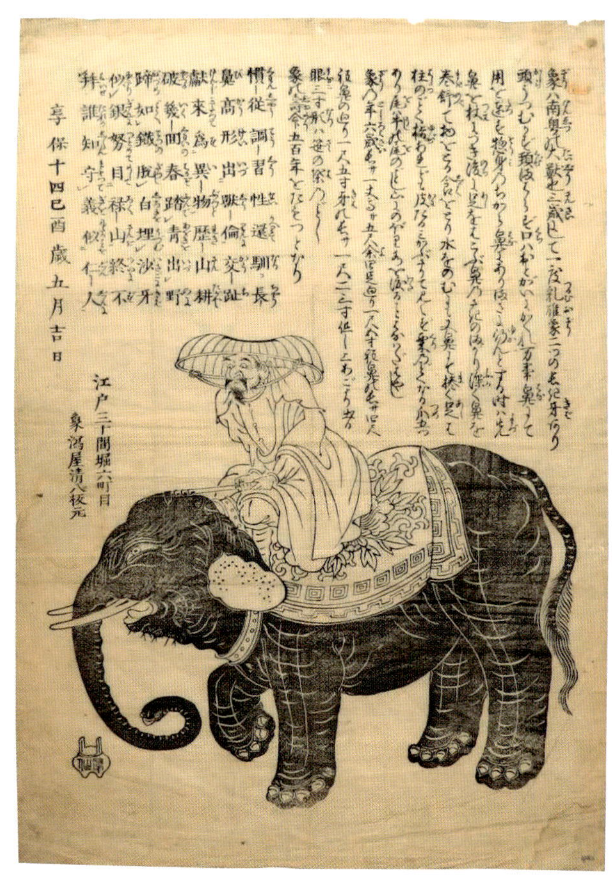

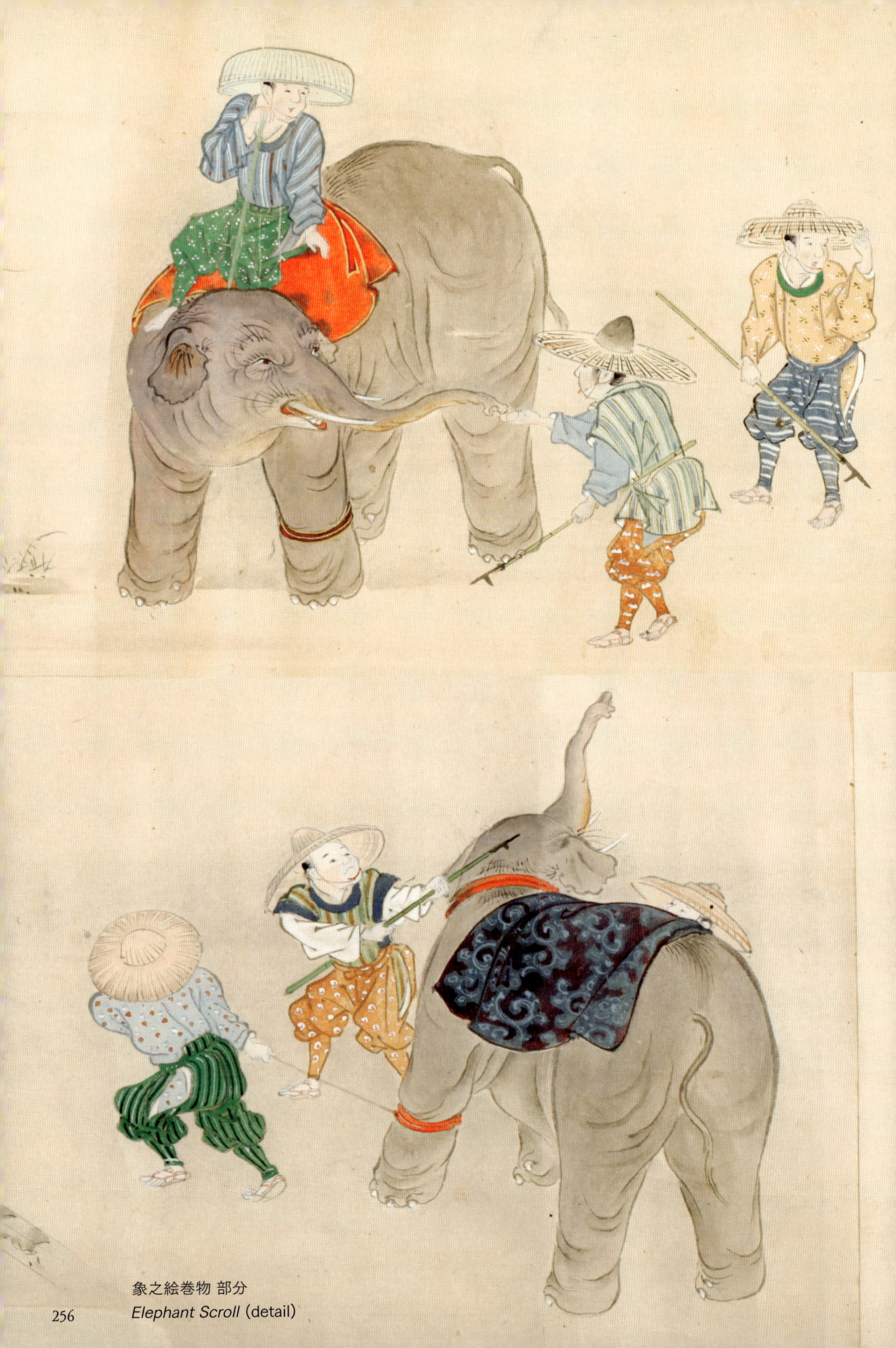

象之絵巻物 部分
Elephant Scroll (detail)

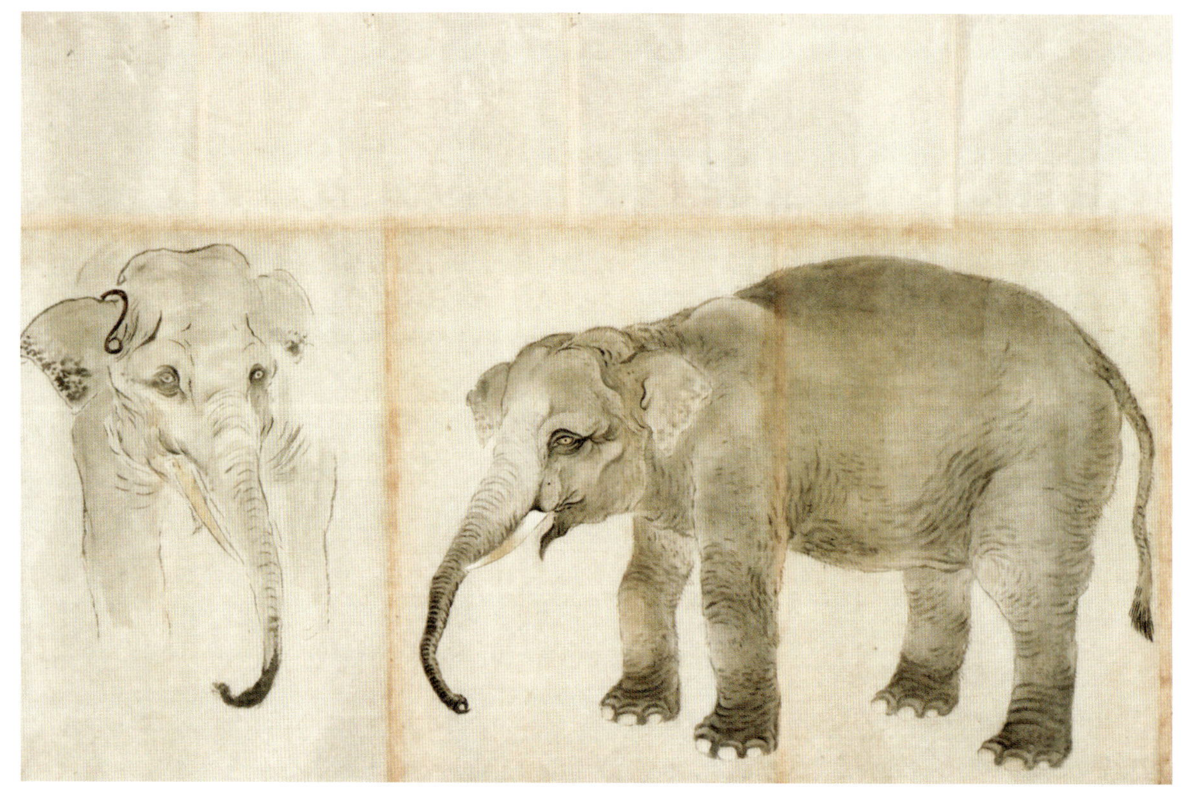

鳥獣鷹象写生図巻・象巻

狩野古信
享保14年(1729)
東京国立博物館

享保年間(1716〜36)に上陸した象はもともと、8代将軍吉宗が2年前に舶載を命じたものだった。求めた理由の一つは、交趾国では軍用に用いられたとのことから、海外文物の実用性に強い関心のあった吉宗がその効果を期待したためだったともいう。江戸の浜御殿に落ち着いた象は、時を置かずに江戸城内に入り、待ちわびた吉宗は大広間の車寄で実見を果たした。吉宗がその後、将軍家お抱えの狩野古信(1696〜1721)に命じ象の諸態を詳細に記録させたのが本図である。

Scrolls of Birds and Animals, Falcon and Elephant Painted from Life: Elephant Scroll

Kano Hisanobu
1729
Tokyo National Museum

The elephants that arrived during the Kyōhō era (1716-36) were the ones that eighth shogun Yoshimune had originally ordered two years earlier. It is also said that one of the reasons he requested them was because elephants were used as part of the military in Jiaozhi, and Yoshimune, who saw the importance of adopting the usage of foreign technologies and objects, hoped to use them for that purpose. The elephant, which had been settled in a palace in Edo Bay, was immediately brought to Edo Castle, and Yoshimune, who was tired of waiting, looked at the beast from the entranceway of the reception hall. After that, Yoshimune ordered his shogunal painter Kano Eisen Hisanobu (1696-1721), to make a detailed recording of the various appearances of the elephant, and this is that drawing.

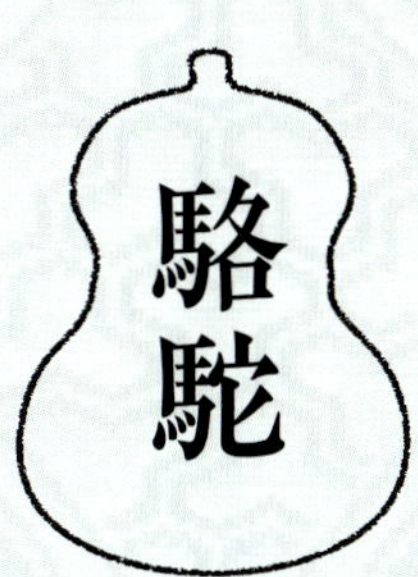

象についで社会現象と言えるほどの人気ぶりを見せたのが駱駝である。長崎にアラビア産の雌雄2頭の駱駝が到着したのは1821年(文政4)。入手した当時のオランダ商館長が幕府への献上を願い出たが断られたため、寵愛する遊女に与えたという。この駱駝はやがて興行師の手に渡り、全国を巡回することになる。駱駝には、中央アジア産のフタコブラクダ(双峰駱駝)と、アフリカ北部から中近東にかけて活動するヒトコブラクダ(単峰駱駝)の2種がある。地理的理由からも、古くから日本に馴染みのあった駱駝は前者であり、正倉院宝物にもフタコブの方がモチーフに採用されている。

The Camel

Following the elephant, the next animal that became a popular topic of conversation to the point of becoming a social phenomenon was the camel. In 1821 (Bunsei 4), a male and female pair of camels from Arabia arrived in Nagasaki. Supposedly the Dutch trade delegation visiting Edo at the time acquired them, and though they petitioned to present them as a gift to the shogunal government, their request was refused; instead, they gave them to a sex worker they favored. Later, these camels were given to a show manager, and they toured all over Japan. There are two kinds of camels: the Bactrian camel (the two-humped camel) of Central Asia, and the Dromedary camel (the single-humped camel) found in the area from Northern Africa to the Near and Middle East. Perhaps it was a matter of geography, but it was always the Bactrian camels that were familiar to Japan since long ago, and it was those that were used as motifs on Shōsō-in treasures.

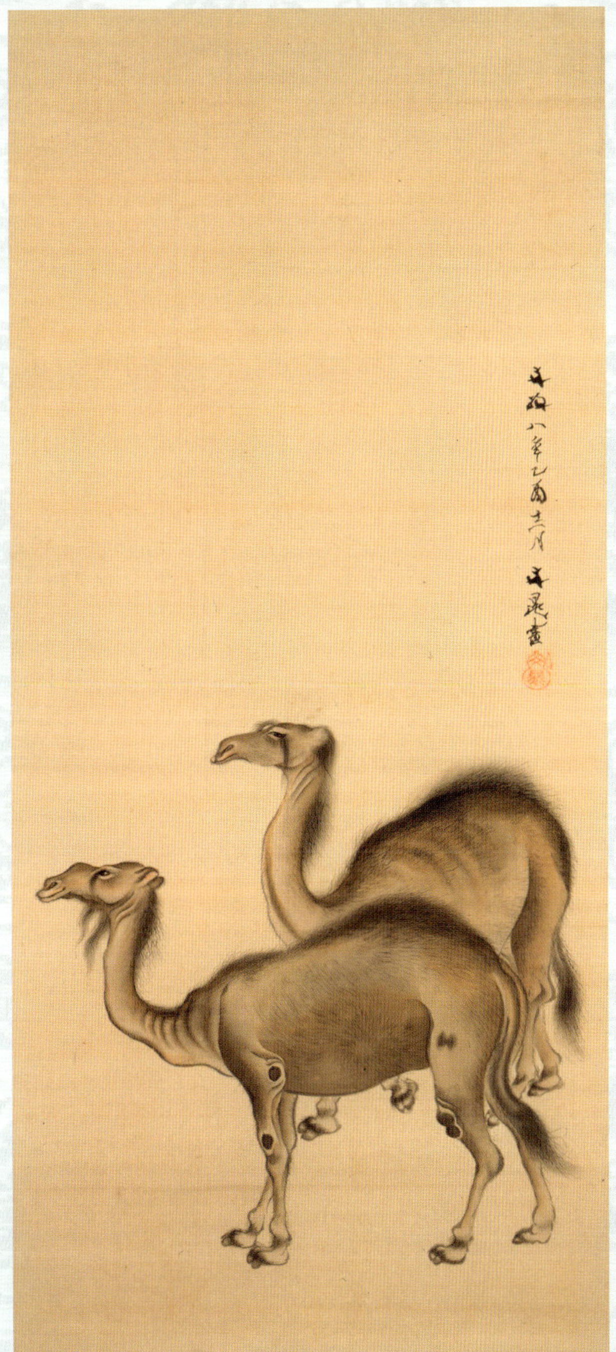

駱駝図

谷文晁
文政8年(1825)
摘水軒記念文化振興財団

Camel

Tani Bunchō
1825
Tekisuiken Memorial Foundation of Culture

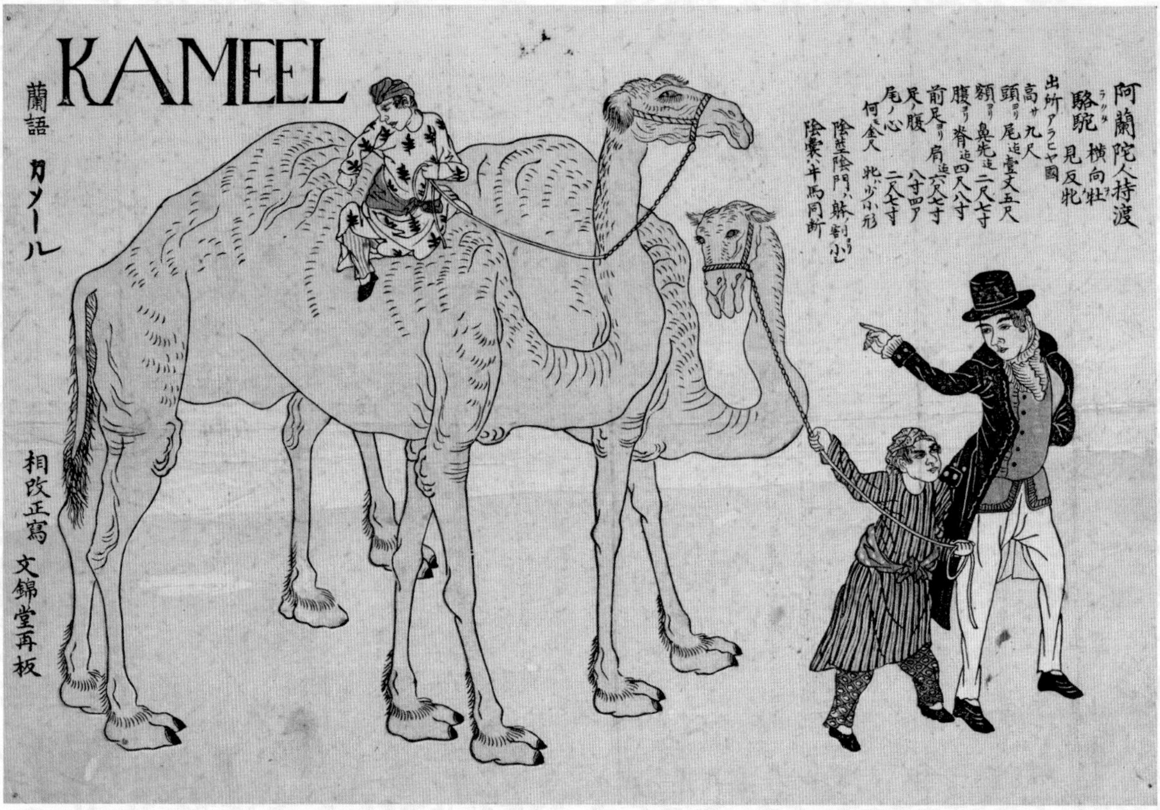

長崎版画「KAMEEL」(文錦堂版)

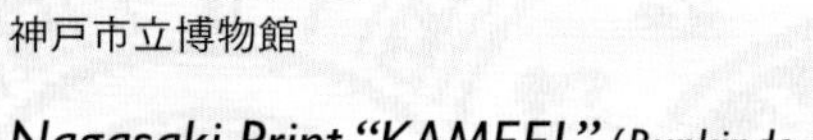

江戸時代後期(19c)
神戸市立博物館

Nagasaki Print "KAMEEL" (*Bunkindo print*)

19th century
Kobe City Museum

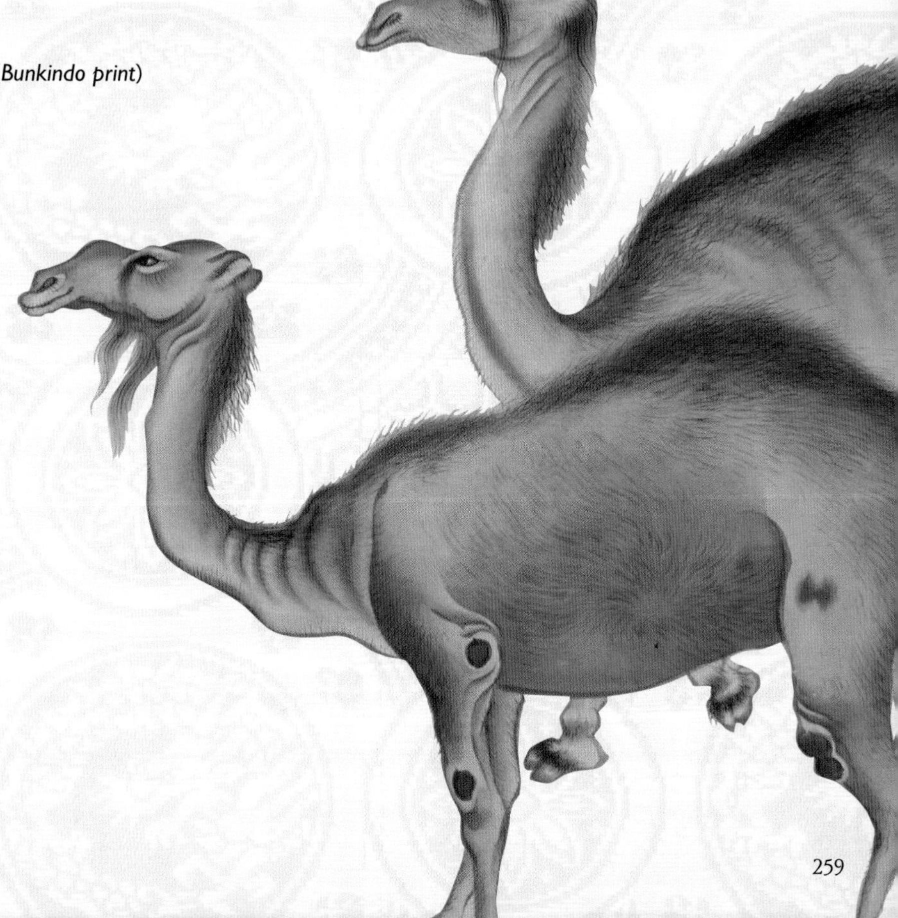

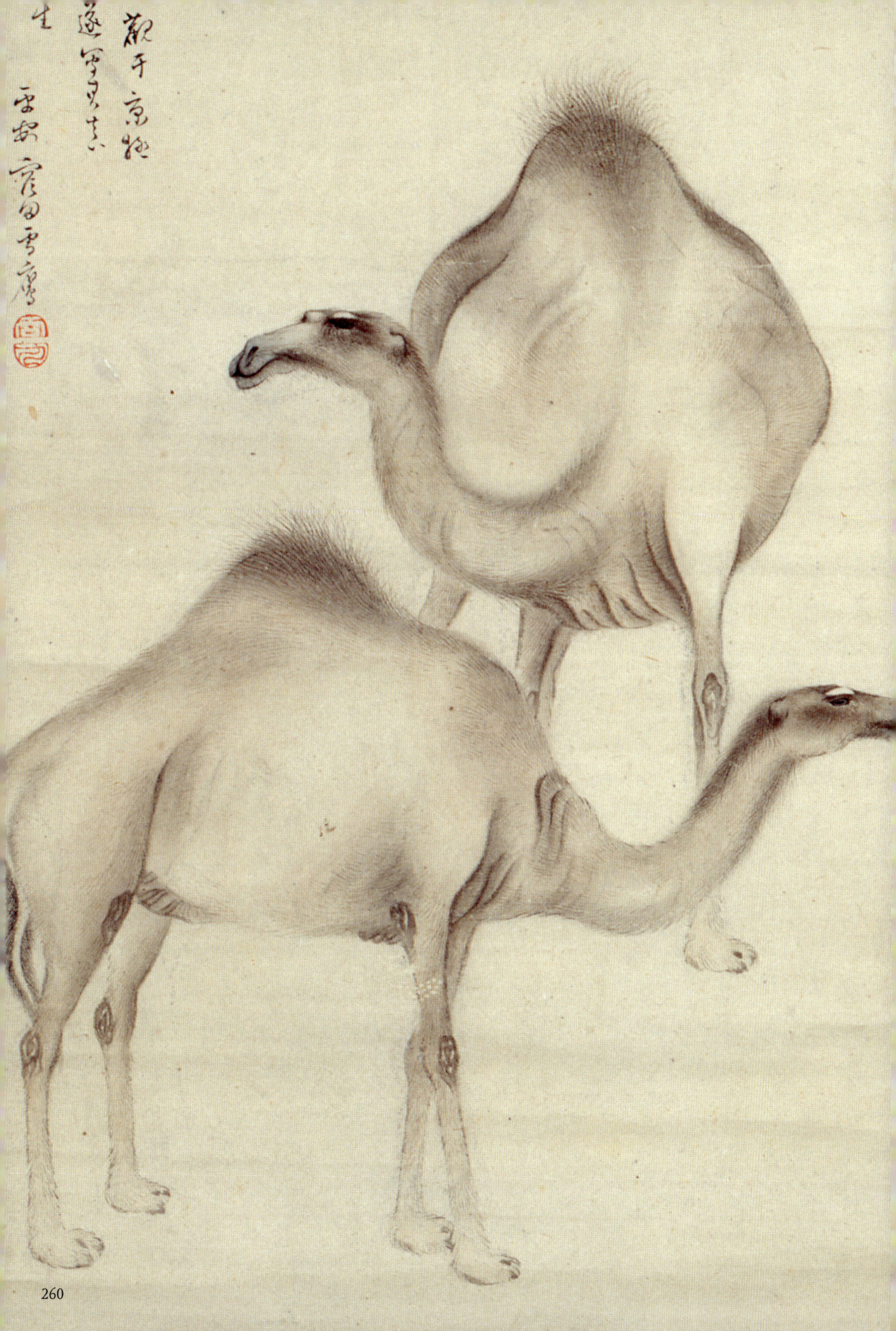

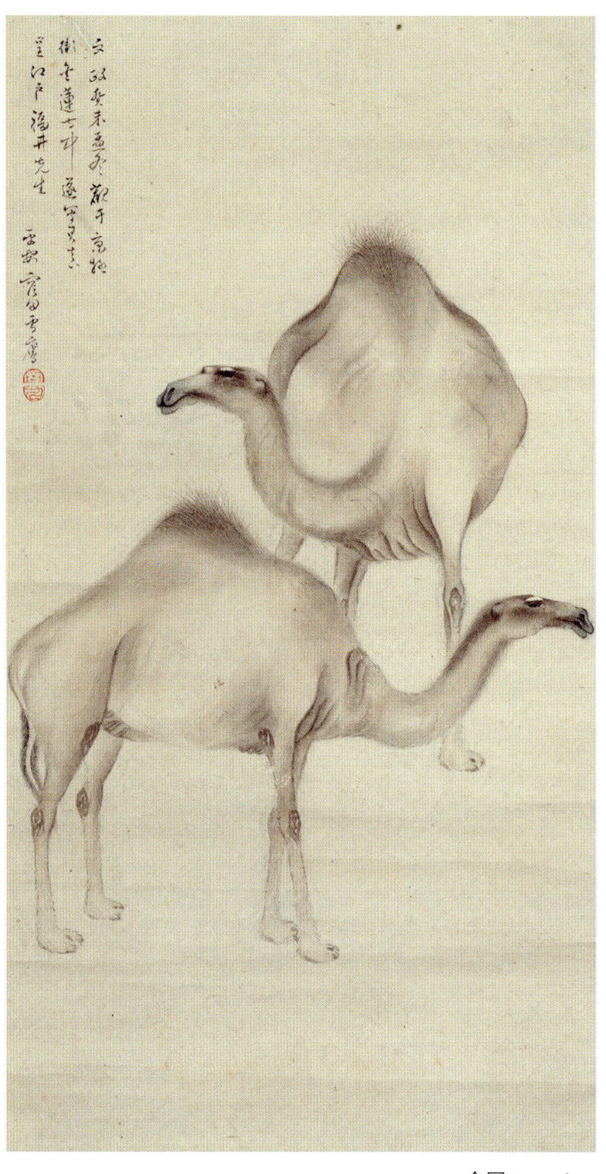

全図 overview

双駱駝図

窪田雪鷹
文政6年（1823）
神戸市立博物館

京都の四条京極にあった金蓮寺における見世物での写生。駱駝図には相当な需要があったらしく、この画家は同図様の作を何点も残している。

Pair of Camels

Kubota Setsuyō
1823
Kobe City Museum

This is a sketch of a public showing at Konrenji in Kyōgoku, Kyoto. It seems that camel pictures were in great demand, and many of these types of works by this artist still remain.

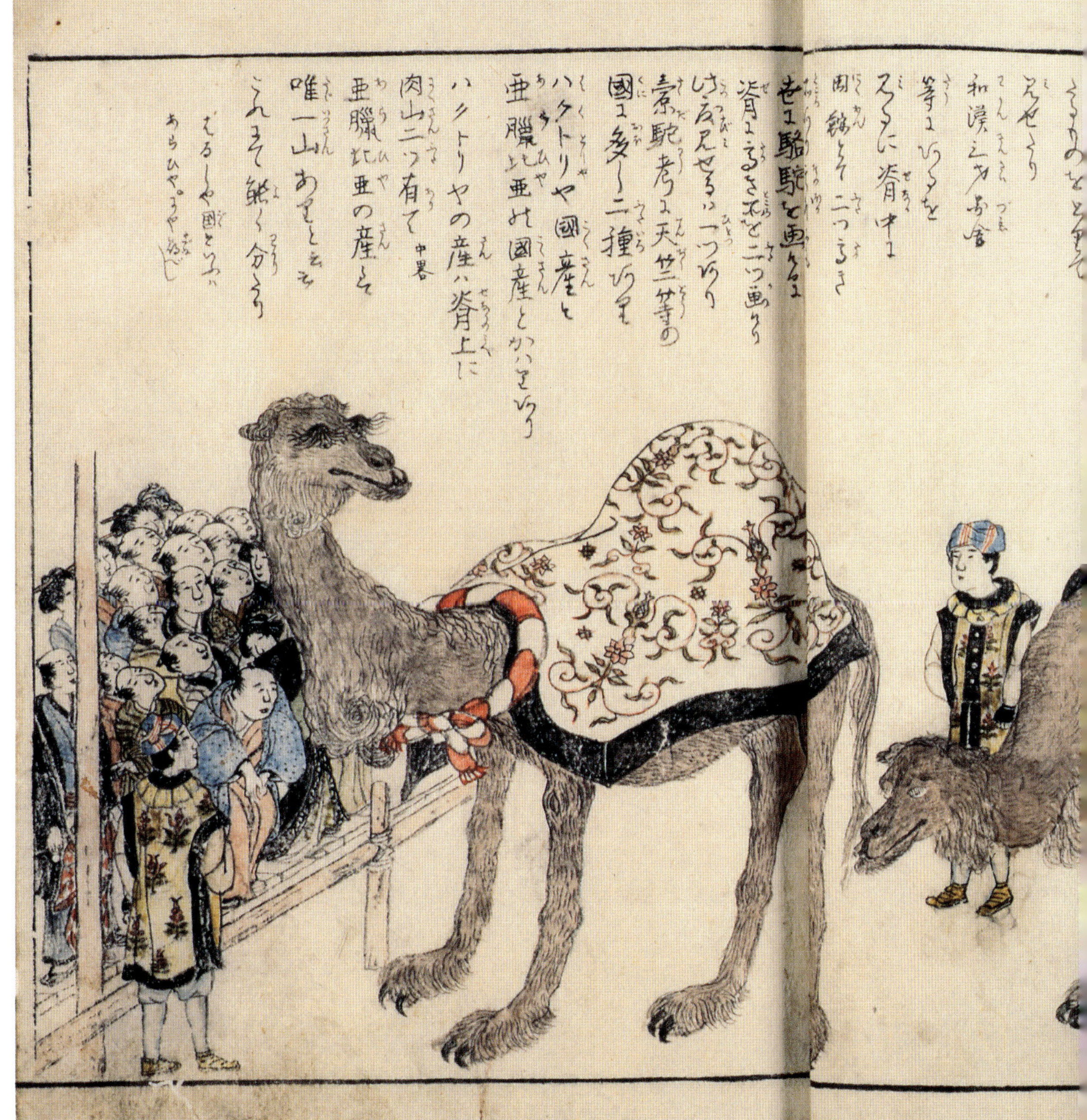

『絵本駱駝具誌』(えほんらくだぐし)

高力猿猴庵
文政10年(1827)
神戸市立博物館

駱駝は1826年(文政9)に名古屋で見世物になった。その時の人気ぶりを具体的に教えてくれるのがこの資料である。駱駝の玩具や駱駝を描いた扇子・煙草入れ・駱駝双六・駱駝の雛人形・駱駝凧・駱駝の水入れといったものまで売り出されたという。現代のキャラクターグッズさながらの、商魂たくましい商品開発が行われていたのである。

Illustrated Record of Camel Merchandise

Kouriki Enkou'an
1827
Kobe City Museum

This is a useful document that concretely demonstrates to us just how popular camels were during their time as public sideshows in Nagoya in 1826 (Bunsei 9). It says that all kinds of camel merchandise were sold, such as camel toys, folding fans and tobacco pouches decorated with images of camels, camel board games, camel *hina* dolls, camel kites, and even camel water jugs. Just like with modern character merchandise, there was an indomitable commercial spirit present in the development of new products.

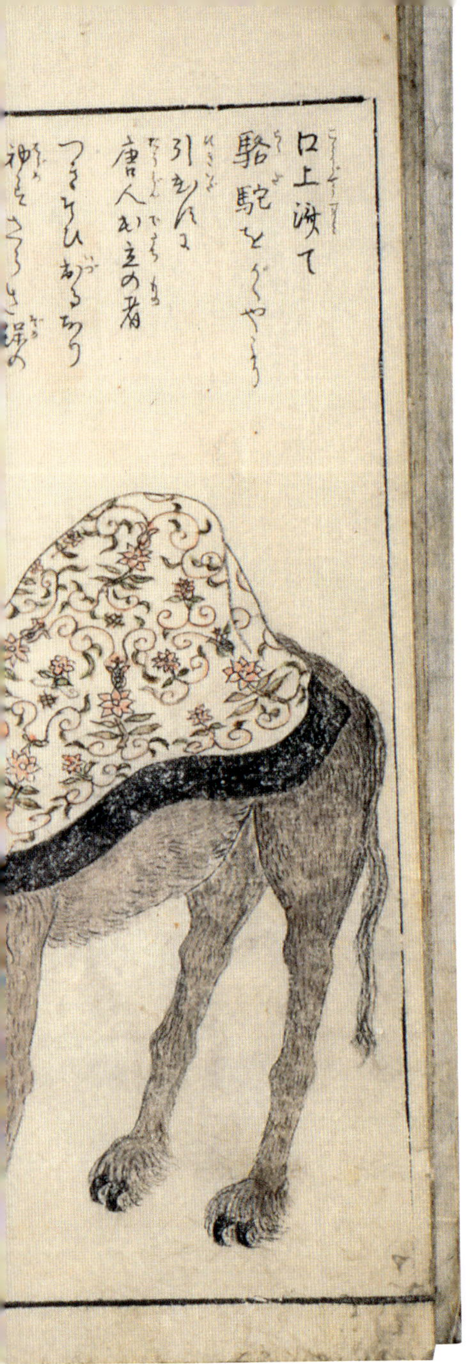

駱駝櫛 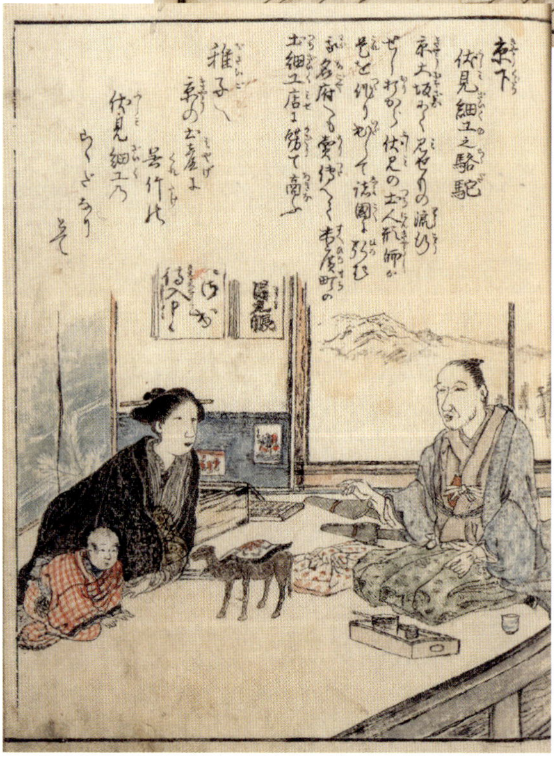
上方より流行り来り
名古屋ニても文政七八
はやりしなり
櫛のむねを駱駝の脊中に
肉鞍の形ちに作りて頂きは
角を張りかゞりある
木地の櫛なり

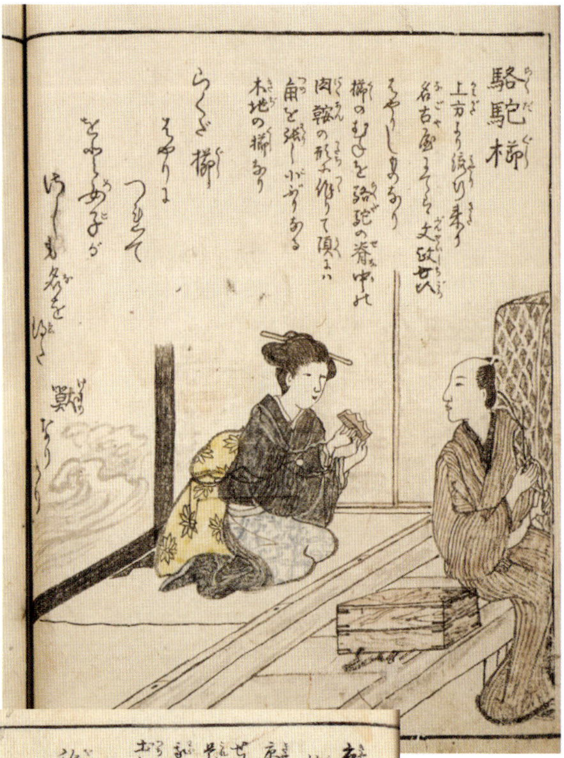

京下
伏見細工之駱駝

Column 3

こりゃ、めずらし！　大陸からの動物上陸

象、駱駝、火喰鳥

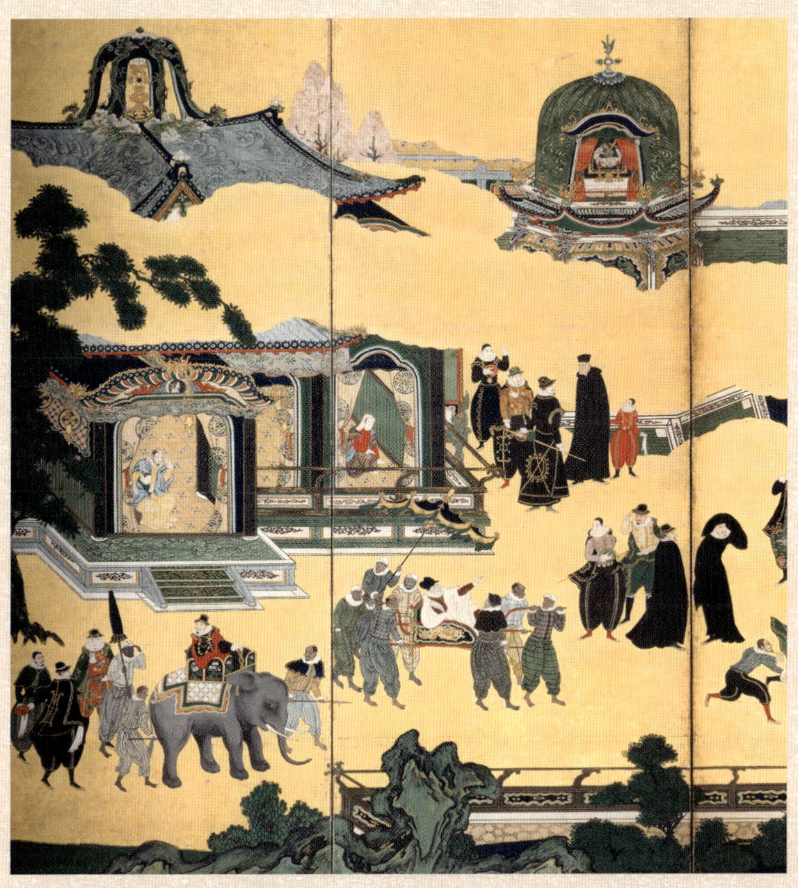

[1] 狩野内膳「南蛮屏風」部分
Detail of *Nanban (Southern Barbarian) Screen* by Kano Naizen

記録によれば日本への象の渡来は1408年（応永15）、南蛮船が若狭国小浜に来航し、亜烈進卿（アラジン）より日本国王（足利義持）への進物として贈ったのが最初という。その後1575年（天正3）明船が豊後国臼杵に来航、大友義鎮に虎・象・孔雀・鸚鵡・麝香猫等を贈ったという。そして3度目に渡来したのが1597年（慶長2）、マニラ総督が秀吉に贈った黒象で、「ドン・ペドロ」の名が付けられていた。象は禁裏で上覧に供された後、京都の人々にも披露されたのだが、象を見ようと群衆が殺到し死者が出るほどだったという。この象が、当時の交易風景を描いた南蛮屏風[1]に登場する。その5年後の1602年（慶長7）、交趾（現ベトナム北部）船が長崎に象をもたらし、今度は徳川家康に贈られた。秀吉なきあとの権力は家康に帰していたからである。家康は、それを上京させ大坂の豊臣秀頼に贈ったという。象は時の権力者に贈られるべき特別な存在だったと思われる。

そして、泰平の世を迎えて1世紀あまりが経過

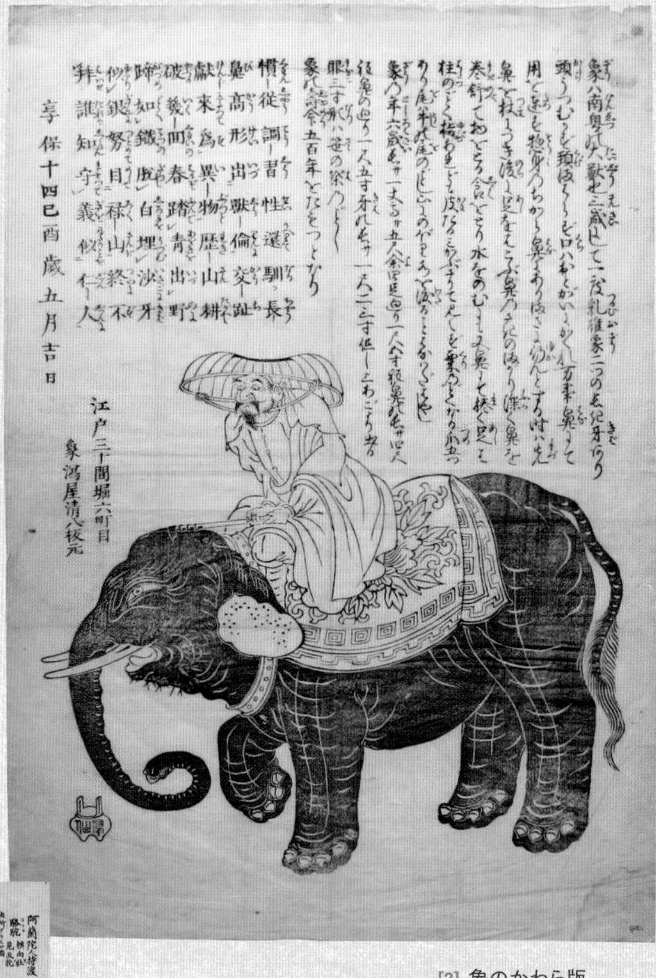

[2] 象のかわら版
Elephant Broadside

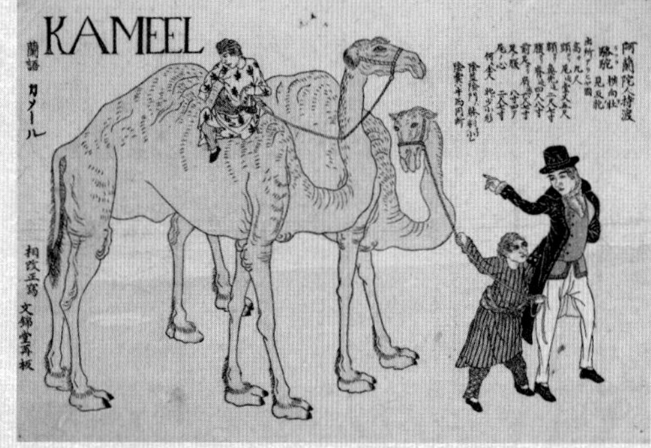

[3] 長崎版画「KAMEEL」(文錦堂版)
Nagasaki Print "KAMEEL" (Bunkido print)

した1728年(享保13)、同じ交趾国から中国商人の手で長崎に雌雄2頭の象がもたらされた。5度目の渡来である。雌象は残念なことに3カ月後、長崎で病死してしまったため、翌年3月に残された雄象だけが江戸へ向け2カ月以上にわたる陸路の旅に出ることになった。

京都では、この象を御所内で中御門天皇らが上覧することになったものの、無位無官では謁見がかなわないとの理由から、「広南従四位白象」という位まで賜ったという。また、多くの関連出版物が出され、糞からは疱瘡麻疹に効能があるという「象洞(ぞうぼら)」なる薬が作られるなど、象にまつわる騒動は一種の社会現象ともなった。当時制作された絵画や各種の刷物[2]には、全体の大きさや重量と各部の寸法、さらには飼料の内容と量までが細かく記入された。象の実像をはじめて眼にした人々の驚きが伝わってくる。

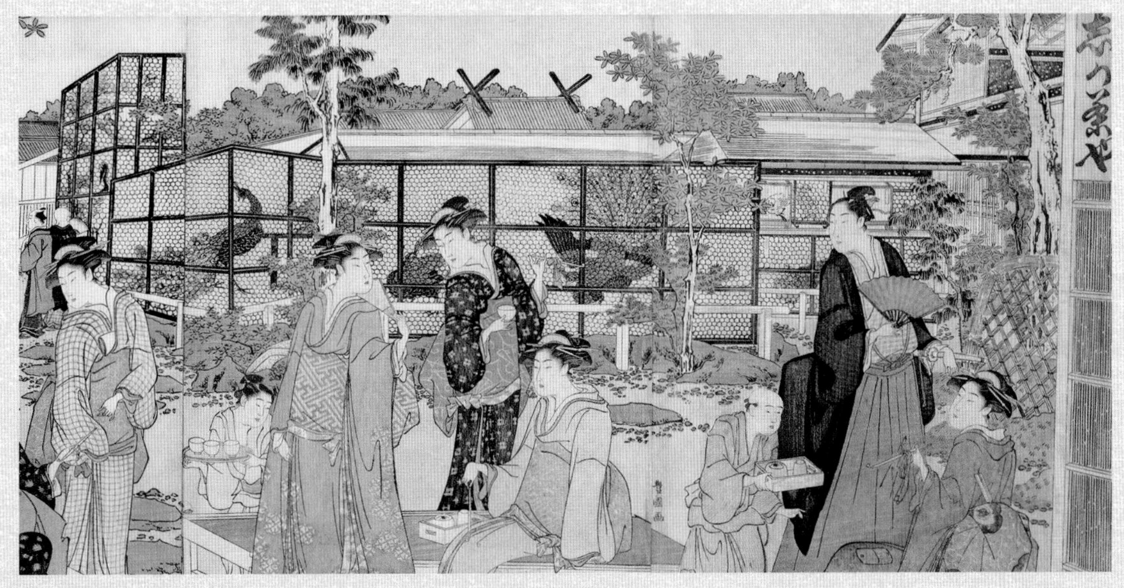

[4] 歌川豊国「しか茶屋」部分
Detail of *Shika Chaya* (*Teahouse for Showing Rare Animals and Birds*)
by Utagawa Toyokuni I

それから1世紀後、象について社会現象と言えるほどの人気ぶりを見せたのが駱駝である。長崎にアラビア産の雌雄2頭の駱駝が到着したのは1821年（文政4）。入手した当時のオランダ商館長が幕府への献上を願い出たものの断られ、寵愛した遊女に与えたという。やがて興行師の手に渡った駱駝は、全国を巡回することになった。駱駝には、中央アジア産のフタコブラクダ（双峰駱駝）と、アフリカ北部から中近東にかけて活動するヒトコブラクダ（単峰駱駝）の2種がある。地理的な理由からも、古くから日本に馴染みのあった駱駝は前者であり、正倉院宝物にもフタコブの方がモチーフに採用されている。1646年（正保3）オランダ商館長から将軍に献上された2頭も、1803年（享和3）通商を求めたアメリカ船がもたらし、結局は陸揚げされずに戻されたのもフタコブの方だったらしい。前宣伝用の引札（チラシ）にも、もちろんフタコブの駱駝が描かれていた[3]。そのため、背中の肉峰が1つしかないのを人々は不思議がり、駱駝自体が贋物と疑われたこともあったようだが、3年後（1824年）江戸での見世物においては空前の大当たりとなった。「駱駝節」なる流行歌や狂歌にもうたわれ、錦絵類に加えて『駱駝考』『和合駱駝之世界』といった書まで刊行されている。

引札に「牝牡とも性質柔和にして夫婦中むつまじき事此上なし、一度是を見れば其気を得てともに中むつまじく成と言伝ふ」と記されるように、2頭の睦まじい姿が夫婦円満の象徴と宣伝され、駱駝は仲良く連れだって描かれるのを常としたようだ。

鳥類では、孔雀などが早くからもたらされ、孔雀茶屋・鹿茶屋などといった檻を設けた仮設動物園のような施設で見学させるとともに、茶菓を提供した[4]。大田南畝（蜀山人）は、その随筆『芦の若葉』において、1801年（享和元）に四天王寺参詣の帰途に孔雀茶屋に立ち寄り、金鶏や灰鶴（マナヅル）・孔雀・羊を見たと記録している。火喰鳥（ヒクイドリ）はとくに人気の鳥だった。江戸時代に駝鳥の舶載例はほとんどないが、火喰鳥はしばしば舶載され見世物にもなった。当時は両者が混同されていたようだが[5]、火喰鳥は「八相涅槃図」[6]に描かれた動物群のなかにま

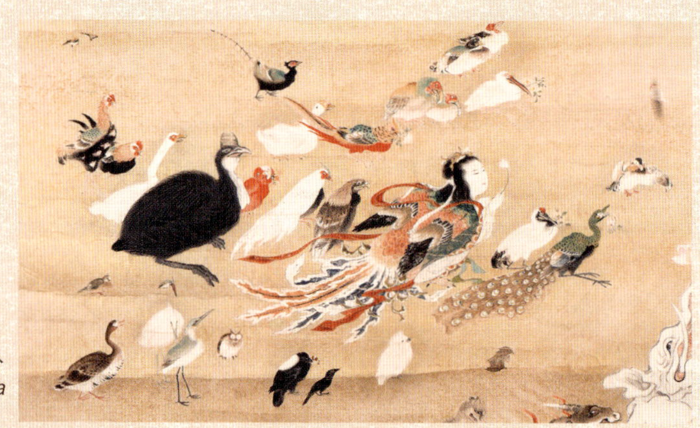

[6] 根元常南・菅井梅関筆「八相涅槃図」部分
Detail of *The Eightfold Path to Nirvana* by Nemoto Jōnan and Sugai Baikan

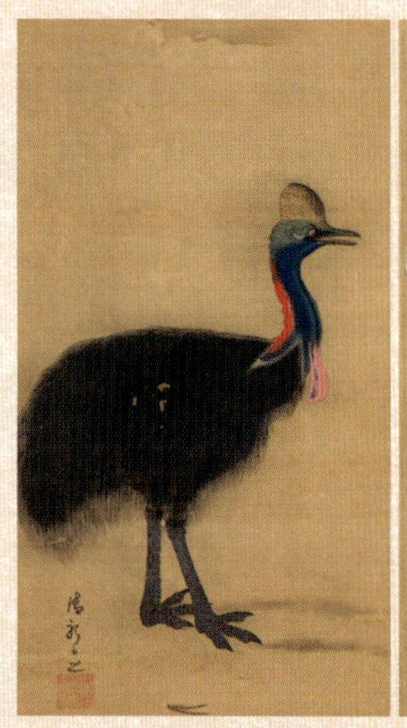

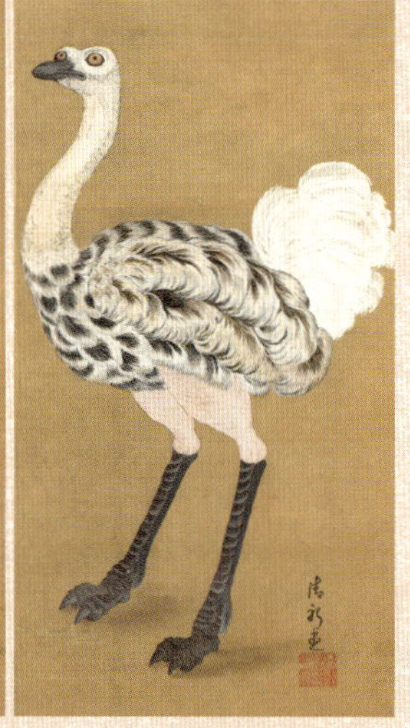

[5] 清躬「駝鳥・火喰鳥図」部分
Detail of *Ostrich and Cassowary* by Seikyū

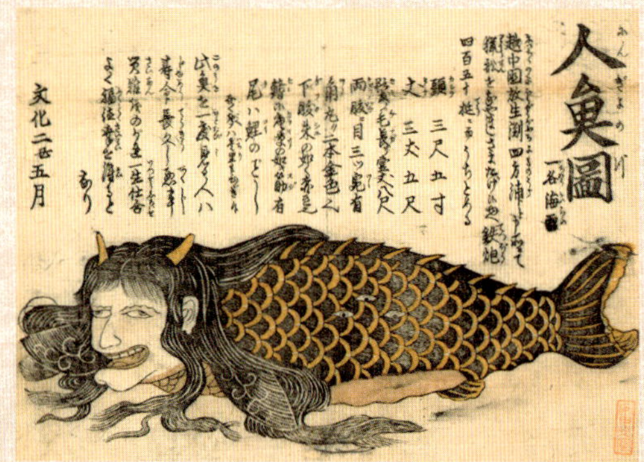

[7]「瓦版 人魚図」
Broadside Picture of a Mermaid

で登場し、その流行の様子を伝えている。

∽

実在の動物とは言い難いが、最後に人魚についても紹介しておきたい。その肉を食えば800歳の長寿を約束されるという人魚。古くはオオサンショウウオなどを人魚とみなした時期もあったようだが、とくに北陸から東北地方にかけての日本海側に多くの目撃情報が寄せられてきた。八郎潟近くの遺跡からは、人面と手足を持った人魚が供養する僧とともに描かれた13世紀後半頃の杉板が出土している。時代は下って18世紀後半、男鹿や津軽地方での見聞記録が『六物新志』(1786年刊)に紹介されている。多くの蘭書を駆使して本書を編んだのは大槻玄沢だが、知の最前線にいた当代一流の蘭学者でさえ人魚の実在を信じ、その肉を貼れば皮膚の黒色斑は消え、骨は止血に有用な霊薬であると報告したのである。

1805年(文化2)に越中の放生渕(今の富山湾内)で捕獲された人魚の姿はすさまじいものだった。そのとき出された刷物[7]によると頭は3尺5寸、丈は3丈5尺あったと記されるから、10メートルにも及ぶ巨大生物だったことになろう。さらに5メートル以上もの髪の毛をたくわえ、両腹には3個ずつの目、金色の2本の角、下腹は赤く鰭には唐草のような筋があった。そして尾は鯉に似ていたという。

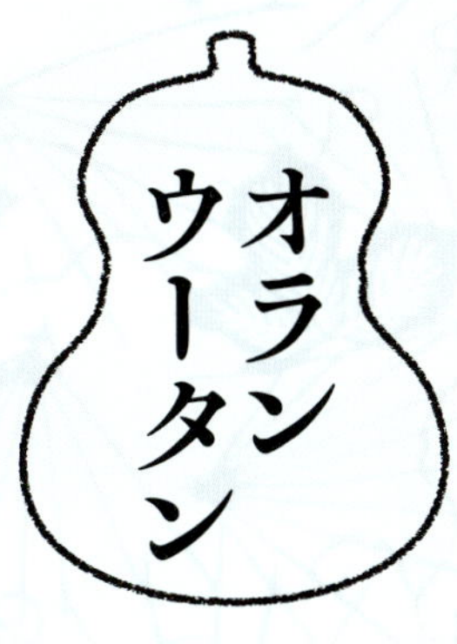

オランウータンが日本にもたらされたのは1792年（寛政4）と1800年（同12）の2度で、『唐蘭船持渡鳥獣之図』や『博物館獣譜』等に写生図が残されている。いずれも長崎で病死してしまったため、長崎以外で生きた姿を目にする機会はなかったのだが、1817年（文化14）に刊行された大槻玄沢編『蘭畹摘芳』において図入りの詳細な解説がなされ、さらにその内容が大田南畝の『一話一言』に収録されるなど、情報自体は確実に伝達されていった。一般に流布したオランウータンの図は1800年渡来時のもので、長崎の唐絵目利でもあった荒木如元（1765～1824）の写生図がその原図となったらしい。

一方、平戸藩主・松浦静山の随筆『甲子夜話』にある図は、皆川淇園が所持していた1792年渡来時の原図を2年後に転写したものという。注記には、毛色は猿よりも赤く人語を話し、大酒を飲み、寝るときは枕や布団を用いるなどといった記述も見える。『本草綱目』などにある記述とも近似しており、また日本で能の演目ともなった「猩々」と重ね合わせ、想像を膨らませていったようである。

The Orangutan

Orangutans first appeared in Japan as illustrations in *Animals Brought on Chinese and Dutch Ships* and *Natural History Museum Record of Beasts* and *Zoological Genealogy of Animals*, published in 1792 (Kansei 4) and 1800 (Kansei 12) respectively. The images were based of two living orangutans that were shipped to Nagasaki but had died after arrival. For that reason, orangutans could not be seen outside of Nagasaki except in printed form. The books *Compendium on Foreign Things* by Ōtsuki Gentaku and the novella *Words Said* by Ōta Nanpo, both published in 1817 (Bunka 14), render orangutans and explain their characteristics. The most widely circulated orangutan picture dates from the first specimens' 1800 arrival in Japan, and it seems that the source for this image was the sketch done by Araki Jogen (1765-1824), a fine arts appraiser and cataloguer (*karae mekiki*) in Nagasaki.

The publication *Nightly Chats in the Year of the Rat* by the lord of Hirado Domain, Matsuura Seizan features an image of an orangutan that is based on a work owned by the painter Minagawa Kien that had arrived from overseas in 1792. In the picture's explanatory text, the author notes that the primate's fur is redder than that of other monkeys. It further mentions that orangutans can talk like humans, are prone to drinking much alcohol, and use pillows and futons when sleeping. *Compendium of Materia Medica* contains a similar explanation, an interpretation that finds its reflection in such Noh theater plays as *Shōjō* which features a red-furred drunken monkey.

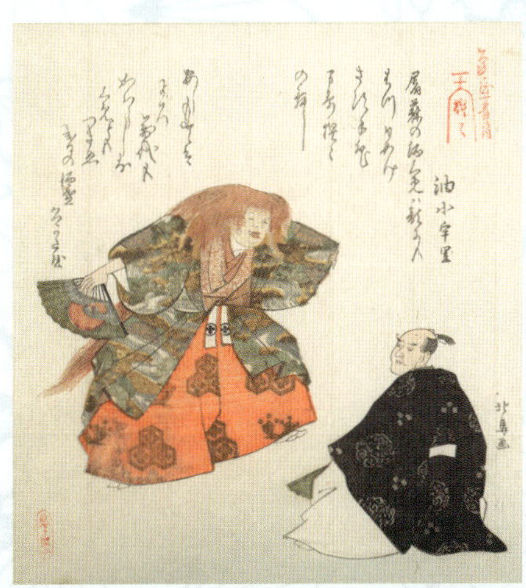

猩々の舞
蹄斎北馬
江戸時代（19c）
メトロポリタン美術館

Scene from the Noh Dance "Shōjō"
Teisai Hokuba
19th century
The Metropolitan Museum of Art

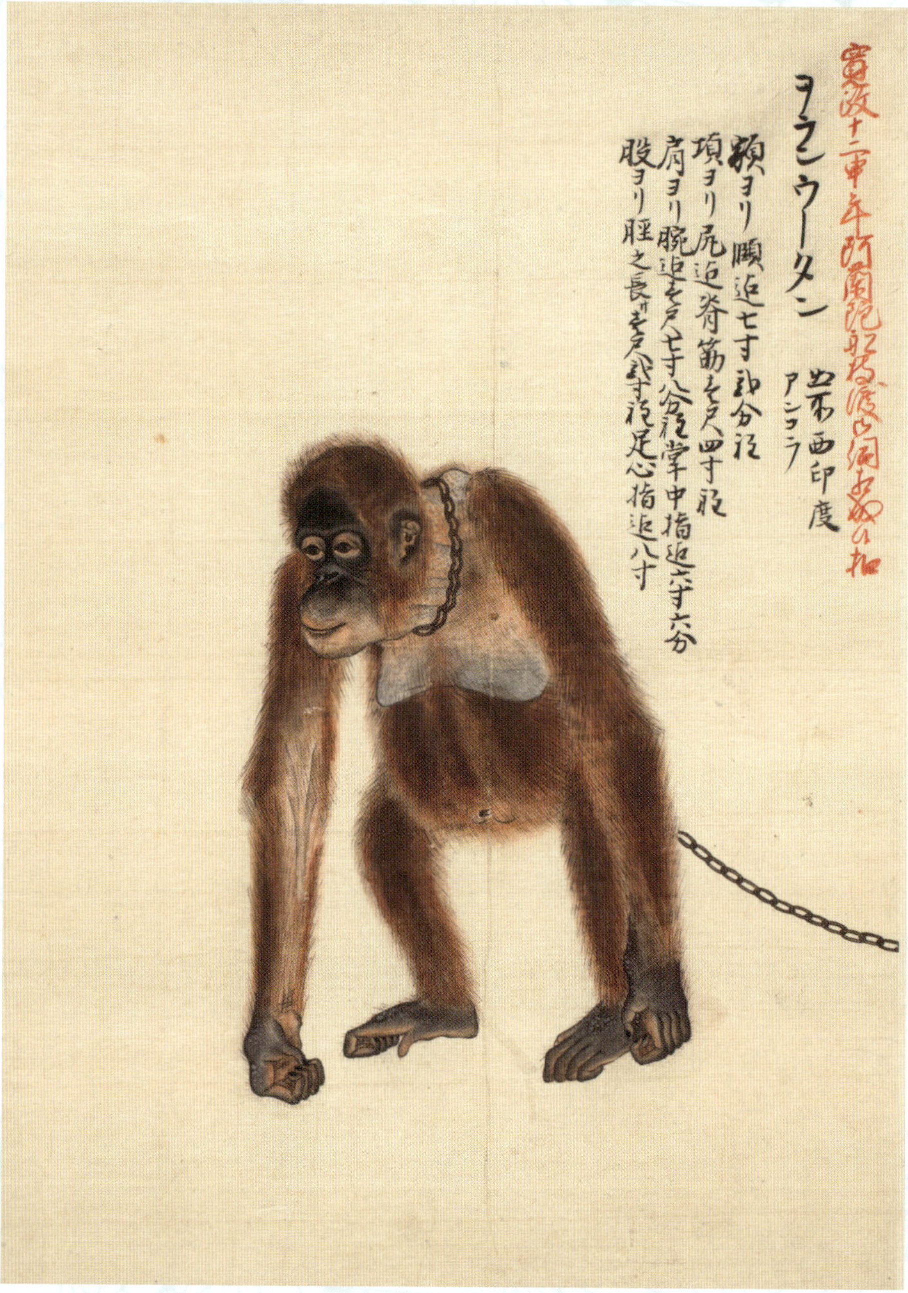

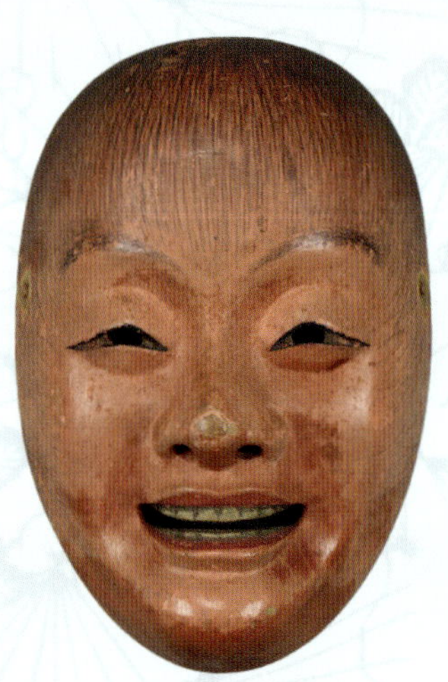

重要文化財
能面 猩々
室町時代（15～16c）
東京国立博物館

Important Cultural Property
Noh Theater Mask: Shōjō
15th-16th century
Tokyo National Museum

唐蘭船持渡鳥獣之図・獣類之図
江戸時代後期（18～19c）
慶應義塾図書館

Animals Brought on Chinese and Dutch Ships: Various Types of Animals
18th-19th century
Keio University Library

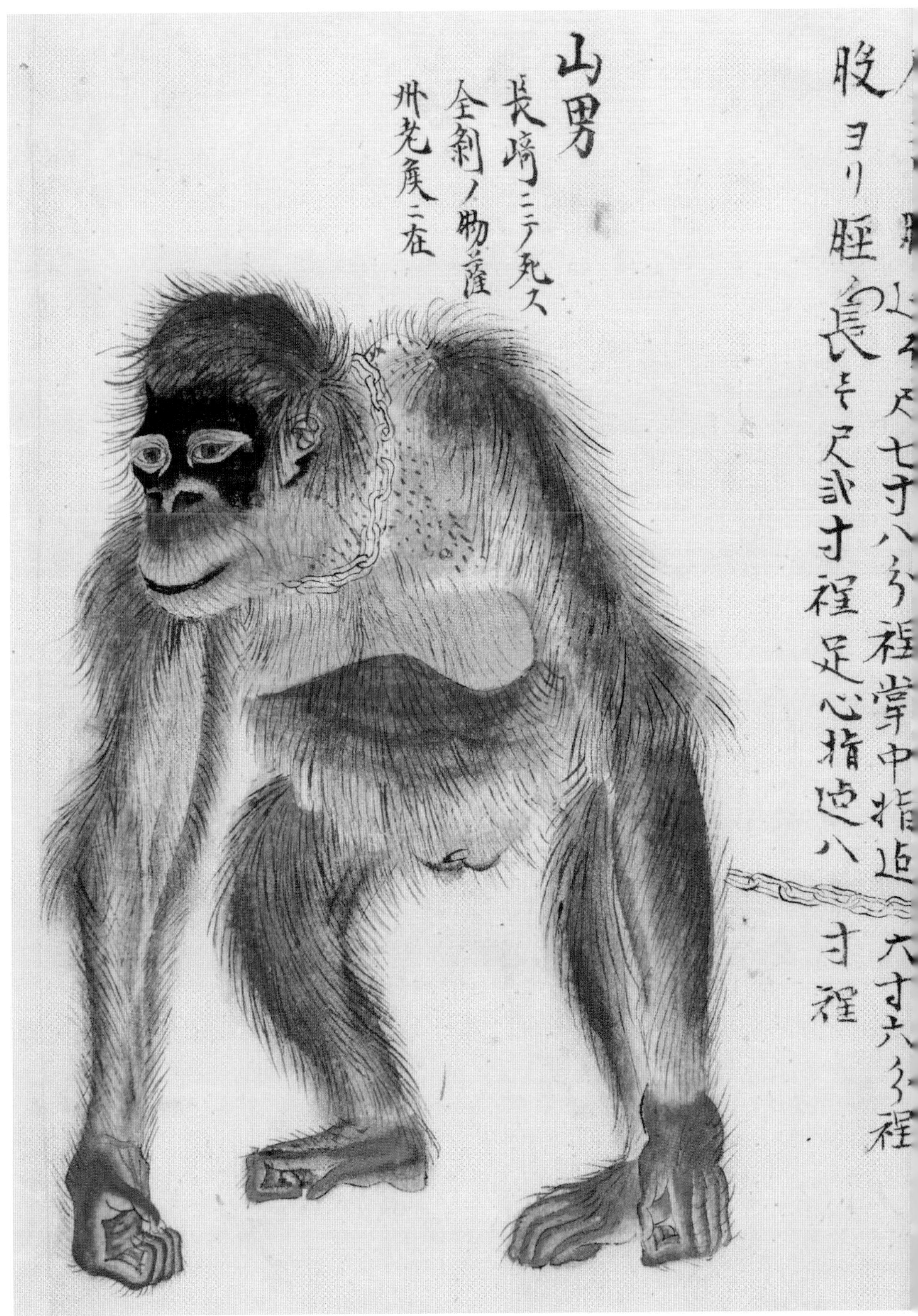
山男
長崎ニテ死ス
全剝ノ物薩
州老侯ニ在
股ヨリ脛迄長壱尺弐寸程足心指迄八寸程

ヲーランウータンノ圖
寛政十二庚申夏出所 西印度アンゴラ
額ヨリ頤迄七寸貳分程

「ヲーランウータンノ図」
(『惜字帖』より)

森島中良編
文化元年(1804)頃
早稲田大学図書館

本図には、「全剝ノ物薩州老侯ニ在」と記されており、島津重豪がオランウータンの全身剝製を所持していたことが確認できる。

Picture of an Orangutan
(from Sekijijō Scrapbook)

Edited by Morishima Chūryō
ca. 1804
Waseda University Library

This work has an inscription saying that this was a full-body taxidermy orangutan in the possession of Shimazu Shigehide.

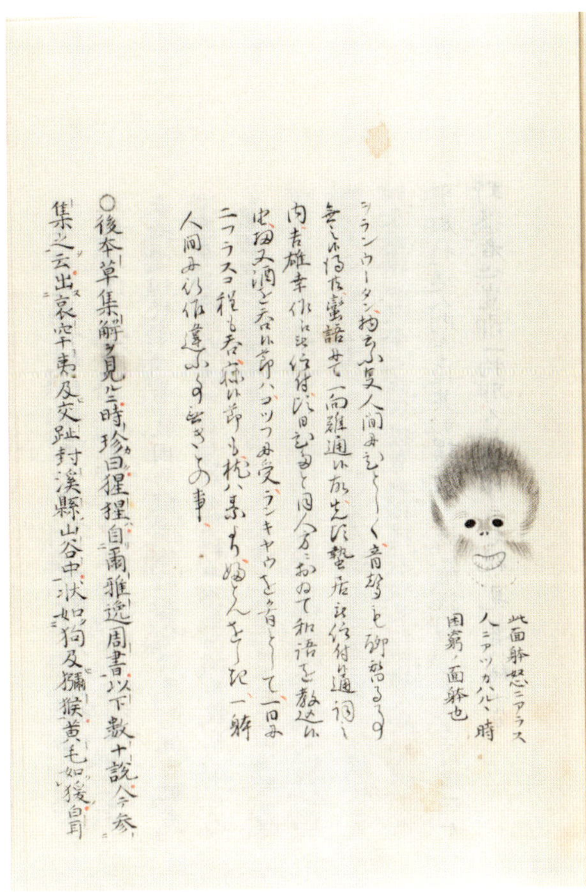

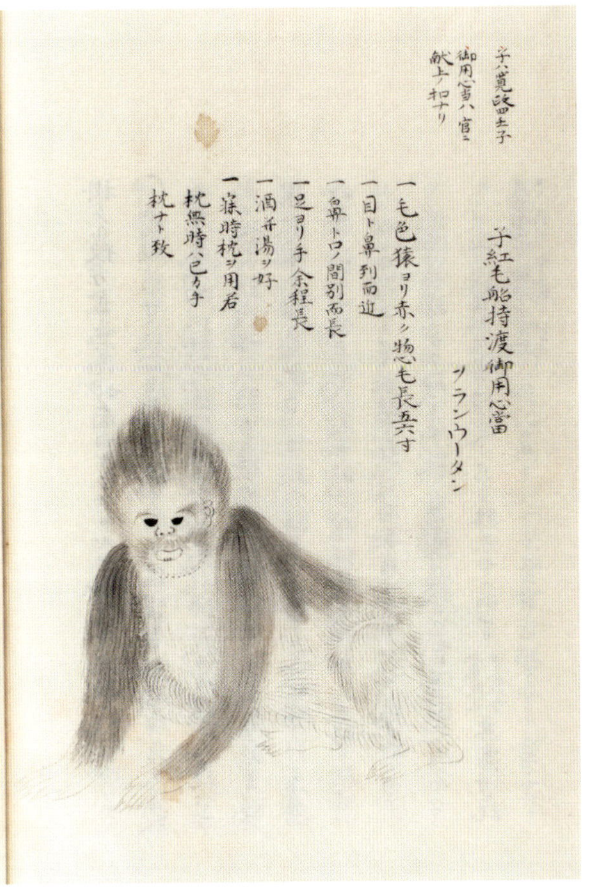

ヲランウータン図
（『甲子夜話』より）

松浦静山
文政4年～天保12年（1821～41）
長崎・松浦史料博物館

Orangutans
(from *Nightly Chats in the Year of the Rat*)

Matsura Seizan
1821-41
Matsura Historical Museum, Nagasaki

阿郎烏烏当写真図
(『蘭畹摘芳』より)

大槻玄沢編
文化14年(1817)刊
国立国会図書館

Orangutans
(*from Compendium on Foreign Things*)
Edited by Ōtsuki Gentaku
Published in 1817
National Diet Library, Japan

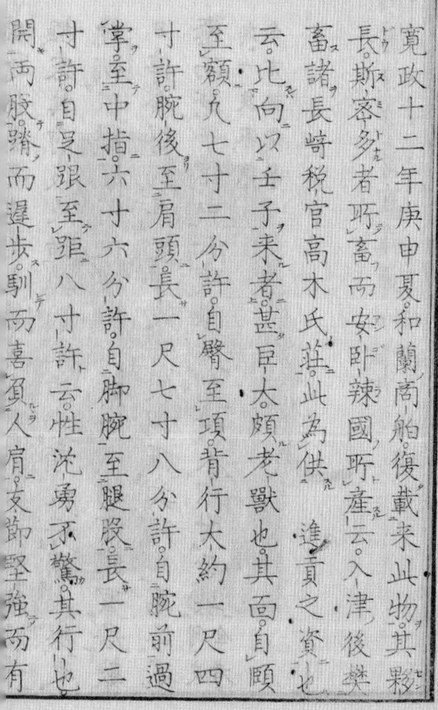
寛政十二年庚申夏和蘭商舶復載来此物其[illegible]
長斯容多者所畜而安卧辣國所産云入津後樊
畜諸長崎税官高木氏莊此為供　進貢之資也
云比向以壬子来者甚巨太頗老獸也其面自頤
至額九七寸二分許自臀至項背行大約一尺四
寸許腕後至肩頭長一尺七寸八分許自腕前過
掌至中指六寸六分許自脚腕至腿股長一尺二
寸許自足跟至距八寸許云性沈勇不驚其行也
開両股蹯而遲歩馴而喜負人肩支節堅強而有

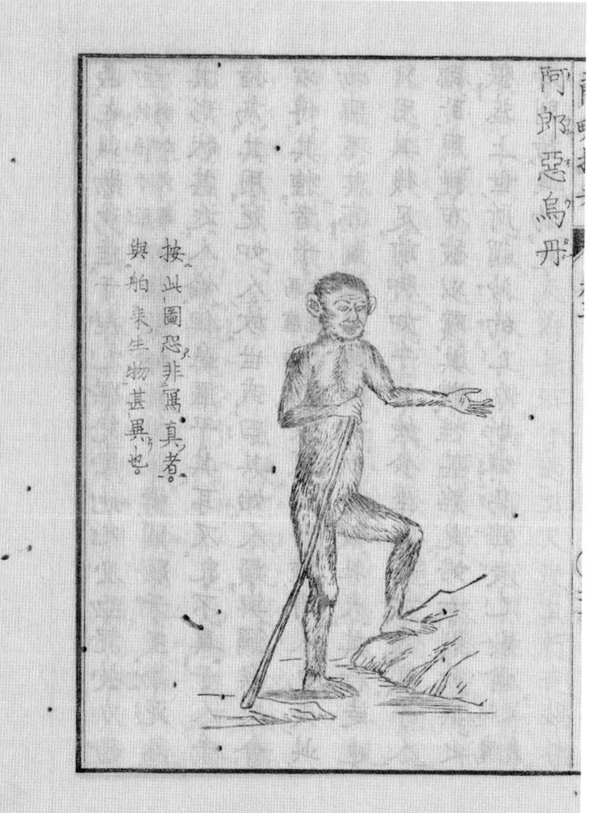

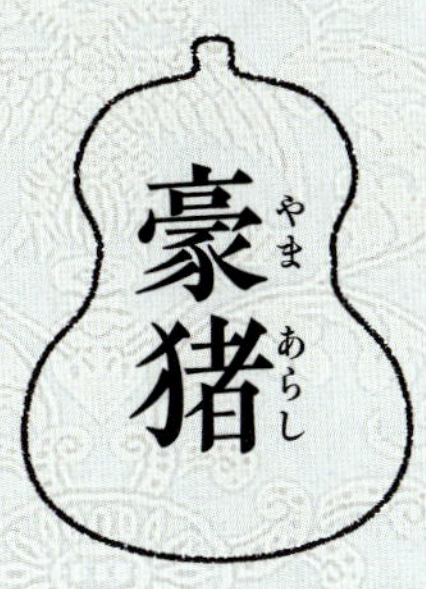

アフリカやヨーロッパ南部、インド、東南アジアに分布する豪猪（やまあらし）は、外敵から身を守るための背中の針毛が大きな特徴。江戸初期にさかのぼる「四条河原遊楽図屏風」にいち早く見世物として登場し、水戸光圀（1628～1700）がこの動物を山林に放したことも伝えられるなど日本への渡来の歴史は古いようだが、記録から舶載が最初に確認されるのは1772年（安永元）のこと。その後、1787年（天明7）、1832年（天保3）の渡来記録があるという。

The Porcupine

The porcupine can be found in Africa, Southern Europe, India, and Southeast Asia, and its most notable characteristic is that it has sharp quills on its back to protect itself from enemy attacks. It first appeared in the early Edo period *Amusements at Shijō Kawara* screens as the subject of a public exhibition, and it is said that Mito Mitsukuni (1628-1700) released this animal into a mountain forest; from these, it would seem that there is a long history of porcupines being brought to Japan, but the earliest importation date that we can confirm in the records is 1772 (An'ei 1). Subsequently, there are also records of porcupines being imported in 1767 (Tenmei 7) and 1832 (Tenpō 3).

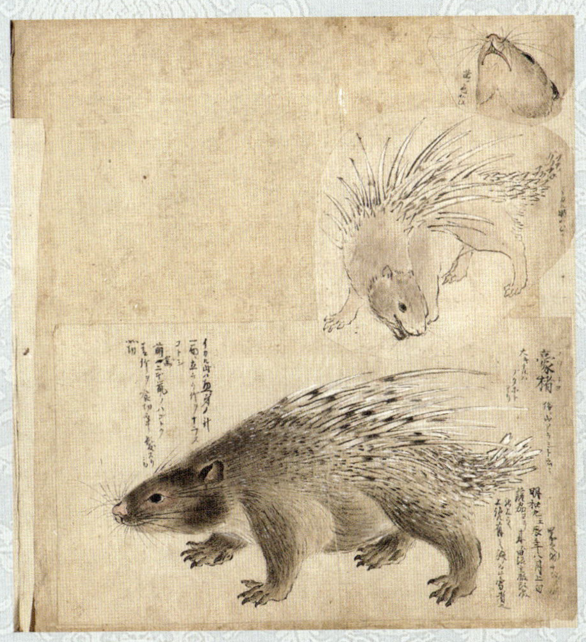

図案ほか粉本貼り込み画帖

板谷派
江戸時代(17-19c)
東京国立博物館

1772（安永元）年薩摩藩がオランダ商館からヤマアラシ2匹を購入した。うち1匹が田沼意次に献上され、さらに将軍が上覧した後に本草・博物学をもって幕府に仕えていた田村藍水（1718～76）に下賜されたという。幕府お抱えの板谷派絵師の手になる本帖には、ヤマアラシの写生図とともにその経緯が記され、上覧直後に写生されたものと知れる。やがて、この図様はいくつかの転写を経て「鳥獣花木図屏風」（p.345）のヤマアラシとして登場することになるのである。

Picture Album of Pasted Sketches

Itaya school
17th-19th century
Tokyo National Museum

In 1772 (An'ei 1), the Satsuma domain purchased two porcupines from a Dutch trading company. Of those, one of them was presented to Tanuma Okitsugu, and the other, after being shown to the shogun, was supposedly bestowed upon Tamura Ransui (1718-76), who in addition to studying natural history and herbal medicine, worked for the government. In this booklet by an Itaya School painter, an employee of the shogunal government, the details are recorded along with an image of a porcupine, and we can understand that this was sketched immediately following the shogunal inspection. Eventually, by way of several copies of this image, a version of this porcupine appears in the *Birds and Animals in the Flower Garden* screens (p.345).

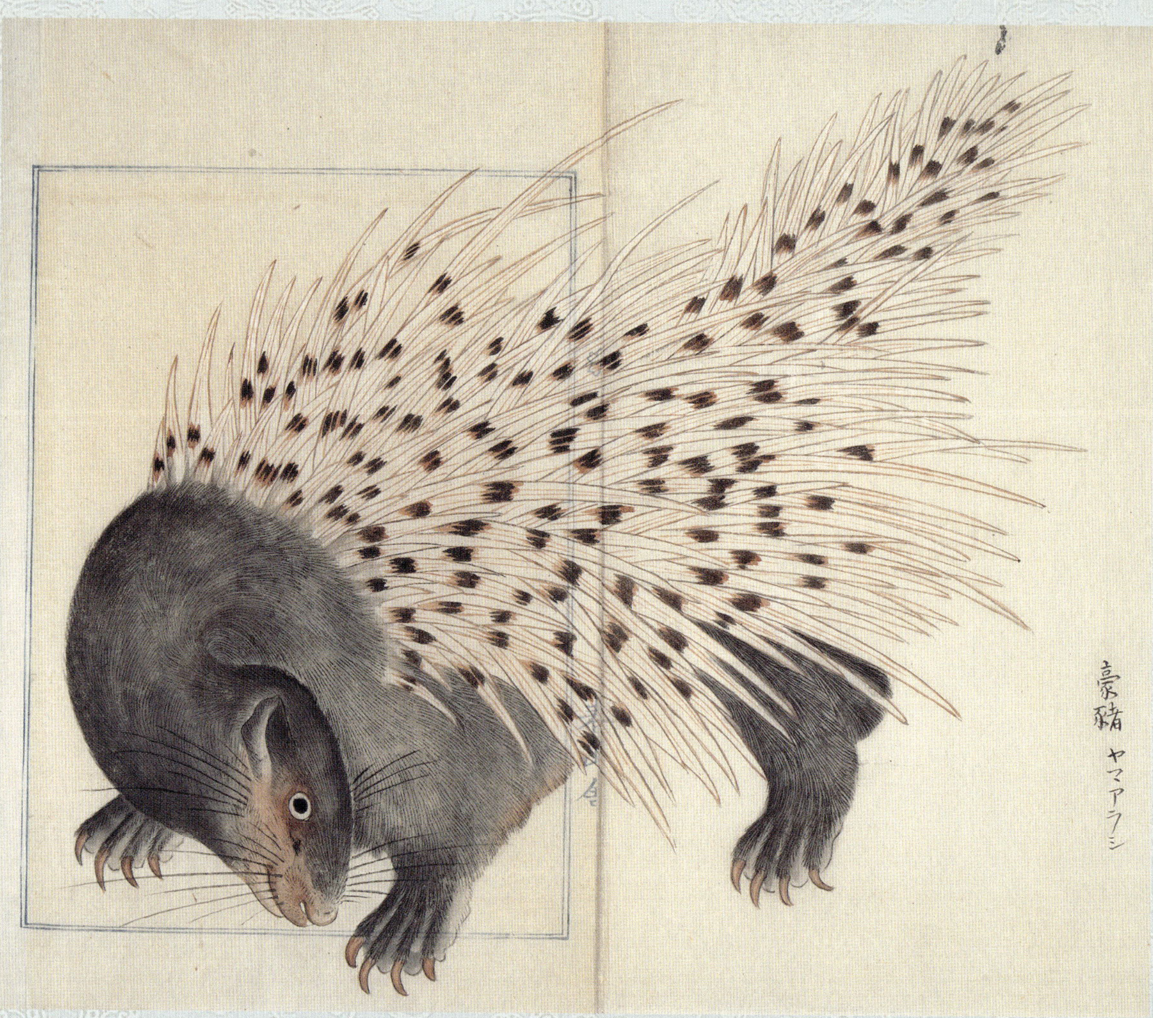

豪猪図
(『本草図説』より)

江戸時代(19c)
西尾市岩瀬文庫

『本草図説』は、江戸の本草家・高木春山(?～1852)が、20年以上の歳月と莫大な私財を投じて作り上げげた、全195巻に及ぶ総合図鑑。おびただしい数の彩色図のなかに、板谷派の図を祖型とする豪猪図が含まれている。

Porcupine
(*from Honzō Zusetsu*)

19th century
Iwase Bunko Library

The *Honzō Zusetsu* is a comprehensive field manual that comprises one hundred and ninety-five scrolls, and was the result of an immense investment of private funds – and over twenty years of labor – on the part of the herbalist Takagi Shunzan (?-1852). The supposed prototype for the Itaya School porcupine painting is also included among its innumerable color pictures.

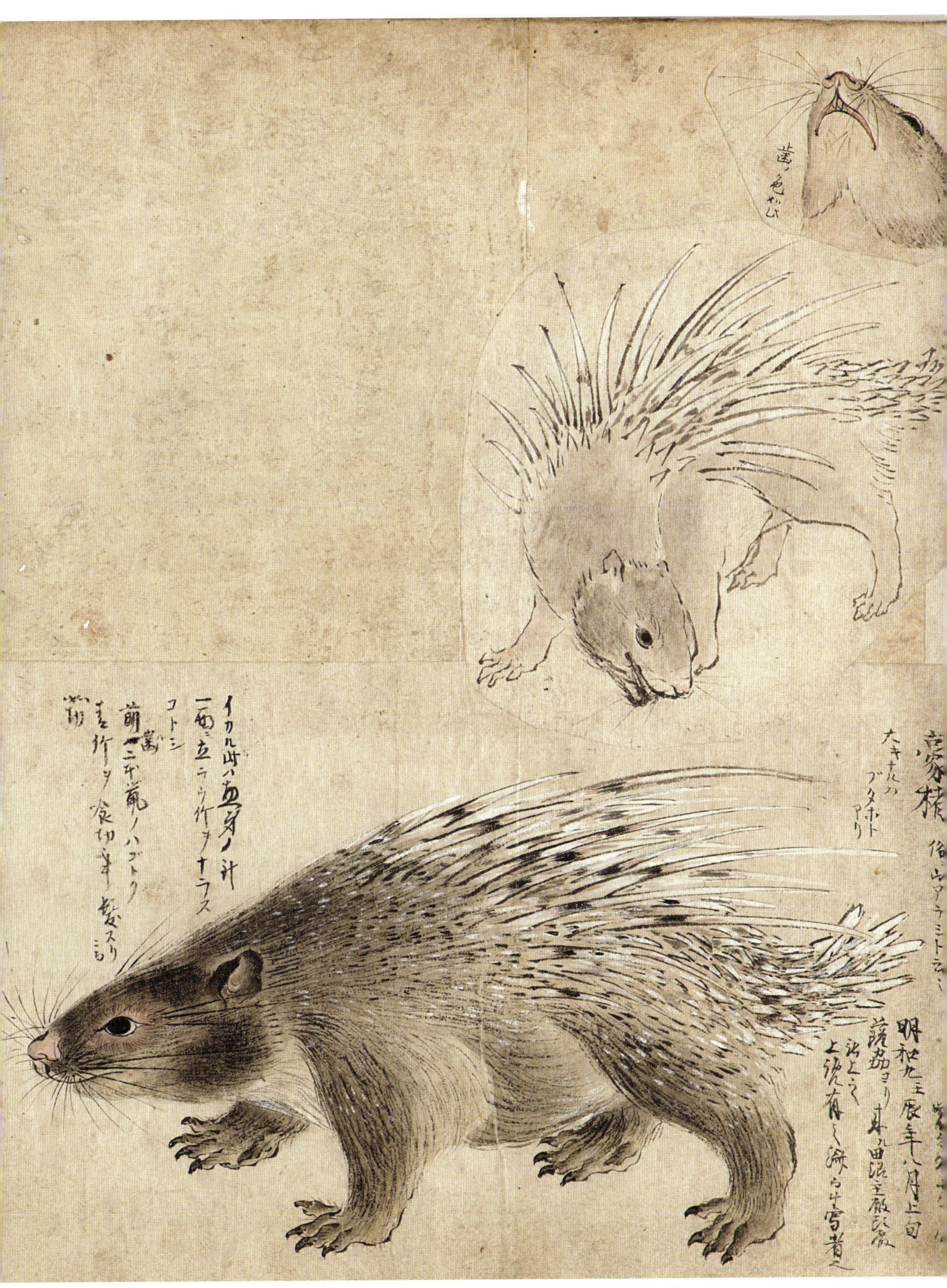

図案ほか粉本貼り込み画帖 部分　*Picture Album of Pasted Sketches* (detail)

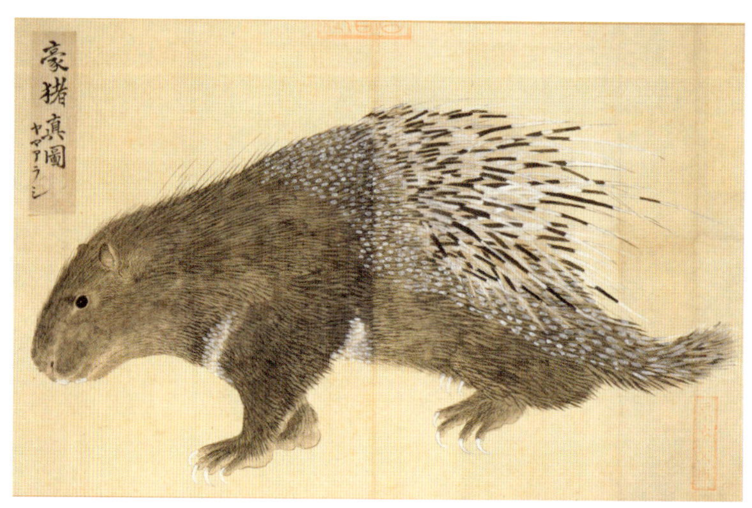

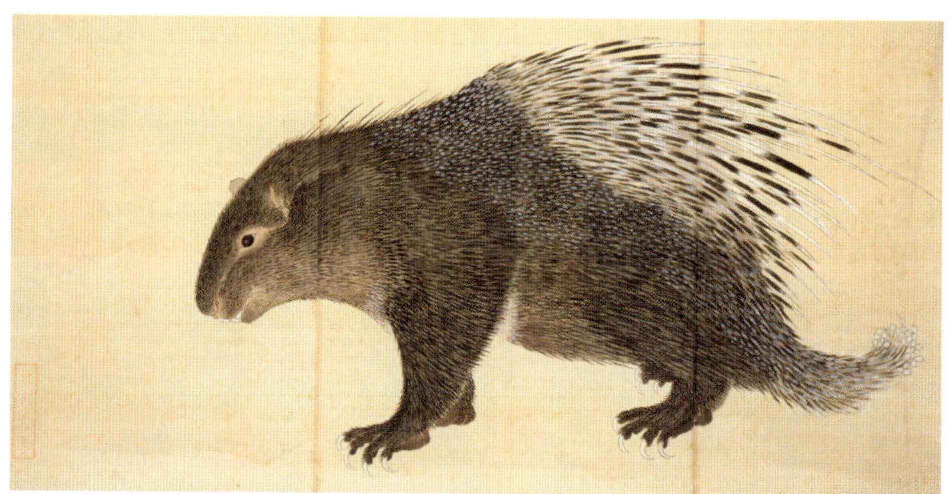

豪猪

(『鳥獣魚写生図』より)

栗本丹洲
江戸時代後期(18〜19c)
国立国会図書館

Porcupines

(from Sketches of Birds, Wild Animals and Fishes)

Kurimoto Tanshū
18th-19th century
National Diet Library, Japan

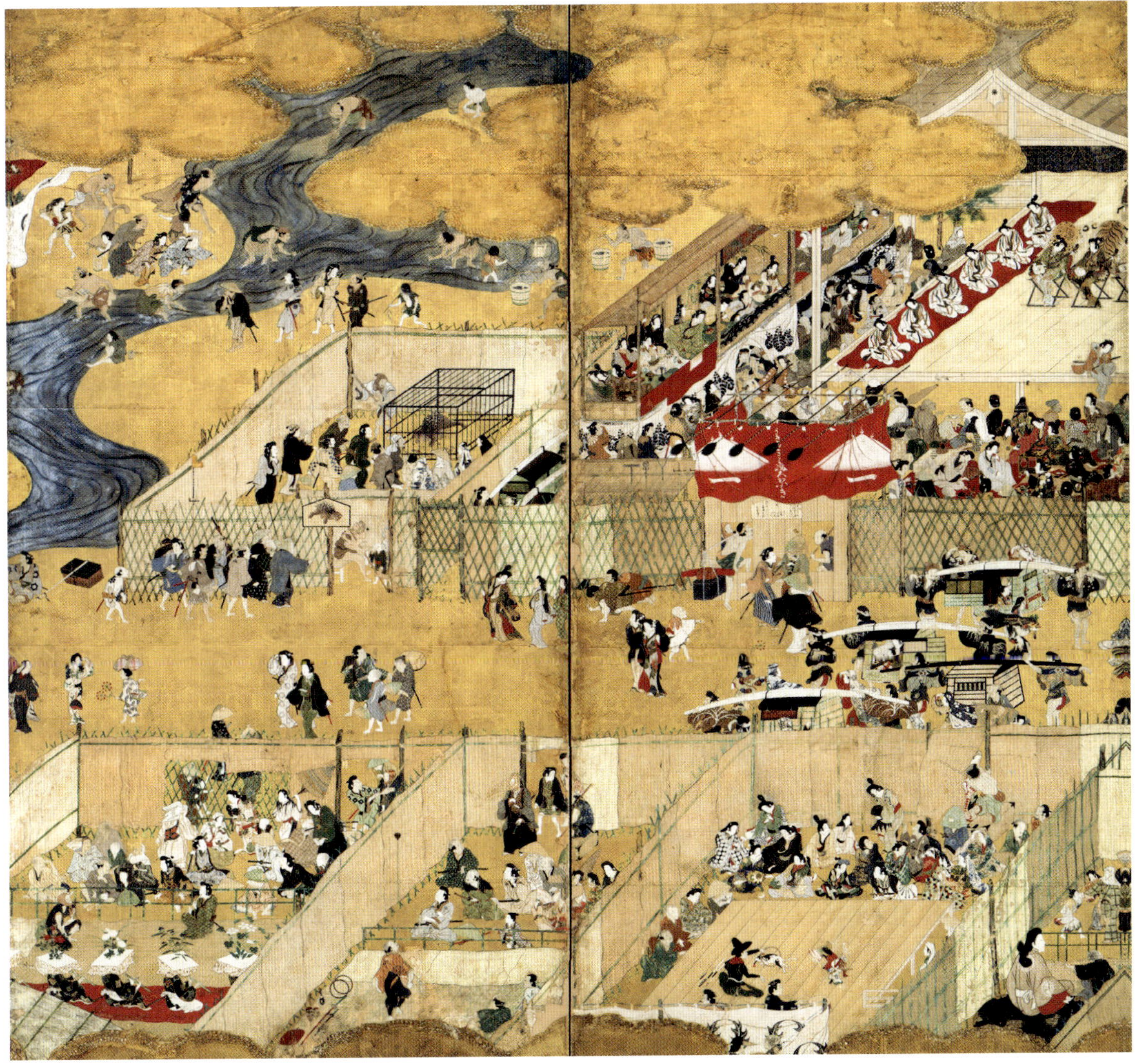

重要文化財

四条河原遊楽図屛風 (右隻)

江戸時代初期(17c前半)
静嘉堂文庫美術館

江戸時代初めの京都四条河原で遊興する人々の様子を描き出した屛風。画面中央左寄りの見世物小屋には、檻に入れられた豪猪のまわりを見物客が囲み、賑わいを見せている。

Important Cultural Property

Amusements at Shijō Kawara Screen (Right Screen)

First half of 17th century
Seikado Bunko Art Museum

This is a folding screen from the early Edo period that depicts a scene of people making merry at Shijō Kawara, Kyoto. In the show tent to the left of the center of the painting, we can see the bustling crowd of spectators surrounding a porcupine in a pen.

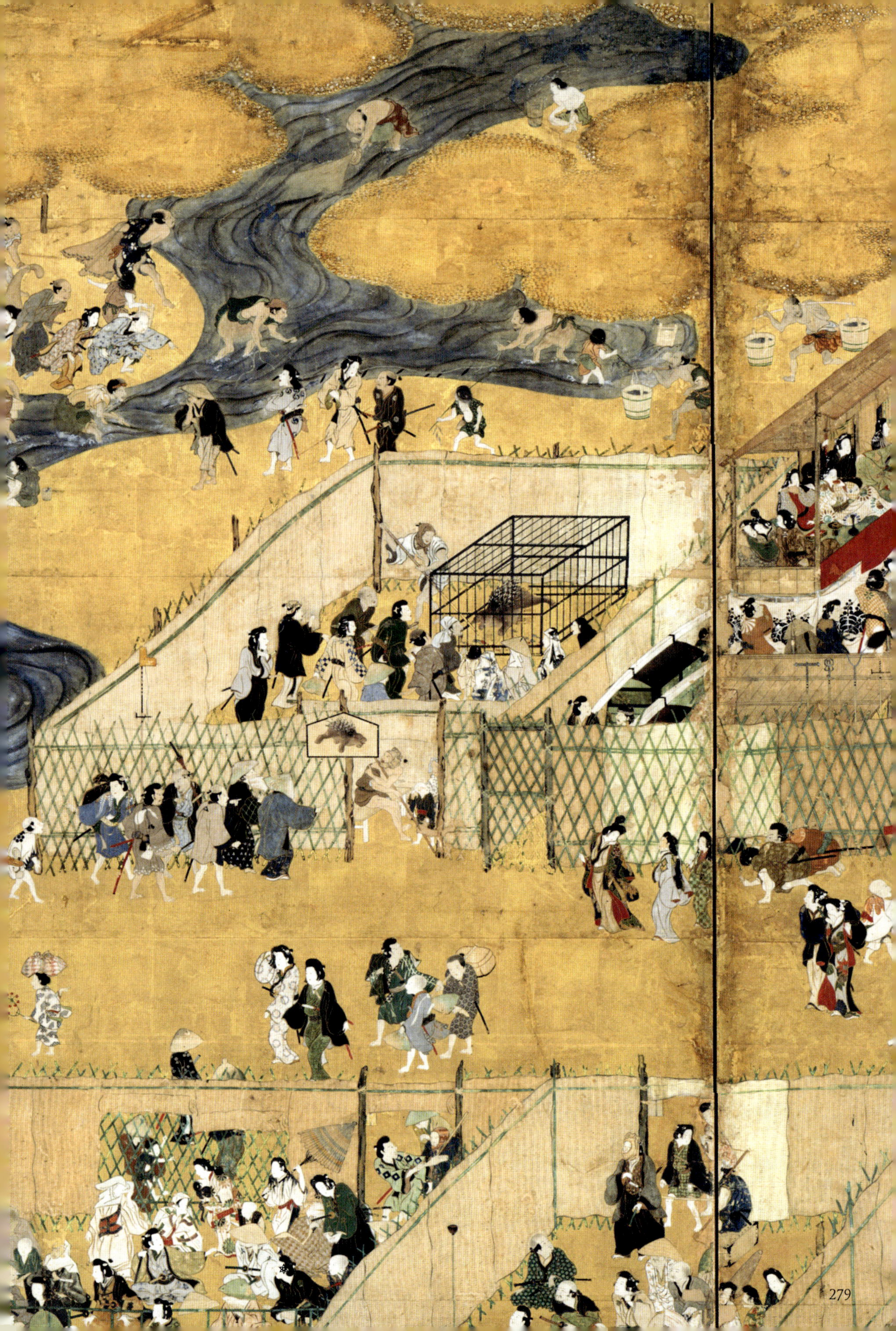

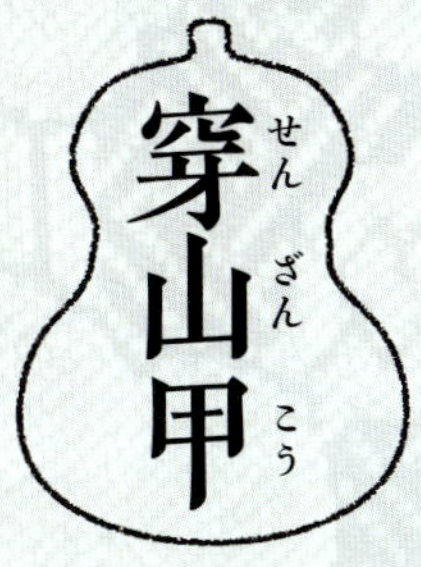

穿山甲（せんざんこう）

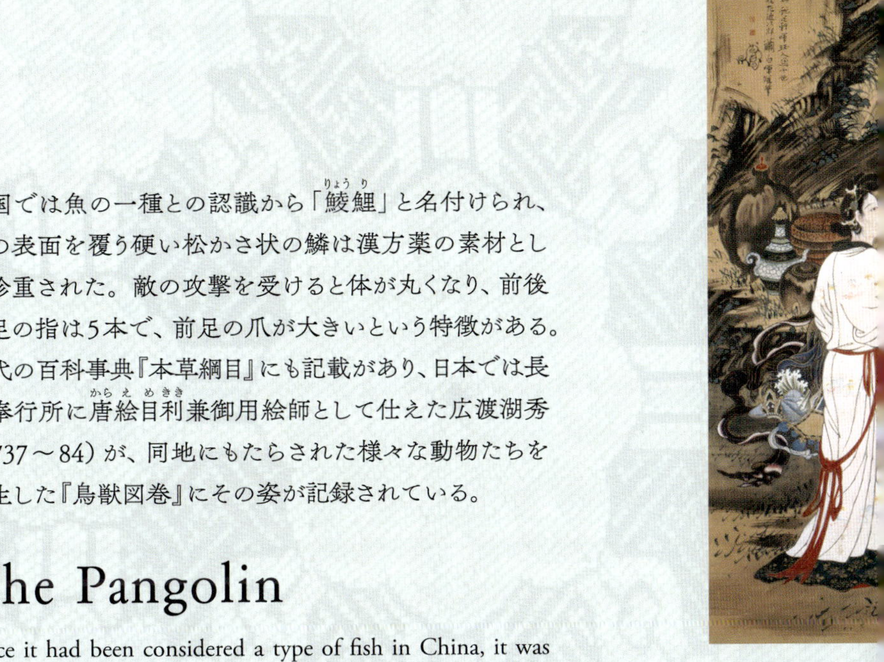

中国では魚の一種との認識から「鯪鯉（りょうり）」と名付けられ、体の表面を覆う硬い松かさ状の鱗は漢方薬の素材として珍重された。敵の攻撃を受けると体が丸くなり、前後の足の指は5本で、前足の爪が大きいという特徴がある。明代の百科事典『本草綱目』にも記載があり、日本では長崎奉行所に唐絵目利（からえめきき）兼御用絵師として仕えた広渡湖秀（1737～84）が、同地にもたらされた様々な動物たちを写生した『鳥獣図巻』にその姿が記録されている。

The Pangolin

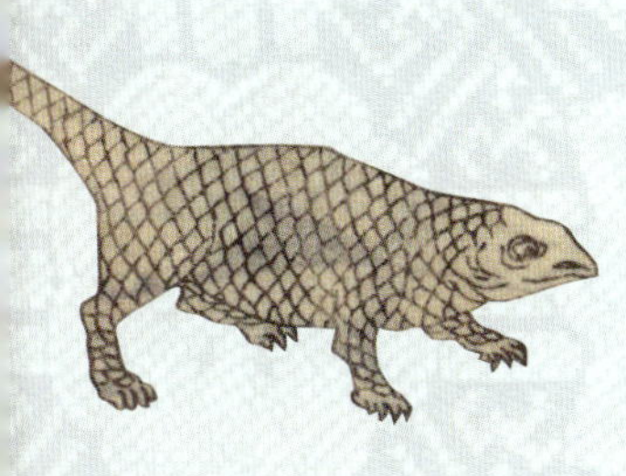

Since it had been considered a type of fish in China, it was known as a type of carp, and the hard pine cone type scales that covered the exterior of its body were highly prized as ingredients in Chinese medicine. Its characteristics are that it curls its body into a round shape when it is attacked by an enemy, it has five toes on its front and back legs, and the claws on its front legs are quite large. The pangolin is also mentioned in the Ming encyclopedia, the *Compendium of Materia Medica*, and in Japan, it appears in the *Birds and Beasts Scroll* by Hirowatari Koshū (1737-84), who was a painter for the government and also the arts appraiser and cataloguer at the Nagasaki magistrate's office. The *Birds and Beasts Scrolls* was where he recorded all the various animals that were brought there, and the pangolin is recorded there as well.

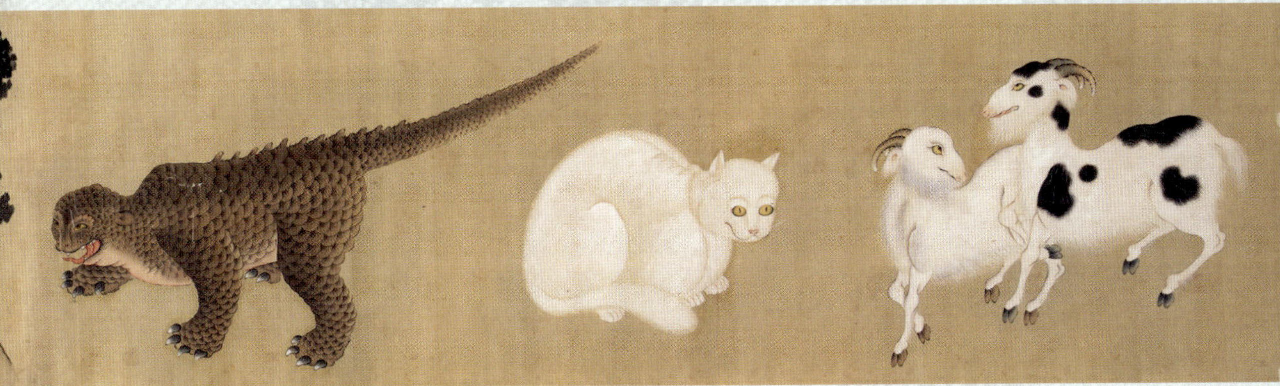

穿山甲（せんざんこう）（『鳥獣図巻』より）
広渡湖秀
江戸時代中期（18c）
長崎歴史文化博物館

Pangolin *(from the Birds and Beasts Scrolls)*
Hirowatari Koshū
18th century
Nagasaki Museum of History and Culture

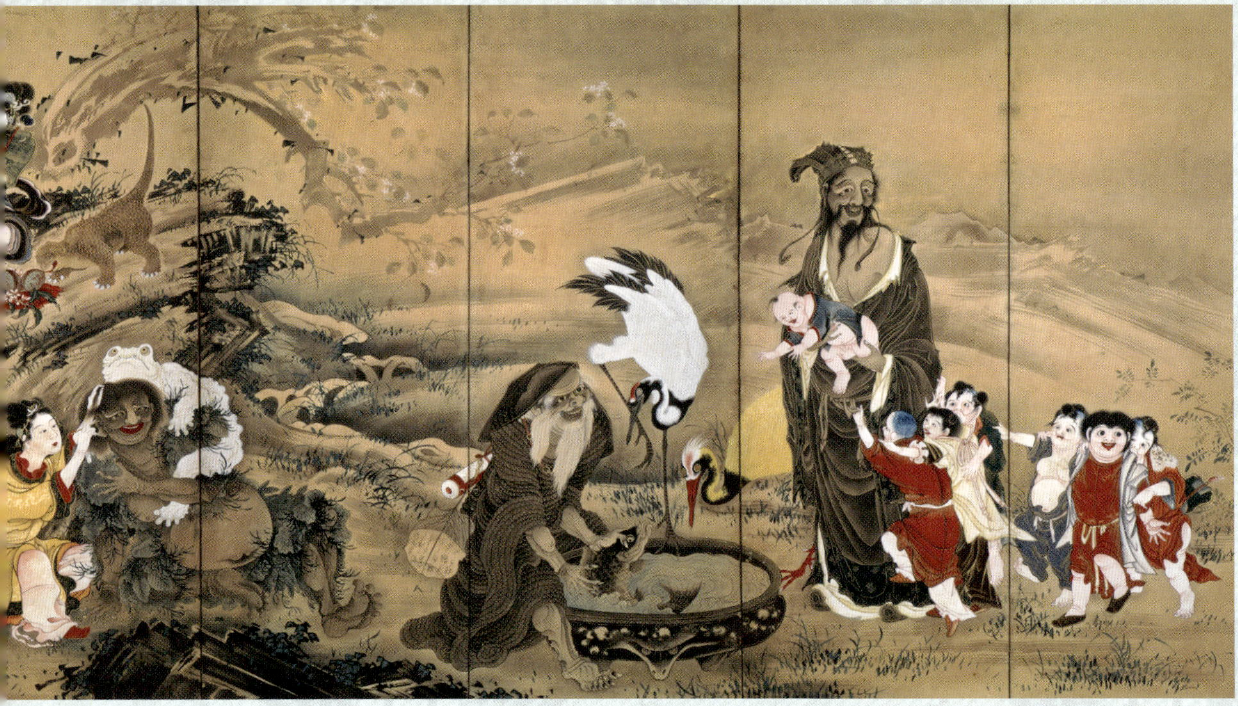

重要文化財

群仙図屏風（左隻）

曾我蕭白
明和元年（1764）
国（文化庁保管）

蕭白が、その奇矯さを存分に発揮した渾身のスペクタル大作。仙人の表現も、動物の姿も奇妙さに溢れる。西王母の仙桃を狙う不思議な動物が目を引く。広渡湖秀の「鳥獣図巻」にある穿山甲図の転用と考えられているが、実は本図制作の前年、京都東山で開催された物産会に植木屋助五郎なる人物により穿山甲が出品されていたことが記録にある。蕭白の作品には、その際の衝撃が反映されているのではあるまいか。

Important Cultural Property

Chinese Immortals Screen (Left screen)

Soga Shōhaku
1764
Japan (Agency for Cultural Affairs)

This is a spectacular masterpiece that fully demonstrates Shōhaku's eccentricity. The depictions of the immortals and the animals overflow with a bizarre quality. Our eyes are drawn to a mysterious animal that looks at the peaches of immortality of the Queen Mother of the West. It is thought that this is based on the depiction of the pangolin in Hirowatari Koshū's *Birds and Beasts Scroll*, but actually, we have a record that a pangolin was put on display by the gardener Sukegorō at a natural history exhibition held in Higashiyama, Kyoto the year before this image was produced. Doesn't Shōhaku capture the shock they must have felt upon seeing this animal?

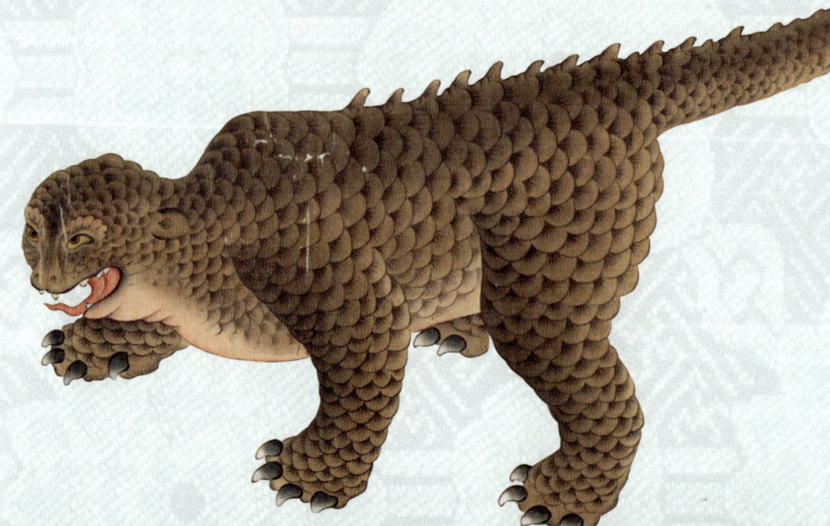

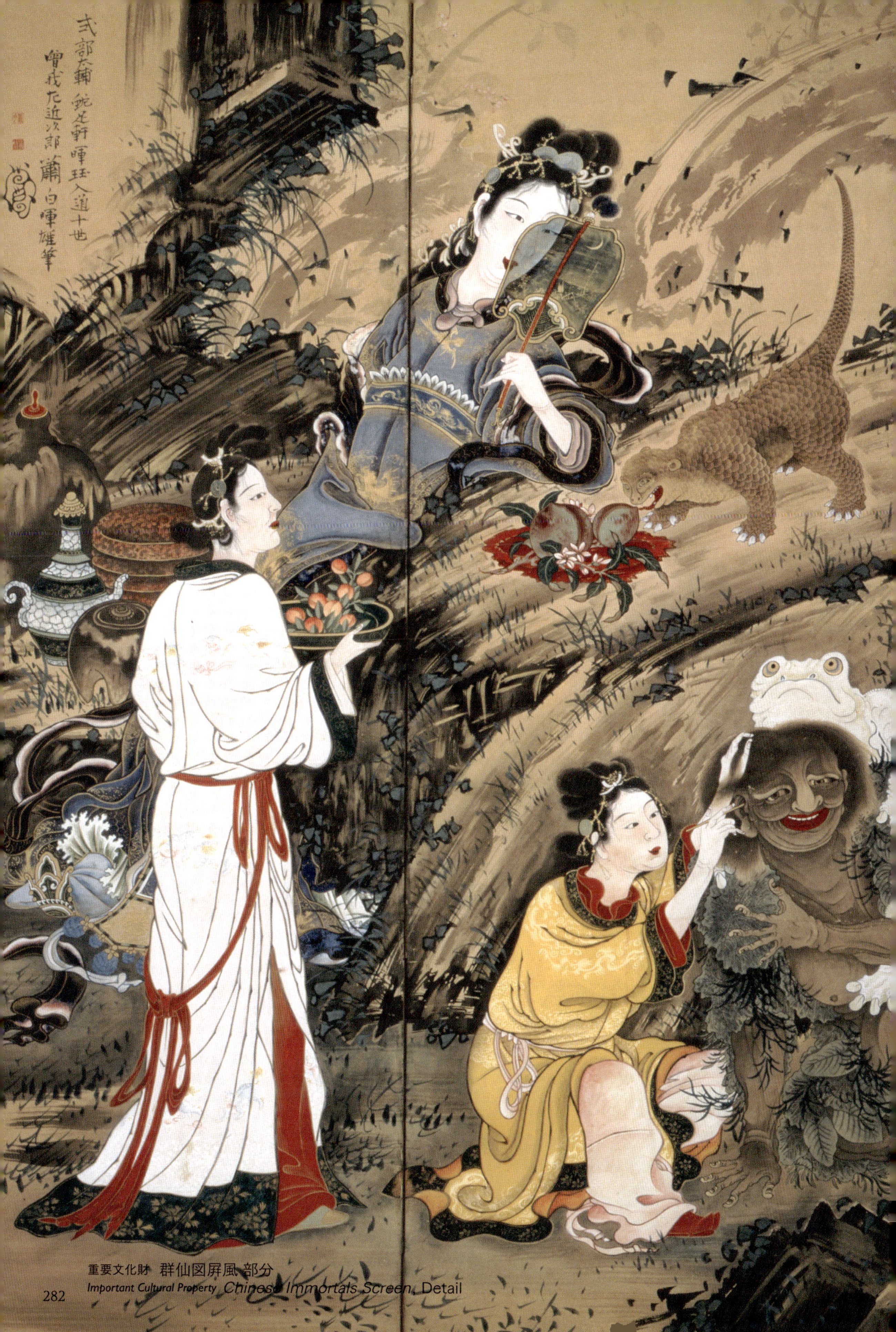

重要文化財 群仙図屏風 部分
Important Cultural Property Chinese Immortals Screen, Detail

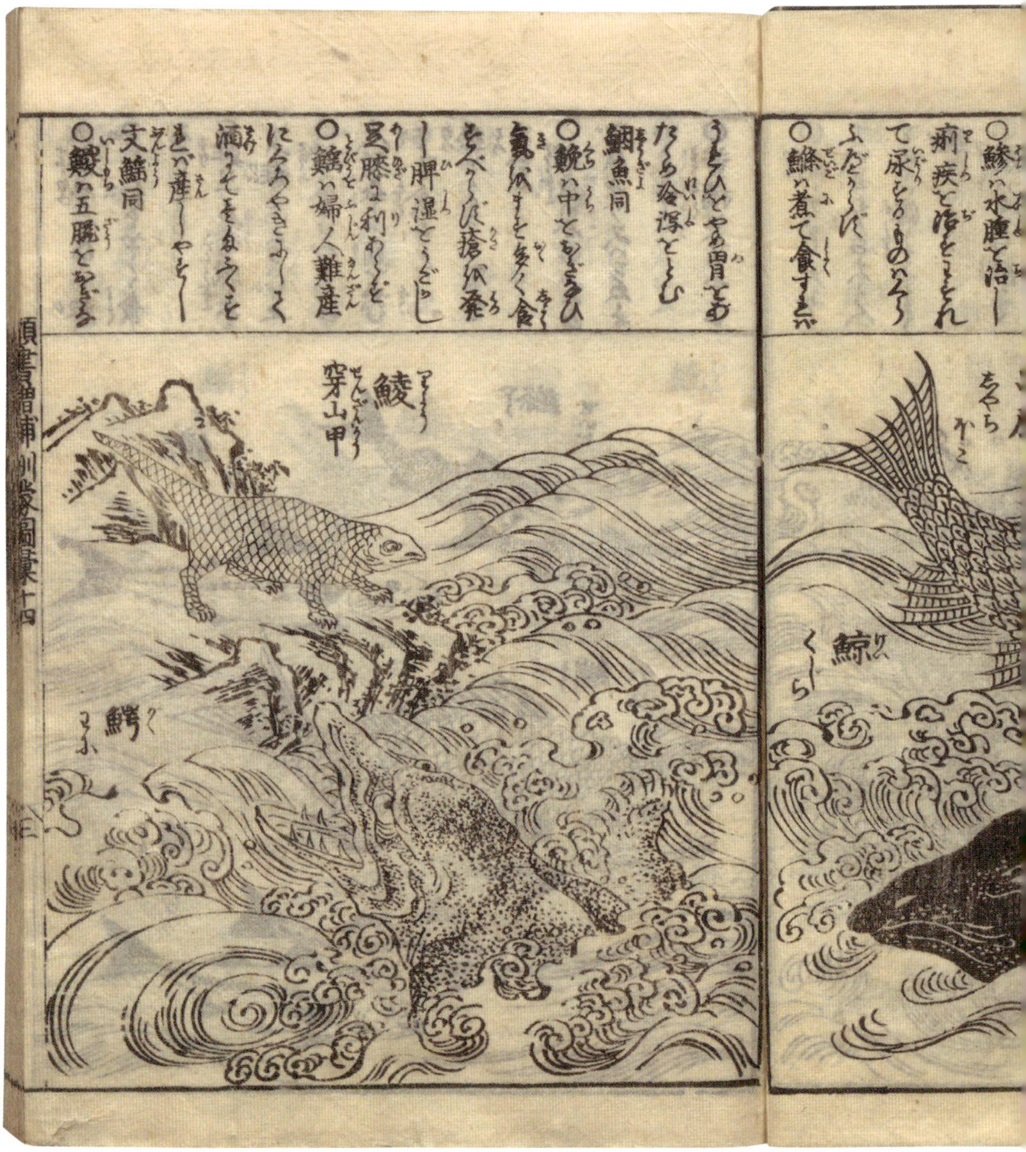

穿山甲
(『頭書 増補訓蒙図彙』より)

中村惕斎
寛政元年(1789)刊
国立国会図書館

Pangolin
(*from Kashiragaki zōho kinmōzui*)

Nakamura Tekisai
Published in 1789
National Diet Library, Japan

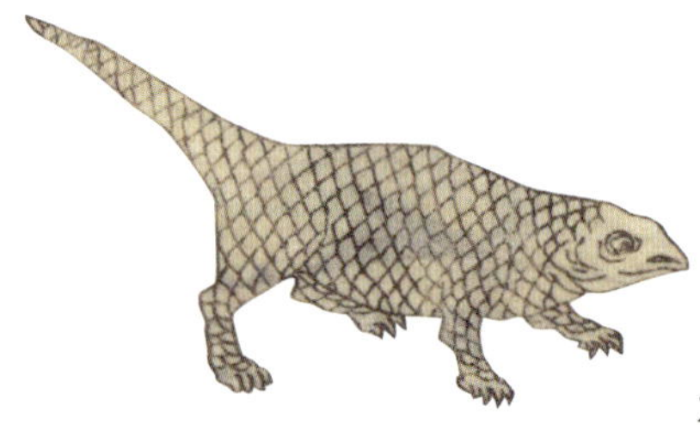

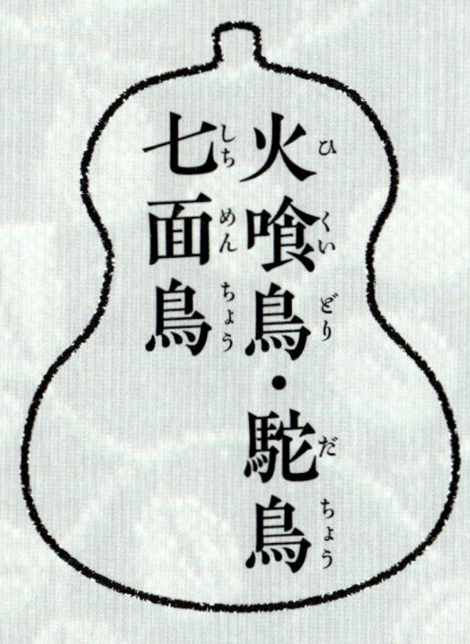

アフリカ産の駝鳥とオーストラリアやニューギニア周辺に棲息する火喰鳥。日本では長らく両者が混同され、後者を誤って駝鳥と呼んできた。駝鳥自体の渡来は1658年(万治元)が唯一の例という。火喰鳥の初渡来は1612年(慶長17)で、その後たびたび移入され見世物にもなった。喉の赤い肉垂が火を食うように見えたのが名の由来といい、金属や石、焼けた炭なども食すと宣伝された。一方、北米原産で16世紀には西欧各国で食用とされていた七面鳥は、オランダ名から日本では「カラクン」と呼ばれ、1639年(寛永16)の初渡来以来、何度か舶載され江戸城内や市中で飼育されることもあったという。

The Cassowary, Ostrich, and Turkey

This is an ostrich from Africa, and a cassowary which inhabits the areas of Australia and New Guinea. These two birds had long been conflated in Japan, and being mistaken for the former, the cassowary also came to be called an ostrich. Supposedly, the only example of an actual ostrich coming to Japan was in 1658 (Manji 1). The first time a cassowary was brought to Japan was in 1612 (Keichō 17), and after that point, they were often imported and shown at sideshows.

It is said that the origin of the name for the cassowary in Japanese ("fire-eating bird") comes from how the red wattle of the throat looks like the bird eats fire, and it was further rumored that the cassowary also ate things like metal, stone, and burnt charcoal. On the other hand, we have the turkey, whose original habitat is in North America, but came to be eaten all over Western Europe in the sixteenth century. It was called "*karakun*" in Japan based on its Dutch name, and since turkeys were first brought to Japan in 1639 (Kan'ei 16), they were imported several times after; turkeys were also raised in Edo Castle and within the city itself.

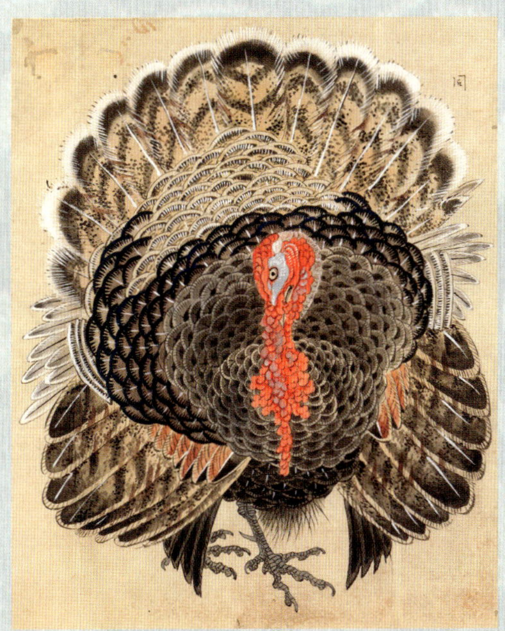

七面鳥(『禽譜』より)

堀田正敦編
江戸時代後期(18〜19c)
宮城県図書館

『禽譜』は、近江堅田藩主で若年寄を長らくつとめた堀田正敦(1755〜1832)の編んだ江戸鳥類学の集大成。多くの大名や旗本らの図譜から転写した図も多数収録されている。正面からとらえた七面鳥の描写が目を引くが、このイメージは枡目描きの「鳥獣花木図屏風」(p.344)にも登場する。

Turkey (*from the Catalogue of Birds*)

Edited by Hotta Masa'atsu
18th-19th century
Miyagi Prefectural Library

The *Catalogue of Birds* is a massive compilation of Edo period ornithology compiled by Hotta Masaatsu (1755-1832), who was the head of Katata in the Ōmi Domain and had a long career as an aide to the Council of Elders. This book also reproduced a large number of images copied from the illustrated catalogues of many daimyo and shogunal retainers. The depiction of the turkey seen from the front draws our attention; that image also appears in the grid pattern painting *Birds and Animals in the Flower Garden Screens* (p.344).

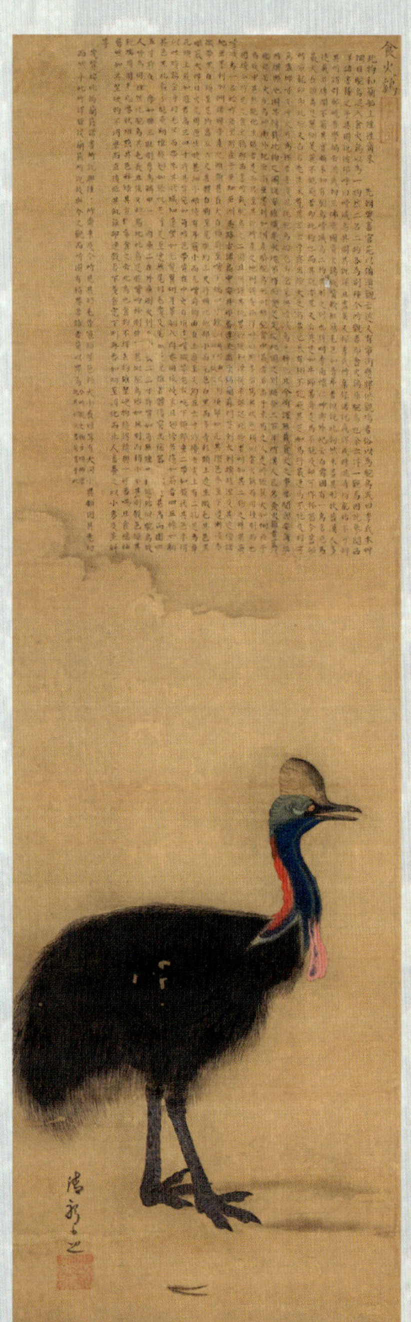
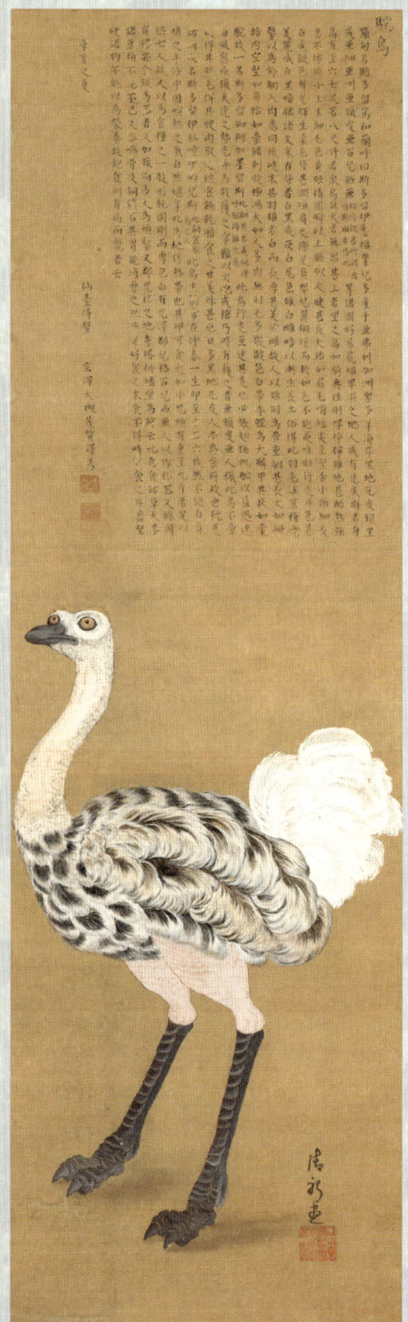
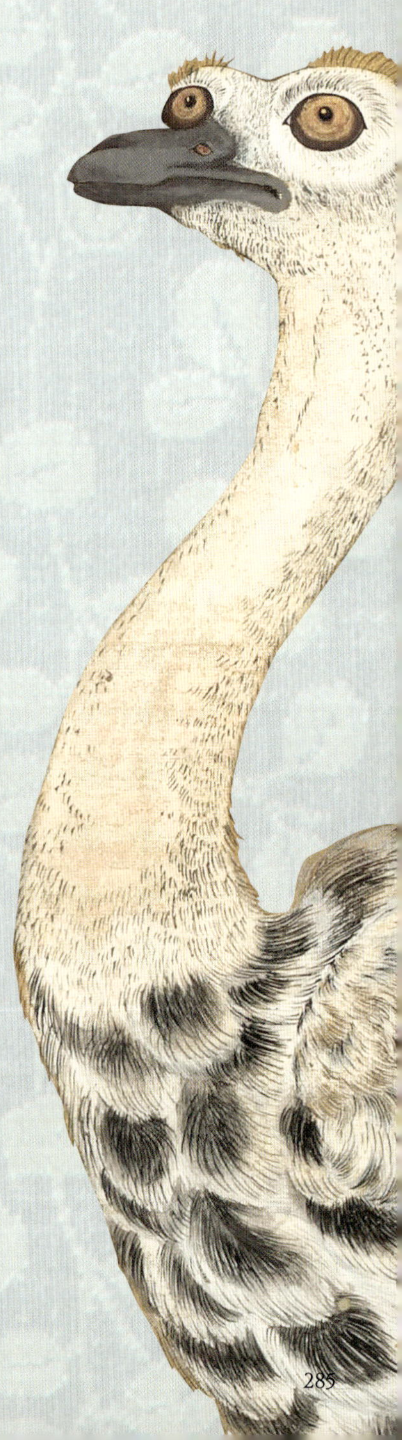

駝鳥・火喰鳥図

清躬筆、大槻玄沢賛
寛政3年（1791）
神戸市立博物館

当代随一の蘭学者であった大槻玄沢は、混同されていた駝鳥と火喰鳥との違いを本図で明確に指摘し、さらに1817年（文化14）出版の『蘭畹摘芳』に図入りで広く紹介した。

Ostrich and Cassowary

Painted by Seikyū, Inscribed by Ōtsuki Gentaku
1791
Kobe City Museum

In this image, Ōtsuki Gentaku, who was the leading scholar of Western studies at the time, clearly indicates the differences between the ostrich and cassowary (which were often mistaken for each other). Furthermore, in 1817 (Bunka 14), this image became widely introduced as an illustration in his Western studies publication *Ran'entekihō*.

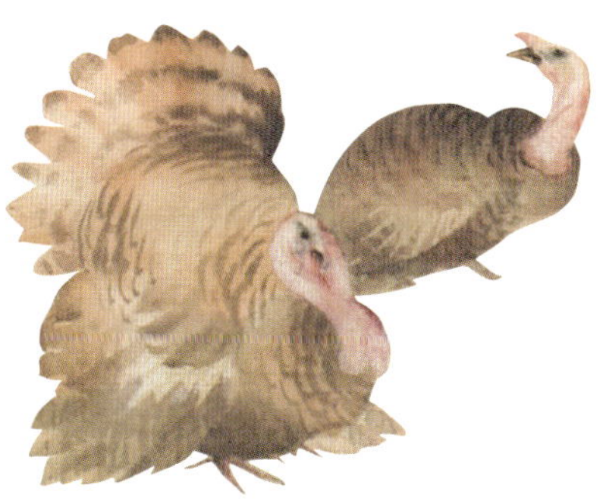

花鳥図

墨江武禅
江戸時代(18〜19c)

七面鳥をはじめとする鳥たちが水辺に憩う。一見すると洋風画のような趣があり、おそらく舶載された銅版画などに倣ったものであろう。筆者は大坂の浮世絵師で諸派も学んだ多彩な画人。西洋のタピスリーなどの質感も感じさせる異国趣味あふれる作品は、いかなる経緯で描かれたのだろうか。

Birds and Flowers

Suminoe Buzen
18th century

Various birds relax on a waterfront, most notably, a turkey. At first glance, this may seem like a Western style painting, and it was probably based off of an imported copperplate engraving. The artist was a specialist of images of the floating world in Osaka, in addition to being a versatile painter who studied various styles. I wonder how he rendered such an exotic work, that captures the feel of something like a Western tapestry.

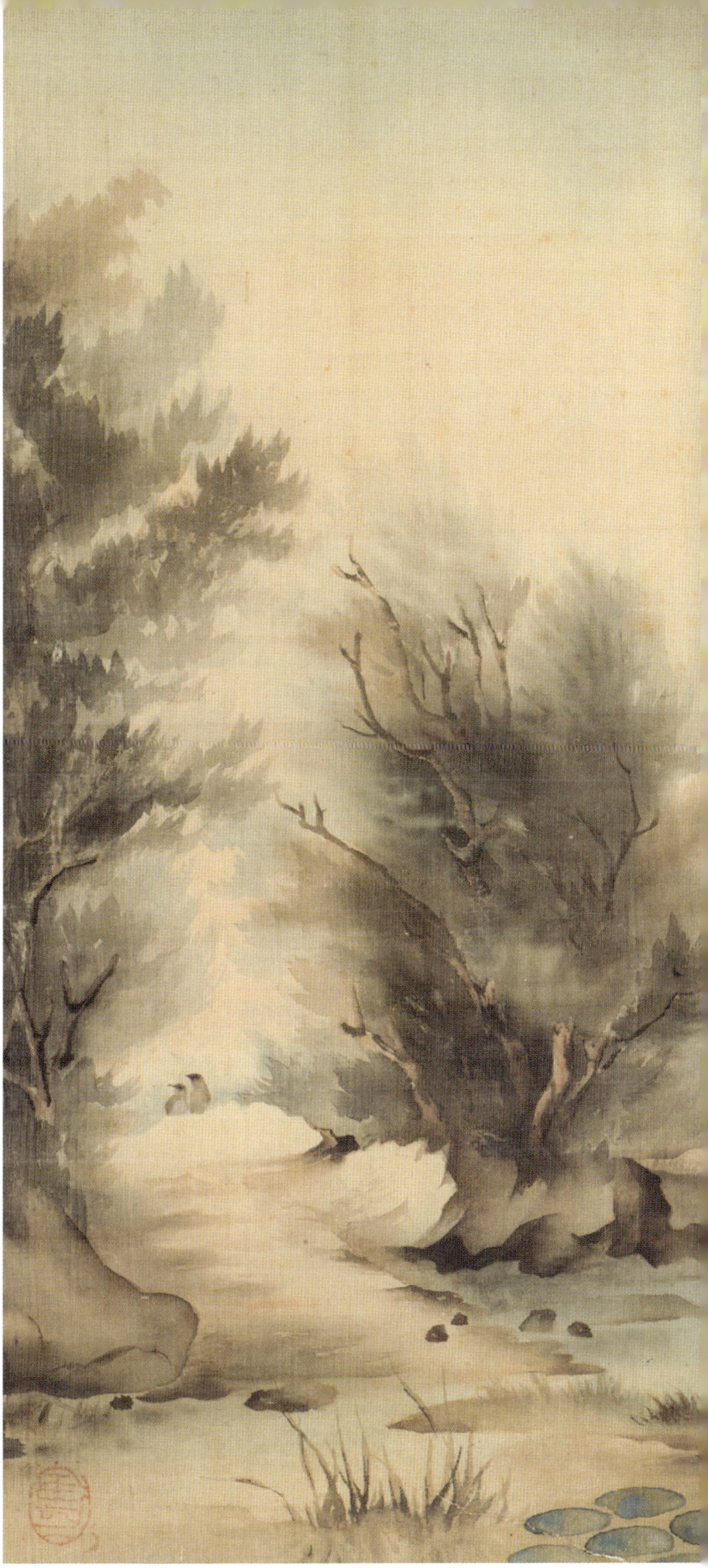

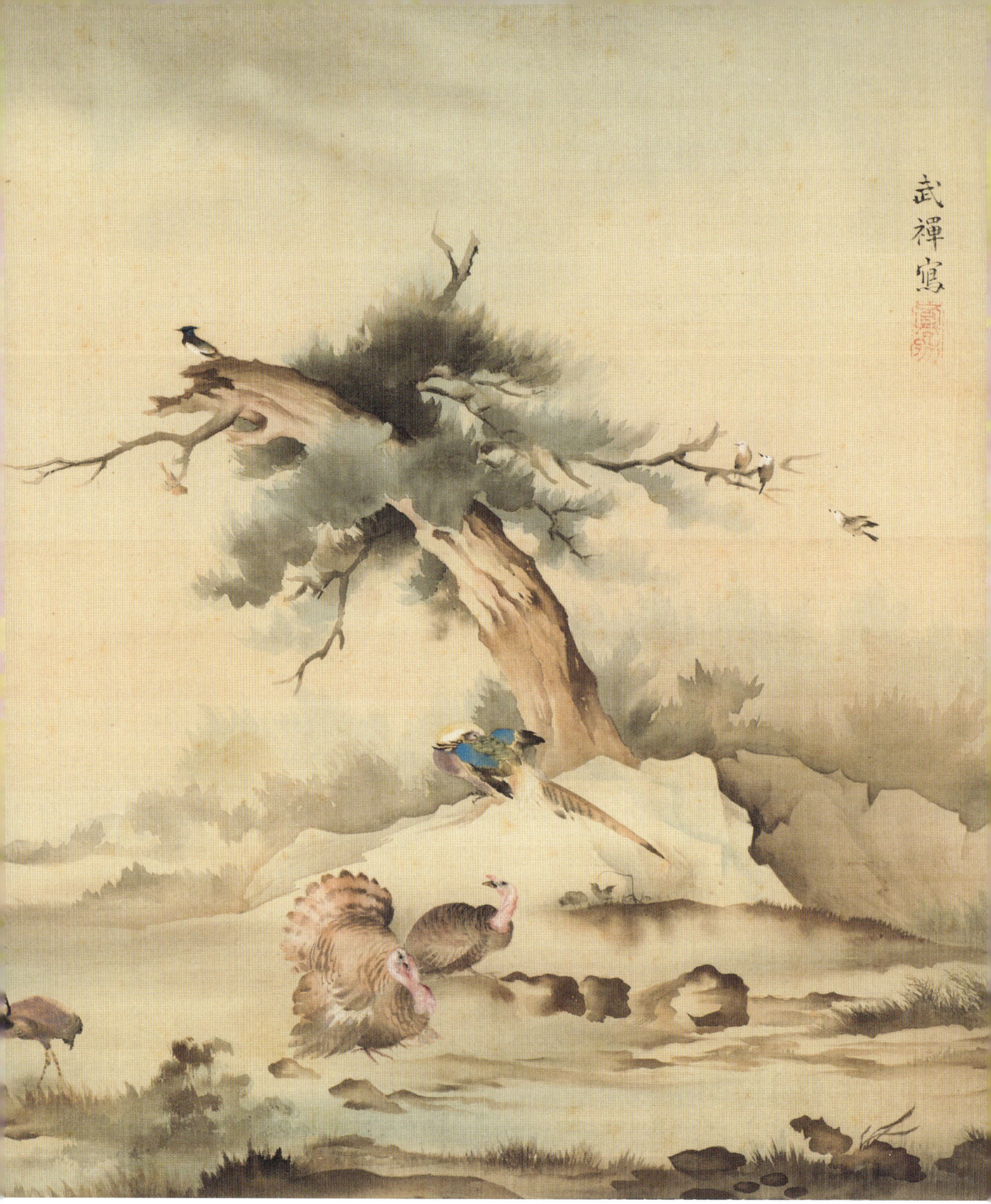

武禪寫

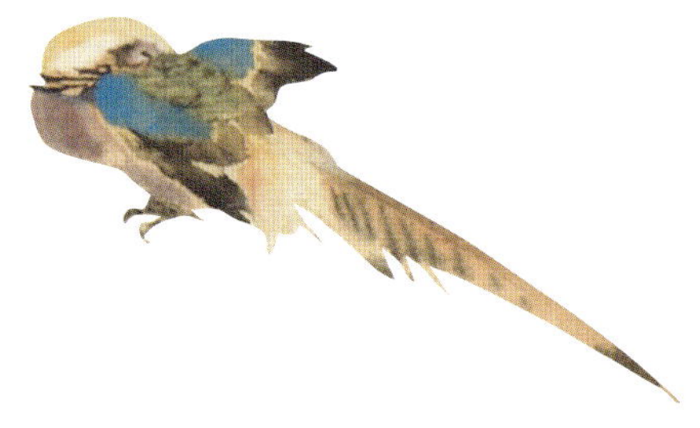

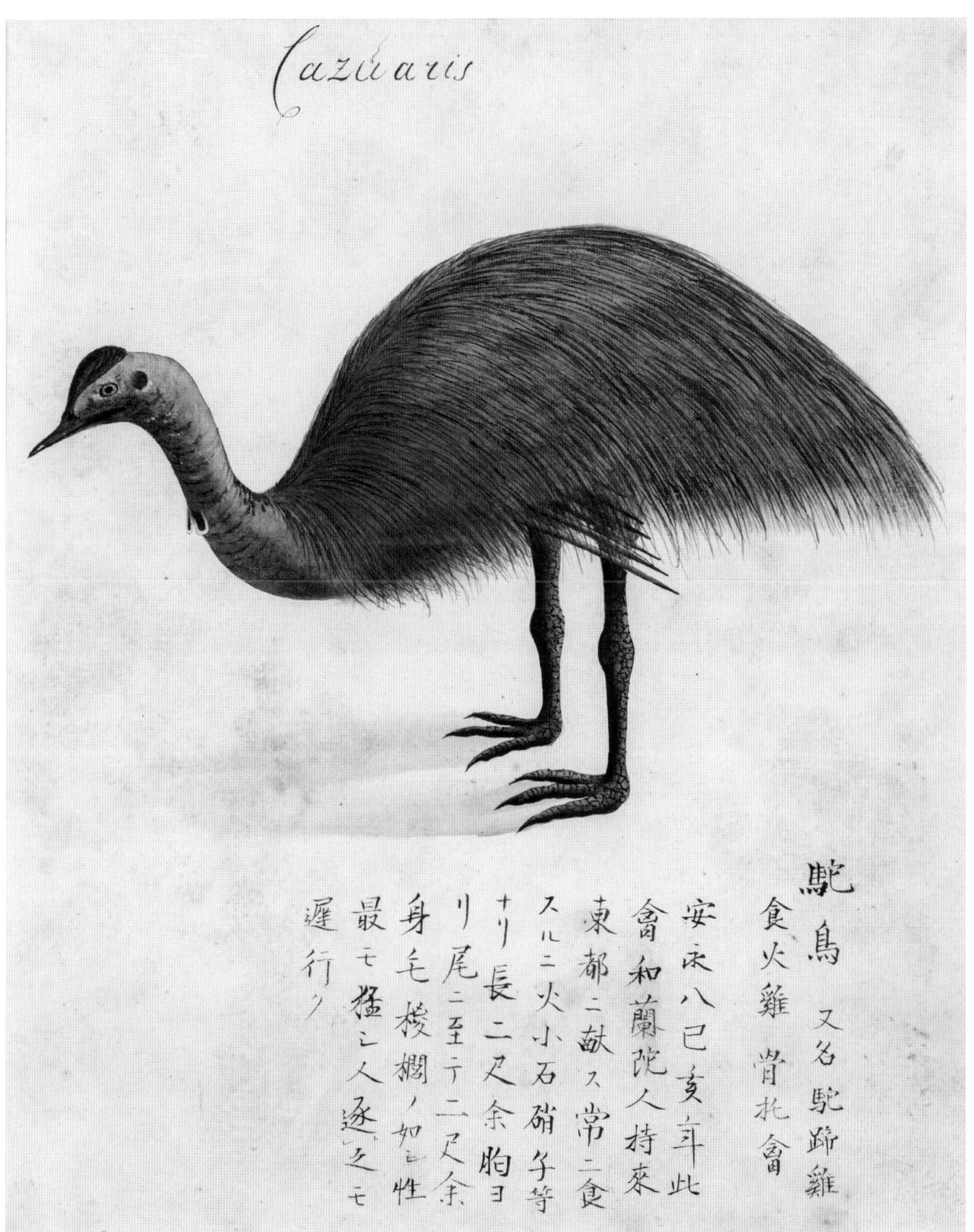

県指定文化財

火喰鳥図（『佐竹曙山写生帖』より）

安永8年(1779)頃
秋田市立千秋美術館

Prefectural Cultural Property

"Cassowary" *(from the Satake Shozan Book of Sketches)*

ca.1779
Akita Senshu Museum of Art

火喰鳥図

石川孟高
江戸時代後期（18〜19c）
帰空庵コレクション

"Cassowary"

Ishikawa Mōkō
18th-19th century
Kikū'an collection

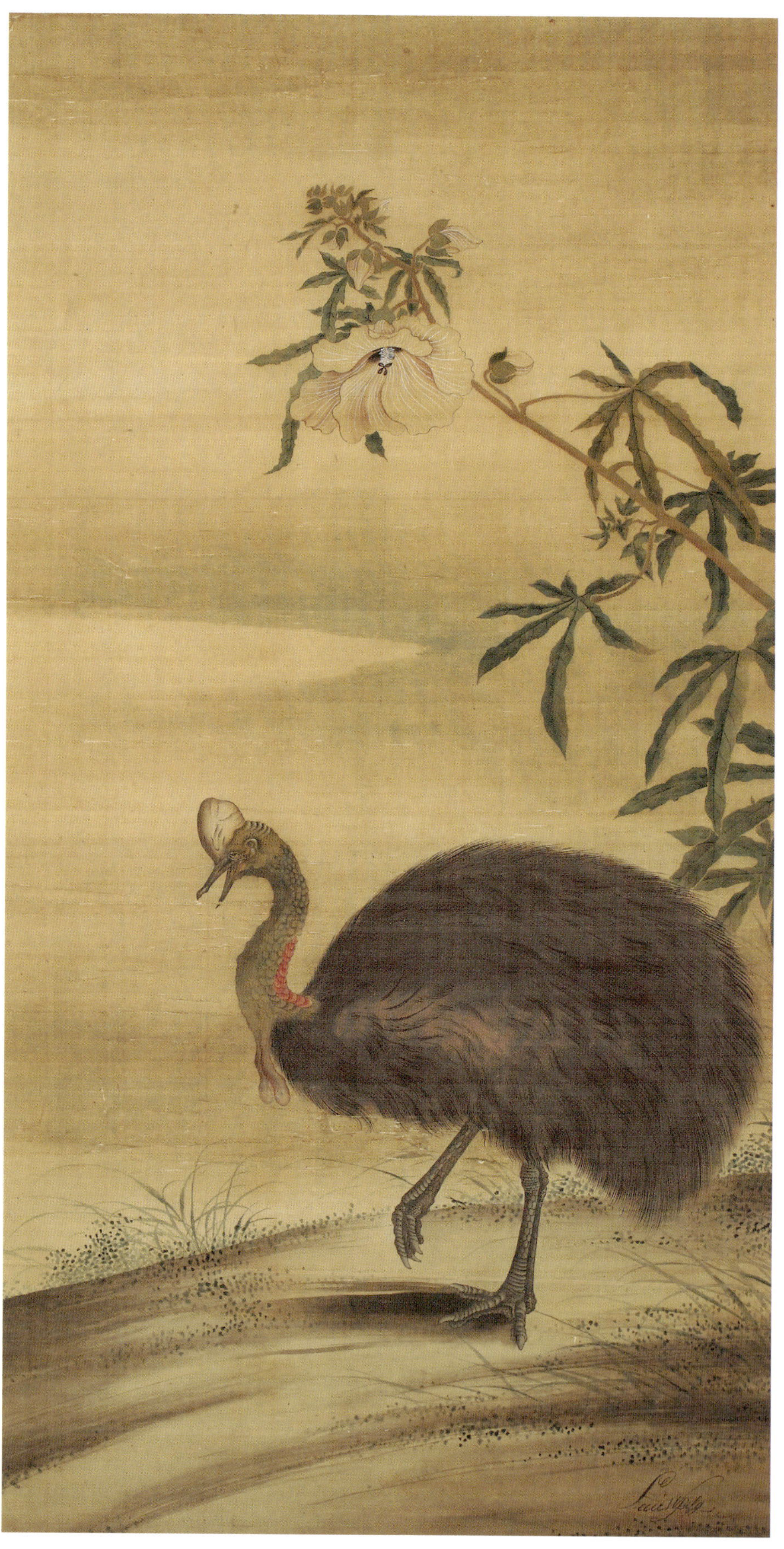

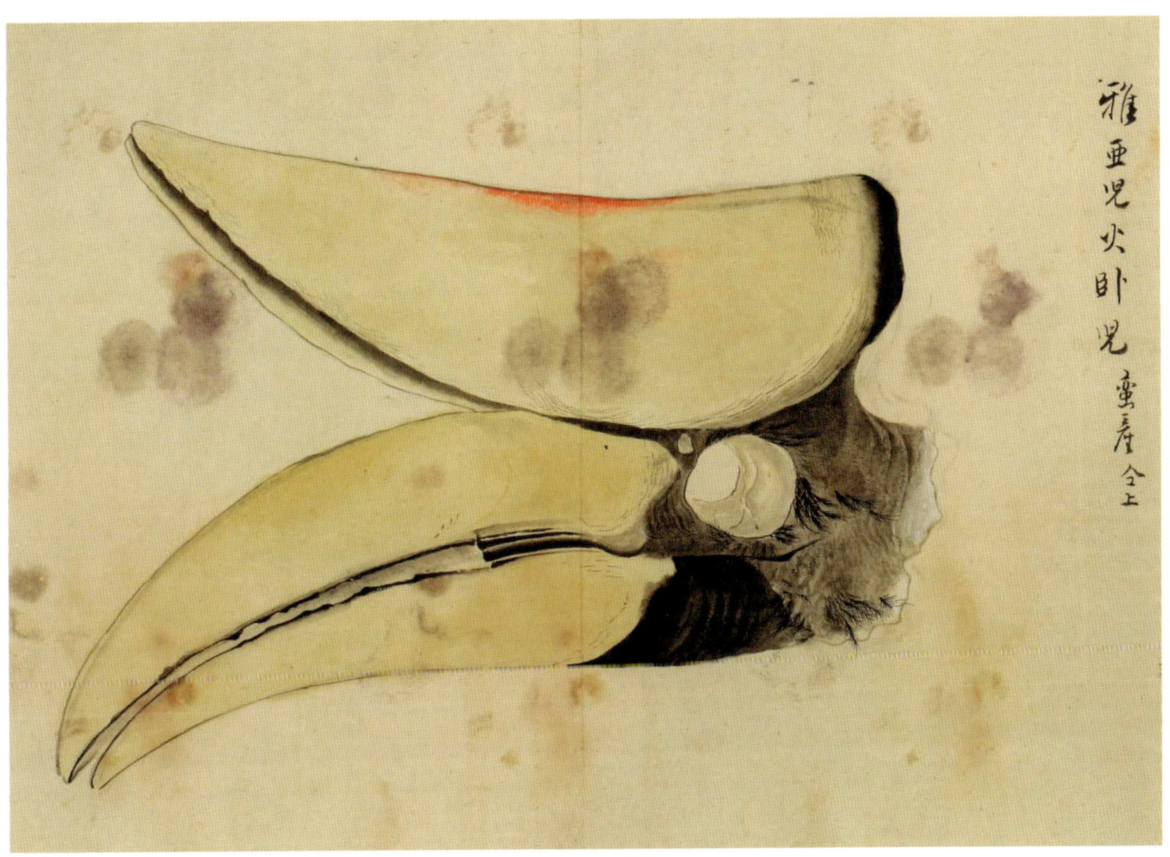

外国産動物図巻（部分）

桂川甫周
江戸時代後期（18c末〜19c初め）
早稲田大学図書館

異国の動物は、大名たちにより飼育され、また標本として保管された。とくに「蘭癖」と呼ばれた蘭学マニアの大名たちが財と手間暇とを費やして編纂した多くの写生図巻や写生帖などに、その成果が披露されている。とりわけ際だった内容を見せるのが、薩摩藩8代藩主・島津重豪（1745〜1833）所有の動物標本類を収録した「外国産動物図巻」である。薩摩藩は、琉球との交易を通じて異国の情報や文物に恵まれていたが、重豪の異国産動物に対する執心ぶりは別格で、シーボルトから直接に鳥や獣を剝製にする方法を教わったというエピソードもある。この図巻は、海亀（玳瑁）やイグアナ、フウチョウ、サイチョウの嘴、犀蹄や犀尾など重豪所有の動物を写したものだが、特にサイチョウについては生体で飼育していたことがわかっている。サイの蹄と尾も目を引くが、さらにオランウータンの剝製や豪猪も所持していたことが別の資料から判明する。薩摩藩の江戸藩邸はまさしく、私設動物園の様相を呈していたはずだ。

Foreign Animals Scroll (*detail*)

Katsuragawa Hoshū
Late 18th century–early 19th century
Waseda University Library

Foreign animals were raised by daimyo, and also kept as specimens. These results were often shown off in works like scrolls and booklets portraying animals drawn from life, especially in those compiled by the "*ranpeki*" daimyo who participated in the mania for western studies and spent considerable time and money on this hobby. One work with especially notable content is the *Foreign Animals Scroll*, a compilation of specimens of various animals, which was reportedly in the collection of Shimazu Shigehide (1745-1833), the eighth ruler of the Satsuma Domain, and an avid natural history enthusiast. The animals Shigehide owned are depicted in this scroll, and they include a sea turtle, a hawksbill turtle, a monitor lizard, an iguana, the bills of a bird-of-paradise and rhinoceros hornbill, and a rhinoceros hoof and tail, but we can understand that the rhinoceros hornbill in particular was taken care of while it was still alive. We can confirm from separate documents that Shigehide also owned a taxidermy orangutan and taxidermy porcupine. The Edo residence of the Satsuma Domain probably looked just like a private zoo.

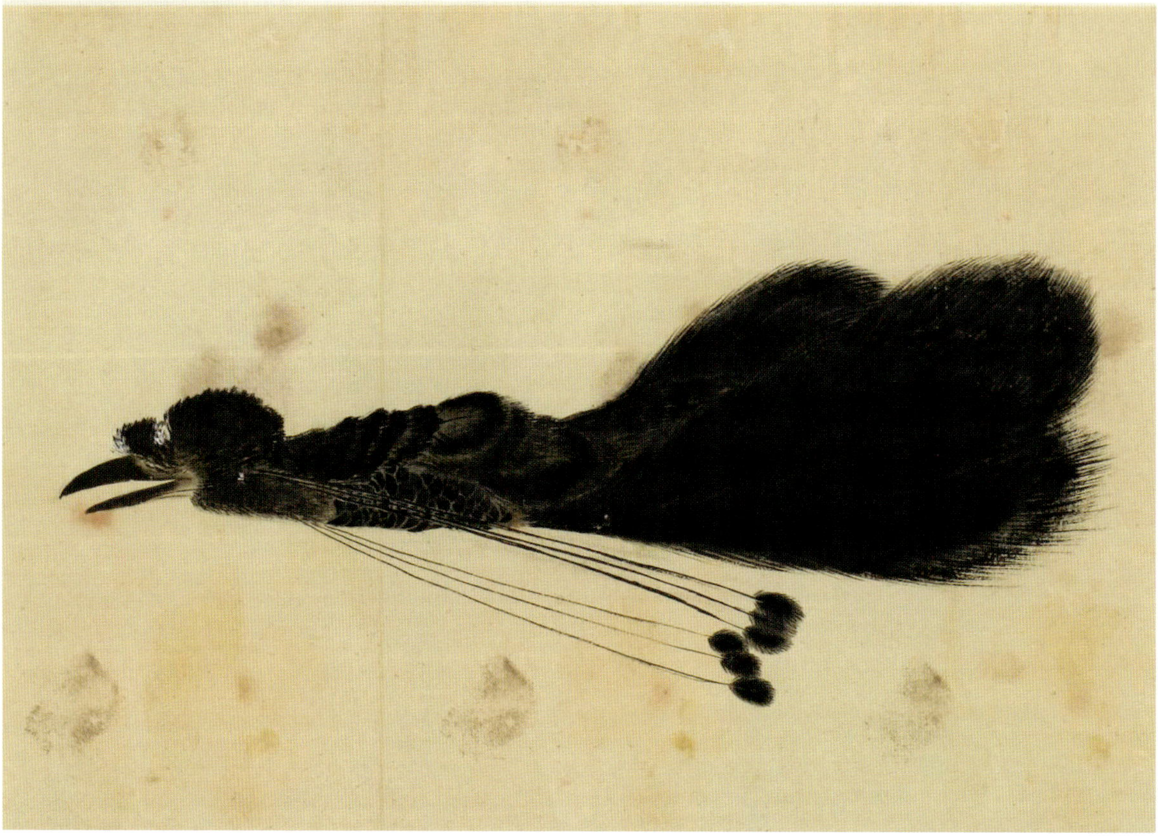

大頭鳥の觜
（松平信綱寄進の宝物のうち）

万治元年（1658）奉納
埼玉・三芳野神社

「知恵伊豆」と呼ばれ江戸幕府の老中として辣腕をふるった松平信綱（1596～1662）が島原の乱で島原半島に赴いた際、当地から持ち帰ったものと伝える。箱裏書から、これらは1658年（万治元）に信綱自身により三芳野神社に奉納されたことがわかる。南洋の貝殻や化石らしきものに交じって、「鳳凰・比翼の鳥」の羽毛や「大頭鳥の嘴」なども含まれる。とくに後者は、サイチョウの嘴であり、宝物として扱われてきたことが興味深い。

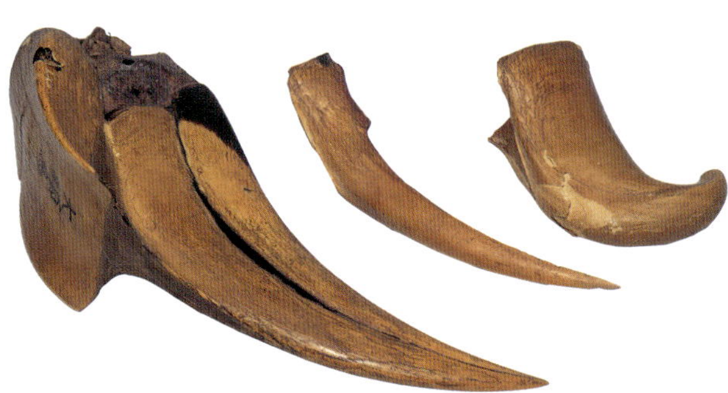

“Beak from a Large-headed Bird,”
(from the Treasures Donated by Matsudaira Nobutsuna)

Offered in 1658
Miyoshino shrine, Saitama

Matsudaira Nobutsuna (1596-1662), known as “Izu the Wise,” was a shrewd member of the Shogun’s council of elders, and it is said that when he went to the Shimabara Peninsula during the Shimabara Rebellion, he brought this back with him. From the note on the box, we can understand that this was donated to Miyoshino Shrine by Nobutsuna himself in 1658 (Manji 1). Mixed in with the seashells and fossils from the south seas, were also items like the feathers from a “A Mated Pair of Phoenixes” and “Beak from a Large-headed Bird.” Regarding the latter, it is the beak of a rhinoceros hornbill, and it is interesting that this was regarded as a treasure.

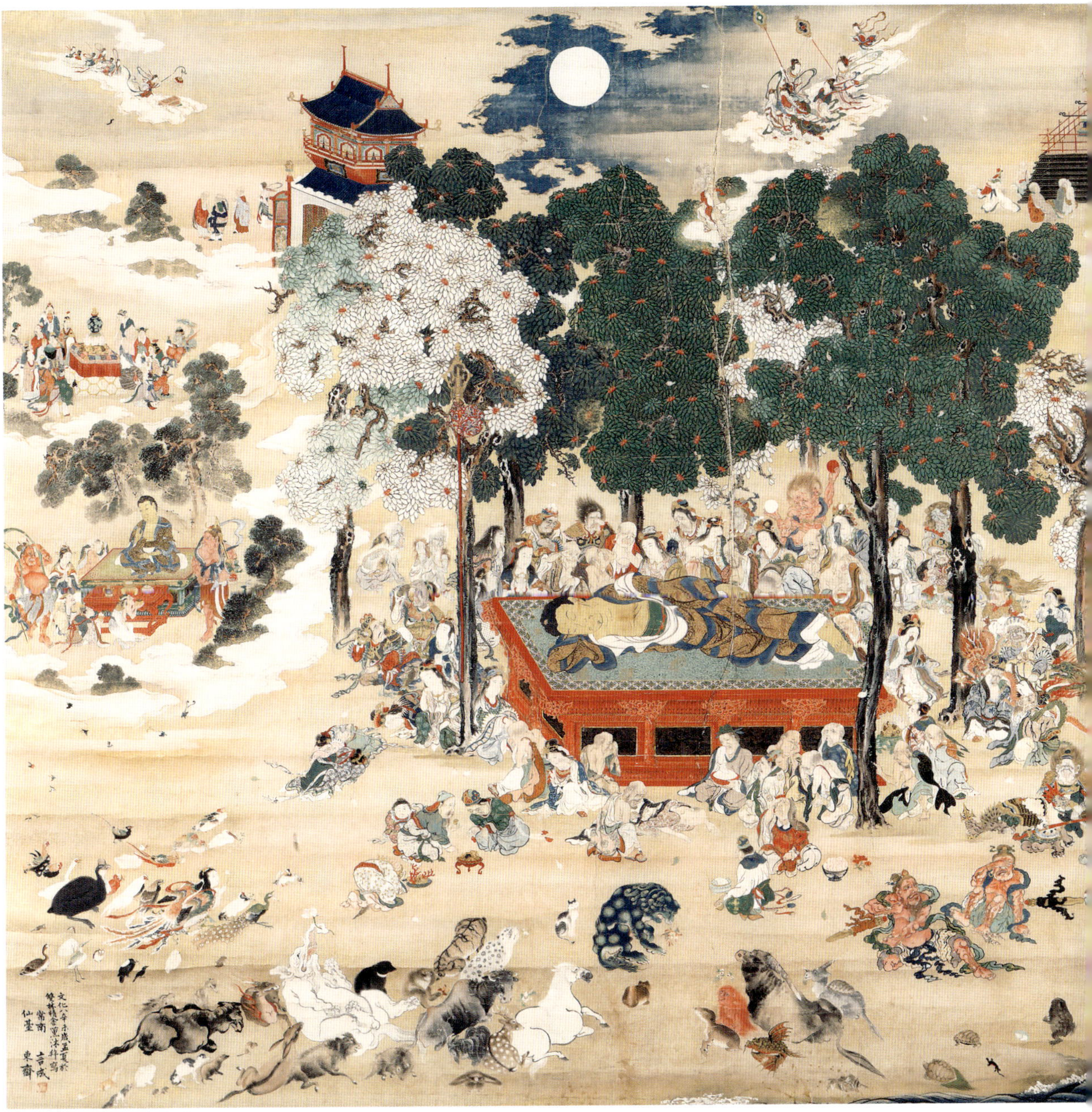

八相涅槃図

根元常南・菅井梅関
文化8年（1811）
群馬・雙林寺

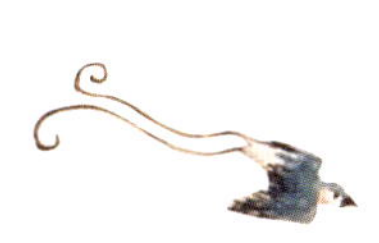

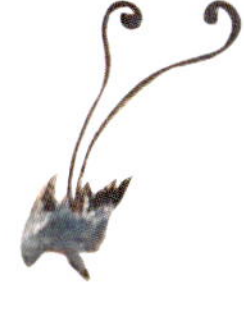

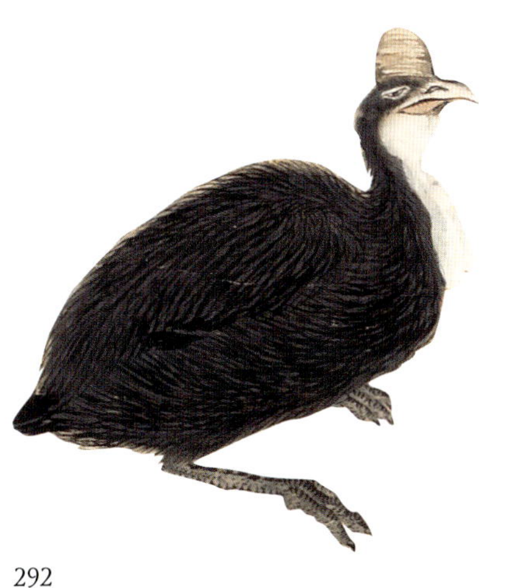

涅槃前後に起こった7つの出来事を画面の左右に加えた形式の涅槃図。28歳の菅井梅関（1784～1844）が、師であった病身の根元常南（1763～1811）に助力して完成させた大幅である。釈迦や衆生などの人物群像を常南が、動物群を梅関が手がけたものであろう。通例見るような動物に加えて、アシカや洋犬、さらには火喰鳥・鸚鵡・インコなど異国の鳥たちが描かれるのが特徴である。そして、空中を舞っているのはフウチョウ。この鳥は当時、脚のない状態で舶載されたため、常に飛んでいて地上に降りることがないと信じられていたのである。

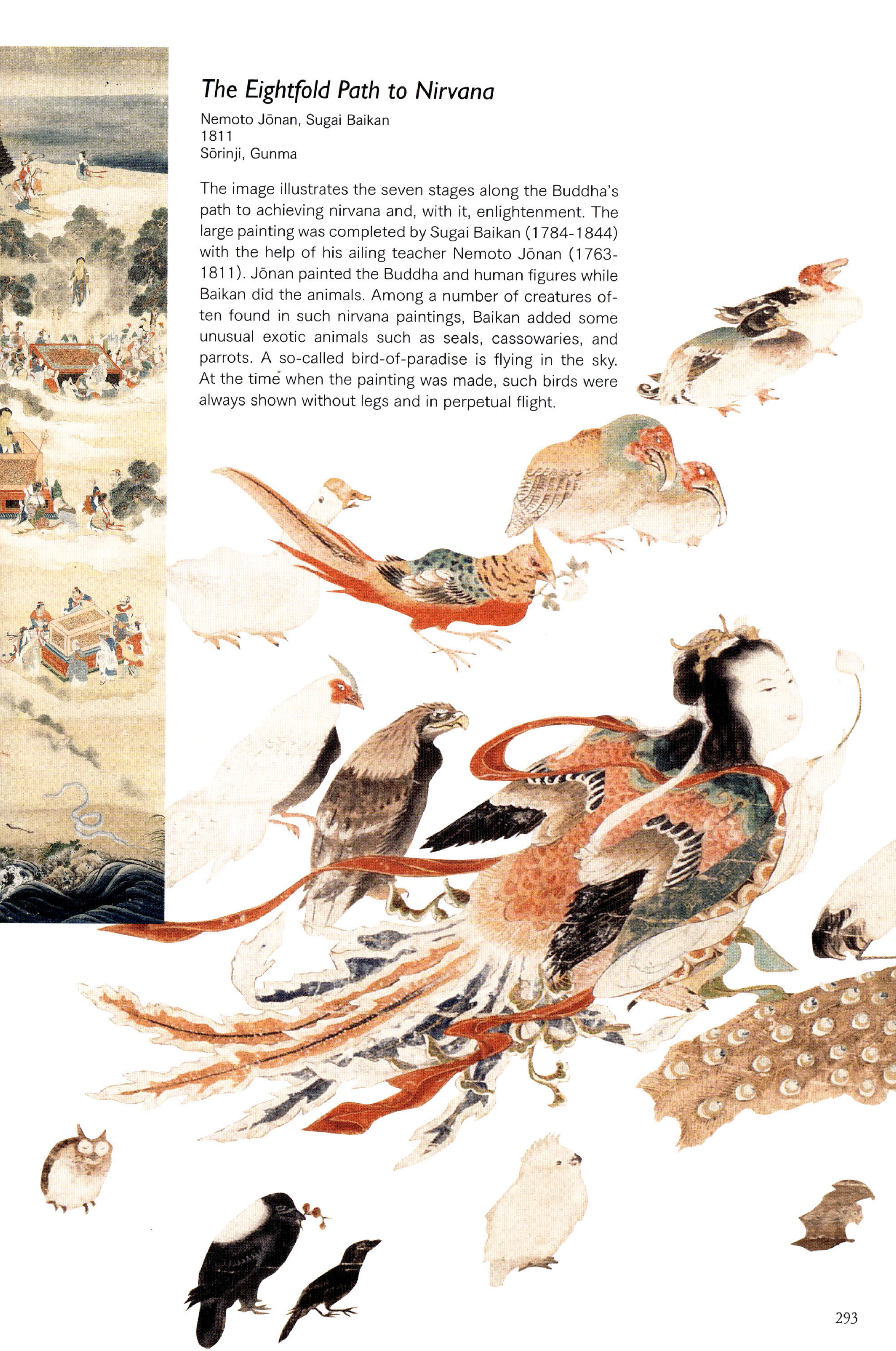

The Eightfold Path to Nirvana

Nemoto Jōnan, Sugai Baikan
1811
Sōrinji, Gunma

The image illustrates the seven stages along the Buddha's path to achieving nirvana and, with it, enlightenment. The large painting was completed by Sugai Baikan (1784-1844) with the help of his ailing teacher Nemoto Jōnan (1763-1811). Jōnan painted the Buddha and human figures while Baikan did the animals. Among a number of creatures often found in such nirvana paintings, Baikan added some unusual exotic animals such as seals, cassowaries, and parrots. A so-called bird-of-paradise is flying in the sky. At the time when the painting was made, such birds were always shown without legs and in perpetual flight.

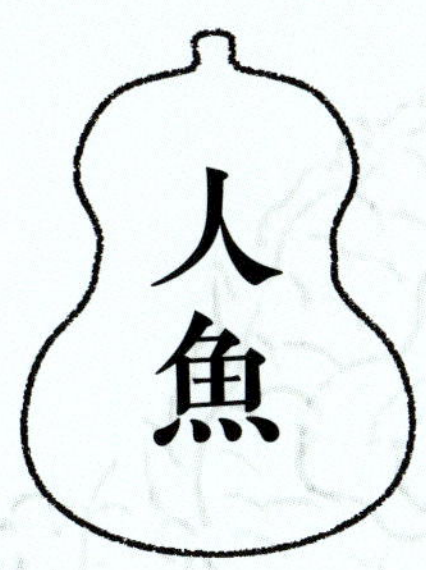

その肉を食えば800歳の長寿を約束されるという人魚。古くはオオサンショウウオなどを人魚とみなした時期もあったようだが、とくに北陸から東北地方にかけての日本海側に多くの目撃情報が寄せられてきた。八郎潟近くの遺跡からは、人面と手足を持った人魚が供養する僧とともに描かれた13世紀後半頃の杉板が出土している。時代は下って18世紀後半、男鹿や津軽地方での見聞記録が『六物新志』（1786年刊）に紹介されている。

The Mermaid

This is a mermaid, and according to legend, you will live a long life of eight hundred years if you eat its flesh. It seems that there was a time long ago when people regarded creatures like the Japanese giant salamander as mermaids, but there were many eyewitness reports, especially on the seaward side of Japan from the Hokuriku to the Tōhoku region. Excavated from the ruins near Hachirō Lagoon, along with monks that held memorials for mermaids that had human faces, hands and feet, were portrayals on cedar doors from the late thirteenth century. Moving forward in time to the late eighteenth century, information records from Oga and the Tsugaru region, were introduced in the *Rokubutsu shinshi* (published 1786).

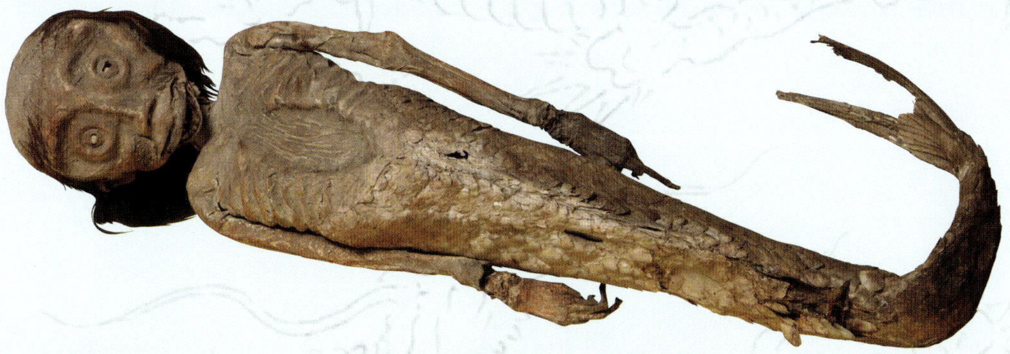

人魚のミイラ

江戸時代後期（19c）
大阪・瑞龍寺

人魚の見世物について、名古屋の小寺玉晁は1819年（文政2）のこととして『見世物雑志』に次のように記している。「人魚の作り物をミする。よき細工也。店先にて人魚の図を拾弐文づつニて売、是を木戸銭とす。」。見世物用のミイラは中国広東地方で製作されたというが、国産化もされていたことが喜多村筠庭（1783～1856）の随筆『きゝのまにまに』の記述からも確認できる。それによれば、宇禰次という細工人が浅草奥山に出した5尺ほどの人魚の見世物は、獣の皮や魚の皮をつなぎ合わせて作ったものだった、というのである。大阪の瑞龍寺をはじめ各地に伝来したものは、往時の人気ぶりを伝える貴重なもの。

Mermaid Mummy

19th century
Zuiryūji, Osaka

Kodera Gyokuchō from Nagoya wrote the following in *Misemono zasshi* about a public showing of a mermaid in 1819 (Bunsei 2): “I saw an artificial mermaid. It was very well-made. At the storefront, they were selling mermaid pictures for twenty-two *mon* apiece, which also served as the admission fee.” The mummy used for the exhibition was supposedly manufactured in the Guangdong region of China, but we can also confirm from the records in *Kikinomanimani*, a set of essays by Kitamura Intei (1783-1856), that they had also started to be produced in Japan as well. According to that source, there was an exhibition held on Asakusa Okuyama of a mermaid five *shaku* (about 150 cm) long made by a craftsman named Uneriji, and he had been manufactured it by connecting the skin of an animal with the skin of a fish. The mermaid mummy toured all over, most notably to Zuiryūji in Osaka, and it is a precious artifact that tells us about how popular it was back then.

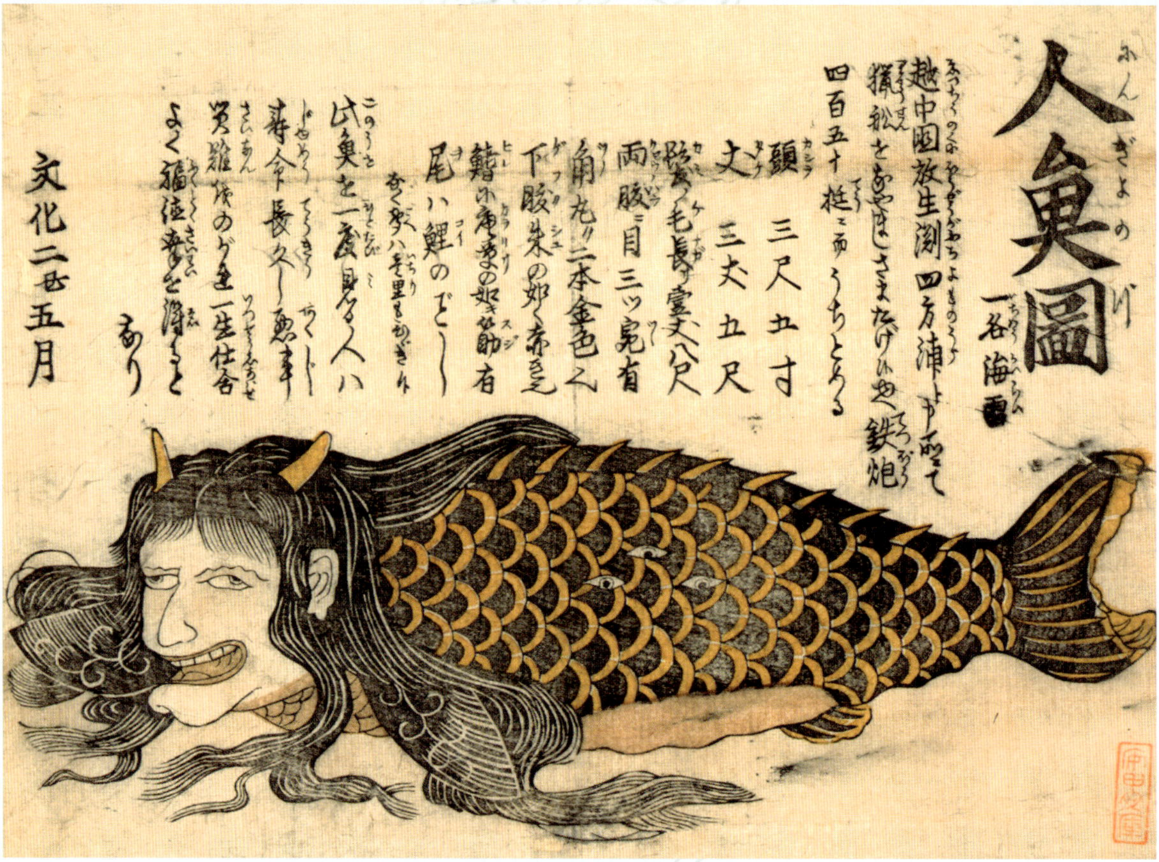

瓦版 人魚図

文化2年（1805）
早稲田大学演劇博物館

1805年（文化2）越中国放生渕（富山湾内）で捕獲された人魚の刷物。「此魚を一度見る人ハ、寿命長久し悪事災難をのがれ、一生仕合よく福徳幸を得るとなり」といった効能が記されている。今ではこの人魚を、紐体類（ちゅうたいるい）に属する深海魚リュウグウノツカイに比定する説が有力視されている。

Broadside Picture of a Mermaid

1805
The Tsubouchi Memorial Theatre Museum,
Waseda University

This is a print of a mermaid that was captured in Hōjōgafuchi, Etchū Province (in Toyama Bay) in 1805 (Bunka 2). It records the following benefits: "people who look at this fish even once will live for a very long time; they will be spared from calamity and misfortune and will receive happiness and good fortune for their entire lives." Currently, there is a very likely theory that hypothesizes that this mermaid was a deep sea giant oarfish, which belongs to the class of ribbon-bodied fish.

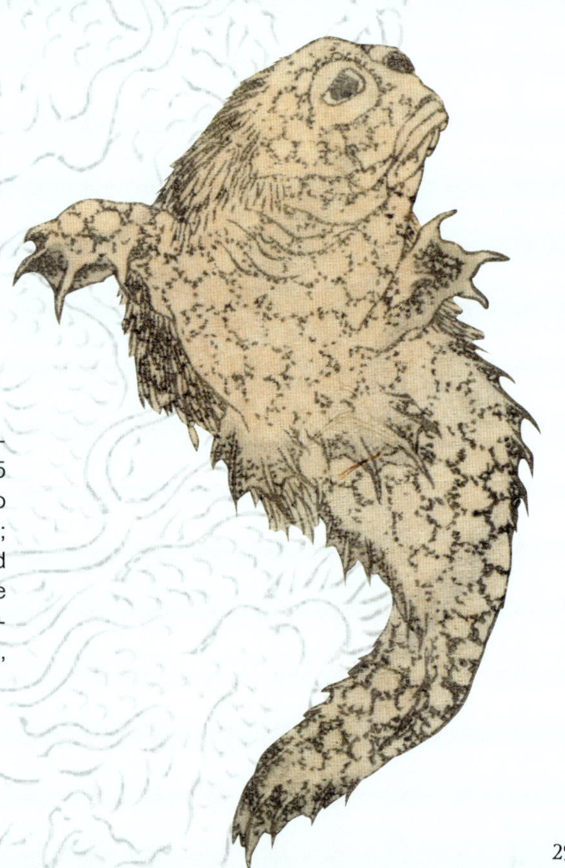

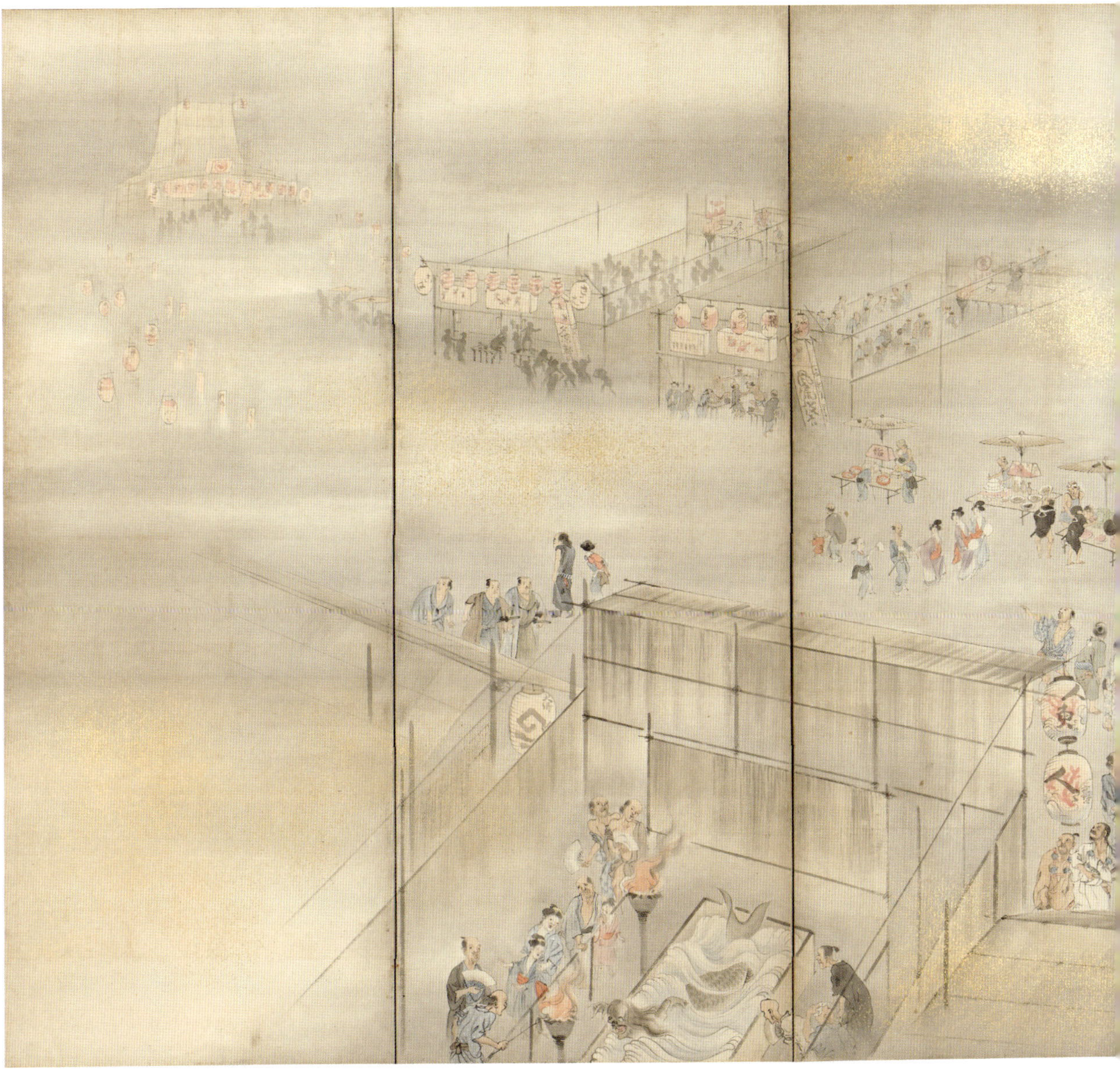

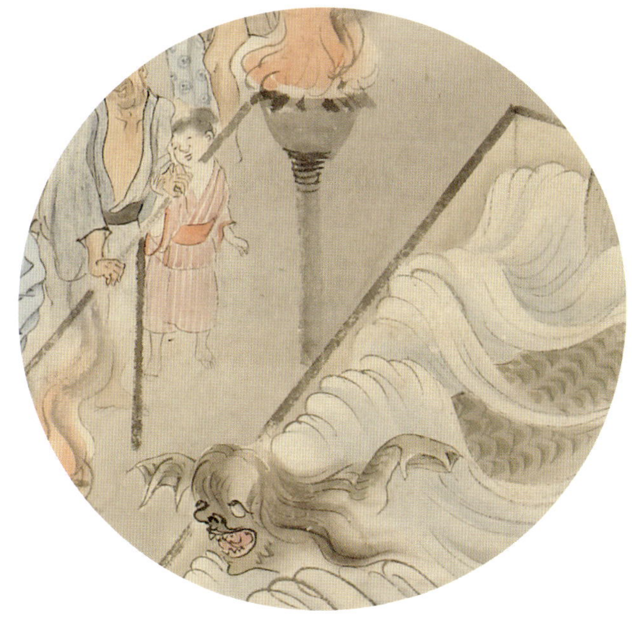

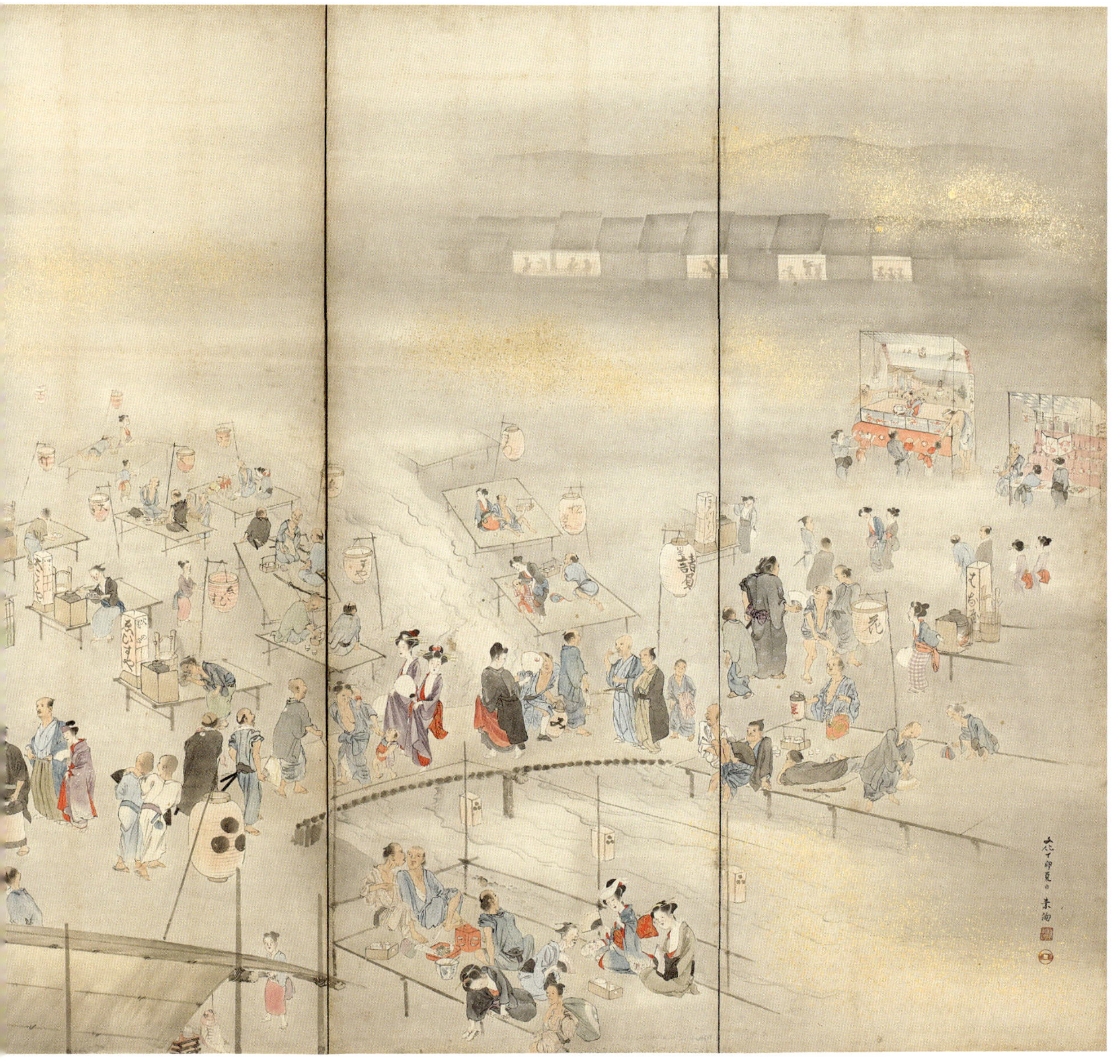

四条河原夕涼図屏風

山口素絢
文化4年（1807）

人魚は見世物としても人気を博したらしく、応挙門人の山口素絢（1759～1818）は本図に水槽の中で泳ぐ人魚の姿を描きとめている。下半身着ぐるみのパフォーマンスだったろうか。

The Cool of the Evening at Shijō Kawara Screen

Yamaguchi Soken
1807

It seems that the mermaid achieved great popularity as a public spectacle, and Yamaguchi Soken (1759-1818), a student of Ōkyo, records the sight of a mermaid swimming in a fish tank in this image. It was probably a performance with someone wearing a costume over the lower half of their body.

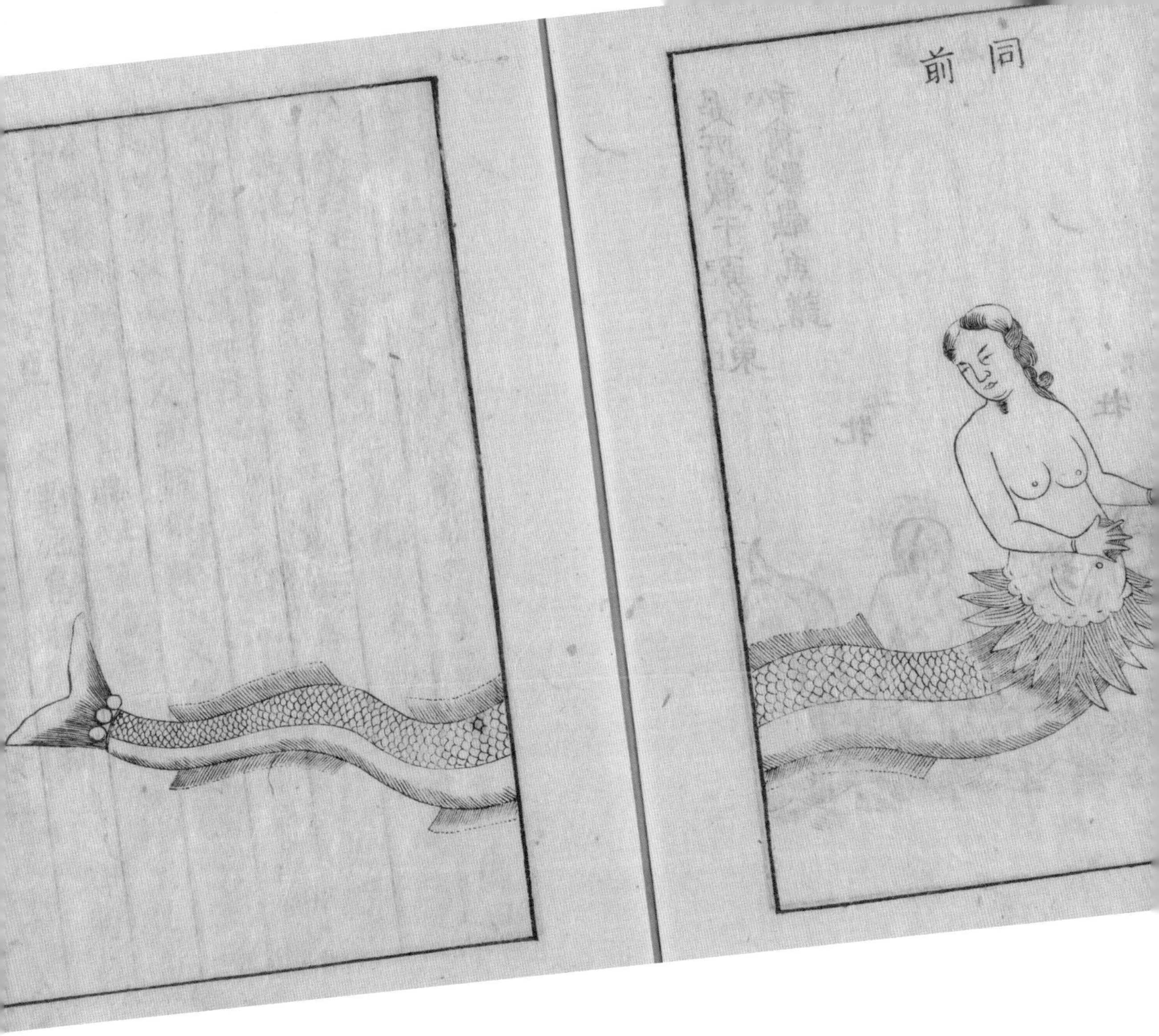

『六物新志』

大槻玄沢著
天明6年(1786)
国立国会図書館

多くの蘭書を駆使して本書を編んだのは大槻玄沢だが、知の最前線にいた当代一流の蘭学者でさえ人魚の実在を信じ、その肉や骨を霊薬であると報告していた。

Rokubutsu shinshi

Ōtsuki Gentaku
1786
National Diet Library, Japan

Ōtsuki Gentaku was the editor for this book, which drew from many Western sources, but even scholars of Western studies, who were on the frontline of knowledge that was the most advanced for its time, believed in the existence of mermaids, and this book reported that a mermaid's flesh and bones were miracle cures.

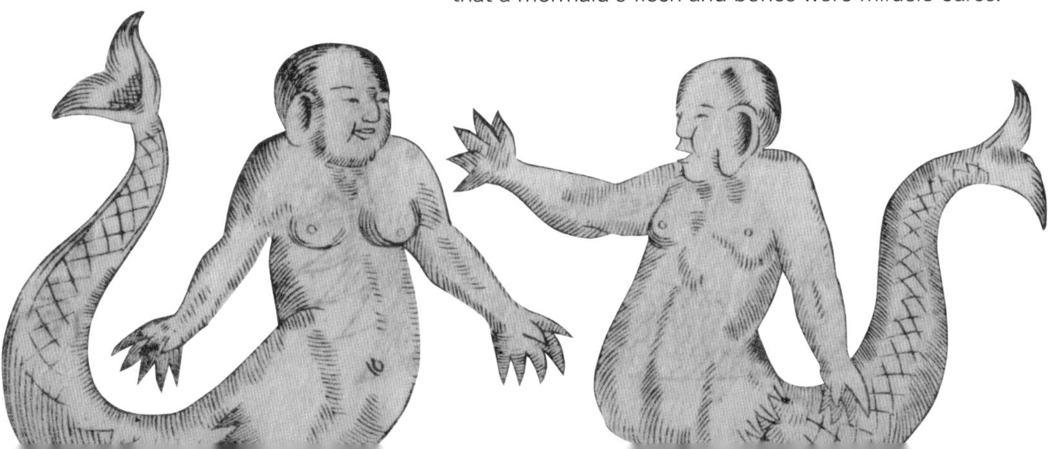

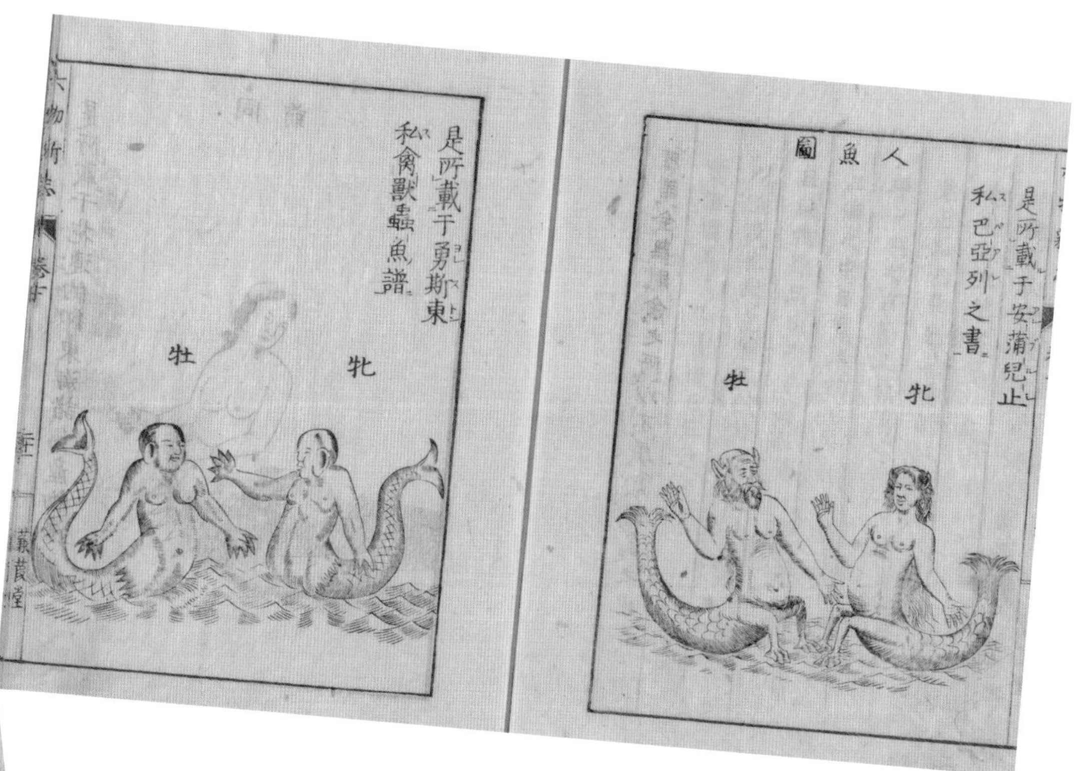

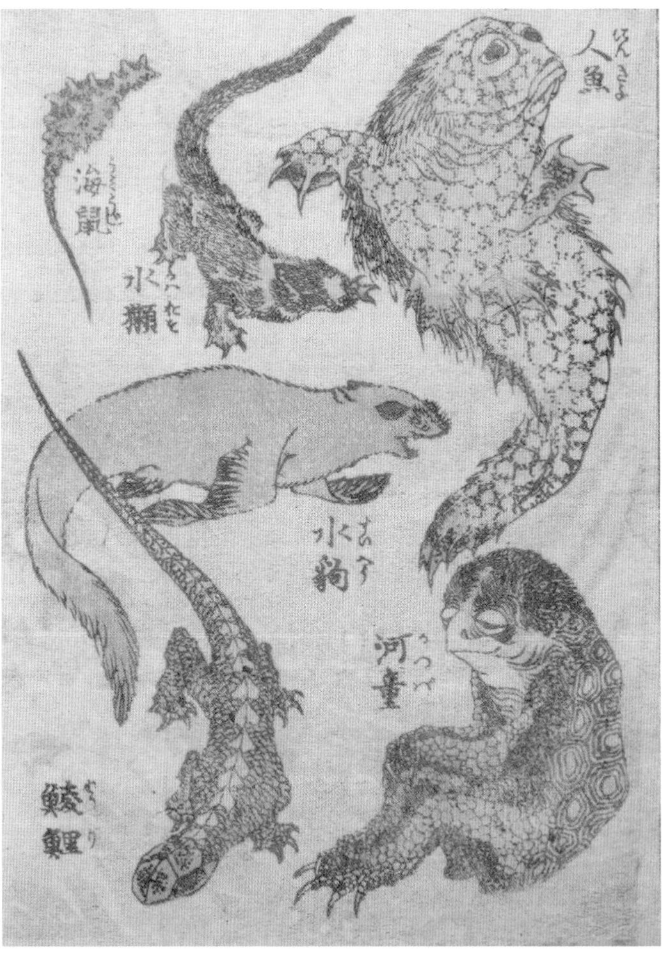

人魚図
（『北斎漫画』三編より）

葛飾北斎
天保5年(1834)頃
メトロポリタン美術館

Mermaid
(from Random Sketches by Hokusai Vol.3)

Katsushika Hokusai
ca. 1834
The Metropolitan Museum of Art

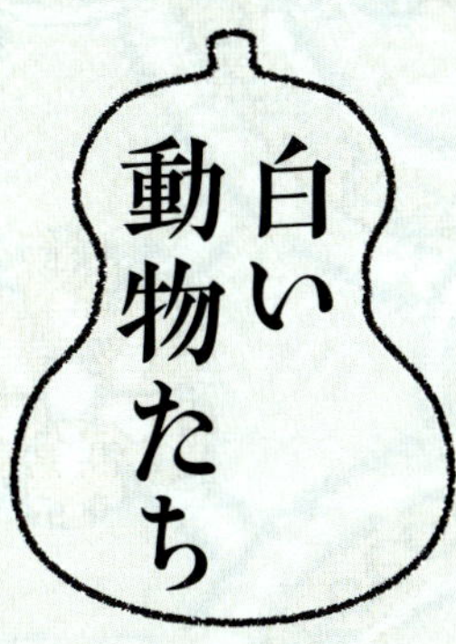

白い動物たちは古来「祥瑞」として改元を促すほどの吉兆であり、これまでの各テーマにおいてもしばしば登場してきた。それらを尊崇する心情は江戸時代になっても、根強く残っていたようで、多くの作例を見い出すことができる。

The White Animals

From time immemorial, white animals were viewed as auspicious omens that could even prompt a change of era. Even in the Edo period, it seems that the feeling of veneration for these animals was still firmly rooted in the public consciousness.

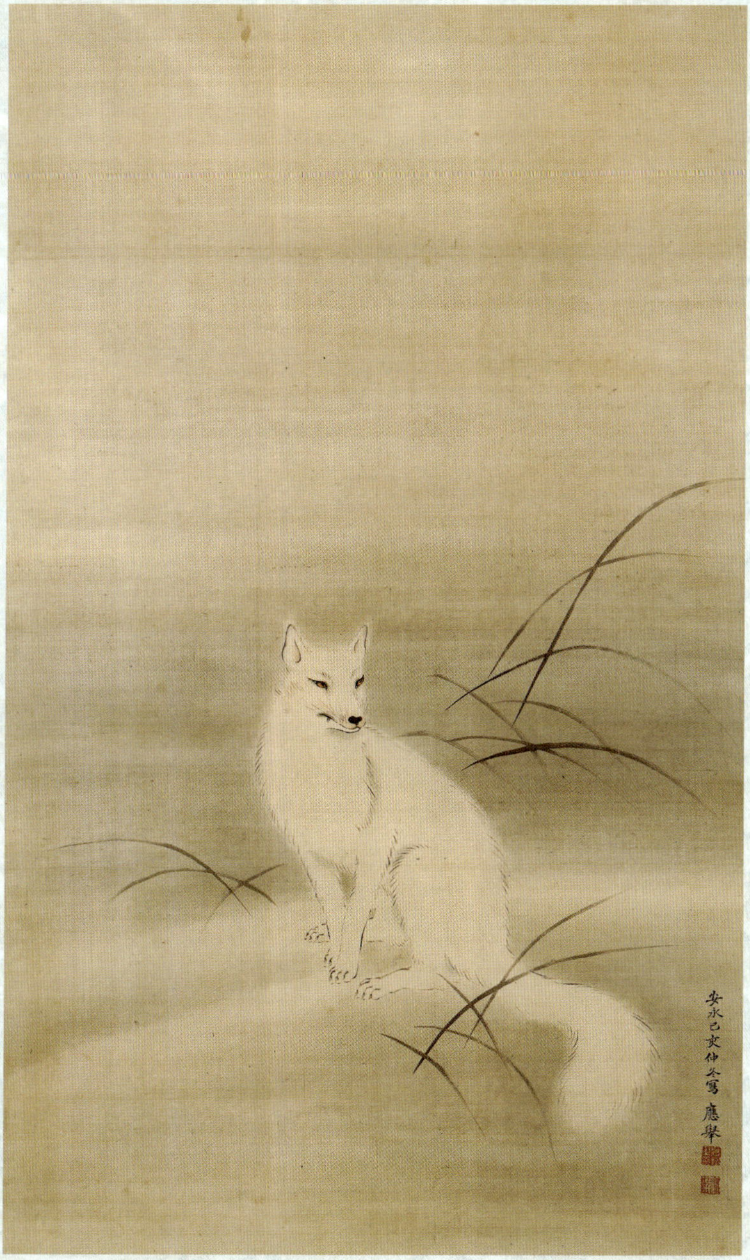

白狐図
円山応挙
安永8年(1779)

White Fox
Maruyama Ōkyo
1779

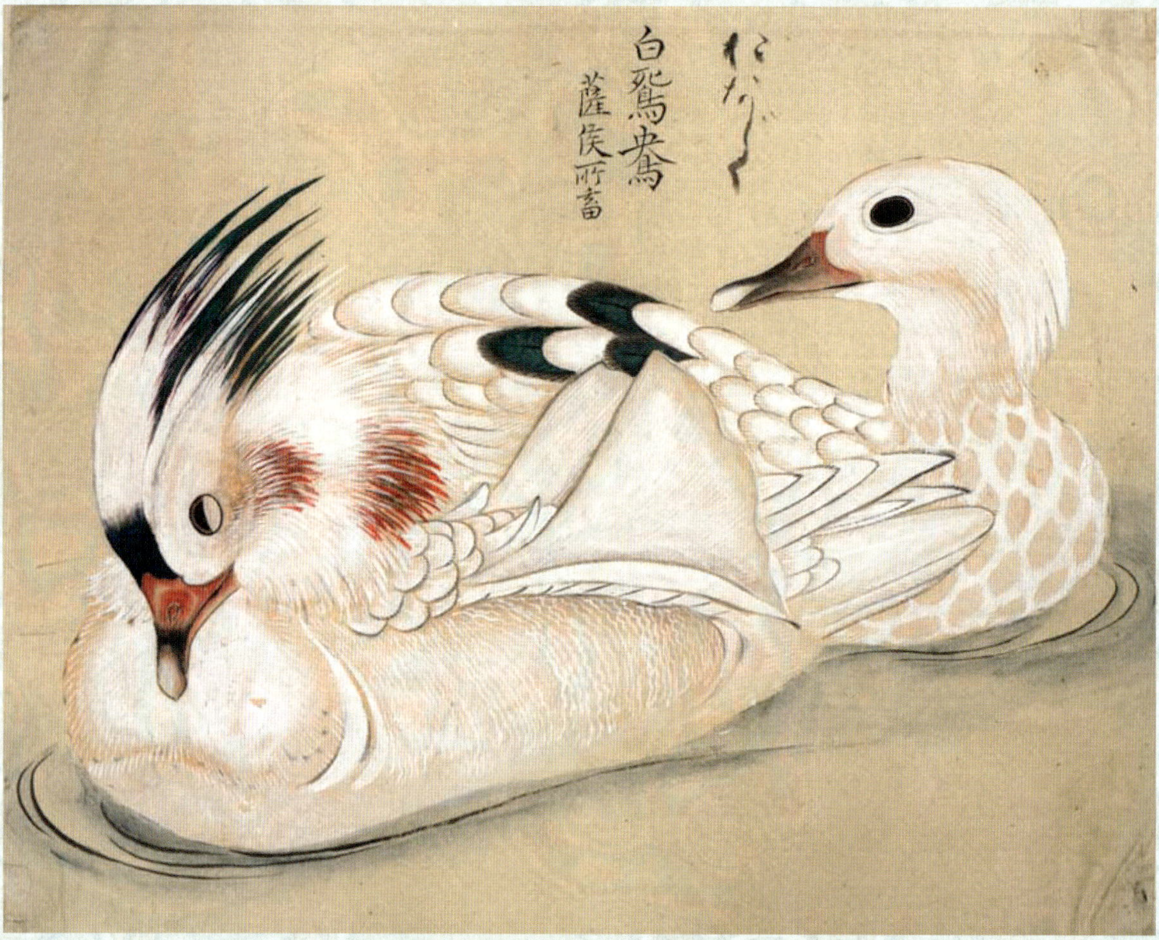

白鴛鴦(『禽譜』より)

堀田正敦 編
江戸時代後期(18〜19c)
東京国立博物館

蘭癖大名の島津重豪が飼育していた白鴛鴦。鴛鴦は婚姻の象徴でもあったが、白い個体はなおさら祝祭の意味合いが強かったであろう。

"White Mandarin Duck"

(from The Catalogue of Birds)

Edited by Hotta Masa'atsu
18th-19th century
Tokyo National Museum

This is a white mandarin duck that was raised by Shimazu Shigehide, a daimyo obsessed with all things Western. Mandarin ducks were also a symbol of marriage, but a white one likely had an even deeper nuance of celebration.

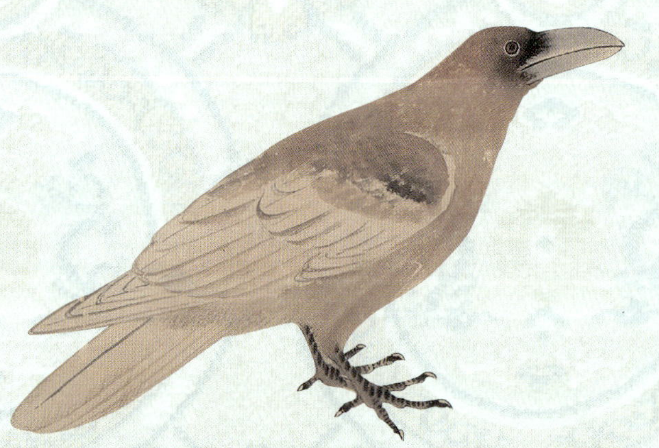

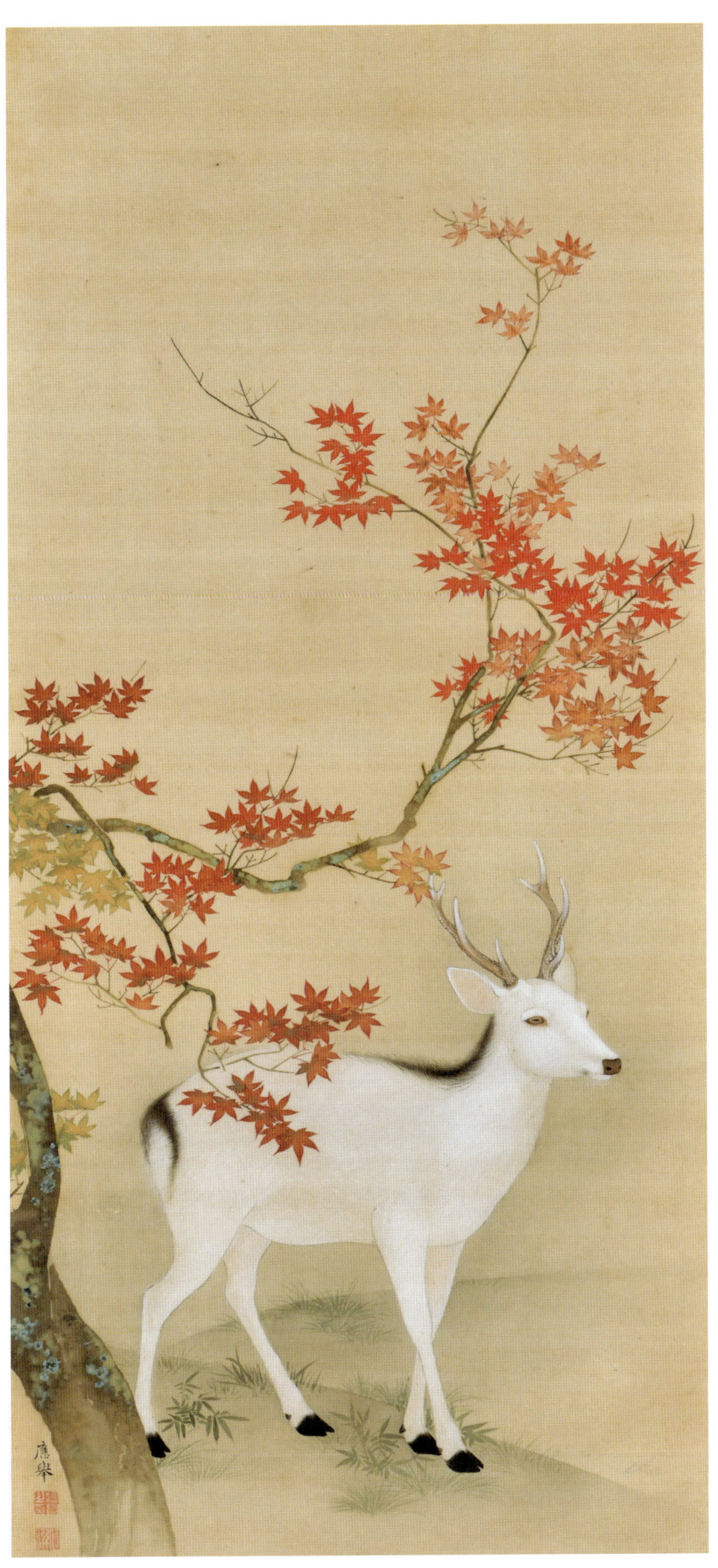

紅葉白鹿図

円山応挙
江戸時代(18c)
敦賀市立博物館

本図は、鮮やかな紅葉の下にたたずむ神々しいまでの白鹿を描くが、毛描きを駆使した体軀の立体感に富む表現や角の質感表現には、写生画家・応挙ならではのものがある。

White Deer Beneath Maple Trees

Maruyama Ōkyo
18th century
Tsuruga Municipal Museum

This image portrays a white deer solemnly standing under vivid autumn foliage. The texture of the horns and the convincing three-dimensionality of a body covered in fur is distinctive of Ōkyo, who was a master of realistic paintings done from life.

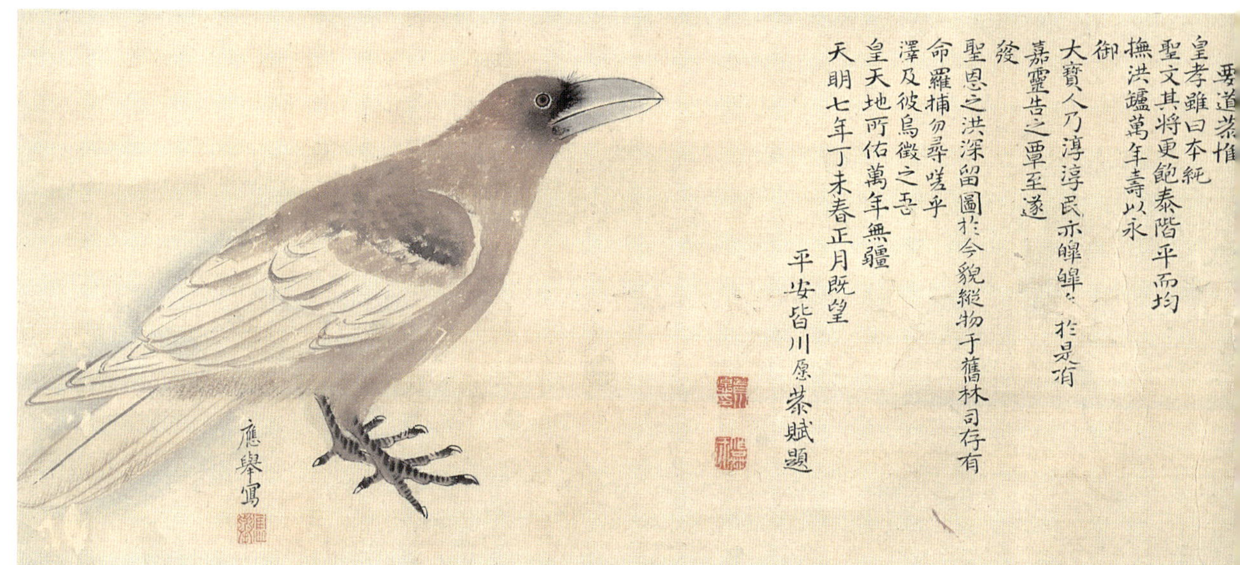

白烏図（部分）

円山応挙筆、皆川淇園賛
天明7年（1787）
本間美術館

1786年（天明6）に京都山科郷で白烏が捕獲され、当時の妙法院門跡・真仁法親王（1768～1805）を経由して光格天皇（1771～1840）の叡覧に至った。この白烏は、真仁法親王の命により応挙門下で写生した上で放たれたのだが、この写生図を応挙が浄写したのが本図である。

White Crow (*detail*)

Painted by Maruyama Ōkyo,
Inscribed by Minagawa Ki'en
1787
Homma Museum of Art

In 1786 (Tenmei 6), a white bird was caught in the Yamashina ward of Kyoto, and the head priest of Myōhō-in, Shinnin Hosshinnō (1768-1805), arranged for it to be delivered for the personal inspection of Emperor Kōkaku (1771-1840). Under the orders of Shinnin Hosshinnō, this white bird was set free after it was sketched by a pupil of Ōkyo's, but this image is the final copy that Ōkyo produced based on that sketch.

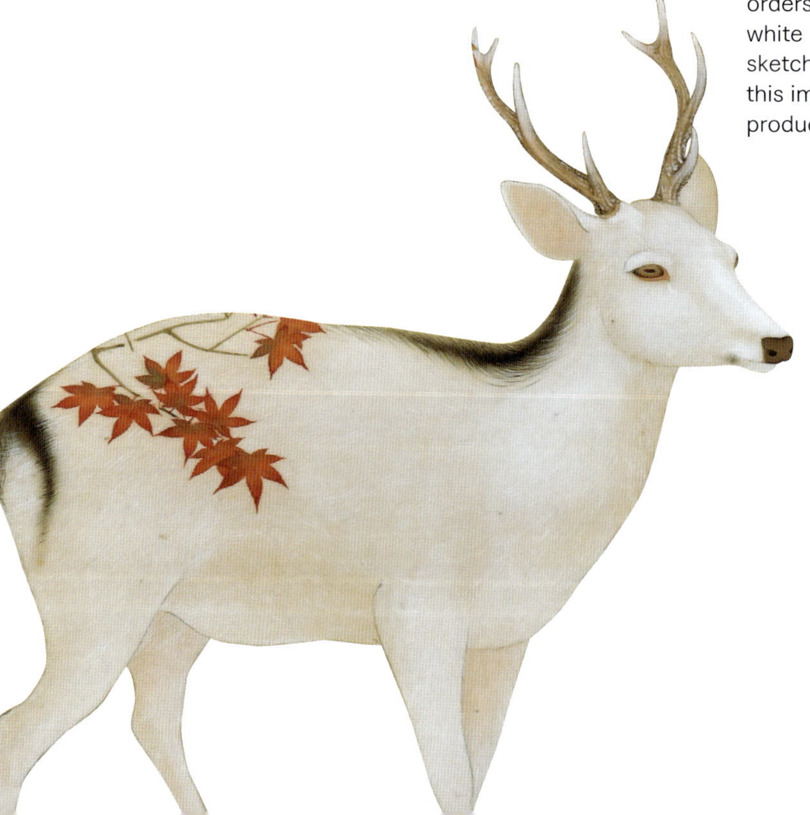

釈迦の臨終に悲嘆する動物たちがひしめくように描かれる「涅槃図」は動物画の宝庫と言えるが、それ以外にも「獣尽図」や「群獣図」などと呼ばれる画巻や屏風仕立ての作品、さらには十二支図のなかに多くの動物群が登場する。とくに江戸時代に写実性が重視されるようになると、個別の動物画を得意とする絵師たちの出現により、豊穣や子孫繁栄など様々な願いの託された作品が生み出されてゆくことになった。

Large Collections of Animals:

The Twelve Signs of the Chinese Zodiac

You can say that "Nirvana of the Historical Buddha" paintings that depict the crowd of animals grieving at Shakyamuni's deathbed are like a treasure trove of animal paintings, but even aside from these, there are works on folding screens and handscrolls that depict birds and beasts; moreover, in the depictions of the zodiac as animals we see large groups of animals as well. Especially in the Edo period, where realism had come to be so prized, the emergence of painters who excelled at painting specific animals gave rise to works that used animals to convey various desires, such as for a good harvest or the perpetuation of one's descendants.

十二支牙彫根付
江戸時代(19c)
メトロポリタン美術館

Netsuke of Group of Animals
19th century
The Metropolitan Museum of Art

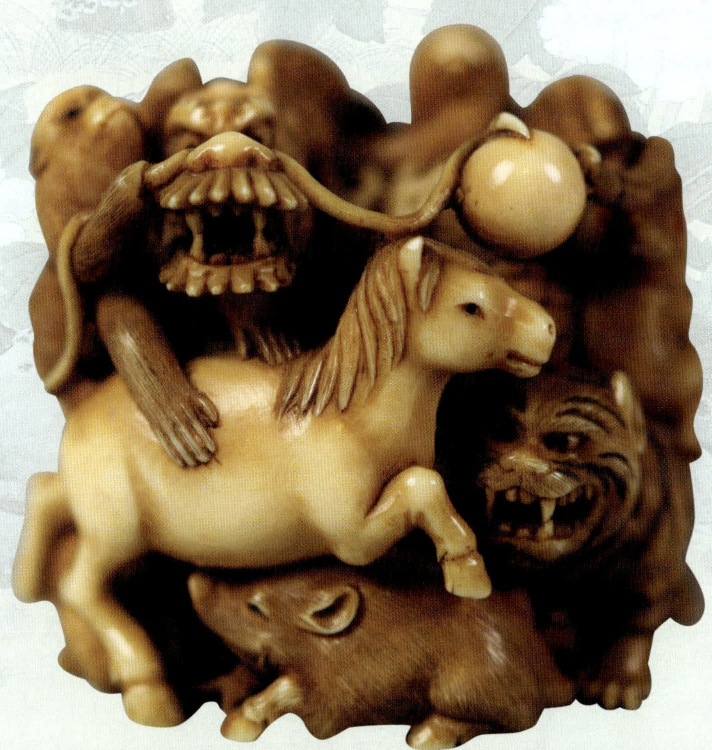

十二支図

渡辺南岳
江戸時代後期(18〜19c)
東京国立博物館

十二支は動物を群として描写する格好の画題であった。12種の動物で完結することから、6曲1双の屏風各扇に1枚ずつ(計12枚)貼り込んだ押絵貼形式のものが一般的で、略画風のタッチのものが多いようだ。それに対し、本図は掛軸に12種すべての動物をまとめ上げた作品。応挙の高弟だった南岳は、画家の構成力が試される主題を苦もなくこなしているように見える。

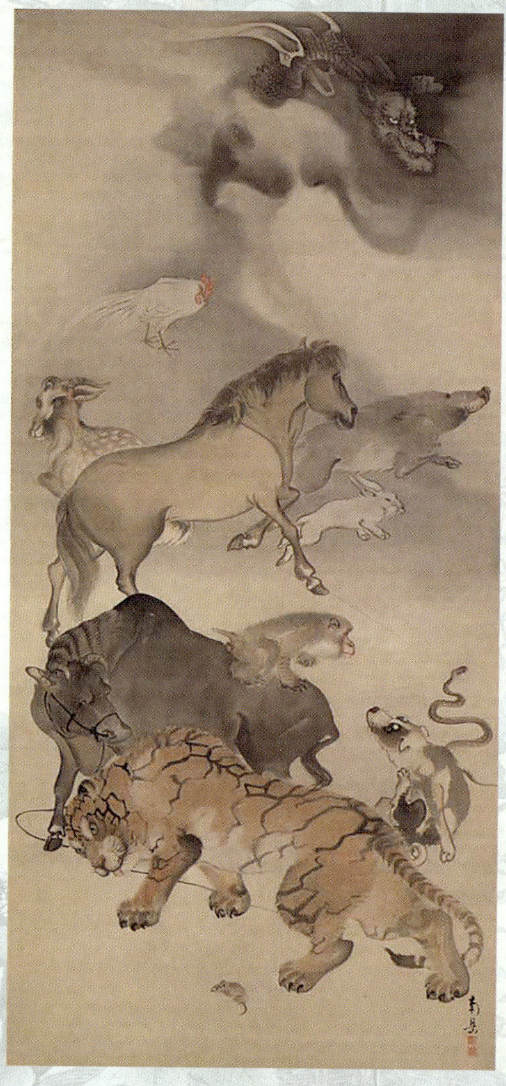

Animals of the Zodiac

Watanabe Nangaku
18th–19th century
Tokyo National Museum

The “twelve animals of the zodiac” was a set painting subject of the zodiac represented as a group of animals. Since it is composed of twelve types of animals, the typical format on a pair of six-panel folding screens is to have a cloth image depicting one figure pasted to each panel (for a total of twelve), and many of these were done in an abbreviated style. In contrast to that, this image is a hanging scroll where all twelve animals are portrayed as a collective. It seems that Ōkyo’s leading disciple Nangaku easily handled the portrayal of this subject, which would normally test the compositional acumen of any artist.

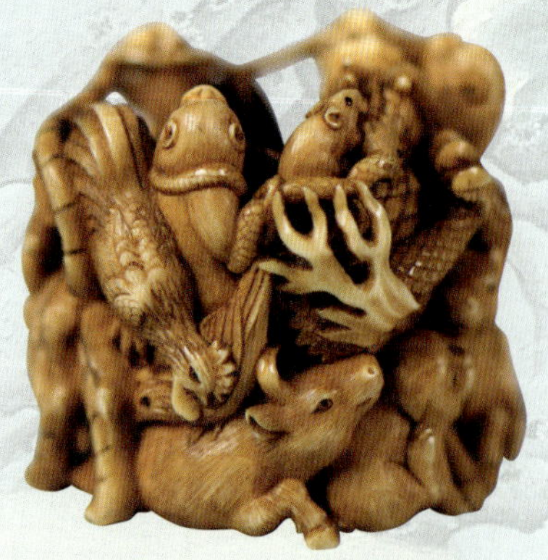

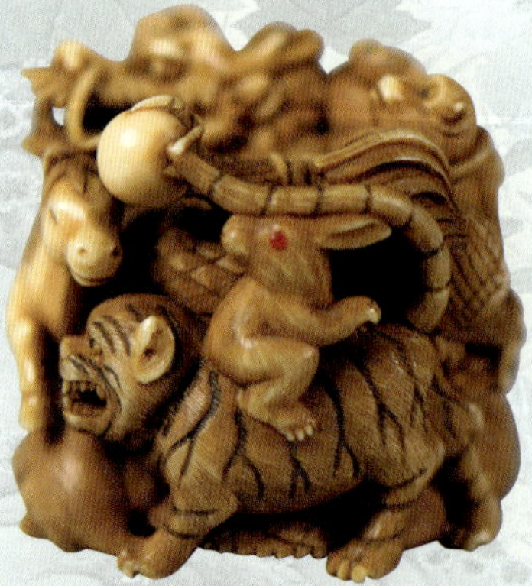

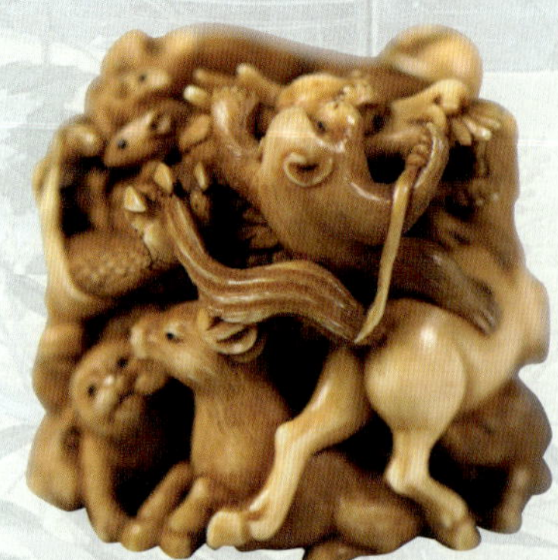

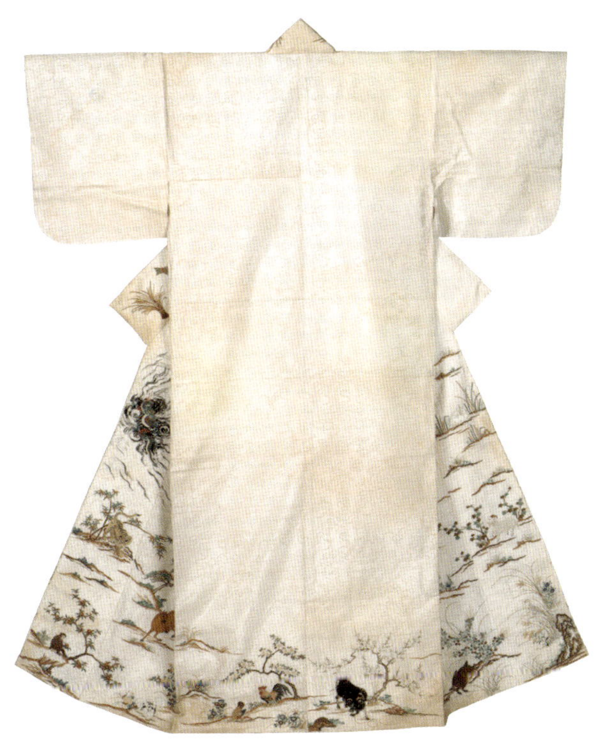

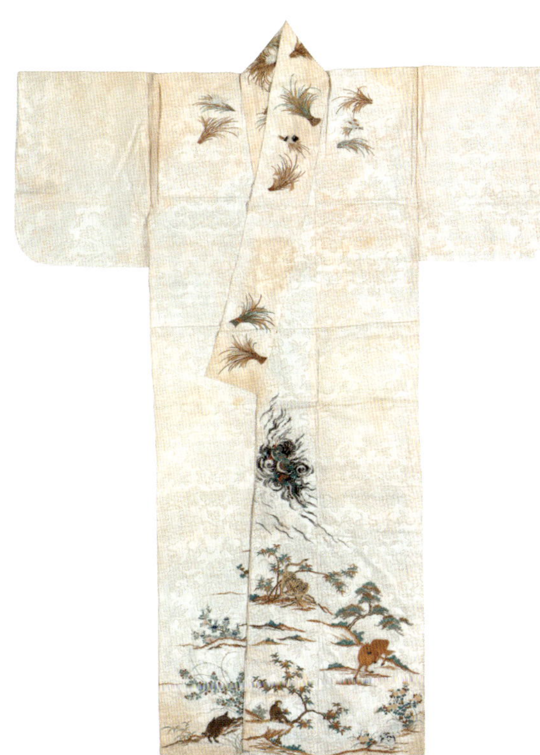

十二支図小袖

江戸時代後期(19c)
国立歴史民俗博物館
(野村正治郎衣裳コレクション)

白の紗綾地を画面として、前見頃から裾にかけて十二支の動物のいる情景を刺繍だけで表現した小袖。武家の夫人が打掛の下に用いた間着と考えられている。十二支そのものの吉祥性を物語る資料と言える。

Animals of the Zodiac Kosode Robe

19th century
Nomura Shōjirō Collection of Clothing and Accessories,
National Museum of Japanese History

This is a *kosode* robe that portrays a scene of the twelve animals of the zodiac embroidered on white *sha'aya* silk, extending from the *maemigoro* front panels down to the hem. It is thought that this would have been worn under an *uchikake* overrobe in the spring or autumn by a married woman of the warrior class. We can see this as a demonstration of the auspicious quality of the zodiac animals.

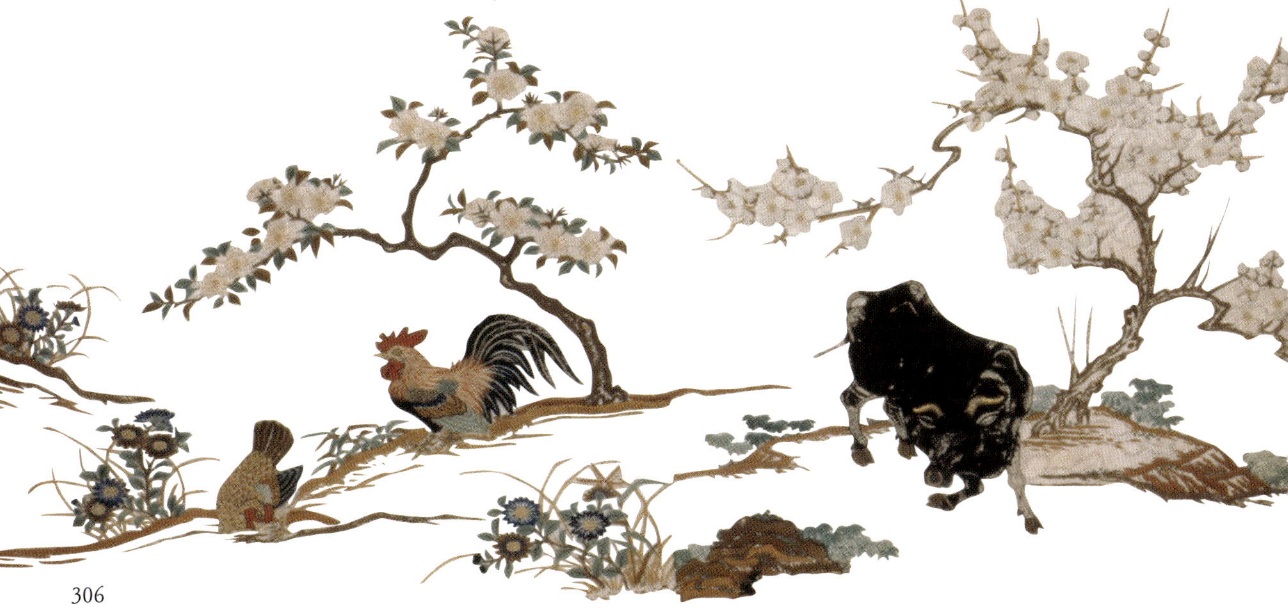

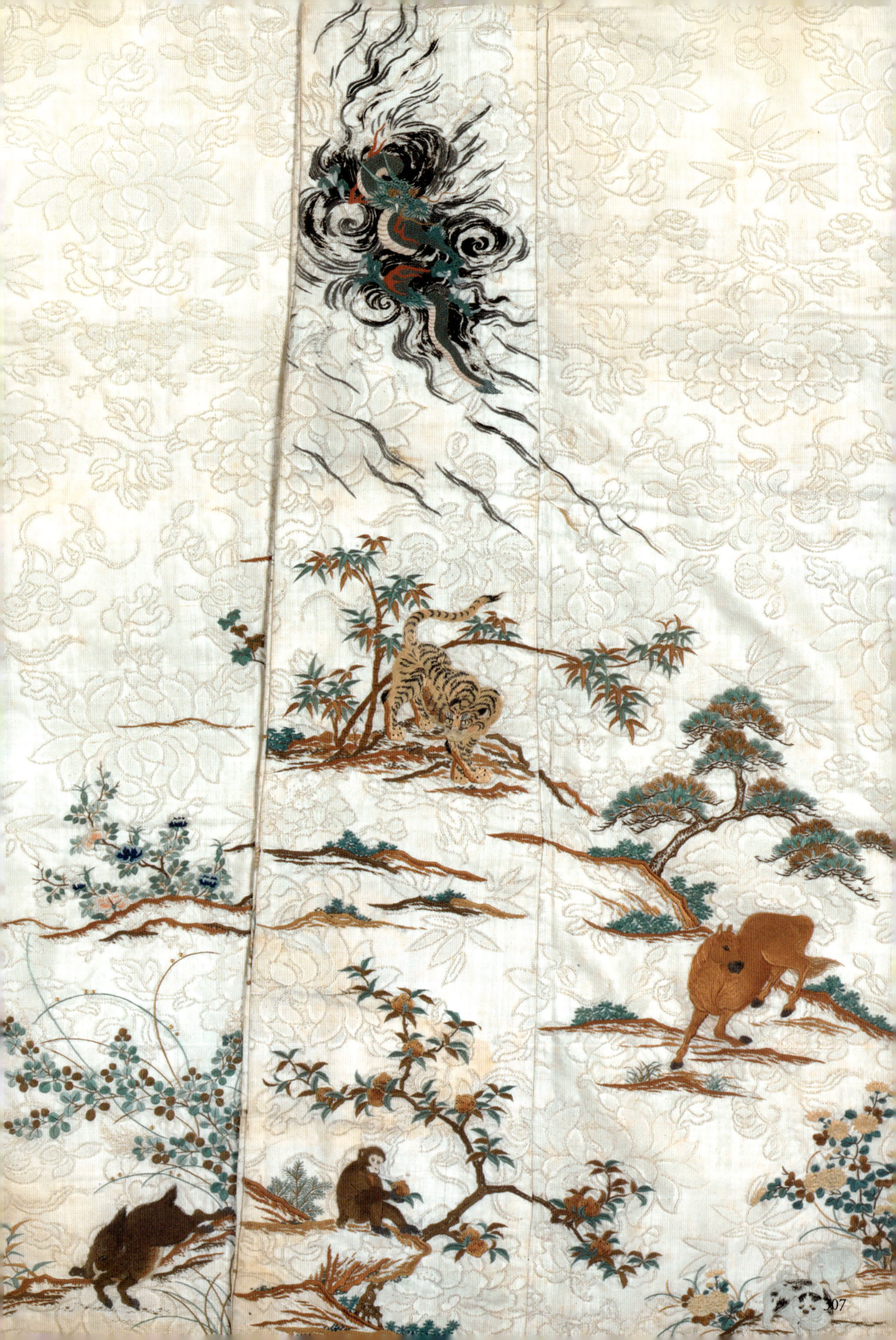

動物大集合

涅槃図の動物たち

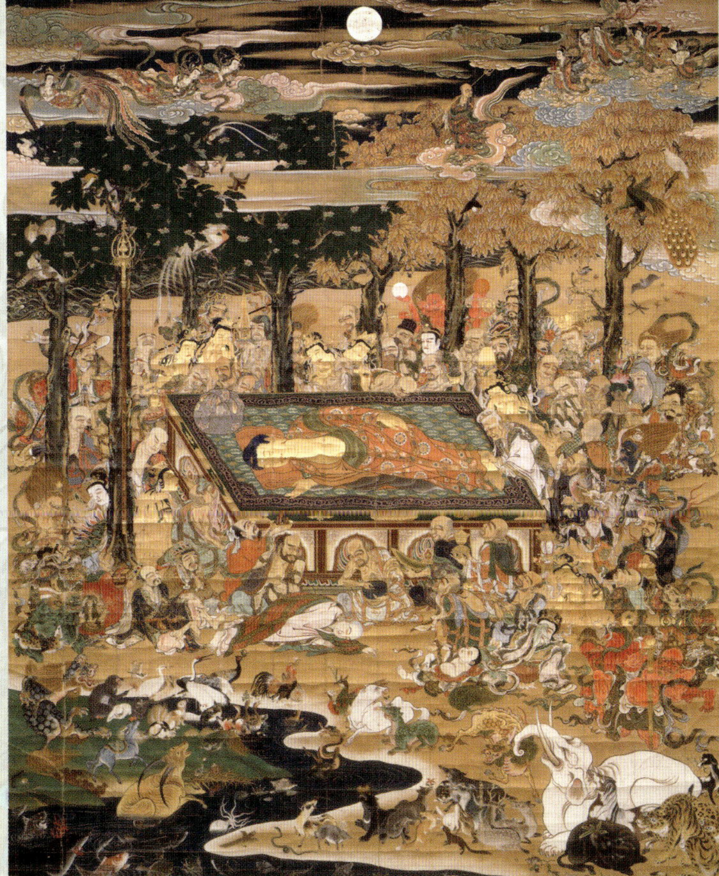

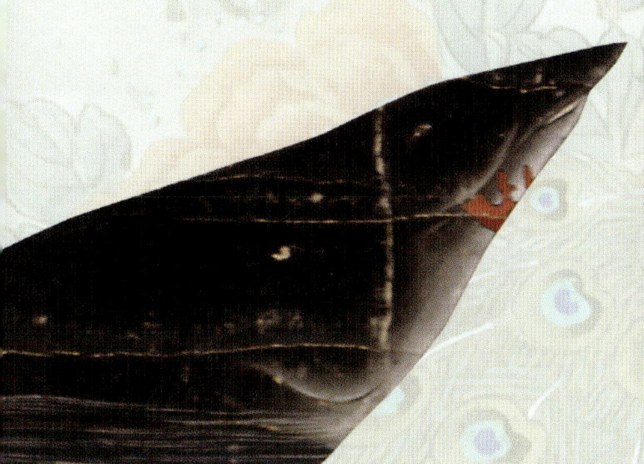

Large Collections of Animals:

The Animals at the Nirvana of the Historical Buddha

釈迦涅槃図

海北友賢
宝永6年（1709）
京都・真正極楽寺（真如堂）

鯨が登場する現存最古の涅槃図と考えられる。友賢は以後も同様の作例を手がけており、彼の得意とした図様だったと思われる。登場する動物（魚介や昆虫も含め）数は127種で、涅槃図中最多を誇る。裏面の墨書から、1709年（宝永6）11月15日三井家の女性たちによる奉納と知れる。

Nirvana of the Historical Buddha

Kaihoku Yūken
1709
Shinshōgokurakuji (Shin'nyo'dō), Kyoto

It is thought that this is the oldest extant painting on this subject where a whale is present. Yūken continued to do many of these types of death of the historical Buddha paintings, and it is considered a subject he was especially skilled at. The number of animal types that appear (including the bugs and marine animals) is one hundred and twenty-seven, and this image boasts the largest number of animals of any painting of this subject. From the ink inscription on the back of the painting, we can tell that this was an offering made by the women of the Mitsui clan on the fifteenth day of the eleventh month of 1709 (Hōei 6).

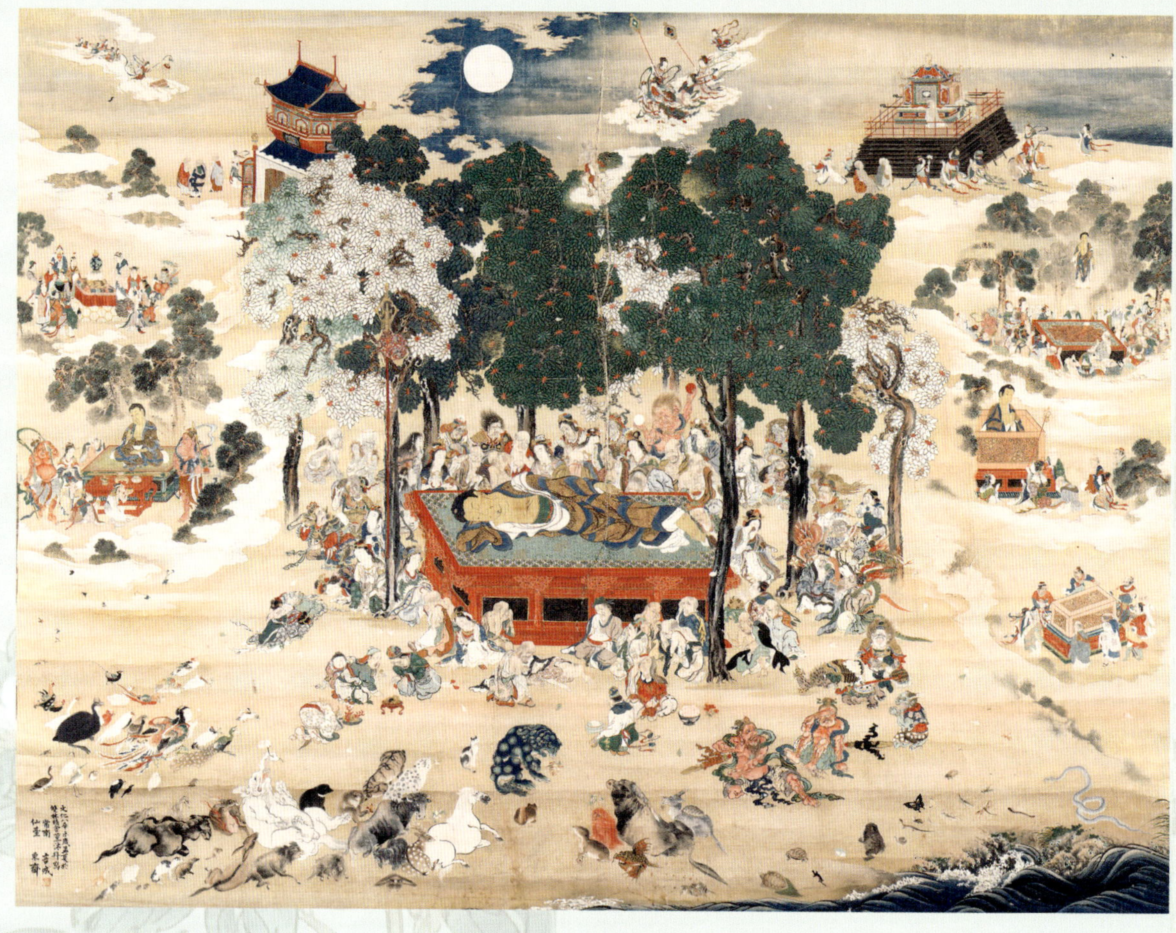

八相涅槃図

根元常南・菅井梅関
文化8年（1811）
群馬・雙林寺

見世物などを通じて、年ごとに目の前に現れる不思議な様相の動物たち、それはある意味で涅槃図の動物世界が現実に存在することを実証するものでもあった。また、そのような意識が逆に、当時の涅槃図における動物の選択に変化をもたらすといった現象をも生み出していたらしい。

The Eightfold Path to Nirvana

Nemoto Jōnan, Sugai Baikan
1811
Sōrinji, Gunma

The exotic animals appearing before people's eyes year by year at sideshow exhibitions served as a manner of proof that these creatures truly existed outside the world of animals portrayed in paintings of the death of the historical Buddha. Also, it seems that, converse to that type of thinking, these sideshow exhibitions also gave rise to changes in the selection of animals portrayed in contemporary death of the historical Buddha paintings.

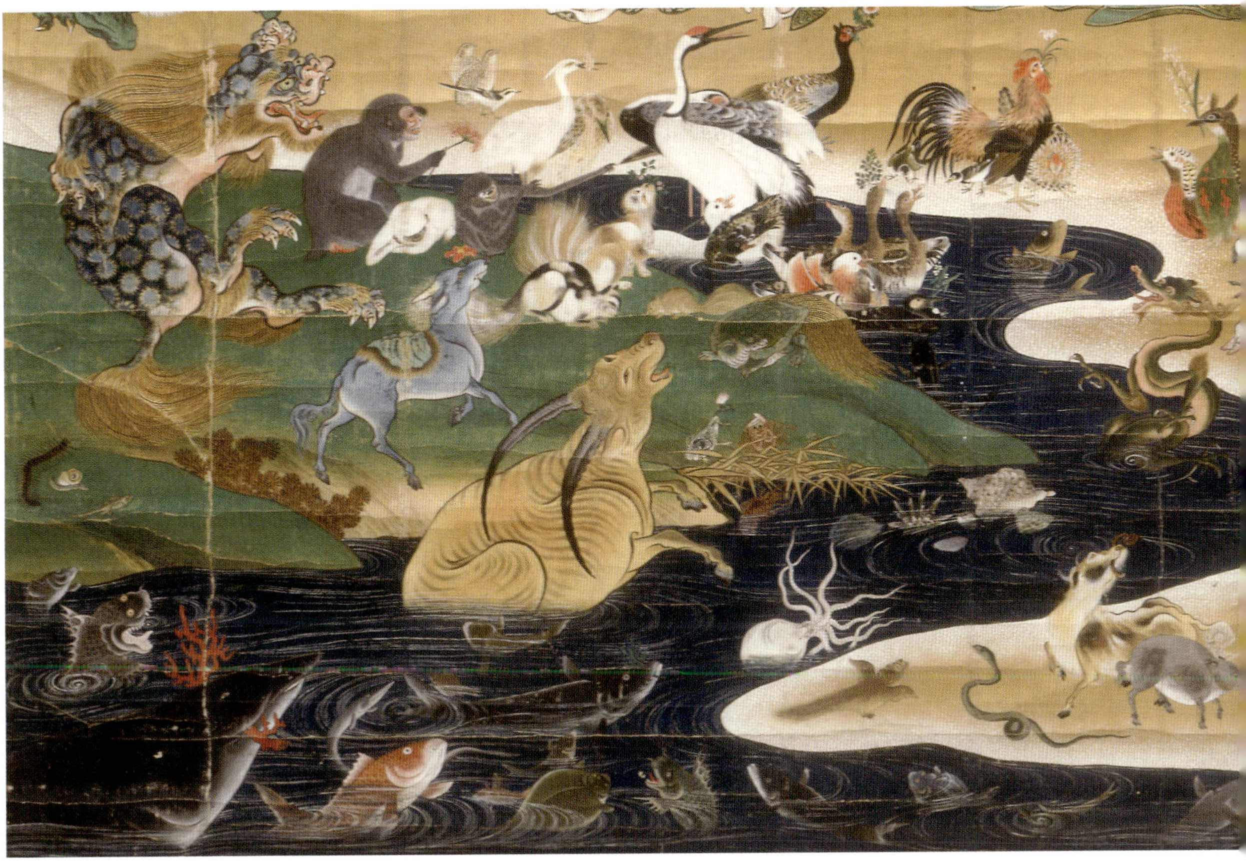

釈迦涅槃図 部分　*Nirvana of the Historical Buddha* (detail)

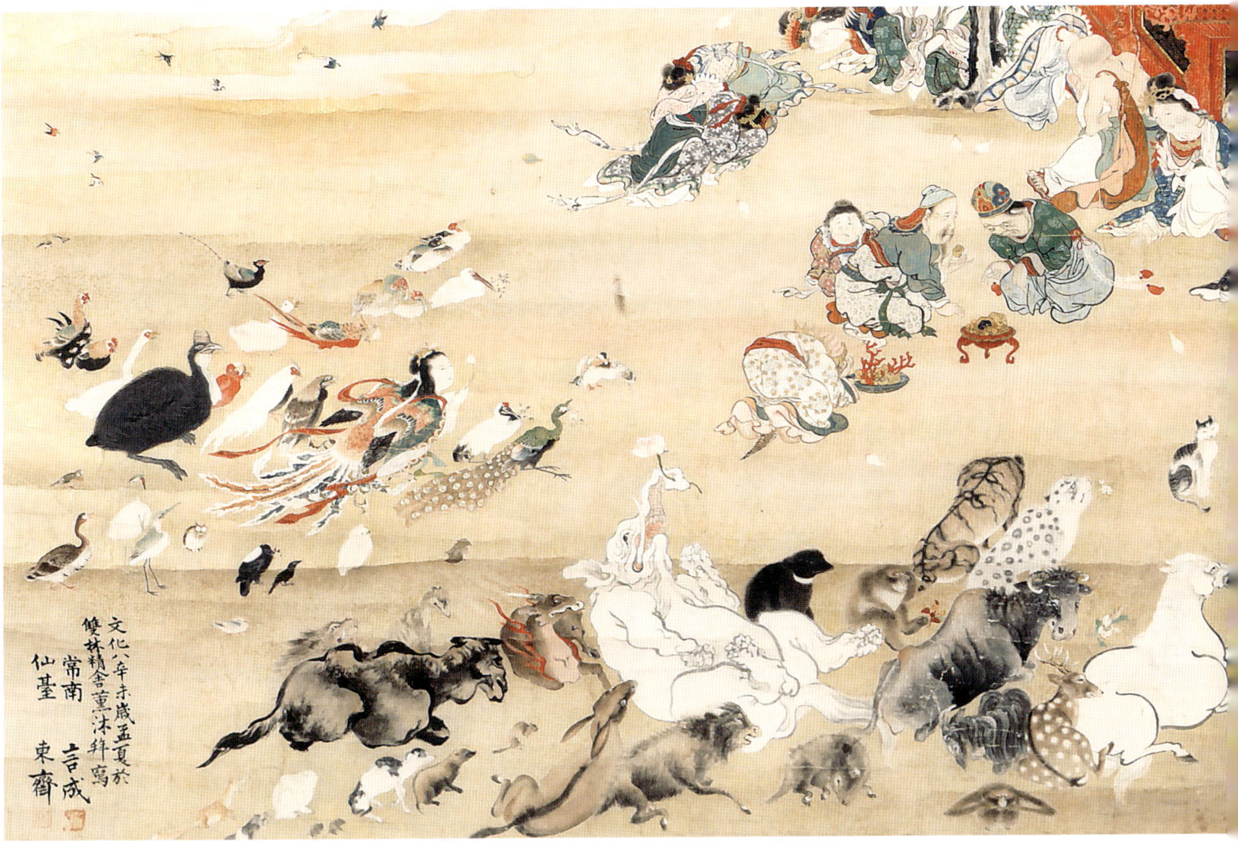

八相涅槃図 部分　*The Eightfold Path to Nirvana* (detail)

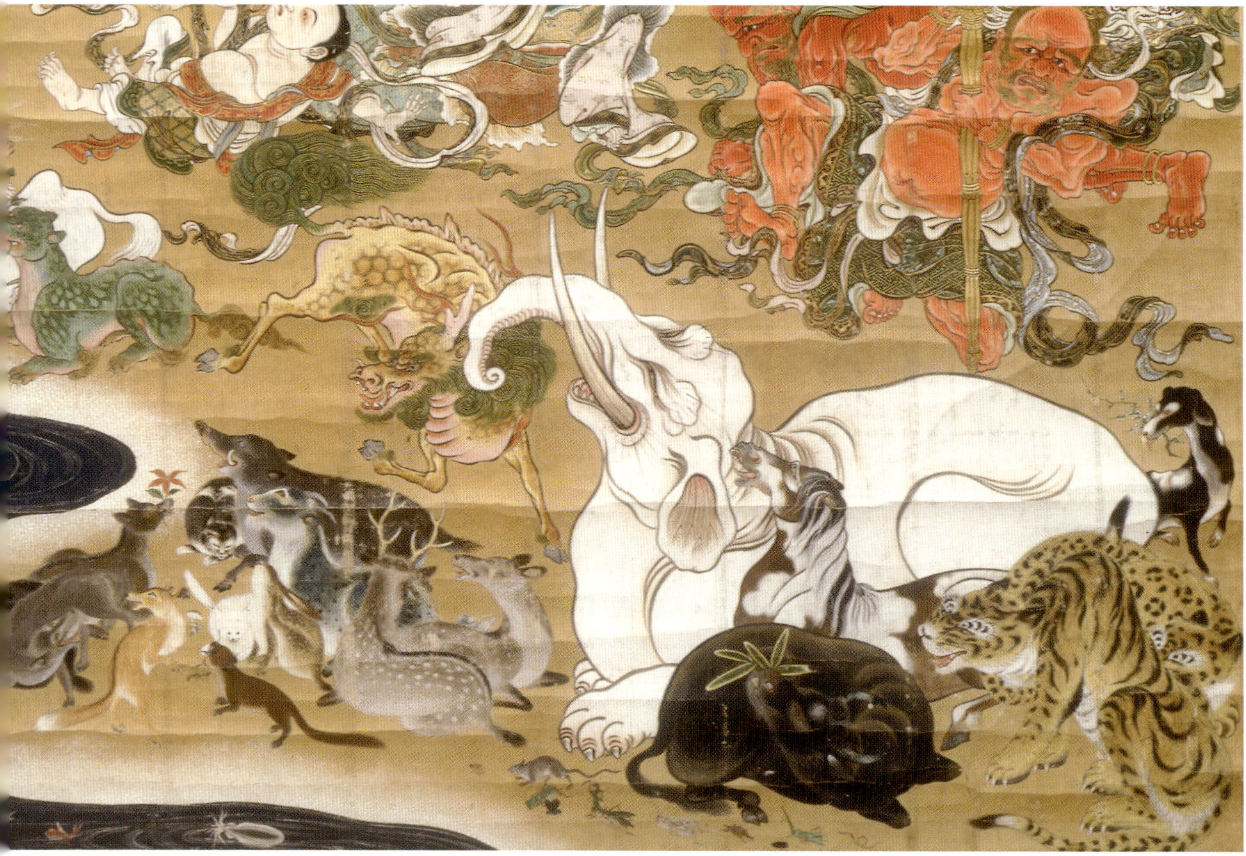

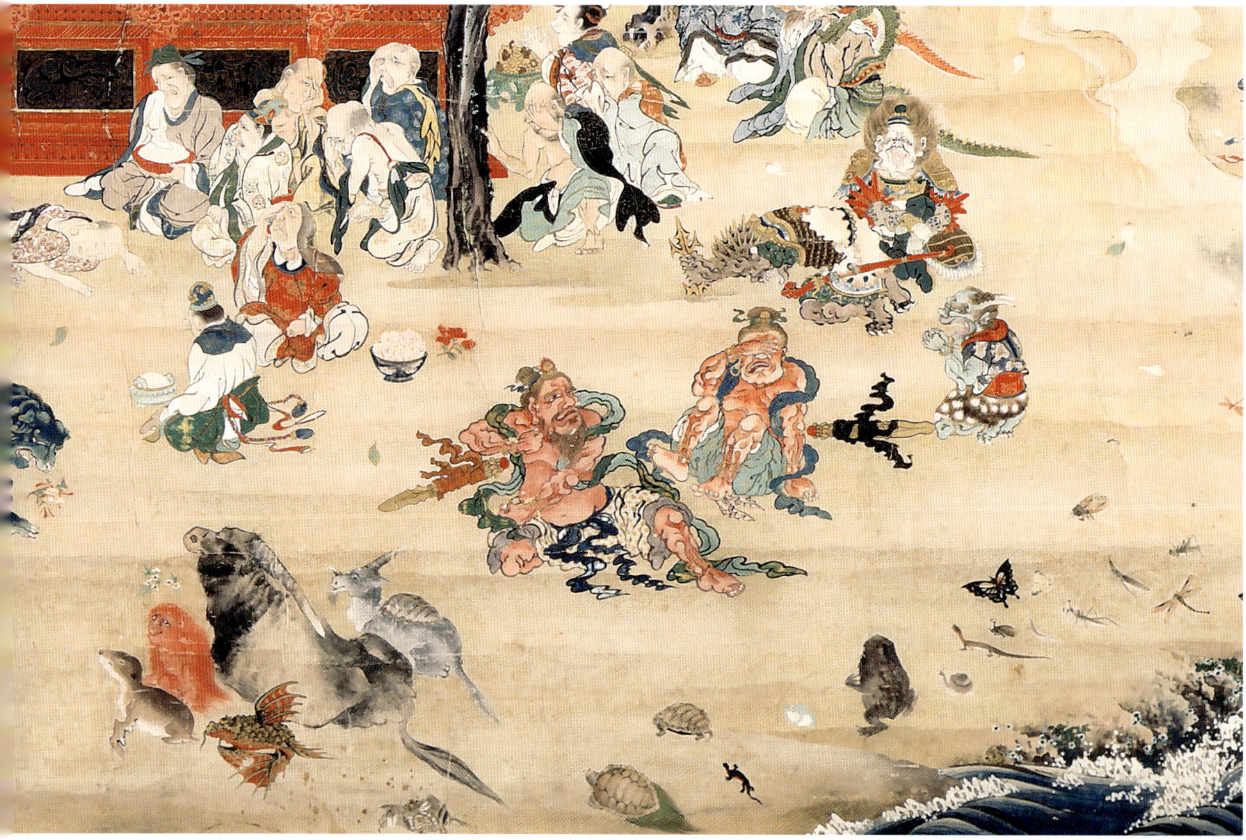

Column 4

動物大集合

涅槃図から楽園へ

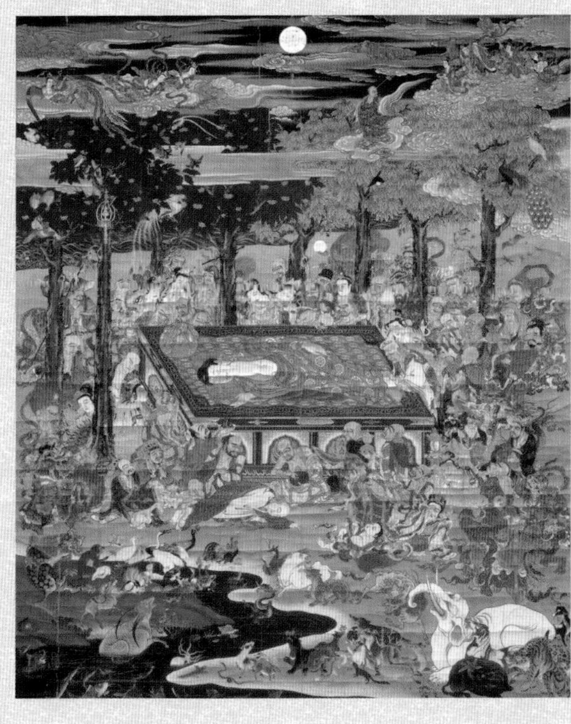

[1] 海北友賢「釈迦涅槃図」
Nirvana of the Historical Buddha by Kaihoku Yūken

動物は古くから宗教との関わりにおいて描かれることが多かったが、とくに釈迦が亡くなる場面を描く「涅槃図」は動物画の宝庫といえよう。横たわる釈迦を中心として、周囲にはその死を嘆き悲しむ仏菩薩や仏弟子たち、そして多くの動物群が下方にひしめいているのである。涅槃図が典拠とする経典には、龍・象・獅子以下、鳥や昆虫までも含めた動物たちが涅槃の場に集った動物として列挙されるのだが、日本においてはそこに現れない虎や猪・鹿・猿・犬などが追加され、時代とともにその種類も増加していった。

涅槃図は、宗派を問わず毎年2月15日の涅槃会(ねはんえ)において各寺院で展観されるため、このような図様は画家たちにとって親しみ深いものだったであろう。加えて、大幅の懸幅を本堂の梁などに掛けた場合、画面下方の動物群は衆目のもっとも近くに位置することになるため、ある程度の選択の自由さも手伝ってか、描かれる動物たちは画家にとり格好の腕の見せ所となったようである。

動物が増えたとはいえ、ほとんどが陸上の生物か鳥類に限定されていた涅槃図のなかにあって、鯨をはじめとする水棲生物が加えられた作品がある。その最初期の作例が、1709年（宝永6）に描かれた海北友賢筆「釈迦涅槃図」（京都・真正極楽寺蔵）[1]である。描かれた動物の数は127種にものぼり、まさに動物図鑑の様相を呈するに至ったのである。その背景には、わが国における最初期の絵入り百科事典として知られる中村惕斎（1629～1702）編『訓蒙図彙』（初版1666年刊）が1695年（元禄8）に増補され、

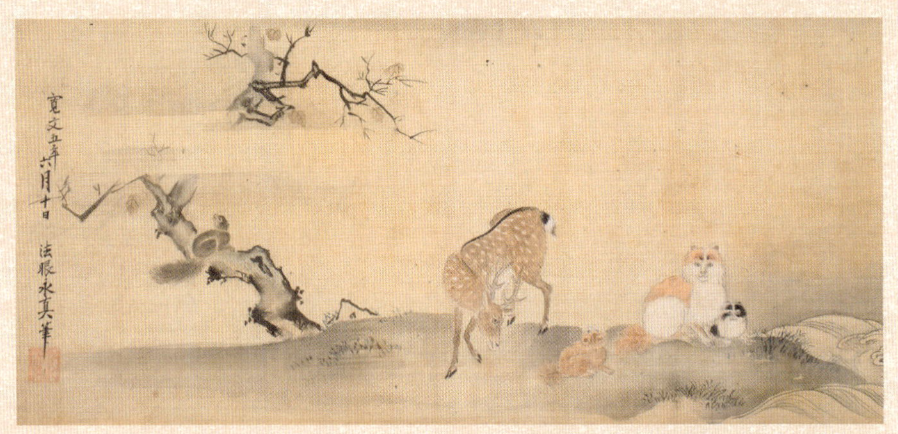

[2] 狩野探幽ほか「獣尽図巻」部分
Detail of *Beasts Scroll* by Kano school

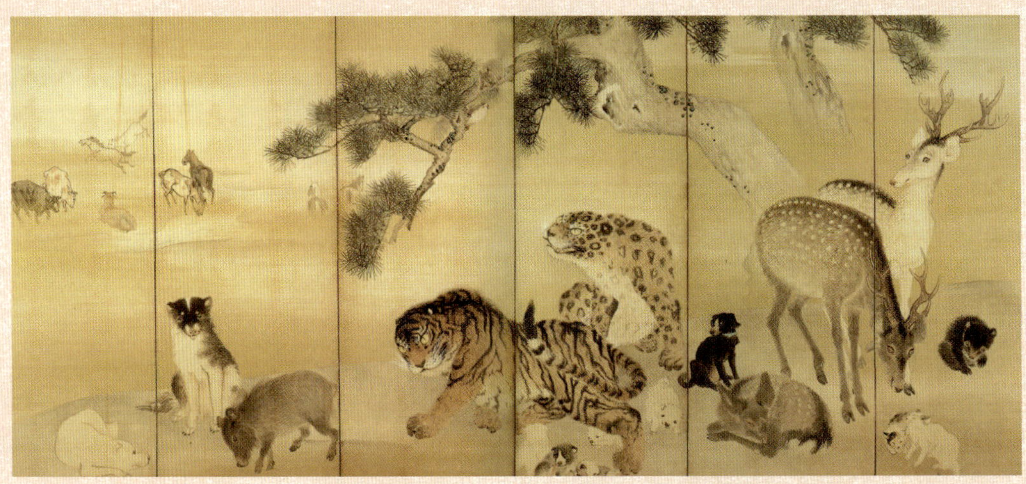

[3] 円山応挙「群獣図屏風」部分
Detail of *Beasts Screen* by Maruyama Ōkyo

1709年（宝永6）に貝原益軒（1630〜1714）編『大和本草』が刊行、さらに1712年（正徳2）には寺島良安（1654〜？）編『和漢三才図会』（105巻）が成立、といった動向に連動したものだろうか。それとも、捕鯨や水産関係の檀越（だんおつ）の関与などがあったものか、興味深い現象といえよう。

涅槃図と並んで、「獣尽図巻」[2]や「諸獣図巻」などと題される一群がある。霊獣から実在の動物までが同居するかたちで山野や渓間に遊ぶ様子を描き出した、動物の見本帳のような趣のものである。このような動物画の豊富な遺産を下敷きに制作されたのが、円山応挙の「群獣図屏風」[3]であろう。両隻に配された常緑の松と檜のもと、象から鼠まで大小さまざま19種53体の動物たちが、多くの場合つがいで登場する。さらに、安産の象徴である犬の親子や繁殖力の強い兎や鼠までが描き出される点に、豊穣あるいは子孫繁栄といった吉祥的な意味合いを読み取ることができる。涅槃の場から解放された動物たちは、もはや嘆き悲しむことも争うこともなく安心してくつろいでいる。まさしく動物の楽園である。

では、応挙の高弟・長沢芦雪の「白象・黒牛図屏風」[4]は、どう考えればよいのだろう。屏風いっぱいに体軀を描き込むことで、その巨大さを印象づける効果を狙ったに違いないのだが、膝を折って地にひれ伏すような姿勢そのものは、釈迦の臨終に悲嘆しうずくまる涅槃図の動物たちを強く連想させる。そのような動物群のなかで、とくに目を引くのが常に中央付近に配される白象

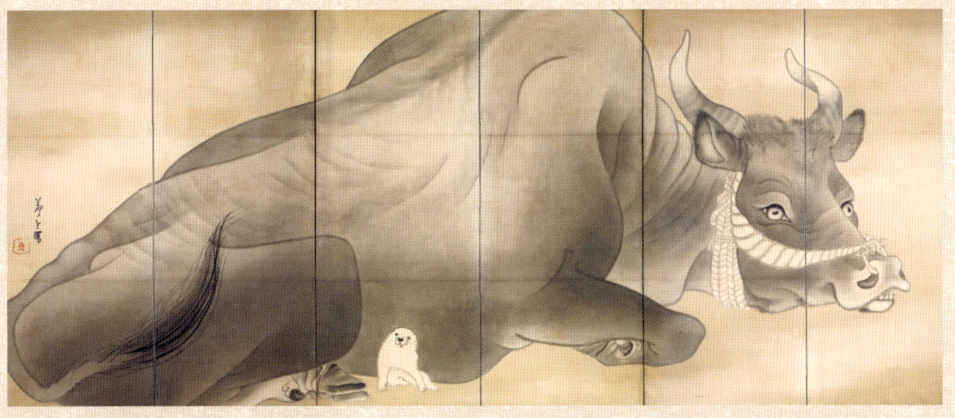

[4] 長沢芦雪「白象・黒牛図屏風」部分
White Elephant and Black Bull Screens by Nagasawa Rosetsu

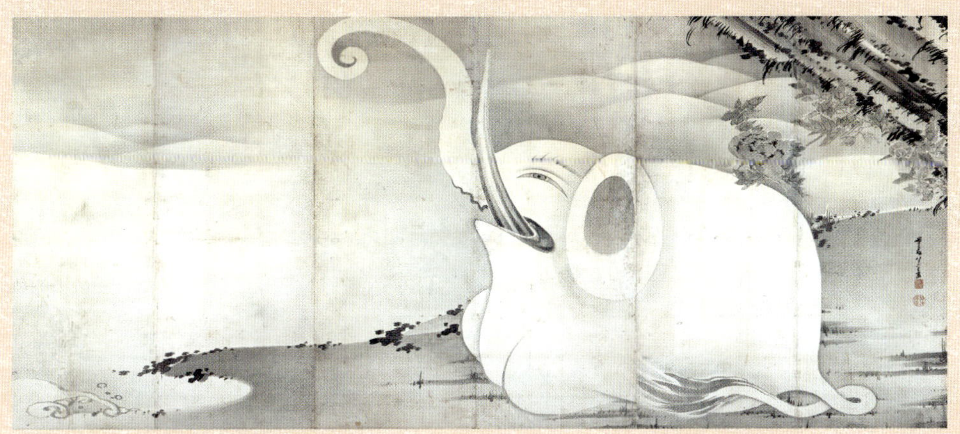

[5] 伊藤若冲「象と鯨図屏風」部分
Elephant and Whale Screens by Itō Jakuchū

と獅子なのだが、白象と黒牛が対峙するように描き出された作例も残されている。芦雪は、このような遺品に刺激されながら、黒白の対比に好都合で大きな体軀を誇る白象と黒牛とを選択したものであろう。

これとほぼ同時期の作と考えられる伊藤若冲の「象と鯨図屏風」[5]は、陸・海それぞれの世界における最大の生物を、白と黒とで対比させた大作である。芦雪画の黒牛を鯨に置き換えたような趣向とも言えようが、先に見たような白象と鯨とが登場する涅槃図にモチーフの淵源をたどれるのであろう。口元を震わせる白象と、潮を勢いよく吹き上げる鯨とが発する音声(現実には聞こえないが)からは、どこか哀愁を帯びた気配さえ漂うのだが、その理由の一端は涅槃図のイメージによるのであろう。本図は1795年(寛政7)若冲80歳の作と考えられているが、この年は実母の十七回忌にあたる。さらに若冲はこの年、母の享年を迎えていた。熱心な仏教徒だった若冲は、涅槃図から抽出した白象と鯨に母への追慕の思いを託したのではなかったか。

一方、この若冲が開発した「枡目描き」技法で表現された鳥獣世界(p.344)は、何に由来するのだろうか。この点に関しては近年、ゴットフリート著『史的年代記』(1630年刊)[6]との関連が指摘されている。18世紀後半には蘭学者や複数の藩主らが所持していたことが確認され、識者の間では知られた存在だったようだが、同書には『旧約聖書』「創世記」に登場するエデンの園が銅版画で掲載されているのである。描かれるのは、弱肉強食を超えた平和な楽園世界そのもので、アダムとエヴァを取り去れば確かにそのまま

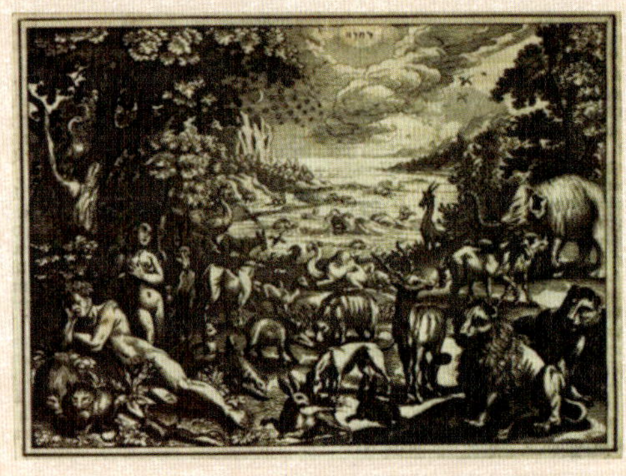

[6] ゴットフリート著『史的年代記』より
Historische Chronica
by Johann Ludwig Gottfried

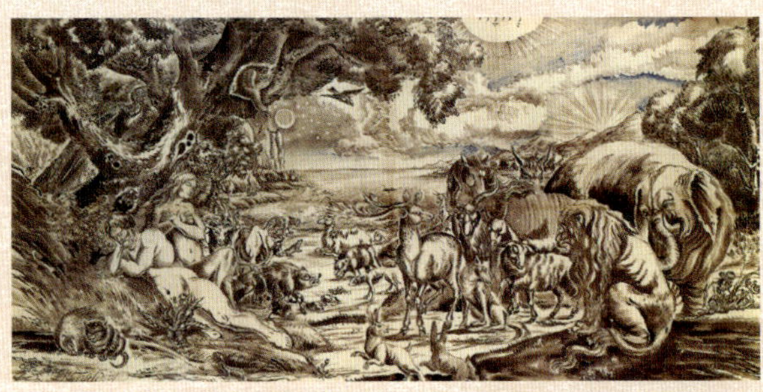

[7] 石川大浪「天地開闢之図」
Genesis by Ishikawa Tairō

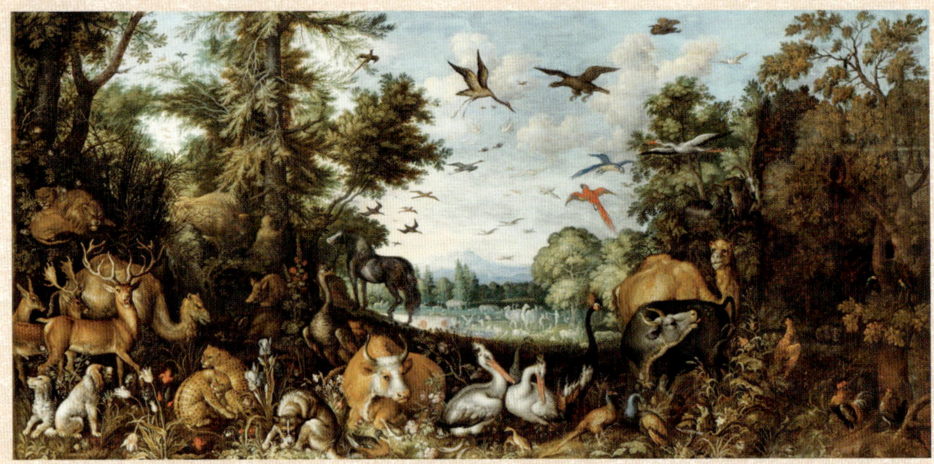

[8] ルーラント・サーフェリー「動物のいる風景」
Landscape with Wild Beasts by Roelant Savery

「樹花鳥獣図屏風」や「鳥獣花木図屏風」の図様になるとも言える。この図にもとづき、1800年（寛政12）頃に洋風画家・石川大浪が「天地開闢之図」[7]を制作しており、交友関係にあった大坂の木村蒹葭堂などを通じて若冲のもとにこの図様の情報が届いていた可能性はあろう。

これと同様、動物の集う情景を描くものに、『旧約聖書』の「ノアの箱舟」やギリシア神話に登場する詩人で奏楽の名手だったオルフェウスを主題とした作品群がある。とくに後者は、鳥獣画を得意としたオランダの画家ルーラント・サーフェリー（1577頃～1639）が多く手がけた主題で、主人公は往々にしてきわめて小さく扱われ、一見動物だけで画面が埋め尽くされたかのような印象を与えるものだ[8]。動物の楽園を思わせるこの種の絵画（銅版画）などが、当時の日本にもたらされていた可能性は考えられないものだろうか。

屏風の画面に目を戻せば、そこには豪猪（ヤマアラシ）や麝香猫・オランウータン・驢馬・豹・孔雀・火喰鳥・鸚鵡など、中国船やオランダ船に乗ってやってきた多彩な動物たちが描き込まれており、見る者は「異国」イメージを強烈に印象づけられたはずである。当時は、幕府への献上品や諸藩からの注文に応じた鳥獣のほか、興行師の手にわたり見世物にされる動物も多く、孔雀茶屋や鹿茶屋と呼ばれた簡易な動物園も市中に設営されるような時代であった。年ごとに目の前に現れる不思議な姿の動物たち、それはある意味で涅槃図の動物世界が現実に存在することを実証するものでもあったわけである。

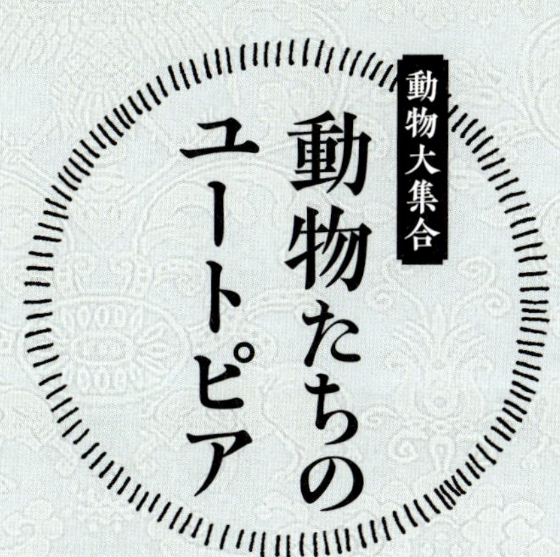

Large Collections of Animals:

Utopia of Animals

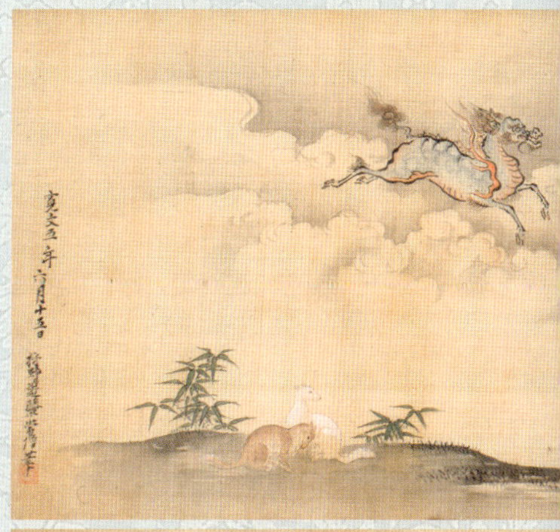

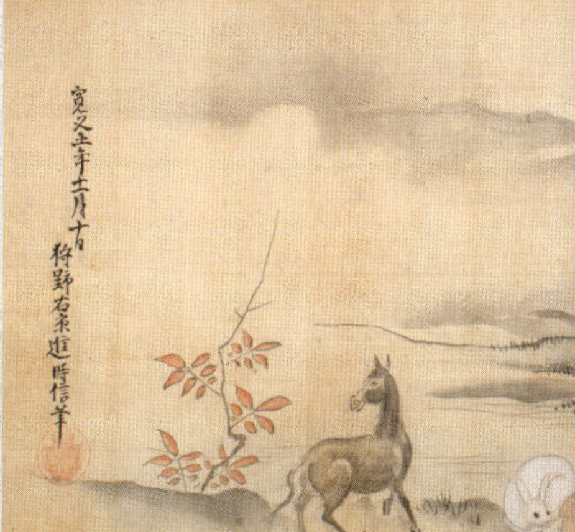

獣尽図巻（部分）

狩野安信・常信・益信・時信・春雪・氏信・
勝田貞寛・狩野探幽
寛文5年（1665）

狩野探幽（1602～74）一門により制作された「獣尽図巻」。獅子や白象・麒麟・水犀・獏などの霊獣のほか、虎や駱駝・驢馬・麝香猫といった異国の動物、あるいは牛馬や鹿・山羊・猿、さらには鼠や栗鼠・兎・猫・犬など30余種の動物群が思い思いの姿で活動する。さながら動物たちの理想郷である。

Beasts Scroll (*detail*)

Kano Yasunobu, Tsunenobu, Masunobu,
Tokinobu, Shunsetsu, Ujinobu, Katsuta Sadahiro,
and Kano Tan'yū
1665

This is a handscroll of various beasts done by a follower of Kano Tan'yū (1602-74). Over thirty types of animals appear in this scroll; in addition to sacred beasts like the lion, white elephant, *kirin*, water rhinoceros, and tapir, there are exotic animals such as the tiger, camel, donkey, and civet; there are even animals like the horse, cattle, deer, goat, and monkey, down to the mouse, squirrel, rabbit, cat and dog. It is just like an animal utopia.

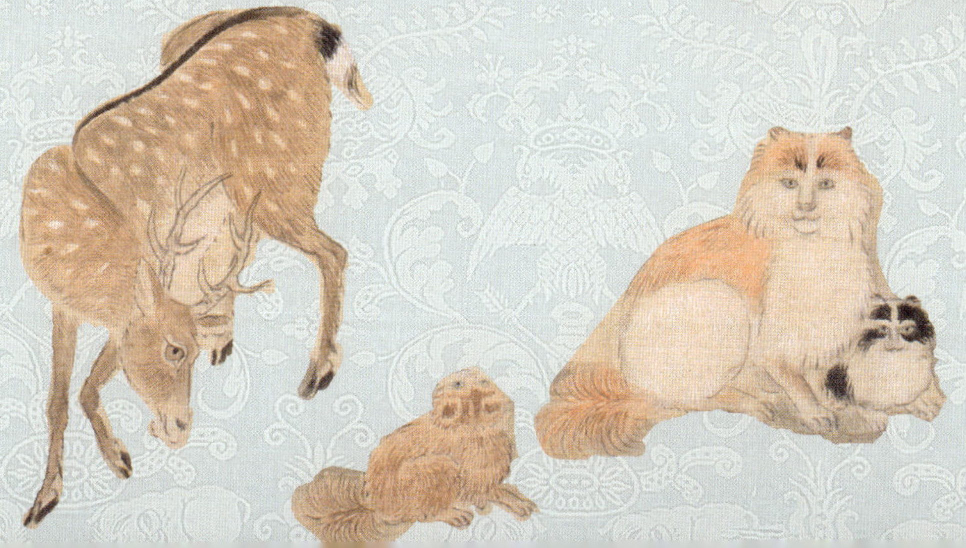

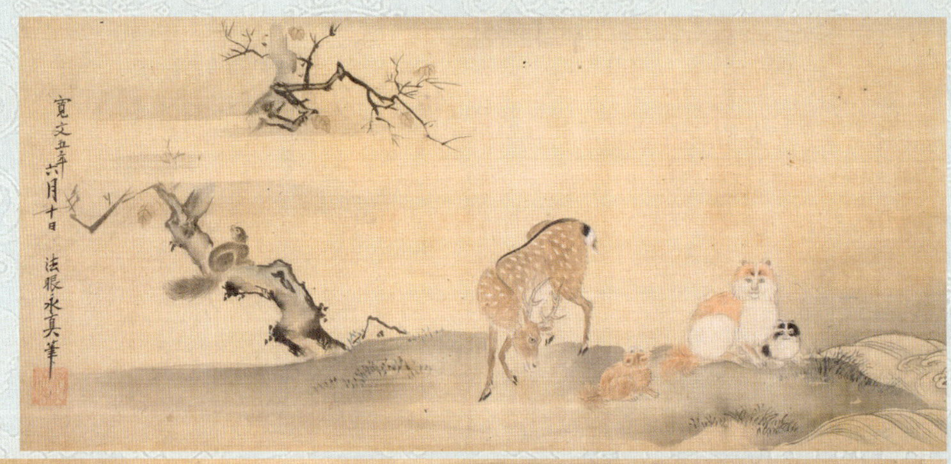
寛文五年
六月十日
法眼永真筆

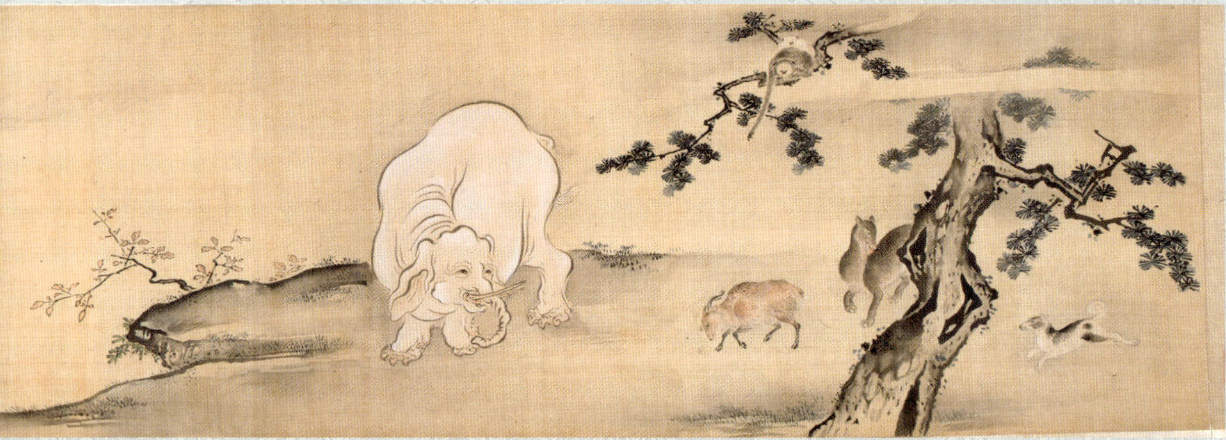

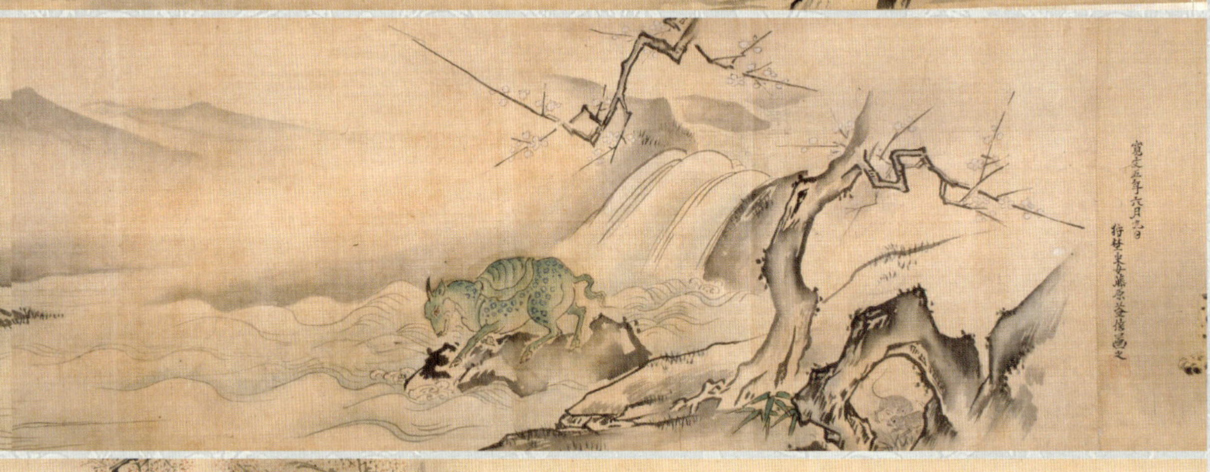
寛文五年六月

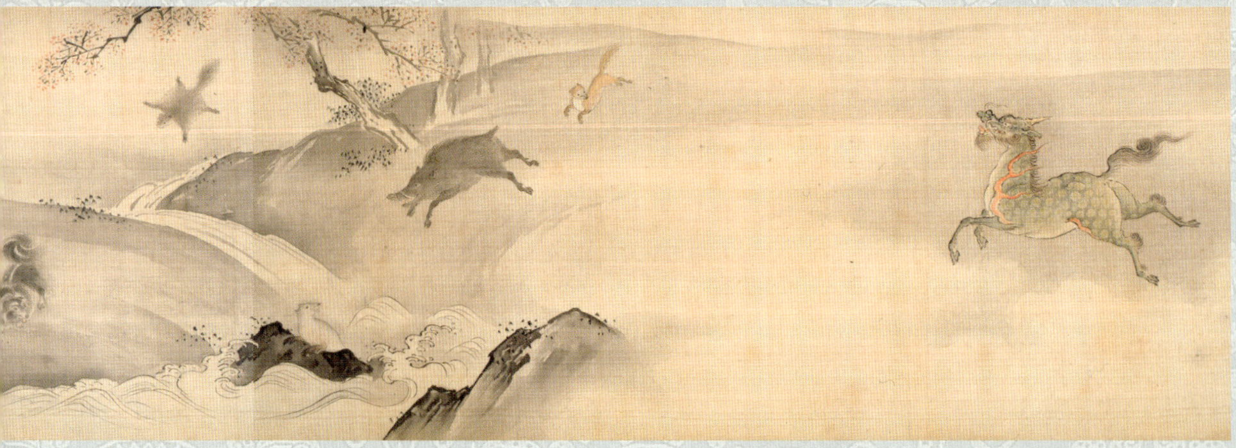

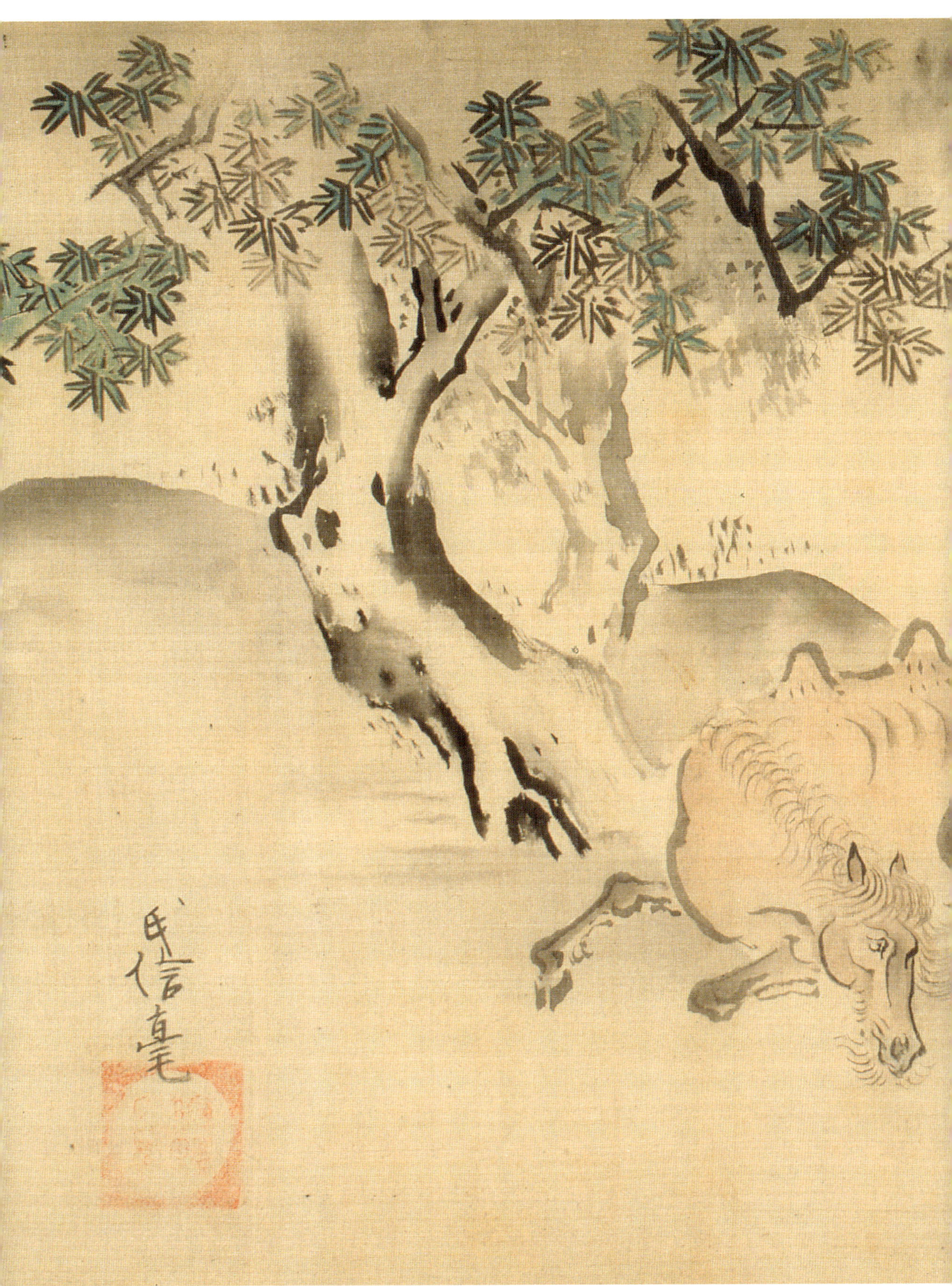

318　獣尽図巻 部分 *Beasts Scroll* (detail)

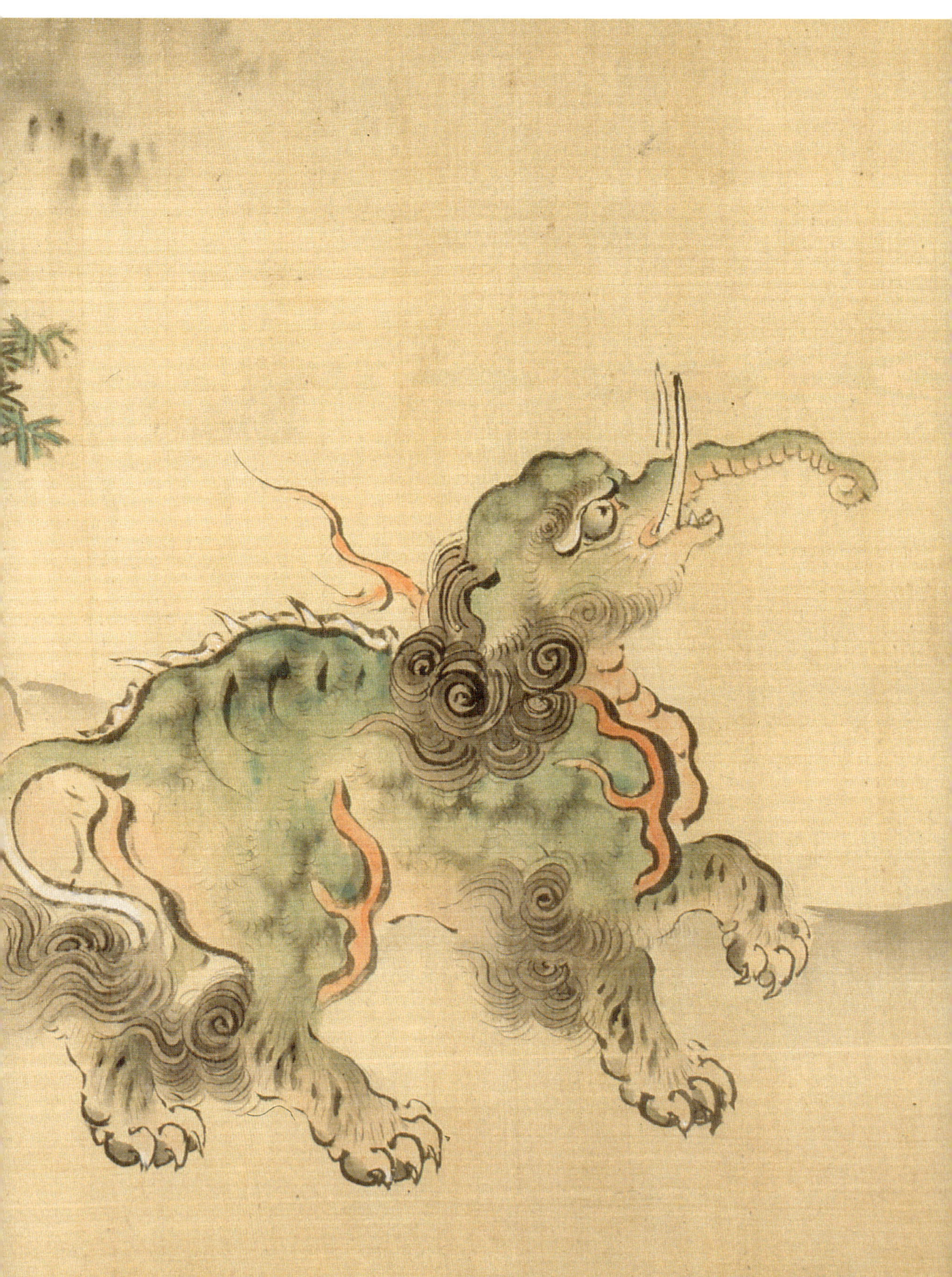

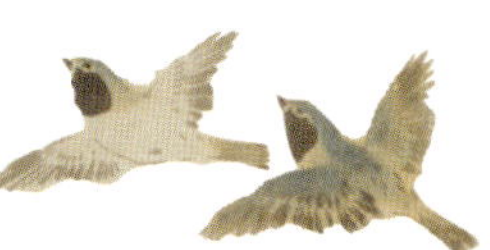

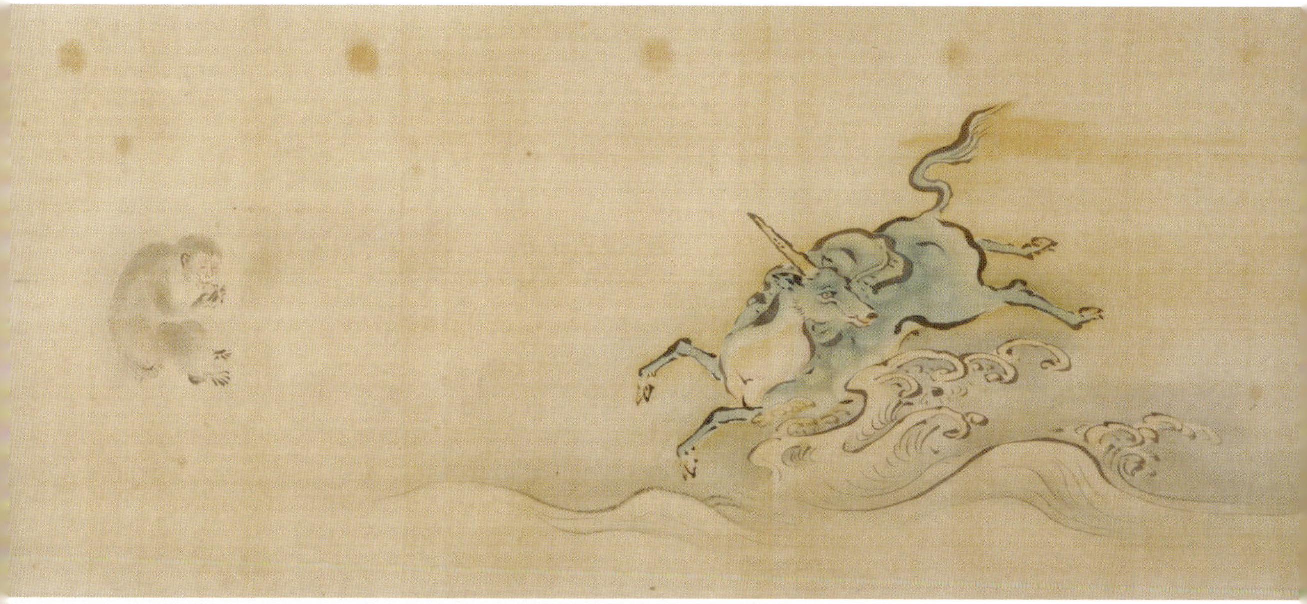

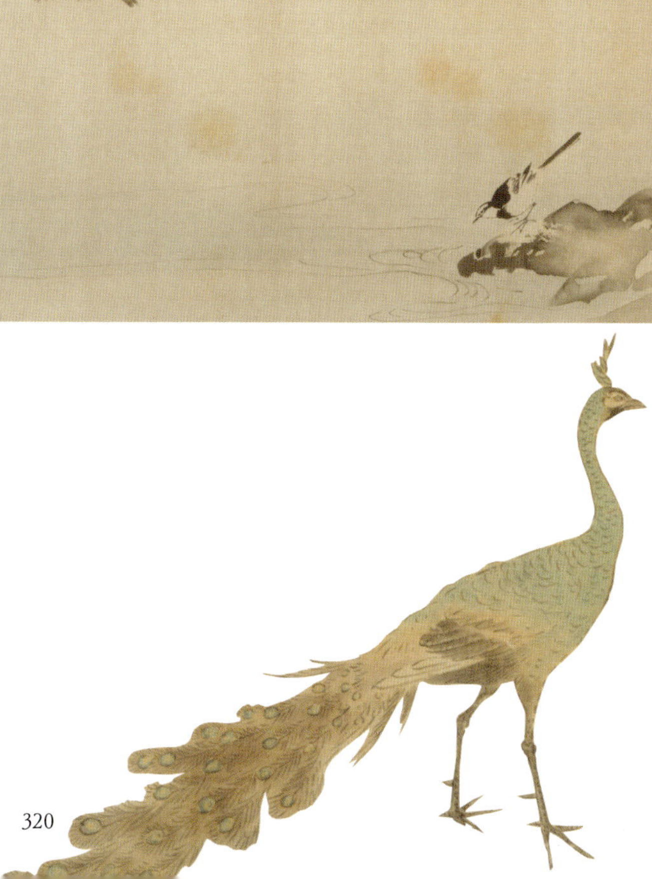

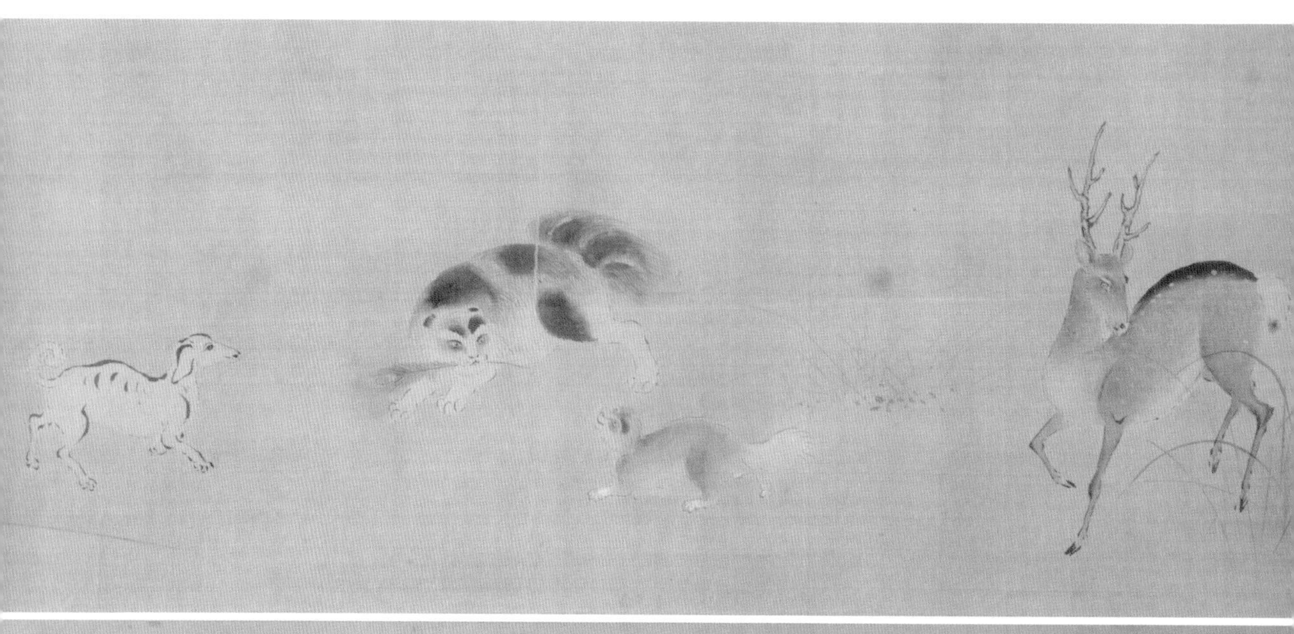

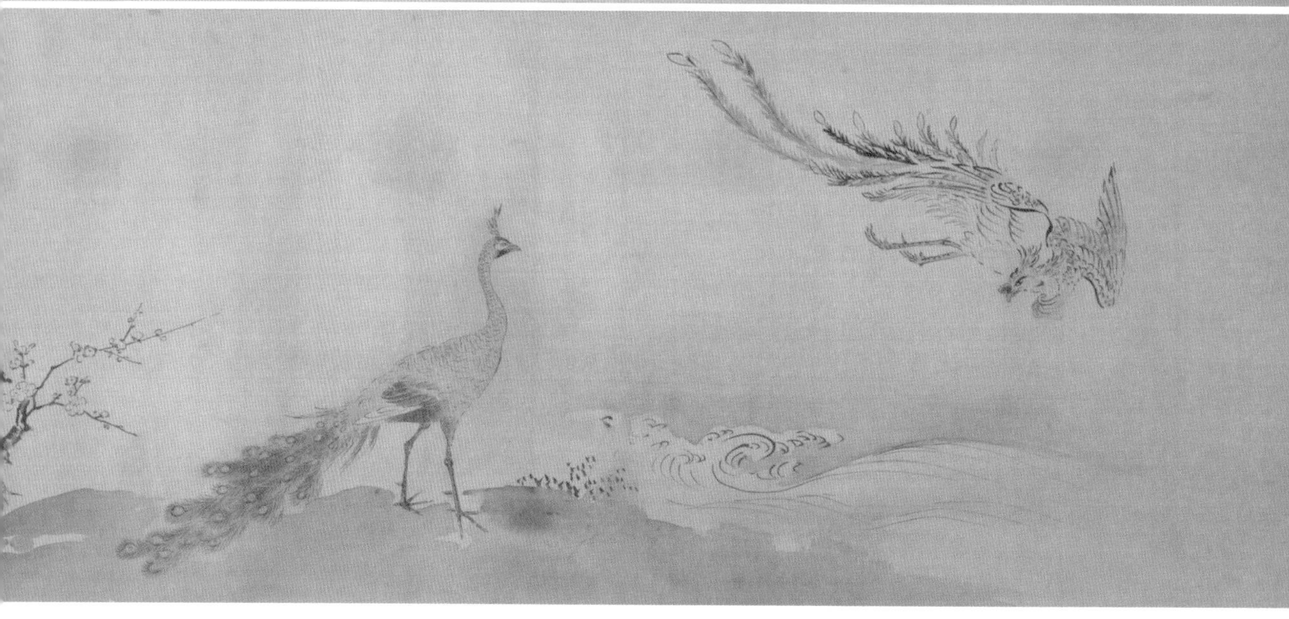

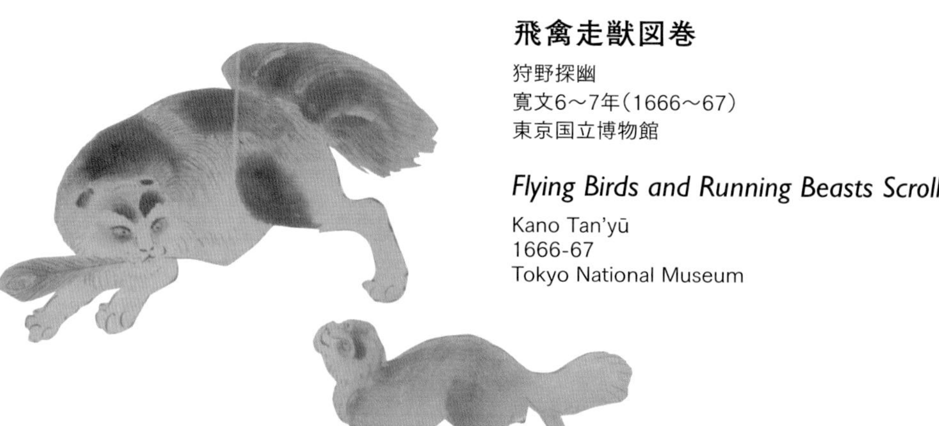

飛禽走獣図巻

狩野探幽
寛文6〜7年(1666〜67)
東京国立博物館

Flying Birds and Running Beasts Scroll

Kano Tan'yū
1666-67
Tokyo National Museum

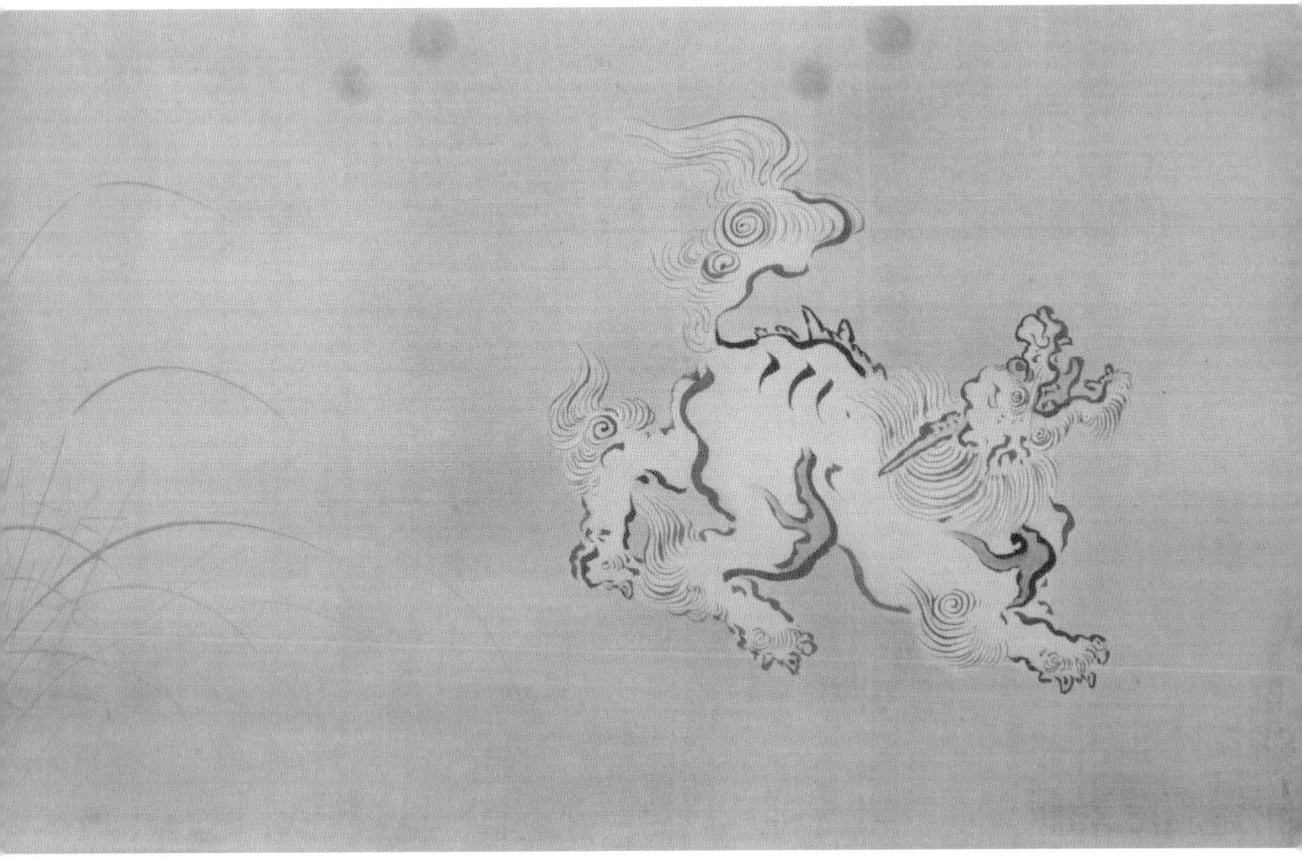

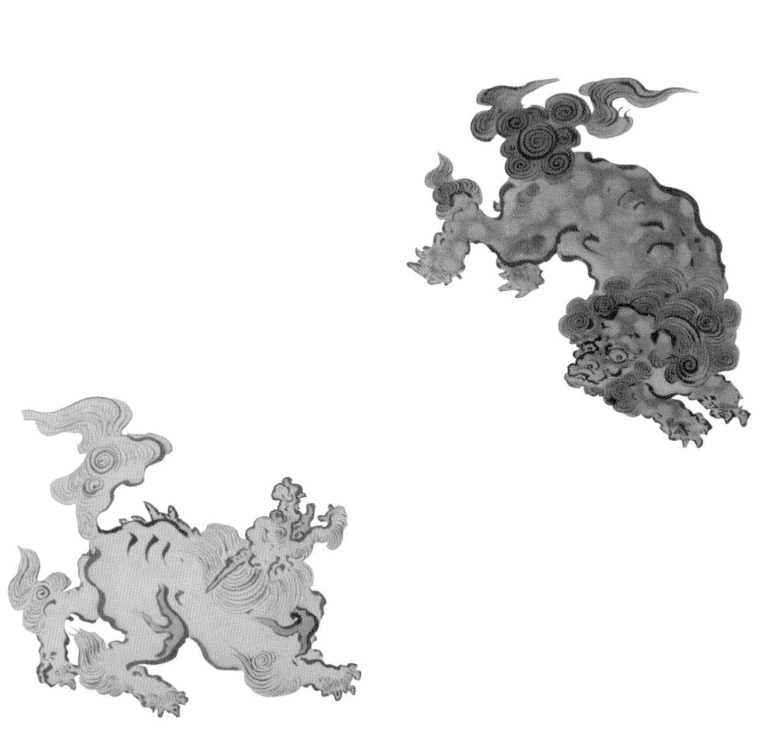

飛禽走獣図巻 部分
Flying Birds and Running Beasts Scroll（detail）

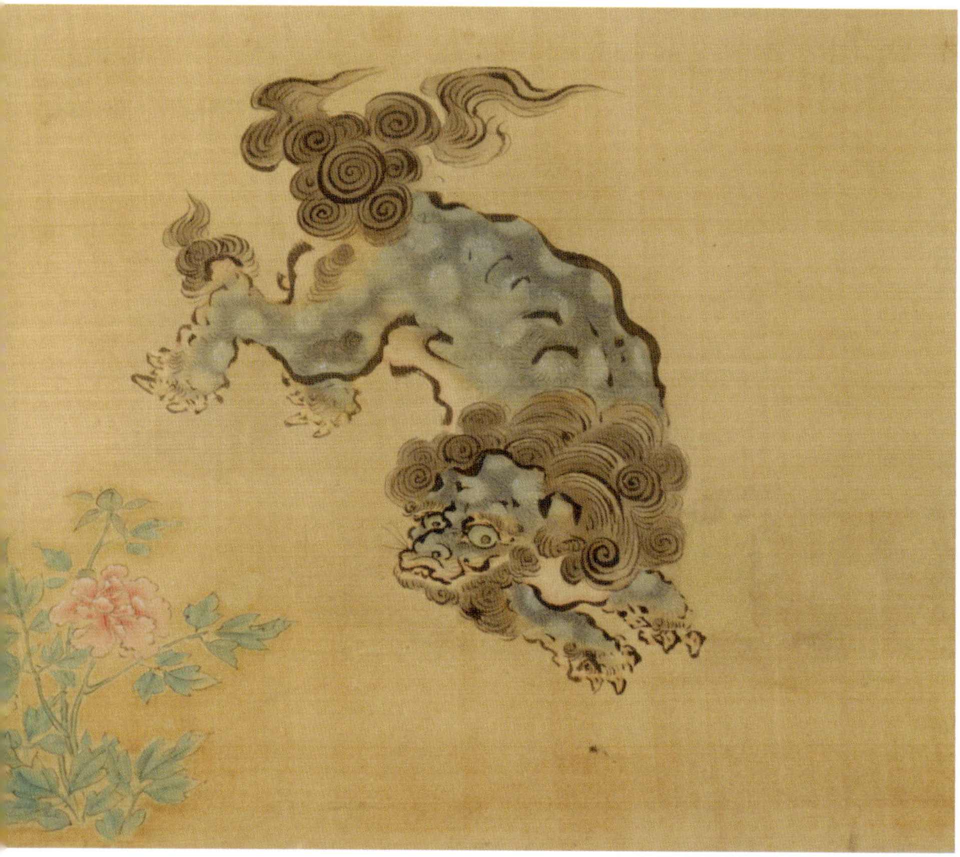

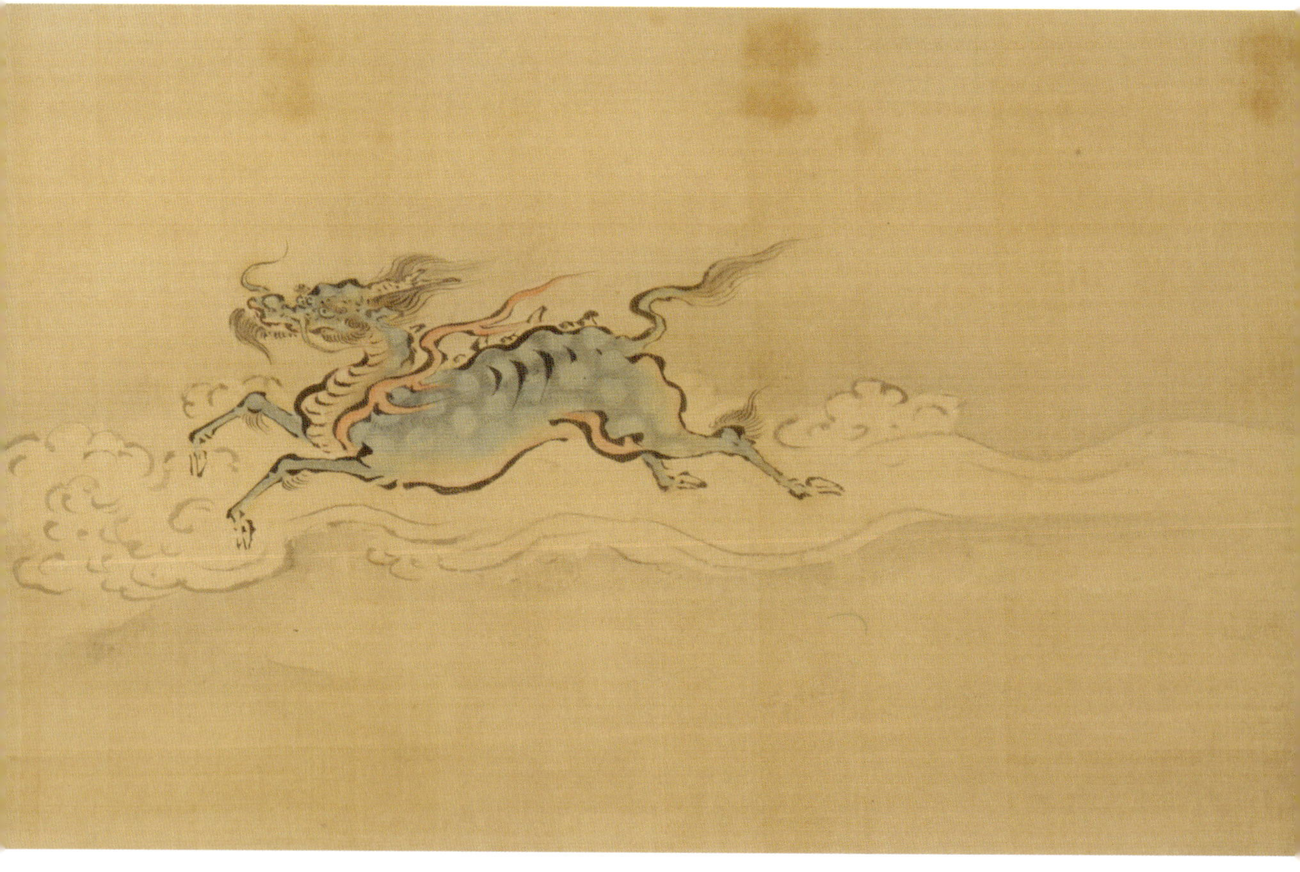

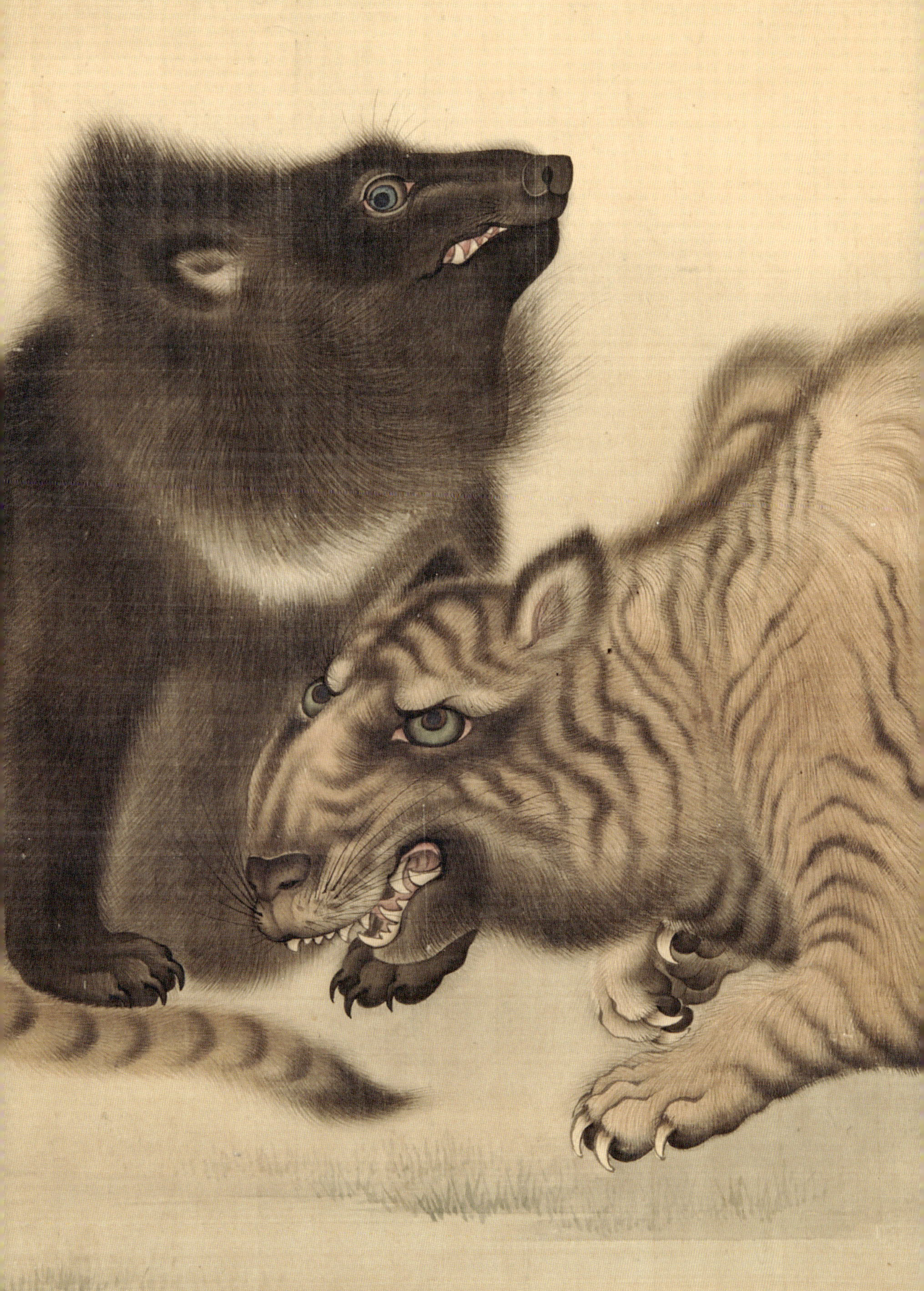

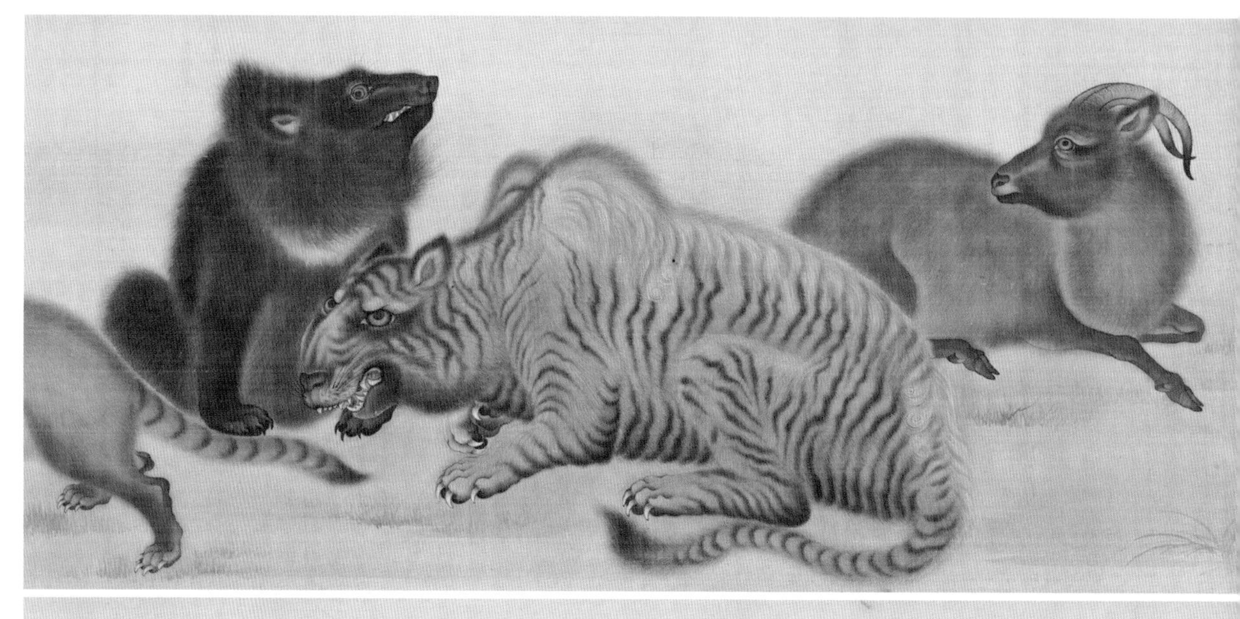

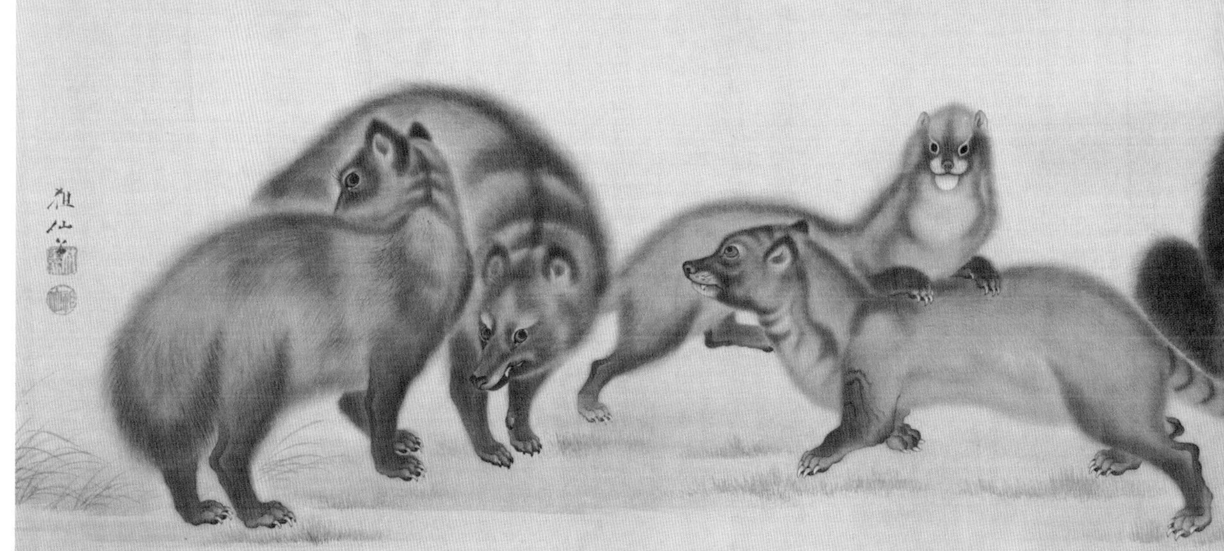

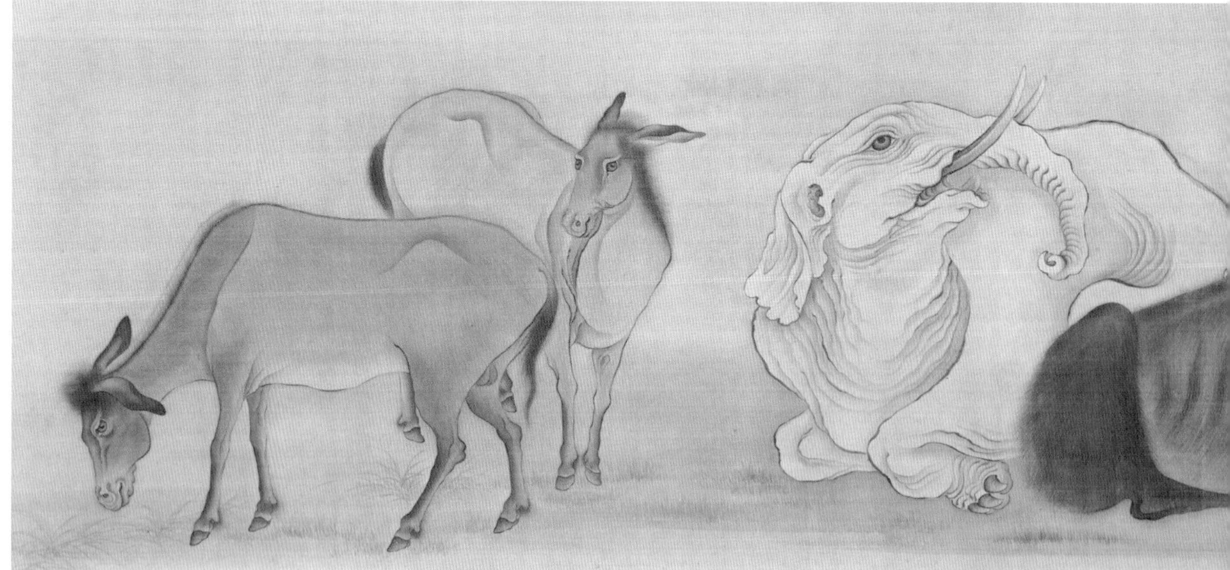

群獣図巻 部分 *Beasts Scroll* (detail)

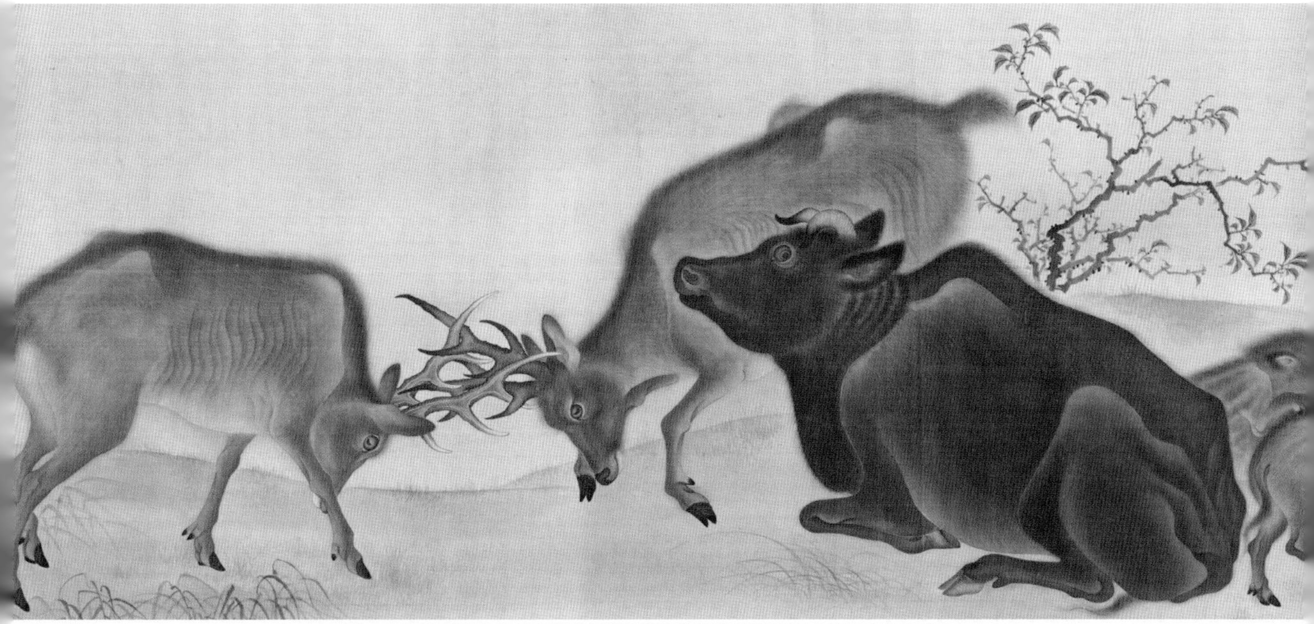

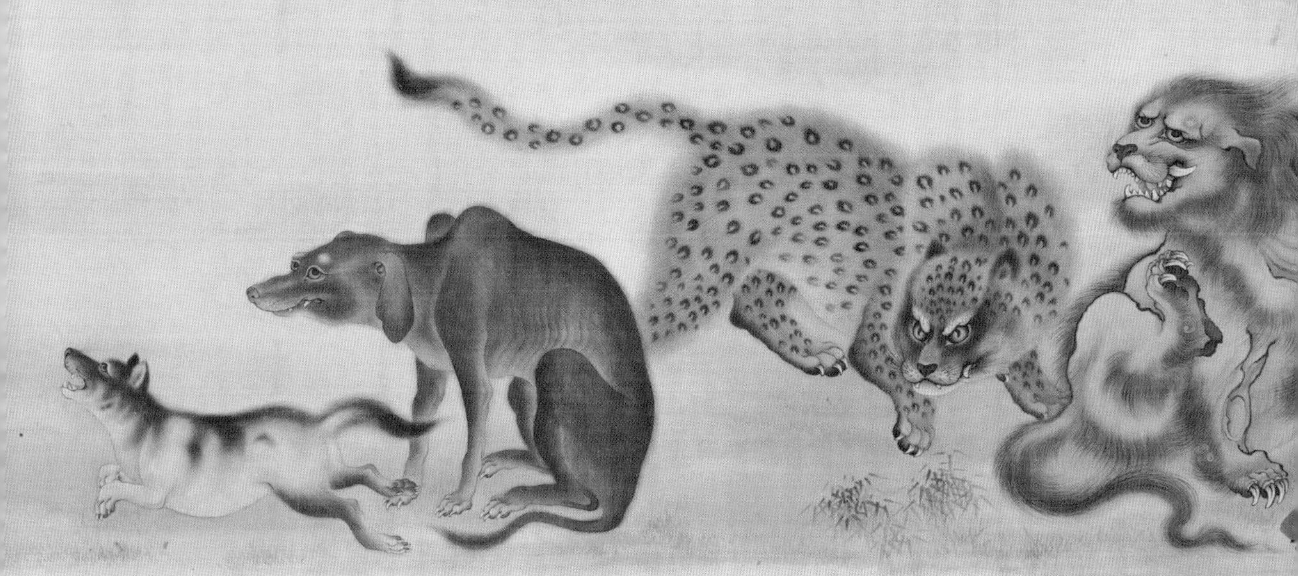

群獣図巻

森狙仙
江戸時代後期（18〜19c）

猿や鹿の絵をはじめ、動物画を得意とした毛描きの名手・森狙仙（1747？〜1821）による作品。十二支に含まれないものや異国の動物も多く、獣の見本帳のような趣である。狩野探幽らによる「獣尽図巻」（p.316-317）からほぼ1世紀半が経過し、動物の描写はここに極まった感がある。極端な陰影を施した立体感あふれる表現に目を奪われるが、描法の違いに時代の求めたものの変化を読み取るべきかもしれない。

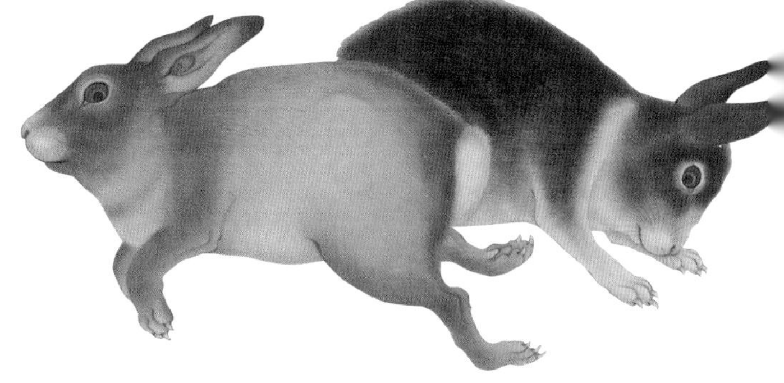

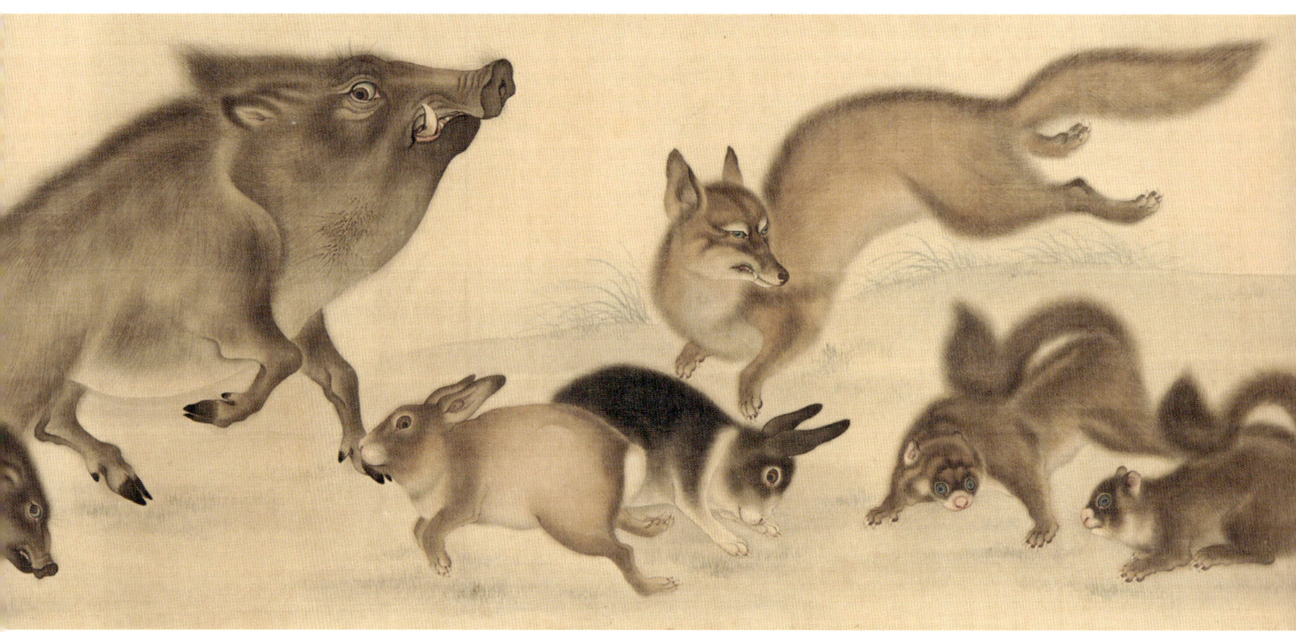

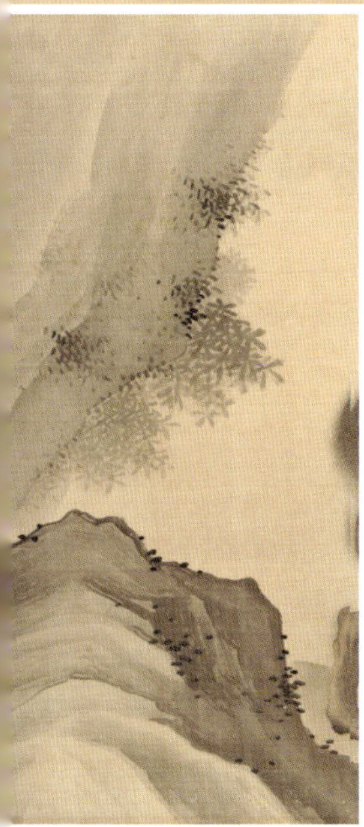

Beasts Scroll

Mori Sosen
18th–19th century

This is a work by Mori Sosen, a master of depicting fur who was especially adept at painting animals, particularly monkey and deer. There are many exotic animals and animals not included in the zodiac here; this work has the air of a sample catalogue, but the artist's intention is unclear. The eye is captivated by this type of painting that overflows with a sense of three-dimensionality in the extreme shading. About a century and a half after Kano Tan'yū created his sketches of various beasts (p.316-317), the depiction of animals had reached a new stage that is represented in images like this one. The skillful use of shading endows the creatures with a sense of plasticity, heralding in a new age of depicting animals.

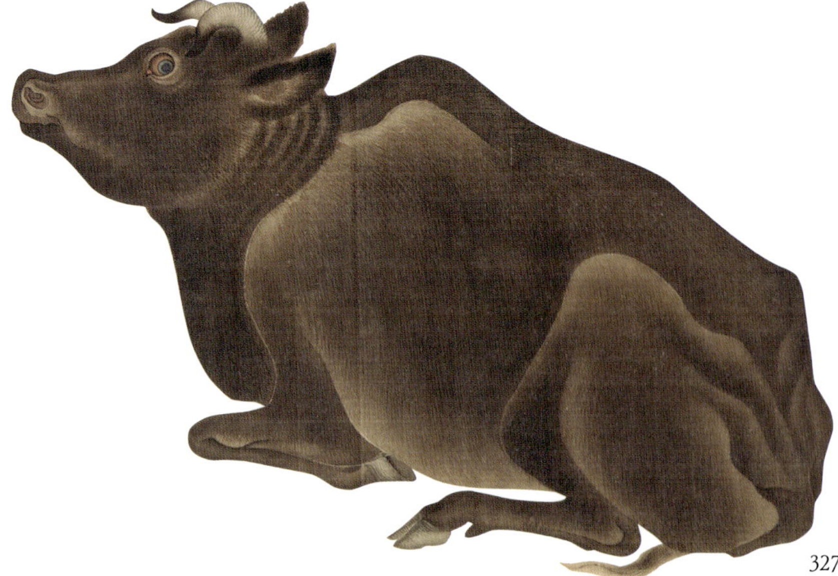

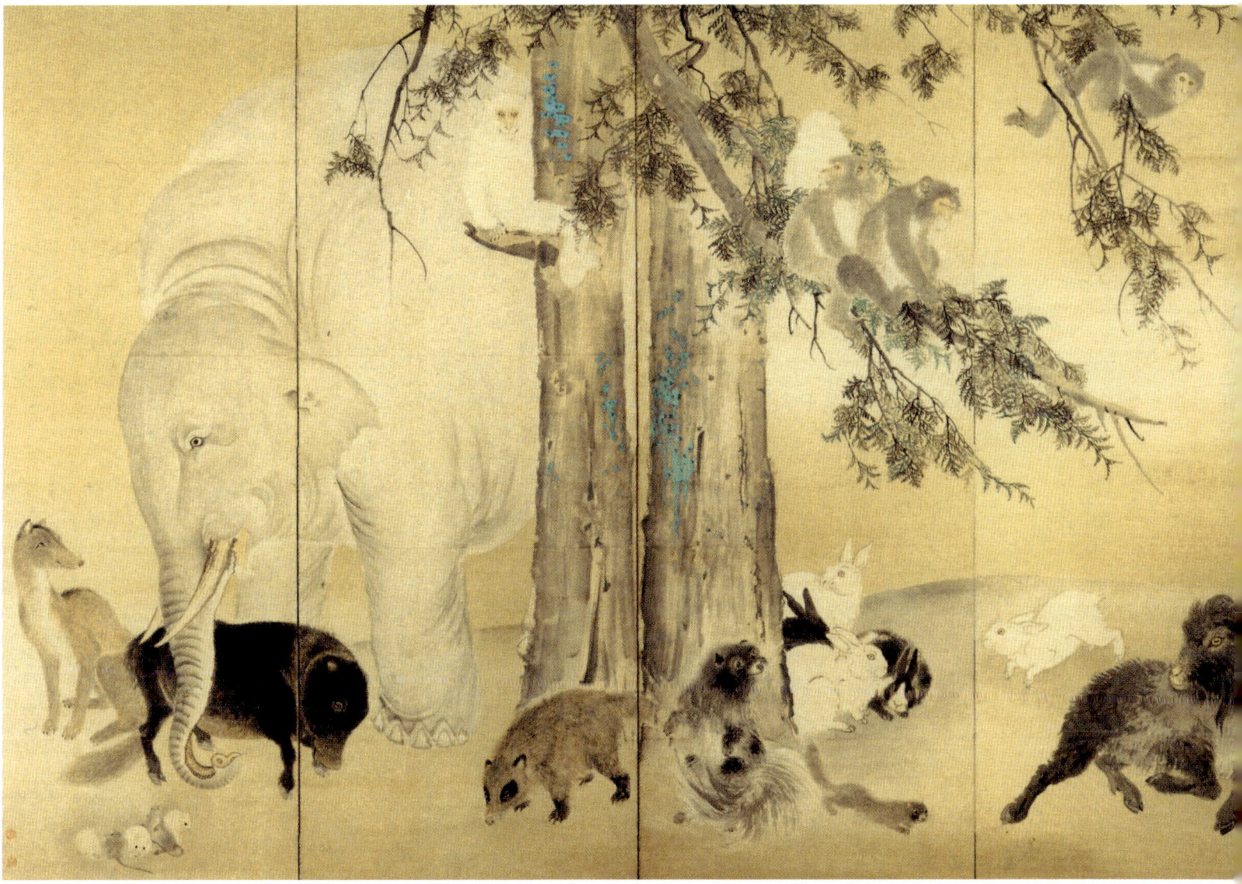

Beasts Screens

Maruyama Ōkyo
1789-95
Sannomaru Shozokan
(The Museum of the Imperial Collections)

This depicts nineteen types and fifty-three animals total. From the auspicious scene of evergreen pines and cypresses (two each), albino animals, which are extremely auspicious, a tiger-leopard pair, a pair of dogs, symbols of the perpetuation of one's descendants (the mouse, the rabbit, the dog), all further decorated by ornate gold paint, it is thought that this is a celebratory folding screen meant to decorate an auspicious and sacred space like that for a wedding or celebration of longevity. Regarding the elephant, we can also interpret it as being derived from life drawings in catalogues, such as the image of the elephant that came during the Kyōhō era that Kano Eisen Hisanobu painted in Edo in the *Scrolls of Birds, Animals, Falcon and Elephant Painted from Life*. It is said that the results of Ōkyo challenging himself to do life drawings from a young age were that he put his skills to good use in drawings of animals like goats, deer and tigers, and it is possible that this was considered to be composed from the copybooks preceding this folding screen.

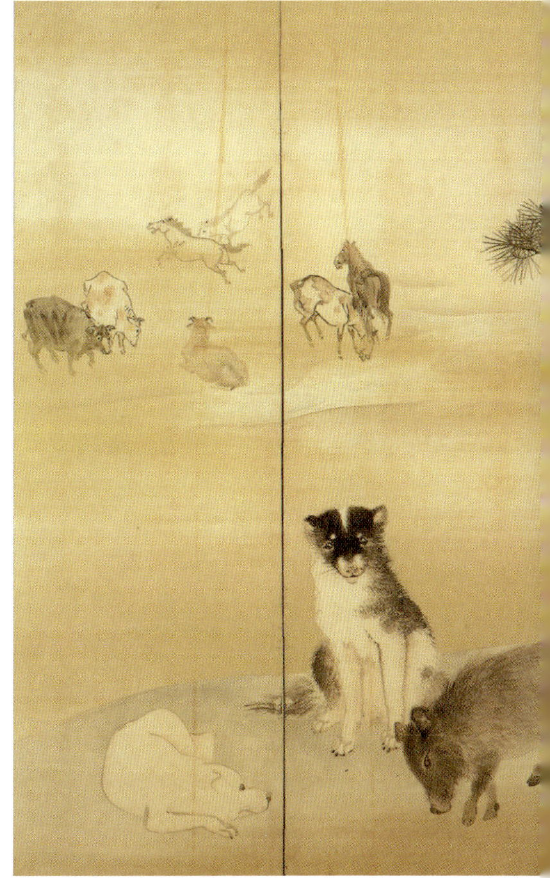

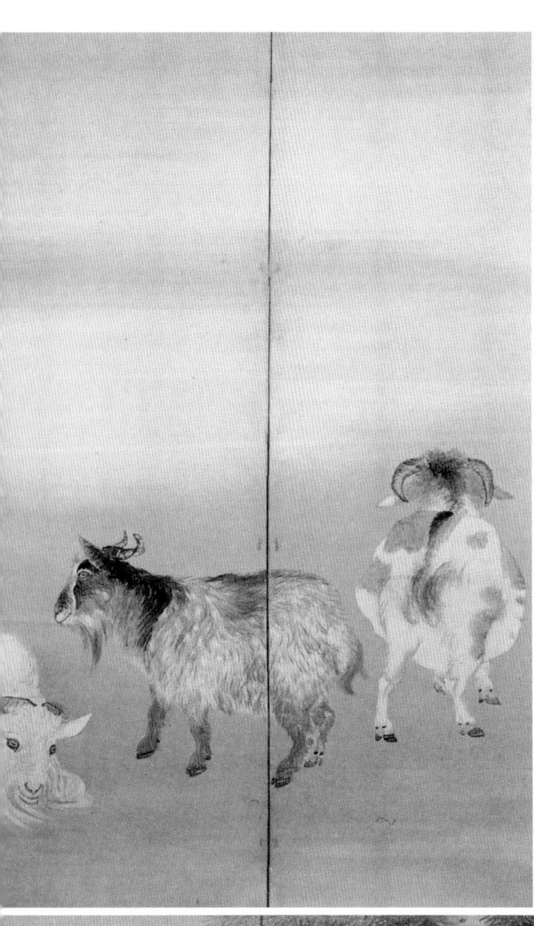

群獣図屏風

円山応挙
寛政年間前期（1789～95）
宮内庁三の丸尚蔵館

19種53体の動物を描く。金泥による華やかな加飾、2本ずつの常緑の松と檜、吉祥性の強い白い動物、つがいや親子の虎豹や犬、子孫繁栄のシンボル（鼠・兎・犬）から、婚礼や長寿などのハレの場を飾るための賀の屏風と考えられる。象については、享保期の渡来象を狩野古信が江戸で描いた「鳥獣鷹象写生図巻」収載図をもとにした一連の写生図からの転用とも解釈できる。応挙が若い頃から挑んだ写生の成果が山羊や鹿・虎などに活かされているとはいえ、この屏風が先行する粉本類から構成されたと見なすことも可能なのである。

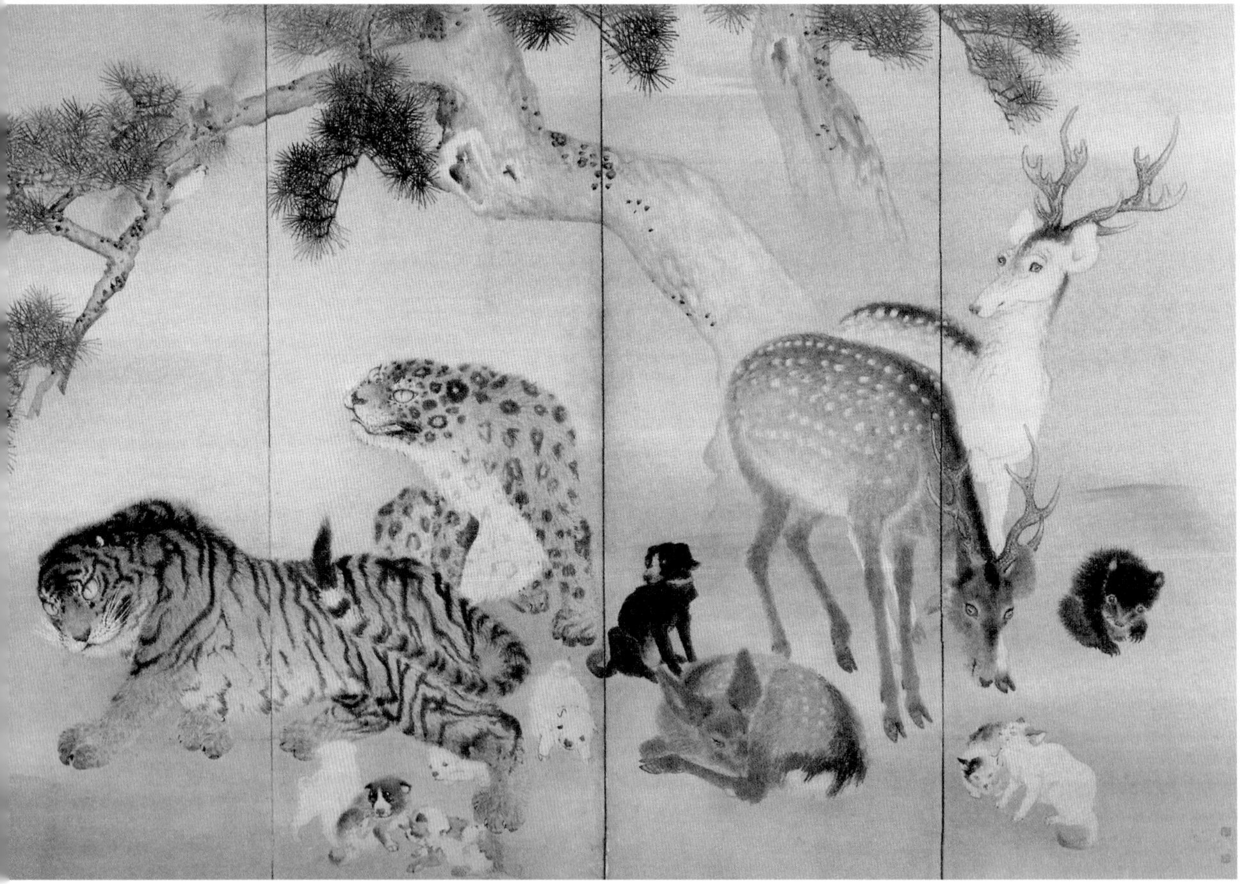

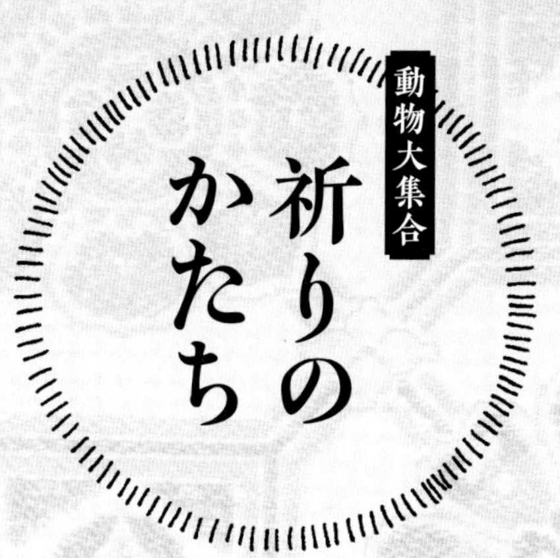

Large Collections of Animals:

Visualizing Prayers

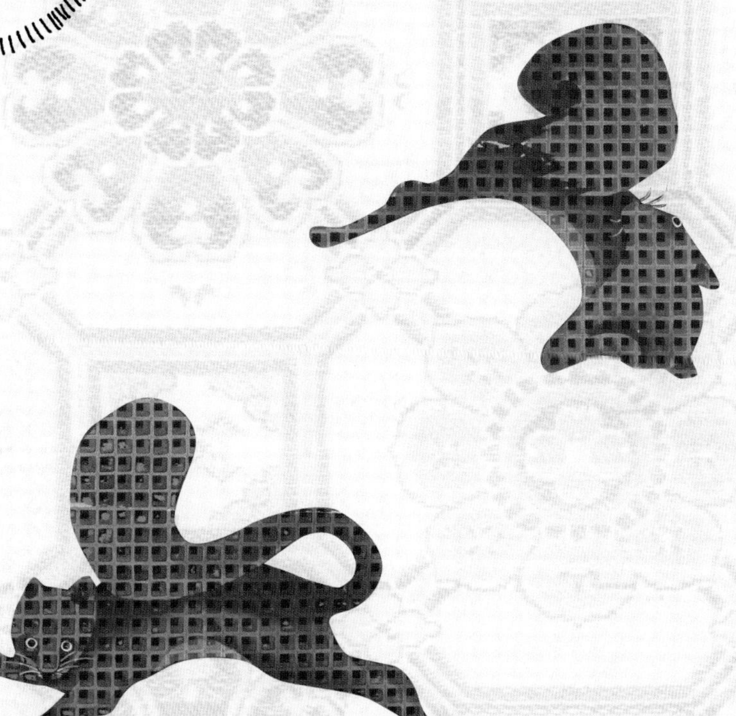

白象群獣図

伊藤若冲
江戸時代後期(18c)

いわゆる「枡目描き」を試みた若冲の試行的作品と考えられている。枡目の数は約6,000個。捺された印章が1794年(寛政6)以降の特徴を示すとされ、晩年期の作と知れる。年老いてなお、新たな絵画表現の可能性に挑戦する若冲のエネルギーに圧倒される。

White Elephant and Beasts

Itō Jakuchū
18th century

It is thought that this painting was a trial attempt by Jakuchū, who pioneered the so-called "mosaic-type grid pattern." There are about six thousand squares in this image. The seal that he used here is characteristic of his work from after 1794 (Kansei 6), so we can tell that this is a work he did in his twilight years. The viewer is overwhelmed by Jakuchū's energy in challenging himself to experiment with this innovative type of painting despite his advanced age.

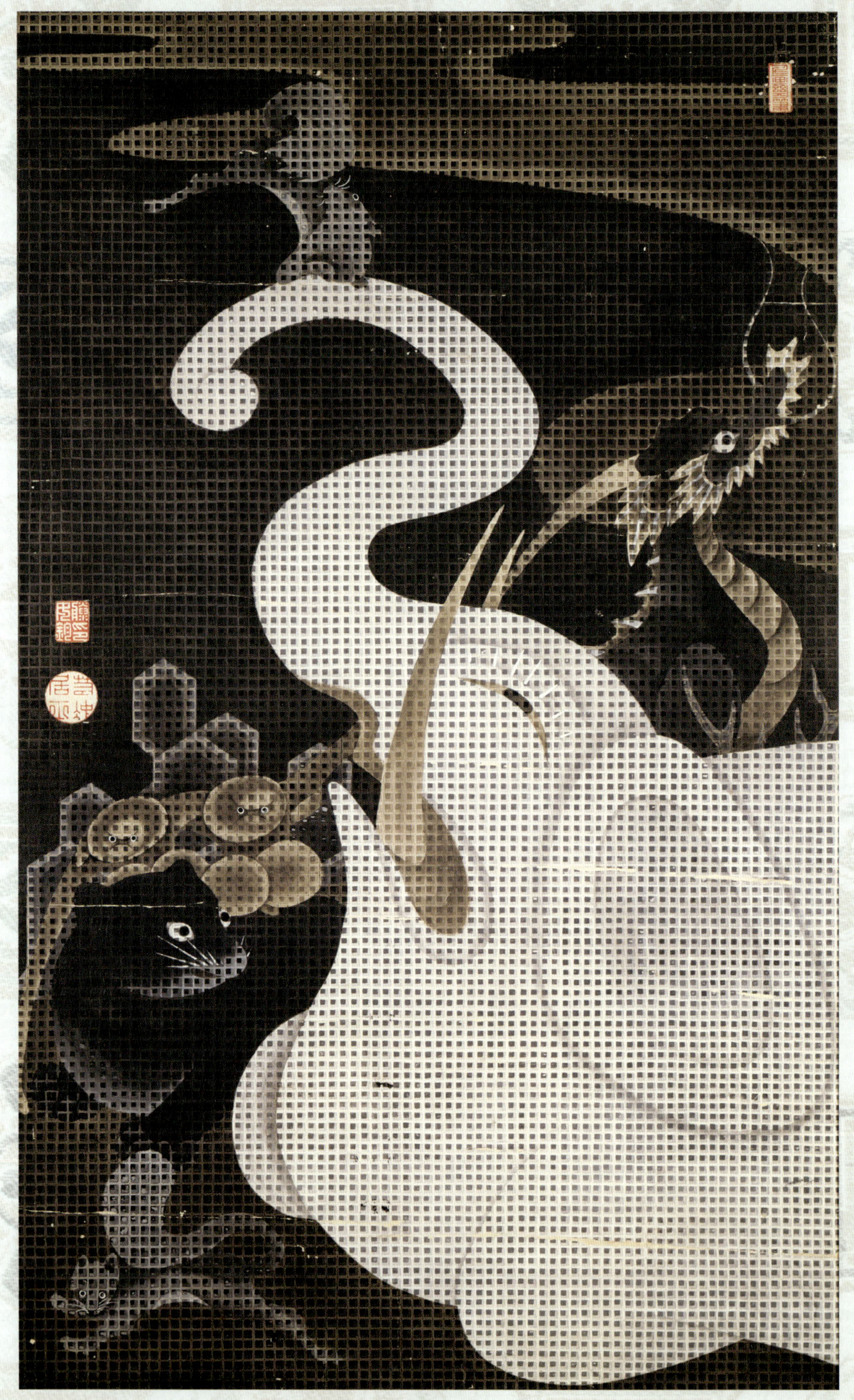

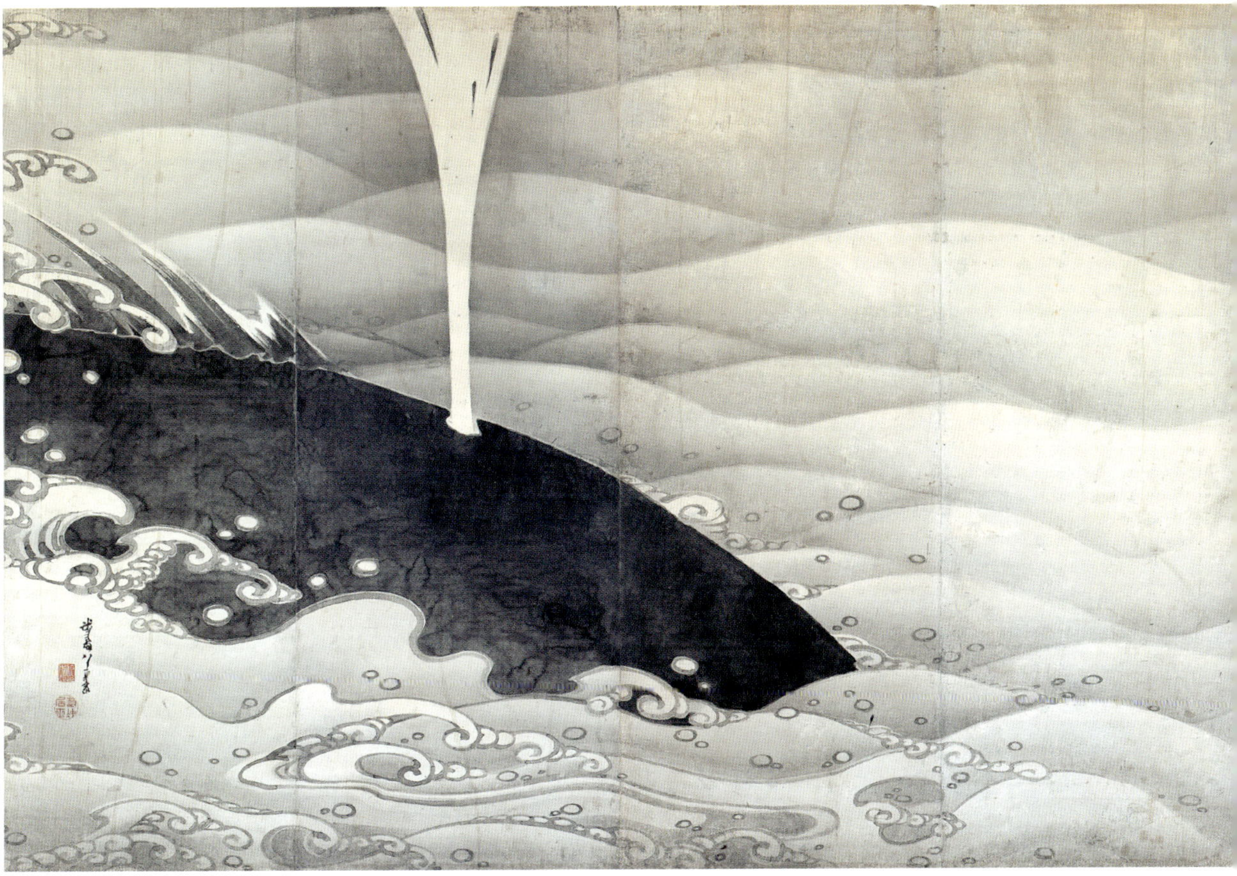

象と鯨図屏風

伊藤若冲
寛政7年（1795）
MIHO MUSEUM

陸・海それぞれの世界で最大の生物を、白と黒とで対比させた作品。落款に82歳の筆であることを記すが、若冲の記年について還暦以後は改元ごとに1歳加算したという狩野博幸氏の提言がある。それに従えば、本図制作時の若冲の実年齢は80歳で、1795年（寛政7）の作となる。この年は実母の十七回忌にあたり、加えて若冲はその母の享年を迎えていた。熱心な仏教徒だった若冲にとって、この年は特別なものだったはずで、おそらく母への追慕の念を表した作品を制作したことであろう。ちょうど、この母が亡くなった際に描かれたとされる「果蔬涅槃図」のように。そして、その作品こそが本図ではなかったかと思えるのである。口元を震わせる白象と、潮を勢いよく吹き上げる鯨とが発する音声（現実には聞こえないが）は、母の慈愛に対する思慕と哀悼の叫びだったのではあるまいか。水墨だけで描かれた本図の見せる、どこか哀愁を帯びた気配は、そのような背景を踏まえてこそ納得できるように思う。

Elephant and Whale Screens

Itō Jakuchū
1795
MIHO MUSEUM

This is a work where the largest animals of the land and sea are contrasted in black and white. The signature states that this work was done when Jakuchū was eighty-two years old, but Kano Hiroyuki suggests that after his sixtieth birthday, following the change of era, one year was added, making Jakuchū's signature inaccurate. Assuming this was indeed the case, Jakuchū was actually eighty when he painted this work, and it was painted in 1795 (Kansei 7). This year corresponded to the sixteenth anniversary of his biological mother's death; additionally, Jakuchū was approaching the age that his mother had died at. Ever the avid student of Buddhism, this year had special meaning to Jakuchū. It seems that the work was created in memory of his mother. Jakuchū made it around the same time as his *Vegetable Nirvana*, which coincided with his mother's death. It is easy to imagine that Jakuchū considered this work to be the main image in her honor. Aren't the sounds (that we cannot actually hear) created by the white elephant with the quivering mouth and the whale that vigorously spouts seawater into the air expressions of Jakuchū's longing affection for his mother and a scream of lament in her absence? To fully understand this ink painting, I think that touching on that kind of background will give the viewer an indication of how deeply this work is tinged with sorrow.

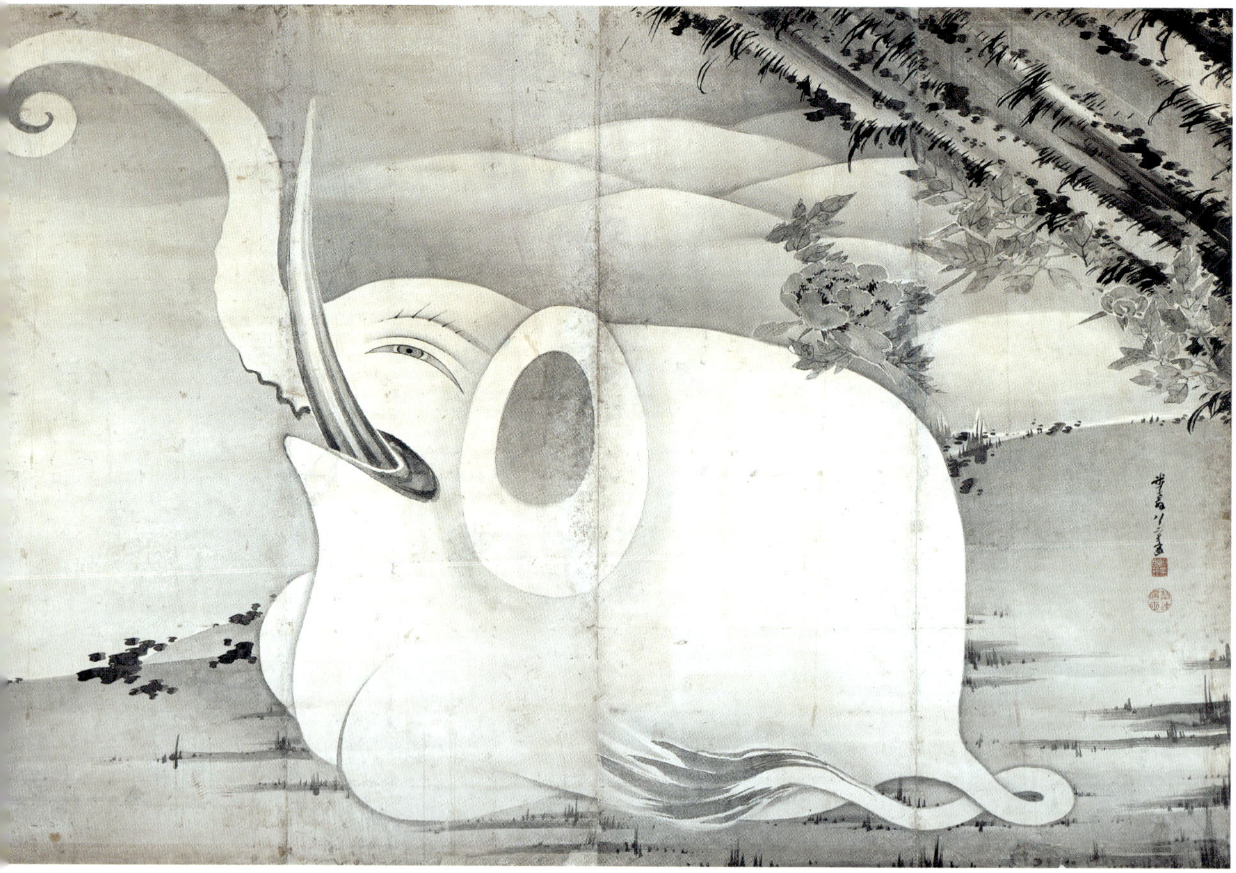

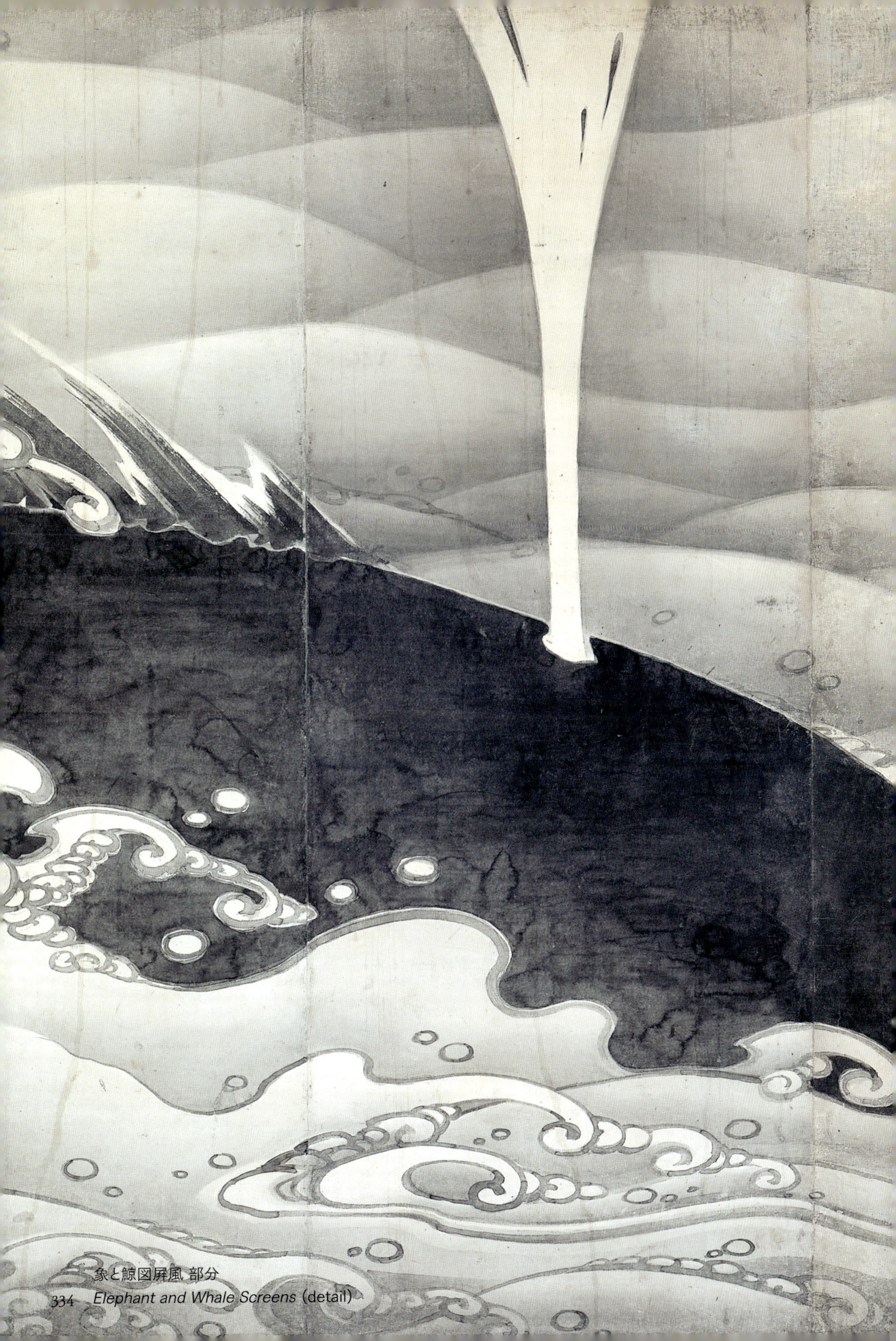

象と鯨図屏風 部分

Elephant and Whale Screens (detail)

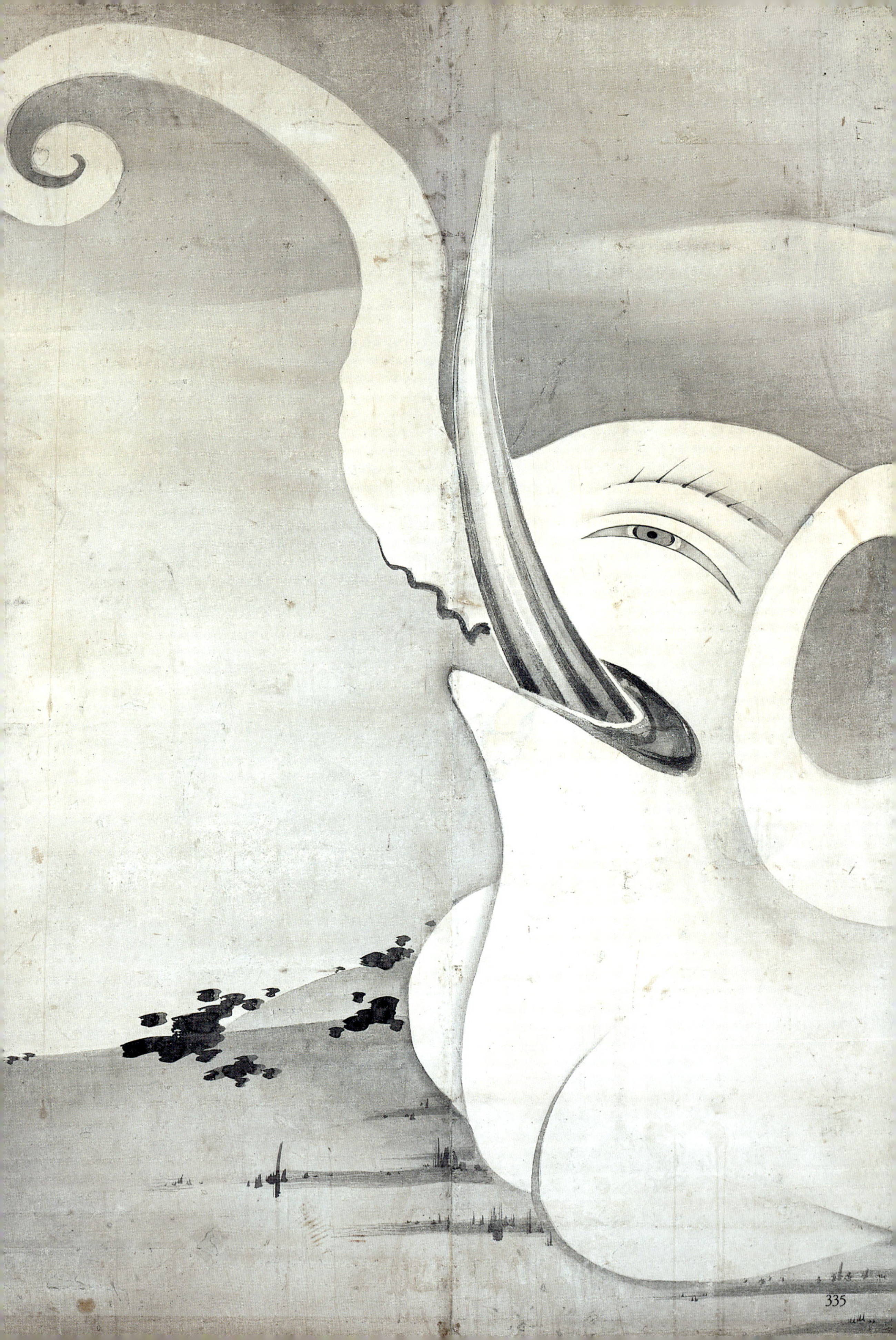

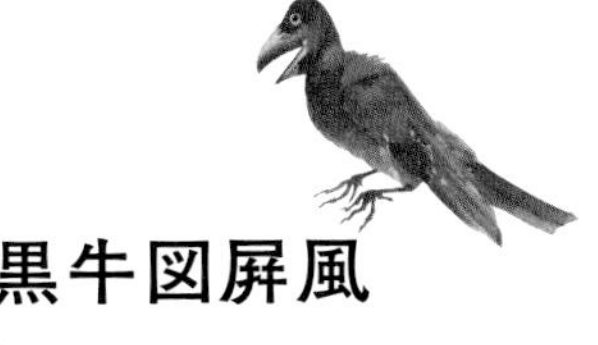

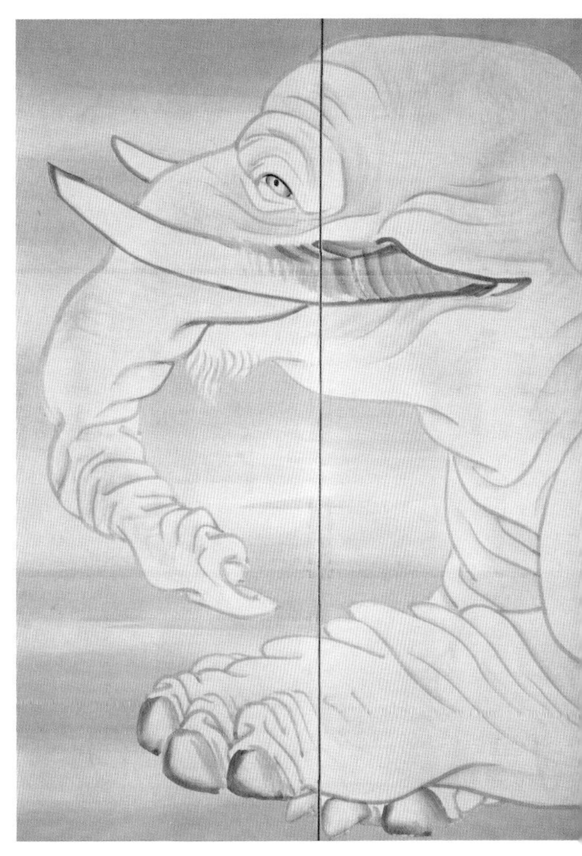

白象黒牛図屏風

長沢芦雪
江戸時代後期（18c）
エツコ＆ジョー・プライスコレクション

屏風の大画面から、はみ出すほどの象と牛。よく見ると、白象の背に黒いカラス、黒牛の腹下には白い子犬が描かれている。黒と白の対比をねらった作品を一般に「黒白（こくびゃく）図」と称するが、本図はそれに大小の対照も加えたもの。描かれたモチーフのすべてが対照の妙に貢献しているのである。

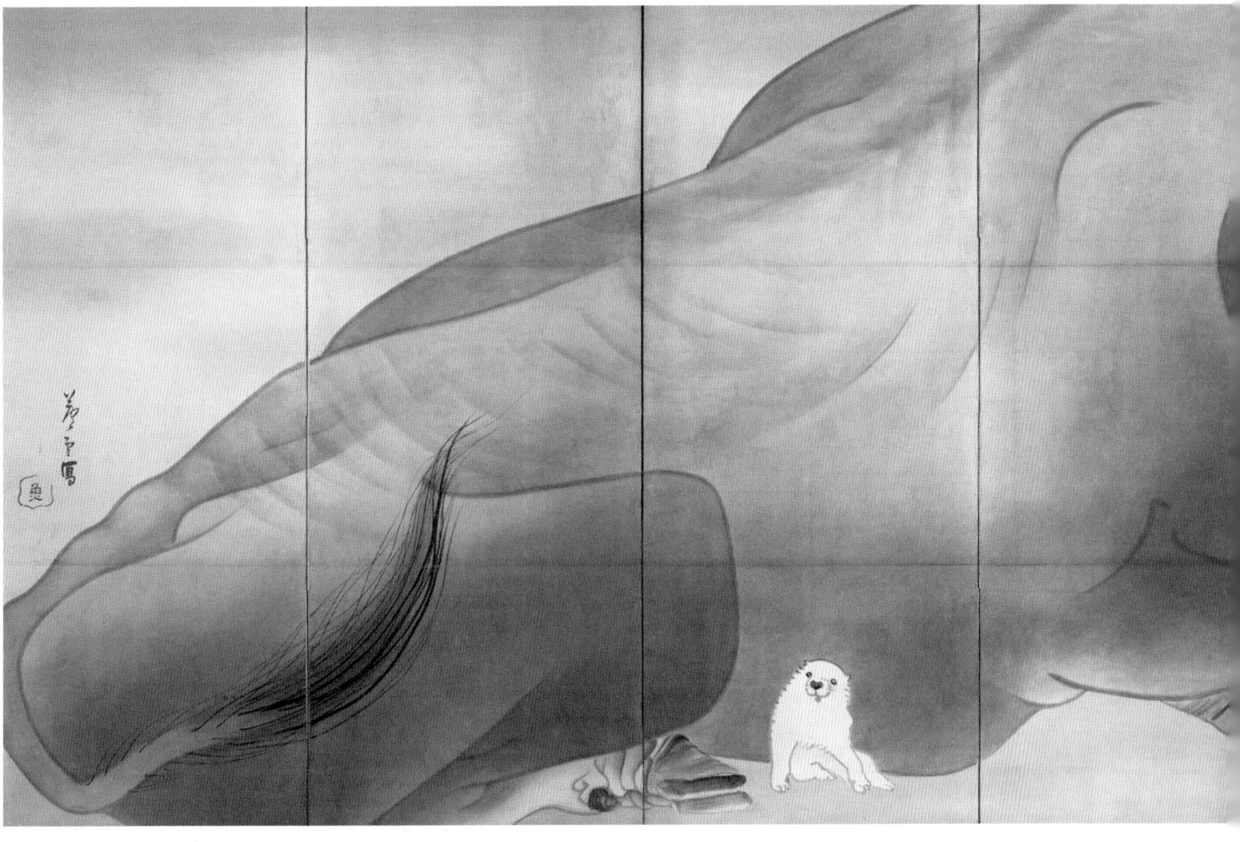

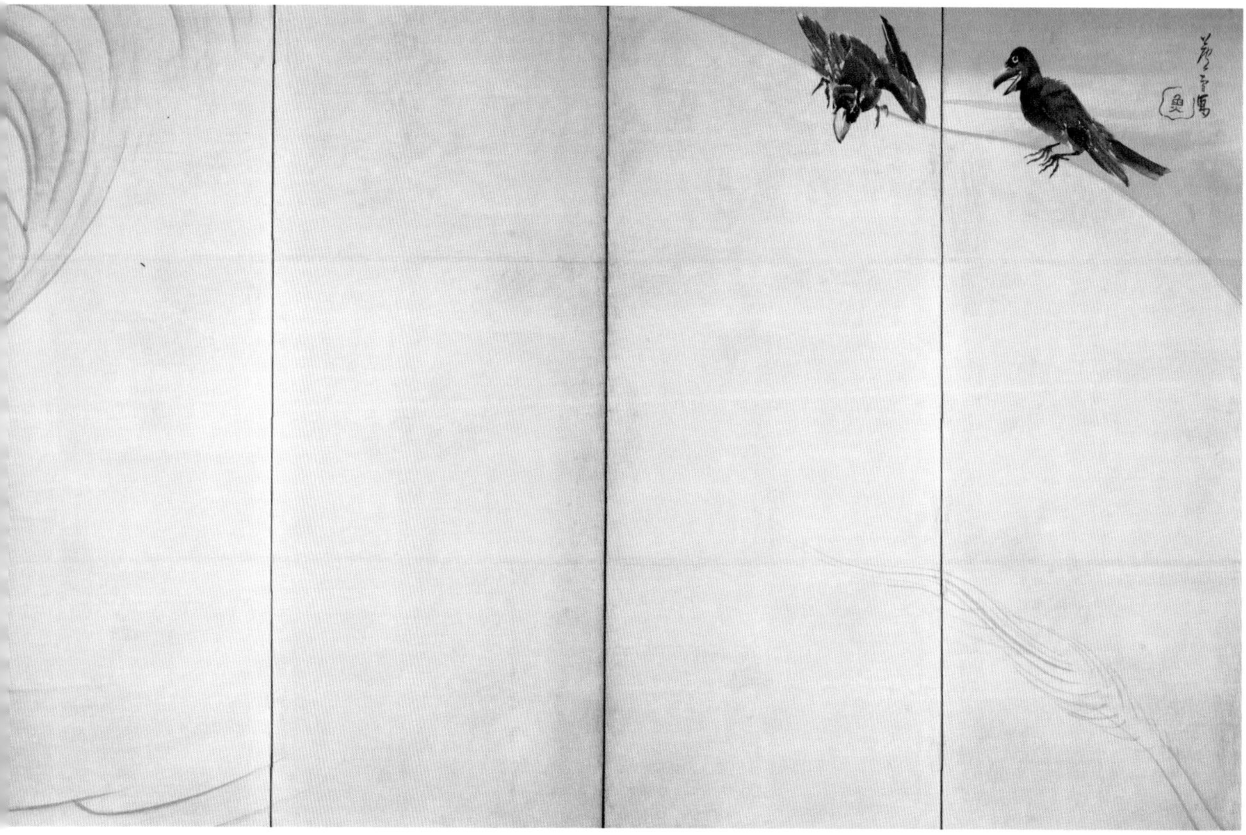

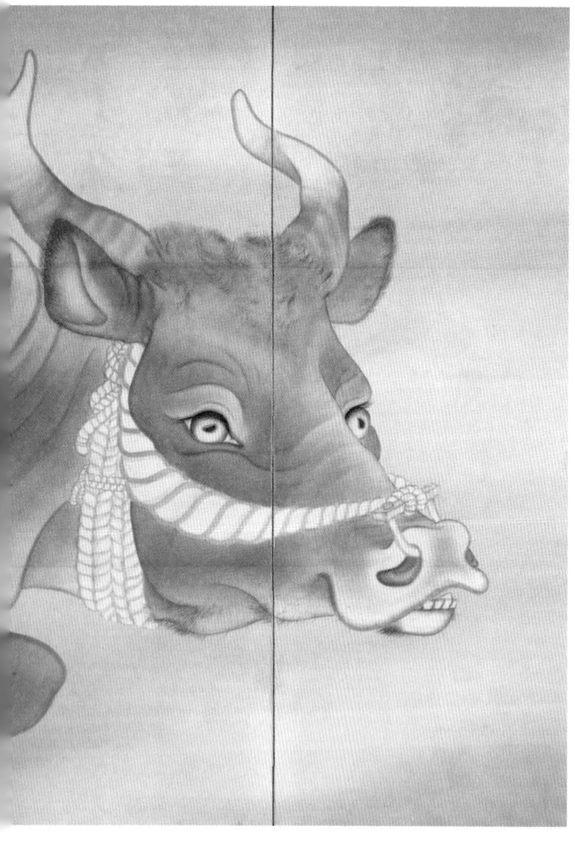

White Elephant and Black Bull Screens

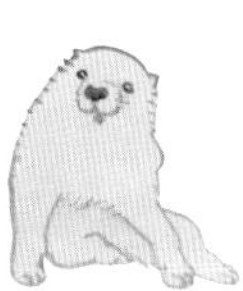

Nagasawa Rosetsu
18th century
Etsuko and Joe Price collection

This work depicts an elephant and bull so large that they even clear the frame of the large-scale screens. Looking at it carefully, there is a black crow on the back of the white elephant, and there is a white puppy under the belly of the black bull. Works that focus on the contrast between black and white are commonly titled *Monochrome Painting*, but this work also adds the opposing elements of large and small. All the motifs painted here contribute to a sense of clever contrast.

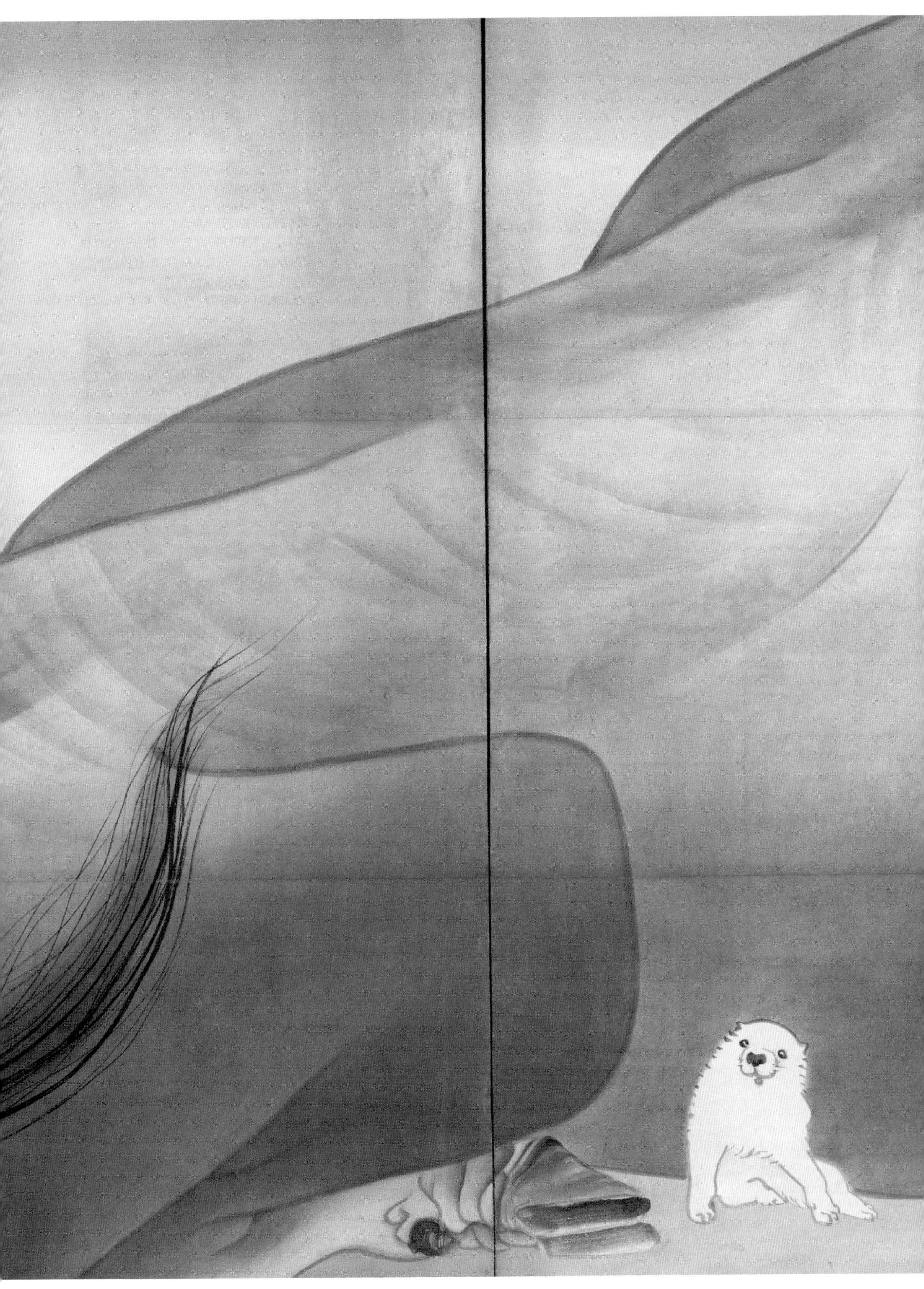

338 白象黒牛図屏風 部分 *White Elephant and Black Bull Screens* (detail)

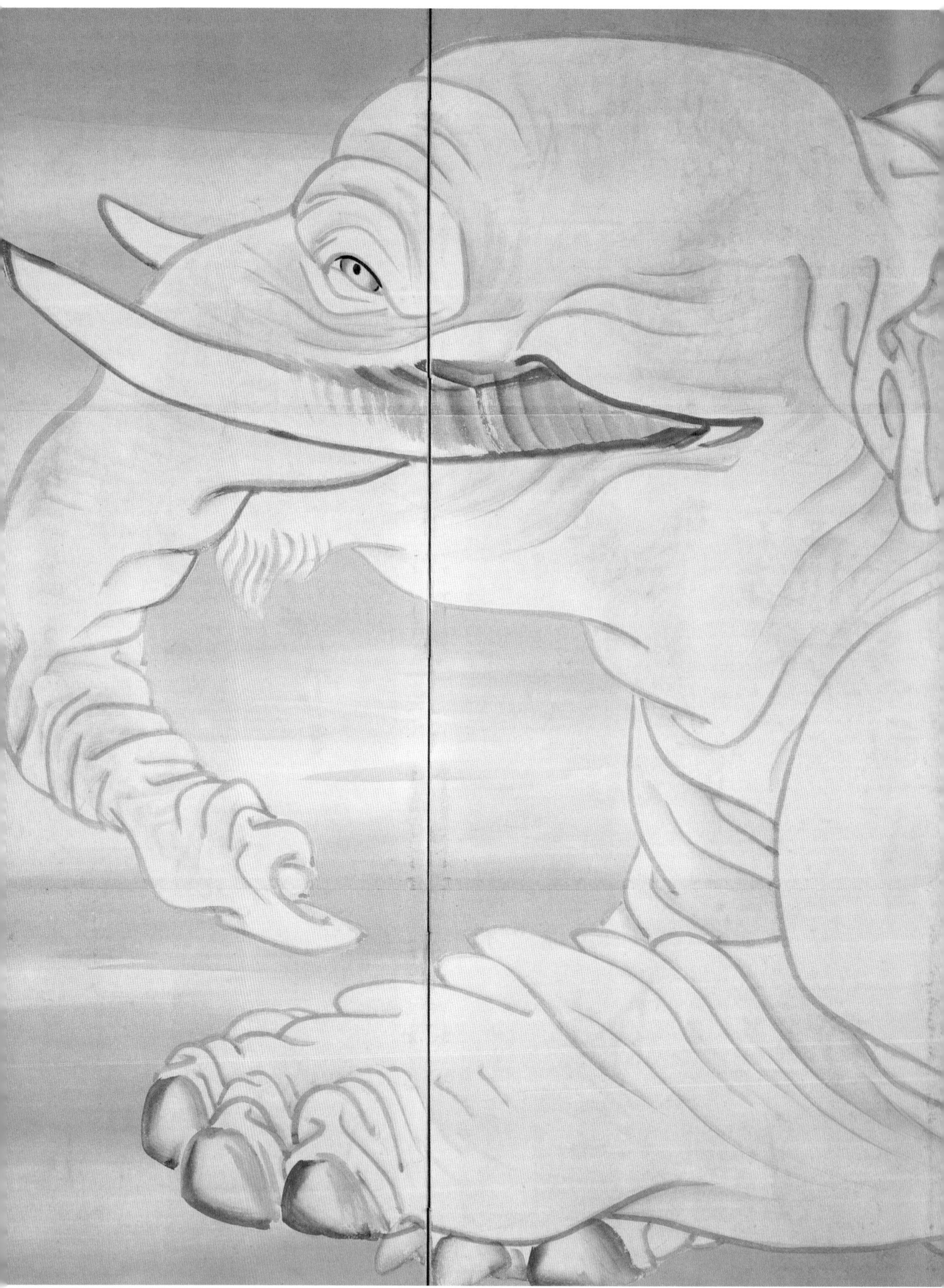

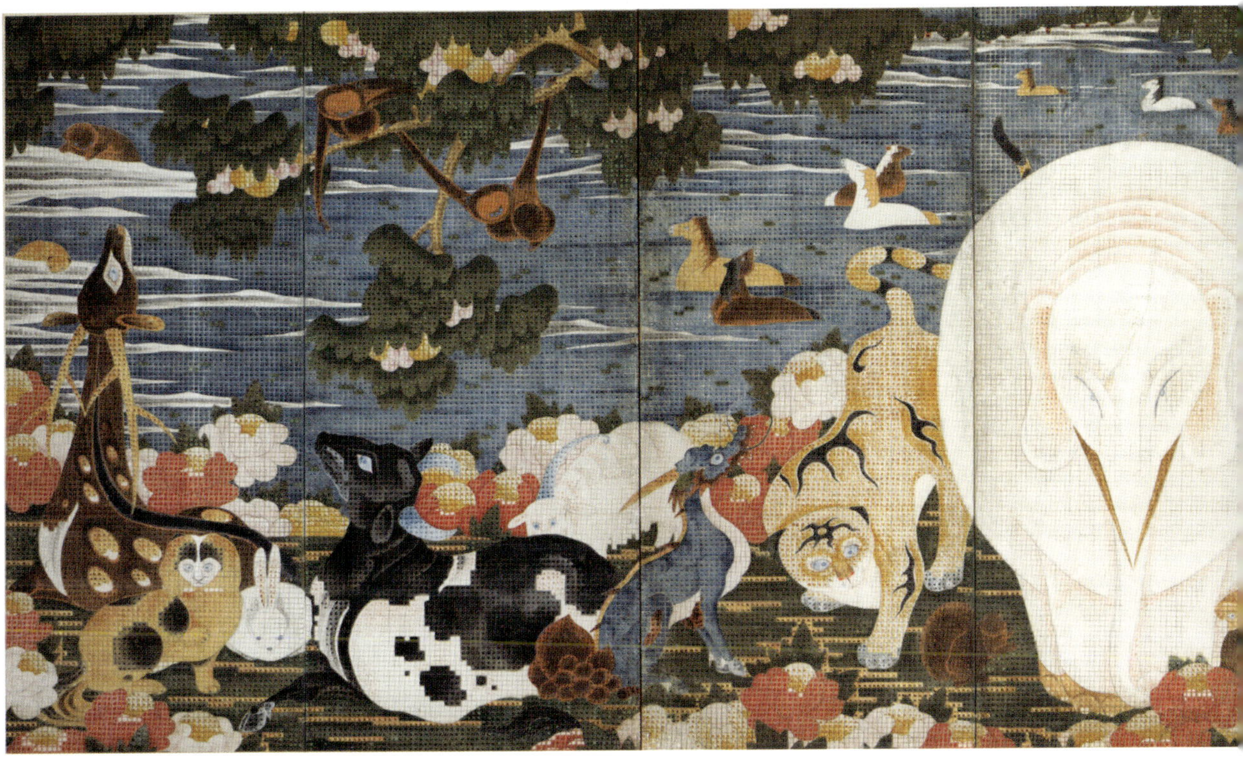

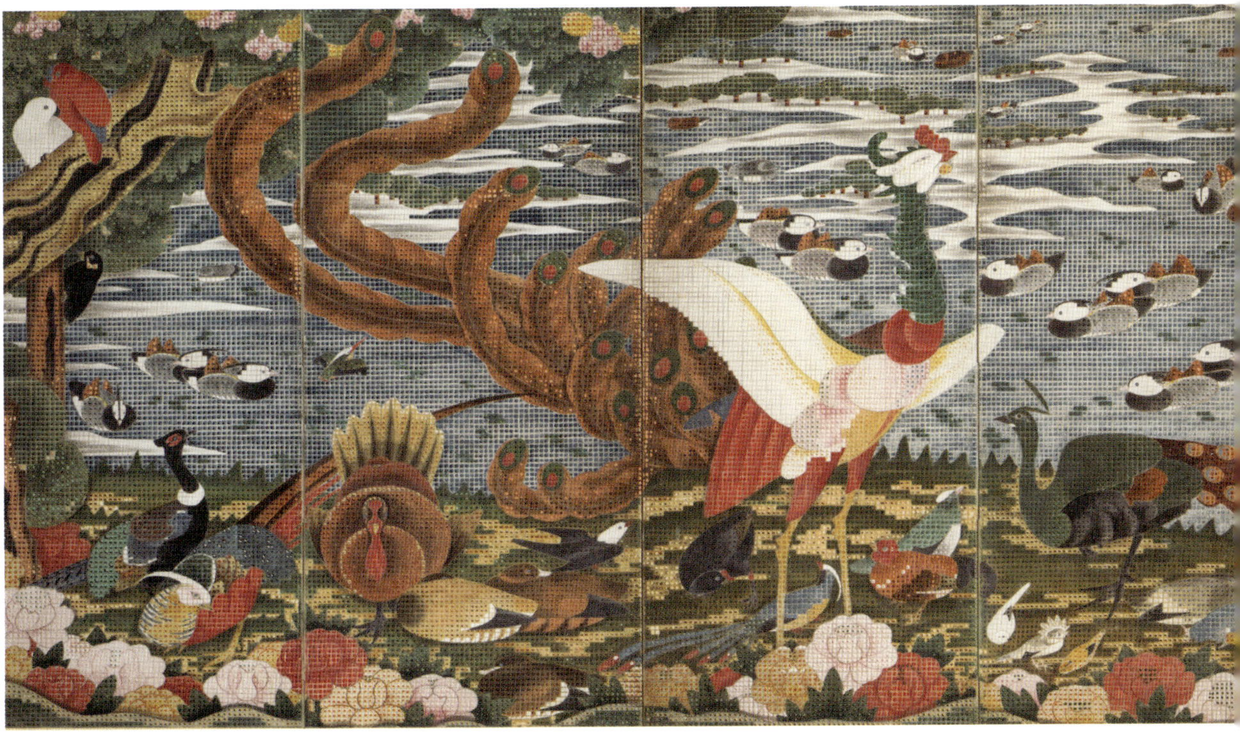

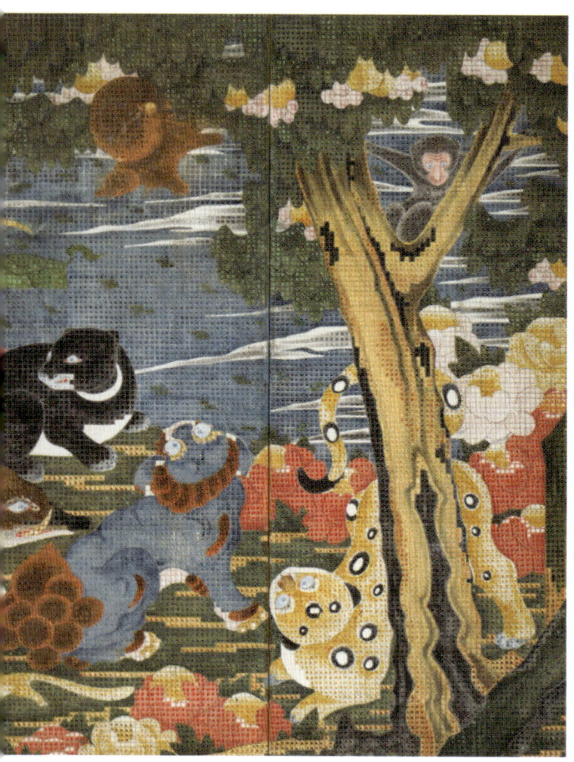

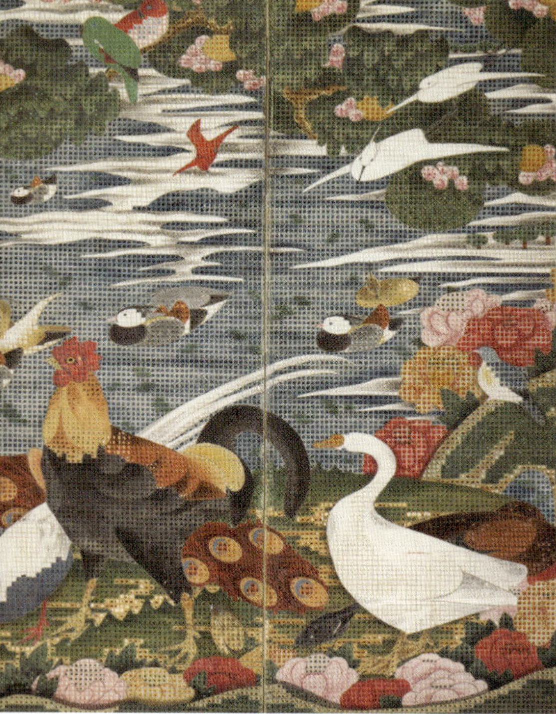

樹花鳥獣図屏風

江戸時代後期(18c)
静岡県立美術館

右隻においては、主役である正面向きの白象を要として、動物たちと花樹の競演がくり広げられている。描かれるのは、十二支を中心に全23種の獣類。対する左隻には、鳳凰を中心に延べ35種の鳥たちが描かれ、同じ豊穣の世界が現出する。枡目は9ミリ四方で、両隻合わせて約60,000個。

Birds and Animals in the Flower Garden Screens

18th century
Shizuoka Prefectural Museum of Art

On the right screen, a pageant of animals and flowering trees surrounds a white elephant facing forward. Twenty-three types of animals are portrayed here, including the zodiac animals. On the contrasting left screen, a world of the same abundance unfolds in the scene of a phoenix surrounded by thirty-five types of birds. Each grid box is nine millimeters square, and both screens together are made up of about sixty thousand squares.

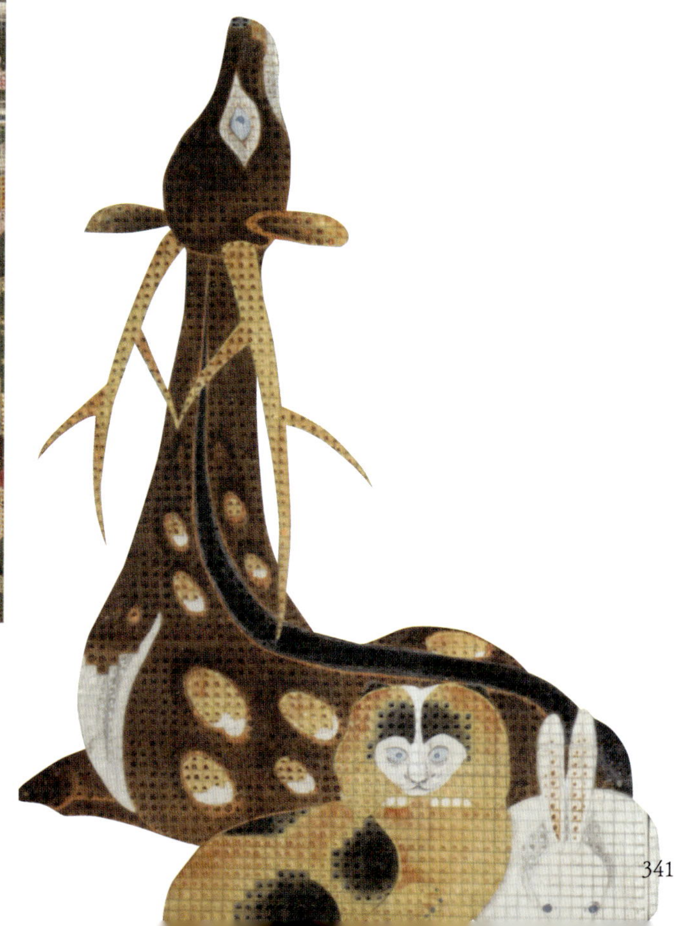

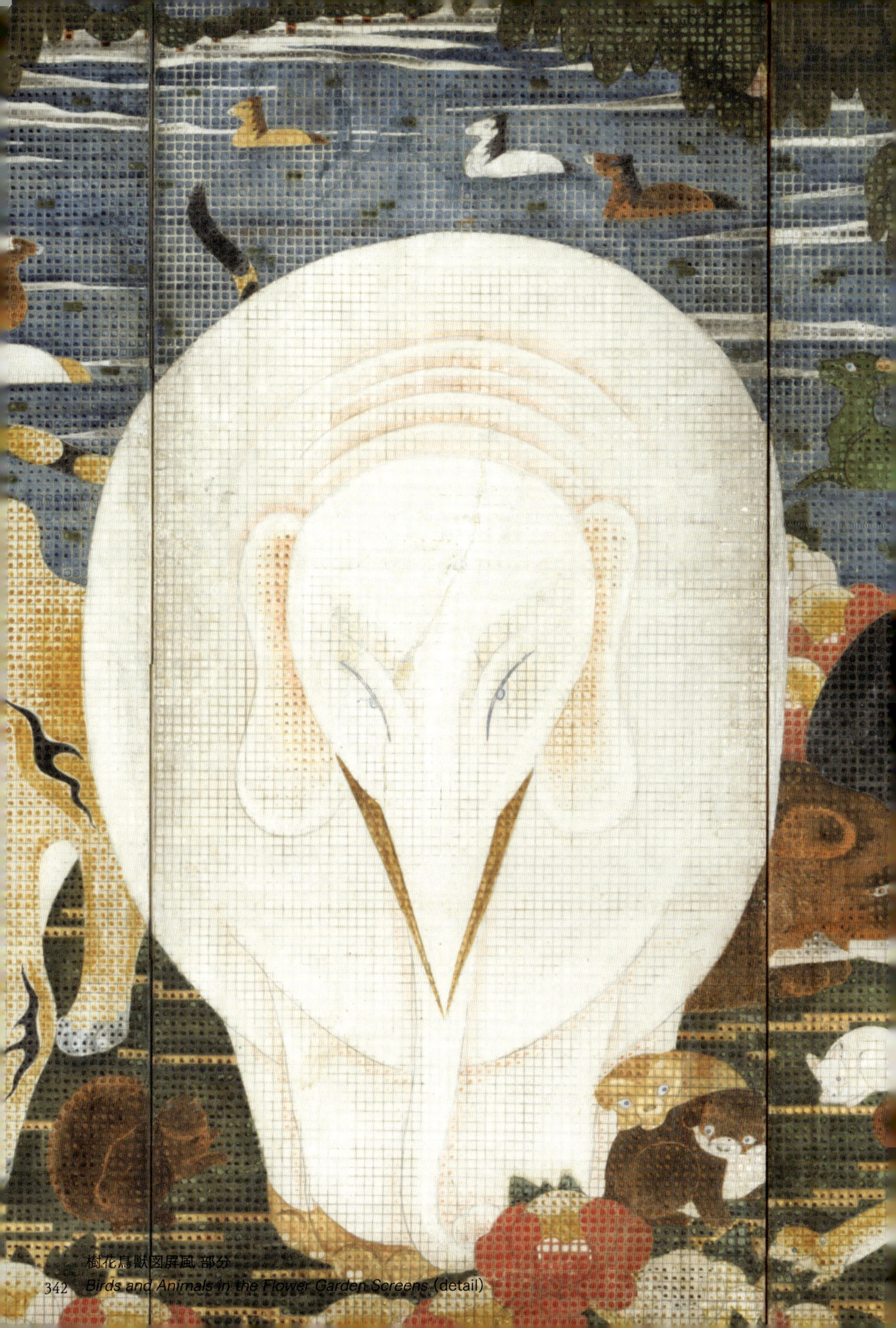

樹花鳥獣図屏風 部分
Birds and Animals in the Flower Garden Screens (detail)

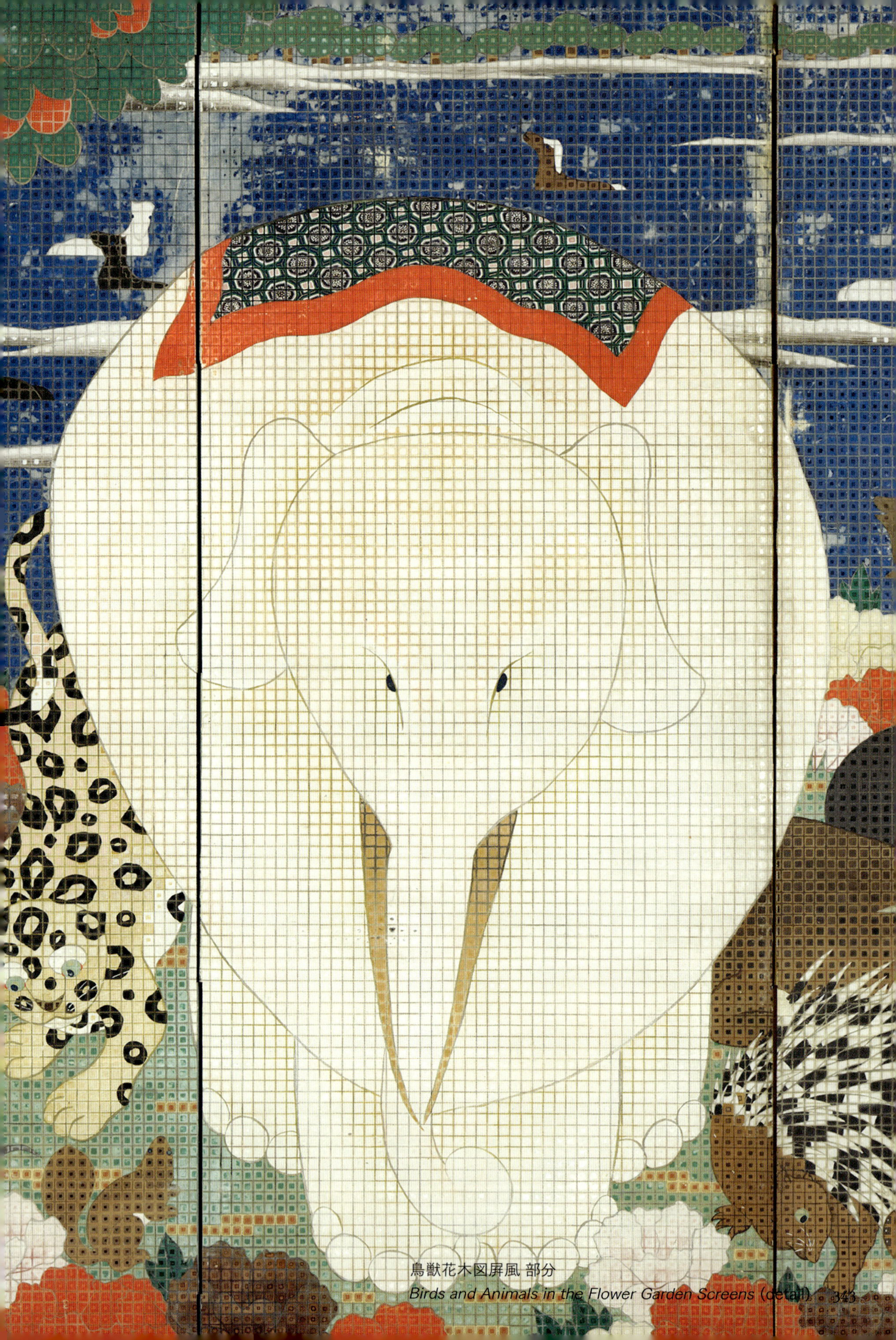

鳥獣花木図屏風 部分
Birds and Animals in the Flower Garden Screens (detail)

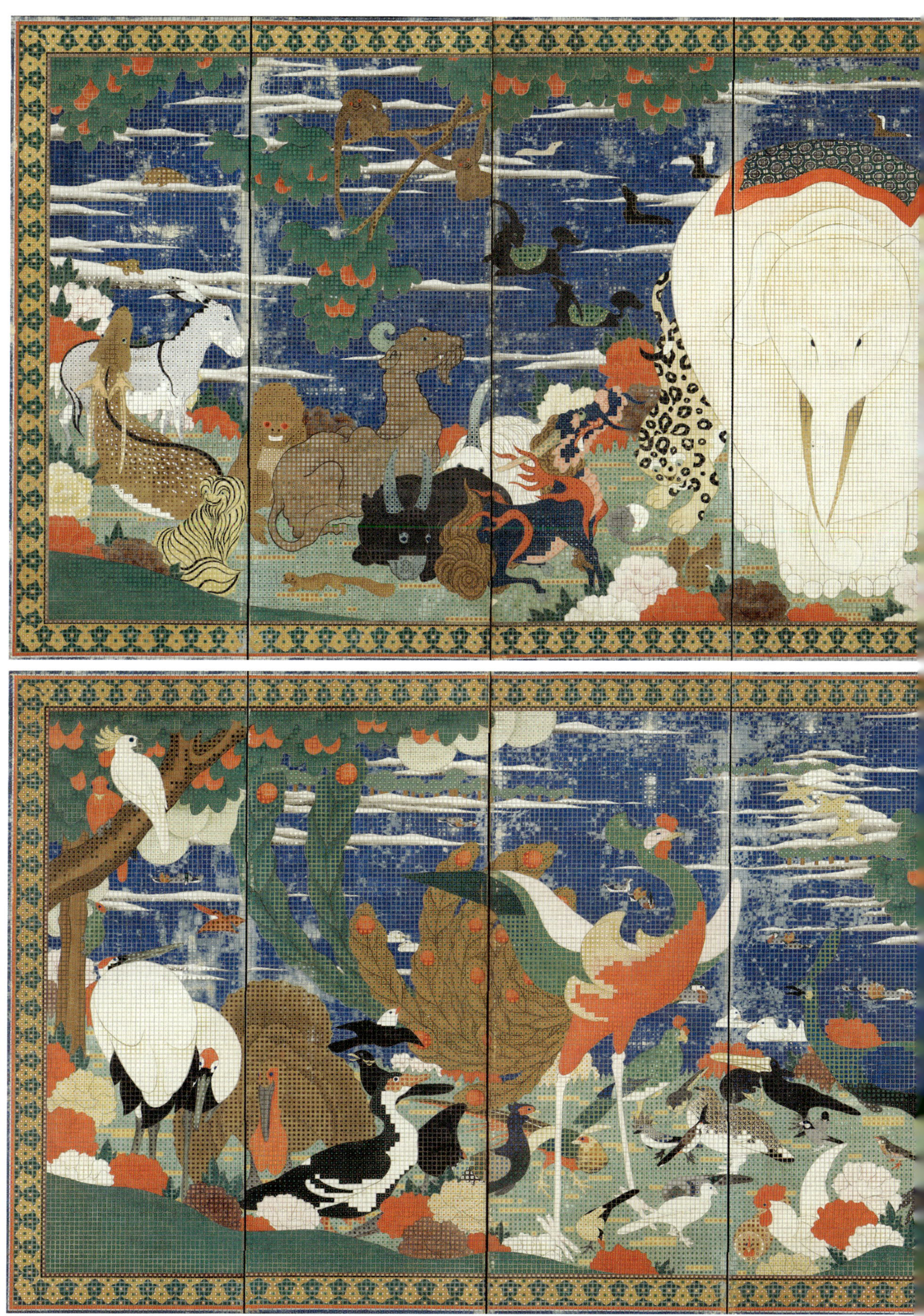

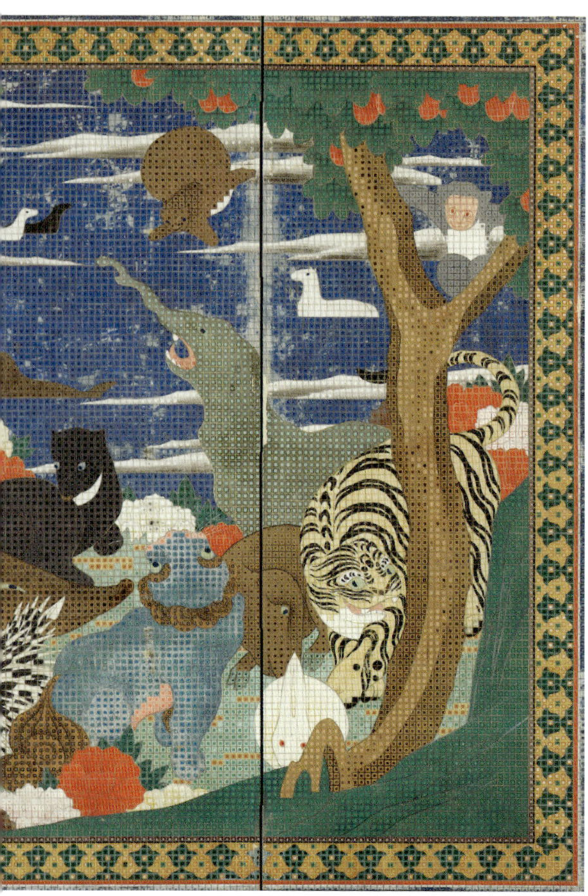

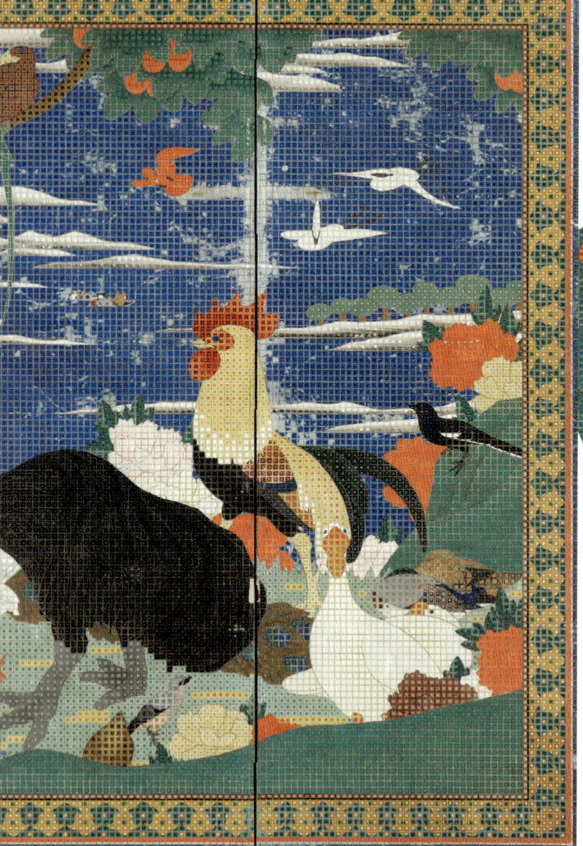

鳥獣花木図屛風

江戸時代後期（18c）
出光美術館

一見、静岡県立美術館本と近似した内容に見えるが、動物の種類が23から29種へ、鳥類は35から45種へと増加。さらに、前者が造形的な面白さを重視するのに対し、本図では異国動物の多さが際立っており、異国性をさらに高めている点が大きく異なる。ここに登場する異国動物の多くが、当時流行した博物学の最新の情報を反映しているのである。枡目は12ミリ四方で、両隻合わせて約86,000個。

Birds and Animals in the Flower Garden Screens

18th century
Idemitsu Museum of Arts

At first glance, this work looks just like the one at the Shizuoka Prefectural Museum of Art, but in this version, the amount of animal types goes from twenty-three to twenty-nine, and the amount of bird types increases from thirty-five to forty-five. Moreover, in contrast to how the former emphasizes the cleverness in the way the animals are modeled, this image focuses more on the variety of foreign animals, and the sense of exoticism here is noticeably more pronounced. Many of the exotic animals that appear here reflect the latest natural history information that was in vogue at the time. Each grid box is twelve millimeters square, and both screens together are made up of about eighty-six thousand squares.

掲載作品を所蔵する施設等のご案内

休館日等は変更する場合があります。各施設にお問い合わせください。

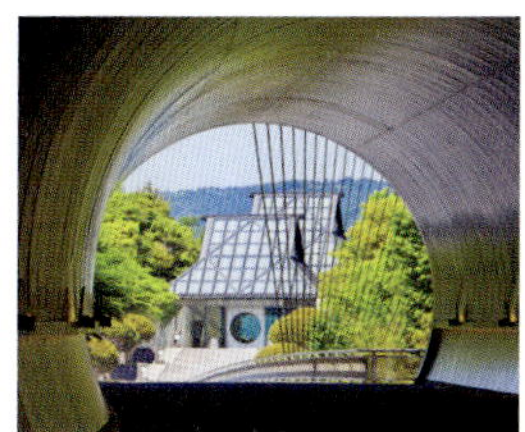
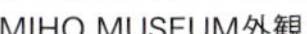
MIHO MUSEUM外観

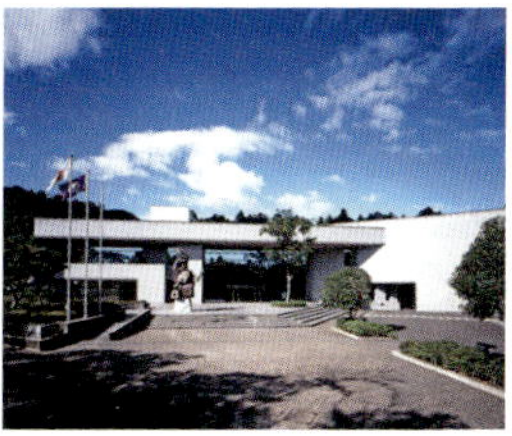
仙台市博物館外観

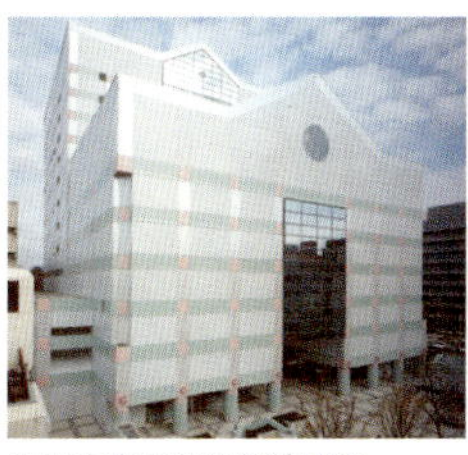
秋田市立千秋美術館外観

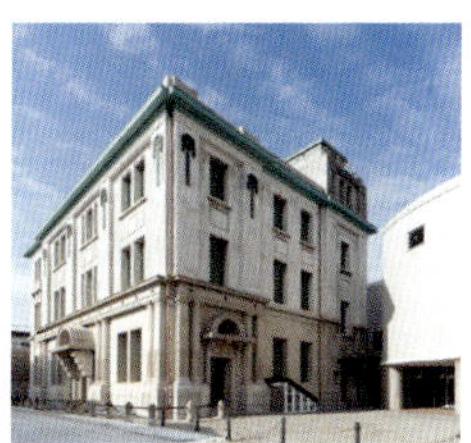
敦賀市立博物館外観

東北	**秋田市立千秋美術館** Akita Senshu Museum of Art 018-836-7860	〒010-0001 秋田県秋田市中通二丁目3-8（アトリオン） ㊡年末年始、アトリオン全館点検日、展示替・施設整備期間	JR秋田駅西側のアトリオン内にある美術館。佐竹曙山、小田野直武らの秋田蘭画や、平福穂庵・百穂父子、寺崎廣業、木村伊兵衛など秋田ゆかりの作家作品を収蔵。洋画家・岡田謙三の記念館も併設。
	帆風美術館 Vanfu Museum 0178-20-1335	〒039-2245 八戸市北インター工業団地1-5-2 株式会社帆風八戸センター1F ㊡月曜・火曜・土曜（祝日の場合は開館）※祝日開館した場合は水曜休館。ほか展示替期間・年末年始	株式会社帆風が青森県八戸市への地域貢献として設立。同社が長年培ったカラーマネジメント技術を、美術の領域で利用した技法「デジタル光筆画」によってつくられた作品を展示する、複製画専門の美術館。江戸時代の日本画を主に扱う。
	本間美術館 Homma Museum of Art 0234-24-4311	〒998-0024 山形県酒田市御成町7-7 ㊡12月~2月、火曜・水曜（祝日の場合はその翌日）、展示替期間	1947年、酒田の豪商として知られた本間家が創始者として開館した美術館。展覧会を年に8回ほど開催するほか、収蔵品をテーマに沿って展示。古美術から現代美術までの幅広いジャンルのコレクションを約3,000件所蔵。
	仙台市博物館 SENDAI CITY MUSEUM 022-225-3074	〒980-0862 宮城県仙台市青葉区川内26番地 ㊡月曜日（祝日・振替休日は開館）、祝日・振替休日の翌日（土・日曜日、祝日は開館）、年末年始	仙台伊達家からの寄贈資料をはじめ、仙台に関わる歴史・文化・美術工芸資料など約9万8千点を収蔵。常設展示では、季節ごとに展示替えを行い、随時1,000点の資料を展示し、特別展・企画展も年3~4回開催している。
関東	**角匠** Sumisho Art Gallery 03-3593-0777	〒100-0006 東京都千代田区有楽町1-2-15-3F ㊡土曜・日曜・祝日	創業以来40年、江戸時代に活躍した諸派の絵画、特に浮世絵肉筆画を中心として日本近世絵画全般を扱っているギャラリー。
	早稲田大学坪内博士記念演劇博物館 The Tsubouchi Memorial Theatre Museum, Waseda University 03-3202-6579	〒169-8050 東京都新宿区西早稲田1-6-1 ㊡不定休	世界各地の演劇に関する資料をおよそ100万点所蔵しているアジアで唯一の演劇・映像専門総合博物館。膨大な所蔵資料から様々な展覧会や演劇講座等を無料で開催。また一般利用できる図書室やAVブースも併設している。
中部・北陸	**岩松院** Gansho-in Temple 026-247-5504	〒381-0211 長野県上高井郡小布施町雁田604 ㊡3/15, 4/20, 秋分の日,12/8	長野県小布施町の古刹。葛飾北斎が描いた天井画『八方睨み鳳凰図』を所蔵する他、俳人小林一茶が俳句を詠んだ『蛙合戦の池』や、戦国武将福島正則の霊廟や遺品がある。
	敦賀市立博物館 Tsuruga Municipal Museum 0770-25-7033	〒914-0062 福井県敦賀市相生町7-8 ㊡月曜日（祝日・振替休日は開館）、祝日・振替休日の翌日（土・日曜日、祝日は開館）、年末年始	昭和2(1927)年に竣工した旧大和田銀行本店建物を活用したレトロで趣ある博物館（重要文化財）。年1回の特別展をはじめ、敦賀の豊かな歴史文化を物語る資料や美術工芸作品などを展示している。
近畿	**朝田寺** Choudenji 0598-51-8661	〒515-0027 三重県松阪市朝田町427 ㊡なし ※曽我蕭白の寺宝公開：4月20日～5月5日。本尊地蔵菩薩像の拝観については要問合せ。	御本尊は地蔵菩薩像（重要文化財）。「道明供養」のため宗派を問わず故人の衣類を持参して参拝者が訪れる。御本尊や僧形坐像（県指定文化財）など平安期の仏像が多数安置され、蕭白の作品は11点伝わる。牡丹、紫陽花、朝田寺紅蓮が境内を彩る。
	MIHO MUSEUM 0748-82-3411	〒529-1814 滋賀県甲賀市信楽町田代桃谷300 ㊡月曜（祝日の場合は翌平日）、春・夏・秋の季節閉館	ルーヴル美術館のガラスのピラミッドで知られるI. M. ペイが、自然・建物・美術品の融合をテーマに設計した美術館。南館では世界の古代美術の名宝を、北館では春・夏・秋の開館毎にテーマ性を持った特別展を開催。
	瑞龍寺 Zuiryūji 06-6641-4650	〒556-0016 大阪府大阪市浪速区元町1-10-30 ㊡不定休	寺宝のミイラは非公開。 黄檗宗末寺。開山は鉄眼道光禅師（寶藏國師）。鉄眼は大蔵経の開刻出版を庶民の捐金によって果たそうと活動したが、大飢饉が発生し、資財を難民救済に充てたことから、人々は彼を称え鉄眼寺とも称する。

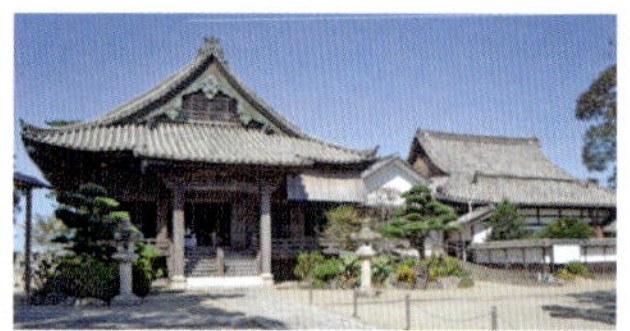
朝田寺 本堂 書院

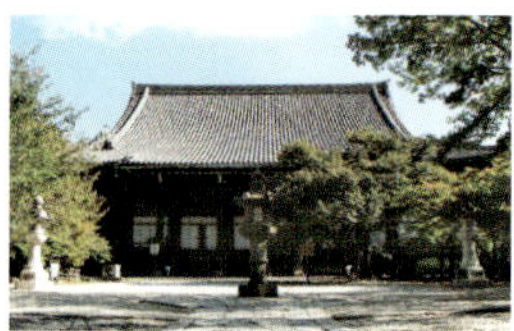
真正極楽寺外観

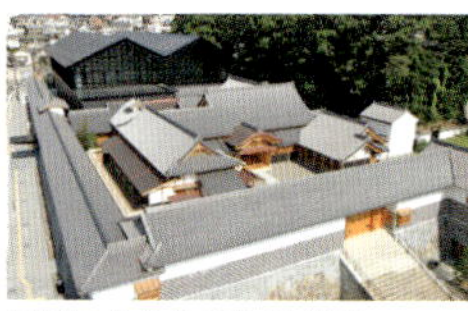
長崎歴史文化博物館外観

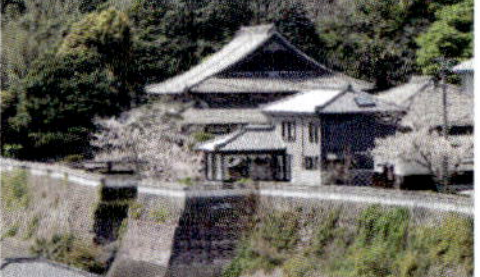
松浦史料博物館外観

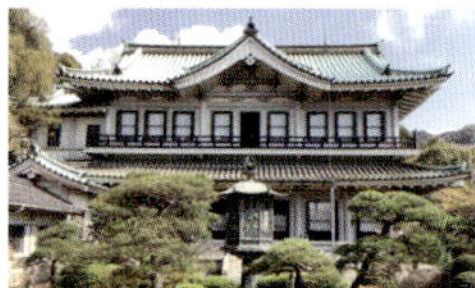
白鶴美術館外観

地域	名称	所在地・休館日	概要
	相国寺承天閣美術館 Shokokuji Jotenkaku Museum 075-241-0423	〒602-0898 京都府京都市上京区今出川通烏丸東入相国寺門前町701 ㊡年中無休（ただし年末年始・展示替え期間を除く）	相国寺創建600年記念事業の一環として建設され相国寺・鹿苑寺（金閣）慈照寺（銀閣）他塔頭寺院に伝わる美術品を受託し、保存及び展示公開している。国宝5点、重要文化財145点を収蔵。
	千總ギャラリー（株式会社千總） CHISO Co., Ltd. 075-253-1555	〒604-8166 京都府京都市中京区三条通烏丸西入御倉町80 ㊡火曜・水曜	京友禅の千總が所蔵する小袖をはじめとした染織品や絵画作品、古文書など約2万点の作品を展覧会で紹介。また千總の美を歴史、職人技、アート性など多角的な切り口から体験できる企画を通して、ブランドの世界観を発信している。
	株式会社 古美術 瀬戸 Kobijutsu SETO Co.Ltd. 075-762-0550	〒605-0037 京都府京都市東山区三条通神宮道西北角西町151-1 ㊡年末年始・夏期休業あり	2012年より京都岡崎の平安神宮近くに店舗を構える古美術商。古書画などの掛軸をはじめとし、屏風・額・彫刻など幅広く取り揃える。併設のギャラリースペースでは常設展示の他、若手作家の展示なども行っている。
	鷲峰山 高台寺 Kodaiji Zen Temple 075-561-9966	〒605-0825 京都府京都市東山区高台寺下河原町526 ㊡なし ※法務がある場合一部堂宇閉堂の場合あり	臨済宗建仁寺派の禅宗寺院。豊臣秀吉没後、その菩提を弔う為正室の高台院が1606年建立。伝小堀遠州作の庭園（国史跡名勝指定）には秀吉の城、伏見城の遺構など開創時の堂宇が残る。高台院の命日には茶会も行われる。
	養源院 Yogenin 075-561-3887	〒605-0941 京都府京都市東山区三十三間堂廻り町656 ㊡不定休	養源院は淀殿が創建し、お江が父 浅井長政公の菩提寺として再建された寺院である。堂内には俵屋宗達が描いた杉戸絵があり、表現内容豊かな霊獣たちが描かれている。
	真正極楽寺 SINSYOO GOKURAKUJI 075-771-0915	〒606-8414 京都府京都市左京区浄土寺真如町82 ㊡原則として拝観日以外。	永観2年（984）に戒算上人が開創した、比叡山延暦寺を本山とする天台宗寺院。「うなずきの弥陀」を御本尊とし、江戸時代再建の本堂や三重塔、仏像・文化財を数多く所蔵。特別拝観日は3月1日～3月31日。
	栂尾山高山寺 Toganoosan Kosanji 075-861-4204	〒616-8295 京都府京都市右京区梅ケ畑栂尾町8 ㊡なし	建永元年(1206)、明恵上人が後鳥羽上皇の勅願により華厳宗の道場として開山した寺。学問寺として発展し、今も国宝8点、重文1万点余りを所蔵している。また、明恵上人が栽培した茶が宇治へと伝わったことから茶の発祥地ともいわれている。国の史跡と世界文化遺産に登録されている。
	無量寺・串本応挙芦雪館 Muryoji Kushimoto Okyo Rosetsukan 0735-62-6670	〒649-3503 和歌山県東牟婁郡串本町串本833 ㊡年中無休。但し、陳列替えその他都合により臨時休館あり。	本州最南端の「芦雪寺」の別名を持つ無量寺にある日本一小さい美術館「串本応挙芦雪館」は江戸時代の奇才・長沢芦雪とその師・円山応挙の作品を収蔵する。中でも芦雪筆「竜虎襖絵」は日本水墨画の優品として国内外で評価が高い。
	白鶴美術館 Hakutsuru Fine Art Museum 078-851-6001	〒658-0063 兵庫県神戸市東灘区住吉山手6-1-1 ㊡夏季・冬季および春季・秋季開期中の月曜（祝日の場合は翌日）	昭和9(1934)年開館。白鶴酒造七代嘉納治兵衛が蒐集した中国古代青銅器・銀器・鏡や陶磁器、奈良・平安時代の経巻、鎌倉から江戸時代の絵画などを所蔵展示する。平成7(1995)年、十代嘉納秀郎蒐集の近代中東絨毯展示館を併設。
九州	**長崎歴史文化博物館** Nagasaki Museum of History and Culture 095-818-8366	〒850-0007 長崎県長崎市立山1-1-1 ㊡毎月第3月曜日（祝日の場合は翌日）	近世長崎の海外交流史を主なテーマとする博物館。江戸時代にあった奉行所の跡地に当時の建物が復元されている。また、多彩なコレクションの中から、貴重な歴史資料や美術工芸品を見ることができる。
	松浦史料博物館 Matsura　Historical Museum 0950-22-2236	〒859-5152 長崎県平戸市鏡川町12 ㊡年末年始	長崎県で最も歴史のある私立博物館。平戸藩主松浦家に伝来した文物を展示公開する。特に9代藩主松浦清（静山）がコレクションした楽歳堂旧蔵の資料は貴重である。

（各地域内の郵便番号順）

掲載作品を所蔵する施設等のご案内（つづき）

東北	**宮城・松島町** Matsushima-chō, Miyagi	〒981-0215 宮城郡松島町高城字帰命院下一19-1
	宮城県図書館 Miyagi Prefectural Library	〒981-3205 宮城県仙台市泉区紫山1-1-1
関東	**出光美術館** Idemitsu Museum of Arts	〒100-0005 東京都千代田区丸の内3-1-1　帝劇ビル9階
	宮内庁三の丸尚蔵館 Sannomaru Shozokan (The Museum of the Imperial Collections)	〒100-8111 東京都千代田区千代田1-1
	国立国会図書館 National Diet Library	〒100-8924 東京都千代田区永田町1丁目10-1
	国立公文書館 National Archives of Japan	〒102-0091 東京都千代田区北の丸公園3-2
	ギャラリー紅屋 GALLERY BENIYA	〒107-0062 東京都港区南青山3-10-41ジュエル青山501
	慶應義塾図書館 Keio University Library	〒108-8345 東京都港区三田2-15-45
	東京国立博物館 Tokyo National Museum	〒110-8712 東京都台東区上野公園13-9
	国立科学博物館 National Museum of Nature and Science	〒110-8718 東京都台東区上野公園7-20
	静嘉堂文庫美術館 Seikado Bunko Art Museum	〒157-0076 東京都世田谷区岡本2-23-1
	早稲田大学図書館 Waseda University Library	〒169-8050 東京都新宿区西早稲田1丁目6-1
	摘水軒記念文化振興財団 Tekisuiken Memorial Foundation of Culture	〒277-0005 千葉県柏市柏4丁目5-3
	国立歴史民俗博物館 National Museum of Japanese History	〒285-8502 千葉県佐倉市城内町117
	日光東照宮 Nikko Toshogu Shrine, Tochigi	〒321-1431 栃木県日光市山内2301
	埼玉・三芳野神社 Miyoshino Shrine, Saitama	〒350-0053 埼玉県川越市郭町2丁目25-25-11
	太田市立新田荘歴史資料館 Ōta Municipal Nittanoshou History Museum	〒370-0426 群馬県太田市世良田町3113-9
	群馬県立近代美術館（戸方庵井上コレクション） Kohoō'an Inoue Collection, The Museum of Modern Art, Gunma	〒370-1293 群馬県高崎市綿貫町992-1群馬の森公園内
	群馬・雙林寺 Sōrinji, Gunma	〒377-0202 群馬県渋川市中郷2300
中部	**長野・北斎館** The Hokusai-kan Museum	〒381-0201 長野県上高井郡小布施町大字小布施485
北陸	**長野・真田宝物館** The Sanada Treasures Museum	〒381-1231 長野県長野市松代町4-1
	静岡県立美術館 Shizuoka Prefectural Museum of Art	〒422-8002 静岡県静岡市駿河区谷田53-2
	西尾市岩瀬文庫 Iwase Bunko Library	〒445-0847 愛知県西尾市亀沢町480
	名古屋城総合事務所 Nagoya Castle	〒460-0031 愛知県名古屋市中区本丸1-1
	岐阜・内藤記念くすり博物館 The Naito Museum of Pharmaceutical Science and Industry, Gifu	〒501-6195 岐阜県各務原市川島竹早町1
	富山市郷土博物館 Toyama Municipal Folk Museum	〒930-0081 富山県富山市本丸1-62
	富山市佐藤記念美術館 Toyama city Satō Memorial Museum	〒930-0081 富山県富山市本丸1-33
近畿	**三重県総合博物館** Mie Prefectural Museum	〒514-0061 三重県津市一身田上津部田3060
	関西大学図書館 Kansai University Library	〒564-8680 大阪府吹田市山手町3-3-35
	京都・相国寺 Shōkokuji, Kyoto	〒602-0898 京都府京都市上京区相国寺門前町701
	京都・建仁寺 Ken'ninji, Kyoto	〒605-0811 京都府京都市東山区小松町584
	京都国立博物館 Kyoto National Museum	〒605-0931 京都府京都市東山区茶屋町527
	国際日本文化研究センター International Research Center for Japanese Studies	〒610-1192 京都府京都市西京区御陵大枝山町3-2
	京都・平等院 Byōdōin, Kyoto	〒611-0021 京都府宇治市宇治蓮華116
	京都・石清水八幡宮 Iwashimizu-hachimangū Shrine, Kyoto	〒614-8588 京都府八幡市八幡高坊30
	宮内庁正倉院事務所 The Office of Shosoin Treasure House	〒630-8211 奈良県奈良市雑司町129
	奈良県立美術館 Nara Prefectural Museum	〒630-8213 奈良県奈良市登大路町10-6
	奈良国立博物館 Nara National Museum	〒630-8213 奈良県奈良市登大路町50
	奈良・薬師寺 Yakushiji, Nara	〒630-8563 奈良県奈良市西ノ京町457
	大和文華館 THE MUSEUM YAMATO BUNKAKAN	〒631-0034 奈良県奈良市学園南1-11-6
	奈良・安倍文殊院 Abe-monjuin, Nara	〒633-0054 奈良県桜井市大字阿部645
	神戸市立博物館 Kobe City Museum	〒650-0034 兵庫県神戸市中央区京町24
中国	**島根県立美術館（永田コレクション）** Nagata Collection, Shimane Prefectural Museum	〒690-0049 島根県松江市袖師町1-5
九州	**福岡市美術館** Fukuoka Art Museum	〒810-0051 福岡県福岡市中央区大濠公園1-6
	九州国立博物館 Kyushu National Museum	〒818-0118 福岡県太宰府市石坂4-7-2
	熊本県立美術館 Kumamoto Prefectural Museum of Art	〒860-0008 熊本県熊本市中央区二の丸2-2
	沖縄美ら島財団 Okinawa Churashima Foundation	〒905-0206 沖縄県国頭郡本部町字石川888
海外	**國立故宮博物院** National Palace Museum, Taipei	No. 221, Sec 2, Zhi Shan Rd, Shilin District, Taipei City
	ベルリン州立図書館 Berlin State Library	Unter den Linden 8, Potsdamer Strasse 33, Westhafenstrasse 1, Berlin, Germany
	ボストン美術館 Museum of Fine Arts, Boston	465 Huntington Avenue, Boston, MA 02115 U.S.A.
	メトロポリタン美術館 The Metropolitan Museum of Art (The Met Fifth Avenue)	1000 Fifth Avenue, New York, NY 10028 USA
	クリーブランド美術館 The Cleveland Museum of Art	11150 East Boulevard, Cleveland, OH 44106 U.S.A.

掲載作品の基本情報

以下の項目を記載しています(不明な情報は割愛)。
作品名(⦿は国宝、◎は重要文化財、○は重要美術品、□は県指定文化財)、
作者、員数、品質形状、寸法(縦、横または長さ、高さの順。単位は記載がなければcm。)、時代、所蔵、クレジット

1章

四神と霊獣

⦿キトラ古墳壁画のうち朱雀・白虎・玄武　3面　漆喰・彩色　西壁（白虎）112.8×204.2、南壁（朱雀）95.7×72.8、北壁（玄武）112.2×105.7　飛鳥時代（7c末〜8c初頭）　国（文部科学省所管）
⦿高松塚古墳壁画のうち青龍　1面　漆喰・彩色　東壁（青龍）113.4×265.5　飛鳥時代（8c初頭）　国（文部科学省所管）
⦿薬師寺金堂薬師如来坐像台座（玄武）　1基　銅製鋳造　白鳳時代（7c末〜8c初頭）　奈良・薬師寺
十二霊獣図巻　1巻　紙本着色　35.9×513.2　室町時代（16c）　東京・静嘉堂文庫美術館　静嘉堂文庫美術館イメージアーカイブ/DNPartcom

鳳凰

旭日鳳凰図　伊藤若冲（1716〜1800）　1幅　絹本着色　185.5×113.8　江戸時代後期（18c）　宮内庁三の丸尚蔵館
⦿鳳凰　1対のうち　銅造鍍金　高98.9　天喜元年（1053）　京都・平等院
八方睨み鳳凰図（天井画）　葛飾北斎（1760〜1849）　1面　板絵着色　間口6.3m、奥行5.5m　弘化2年（1845）頃　長野・岩松院
□鳳凰図屏風　狩野左京（1581〜1657）　4曲1隻　紙本金地着色　160.6×319.0　慶長15年（1610）　宮城・松島町
百鳥図　伝・銭選　1幅　絹本着色　152.0×185.0　中国・明時代（16c）　宮内庁三の丸尚蔵館
百鳥画冊　3冊のうち　紙本着色　各48.0×35.8　江戸時代後期（18c末〜19c前半）　ベルリン州立図書館
白麻地桐鳳凰文帷子　1領　麻 絹刺繍　江戸時代（19c）　東京国立博物館　ColBase

獅子

唐獅子図屏風　狩野永徳（1543〜90）　6曲1隻　紙本金地着色　224.2×453.3　桃山時代（16c）　宮内庁三の丸尚蔵館
獅子牡丹蒔絵鏡箱　1合　木製漆塗金蒔絵　南北朝時代（14c）　東京国立博物館　ColBase
⦿文殊菩薩騎獅像　快慶　5軀のうち　木造 金泥塗 彩色 截金　像高198.0　建仁3年（1203）　奈良・安倍文殊院
◎唐獅子図杉戸　俵屋宗達（?〜1640頃）　4面　板地着色　各182.0×122.5　元和7年（1621）以降　京都・養源院
獅子図軸　周全　1幅　絹本着色　123.2×198.4　明時代（16c）　東京国立博物館　ColBase
五彩獅子文有蓋壺　1個　磁製　景徳鎮窯　総高34.0、口径12.0、底径14.0　中国・清時代（17〜18c）　東京国立博物館　ColBase
獅子戯児図　沈南蘋（1682〜?）　1幅　絹本着色　196.0×96.6　乾隆21年（1756）　神戸市立博物館　Photo: Kobe City Museum/DNPartcom
獅子図（『ヨンストン動物図譜』より）　ヤン・ヨンストン（1603〜75）著　1冊　紙本銅版　39.5×26.0　1660年アムステルダム刊　仙台市博物館
獅子図　宋紫石（1715〜86）　1幅　絹本着色　103.0×36.4　明和5年（1768）　大和文華館
『紅毛雑話』　森島中良（1756？〜1810）著　5冊のうち　紙本墨摺　23×16　天明7年（1787）刊　国立国会図書館
サムソンと獅子図　岸駒（1749〜1838）　1幅　絹本着色　40.8×56.0　天明2年（1782）
獅子図　石川孟高　1幅　絹本着色　17.9×27.3　江戸時代（19c）　歸空庵コレクション
◎日新除魔図　葛飾北斎（1760〜1849）　219枚のうち　紙本墨画　各縦13.0〜40.2、横13.5〜40.3　天保13〜14年（1842〜43）　九州国立博物館　ColBase
唐獅子図　吉村孝敬（1769〜1836）　1幅　絹本着色　117.2×141.8　天保2年（1831）　エツコ＆ジョー・プライスコレクション

龍

⦿竜首水瓶（法隆寺宝物）　1口　銅製 鋳造鍍金・鍍銀　全高49.9、胴径18.9　飛鳥時代（7c）　東京国立博物館　ColBase
◎五龍図巻　伝・陳容　1巻　紙本墨画　淡彩　45.2×299.5　南宋時代（13c）　東京国立博物館　ColBase
雲龍図襖　海北友松（1533〜1615）　8面　紙本墨画　西側 各198.0×187.0、北側 各186.0×133.0　桃山時代（16c）　京都・建仁寺
雲龍図襖　曾我蕭白（1730〜81）　8面　紙本墨画　各165.6×135.0　宝暦13年（1763）　ボストン美術館　Photograph © 22/11/2020 Museum of Fine Arts, Boston William Sturgis Bigelow Collection
◎雲龍図屏風　円山応挙（1733〜95）　6曲1双　紙本淡彩　各176.0×365.0　安永2年（1773）
昇龍図　菅井梅関（1784〜1844）　1幅　絹本墨画淡彩　108.1×36.7　天保6年（1835）　仙台市博物館
龍骨之図　上田耕夫筆、皆川淇園賛　1巻　紙本墨画淡彩　天地73.5　文化2年（1805）賛
龍のミイラ　1体　体長約100　江戸時代（19c）　大阪・瑞龍寺
トウヨウゾウの化石（近江国滋賀郡南庄村出土）　1組　文化元年（1804）出土　国立科学博物館

飛龍

飛龍図（『魚類譜』より）　長谷川雪旦（1778〜1843）、雪堤（1813〜82）　1帖　紙本墨画淡彩　30.0×21.7　江戸時代（19c）　国立公文書館
飛龍図　原在中（1750〜1837）　1幅　絹本墨画金泥　105.6×39.6　文政12年（1829）
⦿飛龍彫刻（御水舎）　1対　木造彩色　寛永13年（1636）　日光東照宮

コラム1

龍の図（□『佐竹曙山写生帖』より）　佐竹曙山（1748〜85）　3帖のうち　紙本着色　安永7年（1778）頃　秋田市立千秋美術館
鯱図（『魚類譜』より）　長谷川雪旦（1778〜1843）、雪堤（1813〜82）　1帖　紙本墨画淡彩　30.0×21.7　江戸時代（19c）　国立公文書館

虎

虎牙彫根付　1個　象牙製　高3.5　江戸時代（19c）　メトロポリタン美術館　Bequest of Susan Dwight Bliss, 1966
虎図　伊藤若冲（1716〜1800）　1幅　絹本着色　129.7×71.0　宝暦5年（1755）　エツコ＆ジョー・プライスコレクション
◎竹林豹虎図（名古屋城本丸御殿　玄関一之間）　狩野派　4面　紙本着色　各約200×150　慶長19年（1614）　名古屋城総合事務所
虎皮写生図　円山応挙（1733〜95）　2曲1隻　紙本着色　150.5×178.2　江戸時代後期（18c）　本間美術館
虎嘯生風図　円山応挙（1733〜95）　1幅　絹本着色　120.9×56.9　天明6年（1786）　東京国立博物館　ColBase
猛虎図　岸駒（1749〜1838）　1幅　絹本着色　139.0×222.5　江戸時代後期（18〜19c）　本間美術館
虎前脚後脚　岸駒旧蔵　1頭分　江戸時代後期（18c）　富山市佐藤記念美術館
竹に虎図　尾形光琳（1658〜1716）　1幅　紙本墨画　28.3×39.0　江戸時代（17c）　京都国立博物館　ColBase
虎図襖　長沢芦雪（1754〜99）　6面　紙本墨画　各183.5×115.5、180.0×87.0　天明6年（1786）　和歌山・無量寺串本応挙芦雪館

獏

獏図（⦿鳥獣人物戯画・乙巻部分）　1巻　紙本墨画　30.7×1215.9　平安時代後期（12c）　京都・高山寺
獏木彫根付　1個　象牙製　高5.1　江戸時代（18世紀）　メトロポリタン美術館　Gift of Mrs. Russell Sage, 1910
◎獏蒔絵枕　1個　12.4×33.3×10.6　桃山時代（17c）　京都・高台寺
獏図印籠　1個　漆塗　6.6×6.4×2.6　江戸時代（18c）　メトロポリタン美術館　H. O. Havemeyer Collection, Bequest of Mrs. H. O. Havemeyer, 1929
獏牙彫根付　1個　象牙製　高3.8 江戸時代（19c）　メトロポリタン美術館　Gift of Mrs. Russell Sage, 1910
獏牙彫根付　1個　象牙製　高7.0 江戸時代（18c）　メトロポリタン美術館　Gift of Mrs. Russell Sage, 1910
獏図杉戸　曾我蕭白　2面　板地着色　各190×90.2　明和元年（1764）頃　三重・朝田寺
獏図（『北斎漫画』二編）　葛飾北斎（1760〜1849）画　1冊　紙本墨摺　22.9×15.9 文化12年（1815）刊　メトロポリタン美術館　Bequest of W. Gedney Beatty, 1941

瑞獣の宝庫：日光東照宮の建築彫刻

⦿獅子彫刻（陽明門）　木造彩色　寛永13年（1636）　日光東照宮
⦿獅子彫刻（陽明門）　木造彩色　寛永13年（1636）　日光東照宮
⦿麒麟彫刻（陽明門）　木造彩色　寛永13年（1636）日光東照宮
⦿獏彫刻（表門）　木造彩色　寛永13年（1636）　日光東照宮
⦿麒麟彫刻（表門）　木造彩色　寛永13年（1636）　日光東照宮
⦿象彫刻（上神庫）　木造彩色　寛永13年（1636）　日光東照宮
⦿犀彫刻（幣殿）　木造彩色　寛永13年（1636）　日光東照宮

コラム2

獅子の洞窟にいるダニエル　ピーター・ルーベンス（1577〜1640）　1面　キャンバス油彩　48×63.8　1615-1620 ウィーン美術史美術館

麒麟

麒麟紋章（一品武官麒麟補子）　1枚　紗刺繍　34.3 × 34.3 明時代後期（17c後半）　メトロポリタン美術館　Gift of Mrs. Russell Sage, 1910
麒麟図（⦿鳥獣人物戯画・乙巻部分）　1巻　紙本墨画　30.7×1215.9 平安時代後期（12c）　京都・高山寺
麒麟牙彫根付　1個　象牙製　高7.3 江戸時代（18c）　メトロポリタン美術館　Gift of Mrs. Russell Sage, 1910
瑞応麒麟図（画麒麟沈度頌）明人　1幅　絹本着色　90.4×45.0 明・永楽12年（1414）頃　台北・国立故宮博物院
◎波と麒麟図杉戸（水犀）　俵屋宗達（?〜1640頃）　2面（8面のうち）　板地着色　各182.0×122.5 元和7年（1621）以降　京都・養源院
麒麟・鳳凰図　狩野典信（1730〜90）　双幅　絹本着色　各166.5×117.5　江戸時代（18c）　兵庫・白鶴美術館
麒麟図　沈南蘋（1682〜?）　1幅　絹本着色　138.9×161.1 中国・乾隆14年（1749）　長崎歴史文化博物館
麒麟図　桂川甫周（1751〜1809）　1幅　紙本着色　105.1×28.4 江戸時代後期（18c）
キリン図（『ヨンストン動物図譜』より）　ヤン・ヨンストン（1603〜75）著　1冊　紙本銅版　39.5×26.0 1660年アムステルダム刊　仙台市博物館
麒麟・鳳凰図　増山雪斎　双幅　紙本着色　各120.8×33.3

犀

犀図（⦿鳥獣人物戯画・乙巻部分）　1巻　紙本墨画　30.7×1215.9 平安時代後期（12c）　京都・高山寺
平螺鈿背円鏡　1面　銅製 鋳造 螺鈿 玳瑁　径35.5 奈良時代（8c）　宮内庁正倉院事務所
犀図　谷文晁（1763〜1841）　1面　紙本着色　39.0×63.0 寛政2年（1790）
犀図（『ヨンストン動物図譜』より）　ヤン・ヨンストン（1603〜75）著　1冊　紙本銅版　39.5×26.0 1660年　アムステルダム刊　仙台市博物館
外国産動物図巻（犀蹄・犀尾）　桂川甫周（1751〜1809）　1巻　紙本着色　27.0×528.5　江戸時代（18c）　早稲田大学図書館
犀図　作者不詳　1幅　紙本着色　113.3×109.8　江戸時代（18c）　神戸市立博物館　Photo: Kobe City Museum/DNPartcom

白澤

白澤・唐木図杉戸　狩野派　4面のうち　板絵金地着色　寛永13年（1636）　日光東照宮
『旅行用心集』　八隅盧庵著　1冊　紙本墨摺　18.5×12.5 文化7年（1810）刊　国立国会図書館
白澤之図　城間清豊（1614〜44）　1幅　紙本着色　80.0×35.6　17c　沖縄美ら島財団

白澤図　守節　1幅　紙本着色　60×29　江戸時代（18c）　国際日本文化研究センター
白澤像（枕屏風）　4曲1隻　紙本着色　92×192cm 江戸時代（19c）　岐阜・内藤記念くすり博物館
白澤図（『北斎漫画』二編）　葛飾北斎（1760〜1849）画　1冊　紙本墨摺　22.9×15.9 文化12年（1815）刊　メトロポリタン美術館　Bequest of W. Gedney Beatty, 1941

蝙蝠

蝙蝠牙彫根付　1個　象牙製　高3.2 江戸時代（19c）　メトロポリタン美術館　Gift of Mrs. Russell Sage, 1910
桃蝠文皿　1枚　磁性　直径20.7 雍正年間（18世紀）　メトロポリタン美術館 Gift of Stanley Herzman, in memory of Gladys Herzman, 1997
納涼美人図　歌川豊国（1769〜1825）　1幅　絹本着色　84.7×36.6 群馬県立近代美術館（戸方庵井上コレクション）
百蝠文刺繡袍　1領　絹地刺繡　137.2 × 190.5 清時代（18c）　メトロポリタン美術館　Anonymous Gift, 1943
蝙蝠文紗刺繡袍　1領　紗絹刺繡　140.7 × 226.7 清時代（18c）　メトロポリタン美術館　Purchase, Joseph Pulitzer Bequest, 1932
麻姑仙人図　石川大浪（1762〜1817）　1幅　絹本着色　95.7×31.8 江戸時代（18c後半〜19c初め）歸空庵コレクション
鹿図鐔　1個　赤銅地 色絵　7×6 江戸時代（19c）　メトロポリタン美術館　H. O. Havemeyer Collection, Bequest of Mrs. H. O. Havemeyer, 1929
蝙蝠図（団扇絵判）　長谷川雪旦（1778〜1843）、雪堤（1813〜82）　1枚　錦絵　小判　江戸時代（19c）　東京国立博物館　ColBase
鳥獣画巻　河鍋暁斎（1831〜1889）　1巻　紙本着色　27.3×516.9 江戸時代末期（19c後半）　メトロポリタン美術館　Fletcher Fund, 1937

2章

鹿

◎春日鹿曼荼羅　1幅　絹本着色　76.5×40.5 鎌倉時代（14c）　奈良国立博物館　ColBase
神鹿（春日神鹿舎利厨子安置）　1幅　木製 黒漆塗 / 銅製 鍍金（神鹿、金具）鎌倉〜南北朝時代（14c）　奈良国立博物館　ColBase
鹿図目貫　1対のうち　金 彫金　幅1.3 江戸時代（18c）　メトロポリタン美術館　Purchase, Joseph Pulitzer Bequest, 1938
○萩に鹿図屏風　狩野左京（1581〜1657）？　4曲1双のうち　紙本金地着色　各159.0×346.8 寛永5年（1628）　仙台市博物館
鹿木彫根付　1個　木製　高3.8 江戸時代（19c）　メトロポリタン美術館　Gift of Mrs. Russell Sage, 1910
双鹿図屏風　円山応挙（1733〜95）　2曲1隻　紙本金地着色　157.2×160.8 天明3年（1783）　京都国立博物館　ColBase
鹿図小柄　1本　四分一・赤銅・銅・金・銀製　9.8×1.4 江戸時代（18c）　メトロポリタン美術館　The Howard Mansfield Collection, Gift of Howard Mansfield, 1936
鹿鶴図屏風　沈南蘋（1682〜?）　6曲1双　絹本着色　各144.2×280.4 中国・乾隆4年（1739）　東京国立博物館　ColBase
寿老人図　狩野探信（1653〜1718）　1幅　絹本着色　93.2 × 38.1　江戸時代（19c）　メトロポリタン美術館　The Harry G. C. Packard Collection of Asian Art, Gift of Harry G. C. Packard, and Purchase, Fletcher, Rogers, Harris Brisbane Dick, and Louis V. Bell Funds, Joseph Pulitzer Bequest, and The Annenberg Fund Inc. Gift, 1975
双鹿図　長沢芦雪（1754〜99）　1幅　紙本着色金泥　79.2×88.7 天明3年（1783）　京都国立博物館　ColBase
秋草鹿蒔絵印籠　1個　金銀研出螺鈿象嵌蒔絵　11.4×5.2×2.7 江戸時代（19c）　メトロポリタン美術館　H. O. Havemeyer Collection, Bequest of Mrs. H. O. Havemeyer, 1929

猿

日吉山王本地仏曼荼羅図　1幅　絹本着色　85.4×40.7 鎌倉時代（14c）　東京国立博物館　ColBase
旭日猿図　鳥山石燕（1712〜88）　1幅　絹本着色　94.6×32.7 江戸時代（18c）　熊本県立美術館
猿図（◎ 鳥獣人物戯画 断簡）　1幅　紙本墨画　30.6×83.3 平安時代（12c）　東京国立博物館　ColBase
◎巌樹遊猿図屏風　式部輝忠（生没年不詳）　6曲1双　紙本墨画　各149.0×338.0 室町時代（16c）　京都国立博物館　ColBase
百猿図　狩野栄信（1775〜1828）　1幅　絹本着色　124.2×54.0 享和2〜文化13年（1802〜16）　静岡県立美術館
封侯図　森周峰（1738〜1823）・狙仙（1747?〜1821）・徹山（1775〜1841）・雄山（1780〜1851）　1幅　紙本着色　131.3×57.5 文化11年（1814）　画像提供: 東京国立博物館 Image: TNM Image Archives

狛犬

◎狛犬（吽形）　1幅　木造・彩色　像高66.2 鎌倉時代（13c）　奈良国立博物館　ColBase
狛犬（阿形）　1幅　木造・彩色　像高45.7 鎌倉時代（13c）　メトロポリタン美術館　Mary Griggs Burke Collection, Gift of the Mary and Jackson Burke Foundation, 2015
高野四所明神像　1幅　絹本着色　102×49.5 室町時代（16c）　メトロポリタン美術館　Mary Griggs Burke Collection, Gift of the Mary and Jackson Burke Foundation, 2015

狐

狐牙彫根付　1個　象牙製　江戸時代（19c）　東京国立博物館　ColBase
狐図（◎ 鳥獣人物戯画 断簡）　1幅　紙本墨画　30.6×83.3 平安時代（12c）　東京国立博物館　ColBase
荼枳尼天曼荼羅図　1幅　絹本着色　室町時代（16c）　東京国立博物館　ColBase
白狐図　円山応挙（1733〜95）　1幅　絹本墨画淡彩　119.7×71.3 安永8年（1779）
狐牙彫根付　1個　象牙製　高7 江戸時代（19c）　メトロポリタン美術館　Gift of Mrs. Russell Sage, 1910
葛の葉狐木彫根付　1個　木造　高4.1 江戸時代（19c）　メトロポリタン美術館　Gift of Mrs. Russell Sage, 1910
八尾狐図　狩野探幽（1602〜74）　1幅　紙本淡彩　109.3×56.3 寛永14年（1637）
九尾狐文鏡図　春川五七（1776〜1831）　1枚　錦絵　21.7×18.9 江戸時代（19c）　メトロポリタン美術館　H. O. Havemeyer Collection, Bequest of Mrs. H. O. Havemeyer, 1929
白狐図　吉川一渓（1763〜1837）　1幅　絹本着色　99.8×34.0 江戸時代（18c後半〜19c初め）　摘水軒記念文化振興財団
名所江戸百景　王子装束ゑの木　大晦日の狐火　歌川広重（1797〜1858）　1枚　錦絵大判　安政4年（1857）　メトロポリタン美術館　The Howard Mansfield Collection, Purchase, Rogers Fund, 1936
狐の嫁入図　葛飾北斎（1760〜1849）　1幅　絹本着色　96.2×35.0 天保15年（弘化元、1844）　島根県立美術館（永田コレクション）
婚怪草紙絵巻　浮田一蕙（1795〜1859）1巻　紙本着色　29.8×777.2 安政4年頃（1858）　メトロポリタン美術館　Rogers Fund, 1957

鳩

竹鳩図（芙蓉翡翠・梅鳩・竹鳩図のうち）　鶴沢探龍（?〜1855）・探玄（生没年不詳）　3幅のうち　絹本着色　江戸時代（19c）　東京国立博物館　ColBase
孔雀鳩図、銀鳩図（□『佐竹曙山写生帖』より）　佐竹曙山（1748〜85）　3帖のうち　紙本着色　各34.0×26.3 安永7年（1778）頃　秋田市立千秋美術館
松鳩図絵馬　円山応挙（1733〜95）　1面　板地着色　104.3×177.5 天明6年（1786）　京都・石清水八幡宮
鴿図（□『佐竹曙山写生帖』より）　佐竹曙山（1748〜85）　3帖のうち　紙本着色　安永7年（1778）頃　秋田市立千秋美術館
かんむり鳩図　山路探常（1728〜93）　1幅　絹本着色　111.3×42.5 天明8年（1788）　仙台市博物館

鼠

鼠図（『光琳画譜』より）　中村芳中（?〜1819）　2冊のうち　紙本多色摺　27×19.5　文政9年（1826）以降　メトロポリタン美術館　Purchase, Mary and James G. Wallach Foundation Gift, 2013
瓢箪に鼠木彫根付　1個　木製　高3.5 江戸時代（19c）　メトロポリタン美術館　Gift of Mrs. Russell Sage, 1910
三面大黒天画像　真田幸貫（1791〜1852）・谷文晁（1763〜1841）　1幅　紙本着色　天保6年（1835）　長野・真田宝物館
塩鮭と白鼠（『肉筆画帖』より）　葛飾北斎（1760〜1849）　1帖　紙本着色　天地25.0 天保5〜15年（1834〜44）　北斎館
鮭図　蠣崎波響（1764〜1826）・東東洋（1755〜1839）・東寅（1793〜1853）　1幅　紙本墨画　132.8×46.9 文化11年（1814）
鼠と小槌図　葛飾北斎（1760〜1849）　1幅　紙本着色　88.8×28.6 天保15年（1844）　島根県立美術館（永田コレクション）
鼠図目貫　1対　赤銅、金製　金：1.7、黒：2.1 江戸時代（18c）　メトロポリタン美術館　Purchase, Joseph Pulitzer Bequest, 1938
鮑に鼠牙彫根付　1個　象牙製　高2.2 江戸時代（19c）　メトロポリタン美術館　Gift of Alvin H. Schechter, 1985
染付大根鼠図輪花皿　1枚　伊万里焼　高4.6 径29.1 高台径15.6 江戸時代（19c）　東京国立博物館　ColBase

兎

波兎蒔絵旅筆筒　1合　黒漆塗・蒔絵　江戸時代（17c）　東京国立博物館　ColBase
黒麻地波兎牡丹唐草州浜笹文肩衣　1領　麻 染色　丈75.2 裄35.2 江戸時代（19c）　東京国立博物館　ColBase
木賊兎図　円山応挙（1733〜95）　1幅　絹本着色　104.5×42.0 天明6年（1786）　静岡県立美術館
百兎図　円山応挙（1733〜95）　1幅　絹本着色　55.0×86.0 天明4年（1784）
宝珠を搗く月兎　葛飾北斎（1760〜1849）　1幅　紙本着色　82.2×27.8 江戸時代（19c前半）
臼兎牙彫根付　1個　象牙製　高2.7 江戸時代（18c）　東京国立博物館　ColBase
浪兎図　沖探容（?〜1839）　1幅　絹本着色　42.8×67.8 江戸時代（19c前半）

犬

子犬牙彫根付　1個　象牙製　高1.7 江戸時代（18c）　メトロポリタン美術館　Gift of Mrs. Russell Sage, 1910
犬図（『光琳画譜』より）　中村芳中（?〜1819）　2冊のうち　紙本多色摺　27×19.5　文政9年（1826）以降　メトロポリタン美術館　Purchase, Mary and James G. Wallach Foundation Gift, 2013
百犬図　伊藤若冲（1716〜1800）　1幅　絹本着色　142.7×84.2 寛政12年（1800）　京都国立博物館　ColBase
親子犬図　狩野永良（1741〜71）　1幅　紙本着色　39.5×70.8 江戸時代（18c）　静岡県立美術館
朝顔狗子図杉戸　円山応挙（1733〜95）　2面　板地着色　各168.5×81.3 天明4年（1784）　東京国立博物館　ColBase
雪狗子図襖　長沢芦雪（1754〜99）　4面　紙本墨画　各168.7×183 寛政4〜11年（1792〜99）　メトロポリタン美術館　Mary Griggs Burke Collection, Gift of the Mary and Jackson Burke Foundation, 2015

猪

猪牙彫根付　1個　象牙製　高2.2 江戸時代（19c）　メトロポリタン美術館　Bequest of Stephen Whitney Phoenix, 1881
猪図　森狙仙（1747？〜1821）　2曲1隻　紙本墨画淡彩　156.6×172.4 文化4年（1807）以前　株式会社 千總
摩利支天像（『北斎漫画』六編）　葛飾北斎（1760〜1849）画　1冊　紙本墨摺　22.9×15.9 文化12年（1815）刊　メトロポリタン美術館　Bequest of W. Gedney Beatty, 1941
猪図　岸連山（1804〜59）　1幅　紙本着色　89.4×147.0 江戸時代（19c）　東京国立博物館　ColBase

鶴

松梅孤鶴図　伊藤若冲（1716〜1800）　1幅　紙本着色　136.5×60.9 江戸時代（18c）　東京国立博物館　ColBase
鶴形漆筥　1合　木製漆塗　高9.5 横11.4 江戸時代（19c）　メトロポリタン美術館　H. O. Havemeyer Collection, Bequest of Mrs. H. O. Havemeyer, 1929
花菱松双鶴鏡　1面　銅・鋳造　径22.2 室町時代（15c）　東京国立博物館　ColBase
松梅孤鶴図　伊藤若冲（1716〜1800）　1幅　紙本着色　136.5×60.9 江戸時代（18c）　東京国立博物館　ColBase
◎鶴下絵三十六歌仙和歌巻　俵屋宗達下絵・本阿弥光悦書　1巻　紙本金銀泥絵墨書　34.0×1460.0 江戸時代（17c）　京都国立博物館　ColBase
群鶴図屏風　石田幽汀（1721〜86）　6曲1双　紙本金地着色　各156.0×362.6 江戸時代（18c）　静岡県立美術館
四季花鳥図屏風　6曲1双　紙本金地着色　各160.7×360.7 桃山時代（16c後半）　メトロポリタン美術館　Purchase, Mrs. Jackson Burke and Mary Livingston Griggs and Mary Griggs Burke Foundation Gifts, 1987
群鶴図　狩野探信（1653〜1718）　1幅　絹本着色　149.2×76.8 江戸時代（17〜18c）　メトロポリタン美術館　Charles Stewart Smith Collection, Gift of Mrs. Charles Stewart Smith, Charles Stewart Smith Jr., and Howard Caswell Smith, in memory of Charles Stewart Smith, 1914
鶴図　長沢芦雪（1754〜99）　2幅　紙本着色　各156×91.2 江戸時代（1780年代後半）　メトロポリタン美術館　Fishbein-Bender Collection, Gift of T. Richard Fishbein and Estelle P. Bender, 2011

霊亀・亀
紅綸子地末広亀模様夜着　1領　江戸時代（19c）　東京国立博物館　ColBase
岩上亀牙彫根付　1個　象牙製　高1.9 江戸時代（19c）　メトロポリタン美術館　Gift of Alvin H. Schechter, 1985
瑞亀図　葛飾北斎（1760～1849）　1幅　紙本着色　34.9×49.4 寛政8年（1796）頃　奈良県立美術館
瑞亀図　狩野常信（1636～1713）　1幅　絹本墨画淡彩　95.3×168.4 江戸時代（17c）　福岡市美術館　画像提供: 福岡市美術館/DNPartcom
浦島太郎騎亀図　河鍋暁斎（1831～1889）　1幅　絹本着色　98.7×36.2 明治時代（1888年以降）　メトロポリタン美術館　Gift of Edward M. Bratter, 1957
亀図（『楚南画譜』より）　大西椿年（1792～1851）1冊　紙本多色摺　27.5×18.5 天保5年（1834）　メトロポリタン美術館　Purchase, Mary and James G. Wallach Foundation Gift, 2013
亀図（『光琳画譜』より）　中村芳中（?～1819）　2冊のうち　紙本多色摺　27×19.5　文政9年（1826）以降　メトロポリタン美術館　Purchase, Mary and James G. Wallach Foundation Gift, 2013

孔雀
色絵孔雀牡丹太湖石図瓶　1口　磁器　高31.0　口径6.9　底経16.0 江戸時代（17c半ば）　九州国立博物館　ColBase
⦿孔雀明王像　1幅　絹本着色　147.9×98.9 平安時代後期（12c中頃）　東京国立博物館　ColBase
◎鳳凰文戧金経箱（京都・高山寺伝来）　1合　木製 黒漆塗 鎗金 螺鈿　20.2×39.3×25.3 元時代（14c）　奈良国立博物館　ColBase
◎四季花鳥図屏風　狩野元信（1477～1559）　6曲1双　紙本金地着色　各163.0×360.5 天文18年（1549）　兵庫・白鶴美術館
◎牡丹孔雀図　円山応挙（1733～95）　1幅　絹本着色　131.5×191.3 明和8年（1771）　京都・相国寺
扇屋見世奢　鳥高斎栄昌（1793～99）大判錦絵3枚続　紙本多色摺　各38.9×24.4 寛政5～11年（1793～99）　メトロポリタン美術館　Fletcher Fund, 1929
「孔雀茶屋」（『摂津名所図会』東生郡 二　所載）　秋里籬嶌 著　1冊　紙本墨摺　25.5×17.9 寛政10年（1798）　国立国会図書館
花鳥獣蒔絵螺鈿洋櫃　1口　木製 黒漆塗 金銀平蒔絵 螺鈿象嵌　高63.5 横125 長54.5 桃山時代末期～江戸時代初期（16c末～17c初め）　メトロポリタン美術館　Purchase, John and Pauline Gandel Gift and Mary Livingston Griggs and Mary Griggs Burke Foundation Fund, 2016
異国人交易図屏風　6曲1隻　紙本着色　70.2×263.8 江戸時代後期（19c初頭）　メトロポリタン美術館　Rogers Fund, 1957
牡丹に孔雀図　谷文晁（1763～1841）　1幅　絹本着色　153×88.2 文政3年（1820）　メトロポリタン美術館　Charles Stewart Smith Collection, Gift of Mrs. Charles Stewart Smith, Charles Stewart Smith Jr., and Howard Caswell Smith, in memory of Charles Stewart Smith, 1914
鳥類写生図巻　岡本秋暉（1807～62）　1巻　紙本着色　27.2×984.7 江戸時代（19c）　東京国立博物館　ColBase

猫
麝香猫図　右都御史（狩野玉楽か）　1幅　紙本着色　76×46.5　室町時代（16c後半）　メトロポリタン美術館　Mary Griggs Burke Collection, Gift of the Mary and Jackson Burke Foundation, 2015
牡丹に猫図　原在中（1750～1837）　1幅　絹本着色　175.0×90.0 江戸時代（18c後半～19c前半）　仙台市博物館
霊猫図　岸駒（1749～1838）　1面　紙本金地着色　175.0×90.0　天明3年～文化5年（1784～1808）　富山市郷土博物館
群獣人物図巻　河鍋暁斎（1831～1889）　1巻　紙本着色　27.6×629.9 江戸時代（19c）　メトロポリタン美術館　Fletcher Fund, 1937
新田猫絵　岩松徳純（1777～1825）・岩松道純（1798～1854）　2幅　紙本着色（上）40.2×58.0・（下）40.0×63.3　江戸時代（19c）　太田市立新田荘歴史資料館

鯨
六鯨図并捕鯨具　1巻　紙本着色　25.3×600.7　天保15年（1844）　三重県総合博物館
大漁鯨のにぎわひ　歌川国芳（1797～1861）　大判錦絵3枚続　紙本多色摺　大判嘉永4年（1851）ギャラリー紅屋
旭潮鯨波図　根元常南（1763～1811）　1幅　絹本着色　55.0×97.2 寛政9年（1797）
『日本永代蔵』　井原西鶴（1642？～93）著　1冊　紙本墨摺　26×18 貞享5年（1688）　国立国会図書館
『頭書 増補訓蒙図彙』　中村惕斎(1629～1702)編、下河辺拾水画　1冊　紙本墨摺　22.8×16.5 寛政元年（1789）刊　国立国会図書館
『除蝗録』　大蔵永常　1冊　紙本墨摺　23×16 文政9年（1826）刊　国立国会図書館

3章

象
象の鳥獣座（普賢菩薩騎象像部分）　1幅　銅製鍍金　像高18.5 中国・遼時代（10c）　クリーブランド美術館　Andrew R. and Martha Holden Jennings Fund
⦿普賢菩薩像　1幅　絹本着色　159.1×74.5 平安時代（12c中頃）　東京国立博物館　ColBase
◎白象図杉戸　俵屋宗達（?～1640頃）　2面　板地着色　各182.0×122.5 元和7年（1621）以降　京都・養源院
◎南蛮屏風　狩野内膳（1570～1616）　6曲1双のうち　紙本金地着色　各154.5×363.2 桃山時代（16c後半～17c初め）　神戸市立博物館　Photo: Kobe City Museum/DNPartcom
象之絵巻物　尾形探香（生没年不詳）　1巻　紙本着色　27.6 江戸時代中期（19c半ば）　関西大学図書館
象のかわら版　1枚　紙本墨摺　46.5×31.8 享保14年（1729）　関西大学図書館
鳥獣鷹象写生図巻・象巻　狩野古信（1696～1721）　1巻　紙本淡彩　59.7×527.2 江戸時代（18c）　東京国立博物館　ColBase

駱駝
駱駝図　谷文晁（1763～1841）　1幅　絹本着色　97.8×41.9 文政8年（1824）　摘水軒記念文化振興財団
長崎版画「KAMEEL」（文錦堂版）　1枚　木版 合羽摺　30.3×44.0　江戸時代後期（19c）　神戸市立博物館　Photo: Kobe City Museum/DNPartcom
双駱駝図　窪田雪鷹（生没年不詳）　1幅　紙本着色　73.2×38.8　文政6年（1823）　神戸市立博物館　Photo: Kobe City Museum/DNPartcom
『絵本駱駝具誌』　高力猿猴庵（1756～1831）　1冊　紙本墨画淡彩　25.3×18.0　文政10年（1827）　神戸市立博物館　Photo: Kobe City Museum/DNPartcom

オランウータン
猩々の舞　蹄斎北馬（1771～1844）　1枚　紙本墨摺淡彩　21×18.7 江戸時代（19c）　メトロポリタン美術館　H. O. Havemeyer Collection, Bequest of Mrs. H. O. Havemeyer, 1929
唐蘭船持渡鳥獣之図　1枚　紙本淡彩　37.9×25.5　江戸時代後期（18～19c）　慶應義塾図書館
◎能面 猩々　1面　木造彩色　30.3×13.6 室町時代（15～16c）　東京国立博物館　ColBase
ヲーランウータンノ図（『惜字帖』より）　森島中良（1756？～1810）編　1帖のうち　紙本淡彩　28.2×23.8 文化元年（1804）頃　早稲田大学図書館
ヲランウータン図（『甲子夜話』より）　松浦静山（1760～1841）　3編278巻のうち　紙本墨画淡彩　26.6×19.0　文政4年～天保12年（1821～1841）　松浦史料博物館
阿郎烏烏当写真図（『蘭畹摘芳』より）　大槻玄沢（1757～1827）編　3巻のうち　紙本墨摺　25.8×17.6 文化14年（1817）刊　国立国会図書館

豪猪
図案ほか粉本貼り込み画帖　板谷派　1括　紙本墨画・着色　29.5×27.0　江戸時代（17-19c）　東京国立博物館　Image: TNM Image Archives
豪猪図（『本草図説』より）　高木春山（以孝 ?～1853）編・高木正年（1856～1934）増補　195冊のうち　紙本淡彩　26.0×18.9　江戸時代（19c）　西尾市岩瀬文庫
豪猪（『鳥獣魚写生図』より）　栗本丹洲（1756～1834）　1帖　紙本淡彩　（上）：38.8×59.5、（下）：39.2×76.5 江戸時代後期（18～19c）　国立国会図書館
◎四条河原遊楽図屏風（右隻）　2曲1双のうち　紙本金地着色　各164.4×172.8 江戸時代初期（17c前半）　静嘉堂文庫美術館　静嘉堂文庫美術館イメージアーカイブ/DNPartcom

穿山甲
鳥獣図巻（第2巻）　広渡湖秀（初代 1737-1784 または 2代目1766-1820）　3巻のうち　絹本着色　33.9×308.2　江戸時代中期（18c）　長崎歴史文化博物館
◎群仙図屏風（左隻）　曾我蕭白（1730～81）　6曲1双　紙本着色　各172.0×378.0 明和元年（1764）　国（文化庁保管）
『頭書　増補訓蒙図彙』　中村惕斎(1629～1702)編、下河辺拾水画　1冊　紙本墨摺　22.8×16.5 寛政元年（1789）刊　国立国会図書館

火喰鳥・駝鳥・七面鳥
七面鳥（『禽譜』より）　堀田正敦（1755～1832）編　1枚（11帖3巻のうち）　紙本着色　20.4～48.7×41～54 寛政・文政年間（19c）　宮城県図書館
駝鳥・火喰鳥図　清朝筆、大槻玄沢（1757～1827）賛　双幅　絹本着色　各99.0×29.0　寛政3年（1791）　神戸市立博物館　Photo: Kobe City Museum/DNPartcom
花鳥図　墨江武禅（1734～1806）　1幅　絹本着色　35.5×48.5 江戸時代中期（18c）
火喰鳥図（□『佐竹曙山写生帖』より）　佐竹曙山（1748～85）　3帖のうち　紙本着色　安永7年（1778）頃　秋田市立千秋美術館
火喰鳥図　石川孟高（1763～1826）　1幅　絹本着色　98.8×49.6 江戸時代後期（18～19c）　歸空庵コレクション
外国産動物図巻（フウチョウ・サイチョウ）　桂川甫周（1751～1809）　1巻　紙本着色　27.0×528.5 江戸時代後期（18～19c）　早稲田大学図書館
「大頭鳥の觜」（松平信綱寄進の宝物のうち）　一式　万治元年（1658）奉納　埼玉・三芳野神社
八相涅槃図　根元常南（1763～1811）・菅井梅関（1784～1844）　1幅　紙本着色　268.5×335.0 文化8年（1811）　群馬・雙林寺

人魚
人魚のミイラ　1体　約120　江戸時代（19c）　大阪・瑞龍寺
瓦版　人魚図　1枚　紙本色摺　23.5×31.5 文化2年（1805）　早稲田大学演劇博物館
四条河原夕涼図屏風　山口素絢（1759～1818）　6曲1隻　紙本着色　165.1×369.0 文化4年（1807）
『六物新志』大槻玄沢（1757～1827）著　2巻1冊　紙本墨摺　26.5×18.2 天明6年（1786）刊　国立国会図書館
人魚（『北斎漫画』三編より）　葛飾北斎（1760～1849）画　1冊　紙本墨摺　22.9×15.9 文化12年（1815）刊　メトロポリタン美術館　Bequest of W. Gedney Beatty, 1941

白い動物たち
白狐図（前掲）
白鷺鷥（『禽譜』のうち）　堀田正敦（1755～1832）編　1枚（11帖3巻のうち）　紙本着色　20.4～48.7×41～54 寛政・文政年間（19c）　東京国立博物館　ColBase
紅葉白鹿図　円山応挙（1733～95）　1幅　絹本着色　110.0×49.7 江戸時代（18c）　敦賀市立博物館
白鳥図　円山応挙（1733～95）、皆川淇園賛　1幅　紙本淡彩　27.7×124.7 天明7年（1787）　本間美術館

動物大集合：十二支
十二支牙彫根付　1個　象牙製　高3.4 江戸時代（19c）　メトロポリタン美術館　Gift of Mrs. Russell Sage, 1910
十二支図　渡辺南岳（1767～1813）　1幅　絹本着色　150.6×69.7 江戸時代後期（18～19c）　東京国立博物館　ColBase
白唐紗綾地十二支模様縫小袖　1領　袷 白変わり織地（刺繍・金刺繍）　153.0×62.0 江戸時代（19c）　国立歴史民俗学博物館（野村正治郎衣裳コレクション）

動物大集合：涅槃図の動物たち
八相涅槃図（前掲）
釈迦涅槃図　海北友賢　1幅　紙本着色　504.0×396.5 宝永6年（1709）　京都・真正極楽寺（真如堂）

動物大集合：動物たちのユートピア
獣尽図巻　狩野安信・常信・益信・時信・春雪・氏信・勝田貞寛・狩野探幽　1巻　絹本墨画淡彩　縦26.7　寛文5年（1665）
飛禽走獣図巻　狩野探幽（1602～74）　2巻　絹本着色　29.6×651.1 寛文6～7年（1666-67）　東京国立博物館　ColBase
群獣図巻　森狙仙（1747？～1821）　2巻　絹本着色　36.3×352.8、36.3×388.1 江戸時代後期（18～19c）
群獣図屏風　円山応挙（1733～95）　6曲1双　紙本着色　各168.9×364.8 寛政年間（1789～1801）　宮内庁三の丸尚蔵館

動物大集合：祈りのかたち
白象群獣図　伊藤若冲（1716～1800）1面　紙本墨画淡彩　123.0×71.5 江戸時代後期
象と鯨図屏風　伊藤若冲（1716～1800）　6曲1双　紙本墨画　各159.4×354.0 寛政7年（1795）　MIHO MUSEUM
白象黒牛図屏風　長沢芦雪（1754～99）　6曲1双　紙本墨画淡彩　各155.3×359.0　江戸時代後期（18c）　エツコ＆ジョー・プライスコレクション
樹花鳥獣図屏風　6曲1双　紙本着色　各133.0×357.0 江戸時代後期（18c）　静岡県立美術館
鳥獣花木図屏風　6曲1双　紙本着色　各167.0×376.0 江戸時代後期（18c）　出光美術館

著者略歴

内山 淳一（うちやま じゅんいち）

1959年群馬県生まれ。東北大学大学院修了。仙台市博物館において長らく展示活動に従事し、同館館長を経て現在は宮城学院女子大学特任教授（2019～）。著書に『江戸の好奇心－美術と科学の出会い』（講談社、1996、第8回倫雅美術奨励賞受賞）、『動物奇想天外－江戸の動物百態』（青幻舎、2008）など。美術史学会『美術史』論文賞受賞（2017）。江戸時代を中心とした日本の近世絵画史、とくに西洋からの影響を受けて展開した洋風画を専門とする。好きな動物は、うさぎと犬。

めでたし めずらし　瑞獣 珍獣

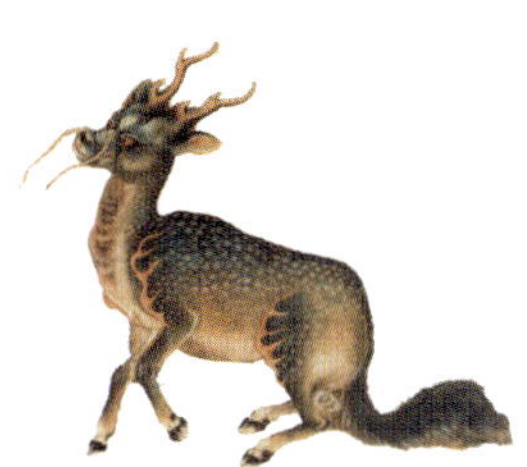

2020年11月22日　初版第1刷発行

著　者　内山淳一

翻　訳　安蘭澄子、ジャニーン・ムルナー
校　正　株式会社 鷗来堂
デザイン　林 陽子（Sparrow Design）
イラスト　芝田知佳
編　集　原 瑛莉子

発行人　三芳寛要
発行元　株式会社 パイ インターナショナル
〒170-0005 東京都豊島区南大塚2-32-4
TEL 03-3944-3981　FAX 03-5395-4830　sales@pie.co.jp

印刷　株式会社 廣済堂

ISBN 978-4-7562-5204-3　C0071

表紙

獏：『北斎漫画』（メトロポリタン美術館）、国宝 鳳凰（平等院）、フウチョウ：八相涅槃図（群馬・雙林寺）、穿山甲：鳥獣図巻（長崎歴史文化博物館）、虎図（エツコ＆ジョー・プライスコレクション）、麒麟図（長崎歴史文化博物館）、七面鳥：『禽譜』（宮城県図書館）、白象：象と鯨図屏風（MIHO MUSEUM）、鶴図（メト
ロ … 国立博物館）、かんむり鳩
図 … 術館）、鼠：『肉筆画帖』（長
野
ナ
蜴 … 秋田市立千秋美術館）、亀：
『 … 物院）と表紙掲載の作品